Sales Force Management

In this latest edition of *Sales Force Management*, Mark Johnston and Greg Marshall continue to build on the tradition of excellence established by Churchill, Ford, and Walker, increasing the book's reputation globally as the leading textbook in the field. The authors have strengthened the focus on managing the modern tools of selling, such as customer relationship management (CRM), social media and technology-enabled selling, and sales analytics. It's a contemporary classic, fully updated for modern sales management practice.

Pedagogical features include:

* Engaging Breakout Questions designed to spark lively discussion.

* Leadership Challenge assignments and Minicases to help students understand and apply the principles they have learned in the classroom.

* Leadership, Innovation, and Technology boxes that simulate real-world challenges faced by salespeople and their managers.

* New Ethical Moment boxes in each chapter put students on the firing line of making ethical choices in sales.

* Role-Plays that enable students to learn by doing.

* A selection of comprehensive sales management cases on the Companion Website.

The Companion Website includes an instructor's manual, PowerPoints, and other tools to provide additional support for students and instructors.

Mark W. Johnston is the Alan and Sandra Gerry Professor of Marketing and Ethics at Rollins College, USA. He is the co-author, with Greg W. Marshall, of *Contemporary Selling,* 5th edition, published by Routledge and the forthcoming *Routledge Companion to Selling and Sales Management.*

Greg W. Marshall is the Charles Harwood Professor of Marketing and Strategy at Rollins College, USA. He is the co-author, with Mark W. Johnston, of *Contemporary Selling,* 5th edition, published by Routledge and the forthcoming *Routledge Companion to Selling and Sales Management.*

Finding academic textbooks that reflect the role of sales managers has been difficult. A gap between corporate sales management tasks and student learning approaches in the classroom has grown. Johnston and Marshall have filled this gap and provided a variety of opportunities to connect student learning, academic requirements, and practitioner realities.

— **Dena H. Hale, Southeast Missouri State University, USA**

This is a comprehensive text that delivers all you need to know about B2B selling from a personal selling and a sales management context. It is instructive with excellent supporting learning materials invaluable in the classroom. I will use this text in both my undergraduate and some postgraduate teaching.

— **Tony Douglas, Edinburgh Napier University, UK**

Sales Force Management

Leadership, Innovation, Technology

Twelfth Edition

*Mark W. Johnston and
Greg W. Marshall*

Routledge
Taylor & Francis Group

NEW YORK AND LONDON

Please visit the companion website for this
title at www.routledge.com/cw/Johnston.

First published 2016
by Routledge
711 Third Avenue, New York, NY 10017

and by Routledge
2 Park Square, Milton Park, Abingdon, Oxon OX14 4RN

Routledge is an imprint of the Taylor & Francis Group, an informa
business

First through tenth edition published by McGraw-Hill.

Eleventh edition published by Routledge, 2013.

Library of Congress Cataloging in Publication Data
A catalog record for this book has been requested

ISBN: 978-1-138-95171-6 (hbk)
ISBN: 978-1-138-95172-3 (pbk)
ISBN: 978-1-315-66806-2 (ebk)

Typeset in Stone Serif
by Swales & Willis Ltd, Exeter, Devon, UK

To Susan and Grace
                    —Mark

To Patti and Justin
                    —Greg

Brief Contents

Detailed Contents

About the Authors

Mark W. Johnston, Ph.D.

Mark W. Johnston is the Alan and Sandra Gerry Professor of Marketing and Ethics at the Roy E. Crummer Graduate School of Business, Rollins College, in Winter Park, Florida. He earned his Ph.D. in marketing from Texas A&M University. Prior to receiving his doctorate he worked in industry as a sales and marketing representative for a leading distributor of photographic equipment. His research has resulted in published articles in many professional journals, such as the *Journal of Marketing Research, Journal of Applied Psychology,* and *Journal of Personal Selling & Sales Management.*

Mark has been retained as a consultant for firms in the personal health care, chemical, transportation, service, and telecommunications industries. He has consulted on a wide range of issues involving strategic sales force structure, sales force performance, sales force technology implementation, market analysis, sales training, and international market decisions. Mark has conducted a number of seminars around the world on a variety of topics, including motivation, managing turnover in the organization, sales training issues, ethical issues in marketing, and improving overall sales performance.

Greg W. Marshall, Ph.D.

Greg W. Marshall is the Charles Harwood Professor of Marketing and Strategy in the Crummer Graduate School of Business at Rollins College, Winter Park, Florida. He also holds an appointment as Professor of Marketing and Strategy in the Aston Business School, Birmingham, UK. He earned his Ph.D. in marketing from Oklahoma State University. Greg's industry experience includes 13 years in selling and sales management, product management, and retailing with companies such as Warner Lambert, Mennen, and Target Corporation. When he left Warner Lambert in 1986 to enter academe, he was the manager of the top-performing sales district in the United States. In addition, he has served as a consultant and trainer for a variety of organizations in both the private and public sectors, primarily in the areas of marketing planning, strategy development, and service quality.

Greg is an active researcher in selling and sales management, having published more than 50 refereed articles in a variety of marketing journals, and he serves on the editorial review board of the *Journal of the Academy of Marketing Science, Journal of Business Research,* and *Industrial Marketing Management.* He is editor of the *Journal of Marketing Theory and Practice* and is past editor of the *Journal of Personal Selling & Sales Management,* currently serving on its senior advisory board. Greg is past president of the Academic Division of the American Marketing Association, a distinguished fellow and past president of the Academy of Marketing Science, and is a fellow and past president of the Society for Marketing Advances.

In addition to working together on *Sales Force Management*, Mark and Greg are the co-authors of *Contemporary Selling,* also published by Routledge/Taylor & Francis Group.

Preface

INTRODUCTION

The twelfth edition of *Sales Force Management* carries on the tradition from previous editions, incorporating the latest research and management practices into an easy-to-read yet comprehensive learning tool.

You will notice that we continue to integrate a variety of innovative learning tools with the latest in sales management theory and practice. At the same time, we have taken great care to preserve the excellent framework and principles from editions one through eleven. In short, we have taken the best from earlier editions and added relevant, real-world student learning tools and up-to-date sales management theory and practice to create this twelfth edition of *Sales Force Management*.

Still without peer, *Sales Force Management* remains the definitive text in the field. Building on the tradition of excellence established by Gil Churchill, Neil Ford, and Orv Walker, in this twelfth edition Mark Johnston and Greg Marshall maintain the quality and integrity of earlier editions while breaking new ground.

WHY WRITE THIS BOOK?

For most of the twentieth century, the practice of sales management was an unfortunate combination of tradition, folklore, personal experiences, and intuition. Sales managers had very little in the way of research or management theory to help better understand the motives and behaviors of their own salespeople. As a result, there was practically no support for the sales manager in the field.

Fortunately, during the 1970s sales academicians and researchers began to conduct empirical studies and develop theoretical models to explain salesperson behavior and motivation. Sales managers found the information invaluable and added their own insights, further refining and enhancing the sales management knowledge base. Today, sales research appears in all the leading marketing journals, and one journal is singularly dedicated to the field of sales management (*Journal of Personal Selling & Sales Management*).

It is not surprising that, as changes were occurring in sales management, the rest of the organization also was experiencing significant transformation. Concepts like strategic alliances, customer relationship management, and value creation brought revolution to every part of the organization, including the sales force. Today, salespeople are expected to have new skills, more information, and instant answers. This makes managing the sales force an even more formidable challenge. Old ways will no longer work—sales force management is undergoing change at an increasing rate, and success in the future will be defined, in part, by how well sales managers learn to manage in this new world.

From the beginning, *Sales Force Management* filled the need for a single, detailed summary of sales management theory, analysis of sales force research, and review of its managerial implications for the organization. Other books provide a cursory appraisal of relevant research or fail to keep pace with current knowledge and trends. Our primary goal in the twelfth edition is the same as it was in the first: offer students a thorough, up-to-date, and integrated overview of accumulated theory and research relevant to sales management.

In writing such a book, however, we know that simply presenting a summary of theories and research would be incredibly dull (we were students, too) and, even worse, would provide little real insight for students interested in learning how a sales manager can *apply* this information in the real world. Put simply, our second goal is to highlight how real managers apply these theories and principles in their own organizations. By identifying recent practices, applications, and the use of state-of-the-art technology, we combine real-world sales management *best practices* with cutting-edge theory and empirical research—all in a single source.

STRUCTURE OF THE BOOK

Over the book's history, a framework has been developed that portrays sales managers' activities as three interrelated, sequential processes, each of which influences the various determinants of salesperson performance. The twelfth edition continues to use this time-tested and insightful structure.

1. *Formulation* of a sales program. This process involves organizing and planning the company's overall personal selling efforts and ensuring that the selling initiative is integrated with the other elements of the firm's marketing strategy.
2. *Implementation* of the sales program. This involves selecting appropriate sales personnel, providing effective training and development, as well as compensation.
3. *Evaluation and control* of the sales program. This involves employing proper metrics to monitor and evaluate sales force performance so adjustments can be made to either the sales program or its implementation as needed.

Chapter 1 introduces the subject of sales management with an overview of the field, including key aspects of the external and internal environment of selling.

The remainder of the book is divided into three sections corresponding to the three processes described earlier.

- **Part One: Formulation of a Sales Program (Chapters 2 through 5)** This section examines the process of buying and selling, including a strong emphasis on selling as a career and the role of organizational buyers; linkages of sales management to business and marketing-level strategies; organizing for success in sales management; and the strategic role of information in forecasting, setting quotas, designing sales territories, and conducting sales analysis. A continuing feature of this edition is emphasis on customer relationship management (CRM) and its link to sales management. New to this edition is a major section linking CRM to the use of data analytics that are relevant to sales organizations.
- **Part Two: Implementation of the Sales Program (Chapters 6 through 11)** This section provides an overview of the determinants of sales performance with the special focus on a salesperson's role perceptions and motivation. It then proceeds to examine decisions involving the recruitment and selection of sales personnel, sales training, and the design of compensation and incentive programs.
- **Part Three: Evaluation and Control of the Sales Program (Chapters 12 and 13)** This section discusses techniques for monitoring and controlling sales force behavior and performance. It examines various approaches for conducting behavioral and other performance analyses.

THE APPROACH OF THE BOOK

Sales Force Management is designed for use in a course on sales management at either the undergraduate or graduate level. It also complements a variety of teaching approaches. Instructors who focus primarily on either a lecture/discussion format or case format will find plenty of material for any teaching calendar in the chapters, enhanced by the end-of chapter Breakout Questions and discussion-centered Leadership Challenges. For those adopting a more case-oriented approach, each chapter contains a short, thoughtful "Minicase" to highlight key learning elements from the chapter along with guiding questions. If you are looking for more comprehensive cases for your course, our Companion Website houses a variety of longer cases in sales management for your use. And, an updated sales management role-play is provided for each chapter.

FEATURES OF THE TWELFTH EDITION

We subscribe to the old adage, "if it isn't broke, don't fix it." The philosophy in creating the twelfth edition was to begin by updating and enhancing the best parts of *Sales Force Management.* As a result, those who have used previous editions will be comfortable with the twelfth edition. But at the same time, with this new edition we have included numerous updates to chapter content, examples, feature boxes, updated data, and more attention to global and ethical aspects of sales force management.

Learning Objectives

Each chapter has succinct learning objectives based on chapter material. Using active language to emphasize the expected student learning outcomes, these objectives enable professors to guide discussions and develop tests so that students get the most out of the book.

Key Terms

Key terms are listed at the end of each chapter and are highlighted in bold within the body of the chapter to help students focus on key ideas and concepts. Professors find these terms can create the basis for assessing students' understanding of the chapter.

Feature Boxes: Leadership, Innovation, and Technology

These three themes drive much of sales management theory and practice today and form the basis for the feature boxes throughout the twelfth edition. These boxes highlight the latest trends in sales management and are designed to illustrate material presented in the chapters in an applied context. Professors will benefit from incorporating these features into class discussion and exercises, and students will find it easier to apply the concepts they are learning in the chapter.

New Feature Box: Ethical Moment

For the first time ever, the twelfth edition of *Sales Force Management* contains an Ethical Moment in each chapter. These interesting and engaging vignettes touch on a variety of ethics-in-sales issues and each one ends with a question to consider that is sure to spark great class discussion.

Breakout Questions

Timely discussion questions, called Breakout Questions, can be found at the end of each chapter. These make for great discussion starters as well as good review questions for exams. And following along with our increased theme of sales ethics, in every chapter a new Ethical Question has been added to the current battery of Breakout Questions.

Leadership Challenge

Leadership is an essential characteristic of successful sales managers. While we include it as a feature box in the text, our goal is to engage the student even more deeply in learning and applying leadership issues. As a result (and not found in any other sales management text), a unique set of short end-of-chapter leadership cases will test the student's ability to make leadership decisions. Short and focused on issues from that chapter, the Leadership Challenges ask students to assess a real situation from a manager's perspective, make decisions, and often develop an implementation strategy.

Role-Plays

Both in the field and classroom, it is widely accepted that role-playing is a valuable tool for helping salespeople and students apply what they are learning. Each Role-Play enables students to work together to employ important sales management concepts they have learned in that particular chapter.

Minicases

Each chapter contains a Minicase enabling students to apply directly what they are learning in the chapter. These Minicases, written specifically for *Sales Force Management,* are short and designed to be used in a variety of ways. For example, they are great for discussion starters in class or as individual assignments. Additionally, student teams can be assigned to analyze the case and make a presentation to the class. Feedback from colleagues was a key driver in creating these shorter, more focused cases that will certainly enhance student learning. Key issues from the chapter will be brought out for the students as they analyze the case. And importantly, most of these Minicases have strong global selling implications. Each Minicase ends with a set of directed, action-oriented questions that force the student to integrate the chapter material.

SUPPLEMENTS

Companion Website

Both instructors and students will appreciate the book's Companion Website (www.routledge.com/cw/Johnston), which has been built specifically for the twelfth edition.

PowerPoint Slides—New and Updated

Many instructors like using PowerPoint to support their in-class presentations, and students have come to find these slide presentations a valuable learning tool. The PowerPoint package for this edition is presented in an effective and interesting graphic design that complements the graphic elements of the book. The slides are flexible enough for instructors to include their own material yet comprehensive enough to stand alone.

Major Cases

For the twelfth edition, a variety of major cases on sales management are available for use on the book's Companion Website.

ACKNOWLEDGMENTS

Books are the result of hard work by many people, and we very much appreciate the efforts of numerous individuals associated with this new edition. First, as this book is built on the research and hard work of sales management academicians and practitioners, we would like to thank the many scholars and colleagues who have contributed to the body of sales force research over the past years. We reference their work and honor their contributions to the field. Chris Richardson (Aston University), Brian Connett (California State University–Northridge), Tony Douglas (Edinburgh Napier University–Craiglockhart Campus), Stephanie Mangus (Michigan State University), Dena Hale (Nova Southeastern University, School of Business & Entrepreneurship), Steve Udrisky (Oklahoma State University, Spears School of Business), Larry Muller (WVU–Parkersburg), Kathy Newton (Purdue University) as well as our anonymous reviewers.

Sharon Golan, Erin Arata, and Scott Sewell. Working with professionals who are also fantastic people makes the task easier and more enjoyable—thanks again to everyone at Routledge/Taylor & Francis. Finally, Sarah Bishop and Phillip Wiseman here at Rollins College, who contributed in an outstanding manner to the updating and integration of literature and references in this edition—your efforts are greatly appreciated. And Phillip deserves additional kudos for his substantial contributions to the new sales analytics section in Chapter 3.

We want to offer a very special thank you to our families and friends. Without their encouragement and support you would not be reading this book. You are special and you are appreciated. Enjoy the book!

Mark W. Johnston, Rollins College
Greg W. Marshall, Rollins College
January 2015

Introduction to Sales Management in the Twenty-First Century

LEARNING OBJECTIVES

Sales management is one of the most important elements in the success of modern organizations. When major trends emerge, such as a shift in the economy toward small- to medium-sized businesses, it is incumbent upon sales managers to react with new selling approaches. And not only is personal selling the most expensive component of the marketing mix for most companies, but it is the firm's most direct link to the customer. While Thoreau may have believed that the world will beat a path to the door of the company with the best mousetrap, the world needs someone to show how that mousetrap is better—and that role usually belongs to the salesperson. Otherwise, that sale may never occur. Therefore, management of the sales force is one of the most important executive responsibilities.

This chapter introduces you to the field of sales management. After reading it you should be able to

- Identify and discuss key trends affecting sales organizations and sales managers today.
- Present a general overview of the sales management process.
- Identify and illustrate the key external and internal environmental factors that influence the development of marketing strategies and sales programs.

SALES MANAGEMENT IN THE TWENTY-FIRST CENTURY

As reflected in the chapter opener, personal selling and, consequently, sales management are undergoing dramatic changes. These changes are being driven by several behavioral, technological, and managerial forces that are dramatically and irrevocably altering the way salespeople understand, prepare for, and accomplish their jobs. Among the behavioral forces are rising customer expectations, globalization of markets, and demassification of domestic markets; technological forces include sales force automation, virtual sales offices, and electronic sales channels; and managerial forces consist of a shift to direct marketing alternatives, outsourcing of sales functions, and a blending of the sales and marketing functions.[1]

Salespeople and those who manage them realize these changes affect every aspect of sales management from the way the sales department is structured to the selection, training, motivation, and compensation of individual salespeople. Sales organizations are being reinvented to better address the needs of the changing marketplace. A number of critical issues have been identified in reinventing the sales organization, including the following: (1) building long-term relationships with customers, which involves assessing customer value and prioritizing customers; (2) creating sales organizational structures that are more nimble and adaptable to the needs of different customer groups; (3) gaining greater job ownership and commitment from salespeople by removing functional barriers within the organization and leveraging the team experience; (4) shifting sales management style from commanding to coaching; (5) leveraging available technology for sales success; and (6) better integrating salesperson performance evaluation to incorporate the full range of activities and outcomes relevant within sales jobs today.[2]

In the broadest perspective, these new-age issues in sales management represent three key themes: (1) innovation—willingness to think outside the box, do things differently, and embrace change; (2) technology—the broad spectrum of technological tools now available to sales managers and sales organizations; and (3) leadership—the capability to make things happen for the benefit of the sales organization and its customers. The chapter opener provides vivid examples of each of these issues at play as firms modify the way they do business to accommodate the twenty-first-century marketplace. Throughout the chapters in this book, you will find highlighted feature boxes calling attention to industry examples of innovation, technology, and leadership among sales organizations. Now we introduce the themes and briefly address their impact on personal selling and sales management. In addition, we will also introduce the issues of globalization and ethics in sales management.[3]

Innovation Fuels Success in Selling Today

For many years the dominant sales approach was transactional selling—a series of transactions, each one involving separate organizations entering into an independent transaction involving the delivery of a product or service in return for compensation. In today's highly competitive environment, however, customers realize there are benefits in building relationships between themselves and their suppliers and have thus turned to relationship selling approaches. For example, Xerox has identified fewer than 500 vendors with which it wants to do business. In contrast, in 1989 more than 5,000 vendors were supplying Xerox. As a result of buyers narrowing their vendor pool, salespeople are being asked to do more, working with customers to solve their problems, improve efficiencies, and, in general, add value to their customers' business. More and more companies have salespeople with offices at or near their customers' facilities. For example, P&G has aggressively reorganized its client teams so they are stationed very close to the company's major accounts. Bentonville, Arkansas, home to Walmart, is also home to a team of several hundred P&G employees!

Offering this level of service is expensive, however, and it cannot be provided equally to all customers across the board. As a result, sales managers must prioritize their customers, creating partnerships with some while seeking to maximize efficiencies with others. In essence, organizations are creating a multilayered sales strategy that seeks to create unique and even more strategic relationships with the best customers while streamlining a transaction-based relationship with others who demand less service.[4] Shell Oil, for example, found that some smaller buyers did not want or have time for personal visits by salespeople. When the company reallocated personal sales efforts to larger accounts and began using only telemarketing to call on smaller accounts, it found that all customers, even those assigned to telemarketing, were more satisfied. Selling costs were reduced, sales increased, and profits soared.

Sales Effectiveness Is Enhanced through Technology

Broadly speaking, technology has had a profound effect on almost every facet of personal selling. Tablets are a great example. Beer salespeople use iPads to show proprietors and customers a video about their brand—say, Heineken—and then ask viewers to answer a question about the video. If you get it right you get a free drink coupon! They also ask if you wanted to provide information, such as e-mail address and age, in order to stay up to date on Heineken news or offers. Such a seamless approach to customers would not be possible without the accompanying technology. Of course, the Internet has taken the interaction between customer and company to a new level, creating the ability to remain in touch with the customer (update information, handle questions, deal with complaints) in ways that have not been possible in the past. Companies are still learning how to best incorporate new technology into the business of selling.

The Internet's ability to inform, persuade, and enhance the personal selling component makes it a critical part of sales management in the twenty-first century. For today's young salespeople and buyers, the Internet is simply a given—they can't imagine what business was like before it! Nearly every company of any size has created an extensive, integrative, and interactive website to sell and service customers. Zappos is a great example of a firm whose sales, customer satisfaction, and loyalty are greatly enhanced by their Web presence. The website has become an important sales tool as account managers work with customers to help them see the benefits of ordering online.

But don't think technology is just about the Internet alone. Electronic data interchange (EDI) systems in manufacturing and efficient consumer response (ECR) systems in retailing enable companies to tie their computers directly to their customers. When a customer's computer recognizes a low inventory, it can generate an order directly to the vendor's computer, which then schedules the product for delivery (and in some cases even schedules the product for manufacturing). Thus, order and delivery systems have become just-in-time delivery systems. In addition, customer relationship management (CRM) systems are driving the overall customer capturing and retention enterprise in many firms.

TECHNOLOGY   Social CRM

In Chapter 3 you will learn the basics of customer relationship management (CRM) and how it fits into the world of selling and sales management. At its essence, CRM provides an organization the opportunity to better manage customer relationships through comprehensive, integrated technology capabilities. Today, with the impact of social media, it is important to integrate data from these social media sites with existing customer relationship management systems.

Social CRM apps help salespeople and companies track customer activity and allow them to engage with customers quicker and more effectively. Social CRM apps are now common among salespeople. Companies' social media presence helps build their brand and build trust among customers. As customers use social media sites to interact with companies, salespeople need to be able to easily communicate with them and track their satisfaction rate.

The social CRM app market is growing, but the apps are only useful if it ties into a company's bottom line. The apps have been shown to help business objectives and increase the productivity of salespeople. Mobility is an important factor today and is considered a reason for the success of social CRM apps. As conversations between salespeople and customers move to the world of social media, salespeople must be equipped with the proper technology to best interact with and understand the customer.[5]

Chapter 3 provides a more extensive discussion of CRM and how it fits into various elements of sales management. For now, take a look at the Technology box for some insights on the status of CRM.

Leadership Is a Key Component in Sales Management Success

In the sales environment of the twenty-first century, traditional work relationships are being questioned and are often replaced with new ones. Nowhere is this more prevalent than in the relationship between salesperson and sales manager. In the traditional top-down bureaucratic style, managers were the supervisors responsible for administering the sales force. Conversely, they were held directly accountable for the actions of their salespeople. Words like *control* and *manage* were used to describe their activities.

The highly dynamic and competitive environment of the twenty-first century demands a more responsive, flexible approach to sales management. Sales forces are becoming less hierarchical with fewer layers of management while more responsibility is being given to the salesperson. Leading versus managing is an important distinction for today's successful sales manager. Effective sales management is now more often defined by how good a leader you are than how good a manager. Effective leadership of salespeople includes (1) communicating with salespeople rather than controlling them, (2) becoming a cheerleader and coach instead of a supervisor or boss, and (3) empowering salespeople to make decisions rather than directing them. Common across these items is an approach of mentoring, rather than directing, salespeople.[6] Being an effective leader requires new and different skills from the traditional manager role. One way to begin the journey toward being a good leader is summarized in the concept of servant leadership, which is discussed in the Leadership box.[7]

Sales Management Is a Global Endeavor

Innovation, technology, and leadership are pervasive themes in sales management today. Because companies now operate in a global marketplace, these themes play out on a global stage. Products are designed in one country, manufactured in another, and marketed around the world. In some cases, competitors in one part of the world are partners in another. Global suppliers have increased the importance of vendor relationships not only around the country but around the world. The internationalization of business was, for many years, considered a process of big multinational corporations. However, in today's global society even small domestic companies are doing business in international markets as a result of independent distributor relationships, trade shows, and the ability of the Internet to generate awareness and interest literally anywhere in the world.

This global focus is driven by a number of factors. As noted earlier, the ability to communicate anywhere in the world with relative ease has opened new markets. Potential customers worldwide can call, fax, or e-mail questions or orders easily. Even more significant is the realization that, for many companies, significant growth opportunities lie outside domestic markets. This is especially true in the United States as companies as diverse as DuPont, Microsoft, and Coca-Cola acknowledge that most of their growth, and consequently much of their investment over the next few years, will be outside the United States. Finally, many companies have become more international because their customers are global.

LEADERSHIP   Servant Leadership

In recent years, approaches to leadership have taken on nearly mystic qualities. One new-age approach is *servant leadership*. Robert Greenleaf, who retired in 1964 from an executive position with AT&T, spent the rest of his life writing and studying about leadership and the characteristics of leaders. Today, the Robert K. Greenleaf Center is located in Indianapolis.

Greenleaf's servant leadership is based on ten key characteristics that he viewed as central to the development of servant leaders: (1) listening, (2) empathy, (3) healing, (4) awareness, (5) persuasion, (6) conceptualization, (7) foresight, (8) stewardship, (9) commitment to the growth of people, and (10) building community. The power of the concept of servant leadership can be stated in five points:

● The servant leader takes his or her people and their work very seriously. The leader believes that the work exists for the people as much as the people exist for the work.
● The servant leader listens to his or her people and takes his or her lead from them. The leader believes that he or she will not have all the answers but that the people who are working with the customers will have the answers.
● The servant leader heals and builds trust. The leader is open with his or her people and lets them vent.
● The servant leader is self-effacing. The leader allocates the rewards and glory to his or her people.
● The servant leader sees him- or herself as a steward. The leader must have a long-term perspective and must be a visionary. The leader leads the conversations, the visions are shared, and a stronger shared vision emerges from the dialogue.

Given the complexities of modern sales organizations and their environment, sales managers can gain substantial insight from learning how to create an environment for success among their salespeople through servant leadership.[8]

All of these changes have led to dramatic transformations in the focus of personal selling and the way the sales force is managed. Diversity in the sales force has created new challenges for sales managers. In addition, managers need to understand a wide range of environmental differences (cultural, legal, behavioral) in the selling process. Indeed, a number of companies require managers to spend time overseas because they believe it is important for the individual to learn an international perspective.[9] The Innovation box provides a nice illustration of the innovations needed for a successful global selling strategy, especially from a cultural perspective.

Ethics Underlies All Selling and Sales Management Activities

Characterizing sales as trending toward more ethical behavior may be unfair to the many ethical salespeople of the past. But it is true that ethical selling practices, just like ethics in all aspects of business, is more prominent due to the seemingly endless business ethics debacles that dominate the news. For example, the U.S. government has developed Federal Sentencing Guidelines that are designed to punish firms that allow salespeople (and other employees) to engage in unethical behavior. Penalties are reduced for firms that have required ethics training and have adopted other policies that encourage ethical behavior.

Even without encouragement from the government, the increasingly long-term nature of business relationships requires higher ethical standards than did earlier transactional selling approaches. A sucker may be born every minute, but if your business depends on repeat purchase and word-of-mouth advertising, you can't sucker customers and hope to stay in business. Put another way, long-term relationships and customer loyalty are impossible to maintain in an atmosphere of distrust brought on by unethical sales approaches. Throughout this book you will notice a strong theme of highly ethical practice in selling and sales management. We encourage all sales organizations to develop a formal code of ethical conduct to attempt to engrain ethical behaviors in their organizational culture.[10]

WHAT IS INVOLVED IN SALES MANAGEMENT

Two key points should be made at the outset about sales management in the twenty-first century. First, modern companies realize that selling is an indispensable component of an effective marketing strategy. In fact, it has become popular to discuss selling as a "boardroom topic." That is, top management acknowledges the critical role of personal selling in building customer relationships, and customers have come to rely on the problem-solving capabilities of a well-trained sales force. As a result, the management of these seller–customer aspects of the firm—sales management—has become a more exciting and challenging career opportunity than ever before.

Second, managing a sales force is a *dynamic* process. Sales management programs must be formulated to respond effectively to a firm's environmental circumstances (both external and internal, or organizational, environment), and they

INNOVATION   Bridging the Culture Gap in Global Selling

To achieve sales success on a global scale, you have to begin by bridging the culture gap.

As technology and transportation make the world smaller and smaller, today's business environment calls for a multicultural selling strategy. Even if your territory is limited to the United States, you may sell to customers with cultural backgrounds very different from yours. With these customers, strong relationships come from understanding and honoring those differences, not denying them.

For instance, in certain parts of Asia, the number four is considered unlucky to a large enough extent that local companies will avoid packaging their products in groups of four. It is imperative that these different customs are embraced and accounted for if selling to these cultures is to be a success.

The approach to selling must also be adapted. While using certain types of humor or platitudes with U.S.-based customers will aid results, it may be difficult for other cultures to comprehend, so care should be taken. This is especially important when dealing with customers from countries such as Germany, where English is a strong second language for most. The temptation is to assume that, because they speak the language, they will understand the humor, which is not the case. With this particular cultural group, it is better to skip the humor and concentrate on business.

A misconception exists that assumes people from other cultures all want to be treated the same and do not want their differences identified or their culture discussed. In fact, discussing the cultural difference, and portraying a genuine interest, can help form the strong relationship that many sales professionals seek with their customers.

must be consistent with the organization's marketing strategies. At the same time, good sales management practices are essential for the successful implementation of a firm's competitive and marketing strategies. To help understand the scope of the sales management task, we define sales management as all activities, processes, and decisions involved in managing the sales function in an organization.

Managing a sales force well involves understanding the complexity of selling activities as well as the decisions involved in managing those activities. The purpose of this book is to provide you with an understanding of the role of the sales management function in marketing and the entire organization, as well as in the marketplace. In addition, the book carefully examines the activities and decisions that comprise an effective sales management program.

Selling Process

Many people have misconceptions about the selling process, the activities carried out by salespeople, and the personal characteristics necessary for a successful sales career. To complicate matters even more, various selling jobs can involve very different tasks and require different skills and abilities. Just imagine the differences involved in selling across the many divisions of a diversified company such as General Electric, which sells an amazingly wide array of products and services from light bulbs to jet engines to home appliances to financial services. Each has its own sales force and its own markets. Selling skills and requirements can vary greatly among the different businesses due to the different buying processes and needs in the various markets, as well as different levels of product complexity.

To reduce misconceptions about personal selling, and to establish a solid foundation of knowledge for our subsequent discussion of sales force management,

Chapter 2 examines buying processes and selling processes in detail. Then, Chapter 3 broadens the sales role to a more strategic level, emphasizing key aspects of customer relationship strategies.

Sales Management Process

The sales management process, or process of effective management of a company's sales force, involves three interrelated sets of decisions or processes.

1. *The formulation of a sales program.* The sales program should consider the environmental factors faced by the firm. Sales executives organize and plan the company's overall personal selling efforts and integrate these with the other elements of the firm's marketing strategy. The formulation process is represented by Part One of this book.

2. *The implementation of the sales program.* The implementation phase involves selecting appropriate sales personnel and designing and implementing approaches that will direct their efforts toward the desired objectives. The implementation process is represented by Part Two of this book.

3. *The evaluation and control of the sales program.* The evaluation phase involves developing methods for monitoring and evaluating sales force performance through appropriate metrics. Evaluation and control allows for adjustment of the sales program or the way it is implemented when performance is unsatisfactory. The evaluation and control process is represented by Part Three of this book.

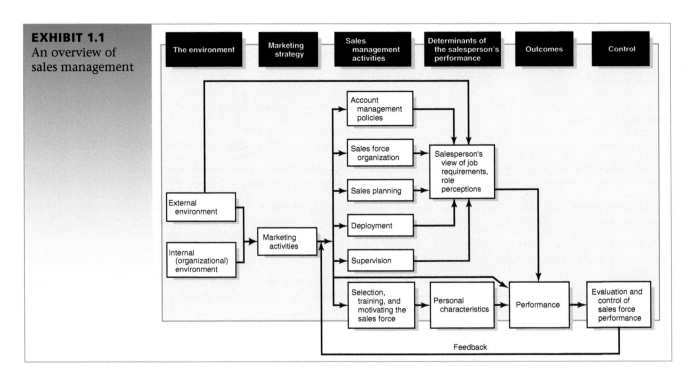

EXHIBIT 1.1
An overview of sales management

The specific activities involved in these three processes, along with the variables that influence those activities, are summarized in the model of sales management in Exhibit 1.1. This model serves as a road map for the overall sales management process: formulation, implementation, and evaluation and control of the sales program for the organization. You will be introduced to each of these three major aspects of sales management at the beginning of each of the three major parts of the book.

For now, peruse the model and get a feel for the flow. You will note that the external and internal (also known as organizational) environments flow into the other aspects of the model. Before we can begin to learn about formulation, implementation, and evaluation and control of a sales program, we first need to gain a clear understanding of the key external and internal (organizational) factors in the environment that may affect the sales manager's ability to execute the remaining aspects of the model. On the external side, the demands of potential customers and the actions of competitors are two obvious environmental factors. Other external environmental factors such as energy prices, technological advances, government regulations, and social concerns can affect a company's selling initiatives. For instance, when gasoline prices spike, you'd better believe sales managers caution their salespeople about making unnecessary trips in company cars.

On the organizational side, environmental factors such as human and financial resources, the firm's production capacity, and its expertise in research and development can either help or hinder the sales force's ability to pursue customers or expand its market share.

ENVIRONMENTAL FACTORS IMPACT SUCCESS IN SELLING

External and internal (organizational) environmental factors influence sales managers in four basic ways.

1. *Environmental forces can constrain the organization's ability to pursue certain marketing strategies or activities.* An example is when the government declares the sale of a product to be illegal or when a well-entrenched competitor makes it unattractive for the firm to enter a new market.

2. *Environmental variables, and changes in those variables over time, help determine the ultimate success or failure of marketing strategies.* The rapid growth in the number of women in the labor force in recent decades, for instance, helped ensure the success of Stouffer's Lean Cuisine, ConAgra's Healthy Choice, and other quality brands of convenient frozen entrées.

3. *Changes in the environment can create new marketing opportunities for an organization,* as when a new technology allows development of new products. The emergence of electronic commerce software, for instance, enabled HP to develop solutions to problems such as security, design, and flow of data over the Internet,

some of the more important challenges that customers face. As one customer said, "There is a lot of value in companies like HP offering to help customers put up electronic commerce sites." Not surprisingly, HP has reorganized to shift its main emphasis from printers to enterprise systems.

4. *Environmental variables are affected and changed by marketing activities*, as when new products and promotional programs help change lifestyles and social values. In view of the increased activity by consumer groups, environmentalists, and other public interest groups and agencies, marketers today must consider how proposed programs will affect the environment as well as how the environment will affect the programs.

Consequently, one of the most important—but increasingly difficult—parts of any sales manager's job is to monitor the environment, predict how it might change, and develop strategies and plans for the sales function that are suited to the environmental conditions. Because selling is but one part of the overall marketing initiatives of the firm, the sales program must be adapted to the environmental circumstances faced by the firm as a whole. Chapter 3 ties the sales manager's role to overall marketing and business planning.

EXTERNAL ENVIRONMENT

By definition, factors in the external environment are beyond the control of the individual manager; however, companies do try to influence external conditions to the extent they can through political lobbying, public relations campaigns, and the like. But for the most part, the sales manager must take the environment as it exists and adapt strategies to fit it.

Markets consist of people. As the demographic, educational, and other characteristics of the population change, market opportunities change. This also affects opportunities in business markets, since an organization's demand for goods and services is derived from the demand for its own products. Further, economic systems are becoming more open, meaning that there is ever-increasing competition from global companies. External environmental factors can affect the way a company competes globally, which will then influence how the company competes locally.

As indicated in Exhibit 1.2, variables in the external environment that affect sales and marketing may be grouped into five broad categories: (1) economic, which includes competition; (2) legal and political; (3) technological; (4) social and cultural, focused on ethics; and (5) natural.

Economic Environment

People and organizations cannot buy goods and services unless they have the money. The total potential demand for a product within a given country depends on that country's economic conditions—the amount of growth, the unemployment rate, and the level of inflation. These factors must be considered when analyzing market opportunities and developing sales forecasts. Keep in mind, though, that global economic conditions also influence many firms' ability to earn a profit. Companies as diverse as Intel, Caterpillar, and DuPont have been adversely impacted at the bottom line in their European operations due to the variability in exchange rates between the U.S. dollar and the euro.

A second aspect of the economic environment is the existing distribution structure in an industry. This includes the number, types, and availability of wholesalers, retailers, and other intermediaries a firm might use to distribute its product. Much of a firm's personal selling effort may be directed at trying to persuade such intermediaries to stock and provide marketing support for the company's products.

Understanding Competitors

Another critical economic variable is the amount of competition in the firm's industry—both the number of competing firms and their relative strengths in the marketplace. Ideally, a company's marketing and sales programs should be designed to gain a differential advantage over competitors. For example, rather than trying to compete with the low prices of foreign competitors such as Komatsu, Caterpillar has been successful in the heavy construction equipment business by providing superior product quality and excellent service, while charging prices as much as

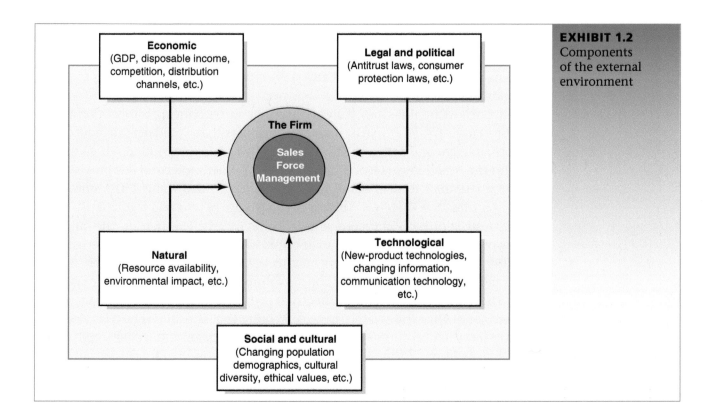

EXHIBIT 1.2
Components of the external environment

10 to 20 percent higher than its competitors. Salespeople go head to head with competitors on a daily basis; as a result, the sales force is often the first to observe changes in competitive strategy and activity. One of the critical issues is getting information from the sales force to strategic planners so that the company can act on those observations. Reports that detail competitive activity, such as analyses of lost sales, can summarize competitive activity for sales and marketing management. Sophisticated customer relationship management (CRM) software systems can greatly aid in facilitating information collection, analysis, and dissemination.

Salespeople are particularly important when exploring market opportunities in other countries. Given the added risks involved when selling in a foreign country, accurate and timely market information may be more important than in domestic marketing. In many cases, foreign salespeople are the only link the company has to the customer. Companies with international sales forces survey their salespeople, with either formal written surveys or informal telephone surveys, in order to assess foreign markets.[11]

Global Legal and Political Environment

Many of the changes in society's values are eventually reflected in new laws and government regulations—that is, where the social–cultural–ethical environment intersects the legal–political environment. In recent years, the number of laws regulating the conduct of business, including personal selling, has increased dramatically at all levels of government. Three broad categories of laws are particularly relevant to sales programs: (1) antitrust, (2) consumer protection, and (3) equal employment opportunity. These laws vary greatly by country and can be very complex. Salespeople themselves can hardly be expected to know all of the legal details, hence most sales organizations of any size employ HR and legal experts to advise sales managers on these matters.

Antitrust laws are aimed primarily at preserving and enhancing competition among firms in an industry. They restrict marketing practices that would tend to reduce competition and give one firm a monopoly through unfair competition. To give you a sense for the issues, several U.S. antitrust and consumer protection law provisions of particular relevance to sales management are outlined in Exhibit 1.3. A number of other countries have their own version of these types of laws and regulations.

The restrictions on anticompetitive behavior spelled out in the antitrust laws apply to firms selling goods or services to intermediaries, business users, or ultimate consumers. When a firm sells to consumer markets, however, it faces additional restrictions imposed by consumer protection laws at all levels of government. These laws are aimed more directly at protecting consumer welfare by setting standards of quality and safety. They also require that consumers be provided with accurate information to use in making purchase decisions. Since personal selling is one means of providing consumers with information, many laws requiring full disclosure and prohibiting deceptive or misleading information have a direct impact on selling activities.

Misrepresentation of a company's product by a salesperson can have both ethical and legal consequences, whether the salesperson is dealing with end-user consumers or organizational customers. Many salespeople are unaware that they assume legal obligations every time they approach a customer. By making certain statements, they can embroil their companies in a lawsuit and ruin the very business relationship they are trying to establish. But recent court cases around the world have held firms liable for multimillion-dollar judgments for misrepresentation or breach of warranty due to statements made by their salespeople, particularly when the sale involved big-ticket, high-tech products or services.

Over the past few years, so-called "no-call" lists have become prevalent, blocking the ability for firms to do telemarketing to customers who choose to be listed. In some countries, severe fines are imposed on sales organizations that violate these no-call lists. While this legal development may not directly affect salespeople in business settings through personal contact, because telemarketing and teleselling are often used to support in-person selling approaches, many companies have had to adjust their overall sales programs to comply with these regulations.

One other type of legislation has a direct effect on sales managers as they attempt to implement their sales programs: equal employment opportunity laws. It is unlawful to discriminate against a person in either hiring or promotion because of race, religion, nationality, sex, or age. For this reason, certain types of aptitude tests are illegal if they are culturally or sexually biased or if they are not valid predictors of a person's job performance. The legal aspects of recruiting and selecting sales representatives, as well as other issues related to the increasing cultural diversity of the labor force, are examined in Chapter 9.

Technological Environment

As mentioned earlier, technology not only influences sales strategies, it often drives the firm's capability to effectively sell. Of course, the impact of technology is obvious with companies like IBM and HP. But in the generally low-tech world of propane sales, Blue Rhino is one company that has used technology to capture significant market share. By improving the processes of filling and storing tanks, the company has begun to dominate a market that was largely populated by small, independent dealers. In one *King of the Hill* episode, Hank Hill's propane company has to reduce its workforce due to the loss in sales to the local MegaLo Mart. While the *King of the Hill* plot may seem made up, that is exactly what Blue Rhino has done. Blue Rhino dominates by distributing through the country's largest and fastest-growing retailers (Walmart, Home Depot, and Lowe's), a distribution strategy made possible by better technology.

The most obvious impact of the technological environment on marketing is in providing opportunities for product development. Technology advances have been occurring at a rapidly increasing rate, and new products are accounting for an increasing percentage of total sales in many industries. For example, historically at 3M more than half of the current sales volume is generated by products that were not in existence five years ago. Most analysts believe the importance of new

EXHIBIT 1.3
Selected U.S.
antitrust and
consumer
protection laws

Antitrust Provisions

Conspiracies among competing firms to *control their prices*, or to *allocate markets* among themselves, are per se illegal under the Sherman Act.

The Robinson-Patman Act prohibits a firm and its representatives from *discriminating in the prices or services* offered to competing customers. The major purpose of this law is to protect smaller customers from being placed at a competitive disadvantage by "key account" programs or price promotions that offer special incentives to larger buyers. However, the law does allow a marketer to grant discounts to larger buyers based on savings in the costs of manufacturing or distributing the product. Thus, some quantity discounts are legal.

Tying agreements, where a seller forces a buyer to purchase one product to gain the right to purchase another, are illegal under the Clayton and Sherman Acts. A personal computer manufacturer, for example, cannot force a customer to agree to buy extra drives, a scanner, a printer, and so forth as a precondition for buying the computer itself.

Reciprocal dealing arrangements, the "I'll buy from you if you buy from me" type of agreements, are illegal where the effect is to injure competition. Such arrangements do tend to be anticompetitive because large companies—which are large buyers as well as large suppliers—tend to have an advantage over smaller firms.

The Federal Trade Commission Act prohibits *unfair methods of competition* in general. Thus, deceptive product claims, interfering with the actions of a competitor's sales representative, and other unfair acts are illegal.

Consumer Protection Provisions

The Fair Packaging and Labeling Act makes *unfair or deceptive packaging or labeling* of certain consumer commodities illegal.

The Truth-in-Lending Act requires *full disclosure of all finance charges* on consumer credit agreements.

State *cooling-off* laws allow consumers to cancel contracts signed with door-to-door sellers within a limited number of days after agreeing to such contracts.

The Federal Trade Commission requires that door-to-door salespeople who work for companies engaged in interstate commerce clearly announce their purpose when making calls on potential customers.

Many cities and towns have so-called Green River Ordinances, which require all door-to-door salespeople to obtain a license.

products and services to the marketing success of many firms will continue to accelerate. Rapid development of new products requires adjusting a firm's sales programs. New sales plans must be formulated, the sales representatives must be retrained, and, in some cases, new reps must be hired.

Advancing technology also affects sales management in more direct ways. Improvements in transportation, communications, and data processing are changing the way sales territories are defined, sales reps are deployed, and sales performance is evaluated and controlled in many companies. New communication technologies—together with the escalating costs of a traditional field sales call—are changing how the personal selling function is carried out.

The satchel full of samples has given way to the laptop computer; and telemarketing, teleconferencing, and computerized reordering have replaced the face-to-face sales call in a growing number of situations. Consequently, the nature of many sales jobs—and the role of the sales manager in supervising the sales force—has changed dramatically in recent years. We will explore the impact of these new technologies in highlighted feature boxes throughout this book.

Social and Cultural Environment: Ethics

The values of a society affect marketing and sales programs in a variety of ways. Firms develop new products in response to trends in consumer tastes and preferences. In the United States, the well-documented demographic trends of an aging society, greater influx of minorities as a percentage of total population, two-income households, greater mobility, and ever-increasing desire for more leisure time and more convenience-oriented products all have greatly affected selling.

In twenty-first-century sales management, nowhere is the impact of societal values more important than in the way social values set the standards for ethical behavior. Ethics is more than simply a matter of complying with the laws and regulations we will discuss later in this section. That is, a particular action may be legal but not ethical. For instance, when a salesperson makes extreme, unsubstantiated statements such as "Our product runs rings around Brand X," the rep may be engaging in legal puffery to make a sale, but many salespeople (and their customers) view such little white lies as unethical.

Ethics is concerned with the development of moral standards by which actions and situations can be judged. It focuses on those actions that may result in actual or potential harm of some kind (e.g., economic, mental, physical) to an individual, group, or organization. Thus, ethics is more proactive than the law. Ethical standards attempt to anticipate and avoid social problems, whereas most laws and regulations emerge only after the negative consequences of an action become apparent.[12]

Two sets of ethical dilemmas are of particular concern to sales managers. The first set is embedded in the manager's dealings with the salespeople. Ethical issues involved in relationships between a sales manager and the sales force include such things as fairness and equal treatment of all social groups in hiring and promotion, respect for the individual in supervisory practices and training programs, and fairness and integrity in the design of sales territories, assignment of quotas, and determination of compensation and incentive rewards. Ethical issues pervade nearly all aspects of sales force management.

The second set of ethical issues arises from the interactions between salespeople and their customers. These issues only indirectly involve the sales manager because the manager cannot always directly observe or control the actions of every member of the sales force. But managers have a responsibility to establish standards of ethical behavior for their subordinates, communicate them clearly, and enforce them vigorously.

One might ask why a manager should be responsible for providing moral guidance to subordinates. One might even question whether setting and enforcing standards of ethical conduct for the sales force infringes on the freedom of its individual members and their right to make their own moral choices. While such questions may be legitimate topics for philosophical debate, there is a compelling and practical organizational reason for a firm to impose ethical standards to guide employees' dealings with customers: Unethical selling practices make buyers reluctant to deal with a supplier and are likely to result in the loss of sales and profits over time.

Not all customers or competing suppliers adhere to the same ethical standards. As a result, salespeople sometimes feel pressure to engage in actions that are inconsistent with what they believe to be right—in terms of either personal values or formal company standards. Such pressures arise because the sales reps, or sometimes their managers, believe a questionable action is necessary to close a sale or maintain parity with the competition. This point was illustrated by a survey of 59 top sales executives concerning commercial bribery—attempts to influence a potential customer by giving gifts or kickbacks. While nearly two-thirds of the executives considered bribes unethical and did not want to pay them, 88 percent also felt that not paying bribes might put their firms at a competitive disadvantage.

Uncertainty about what to do in such situations—often due to a lack of direction from management—may lead to job stress, poor sales performance, and unhappy customers. Many selling situations involving ethical issues are not addressed by management directives, and many sales personnel want more explicit guidelines to help them resolve such issues. Management can help salespeople avoid the stress and inconsistent performance associated with ethical dilemmas by developing written policies that address problem situations.

The important thing, however, is not just to have a formal policy but to have one that is helpful to the sales force. Such policies should provide clear guidelines for decision making and action so that employees facing similar situations will handle them in a way consistent with the organization's goals. To further reduce uncertainty, policies must be clearly communicated to both sales personnel and customers. The most effective way for managers to influence the ethical performance of their salespeople, however, is to lead by example. Formal policies do not have much impact when top management gives lip service to one set of standards while practicing another. Sales managers who expect ethical behavior from their employees should apply high ethical standards to their own actions and decisions.

The level of ethical standards in the sales force ultimately is a reflection of the integrity of the firm, as manifest in its culture and value system.[13]

Natural Environment

Nature influences demand for many products. Of course, natural disasters such as tornados and floods can influence demand for building products and the like. But unseasonable weather can damage or enhance sales, depending on the type of product. Even one snowy Friday during a peak holiday sales season can negatively impact sales for those retailers that rely on the date's usual high customer traffic.

The natural environment is an important consideration in the development of marketing and sales plans. The natural environment is the source of all the raw materials and energy resources needed to make, package, promote, and distribute a product. Over the past three decades, firms in many industries—such as concrete, aluminum, plastics, and synthetic fibers—have encountered resource or energy shortages that have forced them to limit sales of their products. Some of these shortages in developed nations are partly attributable to the extreme growth rate in developing areas of the globe, such as China. One might assume that sales representatives could take life easy under such circumstances, letting customers come to them for badly needed goods. But the sales force often has to work harder during product shortages, and well-formulated account management policies become even more crucial for the firm's success.

During such periods, the sales organization may be engaged in demarketing of part or all of its product line. The sales force is often required to help administer rationing programs, which allocate scarce supplies according to each customer's purchase history. Since shortages are usually temporary, though, sellers have to be sensitive to their customers' problems so they will not lose customers when the shortage is over. Consequently, account management policies must treat all customers fairly, minimize conflict, and maintain the firm's competitive position for the future.

Growing social concern about the possible negative impacts of products and production processes on the natural environment also has important implications for marketing and sales programs. This is increasingly true for firms that sell to organizations as well as for manufacturers of consumer goods. For instance, countries in the European Economic Community have passed legislation requiring manufacturers to take back, and either reuse or recycle, materials used in packaging and shipping their products.[14]

ETHICAL MOMENT **Ethics and the Natural Environment**

One of the key challenges facing everyone today is how to best manage the environment and the earth's limited natural resources. Pollution, climate change, and other environmental challenges require individuals, companies, and countries to make difficult choices. As companies develop and implement a strategic environmental strategy, the impact can be felt throughout the organization. From the office to the production floor companies look to be more energy efficient, more "green," and better resource managers.

Sales may not spring to mind when considering the impact of environmental issues on an organization, but in fact a company's environmental strategy impacts the sales force and, more specifically, sales managers in many ways. For example, as organizations look to reduce their carbon footprint they seek alternatives to having a salesperson use cars and other transportation to meet with the customer. In some cases, outside sales forces are even reduced and replaced with call centers and inside salespeople. Another issue is the concerted effort to make and sell products that are more environmentally friendly. It is the salesperson's job to create a value proposition that reflects not only the product's inherent advantages and benefits but also its environmental impact. Increasingly, companies are asking salespeople to provide an environmental impact assessment of their products before making a purchase decision. These kinds of changes, as well as many others, reflect the impact of environmental issues on strategy and, more specifically, the sales force.

A focus on the natural environment will continue to influence the role of selling and salespeople, thus managers need to understand the many environmental issues facing the company. At the same time, sales managers must train their sales force to adequately deal with customers' environmental concerns.

Question to Ponder:

• Can you identify other environmental issues that impact the sales force and sales managers?

INTERNAL (ORGANIZATIONAL) ENVIRONMENT

The policies, resources, and talents of the organization also make up a very important part of the marketer's environment. Sales managers may have some influence over higher-level organizational factors due to their participation in planning processes, but in the short run, sales programs must be designed to fit within organizational situations and limitations. The variables in the internal (organizational) environment can be grouped into six broad categories: (1) goals, objectives, and culture; (2) human resources; (3) financial resources; (4) production and supply chain capabilities; (5) service capabilities; and (6) research and development and technological capabilities. These variables are portrayed in Exhibit 1.4.

Goals, Objectives, and Culture

Successful management of customer relationships begins with top management's specification of a company mission and objectives that create a customer-centric organization. As the company mission and objectives change, customer management approaches must be adjusted accordingly. A well-defined mission together with a successful corporate history and top management's values and beliefs leads to development of a strong corporate culture. Such cultures shape the attitudes and actions of employees and help determine the kinds of plans, policies, and procedures salespeople and their managers can implement.

EXHIBIT 1.4
Components of the internal environment

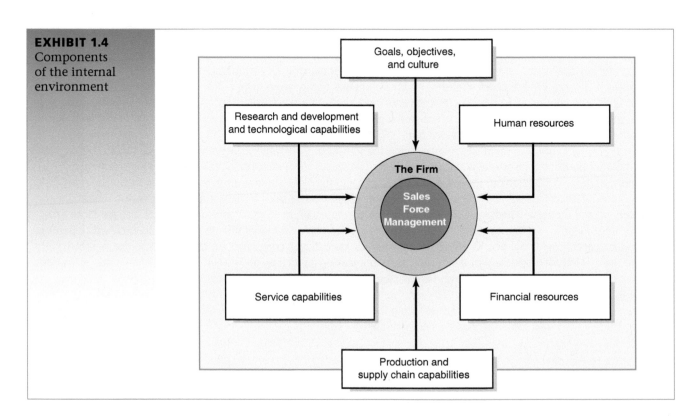

We have already mentioned the central role of ethics and legal considerations in selling today. Much of what drives ethical behavior in sales organizations is the tone set by upper management, as well as the overall culture of the firm.

Human Resources

Modern sales organizations are highly complex and dynamic enterprises, as are their customers' firms. The sheer number of people in many sales organizations, together with the widely varying needs in terms of key success factors in relationship selling creates challenges. In view of the difficulties involved in recruiting highly qualified people for sales positions and the often-lengthy training programs needed to bring new salespeople up to speed on knowledge and skills, it is often difficult to expand a sales force rapidly to take advantage of new products or growing markets. In some cases, however, it may be possible for a firm to compensate for a lack of knowledgeable employees by utilizing outside agencies or specialists on a fee-for-service or commission basis. For example, many companies use distributors when entering new markets, particularly foreign markets, because entering the market can be accomplished so much more quickly by utilizing preexisting sales forces.

Financial Resources

An organization's financial strength influences many aspects of its customer relationship initiatives. It can constrain the firm's ability to develop new value-adding products as well as the size of its promotional budget and sales force. Companies sometimes must take drastic measures, such as merging with a larger firm, to obtain the financial resources necessary to realize their full potential in the marketplace. For example, in the 2000s P&G and Gillette's merger in the highly competitive consumer health products sector provided the latter's product line the benefits of the more extensive global supply chain expertise of the former. Often selling firms and buying firms will form their own partnerships and alliances that create financial benefits for both.

Production and Supply Chain Capabilities

The organization's production capacity, the technology and equipment available in its plants, and even the location of its production facilities can influence the relationship selling initiative. A company may be prevented from expanding its product line or moving into new geographic areas because it does not have the capacity to serve increased demand or because transportation costs make the product's price uncompetitive. Vendors doing business with Walmart are expected to fulfill orders within 24 hours and to deliver the goods to the Walmart warehouses within a two-hour assigned appointment window. Suppliers that don't meet this requirement pay Walmart for every dollar of lost margin. It is no wonder Walmart's vendors are willing to invest the necessary capital to tie their information systems directly in with Walmart's systems so the whole ordering and fullfillment process can be handled seamlessly and at maximum speed. As another example of supply chain efficiency but on the e-commerce side, CEO Jeff Bezos at amazon.com developed a network of distribution centers nationwide long before Amazon's sales volume was sufficient to financially support the warehouse capacity, principally because he wanted to ensure seamless distribution and service after the sale and avoid inventory stockouts.

Service Capabilities

Delivering a high level of service quality is an important organizational capability. Firms that provide great service typically enjoy a strong competitive advantage in the marketplace and make it difficult both for (1) other firms to compete for the same customers and (2) customers to switch to competitor sales organizations, often despite price advantages competitors may have.[15]

Research and Development (R&D) and Technological Capabilities

An organization's technological and engineering expertise is a major factor in determining whether it will be an industry leader or follower in both the development of value-adding products and high-quality service delivery. Excellence in engineering and design can also serve as a major promotional appeal in a firm's marketing and sales programs, as customers are attracted to innovators and industry leaders. Most companies are investing heavily in technology, particularly technology that can help meet relationship selling objectives. In such cases, the firm's salespeople can communicate the R&D and technological sophistication to customers as important value-adding aspects of the company and its products. This capability helps avoid the trap of overrelying on price to get the sale.

SUMMARY

Sales organizations and their managers have been affected by a number of important changes in recent years. It is critical for students of selling and sales management to fully understand these trends and how they affect the success of the sales effort. In this book, we identify and develop three key themes throughout: innovation, technology, and leadership. Along with these themes, we identify important global and ethical issues for twenty-first-century sales managers.

Effective management requires a solid understanding of the activities one is trying to manage. Unfortunately, many people have misconceptions about the selling process, the activities carried out by salespeople, and the personal characteristics necessary for a successful career in professional sales. In part, these misconceptions arise because different types of selling jobs involve different kinds of tasks and require different skills and abilities from the people who do them.

Sales management involves three interrelated processes: (1) formulation of a sales program, (2) implementation of the sales program, and (3) evaluation and control of the sales program. An overarching model of sales management was presented for students' initial perusal in this introductory chapter. Each major section of the book elaborates one process. The remaining parts of this book describe the variables and sales management activities involved in each of these processes: Part One is focused on formulation, Part Two on implementation, and Part Three on evaluation and control.

Environmental factors that can impact sales management are grouped into the two broad categories of external and internal (organizational) environments. The external environment includes the following elements: (1) economic, which includes competition; (2) legal and political; (3) technological; (4) social and cultural, focused on ethics; and (5) natural. The internal environment includes these elements related to the organization itself: (1) goals, objectives, and culture; (2) human resources; (3) financial resources; (4) production and supply chain capabilities; (5) service capabilities; and (6) research and development and technological capabilities. Gaining a thorough and accurate picture of these environmental influencers is essential to successful sales management in the twenty-first century.

KEY TERMS

transactional selling	external environment	internal (organizational)
relationship selling	*economic*	environment
leading versus managing	*legal and political*	corporate culture
sales management	*technological*	
sales management process	*social and cultural*	
formulation	*natural*	
implementation	ethics	
evaluation and control	demarketing	

BREAKOUT QUESTIONS

1. Does the Internet replace the need for salespeople? In what situations is the Internet most likely to replace salespeople? What characteristics of a situation would make the Internet least likely to replace salespeople?

2. A number of organizations that did not consider marketing part of their business activities in the past have found the need to begin to market their services. Nowhere is this more prevalent than in the nonprofit community. While not "selling" a product or service, public service organizations such as the Red Cross have developmental officers who market the organization in the community. How might you "sell" a public service organization in the community? What is different about this versus selling for a for-profit enterprise? What would be your goals and how would you accomplish them?

3. Salespeople are also called *sales representatives*. Define the term *representative*. Whom does the salesperson represent? Why is it important to recognize the different groups that salespeople represent? How does this recognition of who is represented influence sales management?

4. What do you think the differences would be in the selling process for the following products and services? How would managing the sales process differ for each?

   - Selling Planter's Peanuts to your grocer.
   - Selling Planter's Peanuts to Southwest Airlines to be given to its customers.
   - Selling telecommunications equipment costing $1 to $2 million to the U.S. government.
   - Selling telecommunications equipment costing $1 to $2 million to General Electric.
   - Selling five-year leases on prime retail space in Beverly Hills.

5. Changes in the technological environment have the potential to significantly affect the activities of the sales force. Automation can offer the sales force a competitive advantage—if the sales force is motivated to use computers and other technological methods that are part of automation. What steps should management adopt to ensure that the sales force buys into the company's automation system? Especially, what can the sales organization do to promote technology use by more senior salespeople (senior in age, that is)?

6. Ethical Question. Describe the typical salesperson as illustrated in movies, books, and television shows. Why does that image exist as the stereotypical salesperson (be specific)? What role does ethics play in perpetuating the stereotype? Whose responsibility is it to see that a company's code of ethics is carried out?

LEADERSHIP CHALLENGE: THE NEW KID ON THE BLOCK

Grace Hart had established herself as an exceptional salesperson at Digital Medical Instruments (DMI). Only seven years out of college, she had become a sales manager at DMI; then Medical Imaging Technologies (MIT) sought her out to become one of five regional sales managers. MIT was a much larger company than DMI, and Grace knew this was a great opportunity. After several weeks of considering all the options, she took the job at MIT.

She faced several challenges as she arrived for her first day at MIT. Although she had experience in medical imaging equipment, she was not familiar with the specifics of MIT's product line or customers. More significant, Grace did not know many of MIT's sales force, including the 60 salespeople or the three district sales managers in her region. Sales in this region had not been keeping pace with the growth in other parts of the country, and senior management at MIT believed it was time for major changes. They had passed over the district sales managers and gone outside the company to hire Grace.

Grace is considering her first moves at MIT. She knows there is much to learn, and she also knows senior management is expecting sales to increase in her region. As "the new kid on the block," she knows that everyone will be evaluating her. People will be watching to assess her strengths and weaknesses. Salespeople and managers want to know what kind of boss Grace will be. Senior management expects things to improve in the region quickly and have given Grace a great deal of latitude to make whatever changes she feels are necessary. Much is riding on how Grace handles this new job. Her ability to manage the sales force effectively is critical to her success.

Questions

1. You are Grace Hart. What are the first three things you would want to learn about the sales environment at MIT?

2. Consider the elements of sales force management talked about in this chapter. What area of sales management do you think would be *most difficult* for Grace to learn about as "the new kid on the block"?

3. What advice would you give to Grace on her first day at MIT?

ROLE-PLAY: INVENTRON PHARMACEUTICALS

Situation

Karen Tedesco just returned from a three-day trip and picked up a voice mail in her home office from Cindy Cherry, regional sales manager for Inventron Pharmaceuticals. Karen is the district sales manager for the states of Oklahoma, Arkansas, Texas, and Louisiana. Cindy is in charge of all of Inventron's operations west of the Mississippi River. Inventron is a relatively small, specialty pharmaceutical manufacturer with production facilities in Morristown, New Jersey. Its products focus on an array of medicines for the dog and cat market, and its primary customers are veterinarians. Throughout the United States, Inventron has two sales regions, 12 sales districts, and 124 salespeople.

Cindy's message presents a nice opportunity for Karen to help Inventron with some planning for next year's business. Inventron's VP of sales, Hugh Butts, has delegated the task of developing an external environmental analysis to Cindy but with the caveat that she bring one of her best district managers into the process. Cindy has selected Karen for this role. The instructions are for Cindy and Karen to individually prepare a list of the external environmental factors they believe will impact the small animal pharmaceutical business next year and explain why each factor is important and how it might affect business. Then Cindy will travel from the regional office in Denver to Karen's office in Dallas to meet, compare their lists, and come to concensus about what to send to Hugh as input on the plan.

Characters in the Role-Play

Karen Tedesco, district manager for Inventron Pharmaceuticals
Cindy Cherry, regional manager for Inventron Pharmaceuticals (Karen's boss)

Assignment

Break into pairs, with one student playing each character. It doesn't matter what the actual gender mix of your pair is. First, work separately to come up with a list of external environmental factors likely to impact Inventron and its industry over the next year, why each factor is important, and how it might affect business. Then get together and role-play the meeting between Karen and Cindy. Share your lists, being certain you discuss each of the proposed factors. After discussing each factor, come to a concensus on a final list of factors that you would be comfortable forwarding to the VP of sales.

MINICASE: iTEAM, INC.

iTeam, Inc. is a high-tech company based in Walnut Creek, California (26 miles northeast of San Francisco), that produces, markets, and sells computer systems, computer peripherals, and other consumer electronic products to corporate customers and electronics retailers. iTeam, formed as an entrepreneurial start-up by CEO Andrew Taylor along with several of his classmates from business school, has had a charmed life so far. With aggressive pricing and a tremendous internal research and development group, iTeam has grown exponentially in its first five years of existence and has customers throughout the United States. However, a more challenging reality has begun to set in.

At first, iTeam sold its products only locally and on a relatively small scale. But now that it has expanded to selling globally, it is in direct competition with larger, global firms. Because of manufacturing and supply chain efficiencies, these competitors offer equal or lower prices than iTeam with greater product diversity and more value-added services. Although iTeam's past success has been based on lower-than-market prices, it now finds that its costs have increased and that profit margins have shrunk to the point that it cannot price its products any lower.

In addition, sales have been difficult to predict because the high-tech market has fluctuated and corporate high-tech spending has been erratic. Although the high-tech economy has been forecast to increase in the coming two years, Andrew is skeptical.

iTeam has attempted to keep costs low by establishing call centers in India and Ireland and obtaining most of its supply components from China. Although this overseas outsourcing has reduced costs, unfortunately it has also reduced product quality. The firm has also come under fire in the media for laying off U.S. employees in favor of outsourcing the work to foreign workers, and iTeam's board of directors is pressuring Andrew to be more socially responsible in this area.

To further complicate matters, it has come to Andrew's attention that the Environmental Protection Agency has proposed regulations that will greatly restrict levels of lead and mercury levels in electronics products and that will impose disposal obligations on producers of electronic goods.

Andrew thinks the answer to iTeam's growing pains is to expand sales by selling to customers in Europe and Asia. However, such an expansion will require an investment in an expanded supply chain, including new distribution channels and the development of relationships with new customers and suppliers. It will also require changes in iTeam's manufacturing system in order to increase the firm's production capacity.

Most important, iTeam's sales force may need to be developed as well. iTeam grew so quickly that it never established a formal sales program. Consistent with Andrew's personal philosophy of "Who says there is no 'I' in 'team'?", iTeam has been pretty informal in managing its sales force, deferring mostly to aggressive individual salesperson effort and commission-based pay. Also, because of iTeam's former price advantage, the sales reps have never really had to develop relationships with customers or retail partners to generate sales—price seemed to be enough to keep customers satisfied.

Andrew Taylor and iTeam have much to consider as they determine how to move into the future.

Questions

1. What aspects of the external environment are most likely to affect iTeam, Inc.'s future planning, and what impact might each factor have?

2. What aspects of the internal (organizational) environment at iTeam are most likely to affect its future planning, and what impact might each factor have?

3. What advice can you give to Andrew Taylor with respect to iTeam's future sales program? In your opinion, what steps should he take, given the external environment and the company's current circumstances?

PART 1

Formulation of a Sales Program

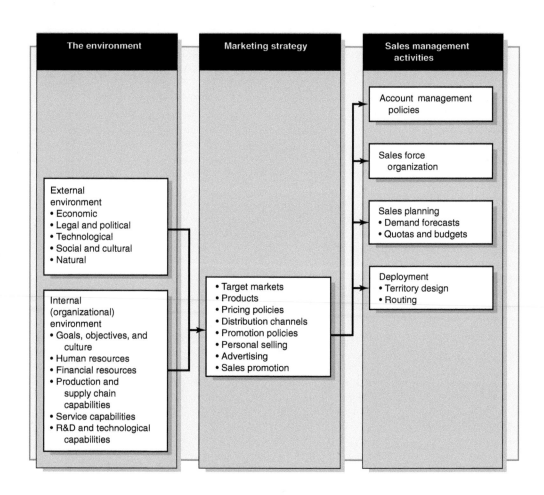

The Process of Selling and Buying

LEARNING OBJECTIVES

This chapter focuses on the process of selling and buying in the organizational marketplace. Many factors are driving the world of professional selling toward a relationship-based approach. This transformation has created a challenging, invigorating, and rewarding environment in which to pursue a career in selling.

Knowledge of the drivers of change in selling, the key success factors required in selling, the activities salespeople perform on the job, and the different kinds of selling jobs available go a long way toward helping a person make a decision if he or she might like to pursue selling as a career path. Successful salespeople always understand the roles that different individuals within the client company play in moving the relationship along, the buying decision process used by their clients, and how their clients go about making different types of purchases and how those differences impact the salesperson's approach to the client.

After reading this chapter you should be able to

- Recognize the key drivers of change in selling and sales management.
- Understand the best practices in selling that lead to exceeding customer expectations.
- Explain the historical basis for stereotypical views of selling in society.
- Point out a variety of reasons why sales jobs can be highly satisfying.
- Identify and explain key success factors for salesperson performance.
- Discuss and give examples of different types of selling jobs.
- List and explain the role of various participants in an organizational buying center.
- Describe the relationship between buying centers and selling centers and the nature of team selling.
- Outline the stages in organizational buyer decision making.
- Point out the nature of different organizational buying situations.

DRIVERS OF CHANGE IN SELLING AND SALES MANAGEMENT

The nature of selling has changed. Sales organizations are being reinvented to better address the needs of the changing marketplace. Six critical drivers of change have been identified in reinventing sales organizations so they can compete successfully in today's selling environment:

1. *Building long-term relationships with customers.* This includes assessing customer value and focusing on high-priority customers.

2. *Creating sales organizational structures that are more nimble and adaptable to the needs of different customer groups.* To compete effectively today, firms must be willing and able to customize the sales effort to meet different customers' preferred ways of doing business. Flexibility is a key asset of modern sales organizations.

3. *Gaining greater job ownership and commitment from salespeople.* This can be accomplished by removing functional barriers within the organization and by leveraging the team experience.

4. *Shifting sales management style from commanding to coaching.* Or, put another way, today's sales managers must create an environment that allows salespeople to use their talents and abilities to successfully secure, build, and maintain relationships with profitable customers. While item 3 implies that in the past, organizational structure was a common stumbling block to salesperson success, item 4 recognizes that sales managers themselves also are often guilty of blocking successful relationship selling. For selling to change, management of salespeople must also change accordingly.

5. *Leveraging available technology for sales success.* Clearly, salespeople today have more types of technological tools at their disposal than ever before. The sales organizations that make the best use of technology will have a strong competitive edge over others.

6. *Better integrating salesperson performance evaluation.* A real weakness of many sales organizations in the past was in how they evaluated and ultimately rewarded their salespeople. The move from transactional selling to relationship selling, coupled with the use of selling teams and a more coaching style of management, necessitates rethinking the performance evaluation and reward process for sales organizations. In Chapters 12 and 13, this critical topic will be discussed in the context of developing a more seamless performance management system that incorporates the full range of activities and outcomes relevant within sales jobs today.[1]

OVERVIEW OF SELLING AS A CAREER

This chapter provides you with important insights to better understand the world of contemporary selling. First, you will have the opportunity to take a look at selling as a potential career path, including the many attractive aspects that explain why selling is such a popular and rewarding job. Sales jobs in the twenty-first century contribute significantly to the world economy and of course to the success of individual firms in the marketplace. But like any other position, misunderstandings exist among people that have never been in selling about what the jobs are really like—and many of these misperceptions are based on stereotypes about selling that are best put out in the open and discussed right now. Then, you will learn about factors that can make one salesperson more successful than another, as well as what activities salespeople perform and different types of sales positions. Finally, we turn the tables and you get to see what organizational buying is all about.

Let's begin by dispelling some myths and mistaken impressions about selling in general. This is a true fact: Well-run selling initiatives can produce enthusiasm and job satisfaction for salespeople, yet despite this, recruiting and keeping excellent salespeople can be very difficult. One reason is that, unfortunately, some college students hold certain negative attitudes toward selling as a career because they think of the field based on old styles of selling where salespeople used hard-sell techniques to get buyers to do things they didn't really want to do and buy products they didn't really need.

Where do these notions come from? For one thing, the old style of selling is embodied in icons of media through the decades including plays, movies, and television shows. Probably the most famous play by an American author is Arthur Miller's Pulitzer Prize–winning *Death of a Salesman,* which most students encounter sometime during their high school or college English courses, Miller immortalized old-style selling through the play's principal character, Willie Loman (as in "low man" on the totem pole of life). Poor Willie left for long sales trips on the road at the beginning of every week, returned a tired and disheartened peddler at the end of every week, and worked his customers based "on a smile and a shoeshine." His family was collapsing in his absence, his self-esteem was at rock bottom, his customers were defecting to other vendors at an alarming rate, and there seemed to be no hope of improvement for Willie on any front. This awful image, while certainly dramatic, has emblazoned on every schoolkid who ever read or acted in the play a sad, demoralizing image of selling.

A classic movie that also dramatically reinforces negative stereotypes about salespeople is 1992's *Glengarry Glen Ross,* adapted from David Mamet's Pulitzer Prize–winning play of the same name. It features a stellar cast, including Al Pacino and Jack Lemmon, and has become an incredible cult favorite as a pay-per-view. In the movie, times are tough at Premier Properties, a boiler-room real estate sales company. Shelly "The Machine" Levene and Dave Moss are veteran salesmen, but only Ricky Roma is on a hot sales streak. Sales leads for the new Glengarry property development could turn everything around, but the front office is holding the leads back until the "losers" prove themselves on the street. Then someone decides to steal the Glengarry leads and leave everyone else wondering who did it. The verbal exchanges among these men desperate to make sales are riveting and very scary to someone interested in sales as a possible career.

Then in the 2000s came the TV show *The Office,* which started in Britain and was exported to the U.S. The "office" that is the subject of the show is a branch of a fictional old-school office supply sales firm Dunder Mifflin. The salespeople use all forms of gimmicks and hard-sell tactics in a desperate struggle to try to stay ahead of the big box retailers like Staples, OfficeMax, and Office Depot as well as the general trend toward a paperless office. If you're into retro TV, you can catch reruns of the classic *WKRP in Cincinnati,* about a lovable cast of characters employed at a third-rate rock-and-roll radio station. One character who was arguably not so lovable was station sales manager Herb Tarleck. Herb was played as a back-slapping, white-shoe-and-polyester-suit-wearing buffoon who exhibited questionable ethics and made sales only through pure dumb luck. Google "Herb Tarleck WKRP" for fun and you'll see what we're talking about!

These images of salespeople have become embedded in the global culture. It is true that some unprofessional and unethical salespeople always have existed and always will exist (just as unprofessional people exist in any profession—witness the crisis in accounting, banking, and housing during the recent global recession). In selling, we seem to have to prove our value to society just a little more than in other professions. But the effort is worth it to those who love the profession, because there's no doubt about it—sales jobs are important to society, they're challenging and invigorating to those who occupy them, and they are also potentially one of the most rewarding career tracks available.

Why Sales Jobs Are So Rewarding

For most professional salespeople, it is precisely the complexity and challenge of their jobs that motivate them to perform at a high level and provide a sense of satisfaction with their choice of careers. A number of satisfaction surveys over the years have found generally high levels of job satisfaction among professional salespeople across a broad cross section of firms and industries. Although these surveys did find some areas of dissatisfaction, that unhappiness tended to focus on the policies and actions of the salesperson's firm or sales manager, not on the nature of the sales job itself.[2]

Why are so many professional salespeople generally quite satisfied with their jobs? Some attractive aspects of selling careers include the following:

1. Autonomy, or the freedom of action and opportunities for personal initiative.

2. Multifaceted and challenging activities as part of the job, sales activities that will be addressed later in this chapter.

3. Financial rewards—salespeople hired right out of college, for example, tend to start at higher salaries than most other professions and also tend to keep up well during their careers with the compensation of their peers outside of sales (due to the nature of sales compensation being linked directly to performance).

4. Favorable working conditions, often via telecommuting with a virtual office, and with less minute-to-minute direct supervision than most other careers.

5. Excellent opportunities for career development and advancement.

High Job Autonomy

A common complaint among workers in many professions is that they are too closely supervised. They complain about the micromanagement of bosses and about rules and standard operating procedures that constrain their freedom to do their jobs as they see fit. Salespeople, on the other hand, spend most of their time working directly with customers with no one around to supervise their every move. They are relatively free to organize their own time and to get the job done in their own way as long as they show good results.

The freedom of a selling career appeals to people who value their independence, who are confident they can cope with most situations they will encounter, and who like to show personal initiative in deciding how to get their job done. However, with this freedom comes responsibilities and potential pressures. Salespeople are responsible for managing their existing customer relationships and developing new ones. Although no one closely supervises the salesperson's behavior, management usually keeps close tabs on the results of that behavior: sales volume, quota attainment, expenses, and the like. To be successful, then, salespeople must be able to manage themselves, to organize time wisely, and to make the right decisions about how to do the job.

High Job Variety

If variety in a job is the spice of life, sales jobs are hot peppers. Most people soon become bored doing routine tasks. Fortunately, boredom is seldom a problem among professional salespeople, as sales positions tend to be high in job variety. Each customer has different needs and problems for which the salesperson can work to develop unique solutions. Those problems are often anything but trivial, and a salesperson must display insight, creativity, and analytical skill to close a sale. Many sales consultants expect creative problem solving to become even more important to sales success in the future.

ETHICAL MOMENT   The Other Side of Autonomy

One of the real advantages of a sales career is the ability to "be your own boss." The autonomy of outside sales offers independence and a sense of entrepreneurship. There is no supervisor looking over your shoulder 24/7 and the ability to meet and work with a variety of customers across many companies and departments provides a dynamic, challenging, and often rewarding work experience.

However, there is another side to autonomy. With the freedom of being outside the company's work environment other distractions, sometimes very legitimate, can create time pressure and conflict. For example, consider the salesperson that gets involved in community-based organizations. As executives rise in an organization they are often asked to take on community service as part of the broader responsibilities. Nowhere is this more prevalent than sales where, because of its outward-looking nature, managers and even salespeople are encouraged to be actively involved in their local community. The challenge is that it is easy to allow these commitments to consume time that could be spent actually selling.

While engaging the local community is a worthwhile and important part of being a good citizen, the sales manager is ultimately responsible for commitment to the company and performance. Autonomy allows a great deal of freedom but also demands a high level of personal ethics and discipline. The "other side" is that the freedom of autonomy allows individuals to put personal choices ahead of work. While everyone can occasionally allow personal commitments to offset work effort the autonomous nature of the sales profession can turn an infrequent event into a significant problem.

Question to Ponder:

- Is there such a thing as too much autonomy for a salesperson? How would you suggest a sales manager regulate the autonomy of their salespeople?

Opportunities for Rewards

To make the sales job even more interesting, as we learned in Chapter 1 the internal and external environment is constantly changing. Salespeople must frequently adjust their sales presentations and other activities to shifts in economic and competitive conditions. For many people in the selling profession, variety and challenge are the most rewarding aspects of their jobs. Sales jobs offer great opportunity for developing a sense of accomplishment and opportunities for personal growth. As we will see in Chapter 6, these are important sources of intrinsic rewards and satisfaction—that is, rewards inherent to satisfaction derived from elements of the job or role itself, as opposed to extrinsic rewards, which are rewards bestowed on the salesperson by the company.

Make no mistake, though, selling can be a very lucrative profession in terms of extrinsic rewards as well. More important, the growth of a salesperson's earnings—particularly the earnings of someone receiving a large proportion of incentive pay—is determined largely by performance, and often no arbitrary limits are placed on the maximum amount a salesperson can earn. Consequently, a salesperson's compensation can grow faster and reach higher levels than that of personnel in other departments at comparable levels in an organization.

According to the Bureau of Labor Statistics, the median annual salary for a sales manager was $105,260 in 2012 with a projected percent change in employment through 2022 of 8 percent.[3]

Favorable Working Conditions

If the stereotypes of sales jobs addressed earlier were true, salespeople would be expected to travel extensively, live on big expense accounts, spend much of their time entertaining potential clients, and consequently have little time for home and family life. Such a situation represents a lack of balance between one's work life and family life such that work is encroaching on family—work–family conflict. Again, this is not an accurate description of the working conditions encountered by most salespeople. Some selling jobs require extensive travel, but the majority of salespeople can secure rewarding positions that allow them to be at home most every night. Indeed, with the increasing use of computer networks, e-mail, video conferencing, and the like, the trend for more than a decade has been for more and more salespeople to telecommute. That is, they work from a remote or virtual office such as out of the home and seldom even travel to their companies' offices.[4]

For all the advantages and attractiveness of telecommuting to the salesperson, as well as the efficiencies and cost-saving aspects to the sales organization, operating out of a virtual office does create a challenge for keeping the sales force fully socialized to the culture of the organization. The Technology box illustrates the benefits and organizational challenges a virtual office environment can create.

Moving up in the Organization

Given the wealth of knowledge about a firm's customers, competitors, and products—and the experience at building effective relationships—that a sales job can

TECHNOLOGY   The Virtual Office—Benefits and Challenges

The decision to permit staff to work from outside the traditional office confines is a complex one. There are numerous advantages to this "virtual office" type of working including a better work–life balance for the employee, cost savings in terms of real estate and overhead for the employer, and even an environmental benefit as the need to travel to work is removed and takes yet another car off the roads.

On the other hand, there is evidence to suggest that the virtual office environment can cause employees to feel isolated and disconnected from their colleagues and their job. A fear of being overlooked for promotion or recognition may arise as a result of the "out of sight, out of mind" philosophy. With modern technology, the virtual office is becoming more connected to the physical office. E-mail, smartphones, and the Internet can keep virtual workers more involved in the daily goings on at their company.

Virtual working has become an essential part of the modern sales job, but sales managers must realize that their staff still need to feel involved and not isolated. Some miss the monitoring and advice given by colleagues and superiors, so this must be continued even when the employee is working virtually.

provide, it is not surprising that often CEOs come up through the sales ranks into the executive suite. For example, Jeff Immelt spent more than 20 years in various sales and marketing positions at General Electric before being named the successor to Jack Welch as CEO. Anne Mulcahy, former president and CEO of Xerox, spent most of her 25 years at the company in sales. She advises that those who climb the corporate ladder from the sales rung need to be willing to take on non-sales-oriented assignments along the way to broaden their experience. And A.G. Laffley, Chairman and CEO of P&G, also came up through the sales ranks and attributes much of his leadership success to the fact that he spent time working directly with customers.

Although salespeople are sometimes reluctant to give up their high-paying jobs to move into managerial positions, most firms recognize the importance of good managerial talent and reward it appropriately, particularly as a person reaches the top executive levels of the sales organization. Total compensation of more than $250,000 a year is not unheard of for vice presidents of sales/chief sales officers (CSOs) in large firms.

Of course, many managerial opportunities are available to successful salespeople at lower levels of the corporate hierarchy as well, most obviously in sales management, product or brand management, and general marketing management. Several possible career tracks salespeople might follow are illustrated in Exhibit 2.1.

Promoting top salespeople into management can sometimes cause problems. Successful selling often requires different personal skills and abilities than does successful management. No guarantee exists that a good salesperson will also be a good sales manager. Also, successful salespeople have been known to refuse promotion to managerial positions—because they enjoy selling, or they can make more money in sales than in management, or both. Finally, recent trends toward corporate downsizing, flatter organizational structures, and cross-functional selling teams have changed the number and nature of managerial opportunities available for successful salespeople. As noted earlier in the chapter, the sales manager of the future is more likely to be a coach or team leader rather than an authority figure isolated in the upper reaches of a corporate hierarchy.

EXHIBIT 2.1
Possible career
tracks for
salespeople

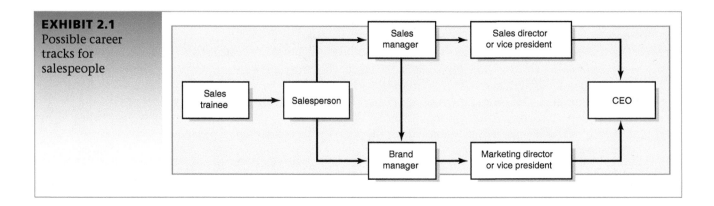

Key Success Factors in Selling

Although certainly many career advancement opportunities are available to the successful salesperson, not all sales recruits turn out to be successful. Some are fired, others quit and seek different careers, and some simply languish on the lower rungs of the sales hierarchy for a long time. Not everyone possesses the key success factors necessary to make it in selling, which raises the question: What personal characteristics and abilities are related to successful sales performance? This is somewhat difficult to answer because different types of sales jobs require different key success factors. Nevertheless, in this section we tackle the issue by presenting a sales manager's perspective on what factors are most important to successful selling today.

Given the shift in selling from transactional to more relationship-oriented approaches, it is reasonable to presume that the factors considered by sales managers to be critical to success in managing customer relationships would be different from those required in former approaches to selling. These success factors take the form of skills, content knowledge, and other attributes sales managers look for when hiring a salesperson. Knowing what sales managers consider important to success in a sales job is very useful information for anyone thinking of selling as a career choice.

An interesting study asked 215 sales managers from a variety of industries to rate the importance of 60 key success factors developed from interviews with salespeople and sales managers.[5] The top 20 factors are presented in Exhibit 2.2. Perusal of Exhibit 2.2 reveals some important trends in the key success factors in selling today. Let's examine the top 10 in more detail.

Listening Skills

The top-rated item is listening skills. Others have found through their own research that buyer–seller relationships are significantly strengthened when salespeople consistently employ effective listening skills, especially using active listening.[6] Ironically, selling courses and sales training seminars almost always focus more on teaching salespeople to speak and write, but not to listen. One of the great things about practicing great listening skills with clients is that it fosters a relationship of trust and respect, as noted in the Leadership box on p. 38.

Follow-up Skills

A key difference between transactional and relationship selling approaches is the effort devoted by the salesperson to the ongoing maintenance and management of the relationship, especially between actual face-to-face encounters with the customer. Remember from Chapter 1 that relationship selling has three components: securing, building, and maintaining the relationship. EMC Corporation, a computer storage company, has a reputation for being obsessed with follow-up. EMC is a major global enterprise, with about 70,000 people worldwide. They are represented by approximately 400 sales offices and scores of partners in 86 countries around the world. Its sales and service teams work hard to anticipate and fix trouble before it's even recognized as a problem by the client. Anything from a toppled storage system to a change in the storage room's temperature causes the boxes to beam home warning messages and activate a response system from EMC reps, often before clients are even aware of the problem. Twenty-three remote locations around the globe position field reps to quickly follow up in person if necessary. Former CEO Mike Ruettgers built a business around responding in person within eight hours in the case of a severe service failure.

Success Factors in Selling	Mean	S.D.	
Highest level of importance			**EXHIBIT 2.2**
Listening skills	6.502	0.683	Sales managers' importance ratings of success factors for professional salespeople
Follow-up skills	6.358	0.772	
Ability to adapt sales style from situation to situation	6.321	0.687	
Tenacity—sticking with a task	6.107	0.924	
Well organized	6.084	0.889	
Verbal communication skills	6.047	0.808	
Proficiency in interacting with people at all levels of a customer's organization	6.000	0.991	
Demonstrated ability to overcome objections	5.981	1.085	
Closing skills	5.944	1.109	
Personal planning and time management skills	5.944	0.946	
Proficiency in interacting with people at all levels of your organization	5.912	0.994	
Negotiation skills	5.827	0.975	
Dresses in appropriate attire	5.791	1.063	
Empathy with the customer	5.723	1.074	
Planning skills	5.685	0.966	
Prospecting skills	5.673	1.209	
Creativity	5.670	0.936	
Ability to empathize with others	5.549	1.105	
Skills in preparing for a sales call	5.526	1.219	
Decision-making ability	5.502	1.023	

Source: Greg W. Marshall, Daniel J. Goebel, and William C. Moncrief, "Hiring for Success at the Buyer–Seller Interface," *Journal of Business Research* 56 (2003), pp. 247–55. Copyright 2003, reprinted with permission from Elsevier.

Note: All items were scaled as follows: 1 = of no importance at all in hiring decisions, 7 = of the utmost importance in hiring decisions. S.D. = standard deviation.

Ability to Adapt Sales Style from Situation to Situation

The practice of adaptive selling is the altering of sales behaviors during a customer interaction or across customer interactions based on perceived information about the nature of the selling situation.[7] This is analogous to the idea discussed earlier of being a nimble firm. Being adaptive allows the salesperson to better practice relationship selling by understanding customer needs and problems and by providing solutions.[8]

Tenacity—Sticking with a Task

Nurturing customer relationships is a long-term proposition. Unlike forms of selling where the objective is to simply close a sale on one client and then move on to the next, managing relationships is a process that requires patience and the willingness to work with a client, often over long periods, before the potential benefits of the relationship to both parties are realized. Great salespeople always keep the big picture while also working on the details. This perspective facilitates tenacity and yields results that are worth the wait.

Well Organized

As the content and responsibilities of sales jobs have increased in complexity and buying organizations have become more complicated to navigate, the ability of a salesperson to skillfully prioritize and arrange the work has increased as a key success factor. Being well organized is a component of effective time and territory management.

LEADERSHIP   Developing Trust and Respect in Sales Relationships

Before a sales prospect will feel comfortable buying from you, they must first respect and trust your company and you. Trust and respect is essential, especially during the early stages of the relationship. Listening is more important than schmoozing; don't just begin telling the prospect about all the benefits of what you are trying to sell. You should ask questions about the prospect's previous experience with what you are trying to sell, and whether or not they were satisfied. Ask if they have ever used your brand and what their feelings are about the brand. Following up is critical to being a successful salesperson. A timely sent e-mail or letter that recaps your meeting and asks if there are any other questions or comments will demonstrate a prompt response to the needs or requests of the prospect.

Here are several ways to earn the respect of your customers and prospects:

- Know your product or service well.
- Be able to express how well your product or service satisfies the wants and needs of your customer.
- Conduct yourself professionally.
- Be a great listener.
- Follow up with prompt responses to customers' needs and requests.

Developing trust is vital in all sales relationships. Trust does not happen overnight and can easily be broken. The easiest way to develop trust is to tell the truth and keep your word. This includes being somewhere when you say you'll be there and doing what you said you would do. Also, it is important to not promise more than you can deliver. Broken promises will diminish trust in any sales relationship.[9]

Verbal Communication Skills

It is of value to note a second time that this factor, while obviously critical to sales success, is rated lower in importance by sales managers than listening skills. Salespeople must be great communicators.

Proficiency in Interacting with People at All Levels of a Customer's Organization

Selling today often involves communication and interaction with many people within the client firm besides the purchasing agent. Later in this chapter we will identify individuals in other roles within firms that may be just as, or even more, important to developing the relationship with the client firm than the buyer or purchasing agent.

Demonstrated Ability to Overcome Objections

A customer may have a number of concerns about any given purchase that the salesperson must work to overcome to the satisfaction of the customer. Objections are a natural and expected part of any sales process. By developing a trusting relationship over the long run with the client, and by working to negotiate win–win solutions, objections can be minimized.

Closing Skills

Obviously, in order for a salesperson to be successful, he or she has to generate business from clients.

Personal Planning and Time Management Skills

As with being well organized, being good at personal planning and managing your time will serve you well in a sales career. Nowadays, both these success factors have been augmented substantially through technology—especially smartphones and tablets.

SELLING ACTIVITIES

Given what we have learned so far about today's world of selling, including the key success factors sales managers believe are important, it should not be too surprising to learn that salespeople spend a large portion of their time collecting information about potential customers, planning, coordinating the activities of other functional departments, and servicing existing customers, in addition to making sales calls. It is difficult to specify the full range of activities in which salespeople engage because they can vary greatly across companies and types of sales jobs. However, in one extensive study, twelve different dimensions, or job factors, were identified.[10] These factors are shown in Exhibit 2.3, along with examples of the specific activities involved in each dimension.

One obvious conclusion from the study is that a salesperson's job often involves a wide variety of activities beyond relationship selling per se. Examination of the various factors paints a picture of a job with wide-ranging activities. The results of another follow-up study aimed specifically at technology-related sales activities are summarized in Exhibit 2.4. Notice in particular the "Impacts" column in the exhibit—not all of the impacts of technology on salespeople are necessarily favorable!

EXHIBIT 2.3
Sales job factors and selected associated activities

Factor 1 Relationship Selling	Factor 2 Promotional Activities and Sales Service	Factor 3 Entertaining	Factor 4 Prospecting
1. Build Trust 2. Ask Questions 3. Build Rapport 4. Listen 5. Consult with Customers 6. Adapt Presentations 7. Sell Value Added 8. Overcome Objections 9. Sell Unique Competencies 10. Close the Sale 11. Work with Key Accounts 12. ID Person in Authority 13. Read Body Language 14. Plan Selling Activities 15. Call on Multiple Individuals 16. Correspond with Customers 17. Help Clients Plan	1. Point of Purchase 2. Set Up Displays 3. Handle Advertising 4. Demonstrate the Product 5. Train Customers with Product 6. Use VCR to Sell 7. Sell Product Accessories 8. Create Newsletters 9. Check Customer Inventory 10. Work Trade Shows 11. Write Up Orders 12. Handle Back Orders 13. Introduce New Products	1. Entertain with Leisure 2. Take Clients to Dinner 3. Take Clients for Drinks 4. Play Golf 5. Take Clients to Lunch 6. Throw Parties	1. Call on Potential Accounts 2. Search Out New Leads 3. Respond to Referrals 4. Submit Bids 5. Make Multiple Calls

Factor 5 Computer	Factor 6 Travel	Factor 7 Training/Recruiting	Factor 8 Delivery
1. Use Internet 2. Work on Web 3. Check E-Mail 4. Learn Software 5. Enter Data on Laptop 6. Collect Database Information 7. Presentation with Laptop	1. Spend Night on the Road 2. Travel Out of Town	1. Train New Sales Reps 2. Mentor Junior Sales Reps 3. Recruit Sales Reps 4. Ride with Reps	1. Deliver Product Samples 2. Deliver Product 3. Stock Shelves

Factor 9 Product Support	Factor 10 Educational Activities	Factor 11 Office	Factor 12 Channel Support
1. Supervise Installation 2. Modify the Product 3. Perform Maintenance 4. Take Clients on Site 5. Expedite Orders	1. Attend Sales Meetings 2. Attend Training Sessions 3. Learn about Products	1. Fill Out Expense Reports 2. Check Voice Mail	1. Establish Relationships with Distributors 2. Train Brokers/Middlemen

Source: William C. Moncrief, Greg W. Marshall, Felicia G. Lassk, "A Contemporary Taxonomy of Sales Positions," *Journal of Personal Selling & Sales Management* 26, no. 1 (January 2006), pp. 56–65.

Factors	Description	Impacts	
1. CONNECTIVITY	The level that salespeople are connected or available to employees and clients	– Technology viewed as matter of course for work – Negative influence on ability to plan – Log in morning and night – Total access expectation	**EXHIBIT 2.4** Technology-related sales job factors and associated impacts
2. RELATIONSHIP	Socialness; social networking and building personal long term contacts	– Younger salespeople are more comfortable building virtual relationships – Technology increasing and changing the way we build relationships – Social not important—technology for building relationships – Clients want less personal contact – Customers have near perfect information – Buyers are driving the mode of relationship	
3. SELLING TOOLS	Technology-based selling techniques used by sellers in creating, building and maintaining relationships	– Technology having revolutionary changes to selling – *Not everyone* embraces the new selling tools, age is a variable to the amount of technology being used – Social media sites (Facebook, LinkedIn) are becoming common – Twitter is being used in a number of ways to sell – Blogs help track competitors and suppliers – The seven steps have become more condensed because of technology	
4. GENERATIONAL	Differences between younger and more experienced reps (roughly above or below 35 years) concerning the use of technology	– Younger reps are shying away from face-to-face contact—younger reps are combining social and work done on job – The two generations are communicating to clients differently	
5. GLOBAL	Building and maintaining worldwide customers and relationships	– Work is waiting on you when you arrive to work—the work has come in from Europe or Asia—answering messages (e-mail) 24 hours a day – Teammates/suppliers are located around the world	
6. SALES/ MARKETING INTERFACE	The merging of sales and marketing strategies	– Branding is being affected by blogs and chatter on the Net – Twitter is becoming a major marketing and selling tool—lines between marketing and sales are blurring because of the use of technology	

Source: Greg W. Marshall, William C. Moncrief, John M. Rudd, and Nick Lee, "Revolution in Sales: The Impact of Social Media and Related Technology on the Selling Environment," *Journal of Personal Selling & Sales Management* 32 (Summer 2012), pp. 351–365.

Several important conclusions can be drawn from this research. First, salespeople have experienced rather substantial job enlargement over the past decade. That is, the sales role today is broader than in the past and contains substantially more activities. One hopes that the efficiencies gained from the technological advances help offset the sheer number of additional activities salespeople perform today. Second, on the technology side of new activities, sales organizations need to work to ensure that all salespeople receive proper training and support on the acceptance and use of the available technology. Finally, it is essential that performance management systems (appraisals, rewards) be updated to properly reflect the dimensions and activities of sales positions today. Otherwise, salespeople will be evaluated and rewarded based on an out-of-date model of their jobs.

The increasing number of nonselling and administrative activities means that many salespeople spend only a small portion of their time actually selling. In firms that sell complicated or customized products or service systems to large customers, the proportion of selling time may be even lower. The increasing involvement of salespeople in nonselling activities is one major reason why the average cost of a sales call has risen consistently in recent years. It takes the performance of many nonselling activities over a long period of time to successfully practice relationship selling. Depending on the industry, the average cost of a sales call today is likely over $500.

High selling costs explain why the search for new ways to improve sales force efficiency has become increasingly urgent in recent years. Using new technologies, reallocating sales effort to customer retention, and purifying the sales job by eliminating nonessential tasks are some of the strategies companies have used to reduce selling costs and increase sales force efficiency.

TYPES OF SELLING JOBS

Not every salesperson engages in all of the activities listed in Exhibit 2.3. Nor does every salesperson devote the same amount of time and effort to the same kinds of activities. The many different types of selling jobs involve widely different tasks and responsibilities, require different types of training and skills, and offer varying levels of compensation and opportunities for personal satisfaction and advancement. And, perhaps most important, different kinds of selling jobs bring different levels and types of opportunities for managing customer relationships. Two broad categories of selling are selling in business-to-consumer markets and selling in business-to-business markets.

Selling in Business-to-Consumer versus Business-to-Business Markets

In terms of sheer numbers, most salespeople are employed in various kinds of retail selling. These jobs involve selling goods and services to end-user consumers for their own personal use. Thus salespeople here are referred to as selling in the business-to-consumer (B2C) market. Examples are direct sellers (Avon, Mary Kay, etc.), residential real estate brokers, and retail store salespeople. However, a much greater amount of relationship selling is accounted for by the business-to-business (B2B) market, which used to be called industrial selling—the sale of goods and services to non-end-user consumers. Selling in B2B markets involves three types of customers:

1. *Sales to resellers*, as when a salesperson for Hanes sells underwear to a retail store, which in turn resells the goods to its customers.

2. *Sales to business users*, as when a salesperson for General Electric sells materials or parts to Boeing, which uses them to produce another product; or when a Xerox salesperson sells a law firm a copier to be used in conducting the firm's business.

3. *Sales to institutions*, as when Dell sells a computer to a not-for-profit hospital or a government agency.

In some instances, the key success factors and sales activities relevant to both B2C and B2B markets, and in managing the two types of sales forces, are very similar. Success in either type of selling requires interpersonal and communications skills, solid knowledge of the products being sold, an ability to discover the customer's needs and solve his or her problems, and the creativity necessary to show the customer how a particular product or service can help satisfy those needs and problems. Similarly, managers must recruit and train appropriate people for both types of sales jobs, provide them with objectives consistent with the firm's overall marketing or merchandising program, supervise them, motivate them, and evaluate their performance.

But B2C and B2B selling also differ in some important ways. Many of the goods and services sold by B2B salespeople are more expensive and technically complex than those in B2C. Similarly, B2B customers tend to be larger and to engage in extensive decision-making processes involving many people. Consequently, the key success factors and activities involved in selling to business buyers are often quite different from those in retail selling. Furthermore, the decisions made in effectively managing a B2B sales force are broader than those required for a B2C sales force. Although some topics in this book apply reasonably well to both types of selling situations, most apply more directly to the B2B. Overall, throughout this book we focus more on the B2B side of sales force management.

Classifying Types of B2B Sales Jobs

Even within the area of B2B selling, many different types of jobs exist requiring different skills. One of the most commonly used, and useful, classification systems for selling jobs is provided next.[11] It identifies four types of B2B selling found across a variety of industries:

1. Trade servicer. The sales force's primary responsibility is to increase business from current and potential customers by providing them with merchandising and promotional assistance. The "trade" referred to in the label is the group of resellers such as retailers or distributors with whom this sales force does business. A P&G salesperson selling soap and laundry products to chain-store personnel is an example of trade selling.

2. Missionary seller. The sales force's primary job is to increase business from current and potential customers by providing them with product information and other personal selling assistance. Missionary salespeople often do not take orders from customers directly but persuade customers to buy their firm's product from distributors or other wholesale suppliers. Anheuser-Busch does missionary selling when its salespeople call on bar owners and encourage them to order a particular brand of beer from the local Budweiser distributor. Similarly, pharmaceutical reps, or detailers, call on doctors as representatives of pharmaceutical manufacturers. When Pfizer first introduced Zyrtec, a top-selling allergy drug, its salespeople communicated with the physicians in their area to alert them to the efficacy of the product, to explain its advantages over other allergy medication such as Allegra and Clarinex, and to influence them to prescribe it to their patients. Note that the Pfizer salesperson normally doesn't "sell" any product directly to the physicians.

3. Technical seller. The sales force's primary responsibility is to increase business from current customers and potential customers by providing them with technical and engineering information and assistance. A sales engineer from the General Electric jet engine company calling on Boeing is engaged in technical selling. The trend nowadays is for most technical selling to be accomplished through cross-functional selling teams. This is because the complexity of many of the products and associated services involved in technical selling make it difficult for any one salesperson to master all aspects of this sale.

4. New business seller. The sales force's primary responsibility is to identify and obtain business from new customers. In relationship selling, this is analogous to a focus on securing and building the customer relationship.

Each type of sales job involves somewhat different activities. The differing nature of each also implies differences in key success factors. In the next section, we see how the sales process often operates in practice.

STAGES IN THE SELLING PROCESS

A popular approach to understanding the stages of the selling process consists of the six steps diagrammed in Exhibit 2.5: (1) prospecting for customers, (2) opening the relationship, (3) qualifying the prospect, (4) presenting the sales message, (5) closing the sale, and (6) servicing the account.

Although the selling process involves only a few distinct steps, the specific activities involved at each step—and the way those activities are carried out—can vary greatly depending on the type of sales position, such as missionary versus trade salesperson, and on the firm's overall selling and customer relationship strategy. Consequently, a firm's sales program should incorporate account management policies to guide each salesperson and ensure that all selling efforts are consistent with the firm's marketing and relationship strategy. We will examine the rationale and content of account management policies in more detail in Chapter 4. The following discussion of the stages in the selling process also mentions some of the more common account management policies used to direct sales representatives.

Prospecting for Customers

In many types of selling, prospecting for new customers is critical. It can also be one of the most disheartening aspects of selling, especially for beginning salespeople. Prospecting efforts are often met with rejection, and immediate payoffs are usually minimal. Nevertheless, the ability to uncover potential new customers often separates the successful from the unsuccessful salesperson.

In some consumer goods businesses, prospecting for new customers simply involves cold canvassing—going from house to house knocking on doors. In most cases, though, the target market is more narrowly defined, and the salesperson must identify prospects within that target segment. Salespeople use a variety of information sources to identify relevant prospects, including trade association and industry directories, telephone directories, other salespeople, other customers, suppliers, nonsales employees of the firm, and social and professional contacts.

Telemarketing is used by many firms to find prospects. Outbound telemarketing involves calling potential customers at their home or office, either to make a sale or

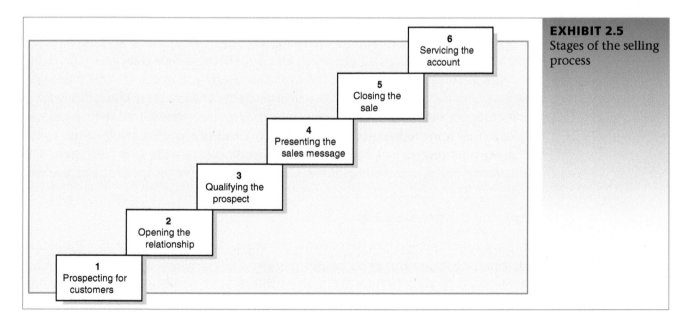

EXHIBIT 2.5
Stages of the selling process

to make an appointment for a field representative. Inbound telemarketing, where prospective customers call a toll-free number for more information, is also used to identify and qualify prospects. When prospects call for more information about a product or service, a representative attempts to determine the extent of interest and whether the prospect meets the company's qualifications for new customers. If so, information about the caller is passed on to the appropriate salesperson or regional office.

The Internet is also proving a useful technology for generating leads to potential new customers. While an increasing number of firms are soliciting orders directly via a home page on the Internet, many—particularly those selling relatively complex goods or services—use their Internet sites primarily to provide technical product information to customers or potential customers. These firms can have their salespeople follow up on technical inquiries from potential new accounts with a more traditional sales call.[12]

A firm's account management policies should address how much emphasis salespeople should give to prospecting for new customers versus prospecting and servicing existing accounts. The appropriate policy depends on the selling and customer relationship strategy selected, the nature of its product, and the firm's customers. If the firm's strategy is transactional, if the product is in the introductory stage of its life cycle, if it is an infrequently purchased durable good, or if the typical customer does not require much service after the sale, sales reps should devote substantial time to prospecting for new customers. This is the case in industries such as insurance and residential construction. Such firms may design their compensation systems to reward their salespeople more heavily for making sales to new customers than for servicing old ones, as we shall see in Chapter 11.

A company that desires strategic partnerships will assign a specific salesperson to each account. Firms with large market shares or those that sell frequently purchased nondurable products or products that require substantial service after the sale to guarantee customer satisfaction should adopt a policy that encourages sales reps to devote most of their efforts to servicing existing customers. Food manufacturers that sell products to retail supermarkets and firms that produce component parts and supplies for other manufacturers fall into this category. Some very large customers may require so much servicing that a sales rep is assigned to do nothing but cater to that customer's needs. In such circumstances, firms have specialized their sales positions so that some representatives service only existing accounts, while others spend all their time prospecting for and opening relationships with new customers. The Innovation box provides some new-age advice on effective prospecting approaches.

Opening the Relationship

In the initial approach to a prospective customer, the sales representative should try to open the relationship by accomplishing two things: (1) determine who within the organization is likely to have the greatest influence or authority to initiate the purchase process and who will ultimately purchase the product, and (2) generate enough

INNOVATION   Different Ways to Prospect

Most prospects do not like cold calling, just like most sales reps do not like making cold calls. Luckily, there are different ways to generate sales leads. Tom Searcy from huntingbigsales.com recommends these approaches to prospect for customers:

- Get involved in the community and associations.
- Write how-to articles in publications that your target clients read.
- Give how-to speeches at prospect industry meetings.
- Provide free or low-cost seminars.

These alternatives are great ways to attract new prospects. How-to articles and speeches can be your chance to display your expertise in the industry you are doing business in. Getting involved in associations and the community and providing free or low-cost seminars allow you to help and build trust among prospects.

Social media is another great way to prospect customers. Two benefits of social media marketing are increased exposure and increased traffic. These benefits can help generate new leads, grow new business partnerships, and improve sales. Of the marketers surveyed in the 2012 Social Media Marketing Report survey by SocialMediaExaminer.com, 85 percent indicated that social media increased exposure and 65 percent indicated increased traffic. Only 40 percent reported that sales were improved and 51 percent reported that they were able to grow business partnerships. Social media is still growing and if companies are able to use it effectively, it can help them generate customers and increase sales.[13]

interest within the firm to obtain the information needed to qualify the prospect as a worthwhile potential customer. An organizational buying center often consists of individuals who play different roles in making the purchase decision. Thus, it is important for the salesperson to identify the key decision makers, their desires, and their relative influence.

Selling organizations can formulate policies to guide sales reps in approaching prospective customers. When the firm's product is inexpensive and routinely purchased, salespeople might be instructed to deal entirely with the purchasing department. For more technically complex and expensive products, the sales representative might be urged to identify and seek appointments with influencers and decision makers in various functional departments and at several managerial levels. When the purchase decision is likely to be very complex, involving many people within the customer's organization, the seller might adopt a policy of multilevel or team selling.

Qualifying the Prospect

Before salespeople attempt to set up an appointment for a major sales presentation or spend much time trying to establish a relationship with a prospective account, they should first qualify the prospect to determine if he or she qualifies as a worthwhile potential customer. If the account does not qualify, the sales rep can spend the time better elsewhere.

Qualification is difficult for some salespeople. It requires them to put aside their eternal optimism and make an objective, realistic judgment about the probability of making a profitable sale. The qualification process involves finding the answers to three important questions:

1. Does the prospect have a need for my product or service?

2. Can I make the people responsible for buying so aware of that need that I can make a sale?

3. Will the sale be profitable to my company?[14]

To answer such questions, the sales rep must learn about the prospect's operations, the types of products it makes, its customers, its competitors, and the likely future demand for its products. Information also must be obtained concerning who the customer's present suppliers are and whether any special relationships exist with those firms that would make it difficult for the prospect to change suppliers. Finally, the financial health and the credit rating of the prospect should be checked.

Because so many different types of information are needed, nonselling departments within the company—such as the credit and collections department—often are involved in the qualification process when large purchases are made. Frequently, however, credit departments do not get involved until after the prospect has agreed to buy and filled out a credit application. In these situations, company policies should be formulated to guide the salesperson's judgment concerning whether a specific prospect qualifies as a customer. These policies might spell out minimum acceptable standards for such things as the prospect's annual dollar value of purchases in the product category or credit rating. Similarly, some firms specify a minimum order size to avoid dealing with very small customers and to improve the efficiency of their order-processing and shipping operations. Issues related to prioritizing customers are discussed in Chapter 3.

Presenting the Sales Message

The sales presentation is the core of the selling process. The salesperson transmits information about a product or service and attempts to persuade the prospect to become a customer.[15] Making good presentations is a critical aspect of the sales job. Unfortunately, many salespeople do not perform this activity very well. Past studies have discovered that 40 percent of purchasing agents perceive the presentations they witness as less than good. In a recent survey of purchasing executives, the following five presentation-related complaints were among the top 10 complaints the managers had about the salespeople with whom they deal:

- Running down competitors.

- Being too aggressive or abrasive.

- Having inadequate knowledge of competitors' products or services.

- Having inadequate knowledge of the client's business or organization.

- Delivering poor presentations.[16]

One decision that must be made in preparing for an effective sales presentation concerns how many members of the buying firm should attend. Since more than one person is typically involved in making a purchase decision, should a sales presentation be given to all of them as a group? The answer depends on whether the members of the buying center have divergent attitudes and concerns, and whether those concerns can all be addressed effectively in a single presentation. If not, scheduling a series of one-to-one presentations with different members of the buying group might be more effective.

In many cases, the best way to convince prospects of a product's advantage is to demonstrate it, particularly if the product is technically complex. Two rules should be followed in preparing an effective product demonstration. First, the demonstration should be carefully rehearsed to reduce the possibility of even a minor malfunction. Second, the demonstration should be designed to give members of the buying center hands-on experience with the product. For example, Xerox's salespeople learn about their clients' office operations so they can demonstrate their products actually doing the tasks they would do after they are purchased.

Different firms have widely varying policies concerning how sales presentations should be organized, what selling points should be stressed, and how forcefully the presentation should be made. Door-to-door salespeople and telephone salespeople are often trained to deliver the same memorized, forceful presentation to every prospect. A person selling computer systems may be trained in low-key selling, in which the salesperson primarily acts as a source of technical information and advice and does little pushing of the company's particular computers.

Today, the proliferation of relationship selling has resulted in salespeople being called on to give more formal presentations to multiple members of a client organization. For example, often selling firms may give quarterly or annual account review presentations to clients. These presentations typically involve the buying team and selling team as well as members of management from both sides. A firm's policy on sales presentations should be consistent with its other policies for managing accounts. To formulate intelligent sales presentation policies, a sales manager must know about alternative presentation methods and their relative advantages and limitations. Space limitations of this chapter make it difficult to present a lengthy discussion of such issues. The interested student is urged to examine a personal selling textbook where a variety of sales presentation methods are discussed and evaluated in more detail.

Closing the Sale

Closing the sale refers to obtaining a final agreement to purchase. All the salesperson's efforts are wasted unless the client "signs on the dotted line"; yet this is where many salespeople fail. It is natural for buyers to try to delay making purchase decisions. But as the time it takes the salesperson to close the sale increases, the profit to be made from the sale may go down, and the risk of losing the sale increases. Consequently, the salesperson's task is to facilitate the client making a timely final decision. Often, this may best be accomplished by simply asking for an order. "May I write that order up for you?" and "When do you want it delivered?" are common closings. Another closing tactic is to ask the client to choose between two alternative decisions, such as, "Will that be cash or charge?" or "Did you want the blue one or the red one?" In B2B buying and selling, organizational buyers and other decision makers have had extensive training in buying and selling techniques and can identify manipulative closing techniques, so care should be used in selecting a natural way to ask for the sale.

Servicing the Account

The salesperson's job is not finished when the sale is made. Many types of service and assistance must be provided to customers after a sale to ensure their satisfaction and repeat business. Excellent service after the sale bolsters customer loyalty and fosters long-term relationships with customers. But this is another area in which some salespeople do not perform well. When a customer stops buying from a company, much of the time it's because the customer thinks the selling firm's salespeople developed an indifferent attitude after the product was delivered. The salesperson should follow up each sale to make sure no problems exist with delivery schedules, quality of goods, or customer billing. In addition, often the salesperson or members of a sales team supervise the installation of equipment, train the customer's employees in its use, and ensure proper maintenance in order to reduce problems that may lead to customer dissatisfaction.

This kind of postsale service can pay great dividends for both the salesperson and the selling firm, leading to the sale of other, related products and services.[17] For instance, in many capital equipment lines, service contracts, along with supplies and replacement parts, account for greater dollar sales revenue and higher profit margins than the original equipment. A firm's selling and customer relationship strategy should dictate what type of postsale or ongoing service should occur.

To truly understand the selling process, why successful salespeople do what they do, and how to most effectively manage their efforts, it is important to also understand how B2B customers make purchase decisions. After all, in relationship selling, the focus by the salesperson and his or her entire organization is aimed at fulfilling customer needs and solving customer problems. Therefore, the next sections shift the focus of our discussion from the selling side to the buying side to examine the participants in the B2B buying process, the stages of this buying process exhibited by many organizations, and finally the nature of organizational buying situations.

PARTICIPANTS IN THE ORGANIZATIONAL BUYING PROCESS—THE BUYING CENTER

In order to make a decision on a technologically sophisticated IT solution, a wide variety of individuals in a client firm may participate in the decision process, including computer analysts, customer service representatives, procurement personnel, users, and others. The various participants in a buying process may be grouped into seven categories: initiators, users, influencers, gatekeepers, buyers, deciders, and controllers.[18] Together, the individuals assuming these roles form the buying center, which represents all the people who participate in buying or influencing the purchase of a particular product. American Airlines operates one of the largest aviation maintenance and equipment base in the world at its Tulsa, Oklahoma, facility. Mechanics there use a wide variety of products purchased by American from hundreds of vendors. A variety of people at American participate in the purchase of these products in one way or another. Participants in that buying process include the following:

- Initiators are the people who perceive a problem or opportunity that may require the purchase of a new product or service and thereby start the buying process. The initiator can be almost anyone at any level in the firm. Complaints from maintenance workers at American Airlines about outmoded and inefficient equipment, for instance, might trigger the purchase of new machinery. Alternatively, the decision to replace the equipment might be initiated through top management's strategic planning deliberations on how to make the airline more cost efficient and effective.

- Users, the people in the organization who must use or work with the product or service, often influence the purchase decision. For example, drill-press operators at American Airlines might request that the purchasing agent buy drill bits from a particular supplier because they stay sharp longer and reduce downtime in the plant. Users often volunteer to initiate a purchase, so it is possible that the same people may play more than one role.

- Influencers provide information for evaluating alternative products and suppliers, and often play a major role in determining the specifications and criteria to use in making the purchase decision. Influencers are usually technical experts from various departments and can include users. At American Airlines, for example, flight engineers or pilots often influence purchase decisions on the basis of their experience with the performance of various vendor options.

- Gatekeepers control the flow of information to other people involved in the purchasing process. A gatekeeper may control information going to the organization's purchasing agents, the suppliers' salespeople, and others on the selling and buying teams. Gatekeepers influence a purchase by controlling the kind and amount of information that reaches the decision makers. Information technology people are frequent gatekeepers because they often hold the *information* that is key to decision making in a firm. There are two types of gatekeepers: screens (like secretaries at American Airlines who can decide whose telephone call is put through to the executive or purchasing agent) and filters (such as the American Airlines purchasing agent who gathers proposals from three different companies and decides what to tell others in the buying center about each company). The purchasing agent filters information, choosing to pass along some, but not all, of the information in order to influence the decision.

- The buyer is the person who actually contacts the selling organization and places the order. In most organizations, buyers have the authority to negotiate purchases. In some cases, they are given wide discretion. In other instances, they are constrained by technical specifications and other contract requirements determined by technical experts and top administrators. At American Airlines, the level of authority to buy is determined by the size and type of purchase involved. As in many organizations, sometimes the decision is referred to a buying committee who may either vote or work to reach a consensus decision on which vendor to buy from or which product to buy.

- The decider is the person with the final authority to make a purchase decision. Sometimes buyers have this authority, but often it is retained by higher executives in the organization. When American Airlines buys a complete, systemwide computer installation and upgrade, for instance, the final decision is likely to be made by the chief executive or a top management committee.

- The controller is the person who determines the budget for the purchase. Sometimes the budget is set independently of the purchase—for example, the administrative office at American Airlines' Tulsa facility may receive a budget for office equipment set by corporate headquarters in Fort Worth at the start of the fiscal year. Then if the copier needs to be replaced or some other unexpected high-dollar expense looms, the cost would have to somehow fit in that budget. At other times, the controller may be an engineer or a line manager who is trying to keep the cost of the new maintenance procedure within a certain budget.

Estimates of the number of people in the buying center for a typical purchase range from 3 to 12. Different members of the buying center may participate, and exert different amounts of influence, at different stages in the decision process.[19] For example, at American Airlines people from engineering, quality control, and R&D often exert the greatest influence on the development of specifications and criteria that a new maintenance product must meet, whereas the purchasing manager often has more influence when it comes time to choose among alternative suppliers.

The makeup and size of the buying center varies with the amount of risk perceived by the firm when buying a particular product. The buying center tends to be smaller, and the relative influence of the purchasing manager greater, when reordering products the firm has purchased in the past than when buying something for the first time or buying something that is seen as risky.[20] Perceived risk is a function of the complexity of the product and situation, the relative importance of the purchase, time pressure to make a decision, and the degree of uncertainty about the product's efficacy. Similarly, customers' buying centers are more likely to involve a wider variety of participants when they are considering the purchase of a technically complex, expensive product, such as a computer system, than when the purchase involves a simpler or less costly product.[21]

Selling Centers and Buying Centers

Given that major customers' buying centers often consist of people from different functional areas with different viewpoints and concerns, those concerns can often be most effectively addressed by a team of experts from equivalent functional departments in the selling firm, or even from different divisions within the company. Recently, companies have begun to look at the existence of a selling center that brings together individuals from around the organization (marketing, customer service, sales, engineering, and others) to help the salesperson do his or her job more effectively. As in a customer's buying center, the selling organization needs to work together to present a unified, well-coordinated effort to the customer.[22] Since different members of the buying center may be active at different stages of the purchase process, an important part of sales planning involves trying to determine whom the sales organization should contact, when each contact should be made, who should make each contact, and what kinds of information and communication each buying center member is likely to find most useful and persuasive.

The key is establishing a team selling structure within the sales organization that best meets customer needs. For example, a common structure would make the salesperson (i.e., account manager) responsible for working with the entire selling team in order to manage the customer relationship. Often, such customer relationship teams include representatives from a number of functional departments within the sales organization such as R&D, operations, and finance. In an increasing number of situations, customer relationship teams maintain offices in or very near to the customer's facilities and one or more members of the customer relationship team are located in close geographic proximity to the customer.

At Oracle, a large global producer of CRM software, the team for a major account such as General Motors is led by an Oracle account executive. The account executive has a global team of salespeople as direct reports but can also draw from the full functional resources of Oracle to provide solutions for GM at any location in the world. Such an approach creates a matrix organization of direct reports and supporting internal consultants at Oracle who bring their collective expertise to bear for this major client.

Team selling can also present some coordination, motivation, and compensation problems. Former IBM Chairman and CEO Lou Gerstner has frequently spoken out publicly on the difficulties of performance management in team selling environments; it is a key theme in the book he released after his retirement.[23] Team selling is expensive and involves a substantial commitment of human resources, including management. Thus, team-based approaches tend to be most appropriate for the very largest customers, especially those with buying centers, where the potential business over time represents enough dollars and entails enough cross-functional interaction between various areas of both firms to justify the high costs of the team approach. Such a customer is often referred to as a key account. Key accounts generally have a senior salesperson assigned as a key account manager who works with a team that is dedicated to serving that large and very important customer.

ORGANIZATIONAL BUYING DECISION STAGES

We have seen that different members of a buying center may exert influence at different stages in the decision process. This raises the question of what stages are involved. One widely recognized framework identifies seven steps that organizational buyers take in making purchase decisions: (1) anticipation or recognition of a problem or need, (2) determination and description of the characteristics and the quantity of the needed item, (3) search for and qualification of potential suppliers, (4) acquisition and analysis of proposals or bids, (5) evaluation of proposals and selection of suppliers, (6) selection of an order routine, and (7) performance evaluation and feedback.[24] These organizational buying decision stages are portrayed graphically in Exhibit 2.6.

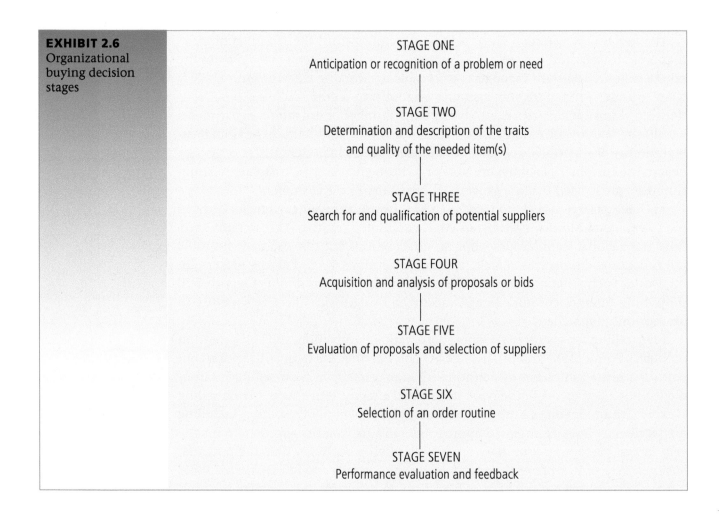

EXHIBIT 2.6
Organizational buying decision stages

STAGE ONE
Anticipation or recognition of a problem or need

STAGE TWO
Determination and description of the traits
and quality of the needed item(s)

STAGE THREE
Search for and qualification of potential suppliers

STAGE FOUR
Acquisition and analysis of proposals or bids

STAGE FIVE
Evaluation of proposals and selection of suppliers

STAGE SIX
Selection of an order routine

STAGE SEVEN
Performance evaluation and feedback

Stage One: Anticipation or Recognition of a Problem or Need

Many organizational purchases are motivated by the requirements of the firm's production processes, merchandise inventory, or day-to-day operations. In such a case, the firm's demand for goods and services is derived demand. Its needs are derived from its customers' demand for the goods or services it produces or markets. For example, the demand for luggage is derived in part from the demand for air travel. The luggage department at Macy's Department Store loses customers, and Samsonite (a leading luggage manufacturer) loses customers, when people don't travel. This characteristic of derived demand can make organizational markets quite volatile, because a small change in the market can result in a relatively large change in the organization's sales.

Many different situations can lead someone to recognize a need for a particular product or service. In some cases, need recognition may be almost automatic, as when the computerized inventory control system at Walmart reports that the stock of an item has fallen below the reorder level. In other cases, a need may arise when someone identifies a better way of operating, such at the American Airlines Maintenance and Equipment Base when an engineer or mechanic suggests a better procedure than what is currently in practice. New needs might also evolve when the focus of the firm's operations changes, as when top management decides to make a new product line. P&G introduced Crest Whitestrips—now Crest 3D White—which sell for considerably more on the grocer's shelf than most any other Crest product, because it wanted to get into the business of more professional products that will raise its average sale and profit per item. In all these situations, needs may be recognized and the purchasing process may be initiated by a variety of people in the organization, including users, technical personnel, top management, and purchasing managers.

Stage Two: Determination and Description of the Characteristics and Quantity of the Needed Item(s)

In organizational buying settings, the types and quantities of goods and services to be purchased are usually dictated by the demand for the firm's outputs and the requirements of its production process and operations. Consequently, the criteria used in specifying the needed materials and equipment must usually be technically precise. Similarly, the quantities needed must be carefully considered to avoid excessive inventories or downtime caused by lack of needed materials. For these reasons, a variety of technical experts, as well as the people who will use the materials or equipment, are commonly involved in this stage.

It is not enough for the using department and the technical experts to develop a detailed set of specifications for the needed item, however. They must also communicate a clear and precise description of *what* is needed, *how much* is needed, and *when* it is needed to other members of the buying center and to potential suppliers. Say Ford Motor Company's design and marketing groups make a decision to change the specifications of a car's interior and electronic systems. This must be communicated effectively to purchasing so that the vendor, often Lear Corporation, can begin the process of changing the parts Ford relies on purchasing from it to satisfy picky customers in this market.

Stage Three: Search for and Qualification of Potential Suppliers

Once the organization has clearly defined the type of item needed, a search for potential suppliers begins. If the item has been purchased before, this search may be limited to one or a few suppliers that have performed satisfactorily in the past. From the seller's perspective, one advantage of relationship selling is that the level of familiarity and trust between the buying and selling firm often results in that seller getting the first opportunity to bid on supplying the needed new products, and often this step of searching for potential suppliers is skipped. Historically, Ford Motor Company has gone with single-source suppliers wherever possible to minimize the variation in quality of production inputs. This approach bodes well for Lear Corporation whenever Ford announces specification changes on aspects of car models on which Lear supplies parts. If the purchase involves a new item, or if the item is complex and expensive (again, if the product represents a risky decision), organizational buyers often search for several potential suppliers to ensure they can select the one with the best product and most favorable terms.

Stage Four: Acquisition of Proposals or Bids

After potential suppliers are identified, the buyer may request specific proposals or bids from each. When the item is a frequently purchased, standardized, or technically simple product (e.g., nails or copier paper), this process may not be very extensive. The buyer might simply consult several suppliers' catalogs or make a few phone calls. For more complicated and expensive goods and services, lengthy and detailed sales presentations and written proposals may be requested from each potential vendor. Governmental and other institutional buyers almost always are required to formally solicit bids.

Stage Five: Evaluation of Offerings and Selection of Suppliers

During this stage of the purchasing process, members of the buying center examine the acceptability of the various proposals and potential suppliers. Also, the buying organization and one or more potential vendors may engage in negotiation about various aspects of the deal. Ultimately, one or more suppliers are selected, and purchase agreements are signed.

The people in the buying organization's purchasing department (i.e., the buyers) usually evaluate offerings and select the supplier. However, others in the buying center, such as technical and administrative personnel, may also play a role in supplier selection, especially when the purchase is complex and costly.

What criteria do members of the buying center use in selecting a supplier? Because organizational buying is largely a rational decision-making process, we would expect "rational" criteria to be considered most important—such as the value-added aspects of the product, the service offered by the supplier, and the like. However, social and emotional factors can also influence this decision. Organizational buyers and other buying center members are, after all, human just like buyers in the B2C marketplace. A number of aspects of difference can be contrasted between consumer versus organizational buyer behavior, as summarized in Exhibit 2.7.

The relative importance of different supplier selection criteria varies across organizations and the types of products or services being purchased. For example, product quality tends to be more important in the purchase of technically complex products, whereas price and customer service are relatively more important for more standardized, nontechnical items, that is, commodity products. Fortunately, firms engaged in relationship selling greatly increase the likelihood that buying firms will look past price as a sole determinant of vendor selection. Instead, because buyers will have much more complete knowledge about you and your products, they will have a better understanding of the overall value to their organization of buying from you versus one of your competitors with whom they do not have a long-standing relationship.

Stage Six: Selection of an Order Routine

Until the purchased item is delivered, it is of no use to the organization. Consequently, after an order has been placed with a supplier, the purchasing department often tries to match the delivery of the goods with the company's need for the product. Other internal activities also must occur when the order is delivered. The goods must be received, inspected, paid for, and entered in the firm's inventory records. These activities represent some of the additional costs that may not be readily apparent to the buying firm. Retailers have become very aggressive in asking vendors to cover these types of costs by charging sales organizations slotting

Aspect of the Purchase	Consumer Buyer	Organizational Buyer
Use	Personal, family, or household	Production, operations, or resale
Buyer motivation	Personal	Organizational and personal
Buyer knowledge of product or service	Lower	Higher
Likelihood of group decision making	Lower	Higher
Dollar amount of purchases	Lower	Higher
Quantity of purchase or order size	Smaller	Larger
Frequency of purchase	More	Less
Number of cyclical purchases	Lower	Higher
Amount of negotiation and competitive bidding	Little	Much

EXHIBIT 2.7
Consumer versus organizational buyer behavior

allowances. Slotting allowances are fees charged by a retailer for the privilege of having them set up a new item in their IT system, program it into inventory, and ultimately make distribution of the item to the stores. Slotting allowances can be costly to manufacturers, and it is not unusual for major retailers to charge slotting fees in the thousands of dollars per new item stocked.

Stage Seven: Performance Evaluation and Feedback

When the goods have been delivered, evaluation by the customer begins. This evaluation focuses on both the product and the supplier's service performance. This is a stage where follow-up by the salesperson is critically important. The goods are inspected to determine whether they meet the specifications described in the purchase agreement. Later, users judge whether the purchased item performs according to expectations. Similarly, the supplier's performance can be evaluated on such criteria as promptness of delivery, quality of the product, and service after the sale. In many organizations, this evaluation is a formal process, involving written reports from the user department and other persons involved in the purchase. The purchasing department keeps the information for use in evaluating proposals and selecting suppliers the next time a similar purchase is made.

THE NATURE OF ORGANIZATIONAL BUYING SITUATIONS

The steps just described apply largely to new-task purchases, where a customer is buying a relatively complex and expensive product or service for the first time (e.g., a new piece of production equipment or a new computer system), or modified rebuy purchase decisions, where a customer is interested in modifying the product specifications, prices, or other terms it has been receiving from existing suppliers and is willing to consider dealing with new suppliers to make these things happen.

At the other extreme is the straight rebuy, where a customer is reordering an item it has purchased many times (e.g., office supplies, bulk chemicals). Such repeat purchases tend to be much more routine than the new-task situation or the modified rebuy. Straight rebuys are often carried out by members of the purchasing department (buyers) with little influence from other members of the buying center, and many of the steps just described (involved with searching for and evaluating alternative suppliers) are dropped. Instead, the buyer may choose from among the suppliers on a "preapproved" list, giving weight to the company's past satisfaction with those suppliers and their products.

Purchasing departments are often organized hierarchically on the basis of these different buying situations. For example, at Walmart's buying office new buyers begin as analysts and assistants, primarily monitoring straight rebuys. New-task purchases and modified rebuys that require more direct vendor contact are handled by more seasoned veterans in the buying office.

From the seller's viewpoint, being an "in" or approved supplier can provide a significant competitive advantage, and the process of relationship selling certainly enhances such favored positions with current customers. For potential suppliers not on a buyer's approved list, the strategic selling problem is more difficult. The objective of an out supplier must be to move the customer away from the automatic reordering procedures of a straight rebuy toward the more extensive evaluation processes of a modified rebuy. Since, as we've already seen, the need to consider a change in suppliers can be identified and communicated by a variety of members of a firm's buying center, an out supplier might urge its salespeople to bypass the customer's purchasing department and call directly on users or technical personnel. The goal is for the salesperson to try to convince users, influencers, and others that his or her products offer advantages on some important dimension—such as technical design, quality, performance, or financial criteria—over the products the client is currently purchasing. Finding someone to play the role of initiator can be difficult, but it is possible if latent dissatisfaction exists.

Kamen Wiping Materials Co., Inc. in Wichita, Kansas, sells high-quality recycled cloth wiping rags to manufacturers. The business essentially consists of banks of huge industrial-sized washing machines. Kamen buys soiled wiping cloths, cleans them, and then resells them to manufacturers in a variety of industries at prices much lower than paper or new cloth rags. Former President Len Goldstein became famous for getting companies such as Cessna, Beechcraft, and other heavy users of wiping materials to change wiping cloth vendors (and even change from paper to cloth, which is a big switch) by scouting out who in the company can benefit the most from the change. This person then becomes the initiator. Here, with most organizational buying decisions, what benefits the company ultimately benefits the members of the buying center, especially the purchasing agent. If buying from Kamen makes various members of the buying center look like heroes for saving money, being environmentally friendly, and so forth, Len Goldstein knew he had a great chance of getting the sale—and keeping the customer.

SUMMARY

Selling is a great career path that can also lead to significant upward mobility professionally, especially into sales management. The drivers of change we talked about in this chapter all translate into opportunities for salespeople to contribute a high level of value to their customers and their own organizations. Salespeople and their managers can and should benchmark their own approaches to managing customer relationships against the best practices of world-class sales organizations.

Selling today is so far removed from the stereotypical societal view of old-style selling as to bear no resemblance whatsoever. The key success factors needed in relationship selling all point to professionalism, strong skills, and broad and deep content knowledge that allow the salesperson to maximize his or her performance and thus rewards. It is especially interesting to examine the sales activities performed by salespeople today. Quite a few new activities have been added in recent years, driven largely by technology and the move from transactional to relationship selling approaches. Then too, understanding the categories of selling jobs available aids in decision making about whether or how to enter the selling profession. It is valuable to understand the process of selling through identification of its six stages.

Because customers are the primary focus of relationship sellers, gaining knowledge about the world of organizational buying greatly enhances the effectiveness of a salesperson in his or her role as a customer relationship manager. Many people in a client firm may influence the buyer–seller relationship and the decision of what to buy, and salespeople must carefully study each of their customers to learn what dynamics are at play within each buying center situation. Often, selling firms form selling centers and initiate team selling approaches to better serve buying centers, especially with large and complex customers (key accounts). Of course, salespeople need to fully understand and appreciate the stages of the organizational buying decision process that each of their customers goes through so the salesperson can work to add value throughout the purchasing process. Different organizational buying decision situations require different communication between buyer and seller, and the seller must be knowledgeable enough about the nature of each purchase to properly manage the process on his or her end.

Overall, the more expertise a salesperson has about how his or her own organization operates and how the customer's firm operates, the more likely the salesperson will be able to sell solutions for the customer and add value to both organizations.

KEY TERMS

drivers of change	business-to-business (B2B) market	perceived risk
autonomy		selling center
sales activities	industrial selling	team selling
job variety	trade servicer	matrix organization
intrinsic rewards	missionary seller	key account
extrinsic rewards	detailer	organizational buying decision stages
work–family conflict	technical seller	
telecommute	new business seller	derived demand
virtual office	buying center	single-source suppliers
adaptive selling	initiator	commodity products
job enlargement	user	slotting allowances
cost of a sales call	influencer	new-task purchases
retail selling	gatekeeper	modified rebuy
end-user consumer	buyer	straight rebuy
business-to-consumer (B2C) market	decider	repeat purchases
	controller	out supplier

BREAKOUT QUESTIONS

1. What does it mean to be "nimble" as a salesperson and as a sales organization? Identify one or more sales organizations that you believe are nimble.
2. Take a piece of paper and draw a line down the middle. Write "Pros" on the top left and "Cons" on the top right. Now, from your own perspective, come up with as many issues as you can on both sides regarding relationship selling as a career choice for you. Be sure to note why you list each item as you do.
3. Creativity is important to sales success. What is creativity? Give a specific example of something or several things you have done that you think are especially creative. How might creativity be taught or trained to salespeople?
4. Telecommuting and using a virtual office are major aspects of many professional sales positions. How do you feel about telecommuting and a virtual office in a job? What aspects of telecommuting and a virtual office are you most and least attracted to?
5. What aspects of sales jobs do you believe provide a strong foundation for moving up in an organization?
6. Review the top 20 key success factors for relationship selling as listed in Exhibit 2.2. Which of these factors are currently your strongest points? Which need the most work? How do you plan to capitalize on the strengths and improve on the weaknesses?
7. Pick any three of the selling activities presented in Exhibit 2.3 that you would most like to perform and then pick any three you would least like to perform. Explain your rationale for listing each as you did.
8. The chapter outlines the roles different members of a buying center play within an organizational buying context. Think of an example of a purchase process you were involved in as an end-user consumer (i.e., not an organizational buyer). Can you come up with examples of people who played these same buying center roles in the context of your example? Try to connect as many specific people to specific buying center roles as you can within the context of your particular purchase.
9. The organizational buying center varies as a function of size of the company and product or service being purchased. How does size of the company influence the composition of the buying center? How might the composition of the buying center differ for each of the following products?

    a. Purchasing a new computer for personal use.
    b. Purchasing a new copy machine for the office.
    c. Selecting a different public accounting firm.
    d. Selecting a new textbook for a sales management course.
    e. Choosing a different source for industrial oils and lubricants.
    f. Purchasing a new machine.
    g. Choosing a marketing research firm.

10. Explain the differences among a new-task purchase, modified rebuy, and straight rebuy. How is each situation likely to alter the way a salesperson approaches a client?
11. In the past, salespeople tended to have the edge over most buyers in terms of information. However, over the past 15 years access to timely and accurate information related to their business has changed how purchasing agents view their jobs. For one thing, they have been able to get a better handle on their costs and can better determine

which items to buy and from whom. How has this proliferation of information affected the relationship, both interpersonally and professionally, between purchasing agents and the sales reps calling on them?

12. Ethical Question. You are the sales manager for a leading services company in a large metropolitan area. Recently you were appointed to the board of directors of a major nonprofit community organization in your city. This brings you and the company a great deal of visibility. The chairman of the board has asked you to take on a special assignment to help define a new strategic plan for this organization. He has told you that this will take at least one day a week for the next year. You know this will expand your contacts with major "players" in the city. What should you do and why? Identify any "downsides" to your decision.

LEADERSHIP CHALLENGE: B2C VERSUS B2B

Charles Renner has been considering the implications of senior management's new growth strategy. As head of sales for Integrity Building Supplies, he had been responsible for a sales force of more than 300 salespeople that sold building supplies to contractors and large developers around the country. He, and more importantly, his sales force, knew how to sell the company's products and services in a business-to-business setting. They had a great reputation in the home-building business and for many contractors Integrity had become their supplier of first choice for many basic building supplies.

Senior management at Integrity, however, had determined there was a real opportunity for company growth by creating a retail (business-to-consumer) channel to target the homeowner wanting to take on home repair projects. The managers believed that they could not compete directly with Home Depot and Lowe's on price or selection but they could compete successfully on service. Charles agreed that the home do-it-yourself market was huge and Home Depot and Lowe's often did not provide adequate postsale service or guidance to individuals wanting to take on these kinds of projects.

The company's board of directors had approved Integrity's move into retail operations and targeted two cities, Atlanta and Dallas, as test markets for the concept. They were both large cities with a significant number of homeowners who enjoyed do-it-yourself projects; in addition, Dallas was the headquarters for Integrity.

Among the many challenges facing Charles as he pondered the future was the sales culture at Integrity. The company had been a B2B organization for its entire 60-year history. Everyone in the organization, including him, knew how to sell to other businesses (contractors, developers) but had no experience selling to consumers who had much less understanding of the products or how to use them. He knew that becoming a B2C company would require a number of changes to the sales culture.

Questions

1. What are the major differences Charles will encounter between a B2B selling environment and a B2C environment?

2. As head of sales for Integrity, what are the two most significant challenges Charles will encounter in putting together a retail sales force?

ROLE-PLAY: EMBLEM FOODS

Situation

Emblem Foods manufactures and sells a wide variety of "healthier" snack products that are typically merchandised in the diet section of supermarkets. Emblem's product line includes salty snacks (such as crackers), sweet snacks (such as cookies and some pastries), and some packaged power bar products. All of Emblem's products are lower in sugar and fat than standard fare.

Bridgette Face has been on the job as a salesperson at Emblem Foods for four weeks. She was hired right out of undergraduate business school at Mercury College, where she majored in marketing. During this first month, she spent the first and fourth weeks in a formal training program at the home office, the second week making sales calls on some of her accounts with her sales manager Geoff Knard, and the third week making sales calls alone. Bridgette really likes her job and the company so far, and she has already impressed Geoff and the trainers at the home office with her enthusiasm and professionalism.

Geoff and a recruiter from the home office are planning to make a recruiting trip to Mercury College next month. Mercury is only 90 miles from Bridgette's home base with Emblem, and Geoff has asked her to join them to help tell the next crop of graduates why careers in selling can be great. The goal is of course to attract good students to interview for careers with Emblem. Bridgette and Geoff are meeting for breakfast in a few minutes to discuss the upcoming trip.

Bridgette has never done any recruiting before, and at age 24 she is only a year older than many of the students she will visit with during the campus visit. She needs to find out what to tell them to convince them that the old stereotypes of selling are not true in today's professional selling situations. She wants to use this meeting to get Geoff to give her ideas on how to "sell" top students on considering a career with Emblem. Geoff comes prepared to help Bridgette overcome resistance she may hear to sales careers from top potential candidates.

Characters in the Role-Play

Bridgette Face, territory manager for Emblem Foods
Geoff Knard, district sales manager for Emblem Foods

Assignment

Break into pairs, with one student playing each character. It doesn't matter what the actual gender mix of your pair is. Before you stage the meeting between Bridgette and Geoff, work separately to come up with a set of the stereotypical bad and good of sales careers. At the meeting, each person should share ideas and the two should work together to prepare for the recruiting trip. Be sure Bridgette is prepared to convey the many rewarding aspects of selling to the students and to deal with questions about the stereotypes.

MINICASE: RISING ACTION BAKERY AND POWER FLOUR, LLC

Joe Reeka is a senior sales representative for Power Flour, LLC, a supplier of flour to private-label brands in supermarkets as well as to bakeries across Europe. Power Flour has developed a new white flour with a nontraditional bleaching agent, which will allow for the baking of bread products with lower carbohydrates but without a change in taste. Joe feels this new flour product would be ideal to sell to Rising Action Bakery and has sent information on the new flour to its purchasing department.

Rising Action Bakery is a small but growing chain of bakeries in Germany, specializing in "home-baked" premium bread products. Its products are baked at a central bakery and shipped to its retail stores. The management team is quite ethnically diverse including talent recruited from multiple global regions. CEO is Ana Paula Gutierrez, and she has a small senior management team consisting of a production and operations manager, Dawn Chiles; a sales and marketing manager, Nimesh Patel; a purchasing manager, Joan Wells; a finance and accounting manager, Matt Simon; and a store coordination manager, Dan Levy. Each manager leads an assistant manager/coordinator and an executive assistant. Rising Action also has a store manager and staff for each of its 24 retail stores.

Ana Paula and her five managers are meeting to discuss the results of the sales and marketing department's recent market research study on the future of low-carbohydrate diets. The results indicated that the trend may not continue, but that low-carb bread products would be in high demand for at least the next two to three years. Sales numbers have been down since the rise in popularity of low-carbohydrate diets, and Nimesh is concerned with maintaining, or hopefully increasing, Rising Action's market share by adding low-carb products to the marketing mix. Dawn's main concern is to produce the low-carb bread efficiently and without having to purchase new equipment. Dawn's assistant manager handles determination of quantities for ordering and would be involved with developing the new bread product and determining the type and amount of flour to be used. Matt is concerned that this will be a large investment in a possibly short-lived product and that the forecasted budgets did not anticipate such an outlay for inventory expense.

Joan is worried about purchasing the right amount of flour for the production needs but also keeping within the budgets determined by finance. Further, Joan is bound by Rising Action's policy of getting three bids on supply purchases. Dan is excited at the prospect of new low-carb products for the retail stores but must make the store managers aware of the changes. The stores would be instrumental in collecting feedback from their customers to determine the success of the new products. Ana Paula trusts the decision making of her management team, but ultimately she is responsible for the new products and especially has a hand in developing recipes that are up to Rising Action's taste standards.

Joan's purchasing assistant, Janice, received the written sales information from Joe Reeka of Power Flour about the new low-carb flour and has called him back for further information.

Questions

1. What participants in the organizational buying process can you identify at Rising Action?

2. Whom should Joe contact and get to know at Rising Action Bakery in order to develop the relationship with the company and achieve a sale and why? What types of information would appeal to each participant in the buying process?

3. Why would a relationship selling approach be more effective than a transactional selling approach for Joe and Power Flour?

4. What stages of the buying process can you identify in this case? Explain.

CHAPTER 3

Linking Strategies and the Sales Role in the Era of CRM and Data Analytics

LEARNING OBJECTIVES

Successful organizations today place the customer at the center of firm strategies and processes. Such customer-centric business models place the sales force in a crucial role, as salespeople are the first line of customer contact in most firms. Thus, salespeople and the selling function are key success factors in modern organizations.

An important comprehensive customer-centric business model is called customer relationship management, or CRM. This chapter provides an overview of CRM and then proceeds to illustrate how the sales force and selling function interface with strategies and processes in market-oriented, customer-centric firms. The process of strategy development and implementation is outlined, and specific guidance is provided on how personal selling can contribute to marketing strategy and what salespeople can do to maximize the success of long-term customer relationships.

After reading this chapter you should be able to

- Understand and outline the key components and goals of CRM.
- Explain the importance of a market orientation and how a market orientation is fostered within a firm.
- Identify the key steps in developing and implementing strategies.
- Describe the role of personal selling in marketing strategy.
- Outline the stages in developing strategic partnership relationships between organizations.
- Discuss the actions salespeople can take to ensure successful long-term buyer–seller relationships.

WHAT IS CUSTOMER RELATIONSHIP MANAGEMENT?

For many years, introductory marketing textbooks have talked about the marketing concept as an overarching business philosophy. At its essence, companies practicing the marketing concept turn to consumers themselves for input in making strategic decisions about what products to market, where to market the products and how to get them to market, at what price, and how to communicate with consumers about the products. These four elements (product, distribution, price, and promotion) are referred to as the marketing mix. The elements of the marketing mix represent the "tool kit" marketers use to develop marketing strategy. Personal selling fits into the marketing mix as part of a firm's marketing communication mix, or promotion mix, along with the other elements of the promotional message used by a firm to communicate with customers: advertising, sales promotion, direct marketing, and public relations and publicity.

Recently, the operationalization or implementation of the marketing concept has become known as a market orientation. That is, the actions taken by a firm that is market-oriented would be focused on aligning all the various organizational processes and functions toward maximizing the firm's success in the competitive marketplace.[1] Not surprisingly, a successful market orientation requires that the firm place the customer in the center of all strategic decisions and firm activities. Thus, a key component of market orientation is exhibiting a customer orientation in all levels and units of an organization. Considerable research indicates that firms with a higher level of customer orientation are usually more successful than less customer-oriented firms. Firms high in customer orientation are often referred to as customer-centric, because they have the customer at the center of their business model.

From a selling function perspective, a customer-centric culture includes, but is not limited to, the following major components:[2]

1. Adopting of a relationship or partnership business model, with mutually shared rewards and risk management.

2. Defining the selling role in terms of the provision of customer business consultation and solutions.

3. Increasing formalization of customer analysis processes and agreements.

4. Taking a proactive leadership role in educating customers about value chain and cost reduction opportunities.

5. Focusing on continuous improvement principles stressing customer satisfaction.

The efforts a firm makes toward cultivating a culture that is market-oriented and customer-centric require a high degree of formalization within the firm. Formalization means that structure, processes and tools, and managerial knowledge and commitment are formally established in support of the culture. With these things in place, strategies and programs may be successfully developed and executed toward the goals related to customer centricity. In general, these goals revolve around establishing and maintaining long-term customer relationships. Today, the most prevalent formalization of a customer-centric culture is customer relationship management (CRM).

CRM is a comprehensive business model for increasing revenues and profits by focusing on customers. More specifically, CRM refers to "any application or initiative designed to help your company optimize interactions with customers, suppliers, or prospects via one or more touchpoints—such as a call center, salesperson, distributor, store, branch office, Web, or e-mail—for the purpose of acquiring, retaining, or cross-selling customers."[3]

PricewaterhouseCoopers Consulting has defined CRM as "a journey of strategic, process, organizational, and technical change whereby a company seeks to better manage its enterprise around customer behaviors. This entails acquiring knowledge about customers and deploying this information at each touchpoint to attain increased revenue and operational efficiencies."[4] Touchpoints are viewed as the intersection of a business event that takes place via a channel using a medium (e.g., online inquiry from a prospect, telephone follow-up with a purchaser on a service issue, face-to-face encounter with a salesperson, etc.). At their essence, touchpoints are where the selling firm touches the customer in some way, thus allowing for information about customers to be collected.

Our discussion of CRM so far leads one to conclude that it is both an overarching philosophy of business that puts the customer at the center of strategic decision making (i.e., a customer-centric enterprise) and a programmatic, integrated implementation system (i.e., software-driven) involving a variety of channels and providers, all of which interact to contribute to the delivery of customer value. Many companies are now adopting CRM as a mission-critical business strategy. These companies are redesigning internal and external business processes and associated information systems to make it easier for customers to do business with them. Because the focus of CRM is aligning the organization's internal and external systems to be customer-centric, marketing as a discipline becomes a core contributor to the success of CRM by virtue of its disciplinary expertise on customers. Specifically, the sales force is a group within most firms that can add substantial value to the success of this process and integrating sales with other organizational functions is critical to firm success.[5]

Many of the concepts underlying CRM are not at all new. One might open a Principles of Marketing textbook from 20 years ago and find a discussion of many of the tenets of what we now refer to as CRM, albeit not particularly integrated or cross-functional in scope. What has changed in the environment to allow for the more integrated approach to customers represented by modern CRM is *technology*. More sophisticated approaches to data management are a key enabler of CRM. Yet, it is a serious mistake to consider CRM as mere software. In fact, many firms are struggling with their CRM initiatives precisely because they have bought the sophisticated software but do not have the culture, structure, leadership, or internal technical expertise to make the initiative successful.

The next section provides a foundation for understanding the concept of CRM. Then, in the remainder of the chapter we expand our discussion of the role of personal selling and the sales force in market-oriented firms and in developing and executing marketing strategies.

From Mass Marketing to One-to-One Marketing

CRM has its evolutionary roots in the progression of marketing, as enabled by advancing technology. Exhibit 3.1 illustrates this evolution from mass marketing, through target marketing, to customer marketing, to one-to-one marketing.

Mass marketing evolved in the early 1900s and dominated marketing management and strategy for decades. In the 1960s, many firms began to apply principles of segmentation, target marketing, and positioning to create different strategies and marketing programs for different consumer groups. A major change in mindset precipitates a shift from targeted consumer marketing (i.e., marketing to big groups of like-minded buyers) to customer marketing, or a focus on developing relationships with individuals. This approach first gained widespread attention in the 1980s. Many of the issues on relationship selling and strategic partnering presented later in this chapter relate to customer marketing.

Ultimately, the sophistication and multiplicity of available technology today enable true one-to-one marketing, as some firms are now able to truly customize offerings for individual users. This concept has been introduced and expanded upon in several books by Don Peppers and Martha Rogers.[6] The Technology box provides excellent examples of how tablets and smartphones can be used to enhance the customer relationship.

As mentioned earlier, CRM enters the picture as a process that provides internal formalization for enabling successful customer marketing and one-to-one marketing. CRM has three major objectives:

1. *Customer retention.* The ability to retain loyal and profitable customers and channels to grow the business profitably.

2. *Customer acquisition.* Acquisition of the right customers, based on known or learned characteristics, which drive growth and increased margins.

3. *Customer profitability.* Increased individual customer margins, while offering the right products at the right time.[7]

EXHIBIT 3.1
Marketing evolution with characteristics and technology attributes

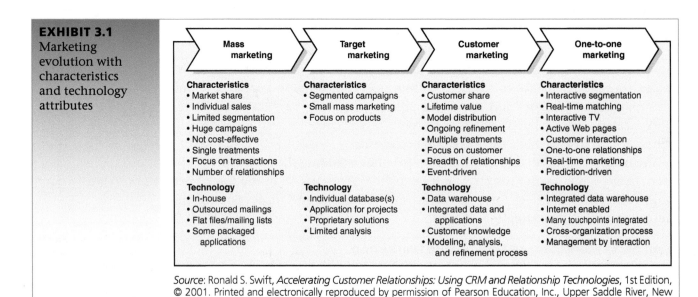

Source: Ronald S. Swift, *Accelerating Customer Relationships: Using CRM and Relationship Technologies*, 1st Edition, © 2001. Printed and electronically reproduced by permission of Pearson Education, Inc., Upper Saddle River, New Jersey.

TECHNOLOGY Sales Mobility and the Emergence of Tablets

The sales industry is always on the go. Upselling customers and finding new customers is a never-ending process. Face-to-face selling continues to have the highest success rate, which means salespeople are constantly meeting with different clients in different places. There is an emerging trend of mobile devices, specifically tablets, being used to empower salespeople who are always traveling. The many features that tablets provide are drastically changing the sales industry and processes.

Tablets are easier to use and more portable than laptops, which makes them perfect for mobile selling. They provide easy access to critical data and streamline the sales cycle for the client or prospect. Salespeople have access to client information 24/7, wherever they are. Tablets and applications are able to provide quick and professional sales quotes, proposals, and other forms that are essential in the selling process. The speed and efficiency that these mobile devices are able to provide greatly increase the chances for closing deals. Customers also appreciate the use of tablets because it adds a degree of transparency to the deal. Customers have full visibility of the process and what is being negotiated. Tablets also eliminate any confusion as salespeople are able to explain and iterate the customer's entire order and options face to face.

Mobile devices provide so many advantages to mobile selling. It is only a matter of time until these devices become the norm. Tablet sales are booming. Salespeople prefer these mobile devices because of their effectiveness and customers appreciate how easily their needs are able to be met. Mobile devices such as tablets allow enterprises to sell more and sell faster.[8]

Thus, a key realization is that CRM involves the process of acquiring, retaining, and growing profitable customers. It requires a clear focus on the service attributes that represent value to the customer and that create loyalty. Simply put, customer value means that when the customer weighs the costs (monetary and otherwise) of a relationship with a seller, the benefits realized from that relationship outweigh the costs. Building customer loyalty is an important goal of CRM processes because loyal customers are typically highly satisfied with the relationship and the product offering and are very unlikely to switch to another company and its products or brands.

CRM has several advantages over traditional mass media marketing, as has been typically used in support of mass marketing and target marketing. The advantages are that CRM

- Reduces advertising costs.

- Makes it easier to target specific customers by focusing on their needs.

- Makes it easier to track the effectiveness of a given promotional (marketing communications) campaign.

- Allows organizations to compete for customers based on service, not prices.

- Prevents overspending on low-value clients or underspending on high-value ones.

- Speeds the time it takes to develop and market a product (the marketing cycle).

- Improves use of the customer channel, thus making the most of each contact with a customer.[9]

One of the most important concepts in CRM is that of the lifetime value of a customer. In his books on customer loyalty, Frederick Reichheld has demonstrated time and again that investment in CRM yields more successful long-term relationships with customers and that these relationships pay off handsomely in terms of cost savings, revenue growth, profits, referrals, and other important business success factors. It is possible to actually calculate an estimate of the projected financial returns from a customer, providing a very useful strategic tool for deciding which customers deserve what levels of investment of various resources (money, people, time, information, etc.).[10] Such analysis has raised the prospects of firing a customer who exhibits a low predicted lifetime value and investing resources elsewhere. Of course, such action assumes other, more attractive customers exist for one's investment.[11]

CRM Process Cycle

The process cycle for CRM may be broken down into the following four elements: (1) knowledge discovery, (2) market planning, (3) customer interaction, and (4) analysis and refinement[12] (see Exhibit 3.2).

Knowledge Discovery

This is the process of analyzing the customer information acquired through the touch-points mentioned earlier. These might include point-of-sale systems, call center files, Internet accesses, records from direct sales, and any other customer contact experiences. A customer-centric data warehouse environment is the optimal approach to handling the data and transforming them into useful information for customer strategy development. A data warehouse environment affords the opportunity to combine large amounts of information and then use data mining techniques to learn more about current and potential customers. A variety of software products are available to help manage the knowledge discovery phase.

Market Planning

This is a key use of the output of the knowledge discovery phase, in that marketing and customer strategies and programs are now developed. These involve the use of the marketing mix and especially the promotion mix in integrated ways. This process will be discussed in detail later in the chapter.

Customer Interaction

This phase represents the actual implementation of the strategies and programs. This includes the personal selling effort, as well as all other customer-directed interactions. These must be aimed at all the customer touchpoints, or channels

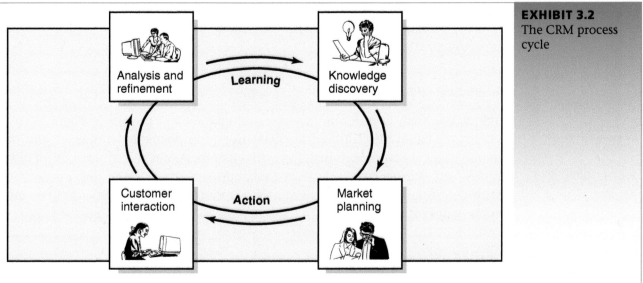

EXHIBIT 3.2
The CRM process cycle

Source: Ronald S. Swift, *Accelerating Customer Relationships: Using CRM and Relationship Technologies*, 1st Edition, © 2001. Printed and electronically reproduced by permission of Pearson Education, Inc., Upper Saddle River, New Jersey.

ETHICAL MOMENT   Ethical Limits of CRM?

Customer Relationship Management (CRM) is a comprehensive business model that enables companies to enhance and extend their customer relationship. Although the impact of implementing a CRM system can be felt throughout the organization, sales in particular is profoundly affected by CRM. The ability to assimilate information, evaluate consumer trends and behavior, and implement comprehensive customer strategies directly affects the salesperson and their relationship with the customer.

Key to the successful development of an effective CRM system is the sales force and its willingness to engage the CRM process. Often this means being an integral part of the data collection process itself, but it can also include properly interfacing with other departments in the organization, delivering prescribed marketing messaging, and other related activities. Of course, all of this takes time away from the salesperson's primary activity—selling. At the same time, the salesperson and by extension the sales manager have access to sensitive customer and company information.

For these reasons, and others, a number of ethical issues are associated with the successful implementation of any CRM system. For example, sales managers must be sensitive to the workload requirement of learning and then implementing a new CRM system. As we will see in later chapters, role stress brought on by an excessive or confusing workload can have a negative effect on salesperson motivation, performance, and job satisfaction. The issue of confidential information also raises ethical issues, as their access to sensitive information requires that salespeople and managers must hold to the highest ethical standards. Breaking the customer's trust via sensitive information collected through a CRM system holds significant ethical and legal implications.

Question to Ponder:

- From the customer's perspective, what do you think would be the greatest concerns from a privacy/security perspective about a vendor's CRM system?

of customer contact, both in person and electronically. Often these touchpoints entail collecting information from customers, which ultimately is stored by the sales organization.

Analysis and Refinement

Finally, the analysis and refinement phase of the CRM process is where learning takes place based on customer response to the implemented strategies and programs. This is a continuous dialogue with customers that is facilitated by all of the inputs for customer feedback. Over time, adjustments made to the firm's overall customer initiatives should yield more and more efficient investment of resources in the endeavor such that return on customer investment is maximized.

Toward a Relationship-Based Enterprise

As stated at the beginning of this section, CRM represents both an overarching business philosophy and a process or tool to facilitate a truly customer-driven enterprise. Facilitating long-term, win–win relationships between buyer and seller firms is a central tenet of CRM. In order to move toward being a relationship-based enterprise, and to improve the effectiveness of CRM initiatives, 10 critical questions must be answered.[13] These questions may be grouped into the following categories: customers, the relationship, and managerial decision making.

Customers

1. Who are our customers?

2. What do our customers want and expect?

3. What is the value potential of our customers?

The Relationship

4. What kind of relationship do we want to build with our customers?

5. How do we foster exchange?

6. How do we work together and share control?

Managerial Decision Making

7. Who are we?

8. How do we organize to move value closer to our customers?

9. How do we measure and manage our performance?

10. How do we increase our capacity for change?

Gaining satisfactory answers to these questions is fundamental to the success of CRM and to becoming a relationship-based firm. The answers guide (1) the evolution of the firm's relationships with customers, (2) the creation of a companywide relationship management game plan, and (3) the selection of solutions with the most appropriate combination and application of supporting technology.[14]

Given the promise of CRM, it is unfortunate that we must report a high failure and abandonment rate for CRM initiatives. The Leadership box provides insight into reasons why CRM fails.

The remainder of this chapter builds on our knowledge of the importance of customer relationships by (1) introducing the concept of market orientation, (2) outlining the process of developing strategies, (3) explaining the role of personal selling in marketing strategy, and (4) providing insights into key issues of personal selling in the relationship era.

LEADERSHIP   CRM Failures Are Often Management's Fault

Here's a mantra worth repeating: CRM software isn't stupid. People are stupid (or they can be)—especially the "management" kind of people. Problems leading to CRM failure often are traced to organizational, not software, issues. The main reason that CRM or any other type of sales force software is not successful is low user acceptance. This acceptance level by those utilizing the system is mainly not a result of technical issues but rather the following organizational issues:

1 Disruption of established routines.
2. The perception of the software as a micromanagement tool.
3. Differences in the expectations for the system from sales staff and management.
4. Perceived lack of management support for the system.

By managing these factors correctly, the software will have a much higher chance of success. Sales staff must be involved in the implementation process so that their own interests can be senselessly integrated with the new software. Management must realize that sales staffs require thorough training and clear communication regarding the expected benefits and pitfalls of the system. It is also essential that management not simply implement the system but also support and promote it until such times when salespeople are fully bought in and can clearly see the benefits for themselves.

CRM-Driven Data Analytics for Sales Manager Decision Making

Customers today are able to gather more information than ever before thanks to the wide array of technological devices that enable an Internet connection. The speed at which information can be gained as well as the sheer amount of information that can be accessed at any point in time has fostered a rapid shift in customer expectations throughout the buying process. According to analysts at Forrester, a leading independent technology and market research company, today's B2B buyer can potentially be anywhere between two-thirds and nine-tenths of the way through their customer process of making a purchase decision before ever reaching out to a vendor.[15]

Such changes in buyer behavior, brought on largely by advances in the physical and digital tools used by buyers and sellers to access and convey information, have led to concurrent changes in the skills required by the sales force to achieve success. The new skills required include heightened capabilities for salespeople to connect with current and potential customers through new and diverse channels, adapt to shifting information from customers and the market on a real-time basis, and take a collaborative and more partnership-oriented approach with customers (many of whom today have comparable or even more information about a given product than the selling organization has).[16]

As customers become more knowledgeable about companies and their products, companies in turn need to become more knowledgeable about customers, their challenges, and their opportunities (think back to the discussion of one-to-one marketing). Having the right type of customer data readily accessible for use by the sales force can be a key source of competitive advantage, and sales managers must lead and manage the process toward greater understanding of customers by ensuring that the right technology is employed and utilized effectively in this pursuit.

You've learned that CRM systems are one key means through which the effort to better understand customers and become customer oriented is enabled. In many cases a CRM system will serve as a strategic hub of valuable customer data, produced both within the system and integrated from external applications and sources. CRM systems can provide a significant amount of the data required for advanced analytics to produce valuable insights about the customers and markets that an organization serves. In addition, CRM systems can provide sales managers with important insights into how their sales force is performing and what kinds of sales outcomes can be reasonably expected from the sales force over different time horizons. CRM systems are well-suited to drive and be driven by the sheer volume of data that is being produced by customers, salespeople, and other internal and external sources.

The term big data is defined by SAS, a leading provider of data analytics software, as "the ever-increasing volume, velocity, variety, variability and complexity of information."[17] Big data, as integrated into the CRM process, provides insights for better understanding current and potential customers from a more in-depth, fact-based viewpoint. CRM systems that are well designed and developed to integrate disparate sources of data enable salespeople and sales managers to make better decisions faster in order to beat the competition in serving customer needs.

This capability is accomplished to a large degree through applying sales analytics, which are defined by Gartner as being "used in identifying, modeling, understanding and predicting sales trends and outcomes while aiding sales management in understanding where salespeople can improve." Adept use of sales analytics provides sales managers with the ability to understand their internal company environment as well as the external environment they compete in, and in turn more effectively influence sales outcomes.

Data Driven Insights into Consumers and Markets

One of the primary advantages of CRM systems and sales analytics is the ability to gain a variety of insights, such as the following.

Insights for Customer Segmentation. The vast amounts of data collected within CRM systems help salespeople and sales managers identify customers with similar needs, interests, and characteristics that may not have been apparent otherwise. These segments can then be used to define selling strategies and tactics by segment that lead to better overall performance.

Insights into the Value of Customers. Existing customers' current and expected value can be examined in terms of present and historical results as those results that are expected to be contributed in the future. For potential customers, advanced sales analytics can provide an estimation of the value of a customer to be acquired by considering factors such as the similarities between a potential customer and a segment of customers the organization has already acquired to create a predictive measure of the value of the customer to be acquired.[18] This enables the sales manager to more effectively direct the activities of the sales force and identify opportunities to maximize delivery of customer value.

Insights into Market Opportunities. Data collected within CRM systems by the sales force, customer service representatives, and digital marketers feeds analytics to better understand the market as a whole. Having a clear view of the market that an organization currently serves or desires to serve helps develop marketing and sales strategies and spot when conditions within the market are changing.

Being able to track the activities that salespeople engage in with customers provides an organization with a clearer understanding of the return on investment (ROI) of selling activities. Organizations that have their salespeople use CRM systems to track the various selling activities they engage in and employ systems that help track the status of a potential customer as that organization or individual moves through the various stages to becoming a customer (e.g., lead to prospect to customer) are in a better position to understand how the sales force is performing and also how to further enhance performance. To help make this objective easier, CRM systems commonly carry the capability to integrate data from e-mail communications and phone calls and correlate the data to the appropriate customer record in the system in order to provide deeper insight into the relationship being nurtured with a potential or current customer and ease the salesperson's burden of data entry for these elements. These capabilities enhance analytic and reporting capabilities for the organization and provide greater insights into how to better support the performance of the sales force. Some of the specific benefits include:

Promote Accountability for the Sales Force. Gaining greater visibility into the actions of the sales force means greater accountability for their actions. Standard procedures and best practices related to selling activities can be tracked within CRM systems and more easily monitored. In order to reward salespeople for timely and diligent inputting of data on their selling activities, organizations can provide incentives in the form of bonuses or other types to salespeople who perform well on this dimension.

An example of where the accountability facilitated by a CRM system comes into play relates to tracking the speed at which a member of the sales force follows up on a lead generated through the organization's website. There is a known relationship between the delay between the creation of a lead and the subsequent follow-up by a member of the sales force and the likelihood that lead will take an appointment with the salesperson who contacted them and ultimately become a customer.[19] In a general sense the longer a lead has to wait to be contacted the less likely they are to ultimately be converted into a customer. CRM systems can provide a record of when a lead was generated and when a salesperson followed up with that lead. A salesperson who understands that this type of data is being tracked in the system and that the expectation is that each lead will be followed up with promptly is more likely to make an effort to do so, especially if appropriate incentives are provided as rewards for this performance.

Provide Greater Decision Clarity and Motivation for the Sales Force. Being able to gain a more holistic view of current and potential customers also provides the sales force with the means to better plan, prioritize, and adjust to shifting conditions. Salesperson decision making is further facilitated by the kind of analytics that enable them to see how close they are to their sales quotas and how they are performing against other metrics that impact evaluation and compensation. In addition, advanced analytical methods can reveal the likelihood of a lead converting to a customer as well as the potential value of that customer. The perspective gained from these kinds of information helps a salesperson understand where they stand in relation to their objectives, and what opportunities remain to help them achieve those objectives. This knowledge makes it easier to determine what steps should be taken next at a given moment, which in turn helps provide greater motivation to continue forward towards achieving those objectives.

Enable Sales Managers to Lead and Manage. CRM based analytics help provide a view into salesperson execution of specific activities that are a part of the selling process. This knowledge enables sales managers to more closely examine the specific steps that salespeople are taking in relation to a current or potential customer and the related result. Thus, sales managers are better able to keep track of the performance of the sales team and the relative status of current and potential customers, providing greater guidance for leading and managing the sales force.

THE IMPORTANCE OF MARKET ORIENTATION

If asked to describe marketing, many people may list activities that describe only selling. And even though some companies call salespeople *marketing representatives*, selling and marketing are not synonymous. As students of marketing know, marketing involves creating products and services that satisfy customer needs, pricing those products and services to meet the customer's budget and make a profit for the firm, placing those products and services so that the customer can access them, and promoting the products and services so that the customer is aware of where they are and what they do. To some degree, the trend toward calling salespeople *marketing representatives* is an accurate portrayal because salespeople often identify customer needs, tailor products and services to meet those needs, negotiate price, and so forth. As mentioned earlier, personal selling is a part of the promotional mix of a firm, which of course represents part of a firm's marketing mix.

The marketing concept states that the key to business success is to identify and satisfy customer needs. Recall that companies that have adopted the marketing concept as a philosophy or way of doing business are considered market-oriented companies. In a market-oriented company, salespeople play a very important role because they not only identify customer needs and satisfy those needs through the sale of a product or service but must also represent the customer to various areas within the sales company. Companies that can adapt quickly to meet changing customer requirements will be successful—it is the responsibility of the sales force to see that those changing requirements are communicated to the right people so that the company can change. Customer centricity, or being customer-centric, is a key element of a market orientation.

So selling is important, not only because of the company's immediate need to generate revenue through the sale of products and services, or because selling often is the largest marketing expense, but because the future of the company depends on salespeople who can carry the voice of the customer throughout the firm. Managing the selling function is one of the most important management functions in any organization, not just because selling is so important (as we saw in Chapter 2) but also because managing selling is unique. Were it not unique, a separate course in sales management would not be necessary!

How Market Orientation Affects Performance

Market-driven companies, or those with a strong market orientation, are superior in two important ways. First, market-driven companies do a better job of market sensing, or anticipating market requirements ahead of the competition. Market sensing is the gathering of information from the market. The sales force should be one important avenue of market sensing, but other avenues include observing competitors' and customers' actions at trade shows, market research, and monitoring customer complaints.

Similarly, the second important difference is that market-driven companies are able to develop stronger relationships with their customers and their channels of distribution. Stronger relationships include more direct lines of communication. Instead of all communication going between a purchasing agent and a salesperson, interaction among engineers, for example, in all three firms (customer, manufacturer, and supplier) can occur. Stronger relationships can result in greater attention to the customer throughout the firm.

Neither important skill (market sensing and relationship building) can develop, however, without the presence of adequate spanning processes, or processes that link internal processes with the customer. Sales management is an important link in the spanning process, as sales managers must represent the sales force and customers to others in the company. For example, salespeople are often the first in the company to run into a new competitor. It takes the sales manager, however, to make sure that those responsible for pricing or product development are aware of the method by which the new competitor is attacking the market. Exhibit 3.3 illustrates the relationship of internal processes with spanning processes to link with customer requirements in market-oriented firms. In this exhibit, internal processes such as financial management are shown to link with spanning processes, such as order fulfillment, which then impact customer-linking processes or other external processes. For internal processes to contribute to the value delivered by the value chain, adequate spanning processes must exist.[20]

Internal Partnering to Create a Market Orientation

Internal and external processes are often in conflict, as different sets of objectives are sought. Sales management wants every potential customer to buy, for example, while the credit department wants only creditworthy accounts. Internal partnering is one spanning process that, when done well, can result in managing such conflict so that it has a positive effect on the firm. Internal partnering, or creating partnering relationships with other functional areas (customers and suppliers within the firm), can also serve to carry market requirements to those managers in charge of internal processes, such as credit approval. Internal partnering is a spanning process that creates a framework or environment for other spanning processes, such as postsale service, new product development, or market penetration and development processes. The result is a market orientation throughout the firm and not just in the sales force.[21]

The customer's voice must be carried to many parts of the firm—internal partnering is one mechanism for carrying that voice. Recognize, though, that it is the sales manager's responsibility to build these internal partnerships. Although a customer focus should pervade the firm, rarely do information systems, employment selection systems, personnel evaluation systems, or other systems encourage departments, other than sales, to take the initiative. In fact, it is more likely that

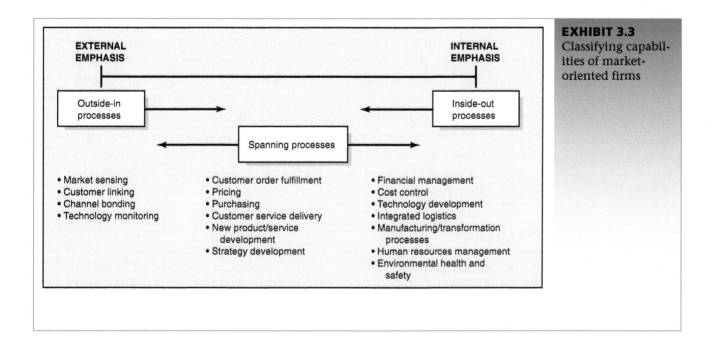

EXHIBIT 3.3
Classifying capabilities of market-oriented firms

just the opposite is true, that incentives abound to not listen to the customer. For example, it costs manufacturing managers to change production from one product to another, yet a sales manager may need to be able to offer different products in order to meet the customer's objectives.

Being market-oriented and customer-centric requires that a firm have a solid foundation of identity. A solid foundation of identity is a clear understanding of what the company is and is striving to be. Too much information is available to try to learn it all, just as too many potential opportunities exist in the marketplace to try to serve them all. A company creates an identity that helps focus learning and market orientation by first creating a sound mission and appropriate goals. Clarity in mission and goals provides the focus, or strategic direction, on which a firm's marketing strategy may be built and implemented. The next section provides a primer on this process.

THE PROCESS OF STRATEGY DEVELOPMENT

Company Mission and Goals

An organization's mission statement attempts to answer the most basic questions about its reason for being. What is our business? What should it be? These seem like simple questions, but they are often difficult for management to answer. Too many mission statements are full of platitudes and attributes that everyone has, rather than focusing on elements that truly define the organization. To illustrate the problem, a group of managers from more than 20 companies identified the same mission statement as being that of their own company![22]

Goals, or objectives, flow from the company's mission and represent more specific targets the firm wishes to meet. Example areas for goal-setting are a firm's financial position, how well it is doing in the marketplace, the quality of its products, and the level of satisfaction of its customers. Objectives are simply more specific than goals. So, for example, P&G might have a goal to maintain its position as number one in market share in the toothpaste category, but flowing from this might be quite a few specific objectives such as increasing global sales on its lucrative Crest Pro-Health line of oral hygiene products by 20 percent in 2016. Generally, good objectives should always be (1) specific, (2) measurable, (3) and realistically attainable.

SBU Strategy

In organizations with multiple divisions or strategic business units (SBUs), each SBU is likely to have its own objectives and a distinct strategy for accomplishing them. For example, General Electric has many global strategic business units competing in quite distinct markets—appliances, aircraft, plastics, and power systems, to name a few. The keystone of a business-level strategy is a decision about how the business will compete in its industry to achieve a sustainable competitive advantage (SCA). An SCA is based on the set of distinctive competencies exhibited by the firm. That is, what quality or attribute of the organization sets it aside from its competitors? How is it, or how will it be, different from the rest of the pack?[23] Hyundai, for example, has as one of its distinctive competencies its unique mix of product quality, desirable features, and reasonable price. As a Korean brand, this combination has made it highly competitive with Japanese models that in the past were viewed as far superior to Korean models. An SBU may contain a number of different products or brands, and its competitive strategy will influence and constrain the marketing goals/objectives, strategies, and functional programs—including the activities of the sales force—appropriate for each of those products.

Several authors have developed classification systems that identify a few common or generic strategies pursued by business units across a variety of industries. The best known of these was developed by Michael Porter. He defined three basic competitive strategies: low cost, differentiation, and niche (or focus).[24] Another popular typology of competitive strategies was developed by Miles and Snow. They classified strategies according to the emphasis placed on growth through new product and market development, and they labeled the resulting categories prospector, defender, and analyzer strategies.[25] Brief definitions of these six generic business strategies are provided in Exhibit 3.4[26] along with some specific implications of different competitive strategies for a business's selling programs and activities.

The strategy process represents a series of steps. These steps are portrayed in Exhibit 3.5. Once a business has decided how it will compete in order to gain a sustainable advantage over other firms, it must then decide where to compete: what specific product markets or market segments it will target. This decision involves assessing the available market opportunities.

Step One: Analyze Market Opportunities

In the broadest sense, a market opportunity exists whenever some human need is unsatisfied. However, an unsatisfied need represents a viable and attractive opportunity for a firm only if:

1. The opportunity is consistent with the mission and objectives of the firm.

2. Enough potential customers exist for the needed product or service so the total potential sales volume is, or will be, substantial.

3. The firm has the necessary resources and expertise to capture an adequate share of the total market.

Evaluating market opportunities involves first evaluating the environmental factors affecting the market and estimating the total market potential for a good or service. Next, the firm must evaluate its capabilities and strengths compared with those of competitors to estimate the share of the total market potential it can reasonably hope to secure. Later, after a specific marketing strategy has been determined, the firm can develop sales forecasts of the actual sales volume it expects to attain over a specified time period.

These estimates of total market potential, company sales potential, and sales forecasts are critical to the firm's sales plans. They provide the basis for defining sales territories, deploying salespeople, and setting sales quotas. Methods for analyzing market opportunities and generating sales forecasts are examined in more detail in Chapter 5.

Market opportunities usually do not involve every consumer or organizational buyer in the marketplace. Market opportunities should be defined, and marketing strategies developed, for specific target markets, which usually consist of only one or a few customer segments with relatively homogeneous preferences and characteristics.

Step Two: Generate Strategies

Strategy generation is a creative task. Typically, several strategies will achieve the same objective. For example, a computer firm interested in increasing its market share might (1) attempt to leapfrog its competitors by introducing a technically superior new generation of computers, (2) attempt to become the low-cost producer and compete aggressively on price, or (3) appeal to customers by developing more convenient distribution.

The key at this stage is to be as creative as possible. The idea is not to evaluate strategies but to generate them. Not only is listing some "far-out" strategies acceptable at this stage, but it is desirable. Later stages in the process will reduce this original

EXHIBIT 3.4
Generic business strategies and their implications for the sales force

Porter's Typology

Low-Cost Supplier

Aggressive construction of efficient-scale facilities, vigorous pursuit of cost reductions from experience, tight cost and overhead control, usually associated with high relative market share.

Differentiation

Creation of something perceived industrywide as being unique. Provides insulation against competitive rivalry because of brand loyalty and resulting lower sensitivity to price.

Niche (or focus)

Service of a particular target market, with each functional policy developed with this target market in mind. Although market share in the industry might be low, the firm dominates a segment within the industry.

Sales Force Implications

Servicing large current customers, pursuing large prospects, minimizing costs, selling on the basis of price, and usually assuming significant order-taking responsibilities.

Selling nonprice benefits, generating orders, providing high-quality customer service and responsiveness, a possibly significant amount of prospecting if a high-growth industry, selecting customers based on low-price sensitivity. Usually requires a high-quality sales force.

Becoming experts in the operations and opportunities associated with the target market. Focusing customer attention on nonprice benefits and allocating selling time to the target market.

Miles and Snow's Typology

Prospector

Attempt to pioneer in product market development. Offer a frequently changing product line and be willing to sacrifice short-term profits to gain a long-term stronghold in their markets.

Defender

Offer a limited, stable product line to a predictable market. Markets are generally in the late growth or early maturity phase of the product life cycle. Emphasis is on being the low-cost producer through high volume.

Analyzer

Choose high-growth markets while holding on to substantial mature markets. Analyzers are an intermediate type of firm. They make fewer and slower product market changes than prospectors, but are less committed to stability and efficiency than defenders.

Sales Force Implications

Primary focus is on sales volume growth. Territory management emphasizes customer penetration and prospecting.

Maintain the current customer base. Very little prospecting for new customers is involved. Customer service is emphasized along with greater account penetration.

Must balance multiple roles—servicing existing customers, prospecting for new customers, uncovering new applications, holding on to distribution of mature products, and supporting campaigns for new products.

Adapted from William L. Cron and Michael Levy, "Sales Management Performance Evaluation: A Residual Income Perspective," *Journal of Personal Selling & Sales Management* 7 (August 1987), pp. 57–66.

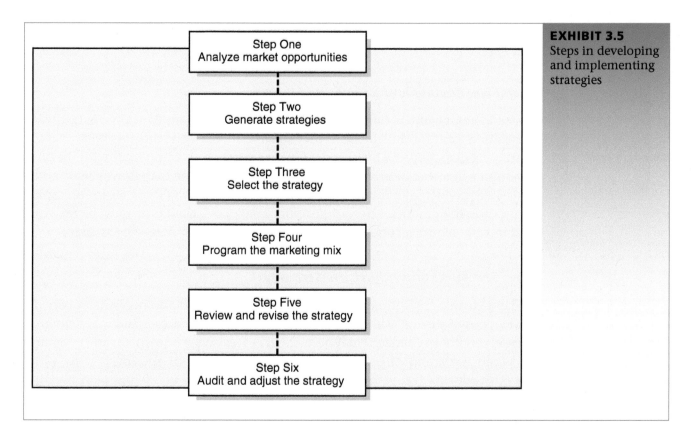

EXHIBIT 3.5
Steps in developing and implementing strategies

list to a more reasonable set. However, generating as many ideas as possible to begin with will ensure that the better strategies are entertained when evaluating alternatives. Even the most sophisticated evaluation procedure cannot select the optimal strategy if no one has thought of it.

Step Three: Select the Strategy

The criteria used to select the most promising marketing strategy should be directly related to the objectives to be accomplished. For example, if the major marketing objective is to increase market share, then those strategies likely to yield high share increases should be scrutinized. Typically, however, a business will have several marketing objectives, and the strategy that is best for one might be detrimental in achieving another. Thus, the best overall strategy may not be the best for any single objective.

Step Four: Program the Marketing Mix

A marketing program combines elements of the marketing mix to implement the strategy. It reflects a particular allocation of financial and human resources. The decision involves three questions: (1) How much is going to be spent on the total marketing effort? (2) How is that expenditure going to be allocated among the elements of the marketing mix? (3) How are the dollars and effort allocated to an element going to be divided among the possible activities? The program level is where the formulation of the firm's sales program often enters the planning picture—it is one part of the firm's overall marketing communications program.

Step Five: Review and Revise the Strategy

Those in charge of the functional areas of the business are typically charged with generating plans for the functions they supervise. This raises the possibility that the marketing plan prepared by a product manager may be incompatible with the business unit's financial or production plans. For example, the cash flows generated by projected product sales might be insufficient or provide too low a return on capital to produce the product. The various functional plans, therefore, must be reviewed and integrated into a cohesive whole at the business-unit and corporate level.

Step Six: Audit and Adjust the Strategy

Today's volatile environment makes planning crucial and also necessitates periodic evaluations of these plans. As competitors adjust their strategies and other environmental conditions change, it may be necessary to revise the firm's plans and programs.

When goals and objectives have been spelled out in specific and measurable terms during the planning process, controlling the marketing plan is rather straightforward. It involves periodic comparisons of actual results with the sales volume, market share, expense budgets, and other objectives specified in the plan. When the results deviate from planned levels, management can attempt to find out why and, if necessary, take corrective action. This could involve adjusting specific elements of the marketing mix, adopting a new marketing strategy, or possibly reevaluating market opportunities.

The sales manager plays a major role in this evaluation and control process since he or she is responsible for evaluating the results of the sales program. Part Three of this book is devoted to a discussion of this control and adjustment process.

THE IMPORTANCE OF INTEGRATING SALES WITH OTHER BUSINESS FUNCTIONS

Looking back in time, it is fair to say that the sales function operated as a stand-alone entity for many years. In truth, the sales force has been something of a mystery to the rest of the organization. Whether because of the widely dispersed footprint of most sales forces or perhaps the renegade image of salespeople as individualists, sales has stood alone and frankly never seemed to mind.

The most classic example of the sales force being at odds with other business functions is the tenuous relationship that has existed over time between sales and marketing. These two functions that are so aligned in their ultimate objectives (i.e., to acquire and retain profitable customers) seemed to have bickered back and forth since the beginning of time. Marketing accuses sales of failing to execute on their elegantly designed marketing strategies, while sales accuses marketing of sitting in an ivory tower unaware of the real-world challenges they face in the field. It has appeared for decades as though the siblings would never move beyond their distrust of one another.

The icy relationship between sales and marketing has now warmed in most top organizations. In part, this improved relationship has been driven by sales' adoption of concepts like customer segmentation and value propositions, which were traditionally in marketing's realm. Similarly, marketing has come under pressure from executives to demonstrate their ability to drive revenue growth, traditionally a metric directly attributable to sales. These trends, along with the implementation of CRM to improve the sharing of information, have contributed to sales' and marketing's decision to join forces.

Marketing is not the only corporate function that has begun to integrate itself with sales, though. With the introduction of technology like sales force automation (SFA) in the 1990s, sales has come to depend heavily on the information technology (IT) department for its mission-critical tools. And as the demand for talented professional salespeople has come to outstrip supply, sales has also developed an intimate relationship with human resources to help them identify, hire, retain, and develop world class sellers and managers.

The willingness of various departments within world class sales companies to link with the sales leaders specifically to work on common initiatives seems to be a direct outcome of progress in building a customer-driven culture. Managers and individual contributors throughout the organization start to judge the value of their contribution by its impact on both internal and external customers. When a common external objective becomes the focus, intra-political positioning begins to diminish in favor of the "bonding" impetus from all parties facing a common "enemy," such as customer dissatisfaction or the competition. The constant refocus of attention on the external goal of delighting customers and surpassing competitors creates an enthusiasm and project momentum that usually dwarfs all but the most imbedded turf issues. In addition, recognition and even key compensation elements that are geared to broader company goals tend to melt the functional silos that occur in most "traditional" organizations.

The incidence of cross-functional meetings increases. Operations meetings routinely include customer service reps and have salespeople participating by teleconference. Human resources and training departments regularly meet with sales to review the tracking associated with the efficiency and effectiveness of the selection, development, and retention processes for customer-interfacing personnel. IT professionals design and develop tools through extensive field study and user input so that the resulting automated processes reduce workload and come across as intuitive and user friendly.

The boundaries between functions blur as more initiatives are collaborative from onset to completion rather than a series of sequential outcomes managed separately within each function. "Team" becomes an adjective attached to the core values of the total organization, and it is not just politically correct corporate speak. In short, leading sales forces no longer view themselves as self-contained entities with all of their required support functions within. Their sales executives have purposefully narrowed their scope so they can concentrate on what they do best—adding value through personal interactions with customers. Marketing, IT, HR, and other corporate peers are more capable in their areas of expertise, and they are being called on to support sales in meaningful ways. The more tightly sales can integrate itself with other parts of the organization, the more leverage they will have to ratchet up their own performance.[27]

PERSONAL SELLING'S ROLE IN MARKETING STRATEGY

As mentioned earlier, a number of choices face strategic planners, choices that include the type of strategy à la Porter or Miles and Snow. Another choice facing strategic marketing planners is the type of relationship desired with the market or segments of the market. The nature of the sales force and its role in carrying out a firm's marketing strategy depend on the type of relationship with the market desired by the organization. Other factors, such as the cost to serve a market, also affect the role of the sales force, as we will discuss.

Role of the Relationship

Most people think of relationships as the bonds that exist between people, and that definition works in many social instances. In business, though, it is more helpful to recognize that relationships occur along a continuum that can be defined by the types of transactions between a buyer and seller. Three basic relationship types exist along this continuum: market exchanges, functional relationships, and strategic partnerships. Exhibit 3.6 summarizes the characteristics of each of these relationship types.

Market Exchanges

At one end of the continuum are market exchanges, or one-shot transactions that occur between a buyer and seller without much thought of future interaction. For example, consider a gasoline purchase. Most people purchase gasoline where it is convenient when they are low on gas. They don't buy gasoline at the same place time after time because they like the clerk and want to do business with that store. Yet, over time, it is possible that a large percentage of purchases are made at the same gas station. These purchases still represent market exchanges because it is the location of the station that drives the purchase—it is on the way to work or closest to the house and so on.

EXHIBIT 3.6 Types of relationships between buyers and sellers		Type of Relationship		
	Characteristics of the Relationship	**Market Exchange**	**Functional Relationship**	**Strategic Partnership**
	Time horizon	Short term	Long term	Long term
	Concern for other party	Low	Medium	High
	Trust	Low	High	High
	Investment in relationship	Low/medium	High	High
	Nature of relationship	Conflict, bargaining	Cooperation	Collaboration
	Risk in relationship	Low	Medium	High
	Potential benefits	Low	Medium	High

Adapted from Stephen B. Castleberry and John F. Tanner, *Selling: Building Partnerships*, 8th ed. (New York: Irwin/McGraw-Hill, 2011).

Do salespeople have a role in market exchanges? Yes, but that role may be different or even uncomfortable for traditional sales forces. Neil Rackham described four different roles for salespeople operating in a market exchange (transactional) selling environment:[28]

1. *Create new value.* Find a way to create a truly distinctive offering, either by product innovation or by developing truly distinctive services that are of real and measurable value to customers and, in so doing, escape a transactional role.

2. *Adapt.* Reengineer your sales approach to succeed in transactional selling by relentlessly stripping out sales and related costs.

3. *Make the market.* Find ways to profit from the transaction itself, either in addition to or in place of the profit you make from the products you sell. A great example of this is the SABRE airline reservation system originally operated by American Airlines' former parent AMR Corporation. While air travel has become increasingly a commodity, SABRE has positioned itself to make money from the transactions a commodity-driven system generates.

4. *Exit.* If you can't figure out a way to succeed in this type of sale, then seriously consider disengaging from the transactional segment of the market, this transactional product or product line, or this transactional customer type.

From the preceding it may be obvious that several characteristics of a market can influence the use of a market exchange relationship strategy. Characteristics such as lack of product differentiation (i.e., commodity products), competition primarily on price, and similar factors can necessitate a market exchange strategy.

Functional Relationships

As we move along the continuum portrayed in Exhibit 3.6, functional relationships reflect the middle area. Functional relationships are long-term relationships between buyer and seller based on close personal friendships. These personal relationships create a climate of cooperation, with open and honest communication.

When functional relationships are appropriate, the salesperson's relationship with the buyer is critical. Examples include financial planning (where the broker becomes a trusted confidant of the client) and contract manufacturing, an industry where salespeople develop strong relationships with product designers so that the sellers' components are included in new products.

Functional relationships can be appropriate when a high level of personal trust is required to manage the business relationship and when the salesperson has special expertise that provides competitive advantage. In these situations, it is in the buyer's best interest to seek a functional relationship. Functional relationships can grow for other reasons that are not strategic.

One danger of functional relationships for the selling organization becomes reality when one party leaves. If the buyer changes jobs, even within the buying organization, a new functional relationship must be created. Similarly, if the salesperson leaves, the relationship is at risk, particularly if the salesperson goes to a competing company. In some industries, it is quite common for salespeople to take their accounts with them—these are industries characterized by functional relationships.

Strategic Partnerships

At the far end of the continuum from market exchanges are strategic partnerships. Strategic partnerships are long-term relationships in which the partners make significant investments to improve the profitability of both companies and jointly achieve strategic objectives. In a true strategic partnership, the relationship is between two organizations and reflects a wide range of personal relationships between members of the two organizations. Thus, the relationship is no longer solely salesperson-centered.

The salesperson still plays an important role, however. This relationship requires direct communication with production, product designers, and others, but the salesperson is responsible for ensuring that the relationship remains strong. Salespeople are both relationship managers and general managers because they are responsible for ensuring the mutual profitability that arises out of the relationship. As relationship managers, they work directly with the buyer to codevelop joint strategic programs and to strengthen the relationship. As general managers, they work within their own organization to see that the strategic programs are carried out.[29]

Strategic partnerships cannot be created with every customer, nor should they be. Strategic partnerships should be created only with customers that are large and can make the investments needed worthwhile, with customers that are innovative and that can provide technology other customers cannot, or with customers that provide access to markets better than any other customer. For example, P&G and Walmart share a well-publicized strategic partnership. Walmart teaches P&G supply chain management methods that enable the firm to be more profitable with all customers. Walmart benefits from P&G's market knowledge and marketing technology. Through this knowledge and technology, Walmart is able to codevelop new markets and new products with P&G so that both companies can capitalize on market opportunities.

PERSONAL SELLING IN THE RELATIONSHIP ERA

The name of the game today for sales organizations is the development of long-term relationships with customers. As we have seen, a CRM model provides internal organizational formalization to support this goal and promote customer loyalty. As we have also learned, often the end result may be a strategic partnership between the seller and buyer firms. What is the role of the salesperson in the era of CRM and customer-centric firms? Some have tried to claim that, given advanced technology,

INNOVATION Building Customer Relationships

Building relationships and maintaining customer loyalty are some of the key goals for organizations today. Following are some of the techniques that may be used to foster strong relationships with customers:

1. Underpromise, overdeliver. This perception of exceeding expectations can result in the customer wanting the same experience in the future.

2. Don't forget the small things. Customers want to know that you care, and showing them that you account for even the smallest concerns they may have will help give them this cared-for feeling.

3. Stay in contact. Even when a sale is not to be made, contact your customers often to thank them. Make this contact genuine and unexpected where possible.

4. Establish a feedback system to monitor your customers' feelings regarding the quality of the service they received. Make sure to act on any negative comments that may later affect their loyalty. These steps should help strengthen the relationship between salesperson and customer and, in turn, strengthen the feeling of loyalty the customer experiences.

electronic channels, and increased tendency for categories of goods and services to be viewed as commodities by customers, the role of personal selling in the twenty-first century will be greatly diminished. However, in our view quite the opposite is true. Certainly, the sales role has changed in modern organizations. But rather than it being diminished, we contend that salespeople have a stronger role than ever before in the success of a firm's customer-centric strategy. The key is, what specifically should salespeople do to maximize the success of long-term-relationship-driven organizations? This section examines some of these sales role issues.

Salespeople have a key role to play in fostering successful relationships. Relationships between organizations that result in strategic partnerships generally go through four stages: awareness, exploration, expansion, and commitment. The focus of the following discussion is on the last three of these stages because these distinguish transactional market exchanges from strategic partnerships vis-à-vis Exhibit 3.6. Remember that a key goal in today's organizations is gaining customer loyalty. The Innovation box explains some of the techniques that can be used to build strong customer relationships and loyalty.[30]

Exploration Stage

In the exploration stage, each side tries to determine the potential value of the relationship. As time goes on, the relationship becomes defined through the development of expectations for each party and the results of individual transactions or interactions. For example, the buyer begins by evaluating the timeliness of follow-ups to requests for information or makes a purchase and tests the seller's product and service. At the same time, trust and personal relationships develop. Building trust is a very important part of developing long-term relationships and represents confidence that a salesperson's word or promise can be believed and that the salesperson has the long-term interests of the customer at the core of his or her approach to doing business.

A strong exploration stage is important for the relationship to flourish over time. When the buyer tries the product for the first time, that customer is excited about receiving the benefits of the product as promised by the salesperson. A poor initial experience is extremely difficult to overcome. Beginning the relationship well requires the salesperson to set the proper expectations, monitor order processing and delivery, ensure proper use of the product, and assist in servicing the customer.

Set Proper Expectations

Many businesspeople try "to underpromise and overdeliver," a catchphrase to encourage salespeople not to promise more than they can deliver, but also to remind salespeople to try to deliver more than was promised in order to pleasantly surprise the buyer. Customer delight, or exceeding customer expectations to a surprising degree, is a powerful way to gain customer loyalty. Overpromising can get the initial sale, but a dissatisfied customer not only will not buy again but also will tell many others to avoid that salesperson and his or her company.

Monitor Order Processing and Delivery

The first expectation the buyer has is that the product will be delivered on time and ready to use. A common temptation is to quote a short delivery time in order to win the sale, even when the rep knows that delivery time can't be met. Giving in to such temptation causes trouble with the customer and with those responsible for the shipping function. Neither will be happy with the salesperson who makes such promises. On the other hand, the salesperson should monitor the order processing and delivery processes to make sure that nothing goes wrong.

Ensure Proper Use

Some buyers may know how to operate the basic features of a product, but if the product is not operating at maximum efficiency, the customer is losing value. Many firms have staffed a customer service department or tasked their technical support group with training customers, but it is still the salesperson's responsibility to make sure that the customer is getting full value of use.

Assist in Servicing

Not all quiet customers are happy. Recent research indicates that users may be dissatisfied long before decision makers are aware of it.[31] Salespeople can learn of such problems by working closely with their company's technical or customer support personnel. Then they can address similar situations in other accounts before the problems grow into complaints.

Complaints may arise at any stage of the relationship, but when complaints arise during the exploration stage, the salesperson has the opportunity to prove commitment to the account. When customers sense that commitment, either through the handling of a complaint or through other forms of special attention, they may be ready to move into the expansion stage.

Expansion Stage

The expansion stage of the relationship process is marked by the opportunity to sell new products or increase the share of the account's business. Trust is developing, allowing the salesperson to focus on identifying additional needs and recommending solutions. Several strategies, including generating repeat sales, cross-selling, and full-line selling, may be used to expand business with current accounts and move them toward loyalty and long-term commitment to the relationship.

Generating Repeat Sales and Upgrading

In some situations, the most appropriate strategy is to generate repeat orders, particularly for supply items and other operating needs. Generating repeat sales requires recognizing buying cycles and being present at buying time. Upgrading is convincing the buyer to use a higher-quality product or newer product and is similar to generating repeat sales. The buyer selects the upgrade because it meets needs better or more efficiently than did the old product.[32]

Full-Line Selling

Selling the entire line of associated products is called full-line selling. Many companies try to get their foot in the door with any sale in order to prove their company's worth as a supplier. The hope is that the buyer will want to purchase the full line after trying out the company. Full-line selling is not the same as full-line forcing, a practice used when a company has one top-selling product that it sells through distributors. Full-line forcing occurs when the company forces distributors to carry the full line in order to be able to sell the top seller. Full-line selling is a sales strategy that involves leveraging the relationship in order to sell the entire line of products. Full-line forcing is a questionable sales tactic, one that got Microsoft a great deal of negative publicity when it bundled its Web browser with its operating system. In contrast, full-line selling is a legitimate method of strengthening the relationship.

Cross-Selling

Cross-selling is similar to full-line selling but reflects selling products that may not be related. Cross-selling works best when the salesperson can leverage the existing relationship with the buyer. Trust in the salesperson and the selling organization already exists; therefore, the sale should not be as difficult if the proper needs exist. If the buying center for the second product line changes greatly, cross-selling becomes more like the initial sale.[33]

Commitment Stage

The basis of expanding a relationship is a solid foundation of customer loyalty. Loyal customers not only exhibit repeat purchase behavior; they also are very reluctant to switch suppliers because of their high level of trust and satisfaction with the salesperson, the selling firm, and its products. As such, customers who are truly loyal are committed to the relationship.

When the buyer–seller relationship has reached the commitment stage, a stated or implied pledge to continue the relationship is in place. Formally, this pledge may begin with the seller being designated a preferred supplier. Although preferred supplier status may mean different things in different companies, in general it means that the supplier is assured a large percentage of the buyer's business and will get the first opportunity to earn any new business.[34] In firms with total quality management (TQM) initiatives in place, all members of the organization are focused on continually working to eliminate errors and defects in all aspects of their products and processes. Sophisticated quality measurement systems and empowerment of employees to take action to fix quality problems are hallmarks of TQM. In such firms, suppliers are typically required to meet rigorous standards in order to be on a preferred supplier list. These standards typically center on making sure the supplier consistently meets the same quality standards as the selling firm. Boeing, Motorola, and Harley-Davidson, for example, all are long-time TQM proponents. Each of these firms closely monitors the quality standards of their parts suppliers and will quickly take a supplier off the preferred list if a pattern of quality problems develops. In the retail field, both Walmart and Target aggressively require that their merchandise suppliers adhere to rigorous quality and product safety standards, and both have active in-house and product testing programs to ensure compliance.

Securing Commitment

Commitment in a relationship should permeate both organizations, supported by a market-oriented and customer-centric culture. Commitment comes from both organizations, and the salesperson must secure commitment not only from the customer but also from the rest of his or her own company. Senior management must be convinced of the benefits of developing a long-term relationship with the account so that the appropriate investments will be made. Additionally, the salesperson has to see that others in the organization are empowered to serve the needs of this customer. For example, if Walmart has a problem with P&G's billing process, P&G's corporate billing department should work directly with Walmart's accounts payable group to resolve the issue and design a more appropriate process. Alignment of billing, shipping, and other key systems is a hallmark of a strong business partnership.[35]

As discussed in Chapter 2, selling activities vary depending on the type of sales job, the firm's relationship strategy, and the stage of the relationship. One element, though, that is common is that a competitive advantage may be gained by matching the selling process to how customers want to buy. Few people exclaim to their friends, "Look at the car I was sold!" Rather they say, "Look at the car I bought!" As we learned in Chapter 2, recognizing how buyers want to buy and creating a selling process that enhances that decision process is an important method of gaining competitive advantage.

PERSONAL SELLING'S ROLE IN THE MARKETING COMMUNICATION MIX

As we have seen, the sales force plays a key role in accomplishing a relationship strategy. A sales force, as we discussed earlier, is just one element in the marketing communication mix. Other elements, such as advertising, sales promotion, direct marketing, and public relations/publicity, are also used to communicate a relationship strategy. Taken as a whole, the various ways the firm strategically communicates its message about its products to the marketplace are referred to as its integrated marketing communication (IMC) strategy. The choice of such elements can influence the role of the sales force, and concurrently the role of the sales force affects other marketing communication choices. This is why effective marketing communication must truly be integrated in the way it uses personal selling, advertising, and the other communication options. The factors that affect the actual role of the sales force include the cost to serve a market segment at the desired service level for the realized market value.

Each customer has a desired service level. In recent years Xerox, who has substantially expanded their business from copying machines to broad document management solutions, has altered its selling options away from just the standard company sales force and into more independent distributors in order to cut costs and increase market coverage. This is possible because a small account for Xerox would not need a Xerox representative assigned to it so long as other sales channels can satisfy the account's needs. Nor would it make sense for Xerox because the realized market value, or profit, of that account would be too low. The challenge for sales managers is balancing the customer's desired service level with the appropriate cost to serve so that a profit is made. In Chapter 5 we address how information may be used to develop and assign sales territories and perform sales analysis.

Advantages and Disadvantages of Selling in Marketing Communication

The advantages of personal selling as a marketing communication tool stem largely from its face-to-face communication with a potential customer. Personal sales messages are often more persuasive than advertising or publicity in the mass media. Another advantage of face-to-face contact in personal selling is that the sales representative can communicate a larger amount of complex information than can be transmitted with other promotional tools. The salesperson can demonstrate the product or use visual aids. And since the salesperson is likely to call on the same client many times, the rep can devote a great deal of time to learning about that client's problems and needs and to educating the client about the advantages of appropriate products or services. The long-term contact in personal selling is particularly important when the product or service can be customized to fit the needs of an individual customer—as is often the case in functional and strategic relationships—or when the terms of sale are open to negotiation.

The primary disadvantage of personal selling as a marketing communication tool is that a sales rep can communicate with only a small number of potential customers. Consequently, personal selling is much more costly per person reached than the other promotional tools. An advertisement in a publication such as *Newsweek* or *Time* costs only pennies per reader, but as we saw in Chapter 2, the cost of a single sales call often costs hundreds of dollars.

Bottom line, personal selling should play a substantial role in a firm's marketing communication mix only when the tasks involved are performed better by face-to-face selling than any other method. Such communication tasks include the following:

1. Transmitting large amounts of complex information about the firm's products or policies.

2. Adapting product offerings or promotional appeals to the unique needs and interests of specific customers.

3. Convincing customers that the firm's products or services are better on at least some dimensions than similar offerings of competitors.

As Exhibit 3.7 indicates, the communication tasks actually faced by a business—and the appropriate amount of personal selling effort to be used in the IMC strategy—depend on the business's objectives, marketing strategy, and resources; the number and type of customers in its target market; and the nature of the other elements of its marketing mix: (1) product characteristics, (2) distribution practices, and (3) pricing policies.

Company Resources, Goals, and Marketing Strategy

Although the costs per person reached are high for personal selling, a successful personal selling effort may require a smaller total financial outlay than either an advertising or a sales promotion campaign. The high costs involved in extensive advertising and sales promotion efforts limit their use by smaller firms. Such firms must often rely on personal selling—perhaps supplemented with less expensive advertising or other forms of communication such as the Internet or trade shows—as their primary promotional tool.

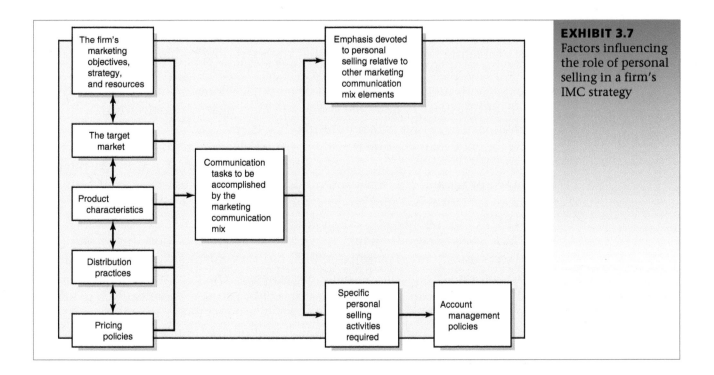

EXHIBIT 3.7
Factors influencing
the role of personal
selling in a firm's
IMC strategy

If the firm's goal is to expand distribution by persuading more wholesalers or retailers to carry the product, then a strong personal selling effort and perhaps a trade promotion program are indicated. The highly persuasive nature of personal selling also makes it an appropriate tool when the objective is to take market share away from established competitors, especially if the product is a relatively complex industrial or consumer durable good. Finally, if the objective is simply to maintain the market share of a well-established product, "reminder" advertising should play the primary role in the marketing communication mix.

Characteristics of the Target Market

Because various marketing communications tools differ greatly in their costs per person reached, the number of potential customers in the firm's target market, their size, and their geographic distribution influence the communications mix. For example, in order to justify the higher costs, personal selling is most often emphasized when the target market contains relatively few customers, the average customer is likely to place a relatively large order, and customers are clustered close together. Firms that sell to industrial markets with few potential customers, and those that distribute their products through a small number of wholesale intermediaries, commonly rely on personal selling as their primary marketing communication mix element. Firms that sell to large, geographically dispersed, consumer markets place primary emphasis on the more cost-efficient advertising and sales promotion methods.

Product Characteristics

Most marketing textbooks suggest that the marketing communication mixes for industrial products concentrate heavily on personal selling; those for consumer durable goods utilize a combination of personal selling and advertising; and producers of consumer nondurable goods rely most heavily on advertising and sales promotion. The reason is that industrial goods and consumer durables tend to be more complex than consumer nondurable goods, so potential buyers need more information to make a purchase decision. Also, industrial goods can often be designed or modified to meet the needs of individual customers, and consumer durables (as well as complex services, such as financial or insurance services) often present the buyer with a range of options.

These generalizations should be viewed with some caution. Industrial goods producers usually stress personal selling, but they might also do extensive advertising and public relations to build awareness of the company and its products so the sales force can gain access to potential customers more easily.[36] Similarly, although a consumer goods producer such as Nabisco might spend large sums on media advertising and sales promotion, it is also likely to field a sales force to call on retailers and build reseller support in its distribution channels.

To make matters even more complicated, the Internet and the whole field of electronic commerce are blurring the distinctions among the various promotional tools. A company's website can (1) communicate large amounts of product information, (2) generate leads for the firm's field sales force to follow up, or (3) allow interested customers to bypass face-to-face contact with a salesperson and order the firm's products electronically.

Distribution Practices

As mentioned, personal selling is often necessary to build reseller support and develop adequate distribution for a product, regardless of whether it is a consumer good or industrial good. The importance of the sales force's role in building a distribution channel is affected by the firm's strategy for influencing resellers to buy its product. When a firm follows a pull strategy, it attempts to build strong customer demand for its brand. The focus is on a strong advertising program aimed at end users. This encourages wholesalers and retailers to carry the product to satisfy their customers and reap the resulting sales and profits.

The manufacturer's sales force often plays a support role in implementing a pull strategy. Because demand is primarily created through advertising to end users, salespeople must ensure that sufficient product is on the shelf, proper shelf signing is up, off-shelf displays are built, and store personnel are familiar with the products.

When a firm uses a push strategy to build reseller support, it offers direct incentives to potential wholesalers and retailers to encourage them to stock the product. When consumers see the product in the store, it is hoped that they will like it and buy it. A wide range of incentives may be offered to resellers, including the following: (1) development of just-in-time reorder and delivery programs that help resellers reduce their investments in inventory and improve inventory turnover, (2) category management programs in which manufacturers work with resellers to maximize sales volumes and margins in the product categories in which the selling firm's products are represented, (3) price promotions, (4) volume discounts, (5) contests for the reseller's salespeople, (6) training programs for resellers, (7) cooperative advertising programs, and (8) point-of-purchase promotional materials.[37]

The manufacturer's sales force plays a principal role in implementing a push strategy. The sales force must explain the advantages of carrying and promoting the supplier's products to prospective channel members, persuade them to stock and aggressively merchandise those products, and maintain cooperative relationships with the firm's channel partners over time.[38]

Pricing Policies

A firm's pricing policies can also influence the composition of its marketing communication mix. Big-ticket items, both industrial goods and consumer durables, typically require substantial amounts of personal selling. Such expensive products are often technically or aesthetically sophisticated, and customers perceive substantial risk in purchasing them. Therefore, potential buyers usually want the kind of detailed information and advice they can get only from a salesperson before making their decisions.

Also, personal selling is essential in marketing products or services where the ultimate selling price is open to negotiation. Although negotiated pricing policies are most commonly found among marketers of industrial goods and services, they are also followed in the sale of some consumer durables, such as automobiles.

Within the marketing communication mix, the importance of personal selling relative to advertising depends on various characteristics of the firm's marketing strategy, including the size and nature of the target market, the complexity and service requirements of the product, and the other elements of the marketing mix. Exhibit 3.8 highlights a number of important questions that must be answered in order to make IMC investment decisions and thus allocate promotional funds effectively and efficiently. In particular, in terms of advertising versus personal selling, the questions in Exhibit 3.8 serve as a guideline toward decision making.

Computerized Ordering and Customer Alliances

To further strengthen relationships with major customers, firms are forming supply chain alliances with those customers involving the development of joint information and reorder systems. For instance, P&G has formed alliances with major supermarket chains, such as Kroger, Publix, and Safeway, to develop a restocking system called efficient consumer response (ECR). Sales information from the stores' checkout scanners is sent directly to P&G's computers, which

EXHIBIT 3.8
Key questions
for investing in
advertising versus
personal selling

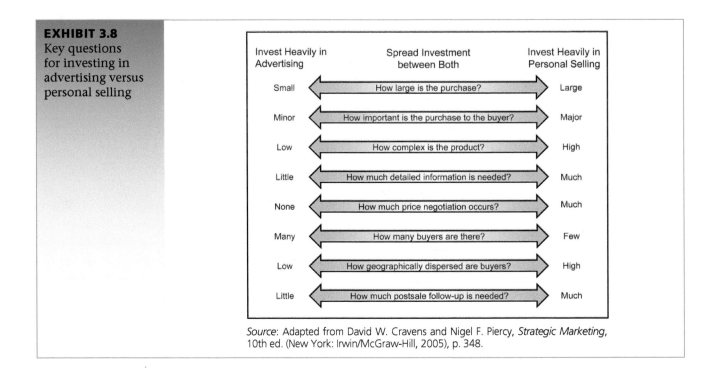

Invest Heavily in Advertising	Spread Investment between Both	Invest Heavily in Personal Selling
Small	How large is the purchase?	Large
Minor	How important is the purchase to the buyer?	Major
Low	How complex is the product?	High
Little	How much detailed information is needed?	Much
None	How much price negotiation occurs?	Much
Many	How many buyers are there?	Few
Low	How geographically dispersed are buyers?	High
Little	How much postsale follow-up is needed?	Much

Source: Adapted from David W. Cravens and Nigel F. Piercy, *Strategic Marketing*, 10th ed. (New York: Irwin/McGraw-Hill, 2005), p. 348.

figure out automatically when to replenish each product and schedule deliveries directly to each store. This paperless exchange minimizes mistakes and billbacks, minimizes inventory, decreases out-of-stocks, and improves cash flow.[39]

IMPROVING CUSTOMER SATISFACTION AND LOYALTY THROUGH FEEDBACK

As discussed in the earlier section on CRM, maintaining the loyalty of major current customers can be crucial for improving a business's profitability as its markets mature and is therefore an important element of any sales strategy. Recall, though, that this chapter also earlier discussed the importance of a market orientation and the role of customer requirements in determining firm success. Maintaining customer loyalty is one outcome of a market orientation. Customer-focused companies, those that cultivate loyal customers with whom a functional or strategic relationship is shared, have substantial advantages across several key performance dimensions versus other companies. Such firms not only avoid the high costs associated with acquiring a new customer but typically benefit because loyal customers (1) tend to concentrate their purchases, thus leading to larger volumes and lower selling and distribution costs, (2) provide positive word-of-mouth and customer referrals, and (3) may be willing to pay premium prices for the value they receive.[40]

Periodic measurement of customer satisfaction is important, then, because a dissatisfied customer is unlikely to remain loyal to a company over time.

Importantly, however, the corollary is not always true: Customers who describe themselves as satisfied are not necessarily loyal. Indeed, one author estimates that 60 to 80 percent of customer defectors in most businesses said they were "satisfied" or "very satisfied" on the last customer survey before their defection.[41] In the interim, perhaps, competitors improved their offerings, the customer's requirements changed, or other environmental factors shifted. The point is that businesses that measure customer satisfaction should be commended—but urged not to stop there. Satisfaction measures need to be supplemented with examinations of customer behavior, such as measures of the annual retention rate, frequency of purchases, and the percentage of a customer's total purchases captured by the firm.

Most important, defecting customers should be studied in detail to discover why the selling firm failed to provide sufficient value to retain their loyalty. Analyzing such failures often provides more useful information than satisfaction measures because they stand out as a clear, understandable message telling the organization exactly where improvements are needed. In fact, gaining feedback from customers on the performance of a selling firm has been institutionalized in many organizations. This idea of 360-degree performance feedback is discussed further in Chapter 13.

Major Account Teams

In Chapter 2, the concept of the buying center was introduced. Sometimes, customers who are strategic partners of a selling organization become so large and complex that a parallel concept to the buying center is implemented on the seller side of the relationship. In such cases, a firm may assign a selling team of representatives from various functional departments of the company to a single customer. The selling team may include representatives from different levels in the company's management hierarchy, too. In fact, it has become increasingly common for executives at the very top of firms, even CEOs, to get directly involved in selling to major strategic partner customers. Such an approach is called top-to-top selling. Legend has it that when Lou Gerstner took over the reins as CEO of IBM, he was shocked by how little the executives in the company actually knew about IBM's customers. Many had apparently not called on a customer in many years. Gerstner immediately instituted a policy that all top-level executives would spend a substantial amount of time in the executive suites of IBM's biggest strategic partners, doing top-to-top selling. This approach has been credited as a major factor in IBM's turnaround and subsequent success in the modern era as a broad-based consulting firm as executives received a clear and direct message about what changes needed to be made to win customers back to IBM.[42]

Implementing a major account management program that includes team selling or top-to-top selling can have important implications for the way a firm organizes its sales force. These issues are discussed in Chapter 4.

SUMMARY

This chapter has highlighted the importance of long-term relationships to organizational success. Firms today strive to create a market-oriented, customer-centric culture. Within such a culture, the role of personal selling is vital to the successful development and implementation of marketing strategies.

CRM provides the firm with necessary formalization for success. That is, a well-implemented CRM business model offers structure, processes and tools, and managerial knowledge and commitment in support of the customer-centric culture. With these things in place, marketing strategies and programs may be successfully developed and executed toward the goals related to customer centricity. In general, these goals revolve around establishing and maintaining long-term customer relationships.

KEY TERMS

marketing concept	data mining	trust
marketing mix	return on customer	customer delight
marketing communication	investment	upgrading
mix (promotion mix)	big data	full-line selling
market orientation	sales analytics	cross-selling
customer orientation	strategic direction	preferred supplier
customer-centric	mission statement	total quality management
formalization	goals	(TQM)
customer relationship	objectives	integrated marketing
management (CRM)	strategic business units	communication (IMC)
touchpoints	(SBUs)	pull strategy
mass marketing	sustainable competitive	push strategy
target marketing	advantage (SCA)	just-in-time reorder and
customer marketing	distinctive competencies	delivery
one-to-one marketing	generic strategies	category management
customer value	market opportunity	supply chain alliances
customer loyalty	marketing program	efficient consumer
lifetime value of a customer	market exchanges	response (ECR)
firing a customer	functional relationships	selling team
data warehouse	strategic partnerships	top-to-top selling

BREAKOUT QUESTIONS

1. One of the great debates in CRM is who should have ownership of the process. In many firms, IT people seem to be the guardians of CRM's secrets. This is because, as we have learned, a key facet of CRM is its information management capabilities. Who do you think should have ownership of CRM in a firm? Is it really necessary that CRM have

an owner? What does ownership of the process imply in terms of actions and behaviors? What is the role of upper management in all this?

2. Is it possible for a firm to be successful without a market orientation? Can you come up with examples of firms that are not very market-oriented but still are leaders in their competitive marketplace?

3. The promotion mix (also known as the integrated marketing communications mix) consists of the various ways the firm communicates with its customers about its product offerings. These include personal selling, advertising, public relations and publicity, sales promotion (sales support of the advertising effort through signage, displays, etc.), direct response, electronic media, and the like. Find an example of a company that you believe does a really good job of actually integrating these approaches to communications. What are the things that make this company's approach so successful?

4. Consider the three basic relationship types described in the chapter: market exchanges (transactional), functional relationships, and strategic partnerships. For each, provide an example of a different sales organization that you believe does a good job with that particular relationship type. What evidence do you have that each is successful?

5. Based on what you have learned about strategic partnerships, what two organizations (either supplier–customer or supplier–supplier) can you identify that are not currently in a partnership but you believe would benefit from one? List the benefits to both parties of forging such an alliance. List any potential problems you believe might emanate from the alliance. What can the firms do to reduce the chances for these potential problems?

6. Strategic partnerships often require direct peer-to-peer communication at the senior executive level between buying firm and selling firm. What are the advantages of having top corporate officers, CEOs in some cases, become directly involved in the selling process? What are the disadvantages? What types of challenges does such direct involvement present to the salesperson and sales manager responsible for the client?

7. Refer to Exhibit 3.4. Using the Miles and Snow typology, how might the marketing strategies and programs of a prospector SBU vary from those adopted by a defender SBU within the same company? Which of these options do you believe would be best: (a) a sales force that sells only for the prospector SBU, or (b) a sales force that is shared between the two SBUs and sells for both the prospector and defender SBU? What are the relevant issues that led to your response?

8. Ethical Question. You are the Sales Manager for a paint manufacturer that sells to various global automobile manufacturers. Your key account manager for a large, global German automobile company has come to you with big news—she has learned from her company contacts that they are planning to introduce a revolutionary new car within six months that will dramatically change the automobile market. She says that the company is demanding total secrecy and to protect confidentiality they specifically don't want your company making this part of its CRM tracking program. Your firm believes that its CRM system database is secure and your salespeople are under strict orders to log all customer information into the system. What will you tell your key account manager? Justify your decision.

LEADERSHIP CHALLENGE: WHOSE CRM IS IT ANYWAY?

Alice Klein wondered what she should do next as she hung up the phone. As vice president of sales for New World Manufacturing, she was responsible for more than 200 salespeople around the country. New World was a manufacturer of precision components for bicycles (gear shift mechanisms). Among the company's clients were Cannondale and Giant Bicycles as well as other leading bicycle companies around the world. In addition to the original equipment manufacturer (OEM) market, New World did a great deal of business selling after-market accessories to bicycle retailers.

Alice had pushed hard for a CRM system to be implemented at New World. Finally, as part of an overall upgrade of the IT system at the company, senior management had purchased a CRM package that included state-of-the-art software and hardware to help New World do a better job of managing its customer relationships. It was expensive to get the package Alice and other executives knew was the best solution. The final cost ran into several million dollars plus additional training time.

It is now six months since the purchase of the system and Elliot Whitney, vice president of information technology, just called Alice to say he still had not received a detailed summary of the information needed by the sales force. He told Alice that senior management was asking about the status of the CRM system. Management wanted the entire company to benefit from the system and were looking forward to its implementation.

The company had a lot of information about its customers as well as other data that could be incorporated into its CRM system (internal billing, price, and production schedules). Alice was well aware of the system's potential and had spent a great deal of time thinking about how the sales force could use it most effectively. After hanging up with Elliot she knew it was time to decide how the new CRM system would be implemented with the sales force.

Questions

1. You are Alice Klein. What critical information do you think would be most helpful for the sales force to be able to access about the relationship between New World and its customers?

2. What technology would you use to deliver this information from the CRM system to the salesperson (tablet, smartphone, laptop, or something else), and why would you choose that technology?

3. What kinds of issues do you think might come up for New World as it implements the CRM system with the sales force, for example, possible salesperson resistance to collecting information for the CRM system?

ROLE-PLAY: SERENDIPITY WIRELESS

Situation

Ellie Rodriguez was puzzled. Sales were just not coming in year-to-date for her area at the forecast rate, despite an improving economy and a solid marketing plan. Ellie had been hired 15 months ago as B2B sales manager for the Boston market for Serendipity Wireless, an up-and-coming player in the overall cell phone market. While many cellular providers focused primarily on the B2C market through retail outlets, Serendipity's focal business was in supplying product and service to small to medium-sized businesses. Ellie has six years of progressively broader sales and sales management experience with a B2C provider in the wireless industry and saw the opportunity at Serendipity as a way to gain experience in B2B.

Over the past few weeks she has spent a lot of time digging into the sales data for the seven salespeople working for her in the Boston district. Also, she has been increasing the amount of time riding with her reps to see how they are handling their territories. As a result, she has become more and more concerned that a couple of the reps are not effectively utilizing Serendipity's in-house CRM system to its fullest potential. For reps Leo Leone and Carla Cadwallader, it seems that they are neither effectively converting leads into customers nor cross-selling the full line of Serendipity products and services to the customers they do sign up. This evidence is a sure sign they are not using the CRM system advantageously. If these two reps could improve their sales by just 8 percent year-to-date, Ellie's whole district would be on plan. Interestingly, these two are Ellie's most senior reps both in age and in length of service with Serendipity.

Ellie calls a meeting with Leo and Carla for tomorrow to discuss the situation and provide ideas on how they can better use Serendipity's CRM system.

Characters in the Role-Play

Ellie Rodriguez, Boston district sales manager for Serendipity
Leo Leone, salesperson for Serendipity
Carla Cadwallader, salesperson for Serendipity

Assignment

Break into groups of three, with one student playing each character. It doesn't matter what the actual gender mix of your group is. Before you stage the meeting, the student playing Ellie should work to prepare a list of benefits of utilizing a CRM system such as Serendipity's. Be mindful that Leo and Carla are senior reps who have been successful in the past; however, you *must* convince them of the ways CRM can help them be successful in the future.

Also before the meeting, the students playing Leo and Carla should work to prepare a list of reasons why they don't want to use the CRM system. Think about both (1) why especially a senior salesperson might be reluctant to utilize such a system and (2) what might be some drawbacks or impediments to CRM in general. Then get together and role-play the meeting. Ellie should lead the discussion, and Leo and Carla should stand firm in their resistance, at least for a while. Ultimately, it will be important for the three to come to agreement about how Leo and Carla will begin to utilize the CRM system. Finish the meeting with a list of specific actions they can take to make this happen, along with what Ellie can do to help.

MINICASE: TRANSSPRECH, A.G.

You are a consultant for an international management strategy consulting firm. Your firm has been approached by Herr (Mr.) Hans Wursching, CEO of TransSprech, A.G., a newly formed cellular phone service and phone provider based in Stuttgart, Germany. TransSprech has a satellite GSM network with complete coverage in Europe and the United States, as well as throughout most countries in the world. The company has established some semblance of a marketing and management strategy, and you have been asked to review the current strategy and help the company go to the next level by growing its sales.

You recently conducted the initial information-gathering meeting with Herr Wursching, and received the following mass of information:

- TransSprech maintains corporate offices in numerous cities around the world. However, its customer service outlets and retail sales are conducted through the company website, as well as through licensed electronics retailers. It does not maintain its own customer service or retail locations.
- Its target markets are both companies and individuals wanting cellular phone service with worldwide coverage and who are willing to pay a premium to get it. It already has about 3,000 customers worldwide and is hoping to grow to 10,000 by year-end.
- Corporate customers are more valuable customers because they are buying in larger volumes. Establishing a customer base is very important as this company attempts to establish itself.
- No sales force has been established. So far the company has received many customers in response to its advertising.
- It offers individual customers four different cost plans with respect to the cellular service, as well as five different phone options. However, corporate customers can negotiate variations within the established options.
- The phones themselves are similar to those used by TransSprech's competitors, but the satellite network providing the coverage is far more advanced.
- The company has retained a Berlin-based advertising and public relations agency to develop a worldwide advertising campaign. Print and television ads have recently saturated the European market and will soon be shown in the U.S. market. The company is currently running several promotions to get its product and name known; however, its long-term goal is to offer a premium, nondiscounted product that is desired because of its value and quality, not low price.
- Because the company and its product are in the early stages of development, there have been technical problems, and the company has had to provide a great deal of service to its customers.
- Herr Wursching understands that it costs more to acquire new customers than to retain existing ones, so he would like to establish a CRM plan at some point to improve customer loyalty and retention. He has a well-trained customer service operator staff in place. However, he does not want to invest in a complicated software system right away. His current technology is giving him enough problems, he says.

Questions

1. What is the company's strategy with respect to each of the four elements of the marketing mix (product, distribution, price, and promotion)?

2. Based on the current marketing strategy, should the company's promotion mix focus be on personal selling or on advertising?

3. What further questions might you ask Herr Wursching to help his company move toward a more relationship-based business and establish CRM initiatives? What other recommendations might you make for him with respect to CRM?

CHAPTER 4

Organizing the Sales Effort

LEARNING OBJECTIVES

Organizing the sales force is one of the most important decisions made by sales management. It has a significant impact on every aspect of the salesperson's performance. Changes in the way selling is done, the increasing importance of effectively managing customer relationships, and the need to assimilate new technologies in the selling function have led to fundamental changes in the organization of today's sales forces.

After reading this chapter, you should be able to

- Identify the purposes of sales organization.
- Understand the different horizontal organizational structures of a sales force.
- Outline the major issues in key account and team selling.
- Discuss key vertical structure issues in sales organizations.
- Identify important issues in starting a new sales force from the ground up.

THE INCREASING IMPORTANCE OF SALES ORGANIZATION DECISIONS

Organizing the activities and management of the sales force is a major part of strategic sales planning. Until recently, however, significant cultural and organizational restructuring was not common among either industrial or consumer goods marketers. Once a firm had an organizational structure in place, its managers tended to take it for granted—at least until performance problems became apparent. But in recent years, increasing rates of change in markets, technology, and competition have forced managers to pay closer attention to their sales organizations and to be more proactive in restructuring those organizations when necessary.[1]

A strong corporate vision and effective strategic market planning are closely linked with how the organization is structured and how it interacts with its customers. This chapter stresses the importance of designing an appropriate organizational framework for the sales force as an integral part of a firm's sales program and examines issues involved in developing such a framework. It begins with a discussion of the purposes of organization—the things a good organizational plan should accomplish. Next, issues related to the horizontal organization of the sales effort are explored. Horizontal organization is concerned with how specific selling activities are divided among various members of the sales force. Finally, the vertical structuring of the sales organization is discussed. Vertical structuring refers to organizing a firm's sales managers and their activities rather than the personnel in the sales force. An understanding of these issues should provide greater appreciation for the crucial role organizational decisions play in developing an effective sales program.[2]

PURPOSES OF SALES ORGANIZATION

An organizational structure is simply an arrangement of activities involving a group of people. The goal in designing an organization is to divide and coordinate activities so the group can accomplish its common objectives better by acting as a group than by acting as individuals. The starting point in organizing a sales force is determining the goals or objectives to be accomplished. These are specified in the firm's overall marketing plan. The selling activities necessary to accomplish the firm's marketing objectives must then be divided and allocated to members of the sales force so the objectives can be achieved with as little duplication of effort as possible. An organizational structure should serve the following purposes:

1. Activities should be divided and arranged in such a way that the firm can benefit from the specialization of labor.

2. The organizational structures should provide for stability and continuity in the firm's selling efforts.

3. The structure should provide for the coordination of the various activities assigned to different persons in the sales force and different departments in the firm.

Division and Specialization of Labor

Two centuries ago, Adam Smith pointed out that dividing any function into its component activities and assigning each activity to a specialist can increase the efficiency with which almost anything is performed. Division and specialization of labor increase productivity because each specialist can concentrate efforts and become more proficient at the assigned task. Also, management can assign individuals only to those activities for which they have aptitude.

In some cases, the personal selling function is so simple and straightforward a firm could gain few if any benefits by applying the principles of division and specialization of labor to its sales force. Salespeople in such companies are expected to carry out all the activities necessary to sell all the products in the company's line to all types of customers within their territories. But in many firms, the selling function is sufficiently complicated that dividing the necessary selling activities can increase efficiency and effectiveness. Different activities are assigned to various specialists, creating two or more specialized sales forces. Today, many firms find that partnering with specialists such as resellers and distributors can enhance the effectiveness of its own sales force.

Management must decide the best way to divide the required selling activities to gain the maximum benefits of specialization within the sales force. Should independent agent intermediaries be used to perform some or all of the firm's selling efforts? Should selling activities be organized by product, by customer type, or by selling function (for example, prospecting for new accounts versus servicing old customers)? As discussed later in this chapter, each basis for horizontally structuring the sales organization has its own advantages and disadvantages. Which one is best depends on the firm's objectives, target market, product line, and other internal and external factors. And a key issue today is the impact of e-commerce and online selling and sales support on organizing the overall sales initiative.

Division and specialization of labor can benefit managerial functions as well as selling functions. Some firms use a simple line organization, a type of vertical organization in which the chain of command runs from the chief sales executive down through levels of subordinates. Each subordinate is responsible to only one person on the next higher level, and each is expected to perform all the necessary sales management activities relevant to his or her own level.

The most common form of vertical organization structure, especially in medium- and large-sized firms, is the line and staff organization. In this form, several sales management activities, such as personnel selection, training, and distributor relations, are assigned to separate staff specialists. This type of specialization, however, raises some questions concerning organizational design, such as

1. What specific functions should be assigned to staff executives?

2. How can staff activities be integrated with those of line sales managers, and should those activities be performed in-house or outsourced to independent contractors, such as personnel agencies and training firms?

These questions are examined further later in this chapter.

Stability and Continuity of Organizational Performance

Although many companies use division and specialization of labor in designing their sales organizations, they sometimes ignore a related caveat concerning good organizational design: Organize activities, not people. In other words, activities should be assigned to positions within the sales organization without regard to the talents or preferences of current employees.

Once an ideal organizational structure has been designed, people can be trained or, if need be, recruited to fill positions within the structure. Over time, those in lower positions should be given the experience and training necessary to enable them to move into higher positions. In athletic terms, the organization should "build depth at all positions." This provides stability and continuity of performance for the organization. The same activities are carried out at the same positions within the firm even if specific individuals are promoted or leave.

Coordination and Integration

The advantages of the division and specialization of labor are clear, but specialization also causes a problem for managers. When activities are divided and performed by different individuals, those activities must be coordinated and integrated so all efforts are directed at accomplishing the same objective. The more an organization's tasks are divided among specialists, the more difficult integrating those tasks becomes. The problem is even worse when outside agents, such as manufacturers' representatives, are used, because the manager has no formal authority over them and cannot always control their actions.

Sales managers must be concerned about the coordination and integration of the efforts of their salespeople in three ways. First, the activities of the sales force must be integrated with the needs and concerns of customers. Second, the firm's selling activities must be coordinated with those of other departments, such as production, product development, logistics, and finance. Finally, if the firm divides its selling tasks among specialized units within the sales force, all those tasks must be integrated.

Consequently, the primary function of the vertical structure of a firm's sales organization is to ensure these three kinds of integration. Questions of vertical organization—such as control for each sales executive, and the most effective use of staff specialists—should be examined with an eye toward effective integration of the firm's overall selling efforts.

HORIZONTAL STRUCTURE OF THE SALES FORCE

There is no best way to divide selling activities among members of the sales force. The best sales organization varies with the objectives, strategies, and tasks of the firm. Furthermore, as the firm's environment, objectives, or marketing strategy changes, its sales force may have to be reorganized. Several key questions are central to this discussion:

1. Should the company employ its own salespeople, or should some or all of its selling efforts be contracted to outside agents, such as manufacturers' representatives?

2. How many different sales forces should the company have, and how should they be arranged?

3. Should separate sales representatives be assigned to different products, types of customers, or sales functions?

4. Who should be responsible for selling to major (key) accounts?

5. How should firms organize their sales and marketing efforts when they enter foreign markets and become global competitors?

Four common bases are used for structuring the sales effort, and each has unique advantages that make it appropriate for a firm under certain circumstances. The first issue to be decided is whether the firm should hire its own salespeople or use outside agents. When the decision is to use a company sales force, alternative approaches include (1) geographic organization, (2) organization by type of product, (3) organization by type of customer, and (4) organization by selling function.

Deciding on a Company Sales Force or Independent Agents

This book focuses primarily on issues associated with managing an internal company sales force, where all of the salespeople and their managers are employees of the firm. In many cases, though, the use of independent agents instead of company salespeople is an important option. IBM, Xerox, and other firms employ both a highly trained sales force and a network of business partners around the world to help market their products and services. In such cases, firms usually rely on agents to cover geographic areas with relatively few customers or low sales potential— territories that may not justify the cost of a full-time company salesperson. It is not unusual for a firm to use both company salespeople and independent agents. Today, the term outsourcing the sales force is popularly used to indicate the use of agents.

Types of Agents

The two most common types of intermediaries a manufacturer might use to perform the selling function are manufacturers' representatives and selling (or sales) agents. Manufacturers' representatives (or reps) are intermediaries who sell part of the output of their principals—the manufacturers they represent—on an extended contract basis. They take neither ownership nor physical possession of the goods they sell but concentrate instead on the selling function. They are compensated solely by commissions.

Reps have no authority to modify their principals' instructions concerning the prices, terms of sale, and so forth to be offered to potential buyers. Manufacturers' reps cover a specific and limited territory and specialize in a limited range of products, although they commonly represent several related but noncompeting product lines from different manufacturers.

These characteristics give reps the advantages of having (1) many established contacts with potential customers in their territories, (2) familiarity with the technical nature and applications of the types of products in which they specialize, (3) the ability to keep expenses low by spreading fixed costs over the products of several different manufacturers, and (4) the appearance as a totally variable cost item on their principals' income statements, since the reps' commissions vary directly with the amount of goods sold.[3] Finding the right rep is a critical business decision for the sales organization. Exhibit 4.1 provides useful guidelines for selecting a rep.

Selling agents are also intermediaries who do not take title or possession of the goods they sell and are compensated solely by commissions from their principals. They differ from reps, however, in that they usually handle the entire output of a principal (operating as the entire sales force for the manufacturer rather than as a representative in a single specified territory). Selling agents are usually granted broader authority by their principals to modify prices and terms of sale, and they actively shape the manufacturer's promotional and sales programs.

Deciding When Outside Agents Are Appropriate

The decision about whether to use independent agents or a company sales force to cover a particular product or market involves a variety of considerations and trade-offs. Four important sets of factors for a manager to consider are (1) economic criteria, (2) control, (3) transaction costs, and (4) strategic flexibility.[4]

EXHIBIT 4.1
Six C's of finding the right rep

Compatible lines

Find a rep with a complementary porfolio, one your product fits into seamlessly. An electrical wiring manufacturer, for example, benefits from having its merchandise sold right alongside conductors and converters.

Compatible territories

Don't hire a rep who sells in barren markets. Look for a seller who moves merchandise in regions saturated with current or potential customers. Find a seller who knows his or her region and knows who to sell your products to in that area.

Compatible customers

Ultimately you want to hire an independent rep who is already selling in your industry and knows about your company and your customers. But regardless, find a rep who knows the types of customers you're looking to target.

Credibility of the rep

The independent sales rep is not only a revenue generator, but he or she is a company ambassador (for you!). Often your rep is the only person associated with your company that certain customers ever meet or talk with. Make sure you send the right ambassador into the field.

Capabilities

Are your products the rep's primary account or a secondary account? Find out how much attention you can expect from the rep. Then you can decide if the right person will be selling your products.

Credits

Check references and do a background check. How long has the rep been selling? For whom? With what success?

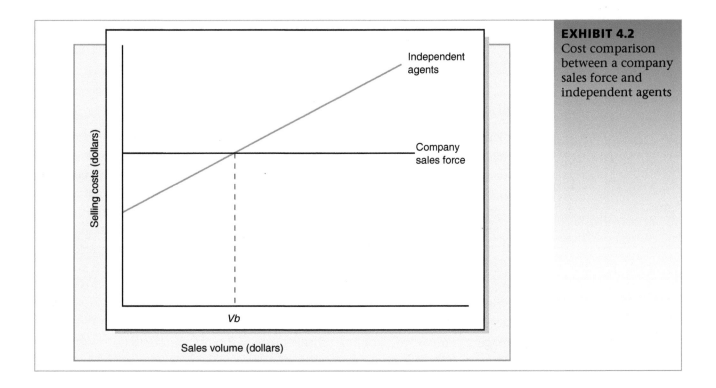

EXHIBIT 4.2
Cost comparison between a company sales force and independent agents

Economic Criteria

In a given selling situation, a company sales force and independent agents are likely to produce different levels of costs and sales volume. A first step in deciding which form of sales organization to use is to estimate and compare the costs of the two alternatives. A simplified example of such a cost comparison is illustrated in Exhibit 4.2.

The fixed costs of using external agents are lower than those of using a company sales force because of less administrative overhead and because agents do not receive a salary or reimbursement for field selling expenses. But costs of using agents tend to rise faster as sales volume increases because agents usually receive larger commissions than company salespeople. Consequently, a break-even level of sales volume exists (Vb in Exhibit 4.2), below which the costs of external agents are lower but above which a company sales force becomes more efficient. This helps explain why agents tend to be used by smaller firms or by larger firms in their smaller territories where sales volume is too low to warrant a company sales force.

Low fixed costs also make agents attractive when a firm is moving into new territories or product lines where success is uncertain. Since the agent does not get paid unless sales are made, the costs of failure are minimized.

The other side of the economic equation is sales volume. The critical question is whether company salespeople are likely to produce a higher volume of total sales than agents in a given situation. Most sales and marketing managers believe they will because company salespeople concentrate entirely on the firm's products, they may be better trained, they may be more aggressive since their future depends on the company's success, and customers often prefer to deal directly with a supplier.

On the other hand, agents' contacts and experience in an industry can make them more effective than company salespeople, particularly when the company is new or is moving into a new geographic area or product line.

Control and Strategic Criteria

Regardless of which organizational form produces the greatest sales in the short run, many managers argue that an internal sales force is preferable to agents in the long run due to the difficulty of controlling agents and getting them to conform to their principals' strategic objectives. Agents are seen as independent actors who can be expected to pursue their own short-run objectives. This makes them reluctant to engage in activities with a long-run strategic payoff to their principal, such as cultivating new accounts or small customers with growth potential, performing service and support activities, or promoting new products. Some research supports this argument, suggesting manufacturers' representatives are more dissatisfied with close supervision and attempts to control their behavior than are company salespeople.[5]

Managers can control a company sales force in many different ways—through the selection, training, and supervision of personnel; establishment of operating procedures and policies; formal evaluation and reward mechanisms; and ultimately transferring or firing salespeople whose performance is not satisfactory.[6]

Independent agents can also be replaced if their performance falls below the manufacturer's expectations. But in many cases, it is difficult for the manufacturer to tell whether an agent's poor performance is due to lack of effort or to factors beyond the agent's control, such as difficult competitive or market conditions. While company salespeople can be monitored on a regular basis, it is usually more difficult and costly—and sometimes impossible—to monitor the behavior of independent agents.[7] Finally, switching costs (such as contractual restrictions on termination) or customer loyalty to the agent may make it difficult for a manufacturer to replace an agent with its own salespeople.[8]

Transaction Costs

Even when a manufacturer decides a poor-performing agent should be replaced, it may be difficult to find an acceptable replacement. This is particularly likely when an intermediary must invest in specialized (or transaction-specific) assets, such as extensive product training or specialized capital equipment, to sell the manufacturer's product or service effectively. It might take a new manufacturer's rep months to learn enough about a technically complex product and its applications to do an effective selling job. The difficulty of finding acceptable replacements for poor-performing agents under such circumstances makes it even harder for the manufacturer to control those agents.

The theory of transaction cost analysis (TCA) states that when substantial transaction-specific assets are necessary to sell a manufacturer's product, the costs of using and administering independent agents (i.e., the manufacturer's transaction costs) are likely to be higher than the costs of hiring and managing a company sales force. This is because TCA assumes independent agents will pursue their own self-interests—even at the expense of the manufacturer they represent—when they think they can get away with it. For instance, they might provide only cursory postsale service or expend too little effort calling on smaller accounts because they are unlikely to earn big commissions from such activities. Because agents are most likely to be able to get away with such behaviors when it is difficult for the manufacturer to monitor or replace them, the transaction cost of using agents under such circumstances is likely to be high.[9]

Recently, however, analysts have questioned TCA's assumption that independent agents will always put their own short-term interests ahead of those of the manufacturer when they can avoid getting caught and replaced. These analysts argue that when both manufacturer and agent believe their relationship can be mutually beneficial for years, norms of trust and cooperation can develop.[10]

Strategic Flexibility

Another important strategic issue to consider when deciding whether to use agents or company salespeople is flexibility. Generally, a vertically integrated distribution system incorporating a company sales force is the most difficult to alter quickly. Specialized agent intermediaries can often be added or dismissed at short notice, especially if no specialized assets are needed to sell the manufacturer's product and the firm does not have to sign long-term contracts to gain agents' support.

Firms facing uncertain and rapidly changing competitive or market environments or those in industries characterized by shifting technology and short product life cycles are often best advised to rely on independent agents to preserve the flexibility of their distribution channels.[11] An example of the use of outsourcing success is presented in the Innovation box.

Most marketing executives argue it is best to use agents in volatile environments, to represent a small company, or for territories with low sales potential where the benefits from scale economies outweigh the difficulties of motivating and controlling the agent's behavior. It is usually preferable to switch to direct salespeople as soon as a company or territory can support the higher fixed costs or when specialized knowledge or other assets are required to do an effective selling job.

Geographic Organization

The simplest and most common method of organizing a company sales force is by geographic organization. Here, individual salespeople are assigned to separate geographic territories. In this type of organization, each salesperson is responsible for performing all the activities necessary to sell all the products in the company's line to all potential customers in the territory. A geographic sales organization is illustrated in Exhibit 4.3.

INNOVATION Outsourcing Success

Traditionally, consumer products sales organizations prided themselves on their service in retail stores. Not long ago, it would not have been unusual for a salesperson for a major packaged goods firm to have a call list with several hundred supermarkets, drugstores, and discount stores on it. Each would be dutifully contacted on a regularly established route, and the salesperson would perform "missionary" duties such as merchandising the shelves and displays, informing clerks and managers of promotions and new products, and putting up sales promotion materials.

For many manufacturers whose primary market is the retail industry, such missionary selling has gone the way of the dinosaur. If the decision to outsource a portion of sales has been made, some factors must be considered to improve the chances of success.

1) Provide an exclusive market—Outsourced staff must be able to trust that the territory assigned is solely theirs and that they can generate income from it.
2) Build trust—The outsourced partners must feel part of the team. For example, never withhold "good" leads for company staff.
3) Make communication easy—Ensure IT is set up so that outsourced staff can access order tracking and other items on the system.

Applying these rules should ensure outsourced sales staff performs to a high standard and feels like part of the team.

The geographic sales organization has several strengths. Most important, it tends to have the lowest cost. Because there is only one salesperson in each territory and territories tend to be smaller than they are under other forms of organization, travel time and expenses are minimized. Also, fewer managerial levels are required for coordination. Thus, sales administration and overhead expenses are kept relatively low.

The simplicity of a geographic organizational structure leads to another advantage involving the firm's relationships with its customers. Because only one salesperson calls on each customer, confusion seldom exists about (1) who is responsible for what or (2) to whom the customer should talk when problems arise.

The major disadvantage of a geographic sales organization is that it does not provide any benefits of the division and specialization of labor. Each salesperson is expected to be a jack-of-all-trades. Each must sell all the firm's products to all types of customers and perform all the selling functions.

Also, this organizational structure provides the individual salesperson with freedom to make decisions concerning which selling functions to perform, what products to emphasize, and on which customers to concentrate. Unfortunately, salespeople are likely to expend most of this effort on the functions they perform best and on the products and customers they perceive to be most rewarding, whether or not such effort is consistent with management's objectives and account management policies.

Management can try to direct the efforts of salespeople through close supervision, well-designed compensation and evaluation plans, and clearly defined statements of policy, but the basic problem remains. Since each salesperson is expected to perform

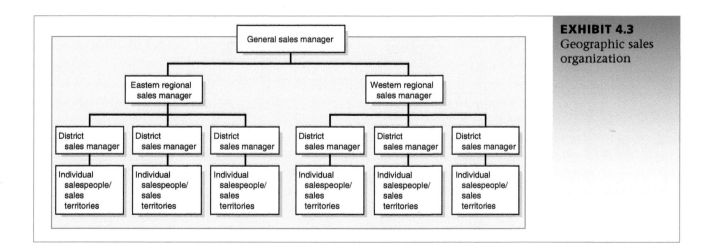

EXHIBIT 4.3
Geographic sales
organization

a full range of selling functions, the sales rep, rather than management, can control the way the selling effort is allocated across products, customers, and selling tasks.

Although a geographic approach to sales organization has its limitations, its basic simplicity and low cost make it very popular among smaller firms, particularly those with limited uncomplicated product lines. Also, while it is unusual for larger organizations to rely exclusively on geographic organization, they do commonly use it in conjunction with other organizational forms. For example, a firm may have two separate sales forces for different products in its line, but each sales force is likely to be organized geographically.

Product Organization

Some companies have separate sales forces for each product or product category in their line, as shown in Exhibit 4.4. A classic example of a product organization is the 3M Company. 3M has more than 50 divisions manufacturing a diverse assortment of products ranging from Scotch tape to abrasives to medical equipment, and many of those divisions have their own separate sales force.

The primary advantage of organizing the sales force by product is that individual salespeople can develop familiarity with the technical attributes, applications, and the most effective selling methods associated with a single product or related products. Also, when the firm's manufacturing facilities are organized by product type—as when separate factories produce each product—a product-oriented organization can lead to closer cooperation between sales and production. This can be very beneficial when the product is tailored to fit the specifications of different customers or when production and delivery schedules are critical in gaining and keeping a customer.

Finally, a product-oriented sales organization enables sales management to control the allocation of selling effort across the various products in the company's line. If management decides more effort should be devoted to a particular product, it can simply assign more salespeople to that product.

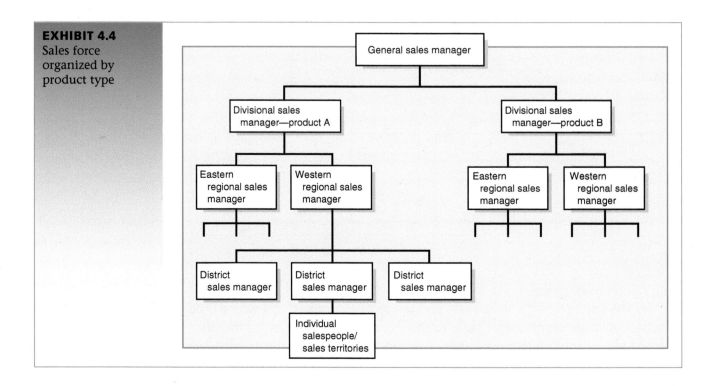

EXHIBIT 4.4
Sales force organized by product type

The major disadvantage of a sales force organized by product type is duplication of effort. Salespeople from different product divisions are assigned to the same geographic areas and may call on the same customers. P&G, historically a product organization, has consolidated product lines under fewer separate selling divisions that employ a team selling approach. This change was precipitated in part because organizational buyers had to deal with too many P&G salespeople. Consumer product marketing folklore is rife with tales about waiting rooms in which every chair was occupied by a P&G rep waiting to see the same buyer. Now at P&G, a team assigned to each major account sells the full product line.

Such duplication leads to higher selling expenses than would be the case with a simple geographic organization. It also creates a need for greater coordination across the various product divisions, which, in turn, requires more sales management personnel and higher administrative costs. Finally, such duplication can cause confusion and frustration among the firm's customers when they must deal with two or more representatives from the same supplier.

Since the major advantage of a product-oriented organization is that it allows salespeople to develop specialized knowledge of one or a few products, this form of organization is most commonly used by firms with large and diverse product lines. It is also used by manufacturers of highly technical products that require different kinds of technical expertise or different selling methods. That is the primary reason some firms, such as 3M, with many different product lines based on widely differing technologies, continue to organize their sales force by product despite the cost disadvantages.[12]

Organization by Customer Type or Markets

It has become increasingly popular for sales forces to use an approach of organization by customer type. This type of customer-oriented sales organization is shown in Exhibit 4.5.

Organizing a sales force by customer type is a natural extension of the marketing concept and reflects a strategy of market segmentation. When salespeople specialize in calling on a particular type of customer, they gain a better understanding of such customer's needs and requirements. They can also be trained to use different selling approaches for different markets and to implement specialized marketing and promotional programs.

A related advantage of customer specialization is that as salespeople become familiar with their customers' specific businesses and needs, they are more likely to discover ideas for new products and marketing approaches that will appeal to those customers. This can be a definite advantage in rapidly changing, highly competitive markets. Finally, this organizational structure allows marketing managers to control the allocation of selling effort to different markets by varying the sizes of the specialized sales forces.

The disadvantages of a customer-oriented sales organization are much the same as those of a product-oriented structure. Having different salespeople calling on different types of customers in the same territory can lead to higher selling expenses and administrative costs. Also, when customer firms have different departments or divisions operating in different industries, two or more salespeople may call on the same customer. This can cause confusion and frustration among customers.

Many firms must believe the advantages of a customer-oriented sales organization outweigh its limitations because it is growing in popularity as an organizational approach. This is particularly true for firms with products that have widely different applications in different markets or firms that must use different approaches when selling to different types of customers, as when a company sells to the government

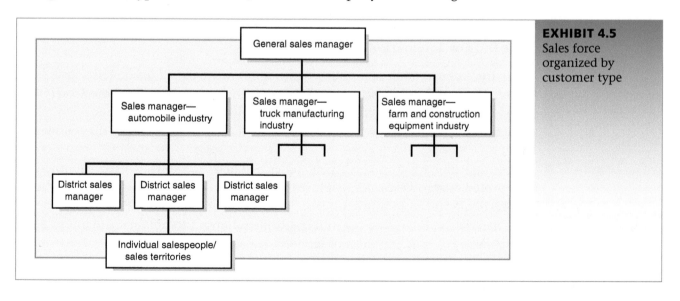

EXHIBIT 4.5
Sales force organized by customer type

as well as to private industry. Also, specialization by customer type is a useful form of organization when a firm's marketing objectives include the penetration of previously untapped markets.[13]

Organization by Selling Function

Different types of selling tasks often require different abilities and skills on the part of the salesperson. Thus, it may be logical under some circumstances to use an approach of organization by selling function so different salespeople specialize in performing different selling functions. One such functional organization is to have one sales force specialize in prospecting for and developing new accounts, while a second force maintains and services old customers.

Such functional specialization can be difficult to implement, however. Since a firm is likely to assign its most competent, experienced, and professionally impressive salespeople to the new-accounts sales force, new customers might object to being turned over from the salesperson who won their patronage to someone else who serves as a maintenance salesperson. It also can be difficult for management to coordinate the development and maintenance functions because feelings of rivalry and jealousy are likely to exist between the two sales forces.

Another form of functional specialization, however, is commonly and successfully used by many industrial product firms: *developmental salespeople* who are responsible for assisting in the development and early sales of new products. Developmental salespeople usually conduct market research, assist the firm's research and development and engineering departments, and sell new products as they are developed. These specialists are often part of a firm's research and development department rather than the regular sales force. Such specialists can help ensure development of successful new products, particularly when they are experienced and knowledgeable about customers' operations and needs as well as about their own firm's technical and production capabilities.

The Role of Telemarketing

One form of specialization by selling function is the use of inside telephone salespeople and outside field salespeople to accomplish separate selling objectives. Obviously, not all selling functions can be performed over the phone, but telemarketing has proven useful for carrying out selected activities, including the following:

- Prospecting for and qualifying potential new accounts, which can then be turned over to field salespeople for personal contact. This function often can be facilitated by including a toll-free phone number in all of the firm's promotional materials so interested potential customers can call to obtain more information about advertised products or services.

- Servicing existing accounts quickly when unexpected problems arise, such as through the use of technical-assistance hotlines.

- Seeking repeat purchases from existing accounts that cannot be covered efficiently in person, such as small or marginal customers and those in remote geographic locations.

- Gaining quicker communication of newsworthy developments, such as the introduction of new or improved products or special sales programs.[14]

The popularity of telemarketing to supplement the activities of the field sales force is growing for two reasons: (1) many customers like it and (2) it can increase the productivity of a firm's sales efforts. And it is especially effective when augmented by an effective online and social media driven sales initiative. From the customers' view, the increased centralization of purchasing, together with growing numbers of product alternatives and potential suppliers in many industries, has increased demands on the time of purchasing agents and other members of organizations' buying centers. Consequently, they like sales contacts over the phone—particularly for routine purposes, such as soliciting reorders or relaying information about special sales programs and price promotions—because telephone sales calls take less time than personal sales calls. However, not all customers may appreciate being shifted from face-to-face selling status to telemarketing.

From the seller's viewpoint, a combination of inside and outside salespeople—together with an appropriate mix of other media, including social media and online

---

ETHICAL MOMENT   Ethical Telemarketing: An Oxymoron?

When you mention telemarketing (or perhaps more properly, "teleselling") to most people they will immediately spout off a long list of negatives—too pushy, unethical, sell products people don't need, take advantage of customers, and the list goes on. Unfortunately, those negative perceptions have too often been true. In much of the world that kind of telemarketing is prohibited or significantly controlled and in the United States the Do Not Call Registry was created to allow consumers to "opt out" of direct telemarketing calls. Of course, not all telemarketers are unethical, but the overwhelming customer perception of unethical behavior is deeply ingrained.

However, most of this perception is based on B2C telemarketing, and in B2B telemarketing sales has a much different—much more respectable—connotation and can be very effective in reaching certain customers (especially smaller firms). Indeed many B2B companies are investing heavily in their inside salesforce, which means sales managers need to understand the ethical implications for their customers of operating this type of selling, especially when it replaces a customer's face-to-face salesperson. As you have learned, a great deal of building a successful customer relationship is based on trust between the customer and seller. When the relationship changes from a face-to-face salesperson to an inside salesperson the company should acknowledge that, at least for some customers, questions may arise that can impact the previous level of trust between the two companies. Enlightened sales managers will proactively work to alleviate customer concerns and maintain and build on the trust in a way that enhances the relationship.

Question to Ponder:

- As a customer who has been successfully serviced by a face-to-face salesperson for many years, how would you react to being told that your account will now be serviced by an inside salesperson? Would you be willing to give it a try or would you be more inclined to consider looking for another supplier? Explain your answers.

TECHNOLOGY Telemarketing Drives CRM

Today, enterprises are relying more and more on technology. It allows for the advancement of specific efforts so that people in the organization can focus on how to expand market share. Telemarketing software is a key technology that can be easily implemented within the sales environment. Telemarketing is a powerful business tool that can help organizations build rapport, identify potential leads, and establish relationships.

Telemarketing software that gathers information about customers should be aligned with the organization's CRM system in order to build business intelligence. These technologies provide keen visibility into the effectiveness of your sales organization. Agents in call centers rely on telemarketing software to gather key information from customers. CRM systems allow organizations to use information gathered from telemarketing software to evaluate the performance of individual agents, sales reps, and the company as a whole. The data also helps prioritize deals, allocate necessary resources, and identify threats and opportunities.

Organizations can use the gathered data to effectively manage the sales pipeline. Benefits of these technologies include: more accurate forecasts, powerful results, ability to build a strong sales team, identify key players, and identify trends occurring within the sales pipeline. It is important to remember that CRM and telemarketing technology can only provide information; they are not built to make decisions. Leaders within the organization are responsible for leveraging the information and making strategic decisions that move the company forward. Telemarketing software and CRM solutions are great tools to help companies improve operations and build better customer relationships.[15]

approaches—offers a way of improving the overall efficiency of the sales force.[16] Moving some salespeople inside and using them in conjunction with other promotional efforts allows the firm to lower the cost of routine sales activities substantially. At the same time, it enables the more expensive outside sales force to concentrate on activities with the highest potential long-term payout, such as new-account generation and the servicing of major customers. The efficiency of telemarketing makes it particularly useful for implementing an account management policy that directs different amounts of effort toward classifications of customers based on differences in size or potential. In the past, some firms prohibited sales forces from calling on very small customers—or told them to visit such accounts infrequently—because their purchase volume was not large enough to cover the cost of a sales call and still contribute to profit. But today, small businesses account for an increasingly large portion of the overall sales volume in many industries—revenue that firms cannot afford to turn away. An inside sales force can call on such customers regularly and with much lower costs than is possible with an outside sales force.

Today, the issue of inside versus outside selling is inextricably linked to a firm's overall customer relationship strategy (see Chapter 3) and technological capabilities. The Technology box provides insights on how CRM and telemarketing are connected.

As we discuss later in this book, however, implementing two or more specialized sales forces, as in the case of inside and outside salespeople, can create interesting challenges for sales managers. Since each specialized sales force focuses on different types of selling activities, separate policies and procedures are often required. For example, some authorities suggest that an effective telemarketing program requires the development of standardized scripts for the salesperson to follow, even though their counterparts in the field might have much more flexibility to tailor their presentations to the needs of individual customers. Such differences in policies and procedures may require recruitment of different types of salespeople for the two sales forces and development of different training and compensation programs for each.[17]

ORGANIZING TO SERVICE KEY ACCOUNTS

Regardless of how their sales forces are organized, many firms are developing new organizational approaches to deliver the customer service necessary to attract and maintain large and important customers—their major or key accounts. Key accounts may be handled on a global basis, or they may be divided up among regions of the world or separate countries. Robert J. Hershock, former corporate vice president, marketing, 3M, said this about 3M's sales approach: "Today, the sales representative needs to be a business manager who is responsible for key accounts. He or she must be able to customize products and services, be knowledgeable about key account strategies and objectives, and be capable of building and implementing key account business plans."[18] As discussed in Chapter 1, the increasing technical complexity of products, industrial concentration, and the trend toward centralized purchasing make a few major accounts critical to the marketing success of many firms in both industrial and consumer goods industries. Moreover, in the ever-increasing global marketplace, key accounts often become global accounts demanding a high degree of coordination with their suppliers. On the customer side, over time Xerox has cut its list of suppliers by 90 percent. Such trends suggest that companies are looking at developing fewer but more substantial relationships with a limited set of global suppliers.[19]

To provide the level of service demanded by key accounts, firms adopt an overall selling philosophy of major account management and partnering. This approach stresses the dual goals of making sales and developing long-term relationships with major customers. Firms believe key account management policies will improve coordination of selling activities and communications with key customers. This should enable the seller to capture a larger share of the purchases made by those customers and to improve profitability.[20] Benefits accrue inside the firm as well. Everyone in the organization works a little harder when they know the customer is significant and has a long-term relationship with the firm.[21]

When a firm decides to implement a key account program, it must address the issue of who in the organization should be responsible for the functions of managing the business of the key accounts. Some firms have no special organizational arrangements for handling their major customers; they rely on members of their regular sales force, supported by other members of their company, to manage accounts. This requires no additional administrative or selling expense.

The disadvantage is that major accounts often require more detailed and sophisticated treatment than smaller customers. Consequently, servicing major accounts may require more experience, expertise, and organizational authority than many salespeople possess. Also, if the sales force is compensated largely by commission, difficult questions may arise about which salesperson should get the commissions for sales to key accounts when one person calls on a customer's headquarters while others service its stores or plants in various territories.

In view of these difficulties, many firms have adopted special organizational arrangements for the major account management function. These arrangements include (1) assigning key accounts to top sales executives, (2) creating a separate corporate division, and (3) creating a separate sales force to handle major accounts.[22]

Assigning Key Accounts to Sales Executives

The use of sales or marketing executives to call on the firm's key accounts is a common practice, especially among smaller firms that do not have the resources to support a separate division or sales force. It is also common when the firm has relatively few major accounts to be serviced. In addition to the relatively low cost of the approach, it has the advantage of having important customers serviced by people who are high enough in the organizational hierarchy to make, or at least to influence, decisions concerning the allocation of production capacity, inventory levels, and prices. Consequently, they can provide flexible and responsive service.

One problem with this approach is that the managers who are given key account responsibilities sometimes develop a warped view of their firm's marketing objectives. They sometimes allocate too much of the firm's resources to their own accounts to the detriment of smaller, but still profitable, customers. In other words, such managers sometimes become obsessed with getting all the business they can from their large customers without paying sufficient attention to the overall impact on sales, operations, or profits.

Another problem is that assigning important selling tasks to managers takes time away from their management activities. This can hinder the coordination and effectiveness of the firm's overall selling and marketing efforts.[23]

A Separate Key Account Division

Some firms create a separate corporate division for dealing with major accounts, usually on a global basis. For example, some apparel companies have separate divisions for making and selling private-label clothing to large global general-merchandise retail. This approach allows for close integration of manufacturing, logistics, marketing, and sales activities. This can be important when one or a few major customers account for such a large proportion of a firm's total sales volume that variations in their purchases have a major impact on the firm's production schedules, inventories, and allocation of resources.

The major disadvantages of this approach are the duplication of effort and the additional expense involved in creating an entire manufacturing and marketing organization for only one or a few customers. It is also risky because the success or failure of the entire division is dependent on the whims of one or a few customers.

A Separate Sales Force for Key Accounts

Rather than creating an entire separate division to deal with major customers, a company may create a separate or key account sales force. A separate sales force has several advantages in dealing with key accounts. By concentrating on only one or a few major customers, the account manager can become very familiar with each customer's problems and needs and can devote the time necessary to provide a high level of service to each customer. Also, the firm can select its most competent and experienced salespeople to become members of the key account sales force, thus ensuring that important customers receive expert sales attention.

Finally, a separate key account sales force provides an internal benefit to the selling company. Because only the most competent salespeople are typically assigned to key accounts, such an assignment is often viewed as a desirable promotion. Thus, promotion to the key account sales force can be used to motivate and reward top salespeople who are either not suited for or not interested in moving into sales management.

In addition to the problem of allocating key account sales to individual members of the field sales force, using a separate sales force for major accounts suffers from many of the other disadvantages associated with organizing sales efforts by customer type. The most troubling problems concern the duplication of effort within the sales organization and the resulting higher selling and administrative expenses.

Team Selling

As we learned in Chapters 2 and 3, today the relationship between customers and sales organizations is complex. Nowadays, salespeople are asked to demonstrate a stronger knowledge of the customer's businesses than ever before as well as provide a more consistent and beneficial interface with the customer—in other words, better service. As we learned in Chapter 3, one way companies deal with these demands is to assign specialists inside the firm to individual customers—team selling. A number of benefits are achieved by allocating more individuals, each with a unique talent, to each customer. First, questions can be answered faster, which reduces the need for the "I will get back to you on that" response to customer inquiries. Second, people with similar interests can speak directly with one another. A technical question from the customer's engineering department can be answered by another engineer in the supplier's support sales team.[24]

The key is identifying a team selling structure that meets the needs of customers. For example, a common structure would make the account manager responsible for working with the entire team selling to and servicing major customers. Often, such major account teams include representatives from a number of functional departments within the firm, such as R&D, operations, and finance. Given that major customers' buying centers often consist of people from different functional areas with different viewpoints and concerns, those concerns can often be most effectively addressed by a team of experts from equivalent functional departments in the selling firm, or even from different divisions within the company. Recently, companies have begun to look at the existence of a selling center that brings together individuals from around the organization (marketing, customer service, sales, engineering, and others) to help the salesperson do his or her job more effectively. These selling centers are analogous to the concept of selling teams discussed in Chapter 3. Just as customers have buying centers, the selling organization needs to work together to present a unified, well-coordinated effort to the customer.[25] In an increasing number of companies, sales organizations maintain offices in the customer's facilities. Lear Corporation, a leading global supplier of automotive interior systems, maintains sales offices on the premises of each of its major customers, who are many of the major automotive firms around the world.[26]

At P&G, the team for a major account such as Tesco (based in the UK) is led by a P&G account executive. The account executive has a global team of salespeople as direct reports, but can also draw from the full functional resources of P&G to provide solutions for Tesco at any location in the world. Such an approach creates a matrix organization of direct reports and supporting internal consultants who bring their collective expertise to bear for the client.

Team selling can also present some coordination, motivation, and compensation problems. Lou Gerstner, former chairman and CEO of IBM, has frequently spoken out on the difficulties of performance management in team selling environments.[27] Team selling is most appropriate for the very largest customers, where the potential purchase represents enough dollars and involves enough functions to justify the high costs. Although team selling is usually used to win new accounts, it is sometimes also used with lower-level personnel for maintenance selling. Production schedulers, expediters, and shipping personnel may join the sales team to keep an existing account satisfied.[28]

A number of important recent trends in team selling are presented in the Leadership box.

LEADERSHIP   **Advantages of Team Selling**

Team selling has two main uses in the modern sales force:

1. Facilitate the sale—When selling to a customer, a salesperson brought into team selling will not be afraid to say "I don't know but I will find out" to the customer. He or she will address questions to production staff, expediters, and so on to ensure that the order the customer is placing can realistically be delivered before it is promised. This will ensure that the team as a whole is helping ensure customer satisfaction.
2. Cross selling—An important part of sales is the cross-selling of other products that may be outside of the normal products that a salesperson would sell. In a team selling environment, salespeople are aware of their customer needs and how to relate these not only to their own product offerings but to other offerings from within the company that may be able to satisfy that need. This cross-selling can be encouraged through incentives and compensation.

Team selling can be a huge benefit for an organization in terms of both revenue and morale. The old "lone wolf" mentality should be discouraged and replaced by a more team-oriented group-goal attitude.

Multilevel Selling

Multilevel selling is a variation of team selling. In multilevel selling, the sales team consists of personnel from various managerial levels who call on their counterparts in the buying organization. Thus, the account manager might call on the customer's purchasing department while the selling firm's vice president of finance calls on the buyer's financial vice president. Sometimes this involves setting up a permanent team to coordinate activities with the customer. Often, however, this is an ad hoc arrangement where individuals at different levels are responsible for maintaining a relationship with the key customer but not as part of an established team.

This approach represents proper organizational etiquette—each member of the selling team calls on a person with corresponding status and authority. Also, it is useful for higher-level executives to participate in opening a relationship with a major new prospect, since they have the authority to make concessions and establish policies necessary to win and maintain that prospect as a customer. When the interaction takes place at the highest levels of both firms, the process is called *top-to-top selling*, as discussed in Chapter 3.

Co-marketing Alliances

In some high-tech industries, such as computers and telecommunications, customers buy systems made up of components manufactured by two or more different suppliers. In some cases, suppliers rely on independent intermediaries, such as value-added resellers (VARs), to combine their components with those from other suppliers to create a system to meet the needs of a particular end user. Increasingly, however, individual suppliers are forming co-marketing alliances and developing joint marketing and sales programs to sell integrated systems directly to the ultimate customer.

In some cases, even competitors develop marketing alliances to maximize their resources. When Warner-Lambert's Parke-Davis pharmaceutical division created the lipid-regulating drug Lipitor, the product offered significant advantages over anything else in the market. However, the firm lacked the sales force necessary to market the drug effectively. Warner-Lambert partnered with Pfizer, a company with a powerful sales force, to create a joint effort managed by a team of individuals from both companies. Salespeople from both firms worked together to maximize the sales of Lipitor in a given territory.[29] Interestingly, a few years later Pfizer acquired Warner-Lambert.

Logistical Alliances and Computerized Ordering

Another popular approach in many industries is the formation of logistical alliances involving the development of computerized information and ordering systems. Such systems enable customers to place an order directly, and often automatically, via a dedicated telephone or satellite link to a supplier's computer. Firms such as P&G and 3M have formed alliances with major supermarket chains and mass merchandisers to develop automatic restocking systems. Sales information from the retailer's checkout scanners is sent directly to the supplier's computers, which figure out automatically when to replenish each product and schedule deliveries directly to each of the retailer's stores. Such paperless exchanges reduce mistakes and billbacks, minimize inventory levels, decrease out-of-stocks, and improve cash flow.[30]

One question that is yet to be answered is: How might computerized reorder systems change the role of the sales force? Will salespeople become largely redundant, or will being freed from the more routine order-taking activities enable firms to refocus personal selling efforts on more complex communications, problem solving, and customer servicing tasks? Years ago when Cisco Systems, a leading producer of Internet working equipment, introduced its website so customers could track and order more efficiently, salespeople were concerned it would have a negative effect on their interaction with customers. The reality was much different. Cisco salespeople quickly realized that they were able to devote more time to actually selling products rather than reordering or tracking existing orders.

VERTICAL STRUCTURE OF THE SALES ORGANIZATION

The beginning of this chapter stressed that the sales organization must be structured vertically as well as horizontally. The vertical organizational structure clearly defines what managerial positions have the authority for carrying out specific sales management activities. This vertical structure also provides for the effective integration and coordination of selling efforts throughout the firm.

Two key questions that must be answered in designing an effective vertical structure for a sales organization are (1) how many levels of sales managers should there be? and (2) how many people should each manager supervise, that is, what is his or her span of control? These questions are related. For a given number of salespeople, the greater the span of control, the fewer the levels of management, and the fewer managers needed.

Major differences of opinion exist about the best policy concerning span of control and the number of vertical levels for a sales organization. Some managers think they have greater control and attain greater responsiveness when the sales force has a "flat" organization with few management levels. They argue that few levels between the top sales executive and the field salespeople facilitate communication and more direct control. But some managers argue that such flat organizations actually limit communication and control because they necessitate large spans of control.

The flat organization with large spans of control has lower administrative costs because of the relatively small number of managers involved. Some argue, however, that such cost savings are an illusion because the lower quantity and quality of management can lead to less effectiveness and productivity.

In view of these disagreements, it is difficult to generalize about the most appropriate number of management levels and span of control for a specific organization. However, managers have a few guidelines to follow. The span of control should be smaller and the number of levels of management should be larger when (1) the sales task is complex, (2) the profit impact of each salesperson's performance is high, and (3) the salespeople in the organization are well paid and professional. In other words, the more difficult and important the sales job, the greater the management support and supervision that should be provided to the members of the sales force.

Another general rule is that the span of control should usually be smaller at higher levels in the sales organization because top-level managers should have more time for analysis and decision making. Also, the people who report to them typically have more complicated jobs and require more organizational support and communication than persons in lower-level jobs.

In addition to deciding how many subordinates sales managers should supervise, another question addresses how much authority each manager should be given in managing subordinates. Where should the authority to hire, fire, and evaluate field salespeople be located within the organization? In some sales organizations, first-level field or district sales managers have the authority to hire their own salespeople. In other organizations, the authority to hire and fire is located at higher management levels.

As a general rule of organization, the more important a decision to the success of a firm, the higher the level of management that should make that decision. In firms that hire many low-paid salespeople who perform relatively routine selling tasks and have only a small impact on the firm's overall profit performance, hiring and evaluation authority is usually given to first-level sales managers. Firms that have professional salespeople who perform complex selling tasks and have a major profit impact usually place the authority to hire and fire at higher levels. This is particularly true when the sales force is viewed as a training ground for future sales or marketing managers.

Selling Responsibilities

In addition to their supervisory and policy-making roles, many sales managers, particularly those at the field or district level, continue to be actively involved in selling activities. Since many sales managers are promoted to their positions only after proving to be competent and effective salespeople, their employers are often reluctant to lose the benefit of their selling skills. Consequently, sales managers are often allowed to continue servicing at least a few of their largest customers after they join the ranks of management.

Some firms rely on their sales managers for selling and servicing key accounts. Sales managers often prefer this kind of arrangement. They are reluctant to give up the opportunities for commissions and direct contact with the marketplace that they gain by being actively involved in selling. The danger is that sales managers sometimes spend too much time selling and not enough time managing their subordinates. Consequently, some firms limit the amount of actual selling in which managers can engage. This is particularly true in large firms where coordinating and supervising a vast sales force requires a great deal of attention by management personnel.

Sales-Related Functions

Many firms face markets that demand high levels of service. Firms that sell capital equipment, for instance, must provide their customers with installation and maintenance service; fashion manufacturers must provide rapid order processing and delivery; and firms that sell electronic components must offer special product design and engineering services. These services must be integrated with the rest of the firm's marketing and selling activities for the company to compete effectively.[31]

The question from an organizational viewpoint, though, is whether sales managers should be given the authority to control such sales-related functions. The answer depends on the function and the characteristics and needs of the firm's customers. Order processing and expediting are low visibility but quite important sales-related functions. In some firms, persons responsible for order processing report to top-level sales management, whereas in other firms they report to operations management, perhaps as part of an inventory control or data processing department. Usually, the more important rapid order processing and delivery are for keeping customers satisfied, the more appropriate it is for sales management to have authority over this function.

Repair and engineering services tend to be responsible to the sales organization in some firms and to the manufacturing or operations department in others. Again, such functions are most likely to be attached to the sales organization when they play a critical role in winning and maintaining customers. This is particularly true when the product must be designed or modified to meet customer specifications before a sale can be made.

The credit function is almost always the responsibility of the firm's controller or treasurer, and it seldom reports to the sales organization because salespeople and their managers may be tempted to be too generous with credit terms to close a sale.

In firms where sales-related functions do not report directly to the sales organization, team selling is often a useful means of coordinating such functions, at least when dealing with major customers where the cost of such an approach is justified. Although the account manager has no formal authority to control the actions of team members from other departments, he or she can coordinate the team's activities at the field level.

The Impact of New Technologies

Many of the preceding conclusions about appropriate spans of control and managerial responsibilities for sales managers must be taken with the caveat that the vertical structure of sales organizations is subject to change in the future due to the impact of ongoing rapid development in new communications and information processing technologies. Companies realize that maximizing the sales effort requires that each salesperson be equipped with an array of technologies. The use of technologies has evolved from productivity enhancers (time management and contact management software; proposal generators) to CRM systems as discussed in Chapter 3, with the capability to drive the entire customer acquisition and retention management process. And today, social networking websites such as Twitter and Facebook in the consumer marketplace, and LinkedIn in the business marketplace, provide new opportunities for customer connectedness.[32]

Staff Support and Outsourcing

Many large sales organizations utilize some staff personnel in addition to their line sales managers. Staff executives are responsible for a limited range of specific activities, but they do not have the broad operating responsibility or authority of line managers. Staff executives commonly perform tasks requiring specialized knowledge or abilities that the average sales manager does not have the time to develop. They may also help collect and analyze information that line managers need for decision making. Thus, the most common functions performed by staff specialists in a sales organization are recruitment, training, and sales analysis. A typical line and staff sales organization is diagrammed in Exhibit 4.6.

The creative use of staff specialists can enable a sales force to function with fewer managers because of the benefits of specialization and division of labor. It can also

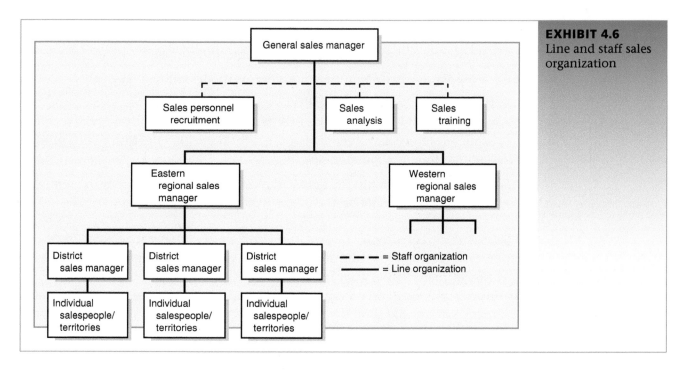

EXHIBIT 4.6
Line and staff sales organization

improve the effectiveness of the sales organization while cutting costs. In addition, staff positions can be used as a training ground for future top-level sales managers.

On the other hand, staff positions are justified only when the sales organization is large enough so staff specialists have enough work to keep them busy. Increasingly, however, even the largest firms are questioning whether in-house staff specialists are really justified. A growing number of firms are outsourcing some staff functions through the use of specialized suppliers, such as recruiting and personnel testing services and training firms. The rationale for this trend is similar to the argument discussed earlier concerning the use of company salespeople versus independent agents. Activities that do not rely directly on a firm's core competencies (i.e., that do not require specialized or transaction-specific assets) often can be performed more effectively and efficiently by outside specialists on a contractual basis.[33]

ADDITIONAL SALES ORGANIZATIONAL ISSUES

Sometimes, the opportunity arises to start from scratch to build a new sales force. Such an opportunity should allow the sales manager to avoid pitfalls and create an initial organizational structure and cultural environment that maximizes the potential for success. The following are six key building blocks to starting a sales force:

- *Start with a strategy*. Define the sales force's mission, skill sets, and customer benefits.
- *Appoint an expansion team*. Get hiring input from human resource executives and the executives who will manage the new sales force.
- *Leverage existing strengths*. Look for new hires within your own ranks, your personal business network, as well as your clients and suppliers.
- *Go to the press*. Articles touting your business model and management team can attract both customers and salespeople.
- *Avoid compensation snafus*. If the new team must work hand-in-hand with the existing sales force, consider paying them both for the sale. Don't kill a million dollar investment by pinching pennies.
- *Provide support*. Get out in the field with your salespeople and show them how to pitch the product. Share best practices in conference calls.[34]

Sales managers assigned to lead the effort of creating a new sales force can employ best practices to create an organization designed for high performance.

Although many issues concerning the strategic organization of the sales force have been examined in this chapter, some related questions have yet to be explored. How many salespeople should a firm hire? How should these people be deployed? How should sales territories be defined? What quota, if any, should be assigned to each sales territory?

The answers to these questions depend on the markets to be served, the potential sales volume in those markets, and the selling effort necessary to capture a desired share of the potential volume. These issues are addressed in Chapter 5.

SUMMARY

This chapter examined important issues in organizing the sales effort. It looked at the benefits a good organizational plan can provide, as well as the major issues involved in deciding on the horizontal and vertical organization of the sales effort.

A good organizational plan should satisfy three criteria. First, it should allow the firm to realize the benefits that can be derived from the division and specialization of labor. Second, it should provide for stability and continuity in the firm's selling efforts. This can best be accomplished by organizing activities and not people. Third, it should produce effective coordination of the various activities assigned to different persons in the sales force and different departments in the firm.

Questions of horizontal organization focus on how specific selling activities are to be divided among members of the sales force. The first issue to be resolved is whether to use company employees to perform the sales function or to rely on outside manufacturers' representatives or sales agents. The cost of using outside agents is usually lower than that of a company sales force at relatively low sales volumes. However, most executives believe company employees will generate greater levels of sales and are easier to control than agents.

When a firm employs its own sales force, four types of horizontal organization are commonly found, structured according to (1) geography, (2) type of product, (3) type of customer, and (4) selling function. Geographic organization is the simplest and most common. It possesses the advantages of low cost and clear identification of which salesperson is responsible for each customer. Its primary disadvantage is that it does not provide the firm with any benefits from division and specialization of labor.

Specializing the sales force along product lines allows salespeople to develop great familiarity with the technical attributes, applications, and most effective methods of selling those products. This can be advantageous when products are technically complex or when the firm's manufacturing facilities are also organized by product type. The major disadvantage associated with organization by product type is duplication of effort.

Organizing a sales force by type of customer or market served allows salespeople to better understand the needs and requirements of the various types of customers. Salespeople are more likely to discover ideas for new products and marketing approaches that will appeal to those customers. However, this scheme also produces duplication of effort, which tends to increase selling and administrative expenses.

A selling function organizational philosophy holds that people should be allowed to do what they do best. Thus, it makes sense to have, say, one sales force specializing in prospecting for and developing new accounts while another maintains and services existing customers. These arrangements are often difficult to implement because of coordination problems.

In addition to deciding on a basic structure, a firm needs to specify how it intends to service key accounts in its horizontal organizational plans. Three arrangements are most commonly found: (1) assigning key accounts to top sales executives, (2) creating a separate corporate division, and (3) creating a separate major account sales force.

Two key questions must be addressed in deciding on an effective vertical structure of the sales organization: (1) How many levels of sales managers should there be? (2) How many people should each manager supervise? The answers are related: For a given number of salespeople, a greater span of control produces fewer levels of management. Although it is difficult to unequivocally state the optimal span of control for a firm, it is generally true that the span of control should be smaller in those firms where (1) the sales task is complex, (2) the profit impact of each salesperson's performance is high, and (3) the salespeople in the organization are well paid and professional.

Another question that must be addressed in designing the vertical structure of a sales organization is, How much authority should be given each manager in the sales management hierarchy, particularly with respect to hiring, firing, and evaluating subordinates? As a general rule, the more important such decisions are to the firm, the higher the level of management that should make such decisions.

Starting up a sales force from scratch requires strong leadership skills and a high degree of experience and preparation on the part of the sales manager. It can be one of the most rewarding assignments in one's career, and it provides the opportunity to take advantage of knowledge of best practices to avoid pitfalls and create a high-performance organization.

KEY TERMS

division and specialization of labor	transaction cost analysis (TCA)	major or key accounts
line organization	geographic organization	team selling
line and staff organization	product organization	selling center
outsourcing the sales force	organization by customer type	matrix organization
manufacturers' representatives	organization by selling function	multilevel selling
selling agents	telemarketing	co-marketing alliances
		logistical alliances
		span of control

BREAKOUT QUESTIONS

1. Intronics Corporation, a manufacturer of electronic circuit boards, reaches the market through the services of 75 manufacturers' agencies. Most of the agencies average two sales agents who call on Intronics customers. The agents also represent seven to eight other manufacturers that produce noncompetitive products. Intronics wants to eliminate the agents and develop its own company sales force. How many salespeople do you think Intronics will have to hire? What issues affect your assessment of how many salespeople are needed?

2. IBM, Xerox, P&G, and many other companies have reorganized to better serve their largest customers. How might a global company reorganize itself to maximize effectiveness with its most important customers? As senior sales management, how

would you define "most important" customer (by current sales, future potential sales, or some other criteria)?

3. The chapter mentions the theory of transaction cost analysis (TCA). What role does TCA play in the decision to use a company sales force rather than independent manufacturers' agents?

4. Telemarketing has resulted in the development of inside sales forces. Some companies assign sales trainees to the inside or telephone sales force as part of the training program in preparation for an outside sales position. Other companies view the two positions as separate. What functions would an inside (telephone) sales force perform? How would these functions differ from those performed by the external sales force? How would compensation plans differ if they differ at all? How might social media and online tools best be used to augment telemarketing/inside sales efforts?

5. LaMarche's Enterprise manufactures both technical and nontechnical products. Its sales forces are organized in the same manner. The technical sales force has 175 people, and the nontechnical group numbers 128. To what extent would such a division affect the following?

   a. Recruiting.
   b. Sales training.
   c. Compensation.
   d. Supervision.
   e. Span of control.

6. Ethical Question. As sales director for On-the-Go Logistics you have been tasked with creating a sales team for a new major account—Gigatron (an online multi-product vendor similar to Amazon). Gigatron is based in London and is fast becoming a world leader in online sales. Your company specializes in creating complex logistics solutions for companies. On-the-Go Logistics is based in Chicago and in the past all their key accounts have been in the U.S., although they have a relatively small sales office in the U.K. to handle the customer base there. Much of their business is in Europe and they would like the On-the-Go key account manager and team to be based in London and comprised entirely of Europeans. Ah, but guess what—your best and most qualified salespeople are all Americans and several would love to move to London. If you promote someone from the company's smaller, less experienced European staff you are certain there will be a problem with some of the more experienced, American based salespeople and you also wonder if anybody promoted from the European office will be able to properly manage such a key account. As sales director, what is the best solution and why?

LEADERSHIP CHALLENGE

Internal or Outsourced Sales Force

Susan Jones was thinking about the future as she drove home from an important day at her company, Satin Organic Products. In a little over nine years, she had taken a small organic milk company and become a major supplier to large health food grocery chains like Whole

Foods and Trader Joe's. During that time, Susan and her vice president of marketing, Sal Clermont, had handled all the sales responsibilities. Working directly with the buyers, Susan and Sal had built an outstanding reputation as people who cared about the quality of their products and their relationship with customers.

Now Susan was faced with a challenge. Susan and Sal would no longer be able to handle the sales responsibilities by themselves. The company had grown too big and needed sales representation in the field. At present, an analysis of the company's current and near-term future plans had determined a need for seven individuals. Four people were required to handle the company's key accounts (Whole Foods and Trader Joe's) and three were needed to call on potential new customers in areas close to the company's expanding operations in the Midwest.

In talking with Sal and others in the food business, Susan realized there were two basic choices and unlimited combinations of those two choices. First, she could hire seven salespeople as employees of the Satin Organic Products. This had certain advantages but was also the most expensive. The second alternative was to hire outside sales agents who knew the food business and the customers. This alternative also had advantages and disadvantages.

Susan knew that she and Sal would have to make a decision soon. Their large customers were demanding more service, and there were a number of new business opportunities that they had not been able to go after because of other responsibilities.

Questions

1. Using the information in this chapter, discuss the advantages and disadvantages of having your own sales force versus hiring outside sales agents.

2. How should Susan set up the sales force for Satin Organic Products and why?

ROLE-PLAY: BLUE TERN MILLS — PART A

Situation

Agnes Klondyke is excited. As chief sales officer (CSO) for Blue Tern Mills, a major manufacturer of traditional salty snacks (nuts, chips, and crackers), she knows that new product development is the lifeblood of the business. But wow . . . the e-mail she got this morning from Blue Tern's CEO Max Pugh really takes the cake (no pun intended of course). Max reports that Blue Tern's acquisition of the Hello brand of healthy grain cereals and packaged healthy snacks has been completed. Beginning in about six months, Blue Tern's sales force will begin selling the new line, which has previously been sold by manufacturers' agents.

Later that afternoon, Agnes got a call from Max to discuss gearing up for selling the new line. Blue Tern's sales force has been organized geographically, with each salesperson selling the entire line of 211 Blue Tern snack products. The problem is that the Hello line adds 117 new products to the mix, and many of these products are sold in different kinds of outlets from Blue Tern items—for example, while some supermarkets, drugstores, and discount stores might sell both Blue Tern and Hello products, the Hello line is also sold in health food stores, in some gyms, and over the Internet. Agnes is quickly realizing that she has a major reorganization task ahead for the company's sales force.

Max has asked for a new organization plan for selling both lines, and he wants the plan on his desk in two weeks. Agnes calls Alan Knorr, West Coast regional manager for Blue Tern, and Penny Pugsley, director of sales for Hello, to a meeting to discuss ideas for the transition and development of a new organizational scheme for Blue Tern's sales force. Penny is cooperative, as in the acquisition she has been promised the vacant East Coast regional manager slot at Blue Tern. Vital facts about Blue Tern's current sales organization: (1) it is organized geographically, with 212 salespeople, 20 district managers, and two regional managers; (2) all the salespeople sell the full Blue Tern product line to all types of retailers; and (3) there are no major account salespeople.

Max has made it clear that he will financially support whatever changes this decision team recommends, including adding some salespeople where needed to support the additional anticipated sales volume from the Hello line. The key question of course is: Is their current simple geographic approach optimal for the new situation?

Characters in the Role-Play

Agnes Klondyke, chief sales officer (CSO) for Blue Tern Mills
Alan Knorr, West Coast sales manager for Blue Tern Mills
Penny Pugsley, currently the director of sales for Hello Healthy Grain Foods and soon to be East Coast sales manager for Blue Tern Mills; note that Penny's job at Hello has been to supervise its network of manufacturers' reprepresentatives (Hello does not have its own sales force).

Assignment

Break into groups of three, with one student playing each character. It doesn't matter what the actual gender mix of your group is. Before you stage the meeting among Agnes, Alan, and Penny, work separately to come up with a proposed new organization plan for Blue Tern's sales force and a transition plan for making the change happen. Remember, Blue Tern must be ready to start selling both lines in six months. Then get together and role-play the meeting. Share your ideas, especially discussing the pros and cons of different new organization schemes for the sales force. After the discussion, come to agreement among yourselves on what will be the best type of sales organization for the firm and list key aspects of implementing the change so that the transition with customers is as smooth as possible.

MINICASE: FONDREN PUBLISHING, INC.

Fondren Publishing, Inc., based in Paris, France, is one of the leading worldwide publishers of academic journals in the area of science and technology. It has more than 2,000 titles in its stable of products and publishes them in both print and electronic formats. Its primary customers are trade customers, who collect academic journal content from several different publisher sources and then package the content and resell it to retail customers. To a lesser extent, Fondren also sells directly to retail customers such as universities, libraries, societies/associations (e.g., Society of Environmental Engineers), and individuals (e.g., professors, scientists).

Fondren's sales force is known for being dynamic and knowledgeable, and some members of its sales team have been with the company for as many as 17 years. It traditionally has had a geographically structured sales force, divided into 14 regions: 6 in the United States, 4 in Europe, 4 in Asia-Pacific. Fondren's largest trade customer, by far, is New York–based AcademCo., which has a 35 percent share in its market and is responsible for 20 percent of Fondren's sales revenues. Therefore, the regional sales team covering the northeastern United States is extra large to accommodate this customer.

Just last week, a deal was reached for Fondren to merge with another journal publisher, Bronson & Sons, which is headquartered in Brussels, Belgium. Bronson specializes in health science titles, which will add more than 750 new titles to those of Fondren. Bronson has fewer trade customers than Fondren and focuses on its direct customers such as societies, universities, and individuals. Bronson's market has previously been limited to Europe, broadly speaking, with no defined territorial sales regions within Europe.

Although the arrangement is a "merger," Fondren has a controlling interest and will blend Bronson's products with its existing products under the Fondren name. Fondren's executives are meeting to decide on how the new merged company will be structured, including how the sales force will be structured.

The executives also want to use this merger and restructuring opportunity to enhance the company's customer service activities. Currently, the customer service department handles the fulfillment and maintenance of new and existing subscriptions (renewals, change of address, and so forth) through telephone operators. Fondren's IT department has plans to implement a new customer service and fulfillment system, which will be able to record and track particular customer information, as well as offer the customer service functions through an online Web interface.

To this point, the sales representatives would make the initial sale, and then turn the customer over to the customer service function for maintenance. Alienor Cointreau, director of customer service and fulfillment, has a vision in which customer service representatives would be able to contribute to sales by up-selling or cross-selling Fondren products when the reps are in contact with customers.

Questions

1. How should Fondren structure its sales force after the merger with Bronson? Why? What are the potential advantages and disadvantages of the structure you chose?

2. How should Fondren treat its key account(s)? Why?

3. What selling approach could Fondren take to coordinate its selling endeavors with its customer service and fulfillment operations?

CHAPTER 5

The Strategic Role of Information in Sales Management

LEARNING OBJECTIVES

Sales managers are both users and generators of information. The sales manager's role with regard to generating, analyzing, and disseminating information is vital to the success of both the firm's marketing strategy and the success of its individual salespeople. Important decisions at all levels of the organization are affected by how well sales managers use information.

This chapter presents a look at several of the key ways sales managers perform this vital information management role including forecasting sales, setting quotas, establishing the size and territory design of the sales force, and performing sales analysis for managerial decision making. Specifically, after reading this chapter, you should be able to

- Discuss the differences between market potential, sales potential, sales forecast, and sales quota.
- Understand the various methods by which sales managers develop sales forecasts.
- Outline the process of setting a sales quota.
- Explain the various types of quotas used in sales management.
- Discuss key approaches to determining sales force size.
- Describe the sales territory design process.
- Understand the importance of sales analysis for managerial decision making.
- Conduct a sales analysis.

USING INFORMATION IN MANAGERIAL DECISION MAKING AND PLANNING

It has been said that information is the fuel that drives the engine in managerial decision making. This is no different in sales management. Sales managers are charged with making decisions and developing plans that impact multifaceted areas of a company. One of these areas, sales forecasting, is directly linked with the overall market opportunity analysis of the firm.

Developing sales forecasts is one of the most important uses of information by sales managers. And concurrently, the sales forecasts they develop become an integral part of an organization's overall planning and strategy development efforts.

Without good sales forecasts, it is impossible for companies to properly invest against their market opportunities. Sales managers must understand the various approaches to forecasting and appreciate the value of utilizing multiple methods of sales forecasting before making a decision on the final forecast to present to the firm.

For the sales manager, the forecast allows for the development of estimates of demand for individual sales territories and subsequently for the establishment of specific sales quotas by territory and by salesperson. Quotas are very important both to the firm and to its individual salespeople. For the firm, the aggregate of sales quotas during a particular performance period represents an operationalization of the sales forecast, and thus progress by the sales organization toward quota achievement is closely monitored by top management. For the individual salesperson, quotas provide specific goals to work toward that are tailored to his or her sales territory. Ordinarily, important elements of compensation and other rewards are linked to quota achievement. Because of the importance of quotas, sales managers must make certain they use the information available to select the proper type of quotas for the situation and to ensure that the level of the quotas is established in a fair and accurate manner.

Another important use of information by sales managers is in determining the optimal size of the sales force. A variety of quantitative analytical approaches are available for making this determination, all of which are driven by information. Once the size of the sales force is set, sales managers turn their analysis toward designing the sales territories. Finally, information is vital to the capability of sales managers to perform sales analyses.

In this chapter, we discuss each of these major strategic uses of information by sales managers and provide a context for sales managers to make better use of the information available to them for decision making.

INTRODUCTION TO MARKET OPPORTUNITY ANALYSIS

Market opportunity analysis requires an understanding of the differences in the notions of market potential, sales potential, sales forecast, and sales quota.

Market potential is an estimate of the possible sales of a commodity, a group of commodities, or a service for an entire industry in a market during a stated period under ideal conditions. A market is a customer group in a specific geographic area.

Sales potential refers to the portion of the market potential that a particular firm can reasonably expect to achieve. Market potential represents the maximum possible sales for all sellers of the good or service under ideal conditions, while sales potential reflects the maximum possible sales for an individual firm.

The sales forecast is an estimate of the dollar or unit sales for a specified future period. The forecast may be for a specified item of merchandise or for an entire line. It may be for a market as a whole or for any portion of it. Importantly, a sales forecast specifies the commodity, customer group, geographic area, and time period and includes a specific marketing plan and accompanying marketing program as essential elements. If the proposed plan is changed, predicted sales are also expected to change.

Naturally, forecast sales are typically less than the company's sales potential for a number of reasons. The firm may not have sufficient production capacity to realize its full potential, or its distribution network may not be sufficiently developed, or its financial resources may be limited. Likewise, forecast sales for an industry are typically less than the industry's market potential.

Sales quotas are sales goals assigned to a marketing unit for use in managing sales efforts. The marketing unit in question might be an individual salesperson, a sales territory, a branch office, a region, a dealer or distributor, or a district, just to name a few possibilities. Each salesperson in each sales territory might be assigned a sales volume goal for the next year. Sales quotas are typically a key measurement used to evaluate the personal selling effort. They apply to specific periods and can be specified in great detail—for example, sales of a particular item to a specified customer by sales rep J. Jones in June.

Exhibit 5.1 shows the relationship between potentials, forecasts, and quotas. Typically the process begins with an assessment of the economic environment. Sometimes this is simply an implicit assessment of the immediate future. Then, given an initial estimate of industry potential and the company's competitive position, the firm's sales potential can be estimated. This in turn leads to an initial sales forecast, often based on the presumption that the marketing effort will be similar to what it was last year. The initial forecast is then compared with objectives established for the proposed marketing effort. If the marketing program is expected to achieve the objectives, both the program and the sales forecast are adopted. That is rare, however. Usually it is necessary to redesign the marketing program and then revise the sales forecast, often several times.

The objectives may also need revising, but eventually the process should produce agreement between the forecast or expected sales and the objectives. The sales forecast is then used as a key input in setting individual sales quotas (goals). In addition, it also serves as a basic piece of information in establishing budgets for the various functional areas.

METHODS OF SALES FORECASTING

The sales forecast is one of the most important information tools used by management and lies at the heart of most companies' planning efforts. Top management uses the sales forecast to allocate resources among functional areas and to control the operations of the firm. Finance uses it to project cash flows, to decide on capital appropriations, and to establish operating budgets. Production uses it to determine quantities and schedules and to control inventories. Human resources uses it to plan personnel requirements and also as an input in collective bargaining. Purchasing uses it to plan the company's overall materials requirements and also to schedule their arrival. Marketing uses it to plan marketing and sales programs and to allocate resources among the various marketing activities. The importance of accurate sales forecasts is exacerbated as companies coordinate their efforts on a global scale.

The sales forecast is also of fundamental importance in planning and evaluating the personal selling effort. Sales managers use it for setting sales quotas, as input to the compensation plan, and in evaluating the field sales force, among other things. Because sales managers rely so heavily on sales forecasts for decision making, and also are integral to the formulation of sales forecasts, it is important that they be familiar with the techniques used in forecast development. The subjective and objective methods discussed in this chapter are listed in Exhibit 5.2.[1]

Each method has advantages and disadvantages, which are summarized in Exhibit 5.3, and the decision of which method to use will not always be clear.[2] In a typical company, the decision will likely depend on its level of technical sophistication, the existence of historic sales data, and the proposed use of the forecast.

Subjective Methods of Forecasting

Subjective forecasting methods do not rely primarily on sophisticated quantitative (empirical) analytical approaches in developing the forecast.

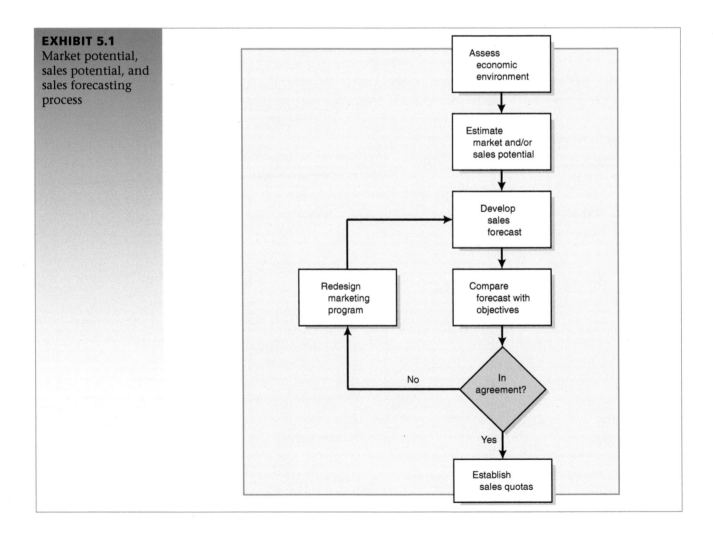

EXHIBIT 5.1
Market potential, sales potential, and sales forecasting process

User Expectations

The user expectations method of forecasting sales is also known as the buyers' intentions method because it relies on answers from customers regarding their expected consumption or purchases of the product.

The user expectations method of forecasting sales may provide estimates closer to market or sales potential than to sales forecasts. In reality, user groups would have difficulty anticipating the industry's or a particular firm's marketing efforts. Rather, the user estimates reflect their anticipated needs. From the sellers' standpoint, they provide a measure of the opportunities available among a particular segment of users.

Sales Force Composite

The sales force composite method of forecasting sales is so named because the initial input is the opinion of each member of the field sales staff. Each person states how much he or she expects to sell during the forecast period. Subsequently, these estimates are typically adjusted at various levels of sales management. They are likely to be checked, discussed, and possibly changed by the branch manager and on up the sales organization chart until the figures are finally accepted at corporate headquarters.

When forecasting via sales force composite, organizations typically use historical information about the accuracy of the salespeople's estimates to make adjustments to the raw forecast data provided by the field sales organization. For various reasons, salespeople may be motivated to either underestimate or overestimate what they expect to sell during a period. For example, if quotas are derived from the forecast, salespeople may underestimate their sales volume in order to "sandbag" business and get assigned a smaller quota. Thus, when their sales results come in they give the appearance of a stronger performance. Alternatively, if certain of the company's products are in short supply (such as in a materials shortage or rapid growth market) or are available to customers in limited quantities (such as a short-term promotion), salespeople may overestimate their sales volume in hopes of securing a greater allocation of scarce products.

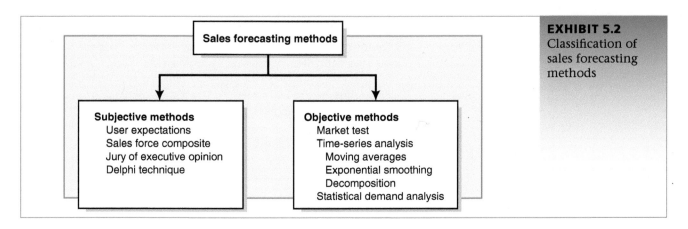

EXHIBIT 5.2
Classification of sales forecasting methods

Jury of Executive Opinion

The jury of executive opinion (or jury of expert opinion) method is a formal or informal internal poll of key executives within the selling company in order to gain their assessment of sales possibilities. The separate assessments are combined into a sales forecast for the company. Sometimes this is done by simply averaging the individual judgments; but other times disparate views are resolved through group discussion toward consensus. The initial views may reflect no more than the executive's hunch about what is going to happen, or the opinion may be based on considerable factual material, sometimes even an initial forecast prepared by other means.

Delphi Technique

In gaining expert opinion, one method for controlling group dynamics to produce a more accurate forecast is the Delphi technique. Delphi uses an iterative approach with repeated measurement and controlled anonymous feedback, instead of direct confrontation and debate among the experts preparing the

EXHIBIT 5.3 Summary of advantages and disadvantages of various sales forecasting techniques	**Sales Forecasting Method**	**Advantages**	**Disadvantages**
	Subjective Methods		
	User expectations	1. Forecast estimates obtained directly from buyers 2. Projected product usage information can be greatly detailed 3. Insights gathered aid in the planning of marketing strategy 4. Useful for new-product forecasting	1. Potential customers must be few and well defined 2. Does not work well for consumer goods 3. Depends on the accuracy of user's estimates 4. Expensive, time-consuming, labor intensive
	Sales force composite	1. Involves the people (sales personnel) who will be held responsible for the results 2. Is fairly accurate 3. Aids in controlling and directing the sales effort 4. Forecast is available for individual sales territories	1. Estimators (sales personnel) have a vested interest and therefore may be biased 2. Elaborate schemes sometimes necessary to counteract bias 3. If estimates are biased, process to correct the data can be expensive
	Jury of executive opinion	1. Easily done, very quick 2. Does not require elaborate statistics 3. Utilizes collective wisdom of the top people 4. Useful for new or innovative products	1. Produces aggregate forecasts 2. Expensive 3. Disperses responsibility for the forecast 4. Group dynamics operate

Delphi technique	1. Minimizes effects of group dynamics 2. Can utilize statistical information	1. Can be expensive and time-consuming	**EXHIBIT 5.3** Summary of advantages and disadvantages of various sales forecasting techniques
Objective Methods			
Market test	1. Provides ultimate test of consumers' reactions to the product 2. Allows the assessment of the effectiveness of the total marketing program 3. Useful for new and innovative products	1. Lets competitors know what firm is doing 2. Invites competitive reaction 3. Expensive and time-consuming to set up 4. Often takes a long time to accurately assess level of initial and repeat demand	
Time-series analysis	1. Utilizes historical data 2. Objective, inexpensive	1. Not useful for new or innovative products 2. Factors for trend, cyclical, seasonal, or product life-cycle phase must be accurately assessed and included 3. Technical skill and good judgment required 4. Final forecast difficult to break down into individual territory estimates 5. Ignores planned marketing effort	
Statistical demand analysis	1. Great intuitive appeal 2. Requires quantification of assumptions underlying the estimates 3. Allows management to check results 4. Uncovers hidden factors affecting sales 5. Method is objective	1. Factors affecting sales must remain constant and be accurately identified to produce an accurate estimate 2. Requires technical skill and expertise 3. Some managers reluctant to use method due to its sophistication	

forecast.[3] Each individual involved prepares a forecast using whatever facts, figures, and general knowledge of the environment he or she has available. Then the forecasts are collected, and an anonymous summary is prepared by the person supervising the process. The summary is distributed to each person who participated in the initial phase. Typically, the summary lists each forecast figure, the average (median), and some summary measure of the spread of the estimates. Often, those whose initial estimates fell outside the midrange of responses are asked to express their reasons for these extreme positions. These explanations are then incorporated into the summary. The participants study the summary and submit a revised forecast. The process is then repeated. Typically, several rounds of these iterations take place. The method is based on the premise that, with repeated measurements (1) the range of responses will decrease and the estimates will converge; and (2) the total group response or median will move successively toward the "correct" or "true" answer.

Objective Methods of Forecasting

Objective forecasting methods rely primarily on more sophisticated quantitative (empirical) analytical approaches in developing the forecast.

Market Test

The typical market test (or test market) involves placing a product in several representative geographic areas to see how well it performs and then projecting that experience to the market as a whole. Often this is done for a new product or an improved version of an old product.

Many firms consider the market test to be the final gauge of consumer acceptance of a new product and ultimate measure of market potential. A. C. Nielsen data, for example, indicate roughly three out of four products that have been test marketed succeed, whereas four out of five that have not been test marketed fail. Despite this fact, market tests have several drawbacks:

- Market tests are costly to administer and are more conducive to testing of consumer products than industrial products.

- The time involved in conducting a market test can be considerable.

- Because a product is being test marketed, it receives more attention in the market test than it can ever receive on a broader/full market scale, giving an unrealistic picture of the product's potential.

- A market test, because it is so visible to competitors, can reveal a firm's hand on its new-product launch strategy, thus allowing competitors time to formulate a market response before full market introduction.

All in all, a market test can be a highly successful sales forecasting technique but one that should not be used unless and until all the positives and negatives have been evaluated by management.

Time-Series Analysis

Approaches to sales forecasting using time-series analysis rely on the analysis of historical data to develop a prediction for the future. The sophistication of these analyses can vary widely. At the most simplistic extreme, the forecaster might simply forecast next year's sales to be equal to this year's sales. Such a forecast might be reasonably accurate for a mature industry that is experiencing little growth or market turbulence. However, barring these conditions, more sophisticated time-series approaches must be considered. Three of these methods, moving averages, exponential smoothing, and decomposition, are discussed here.[4]

Moving Average

The moving average method is conceptually quite simple. Consider the forecast that next year's sales will be equal to this year's sales. Such a forecast might be subject to large error if there is much fluctuation in sales from one year to the next. To allow for such randomness, we might consider using some kind of average of recent values. For example, we might average the last two years' sales, the last three years' sales, the last five years' sales, or any number of other periods. The forecast would simply be the average that resulted. The number of observations included in the average is typically determined by trial and error. Differing numbers of periods are tried, and the number of periods that produces the most accurate forecasts of the trial data is used to develop the forecast model. Once determined, it remains constant. The term moving average is used because a new average is computed and used as a forecast as each new observation becomes available.

Exhibit 5.4 presents a moving average forecast example with 16 years of historical sales data and also the resulting forecasts for a number of years using two- and four-year moving averages. Exhibit 5.5 displays the results graphically. The entry 4,305 for 2004, under the two-year moving average method, for example, is the average of the sales of 4,200 units in 2002 and 4,410 units in 2003. Similarly, the forecast of 5,520 units in 2017 represents the average of the number of units sold in 2015 and 2016. The forecast of 5,772 units in 2017 under the four-year moving average method, on the other hand, represents the average number of units sold during the four-year period 2013–2017. Obviously, it takes more data to begin forecasting with four-year than with two-year moving averages. This is an important consideration when starting to forecast sales for a new product.

Exponential Smoothing

The method of moving averages gives equal weight to each of the last n values in forecasting the next value, where n represents the number of years used. Thus, when $n = 4$ (the four-year moving average is being used), equal weight is given to each of the last four years' sales in predicting the sales for next year. In a four-year moving average, no weight is given to any sales five or more years previous.

Exponential smoothing is a type of moving average. However, instead of weighting all observations equally in generating the forecast, exponential smoothing weights the most recent observations heaviest, for good reason. The

		Forecast Sales	
Year	**Actual Sales**	**Two-Year Moving Average**	**Four-Year Moving Average**
2002	4,200		
2003	4,410		
2004	4,322	4,305	
2005	4,106	4,366	
2006	4,311	4,214	4,260
2007	4,742	4,209	4,287
2008	4,837	4,527	4,370
2009	5,030	4,790	4,499
2010	4,779	4,934	4,730
2011	4,970	4,905	4,847
2012	5,716	4,875	4,904
2013	6,116	5,343	5,128
2014	5,932	5,916	5,395
2015	5,576	6,024	5,684
2016	5,465	5,754	5,835
2017		5,520	5,772

EXHIBIT 5.4
Example of a moving average forecast

EXHIBIT 5.5
Graph of actual and forecast sales using moving averages

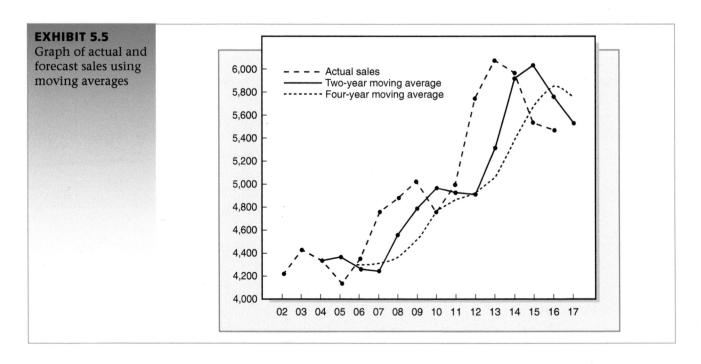

most recent observations contain the most information about what is likely to happen in the future, and they should logically be given more weight.

The key decision affecting the use of exponential smoothing is the choice of the *smoothing constant*, referred to as α in the algorithm for calculating exponential smoothing, which is constrained to be between 0 and 1. High values of α give great weight to recent observations and little weight to distant sales; low values of α, on the other hand, give more weight to older observations. If sales change slowly, low values of α work fine. When sales experience rapid changes and fluctuations, however, high values of α should be used so that the forecast series responds to these changes quickly. The value of α is normally determined empirically; various values of α are tried, and the one that produces the smallest forecast error when applied to the historical series is adopted.

Decomposition

The decomposition method of sales forecasting is typically applied to monthly or quarterly data where a seasonal pattern is evident and the manager wishes to forecast sales not only for the year but also for each period in the year. It is important to determine what portion of sales changes represents an overall, fundamental change in demand and what portion is due to seasonality in demand. For example, Hawaiian Tropic would like to separate out how much of its sales increase in suntan lotion is attributable to the general trend toward increased skin protection from the sun and how much is due to peak seasonal demand in May–September. The decomposition method attempts to isolate four separate portions of a time series: the trend, cyclical, seasonal, and random factors.

- The *trend* reflects the long-run changes experienced in the series when the cyclical, seasonal, and irregular components are removed. It is typically assumed to be a straight line.
- The *cyclical factor* is not always present because it reflects the waves in a series when the seasonal and irregular components are removed. These ups and downs typically occur over a long period, perhaps two to five years. Some products experience little cyclical fluctuation (canned peas), whereas others experience a great deal (housing starts).
- *Seasonality* reflects the annual fluctuation in the series due to the natural seasons. The seasonal factor normally repeats itself each year, although the exact pattern of sales may be different from year to year.
- The *random factor* is what is left after the influence of the trend, cyclical, and seasonal factors is removed.

Exhibit 5.6 shows the calculation of a simple seasonal index based on five years of sales history. The data suggest definite seasonal and trend components in the series. The fourth quarter of every year is always the best quarter; the first quarter is the worst. At the same time, sales each year are higher than they were the year previous. One could calculate a seasonal index for each year by simply dividing quarterly sales by the yearly average per quarter. It is much more typical, though, to base the calculation of the seasonal index on several years of data to smooth out the random fluctuations that occur by quarter.

In using the decomposition method, the analyst typically first determines the seasonal pattern and removes its impact to identify the trend. Then the cyclical factor is estimated. After the three components are isolated, the forecast is developed by applying each factor in turn to the historical data.

Statistical Demand Analysis

Time-series methods attempt to determine the relationship between sales and time as the basis of the forecast for the future. Statistical demand analysis attempts to determine the relationship between sales and the important factors affecting sales to forecast the future. Typically, regression analysis is used to estimate the relationship. The emphasis is not to isolate all factors that affect sales but simply to identify those that have the most dramatic impact on sales and then to estimate the magnitude of the impact. The predictor variables in statistical demand analysis often are historical indexes such as leading economic indicators and other similar measures. For example, a lumber products company might use housing starts, interest rates, and a seasonal shift in demand during summer months to forecast its sales.

CHOOSING A FORECASTING METHOD

The sales manager faced with a forecasting problem has a dilemma: Which forecasting method should be used and how accurate is the forecast likely to be? The dilemma is particularly acute when several methods are tried and the forecasts don't agree, which is more often the norm rather than the exception.

A number of studies have attempted to assess forecast accuracy using the various techniques. Some studies have been conducted within individual companies; others have used selected data series to which the various forecasting techniques have been systematically applied. One of the most extensive comparisons involved 1,001 time series from a variety of sources in which each series was forecast with each of 24 extrapolation methods. The general conclusion was that the method used made little difference with respect to forecast accuracy.[5] Similarly,

EXHIBIT 5.6 Calculation of a seasonal index		Quarter					
Year	**1**	**2**	**3**	**4**	**Total**	**Quarter Average**
2012	82.8	105.8	119.6	151.8	460.0	115.0
2013	93.1	117.6	122.5	156.9	490.1	122.5
2014	92.0	122.4	132.6	163.2	510.2	127.6
2015	95.3	129.0	151.3	185.0	560.6	140.2
2016	120.1	138.1	162.2	180.2	600.6	150.2
Five-year average	96.7	122.6	137.6	167.4	524.3	131.1
Seasonal index*	73.8	93.5	105.0	127.7		

* The seasonal index equals the quarterly average divided by the overall quarterly average times 100; for the first quarter, for example, the seasonal index equals (96.7 ÷ 131.1) × 100 = 73.8.

comparisons of forecast accuracy of objective versus subjective methods gave no clear conclusion as to which method is superior. Some of the comparisons seem to favor the quantitative methods,[6] but others found that the subjective methods produce more accurate forecasts.[7]

In general, the various forecast comparisons suggest that no method is likely to be superior under all conditions. Rather, a number of factors are likely to affect the superiority of any particular technique, including the stability of the data series, the time horizon, the degree of structure imposed on the process, the degree to which computers were used, and deseasonalization of the data. Overall, the best approach seems to be the utilization of multiple methods of forecasting, including a combination of subjective and objective methods, comparing the results, and then employing managerial judgment to make a decision on the final forecast.

Increasingly, firms are turning to scenario planning when developing sales forecasts. Scenario planning involves asking those preparing the forecast a series of "what-if" questions, where the what-ifs reflect different environmental changes that could occur. Some very unlikely changes are considered along with more probable events. The key idea is not so much to have one scenario that gets it right but rather to have a set of scenarios that illuminate the major forces driving the system, their interrelationships, and the critical uncertainties.[8]

DEVELOPING TERRITORY ESTIMATES

Not only must firms develop global estimates of demand, but most also develop territory-by-territory estimates. Territory estimates recognize the condition that the potential for any product may not be uniform by area. Territory demand estimates allow for effective planning, directing, and controlling of salespeople in that the estimates affect the following:

1. The design of sales territories.

2. The procedures used to identify potential customers.

3. The establishment of sales quotas.

4. Compensation levels and the mix of components in the firm's sales compensation scheme.

5. The evaluation of salespeople's performance.

The development of territory demand estimates is typically different for industrial versus consumer goods. Territory demand estimates for industrial goods are often developed by relating sales to some common denominator. The common denominator or market factor might be the number of total employees, number of production employees, value added by manufacturing process, value of materials consumed, value of products shipped, or expenditures for new plant and equipment. Say the ratio of sales per employee is developed for each of several identifiable markets. By then looking at the number of employees in a particular geographic area within each of those identifiable markets, one can estimate the total demand for the product within the area.

The identifiable markets are usually defined using the North American Industry Classification System (NAICS). The NAICS replaced the former system of Standard Industrial Classification (SIC) codes. These systems were developed by the U.S. Bureau of the Census for organizing the reporting of business information such as employment, value added in manufacturing, capital expenditures, and total sales. Each major industry in the United States is assigned a two-digit number, indicating the group to which it belongs. The types of businesses making up each industry are further identified by additional digits.

While firms selling to industrial consumers rely most heavily on identifiable market segments using NAICS codes when estimating territory demand, sellers of consumer goods are more apt to rely on aggregate conditions in each territory. Sometimes this will be a single variable or market factor like the number of households, population, or perhaps the level of income in the area. In other instances, the firm attempts to relate demand to several variables combined in a systematic way. The demand for washing machines, for example, has been shown through statistical demand regression analysis to be a function of the following predictor variables: (1) the level of consumers' stock of washing machines, (2) the number of wired dwelling units, (3) disposable personal income, (4) net credit, and (5) the price index for house furnishings. Since these statistics are published by area, a firm can use the regression equation to estimate demand by area.

Many firms are willing to expend the effort necessary to develop an expression for the relationship between total demand for the product and several variables that are logically related to its sales. Many other firms, however, are content to base their estimates of territory demand on one of the standard multiple-factor indexes that have been developed. A buying power index (BPI) is an index comprised of weighted measures of disposable income, sales data, and market factors for a specific region. Such an index is used by sales organizations to determine the revenue potential for a particular region. If the index does not correlate well with sales of the product, then the firm is probably better off (1) using a single market factor or (2) developing its own index using factors logically related to sales and some a priori or empirically determined weights regarding their relative importance.[9]

PURPOSES AND CHARACTERISTICS OF SALES QUOTAS

As discussed earlier in the chapter, goals assigned to salespeople are called quotas. Quotas are one of the most valuable devices sales managers have for planning the field selling effort, and they are indispensable for evaluating the effectiveness of that effort. They help managers plan the amount of sales and profit that will be available at the end of the planning period and anticipate the activities of the sales team. Quotas are also often used to motivate salespeople and as such must be reasonable. Volume quotas are typically set to a level that is less than the sales potential in the territory and equal to or slightly above the sales forecast for the territory, although they also may be set less than the sales forecast if conditions warrant.

Sales quotas apply to specific periods and may be expressed in dollars or physical units. Thus, management can specify quarterly, annual, and longer-term quotas for each of the company's field representatives in both dollars and physical units. It might even specify these goals for individual products and customers. The product quotas can be varied systematically to reflect the profitability of different items in the line, and customer quotas can be varied to reflect the relative desirability of serving particular accounts.

Purposes of Quotas

Quotas facilitate the planning and control of the field selling effort in a number of ways. Two important contributions of sales quotas are in (1) providing incentives for sales representatives and (2) evaluating salespeople's performance.

Quotas serve as incentives for sales in several ways. In essence, they are an objective to be secured and a challenge to be met. For example, the definite objective of selling $200,000 worth of product X this year, particularly with the opportunity to achieve some desired reward if the quota is met or exceeded, is more motivation to most salespeople than the indefinite charge to go out and do better. It seems one can always do better. Quotas also influence salespeople's incentive through sales contests. A key notion underlying such contests is that those who perform "best" will receive the contest prizes. Quotas can also create incentive via their key role in the compensation systems of most firms. More will be said about these reward and compensation issues in later chapters, but it should be noted here that many firms use a commission or bonus plan, sometimes in conjunction with their base salary plan. In such schemes, salespeople are paid in direct proportion to what they sell (commission plan), or they receive some percentage increment for sales in excess of target sales (bonus plan). Typically, such plans are tied directly to sales quotas. Even when salespeople are compensated with salary only, quotas can provide incentive when salary raises are tied to quota attainment in the previous year. The Leadership box makes a strong case for the importance of strong linkages between sales process and attainment of quota by salespeople.

Quotas also provide a quantitative (objective) standard against which the performance of individual sales representatives or other marketing units can be evaluated. They allow management to recognize salespeople who are performing particularly well and those who may be experiencing difficulty in performance. They provide a basis for developmental actions by the manager and salesperson to ensure a greater level of performance in the future. Issues of performance evaluation of salespeople are discussed in detail in Chapter 13.

LEADERSHIP   Sales Process and Quota Attainment

In recent times there has been much published that devalued the importance of quotas to sales performance. These claims focused on the fact that many companies were concentrating more on customer satisfaction and loyalty. However, in a recent survey of top sales executives, 92 percent claimed that they assign quotas, and 82 percent indicated that quotas are important in gauging sales force success. This illustrates how vital quotas still are in today's sales force.

While setting quotas is important, they are only meaningful if sufficient attainment figures are reached. Following are the findings of a recent study that identified a link between the level of an organization's sales process and quota attainment:

Level 1 Ad Hoc—No clearly defined process and approximately half of sales staff are not attaining quota. Large variation in performance levels.

Level 2 Tribal—Limited process used by certain "tribes" within the company. Still only 50 percent of staff attaining quota but less variation between best and worst performers.

Level 3 Religion—Everyone is using the process but not to its full capability. More salespeople making the quota than not making it.

Level 4 Dynamic World-Class—Fully utilizing people, processes, and technology. Low variation in performance levels of salespeople with very few not attaining quota.

This study provides evidence that assigning quotas is likely to be unproductive unless the process, and *belief in that process*, exists to aid the sales staff to attain their quotas.

Characteristics of a Good Quota

For a quota to be effective, it must be (1) attainable, (2) easy to understand, (3) complete, and (4) timely. Some argue that quotas should be set high so they can be achieved only with extraordinary effort. Although most salespeople may not reach their quotas, the argument is that they are spurred to greater effort than they would have expended in the absence of such a "carrot." Although perhaps intuitively appealing, high quotas can cause problems. They can create ill will among salespeople. They can also cause salespeople to engage in unethical and other undesirable behaviors to make their quotas.[10] The use of very high "carrot" quotas seems to be the exception rather than the rule and is generally not recommended. The prevailing philosophy is that quotas should be realistic. They should represent attainable goals that can be achieved with normal or reasonable, not Herculean, efforts. That seems to motivate most salespeople best.

Quotas should be not only realistic but also easy to understand. Complex quota plans may cause suspicion and mistrust among sales representatives and thereby discourage rather than motivate them. It helps when salespeople can be shown exactly how their quotas were derived. They are much more likely to accept quotas that are related to market potential when they can see the assumptions used in translating the potential estimate into sales goals.

Another desirable feature of a quota plan is that it is complete. It should cover the many criteria on which sales reps are to be judged. Thus, if all sales representatives are supposed to engage in new-account development, it is important to specify how much. Otherwise that activity will likely be neglected while the salesperson pursues volume and profit goals. Similarly, volume and profit goals should be adjusted to allow for the time the representative has to spend identifying and soliciting new accounts.

Finally, the quota system should allow for timely feedback of results to salespeople. Quotas for a sales period should be calculated and announced right away. Delays in providing this information not only dilute the advantages of using quotas but also create ambiguity, as the salesperson gets well into another performance period without knowing how he or she fared in the prior period.

SETTING QUOTAS

In setting quotas, the sales manager must first decide on the types of quotas the firm will use. Then, specific quota levels must be established.

Types of Quotas

There are three basic types of quotas: (1) those emphasizing sales or some aspect of sales volume, (2) those that focus on the activities in which sales representatives

---

ETHICAL MOMENT **Ethical Sales Quotas**

From your reading it should be clear that the sales quota is an essential tool for sales managers. It provides a tremendous incentive by defining specific goals for the salesperson that translate into financial rewards. At the same time, the quota remains a very effective metric for evaluating salesperson performance. Successful sales managers understand how important it is to get the sales quota right—both for the organization and the salesperson.

But such a powerful tool also can be used to punish or coerce salespeople. Why? Put simply, despite the data, discussion, and analysis companies use to develop sales quotas by nature they also have a subjective component. Unethical sales managers can use the subjectivity to create quotas that are unfair and/or unattainable for salespeople, or even manipulative for their own purposes against salespeople. And when a salesperson fails to make the quota, the sales manager can take the position of having a "legitimate" reason to take disciplinary action against that individual.

Most sales organizations have checks and balances in place to prevent this sort of unethical behavior by sales managers, but sometimes it can still happen. One of the keys is to establish a strong sales organizational culture where the quota setting process is clearly defined, transparent, and understood by all. Given that sales quotas drive much of a sales organization's overall performance model, quotas are well ingrained into the sales psyche. This heightens the importance that firms realize there are major ethical implications in the process of creating, implementing, and managing a sales quota.

Question to Ponder:

- As a salesperson, how would you handle a situation in which you were given a sales quota by a manager that you believe is designed to ensure that you fail?

are supposed to engage, and (3) those that examine financial criteria such as gross margin or contribution to overhead. Sales volume quotas are the most popular.[11]

Sales Volume Quotas

The popularity of sales volume quotas, those that emphasize dollar sales or some other aspect of sales volume, is understandable. They can be related directly to market potential and thereby be made more credible, are easily understood by the salespeople who must achieve them, and are consistent with what most salespeople envision their jobs to be—that is, to sell. Sales volume quotas may be expressed in dollars, physical units, or points.

The concept of point quotas deserves explanation. A certain number of points are given for each dollar or unit sale of particular products. For example, each $100 of sales of product X might be worth three points; of product Y, two points; and of product Z, one point. Alternatively, each ton of steel tubing sold might be worth five points, while each ton of bar stock might be worth only two points. The total sales quota for the salesperson is expressed as the total number of points he or she is expected to achieve. The point system is typically used when a firm wants to emphasize certain products in the line. Those that are more profitable, for example, might be assigned more points.

Point quotas can also be used to promote selective emphases. New products might receive more points than old ones to encourage sales representatives to push them. A given dollar of sales to new accounts might be worth more points than the same level of sales to more established accounts. Point quota systems allow sales managers to design quota systems that promote certain desired goals, and at the same time point quotas can be easily understood by salespeople.

Activity Quotas

Activity quotas attempt to recognize the investment nature of a salesperson's efforts. For example, the letter to a prospect, the product demonstration, and the arrangement of a display may not produce an immediate sale. On the other hand, they may influence a future sale. If the quota system emphasizes only sales volume, salespeople may be inclined to neglect these activities. Today, many activities are necessary to support long-term client relationships. It is appropriate that these activities be considered for quota development. Some common types of activity quotas are listed in Exhibit 5.7.

Financial Quotas

Financial quotas help focus salespeople on the cost and profit implications of what they sell. All else being equal, it is easy to understand that salespeople might emphasize products in their line that are relatively easy to sell or concentrate on customers with whom they feel most comfortable interacting. Unfortunately, these

Number of	**EXHIBIT 5.7**
1. Calls on new accounts.	Common types of activity quotas
2. Letters to potential customers.	
3. Proposals submitted.	
4. Field demonstrations arranged.	
5. Service calls made.	
6. Equipment installations supervised.	
7. Displays arranged.	
8. Dealer sales meetings held.	
9. Meetings and conventions attended.	
10. Past-due accounts collected.	

products may be costly to produce and have a lower-than-average return, and these customers may not purchase much and may be less profitable than other potential accounts. Financial quotas attempt to direct salespeople's efforts to more profitable products and customers. Common bases for developing financial quotas are gross margin, net profit, and selling expenses, although most any financial measure could be used.

Administering financial quotas can present difficulties. Their calculation is not straightforward. And the profit a salesperson produces is affected by many factors beyond his or her control—competitive reaction, economic conditions, and the firm's willingness to negotiate on price, for example. Many would argue that in most cases it is unreasonable to hold an individual salesperson responsible for such external influences.

Quota Level

Next, the sales manager must decide the level for each type of quota. In establishing these levels, the sales manager must balance a number of factors, including the potential available in the territory, the impact of the quota level on the salesperson's motivation, the long-term objectives of the company, and the impact on short-term profitability. When discussing quota levels, it is useful to separate sales volume, activity, and financial quotas.

Sales Volume Quotas

Some firms simply set sales volume quotas on the basis of past sales. Each marketing unit is exhorted to "beat last year's sales." Sometimes the standard is the average of sales in the territory over some past time period—five years, for example. The most attractive feature of this quota-setting scheme is that it is easy to administer. One does not have to engage in an extensive analysis to determine what the quotas should be. This makes it inexpensive to use. Also, salespeople readily understand it.

Unfortunately, such quotas ignore current conditions. A territory may be rapidly growing, and the influx of new potential customers could justify a much larger increase than the 7 percent established by the overall company's sales forecast. Alternatively, the territory might be so intensely competitive or the business climate may be so poor that any increase in the assigned sales quota is not justified.

A quota based solely on past sales ignores territory potentials and provides a poor yardstick for evaluating individual sales reps. Two salespeople, for example, might each have generated $300,000 in sales last year. It clearly makes a difference in what one can expect from each of them this year if the market potential in one territory is $500,000 while that in the other is $1 million. The firm may be forgoing tremendous market opportunities simply because it is unaware of them.

A quota based solely on past years' sales can also demoralize salespeople and cause undesirable behaviors. For example, a salesperson who has realized quota for one year may be tempted to delay placing orders secured at the end of the year until the new accounting cycle begins. This accomplishes two things: It makes his or her quota for the next year lower, and it gives him or her a start on satisfying that quota.

Territory potential provides a useful start for establishing quotas for territory sales volume. However, the firm should not adhere strictly to a formula that relates quota to potential, but it should attempt to reflect the special situations within each territory.

Determining how to set territory quotas that reflect the special situations within each territory is often difficult. On one hand, the sales representative who serves the territory should be involved in setting the territory quota, because he or she should have the most intimate knowledge of the conditions in the territory. On the other hand, since the rep will be affected by the quota established, he or she may not be impartial. One might expect sales representatives to understate potential to generate lower, easier-to-reach quotas.

Activity Quotas

The levels for activity quotas are most likely to be set according to the territory conditions. They require a detailed analysis of the work needed to cover the territory effectively. Activity quotas are affected by the size of the territory and by the number of accounts and prospects the salesperson is expected to call on. The size of the representative's customers can also make a difference, as can their purchasing patterns. These factors affect the number of times the salesperson needs to call on them in the period, the number of service calls or calls to demonstrate the use of the firm's equipment he or she must make, and so on.

The inputs for activity quotas can come from at least three sources: (1) discussions between the sales representative serving the territory and the sales manager, (2) the salesperson's reports, and (3) research on the market and its potential.

Financial Quotas

The levels of financial quotas are typically set to reflect the financial goals of the firm. For example, a firm may want a particular net profit or gross margin on all sales in a territory. Suppose the potential for a representative is basically concentrated on two products—one with a gross margin of 30 percent and one with a gross margin of 40 percent. The sales manager could shift the relative attention given to one versus the other by assigning a gross margin goal of 37 percent. The salesperson would then have to sell a greater proportion of the products with 40 percent margin to achieve that goal than if the goal were 34 percent.

DETERMINING SALES FORCE SIZE

Another critical use of information by sales managers is in determining the size of the sales force. Salespeople are among the most productive assets of a company, and they are also among the most expensive. Determining the optimal number to employ presents several fundamental dilemmas. On the one hand, increasing the number of salespeople will increase sales volume. On the other hand, it will also increase costs. Achieving the optimal balance between these considerations, although difficult, is vitally important to a firm's success.

The optimal number of territories depends on the design of the individual territories. Different assignments to salespeople and even different call patterns can produce different sales levels. Of course, the number of calls the sales force must make directly affects the number of salespeople the firm needs. In sum, the number of sales territories and the design of individual territories must be looked at as interrelated decisions whose outcomes affect each other.

The decisions need to be made jointly and not sequentially. Sales force deployment refers to the three interrelated decisions of (1) sales force size or the number of territories, (2) design of the individual territories, and (3) allocation of the total selling effort to accounts. Such simultaneous decisions are implemented through software-driven sales force deployment models. At the same time, it is useful for discussion purposes to separate these issues so as to call attention to the underlying considerations of each. Consequently, the subsequent discussion first addresses the issue of sales force size and then the issue of sales territory design. However, the size of the sales force may need to be revised as a result of the sales territory design.[12]

Several techniques are available for determining the size of the field sales force. Three of the more popular are the (1) breakdown, (2) workload, and (3) incremental methods.

Breakdown Method

The breakdown method is conceptually one of the simplest. An average salesperson is treated as a salesperson unit, and each salesperson unit is assumed to possess the same productivity potential. To determine the size of the sales force needed, divide total forecast sales for the company by the sales likely to be produced by each individual. Mathematically,

$$N = S/P$$

where

N = number of sales personnel needed

S = forecasted sales volume

P = estimated productivity of one salesperson unit

Thus, a firm that had forecast sales of $5 million and in which each salesperson unit could be expected to sell $250,000 would need 20 salespeople. Although conceptually simple and easy to use, the breakdown method is not without its problems. For one thing, it uses reverse logic. It treats sales force size as a consequence of sales volume; instead, determining the number of salespeople needed should be a proactive element of the overall strategic marketing plan. Also, the estimate of productivity per salesperson can be problematic in that it fails to account for differences in (1) ability levels of salespeople, (2) potential in the markets they service, and (3) level of competition across sales territories. Then too, the breakdown method does not take into account turnover in the sales force. New salespeople are usually not as productive as those who have been on the job for several years. The formula can be modified to allow for sales force turnover, but it loses some of its simplicity and conceptual appeal.

Finally, a key shortcoming of the breakdown method is that it does not allow for profitability. It treats sales as the end in itself rather than as the means to an end. The number of salespeople is determined as a function of the level of forecast sales, not as a determinant of targeted profit.

Workload Method

The basic premise underlying the workload method of determining sales force size (or, as it is sometimes called, the *buildup method*) is that all sales personnel should shoulder an equal amount of work. Management estimates the work required to serve the entire market. The total work calculation is treated as a function of the number of accounts, how often each should be called on, and for how long. This estimate is then divided by the amount of work an individual salesperson should be able to handle, and the result is the total number of salespeople required.[13] Specifically, the method consists of six steps, as illustrated in Exhibit 5.8 and discussed next.

1. *Classify all the firm's customers into categories.* Often the classification is based on the level of sales to each customer. A popular approach is to identify and prioritize accounts as A, B, or C based on sales volume. Classification could be based on other criteria also, such as the customer's type of business, credit rating, product line, and potential for future purchases.

Any classification system should reflect the different amounts of selling effort required to service the different classes of accounts and consequently the attractiveness of each class of accounts to the firm. Suppose, for example, the firm had 1,030 accounts that could be classified into three basic types or classes, as follows:

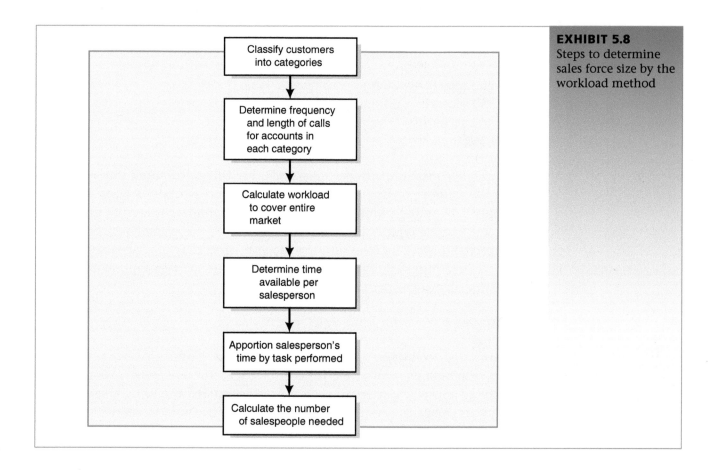

EXHIBIT 5.8
Steps to determine
sales force size by the
workload method

Type A: Large or very attractive—200
Type B: Medium or moderately attractive—350
Type C: Small, but still attractive—480

2. *Determine the frequency with which each type of account should be called upon and the desired length of each call.* These inputs can be generated in several ways. They can be based directly on the judgments of management, or they might be based on more formal analysis of historical information. Suppose the firm estimates that class A accounts should be called on every two weeks, class B accounts once a month, and class C accounts every other month. It also estimates that the length of the typical call should be 60 minutes, 30 minutes, and 20 minutes, respectively. The number of contact hours per year for each type of account is thus calculated as

Class A: 26 times/year × 60 minutes/call = 1,560 minutes, or 26 hours
Class B: 12 times/year × 30 minutes/call = 360 minutes, or 6 hours
Class C: 6 times/year × 20 minutes/call = 120 minutes, or 2 hours

3. *Calculate the workload involved in covering the entire market.* The total work involved in covering each class of account is given by multiplying the number of such

accounts by the number of contact hours per year. These products are summed to estimate the work entailed in covering all the various types of accounts:

Class A: 200 accounts × 26 hours/account = 5,200 hours
Class B: 350 accounts × 6 hours/account = 2,100 hours
Class C: 480 accounts × 2 hours/account = 960 hours
Total = 8,260 hours

4. *Determine the time available per salesperson.* For this calculation, one must estimate the number of hours the typical salesperson works per week and then multiply that by the number of weeks the representative will work during the year. Suppose the typical workweek is 40 hours and the average salesperson can be expected to work 48 weeks during the year, after allowing for vacation time, sickness, and other emergencies. This suggests the average representative has 1,920 hours available per year. That is,

40 hours/week × 48 weeks/year = 1,920 hours/year

5. *Apportion the salesperson's time by task performed.* Unfortunately, not all the salesperson's time is consumed in face-to-face customer contact. Much of it is devoted to nonselling activities such as making reports, attending meetings, and making service calls. Another major portion may be spent traveling. Suppose a time study of salespeople's effort suggested the following division:

Selling   40 percent =   768 hours/year
Nonselling   30 percent =   576 hours/year
Traveling   30 percent =   576 hours/year
              100 percent = 1,920 hours/year

6. *Calculate the number of salespeople needed.* The number of salespeople the firm will need can now be readily determined by dividing the total number of hours needed to serve the entire market by the number of hours available per salesperson for selling. That is, by the calculation

$$\frac{8,260 \text{ hours}}{768 \text{ hours/saleperson}} = 10.75, \text{ or } 11 \text{ salespeople}$$

The workload, or buildup, method is a very common way to determine sales force size. It has several attractive features. It is easy to understand, and it explicitly recognizes that different types of accounts should be called on with different frequencies. The inputs are readily available or can be secured without much trouble.

Unfortunately, it also possesses some weaknesses. It does not allow for differences in sales response among accounts that receive the same sales effort. Two class A accounts might respond differently to sales effort. One may be content with the products and services of the firm and continue to order even if the salesperson does not call every two weeks. Another, which does most of its business with a competitor, may willingly switch some of its orders if it receives more frequent contact. Also, the method does not explicitly consider the profitability of the call frequencies. It does not take into account such factors as the cost of servicing and the gross margins on the product mix purchased by the account.[14]

Finally, the method assumes that all salespeople use their time with equal efficiency—for example, that each will have 768 hours available for face-to-face selling. This is simply not true. Some are better able to plan their calls to generate more direct selling time. Those in smaller geographic territories can spend less time traveling and more time selling. Some more than others simply make good use of the selling time they have available, as the quality of time invested in a sales call is at least as important as the quantity of time spent. The buildup method does not explicitly consider these dimensions.

Incremental Method

The basic premise underlying the incremental method of determining sales force size is that sales representatives should be added as long as the incremental profit produced by their addition exceeds the incremental costs.[15] The method recognizes that decreasing returns will likely be associated with the addition of salespeople. Thus, while one more salesperson might produce $300,000, two more might produce only $550,000 in new sales. The incremental sales produced by the first salesperson is $300,000 but for the second salesperson is $250,000. Suppose the addition of a third salesperson could be expected to produce $225,000 in new sales and a fourth, $200,000. Adding all four would increase sales by $975,000. Suppose further that the company's profit margin was 20 percent, and placing another salesperson in the field cost $50,000 on average. This situation is summarized in Exhibit 5.9.

The analysis in Exhibit 5.9 suggests that two salespeople should be added. At that point, the incremental profit from the additional salespeople equals the incremental cost. Adding more than two salespeople would cause profits to go down, as is seen by subtracting column (6) "total additional cost" from column (4) "total additional profit."

The incremental approach to determining sales force size is conceptually sound. Also, it is consistent with the empirical evidence that decreasing returns can be expected with additional salespeople. Decreasing returns can also be expected with other territory design features such as the number of buyers per salesperson, the number of calls the salesperson makes on an account, and the actual time the representative spends in face-to-face contact.[16]

A key disadvantage of the incremental approach is that it is the most difficult to implement of the three approaches we have reviewed. Although the cost of an additional salesperson can be estimated with reasonable accuracy, estimating the likely profit is difficult. It depends on the additional revenue the salesperson is expected to produce, and that depends on how the territories are restructured, who is assigned to each territory, and how effective they might be. To compound things

EXHIBIT 5.9 Illustration of the incremental approach to determining sales force size	**Number of Additional Salespeople** (1)	**Total Additional Revenue** (2)	**Incremental Revenue Due to Additional Salesperson** (3)	**Total Additional Profit*** (4)	**Incremental Profit Due to Additional Salesperson** (5)	**Total Additional Cost** (6)	**Incremental Cost Due to Additional Salesperson** (7)
	1	$300,000	$300,000	$60,000	$60,000	$50,000	$50,000
	2	550,000	250,000	110,000	50,000	100,000	50,000
	3	775,000	225,000	155,000	44,500	150,000	50,000
	4	975,000	200,000	195,000	40,000	200,000	50,000

* Based on assumption of 20 percent profit margin.

further, the profitability of the new arrangement also depends on the mix of products generating the sales increase and how profitable each is to the company.

DESIGNING SALES TERRITORIES

After the number of sales territories has been determined, the sales manager can address the issue of territory design. Warning: The examples in this section are U.S. focused—however, the concepts and process can be adapted to the needs and information availability of any geographic region of the globe. The stages involved in territory design are shown in Exhibit 5.10. The sales manager strives for the ideal of making all territories equal with respect to the amount of sales potential they contain and the amount of work it takes a salesperson to cover them effectively. When territories are basically equal in potential, it is easier to evaluate each representative's performance and to compare salespeople. (A discussion of the potential problems in integrating territory difficulty differences into performance evaluations of salespeople is presented in Chapter 13.) Equal workloads tend to improve sales force morale and diminish disputes between management and the sales force. While considering these questions, the sales manager should take into account the impact on market response of particular territory structures and call frequencies. Obviously, it is difficult, if not impossible, to achieve an optimal balance with respect to all these factors. The sales manager should do his or her best to ensure the highest degree of fairness and equity in territory design.

Stages in Sales Territory Design

Step 1: Select Basic Control Unit

Some of the terminology in this section is heavily U.S.-centric for purposes of clear example, but those of you in other locales can easily translate the ideas into the context of your own countries. The basic control unit is the most elemental

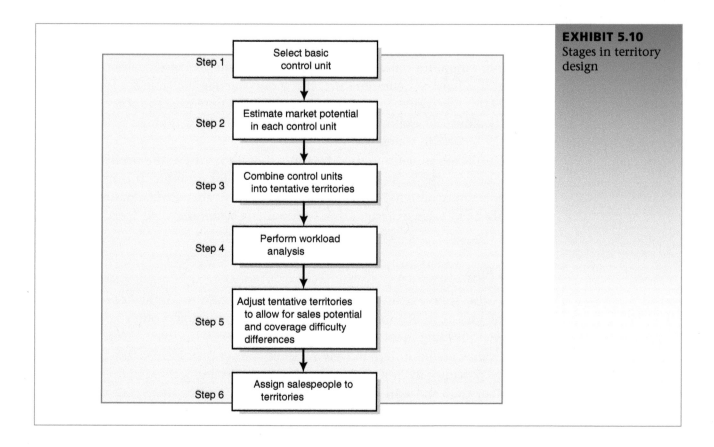

EXHIBIT 5.10
Stages in territory
design

geographic area used to form sales territories—county or city, for example. As a general rule, small geographic control units are preferable to large ones. With large units, areas with low potential may be hidden by their inclusion in areas with high potential, and vice versa. This makes it difficult to pinpoint true geographic potential, which is a primary reason for forming geographically defined sales territories in the first place. Also, small control units make it easier to adjust sales territories when conditions warrant. It is much easier to reassign the accounts in a particular county from one salesperson to another, for example, than it is to reassign all the accounts in a state. Some commonly used basic control units are states, trading areas, counties, cities or metropolitan statistical areas (MSAs), and ZIP code areas.

States

Although it has become less popular, some companies still use states as a basic control because of inherent advantages. State boundaries are clearly defined and thus are simple and inexpensive to use. A good deal of statistical data are accumulated by state, which makes it easy to analyze territory potential.

One primary weakness of using states as control units is that buying habits, or consumption patterns, do not reflect state boundaries because a state represents a political rather than an economic division of the national market. Consumption patterns in Gary, Indiana, for example, may have more in common with those in Chicago than with those in other parts of Indiana. Also, the size of states makes it difficult to pinpoint problem areas. A problem in Ohio may be localized in Cincinnati, but it is hard to determine that if the only figures available are for Ohio as a whole. States also contain great variations in market potential; the potential in New York City alone, for example, might be greater than the combined potential of all the Rocky Mountain states.

State units are sometimes used by firms that do not have the sophistication or staff to use counties or smaller geographic units—for example, firms at the early stages of territory design. States are also used by firms that cover a national market with only a few sales representatives, particularly when they can specify potential accounts by name (e.g., a firm selling dryers to paper mills).

Trading Areas

Trading areas are made up of a principal city and the surrounding dependent area. A trading area is an economic unit that ignores political and other noneconomic boundaries. Trading areas recognize that consumers who live in New Jersey, for example, may prefer to shop in New York City rather than locally. The trading area for a food processor in western Iowa might be wholesalers located in the upper Midwest rather than those in nearby Kansas. As such, trading areas reflect economic factors and are based on consumer buying habits and normal trading patterns.

A major disadvantage of using trading areas as basic control units is that they vary from product to product and must be referred to in terms of specific products. Thus, a company whose salespeople sell multiple product lines may have difficulty defining sales territories by trade areas. Another difficulty is that it is often hard to obtain detailed statistics for trading areas. This in turn makes them expensive to use as geographic control units, although some firms adjust the boundaries of the trading areas so they coincide with county lines. Whether or not a firm formally uses trading areas as basic control units, it should consider the logical trading areas for the products it produces when specifying the boundaries of each sales territory.

Counties

Counties are probably the most widely used basic geographic control unit. They permit a more fine-tuned analysis of the market than do states or trading areas, given that more than 3,000 counties exist and only 50 states and a varying number of trading areas depending on the product. One dramatic advantage of using counties as control units is the wealth of statistical data available by county. For example, the *County and City Data Book*, published biennially by the Bureau of the Census, provides statistics by county on such things as population, education, employment, income, housing, banking, manufacturing output, capital expenditures, retail and wholesale sales, and mineral and agricultural output. This county data is also readily available at the Bureau of Census website. Another advantage of counties is that their size permits easy reassignment from one sales territory to another. Thus, sales territories can be altered to reflect changing economic conditions without major upheaval in basic service. Furthermore, potentials do not have to be recalculated before doing so.

The most serious drawback to using counties as basic control units is that in some cases they are still too large. Los Angeles County, Cook County (Chicago), Dade County (Miami), and Harris County (Houston), for example, may require several sales representatives. In such cases, it is necessary to divide these counties into even smaller basic control units.

Metropolitan Statistical Areas (MSAs)

Historically, when most of the market potential was within city boundaries, the city was a good basic control unit. Cities are rarely satisfactory anymore, however. For many products, the area surrounding a city now contains as much or more potential than the central city. Consequently, many firms that formerly used cities now employ broader classification systems to help them identify and organize their territories. Developed by the U.S. Census Bureau, the control unit is called a metropolitan statistical area, or MSA.

MSAs are integrated economic and social units with a large population nucleus. Exhibit 5.11 ranks the 10 largest population centers in the United States in order of size based on the last U.S. census (2010).

The heavy concentration of population, income, and retail sales in the MSAs explains why many firms are content to concentrate their field selling efforts on them. Some assign all their field representatives to such large areas. Such a strategy minimizes travel time and expense because of the geographic concentration of MSAs.

ZIP Code and Other Areas

Some firms, for which city or MSA boundaries are too large, use ZIP code areas as basic control units. The U.S. Postal Service has defined more than 36,000 five-digit ZIP code areas. An advantage of ZIP code areas is that they are often relatively homogeneous with respect to basic socioeconomic data. Whereas residents within an MSA might display great heterogeneity, those within a ZIP code area are more

Rank	Area	2010 Population (in 000s)
1	New York-Northern New Jersey-Long Island, NY-NJ-PA	18,897.1
2	Los Angeles-Long Beach-Santa Ana, CA	12,828.8
3	Chicago-Joliet-Naperville, IL-IN-WI	9,461.1
4	Dallas-Fort Worth-Arlington, TX	6,371.8
5	Philadelphia-Camden-Wilmington, PA-NJ-DE-MD	5,965.3
6	Houston-Sugar Land-Baytown, TX	5,946.8
7	Washington-Arlington-Alexandria, DC-VA-MD-WV	5,582.2
8	Miami-Fort Lauderdale-Pompano Beach, FL	5,564.6
9	Atlanta-Sandy Springs-Marietta, GA	5,268.9
10	Boston-Cambridge-Quincy, MA-NH	4,552.4

Source: U.S. Bureau of the Census, *www.census.gov*.

EXHIBIT 5.11
Ten largest U.S. MSAs in decreasing order of size

likely to be relatively similar in age, income, education, and so forth and to even display similar consumption patterns. Although the Bureau of the Census typically does not publish data by ZIP code area, an industry has developed to tabulate such data by arbitrary geographic boundaries. The *geodemographers*, as they are typically called, combine census data with their own survey data or data they gather from administrative records such as motor vehicle registrations or credit transactions to produce customized products for their clients.

A typical product involves the cluster analysis of census-produced data to produce homogeneous groups that describe the American population. For example, Claritas (the first firm to do this and still one of the leaders in the industry) used more than 500 demographic variables in its PRIZM NE (Potential Ratings in Zip Markets—New Edition) system when classifying residential neighborhoods. This system breaks the 25,000+ neighborhood areas in the United States into 66 types based on consumer behavior and lifestyle. Each of the types has a name that endeavors to describe the people living there, such as Urban Achievers, Shotguns and Pickups, Pools and Patios, and so on. Claritas and the other suppliers will do a customized analysis for whatever geographic boundaries a client specifies. Alternatively, a client can send a tape listing the ZIP code addresses of some customer database, and the geodemographer will attach the cluster codes.

One disadvantage of using ZIP code areas as basic control units is that the boundaries change over time. However, with the new technology for computerized geographic information systems (GIS), that is less of a problem than it used to be in that the boundaries can easily be reconfigured with the aid of specialized software.

Step 2: Estimate Market Potential

Step 2 in territory design involves estimating market potential in each basic control unit. This is done using one of the schemes suggested earlier in this chapter. If a relationship can be established between sales of the product in question and some other variable or variables, for example, this relationship can be applied to each basic control unit. Data must be available for each of the variables for the small geographic area, though. Sometimes the potential within each basic control unit is estimated by considering the likely demand from each customer and prospect in the control unit. This works much better for industrial goods manufacturers than it does for consumer goods producers. The consumers of industrial goods are typically fewer in number and more easily identified. Furthermore, each typically buys much more product than is true with consumer goods buyers. This makes it worthwhile to identify at least the larger ones by name, to estimate the likely demand from each, and to add up these individual estimates to produce an estimate for the territory as a whole.

Step 3: Form Tentative Territories

Step 3 in territory design involves combining contiguous basic control units into larger geographic aggregates. Adjoining units are combined to prevent salespeople from having to crisscross paths while skipping over geographic areas covered by another representative. The basic emphasis at this stage is to make the tentative territories as equal as possible in market potential. Differences in workload or sales potential (the share of total market potential a company expects to achieve) because of different levels of competitive activity are not taken into account at this stage. It is also presumed that all sales representatives have relatively equal abilities. Importantly, all these assumptions are relaxed at subsequent stages of the territory planning process. The attempt at this stage is simply to develop an approximation of the final territory alignment. The total number of territories defined equals the number of territories the firm has previously determined it needs. If the firm has not yet made such a calculation, it needs to do so now.

Step 4: Perform Workload Analysis

Once tentative initial boundaries have been established for all sales territories, it is necessary to determine how much work is required to cover each territory. Ideally, firms like to form sales territories that are equal in both potential and workload. Although step 3 should produce territories roughly equal in potential, the territories will probably be decidedly unequal with respect to the amount of work necessary to cover them adequately. In step 4, the analyst tries to estimate the amount of work involved in covering each.

Account Analysis

Typically, the workload analysis considers each customer in the territory, with emphasis on the larger ones. The analysis is often conducted in two stages. First, the sales potential for each customer and prospect in the territory is estimated. This step is often called an account analysis. The sales potential estimate derived from the account analysis is then used to decide how often each account should be called on and for how long. The total effort required to cover the territory can be determined by considering the number of accounts, the number of calls to be made on each, the duration of each call, and the estimated amount of nonselling and travel time.

Criteria for Classifying Accounts

Total sales potential is one criterion used to classify accounts into categories dictating the frequency and length of sales calls. A number of other criteria have been suggested as well for determining the attractiveness of an individual account to the firm. The key is to identify those factors likely to affect the productivity of the sales call. Some of these other factors include competitive pressures for the account, the prestige of the account, how many products the firm produces that the account buys, and the number and level of buying influences within the account.[17] The factors that affect the productivity of an individual sales call are likely to change from firm to firm.

Determining Account Call Rates

Once the specific factors affecting the productivity of a sales call have been isolated, they can be treated in various ways. One way is to use the ABC account classification approach discussed earlier in the chapter (see "Workload Method"). Another way is to employ a variation of the matrix concept of strategic planning, which suggests that accounts, like strategic business units or markets, can be divided along two dimensions reflecting the overall opportunity they represent and the firm's abilities to capitalize on those opportunities. In the case of accounts, the division should reflect (1) the attractiveness of the account to the firm and (2) the likely difficulties to be encountered in managing the account.[18] The accounts are then sorted into either a four- or nine-cell strategic planning matrix. For example, Exhibit 5.12 uses the criteria of account potential and the firm's competitive advantage or disadvantage with the account to classify accounts into four cells. It would use different call frequencies in each cell. The heaviest call rates in the sample matrix depicted in Exhibit 5.12 would be on accounts in cells 1, 2, and possibly 3, depending on the firm's abilities to overcome its competitive disadvantages. The lowest planned call rates would be on accounts in cell 4.

Determining Call Frequencies Account by Account

Accounts do not have to be divided into classes and call frequencies set at the same level for all accounts in the class. Rather, the firm might want to determine the workload in each tentative territory on an account-by-account basis. Several approaches may be used to accomplish this. The firm can rate each account on each factor deemed critical to the success of the sales call effort and then develop a sales effort allocation index for each account. The sales effort allocation index is formed by multiplying each rating score by its factor importance weight, summing over all factors, and then dividing by the sum of the importance weights. The resulting sales effort allocation index reflects the relative amount of sales call effort that should be allocated to the account in comparison to other accounts—the larger the index, the greater the number of planned calls on the account.

Another approach is to estimate the likely sales to be realized from each account as a function of the number of calls on the account. Two popular ways exist for estimating the function relating sales to the number of calls on an account: empirical-based methods and judgment-based methods.[19] Empirical-based approaches use regression analysis to estimate the function relating historical sales in each territory to an a priori set of predictors likely to affect sales, including the number of calls. The function so determined represents the line of average sales relationship across all planning and control units.[20]

The judgment-based approaches require that someone in the sales organization, typically the salesperson serving the account but sometimes the sales manager, estimate the sales-per-sales-call function so that the optimal number of calls to be made on each account can be determined. CRM systems provide a wealth of opportunity for data collection toward estimating future sales based on calls on particular customers.

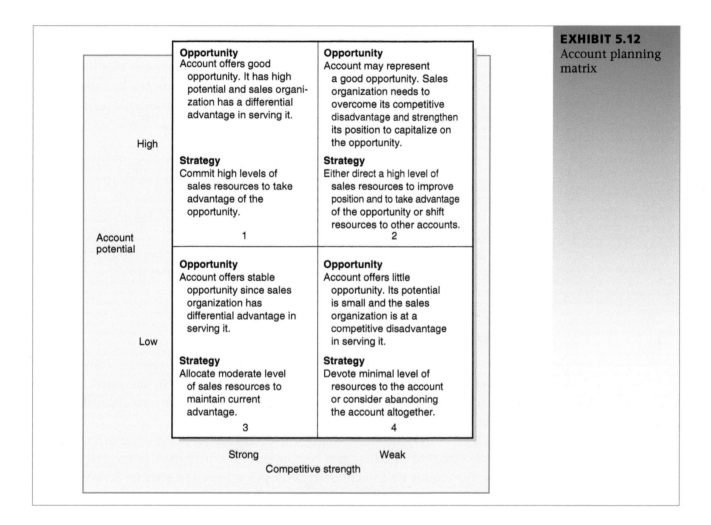

EXHIBIT 5.12
Account planning matrix

Determine Total Workload

When the account analysis is complete, a workload analysis can be performed for each territory. The procedure parallels that discussed earlier in the chapter for determining the size of the sales force using the workload method. The total amount of face-to-face contact is computed by multiplying the frequency with which each type of account should be called on by the number of such accounts. The products are then summed. This figure is combined with estimates of the nonselling and travel time necessary to cover the territory to determine the total amount of work involved in covering that territory. A similar set of calculations is made for each tentative territory.

Step 5: Adjust Tentative Territories

Step 5 in territory planning adjusts the boundaries of the tentative territories established in step 3 to compensate for the differences in workload found in step 4. It is possible, for example, that Washington, Oregon, Montana, Idaho, Wyoming, and Utah together might contain the same sales potential as Ohio. Since considerably less travel time would be necessary to cover the Ohio territory, the workload in the two territories would be far from equal and adjustments will need to be made.

While attempting to balance potentials and workloads across territories, the analyst must keep in mind that the sales volume potential per account is not fixed. It is likely to vary with the number of calls made. Although computer call allocation models consider this, it is not taken into account when, for example, the firm uses the ABC account classification approach and relies exclusively on historical sales when making account classifications. Clearly, reciprocal causation exists between account attractiveness and account effort. Account attractiveness affects how hard the account should be worked. At the same time, the number of calls and length of the calls affect the sales likely to be realized from the account. Yet this reciprocal causation is only implicitly recognized in some schemes used to determine workloads for territories. The firm needs a mechanism for balancing potentials and workloads when adjusting the initial territories if it is not using a computer model.

Step 6: Assign Salespeople to Territories

After territory boundaries are established, the analyst can determine which salesperson should be assigned to which territory. Up to now, it has generally been assumed that no differences in abilities exist among salespersons or in the effectiveness of different salespeople with different accounts or products. Of course, in reality such differences do arise. All salespeople do not have the same ability nor are they equally effective with the same customers or products. At this stage in territory planning, the analyst should consider such differences and attempt to assign each salesperson to the territory where his or her relative contribution to the company's success will be the greatest.

Unfortunately, the ideal match cannot always be accomplished. It would be too disruptive to an established sales force with established sales territories to change practically all account coverage. Changing territory assignments can upset salespeople. If the firm is operating without assigned sales territories, then the realignment might be closer to the ideal. However, the reality is that a firm with established territories typically must be content to change assignments incrementally and on a more limited basis.

The actual assignment of salespeople to sales territories also incorporates personal considerations. The firm may not want to change salesperson call assignments for particular accounts because of the potential for lost business. It may not want to reduce sales force size even if the analysis suggests it should because of morale problems associated with downsizing. Even increasing sales force size can be disruptive. More salespeople mean more sales territories, which means redrawing existing boundaries, changing quotas, and disrupting potential for incentive pay. In sum, sales managers will want to reflect people considerations when they redraw territory boundaries. They will want to minimize disruptions to existing personal relationships between salespeople and customers. Modern sales force technology applications are changing the way sales territories are designed, impacting the various stages of the design process. Examples of these applications are provided in the Technology box.

SALES ANALYSIS FOR MANAGERIAL DECISION MAKING

The process of sales analysis represents another heavy use of information in that it involves gathering, classifying, comparing, and studying company sales data. It may "simply involve the comparison of total company sales in two different time periods. Or it may entail subjecting thousands of component sales (or sales-related) figures to a variety of comparisons—among themselves, with external data, and with like figures for earlier periods of time."[21]

A major benefit of even the most elementary sales analysis is in highlighting those products, customers, orders, or territories in which the firm's sales are concentrated. A heavy concentration is very common and the phenomenon is often called the 80:20 principle, or the concentration ratio. This means it is not at all unusual to find 80 percent of the customers or products accounting for only 20 percent of total sales. Conversely, the remaining 20 percent of the customers or products account for 80 percent of the total sales volume. The same phenomenon applies to orders and territories in that only a small percentage of the total number of orders or a few of the firm's many territories account for the great percentage of its sales. The 80:20 principle describes the general situation, although, of course, the exact concentration ratio varies by company.

Managers wishing to undertake a sales analysis must decide (1) the type of evaluation system, (2) the sources of information, and (3) the type of aggregation of

---

TECHNOLOGY **Territories and Technology**

In a modern sales organization, new technological advancements are changing the way in which sales territories are defined and assigned.

Software exists that will help a sales manager reach a balanced workload between territories, and thus achieve higher sales levels. Brand names of such programs include TerAlign, ProAlign from Mapping Analytics, and Tactician Territory Management. These software programs can identify optimal territories by creating digital road networks and accurately calculating the time spent on the road by each rep. Certain territories can also be tracked and legacy accounts identified and accommodated.

As well as these sophisticated software programs, the rise of the Internet is redefining sales territories. Distance is no option to the Internet so the segmentation and allocation of Internet sales may be better carried out using factors such as language needs or time zones. Internet sales also give rise to a situation where sales and support reps are not dedicated to specific accounts and territories and in this case it is important to have a universal data-base of all customers that can be accessed by all salespeople.

As technology advances, some salespeople will find their territories changing from the traditional geographic approach to a more modern approach in line with the digital age we live in. Thankfully, technology can also help us manage these sometimes more complex territories.

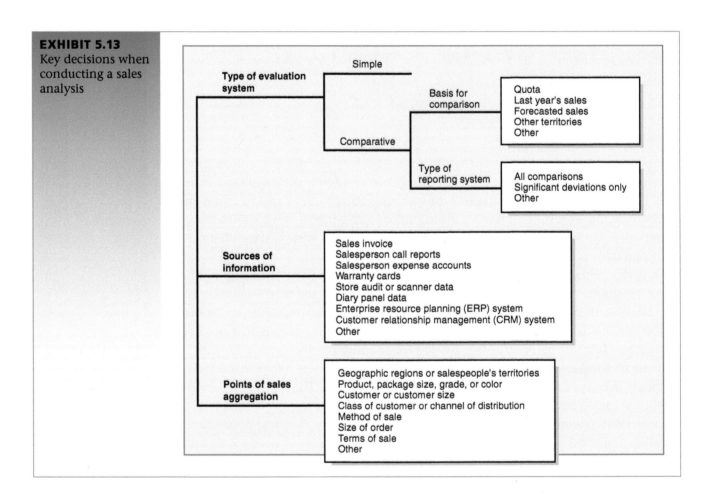

EXHIBIT 5.13
Key decisions when conducting a sales analysis

information that will be used. Exhibit 5.13 provides an overview of the nature of these decisions.

Type of Evaluation System

The first major decision related to sales analysis is the type of evaluation system to use. The type of evaluation system determines how the sales analysis will be conducted. Will it be a simple sales analysis, or a comparative analysis? When it is to be a comparative analysis, two additional questions arise: (1) What is to be the base for the comparison? (2) What type of reporting and control system is to be used?

In a simple sales analysis, the facts are listed and not measured against any standard. In a comparative analysis or, as it is sometimes called, a performance analysis, comparisons are made. Consider, for example, the data in Exhibit 5.14. A simple sales analysis would be restricted to the facts in column 1. These figures suggest Dawson sold the most and Barrington the least. A performance analysis would attempt to go beyond the mere listing of sales to determine where they are greatest

Sales Representative	(1) 2016 Sales ($000)	(2) 2016 Quota ($000)	(3) Performance Index	EXHIBIT 5.14
Diane Barrington	$760.9	$700	108.7	Differences between simple sales analysis and comparative analysis
John Bendt	793.5	690	115.0	
James Dawson	859.2	895	96.0	
Gloria Richardson	837.0	775	108.0	
Walter Keyes	780.3	765	102.0	

and poorest—that is, it would try to make comparisons against some "standard." In Exhibit 5.14, the standard is the quota for each salesperson (column 2), and column 3 provides a performance index for each. This performance index is calculated as the ratio of actual sales to sales quota ($PI = S/Q \times 100$). It suggests Dawson was not the "best" in 2016, but rather Bendt was. In fact, Dawson realized the smallest percentage of total potential as judged by quota.

Bases for Comparison

The comparison with quota is only one type of comparison that can be made. Quota is one of the most common standards because it is very useful, particularly when quotas have been specified well. However, some firms resort to other bases of comparison for a sales analysis, and management must decide which bases of comparison are best for their particular situation. Options might include (1) this year's sales versus last year's sales or the average of a number of prior years' sales; (2) this year's sales versus forecasted sales; (3) sales in one territory versus sales in another, either absolutely or in relation to the ratios in prior years; and (4) the percentage change in sales from one territory to another, as compared with last year.

Such comparisons are certainly better than simply viewing raw sales figures, but they are not generally as productive as a "true" performance analysis. In the latter, variations from planned performance are highlighted, and the reasons for such exceptions are isolated.

Type of Reporting System

The other major issue that arises in a comparative sales analysis is the type of reporting and control system to be used. For example, if one relevant comparison is to be sales as a percentage of quota, this statistic would be provided for each salesperson, branch, district, region, customer, product, and every other unit by which sales are to be analyzed. The problem with this is that it can inundate the sales manager with information. To aid the sales manager, the reports can focus on exceptions, or significant deviations from the norm or from budget. Sales managers can then concentrate on the exceptions while having the full profile of comparisons for assessing the significance of what happened.

Sources of Information for Sales Analysis

A second class of major decisions that must be made with respect to sales analysis is what information is to serve as input to the system and how the basic source documents are to be processed. To address this question, the firm first needs to determine the types of comparisons to be made. A comparison with sales in other territories will require fewer documents than a comparison against market potential or quota or against the average sales in the territory for the last five years. The firm also needs to decide the extent to which preparing the sales report should be integrated with preparing other types of reports. These may include inventory or production reports or sales reports for other company units such as other divisions.

Generally, one of the most productive source documents is the sales invoice. From this, the following information can usually be extracted:

- Customer name and location.
- Product(s) or service(s) sold.
- Volume and dollar amount of the transaction.
- Salesperson (or agent) responsible for the sale.
- End use of product sold.
- Location of customer facility where product is to be shipped or used.
- Customer's industry, class of trade, or channel of distribution.
- Terms of sale and applicable discount.
- Freight paid or to be collected.
- Shipment point for the order.
- Transportation used in shipment.

Other documents provide more specialized output. Some of the more important of these are listed in Exhibit 5.15. As we learned in Chapter 3, CRM systems facilitate the capturing of the customer information referred to in Exhibit 5.15. This customer information can be analyzed and applied to particular sales analysis questions.

Software that links processes such as bid estimation, order entry, shipping, billing systems, and other work processes is called an enterprise resource planning system, or ERP. Boeing uses an ERP system to price out airplanes. Each airline and private customer who buys a jet will fit out each jet differently. As a result, the salesperson's proposal has to account for each different item in order to derive a price. Plus, commission has to be paid on the sale, parts have to be ordered for manufacturing, delivery has to be scheduled—and the ERP helps manage all of these functions. As with CRM, the information generated through enterprise software is an invaluable resource in sales analysis. Yet, ERP implementation must be done properly in order to optimize its value added to the sales organization. The Innovation box on p. 179 illustrates several important risks of ERP implementation.

EXHIBIT 5.15
Other sources of
information for
sales analysis

Cash register receipts
Type (cash or credit) and dollar amount of transaction by department
by salesperson

Salesperson call reports
Customers and prospects called on (company and individual seen;
planned or unplanned calls)
Products discussed
Orders obtained
Customers' product needs and usage
Other significant information about customers
Distribution of salespeople's time among customer calls, travel, and
office work
Sales-related activities: meetings, conventions, etc.

Salesperson expense accounts
Expenses by day by item (hotel, meals, travel, etc.)

Individual customer (and prospect) records
Name and location and customer number
Number of calls by company salesperson (agents)
Sales by company (in dollars or units by product or service by location
of customer facility)
Customer's industry, class of trade, or trade channel
Estimated total annual usage of each product or service sold by
the company
Estimated annual purchases from the company of each such product
or service
Location (in terms of company sales territory)

Financial records
Sales revenue (by products, geographic markets, customers, class
of trade, unit of sales organization, etc.)
Direct sales expenses (similarly classified)
Overhead sales costs (similarly classified)
Profits (similarly classified)

Credit memos
Returns and allowances

Warranty cards
Indirect measures of dealer sales
Customer service

Type of Aggregation of Information to Be Used in Sales Analysis

The third major decision management must confront when designing a sales analysis is which variables will serve as points of aggregation. Without such categories, the firm would be forced to analyze every transaction in isolation or would need to look at sales in the total aggregate. The latter is not particularly informative, and

INNOVATION   **Risks of ERP Implementation**

There is no doubt that ERP systems, when implemented correctly, can deliver improvements to the sales process. This correct implementation, however, can often be a challenge and there are many associated risks to consider:

1. Lack of senior management commitment.
2. Ineffective communication with users.
3. Insufficient training.
4. Failure to receive user support.
5. Ineffective project management.
6. Attempting to reconcile with existing systems.
7. Departmental conflicts.
8. Team composition.
9. Failure to redesign business processes.
10. Confusing change requirements.

As can be seen from the preceding list, all or the most pertinent risk factors are not due to technical difficulties but rather to management and communication.

Several techniques can be used to smooth the implementation process and hopefully eradicate some of these communication issues. For example, user evaluations of the system can be requested and used to trace potential problems or find out why certain groups may be having more problems than others.

the former is almost impossible. The most common and instructive procedure is to assemble and tabulate sales by some appropriate groupings, such as these:

- Geographic regions such as states, counties, regions, or salespeople's territories.
- Product, package size, grade, or color.
- Customer or customer size.
- Market, including class of customer, end use, or channel of distribution.
- Method of sale, including mail, telephone, or direct salespeople.
- Size of order.
- Financial arrangement such as cash or charge.

The classes of information a company may use depend on such things as its size, the diversity of its product line, the geographic extent of its sales area, the number of markets and customers it serves, and the level and type of management for which the information is to be supplied. The firms with a product management form of organization, for example, would be interested in sales by product groups. Product managers might focus on territory-by-territory sales of their products. On the other hand, sales managers will likely be much more interested in territory and customer analyses and only secondarily interested in the territory sales broken out by product.

These sales breakdowns are not necessarily mutually exclusive in that the manager has to choose only one approach. Rather, sales analyses are most productive when they are done hierarchically, in the sense that one breakdown is carried out within another category. The categories are treated simultaneously instead of separately. For example, the analysis may end up showing that customer XYZ in the western region purchased so many units each of products A, B, C, and D. This illustrates a territory, customer, and product hierarchical breakdown.

The advantage of hierarchical breakdowns is illustrated later. For now, you should know that the typical sales analysis results not in a single report but in a family of reports, each reflecting a different level of aggregation, tailored to the person receiving it. Exhibit 5.16, for example, shows the types of sales reports used in a consumer food products company.

Illustration of a Hierarchical Sales Analysis

To illustrate some relevant comparisons and the process used in conducting a sales analysis, consider the example data in Exhibit 5.17 for the XYZ Company.

Report Name	Purpose	Report Access*	
Region	To provide sales information in units and dollars for each sales office or center in the region as well as a regional total.	Appropriate regional manager	**EXHIBIT 5.16** Sales reports in a consumer food products company
Sales office center	To provide sales information in units and dollars for each district manager assigned to a sales office.	Appropriate sales office or center manager	
District	To provide sales information in units and dollars for each account supervisor and retail salesperson reporting to the district manager.	Appropriate district manager	
Salesperson summary	To provide sales information in units and dollars for each customer on whom the salesperson calls.	Appropriate salesperson	
Salesperson customer/ product	To provide sales information in units and dollars for each customer on whom the salesperson calls.	Appropriate salesperson	
Salesperson/ product	To provide sales information in units and dollars for each product that the salesperson sells.	Appropriate salesperson	
Region/product	To provide sales information in units and dollars for each product sold within the region. Similar reports would be available by sales office and by district.	Appropriate regional manager	
Region/ customer class	To provide sales information in units and dollars for each class of customer located in the region. Similar reports would be available by sales office and by district.	Appropriate regional manager	

* To understand the rationale behind who was given access to each report, it is useful to know that salespeople were assigned accounts in sales districts. Salespeople were assigned one or, at most, a couple of large accounts and were responsible for all the grocery stores, regardless of geography, affiliated with these large accounts, or they were assigned a geographic territory and were responsible for all of the stores within that territory. All sales districts were assigned to sales offices or sales centers. The centers were, in turn, organized into regions.

Region	BPI (percentage of U.S.)	Sales Quota ($ millions)	Sales ($ millions)	Difference ($ millions)	Performance Index (PI = S/Q × 100)
New England	5.8193%	$24.44	$25.03	$0.59	102.4
Middle Atlantic	18.3856	77.22	78.19	0.97	101.3
East North-Central	20.1419	84.60	79.48	5.12	94.0
West North-Central	7.3982	31.07	30.51	0.56	98.2
South Atlantic	14.7525	61.96	64.07	2.11	103.4
East South-Central	5.2571	22.08	23.20	1.12	105.1
West South-Central	9.2022	38.65	38.42	0.23	99.4
Mountain	4.2819	17.98	17.73	0.25	98.6
Pacific	14.7613	62.00	64.60	2.60	104.2
Total United States	100.0000%	$420.00	$421.23	$1.23	100.3

EXHIBIT 5.17 Sales and sales quotas for XYZ company

Again, this is a U.S.-centric example but the process can be utilized in any locale in the world for which sufficient information is available. Let's assume the XYZ Company previously determined its sales are highly correlated with population, income, and the general level of retail sales. As such, it has used the Buying Power Index (BPI) published by *Sales & Marketing Management* (S&MM) to determine each region's market potential and has then multiplied these potentials by the company's expected market share to generate the regional quotas in Exhibit 5.17.

Note that although the annual quota was $420 million, total sales in all regions were $421.23 million. Not only has the total company met quota, but also so have most of the regions. The performance index, the ratio of sales to quota, is greater than 100 for five regions. Four regions fell short of their targets, but three of those came very close. Only the east north-central region fell short by any substantial amount (–5.12 percent), but it still had the highest absolute dollar value of sales of any of the major regions. Many sales managers might be tempted from this to assume all is well. At the most, they might send a letter to the manager of the east north-central region, urging him or her to push the salespeople in the region to do better. However, the best approach is to generate the sales breakdown for the east north-central region shown in Exhibit 5.18. The state quotas were determined by multiplying the BPI total U.S. percentages for each state by the $420 million total forecasted sales. In many cases, the firm might wish to convert each percentage to a percentage of the region rather than of the United States as a whole. Thus, the percentage for Illinois would be (6.0037 ÷ 20.1419) × 100 = 29.8. This percentage would then be applied to the $8.60 million quota for the region to get the quota for Illinois. Although the result is the same, this second alternative provides a clearer picture of the concentration of demand in the region. The benefit of this approach holds particularly when one works with smaller and smaller units of analysis.

Exhibit 5.18 shows a problem with sales throughout the region. Referring to the "Performance Index" columns, only the sales representatives in Indiana exceeded

State	BPI (percentage of U.S.)	Sales Quota ($ millions)	Sales ($ millions)	Difference ($ millions)	Performance Index (PI = S/Q × 100)	**EXHIBIT 5.18** Sales breakdown for east north-central region of XYZ company
Illinois	6.0037%	$25.22	$24.30	$0.92	96.4	
Indiana	2.4103	10.12	10.24	0.12	101.2	
Michigan	4.6401	19.49	17.77	1.72	91.2	
Ohio	4.9764	20.90	20.43	0.47	97.8	
Wisconsin	2.1114	8.87	6.74	2.13	76.0	
Total region	20.1419%	$84.60	$79.48	$5.12	94.0	

quota, and then only slightly. Note that the deviations about quota are larger than they were in Exhibit 5.17. This generally happens as one moves to smaller units of analysis. With larger aggregates—for example, regions versus states—the statistician's law of large numbers seems to apply in that the pluses and minuses about quota tend to balance each other. Thus, the performance indexes in the larger analysis tend to be closer to 100. A smaller deviation from quota should initiate further investigation when the analysis is based on large aggregates (regions) rather than on small ones (salespeople). Although some negative deviation in actual sales from standard is evident in Exhibit 5.18 among four of the five states, the deviation in Wisconsin is most pronounced. Only 76 percent of the quota was realized here.

Again, after examining this Wisconsin information, it would be very easy for a sales manager to take some immediate action. However, the savvy manager would recognize that more analysis is needed to uncover what is truly going on. The sales manager should review the tabulation of sales by sales representatives in the Wisconsin district. The eight areas into which the state is divided are shown in Exhibit 5.19, and the results of the tabulation of sales by representative are shown in Exhibit 5.20. Sales are below quota in all sales areas in the state. This suggests that something may be fundamentally wrong. Perhaps economic conditions are poor and unemployment is high; perhaps competition is more intense than in other areas; or perhaps a problem exists with sales force morale and motivation. Although numerous plausible explanations exist for the sales manager to check, the core problem seems to be Hutchins. If he had done as well as the other sales reps in the state, sales for the district would have been much closer to target. The problem is particularly acute because Hutchins has the prime Milwaukee market for a sales territory. Before taking action about Hutchins, the sales manager should examine more specific information on his sales. Hutchins's sales by product are shown in Exhibit 5.21. Hutchins is below quota on the entire product line, but seems to be having the most problem with coffee makers and blenders/mixers/food processors.

So the fundamental question for the sales manager is the following: Is the problem Hutchins or these products? A further analysis of sales of these products by customer indicated the problem was concentrated among large department store

EXHIBIT 5.19
XYZ company
sales territories in
Wisconsin

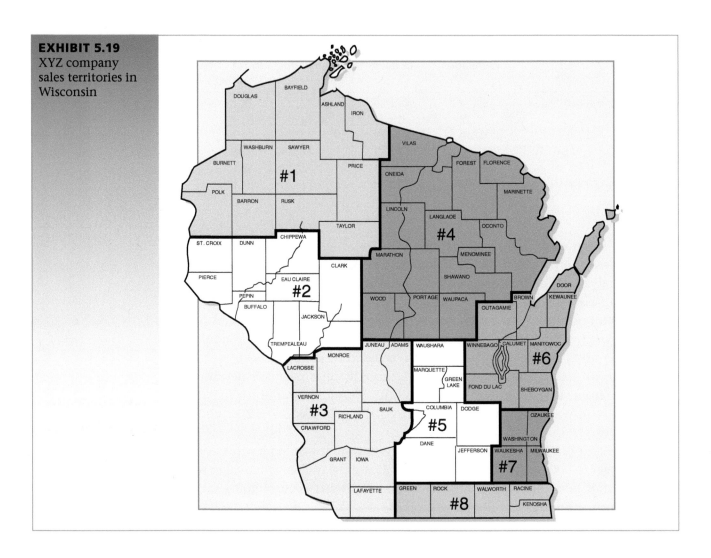

EXHIBIT 5.20
Sales by
representative in
the Wisconsin
district of XYZ
company

Area Representative	BPI (percentage of U.S.)	Sales Quota ($000)	Sales ($000)	Difference ($000)	Performance Index (PI = S/Q × 100)
1. T. Tate	0.0953%	$ 400.2	$ 392.6	$ 7.6	98.1
2. T. Bir	0.1332	559.4	501.0	58.4	89.6
3. C. Holzem	0.1325	556.5	512.4	44.1	92.1
4. A. Elliott	0.2021	848.8	768.7	80.1	90.6
5. P. Martin	0.2596	1,090.3	969.3	121.0	88.9
6. J. Campbell	0.3384	1,421.3	1,340.3	81.0	94.3
7. L. Hutchins	0.6975	2,929.5	1,285.0	1,644.5	43.9
8. B. Lessner	0.2528	1,061.8	970.5	91.3	91.4
Total Wisconsin	2.1114%	$8,867.8	$6,739.8	$2,128.0	76.0

Product	Sales Quota	Sales	Difference	Performance Index (PI = S/Q × 100)	
Can openers/knife sharpeners	$ 212,000	$ 124,500	$ 87,500	58.7	**EXHIBIT 5.21** Hutchins's sales by product
Toasters	468,000	237,000	231,000	50.6	
Coffee makers	627,000	176,000	451,000	28.1	
Blenders/mixers/food processors	604,000	159,200	444,800	26.4	
Griddles/electric fry pans	573,000	340,000	233,000	59.3	
Other—electric carving knives/popcorn makers/hot trays, etc.	445,500	248,300	197,200	55.7	
Total	$2,929,500	$1,285,000	$1,644,500	43.9	

buyers. Furthermore, the problem was not unique to Hutchins but was common to all reps in the east and west north-central regions. A major competitor had been attempting to improve its position in the north-central region through a combination of heavy advertising and purchase rebate offers on these products. This problem had been obscured in other sales territories because sales of other products had compensated for lost sales in coffee makers and blenders/mixers/food processors. Hutchins's sales of other products did not make up the deficit. The problem was compounded by an economic slowdown in the metal-working industry, a big employer in the Milwaukee area.

The Iceberg Principle

Our sales analysis indicates that the problem is not Hutchins; rather, it is the special competitive situation in the north-central region. This situation would not have come to light without this detailed sales analysis. One important principle illustrated by the preceding example is that aggregate figures can be deceiving. Another principle is that small, visible problems are often symptoms of large, unseen problems. The phenomenon has been linked to an iceberg—the iceberg principle, so named because only about 10 percent of an iceberg's mass is above the water level (analogous to the symptoms of a problem). The other 90 percent of the berg is below the surface (analogous to the real problem), and not always directly below the tip either. The submerged portion can be very dangerous to ships. So it is with much sales, marketing, and business data. Real problems are often obscured by visible symptoms.

The typical business engages in many varied activities and collects large volumes of data to support these activities. Thus, it is very common for difficulties or problems in one area to be submerged. The sales manager in our example would have succumbed to a misperception of the problem had the original aggregate sales analysis in Exhibit 5.17 been the stopping point. At that point, on the surface all appeared basically calm and peaceful, but more careful analysis revealed submerged problems with jagged edges that would continue to suboptimize business results if they are not attended to properly. Those analyzing the information that is collected need to be especially wary that the summaries they produce by aggregating and averaging data do not hide more than they reveal.

The iceberg principle is pervasive. The 80:20 rule or concentration ratio discussed earlier is one manifestation of it. Often, the concentration of sales within certain territories, products, or customers hides specific weaknesses. More than one company has shown satisfactory total sales, but when the total was subdivided by territories, customers, and products, serious weaknesses were uncovered.

The preceding sales analysis example also vividly illustrates the difference between a simple sales analysis and a comparative sales analysis, as well as the advantages of the latter. The simple raw sales analysis would have focused on the raw sales data in Exhibit 5.17—it would not have examined the differences from quota. In fact, simple sales analysis probably would not have generated any detailed investigation of the east north-central region because sales there were higher than in any other region. The comparison with quota, however, emphasized that the potential in this region was also greater than in any other and the firm was failing to get its share. The comparative analysis triggered the more intensive investigation and isolated the primary reason for the sales shortfall. The execution of the process depended on having sales quotas available on a very small basis. They had to be available by customer, by product, and by salesperson or the problem would never have come to light.

Quotas are sometimes difficult to generate on such a small basis. In our example, it was possible because detailed geographic statistics on the BPI were available. In situations where other data should be used, they need to be available by small geographic area. That is one reason the sales planning and sales evaluation questions are so intertwined. One must keep in mind the questions of evaluation and the comparisons needed when designing sales territories and sales quotas.

The Isolate-and-Explode Principle

Another concept the example illustrates is the principle of isolate and explode, in which the most significant discrepancies between actual and standard are identified, or isolated, and then examined in detail, or exploded. The detail this explosion reveals is then analyzed, the most significant discrepancies are again isolated, and these are exploded. The process continues until the "real" problems are isolated. Thus, in the example, the following were all isolated and exploded in turn: the east north-central region, the Wisconsin district, Hutchins's sales by product, and Hutchins's product sales by customer.

An alternative would have been to have masses of data available to the sales manager initially. For example, the information system could have supplied the sales manager with the detailed tabulations of sales by each salesperson of each product to each customer in the beginning. More than likely, such a tabulation would go unused because of its size and the time it would take to decipher its contents. The isolate-and-explode principle makes the task manageable. The sales manager can quickly localize trouble spots by focusing on the most substantial exceptions from standard and then hone in more efficiently on an effective cure.

The principle can also be used to isolate exceptional performances for the clues they might provide to what the firm is doing right. Investigating why the east south-central region was 5.1 percent over quota when the entire company was only 0.3 percent over quota might suggest effective competitive strategies and identify best practices that can be duplicated in other sales units.

The isolate-and-explode principle assumes the company's information system can provide sales data hierarchically. In the example, the sales manager could secure data broken out by customer, by product, by sales rep, by district, and by region. The breakdowns resemble a tree: Total U.S. sales are the trunk, regions are the main limbs, districts the next branches, and so on. Further, all combinations of these branches are possible. For example, it is possible to do a study by product and territory, or by customer and product. These alternative types of analysis can also be productive, as can simple one-way categorizing of sales data. The simple tabulation of sales by product, for example, is very useful in showing a firm's product line strengths. Similarly, the simple tabulation of sales by major classes of customers is often informative about the company's market strengths. Keep in mind that these sales analyses are diagnostics, not decision rules. They do not tell the manager what to do but only offer clues as to causes of problems. And sales analyses are only part of the story.

SUMMARY

We have seen in the chapter that sales managers perform a vital role in the process of both using and generating information. The sales forecasts, quotas, territories, and sales analyses developed under the leadership of sales managers touch most every operational aspect of a firm. Aspects of organizational success at many levels are affected by the proficiency of sales managers in performing these information management roles. From the profitability brought by strategic marketing plans when a forecast proves accurate, to the satisfaction of a customer when a sales territory design allows for proper coverage, to the rewards afforded a salesperson for quota attainment—all these outcomes reflect on the sales manager's capability to effectively use information in the job.

Because of this impact, sales managers have a vested interest in becoming as proficient as possible in the information management aspect of their job as described in this chapter. The greater their mastery of these important facets of the position, the greater will be not only their own professional success but also the success of the firm and its salespeople.

KEY TERMS

market potential
sales potential
sales forecast
sales quotas
subjective forecasting
  methods
  user expectations
  sales force composite
  jury of executive opinion
  Delphi technique
objective forecasting
  methods
  market test

time-series analysis
  moving average
  exponential smoothing
  decomposition
  statistical demand analysis
scenario planning
North American Industry
  Classification System
  (NAICS)
buying power index (BPI)
sales volume quotas
activity quotas
financial quotas

sales force deployment
breakdown method
workload method
incremental method
account analysis
sales analysis
80:20 principle
enterprise resource
  planning (ERP)
Buying Power Index (BPI)
iceberg principle
isolate and explode

BREAKOUT QUESTIONS

1. A common problem faced by those responsible for making sales forecasts is "selling" the predictions to others such as the vice presidents of marketing, production, and human resources, and to the CEO or the CFO. These parties hesitate to use forecasts that can have major implications, especially if they are wrong, on their functional area. What can those responsible for sales forecasting do to better sell their results to management? What forecasting guidelines should be followed to improve the predictions?

2. A survey of local business firms to determine how they forecast sales will produce a variety of answers. Some will claim they do not use any formal techniques to forecast sales. You know they must be using some approach, no matter how loosely defined. How do you know a business firm is making a sales forecast? What are the implications of not making a sales forecast?

3. For the following products, indicate what factor(s) you would use to estimate market potential:

   a. Yoplait yogurt
   b. Rolex watches
   c. Apple iPads
   d. Toro power riding lawnmowers
   e. Ektelon racquetball racquets
   f. Nicole Miller designer ties
   g. SWATCH watches
   h. Tylenol
   i. Mary Kay cosmetics

4. To estimate market potential for the garden tractor division of the M–F Implement Co., Mark Haynes, the statistician, estimated the following relationship using multiple regression analyses:

$$Y = a + b_1X_1 + b_2X_2 + b_3X_3 + b_4X_4$$

where

Y = unit sales of U.S. garden tractors

X_1 = number of single-family homes

X_2 = disposable personal income

X_3 = index of food prices

X_4 = family size

Using data for 2010–2016, R^2 = 65.0 was obtained. Should this method be used to predict market potential?

5. A new cake mix is to be introduced by Miracle Foods. To develop territory potentials, a corollary index has been proposed. The index contains several factors, such as income, population, and retail food sales. Can you justify these factors? Does it make sense to use retail food sales, which means cake sales are a function of food sales?

6. Once a quarter, every six months, or annually, each salesperson should estimate the buying potential of each account for each major product or product line. Such a request usually causes the sales force to panic. What goals are likely to be achieved by having the sales force participate in sales forecasting? What are the potential pitfalls, if any? How could those pitfalls be overcome?

7. Most sales managers hesitate to modify sales territories unless supported by compelling reasons. Likewise, sales managers are reluctant to make major changes in the sales compensation package. On the other hand, reassigning salespeople from one territory to another is fairly common and often reflects a form of promotion. One expert contends that if a company's sales force knows the territory too well, then it's time to reassign territories. What are the pros and cons of this approach? What factors related to the salesperson, the company, and the external environment might drive a company to reassign a sales territory?

8. The chapter describes the process to follow to develop territories. After territories have been developed, changes may occur that indicate the territories need to be realigned. What changes can you identify that indicate the need for realignment? How would you go about the process of realigning territories? How would you implement the changes?

9. In the typical case, management by exception leads to a close examination of below-par situations. Only sales representatives who are not meeting objectives, products that are not selling according to expectations, and customers who are not buying products as predicted are carefully reviewed to determine corrective action. What arguments can be advanced for conducting a close examination of the opposite, above-par situations?

10. The use of scanner data collected at the time of checkout in supermarkets has increased dramatically in sales analysis. One company has recruited families nation-wide to participate in a panel study. When a shopper enters the checkout lane, he or she gives the clerk a plastic card that is passed over the scanner. All items purchased that are scanned are recorded in the shopper's diary. Oscar Mayer, a Wisconsin-based producer of meat, turkey, and seafood, has used different advertising campaigns in

several markets. Oscar Mayer analyzes scanner data to determine which ad campaign was most effective. How else could Oscar Mayer and other manufacturers use scanner data? Of what value would scanner data be to salespeople for a company such as Oscar Mayer? To food retailers? What are other industries that could benefit from the same type of data?

11. The Recall Computer Co. has six territories, each represented by one salesperson. After extensive planning, the company determines that each territory would be expected to achieve the following percentages of total company sales for 2012:

Territory 1	27%	Territory 4	12%
Territory 2	15%	Territory 5	20%
Territory 3	18%	Territory 6	8%

These figures are used as the standard for comparing each sales representative's actual 2016 sales. The company projected sales for 2016 of $18,500,000. Determine which sales representative's territory had the best performance by using the performance index, if the actual sales for 2016 in each territory were $5,425,000, $3,205,000, $3,710,000, $2,400,000, $3,900,000, and $2,000,000, respectively, for territories 1–6.

12. In planning a sales analysis system, one must consider that information needs vary from district sales manager to regional sales manager to vice president of sales. Give specific examples of how information needs vary among managers at these levels.

13. Ethical Question. JUS-GRA Industries is an automotive aftermarket parts distributor based in Munich, Germany. As VP of sales for JUS-GRA industries you have been tasked with opening and staffing the first new sales office for the company's Asian operations, which are forecast to grow nicely over the next several years. Based in Tokyo, one of the challenges of this region are the large distances that must be traveled by air to call on customers in far flung locations like Seoul, Shanghai, Kuala Lumpur, Singapore, and other key cities that JUS-GRA would like to open for business. As you consider assigning salespeople to this new region you are very mindful of these travel demands along with other inherent challenges of opening up in a new region of the world. At the same time, one of your best longtime salespeople in Germany—Angelika Krafft, who is also a close family friend—has asked you if she could be moved to this new area. Angelika sees this as an opportunity to gain visibility in the company and show what she can do. You know, however, that she has a family with three children aged 11–16 and that the demands of the new job may put pressure on her family and her spouse. How would you handle her request? Explain your decision.

LEADERSHIP CHALLENGE: A QUOTA BY ANY OTHER NAME

Ralph Dickerson knew an adjustment was needed. In more than 20 years with Bright Right Plastics, he had been around for many changes, and as director of sales for the company, he had initiated a number on his own. Now Ralph knew that he had to reevaluate the quota system that had been used at Bright Right for more than 15 years.

The system had been revised years ago to focus the sales force on financial goals, specifically sales volume. At the time, business was slow and senior management had wanted salespeople to drive sales for the company. It had worked as the company prospered and was now enjoying great success. Selling to large hardware stores, the company had built a reputation as a good supplier of quality plastic fittings and joints in the retail plumbing industry. At the same time, many aspects of the business environment had changed since the quota system was last revised. Most notably, foreign competitors had come in offering competitive prices and better service. Several of Bright Right's old competitors had been driven out of business, and Ralph knew that part of the problem was the quota system in place at the company.

Essentially, the system in place was based on sales volume. As it had evolved the system focused on unit sales. It involved a complex plan that allowed each salesperson to set unit sales goals for every product in the company's large inventory. Senior management considered quotas a critical element in their strategic planning. At the same time, they were used as motivational tools for the sales force. Each overall quota was set high, but within that the salesperson could develop individual product quotas based on his or her customer's needs.

The problem, as Ralph saw it, was that customers wanted greater coordination and support from their suppliers. Specifically, customers like Home Depot and Lowe's wanted salespeople to offer product demonstrations to their own sales force as well as help in arranging displays for the products. Ralph had heard complaints that Bright Right salespeople were less interested in doing these kinds of activities than salespeople from other companies. Unfortunately, he had heard these complaints for several years and was concerned they might be losing business, or soon would be.

He sat in his office pondering his next move. The CEO of the company had set up a meeting for tomorrow to discuss this issue and was looking to Ralph for answers.

Questions

1. What are the advantages and disadvantages of a sales volume–based quota system?

2. What are the advantages and disadvantages of an activity-based quota system?

3. What quota system would you recommend Ralph present to the CEO and why? What challenges would Ralph face in implementing your recommendation?

ROLE-PLAY: BLUE TERN MILLS—PART B

Situation

This situation is a continuation of the situation presented in the Chapter 4 Role-Play. Go back and read that Role-Play and your notes from it to refamiliarize yourself with the scenario.

Agnes, Alan, and Penny have now had their meeting and have proposed a new sales force organization scheme for Blue Tern Mills postacquisition of the Hello line of healthy grain products. It is now time to begin the process of developing a sales forecast for the first year of operation of the combined companies. In order to begin this process, Agnes calls another meeting of the three for a few weeks later.

In advance of the meeting, she asks that each person come prepared with a set of notes listing their proposed combination of forecasting methods to employ along with their rationale for why each should be a part of the final approach to determining this first-year forecast. As you prepare these notes, keep in mind that especially this first year the forecast will be tricky because it will be difficult to determine in advance the full impact of the transition of the Hello line from the manufacturer's representatives to Blue Tern's own sales force, with the new organization scheme for it you developed earlier. Clearly, multiple methods of forecasting should be applied to reach a final forecasting decision and information will have to be effectively sourced and utilized from both firms.

The purpose of the meeting is to settle on methods to be employed in developing the first-year forecast, justify those methods, and list information needed and the sources of that information.

Characters in the Role-Play

Agnes Klondyke, chief sales officer (CSO) for Blue Tern Mills
Alan Knorr, West Coast sales manager for Blue Tern Mills
Penny Pugsley, currently the director of sales for Hello Healthy Grain Foods and soon to be East Coast sales manager for Blue Tern Mills (note that Penny's job at Hello has been to supervise its network of manufacturers' representatives—Hello does not have its own sales force).

Assignment

Break into groups of three, with one student playing each character. It doesn't matter what the actual gender mix of your group is. Before you stage the meeting among Agnes, Alan, and Penny, work separately to come up with the information required: your ideas for methods to be employed in developing the first-year forecast, justification for those methods, information that will be needed to drive your selected methods, and the sources of that information. Then get together and role-play the meeting. Share your ideas, especially discussing the pros and cons of different forecasting approaches proposed. After the discussion, come to agreement among yourselves on what will be the best mix of forecasting approaches, given the unique situation in the first year after the acquisition, and specify the needed information and sources. Note that you are not developing a forecast in the meeting—you are simply deciding on what approaches are to be used, why, and what information is needed.

MINICASE: LASTING IMPRESSIONS

Lasting Impressions is a small Orlando, Florida, company that provides trade-show marketing solutions to customers of all sizes. The company offers to design a plan for trade-show exhibiting from start to finish, including developing a pre- and postevent marketing plan and branding strategy, creating the exhibit booth and corresponding collateral support materials, packaging and shipping all trade-show materials, and providing boothmanship training services.

Founded by CEO Rajiv Dembla in 2006, the company focuses its own sales efforts on customers within the state of Florida and has a team of four account executives—Mary Beth, Suzanne, Franco, and Syl—who act as the salespeople for the organization. Rajiv relies on the same territory design that he has for the past several years, in which he divides the state geographically into four equal-size regions, and the account executives are responsible for the cities within their respective region.

Rajiv is not an especially quantitative manager by nature, but he did acknowledge the need to do a sales forecast for the upcoming 2016–17 fiscal year. He used the sales force composite method by asking his account executives how much each expected to sell during the coming year and then totaling those estimates. This type of method has worked for the company in the past, but Rajiv is concerned that Syl acts in the spirit of the marketing adage "underpromise and overdeliver" by intentionally underestimating his sales expectations so that his quota will be lower. To be safe, Rajiv also determined the sales forecast by taking a moving average of the previous four years of sales (see Table FY 2016–17 Forecasted Sales and Quotas).

Based on an average of these two sales forecasts, Rajiv set out to develop the yearly sales quota for each of his account executives. As he usually did, he kept the quota as simple as possible by basing it on gross dollars brought into the firm from sales, and he made it equal for each account executive. To ensure that his sales team is aggressive, he set the quotas slightly higher than the forecasted sales. As further motivation, Rajiv put 25 percent of each account executive's compensation in the form of a bonus for meeting or beating sales volume quotas.

John Cook, Rajiv's executive assistant, is more sensitive to the needs of the staff than Rajiv and tends to be the one that people talk to freely. Mary Beth complains to him privately, "This quota system does not reward—and even punishes—me for doing what I do best, building relationships with customers through in-person consultations, field demonstrations, and attending trade-show events to ensure everything goes smoothly." She finds these activities invaluable for serving the customer and keeping her pipeline of business full in the long term, but they do not necessarily generate sales volume in the short term.

While Suzanne tells John, "I have no problem with the quota because my territory includes the home city of Orlando. I know all of the businesses there and have no problem generating sales," Franco comes to John upset. His region includes Tallahassee, Pensacola, and the rest of the Florida Panhandle, which is more rural, is farther away from home, and has fewer businesses. As a result, he says, "I am miserable! I can't meet these unfair quotas!"

Syl tells John, "I have the same problem generating sales at times in my north-central Florida territory because there are fewer large cities. But," he whispers with a smile, "I don't worry about it. I recommend more expensive trade-show supplies and services to my customers at the end of the fiscal year to boost my short-term sales. And if I need more sales to meet my quota, I just do some creative accounting and record sales numbers for this year which should come due at the beginning of next year. It works every time."

John is in a quandary. He normally keeps the staff complaints confidential, but in this case he feels like he needs to tell Rajiv that all is not well at Lasting Impressions.

FY 2016–17 Forecasted Sales and Quotas

Account Executive	Forecasted Sales	Quota
Mary Beth	$180,000	$200,000
Suzanne	180,000	200,000
Franco	180,000	200,000
Syl	180,000	200,000
Total	$720,000	$800,000

Questions

1. Based on the facts given, evaluate Rajiv's territory design. What other basic control unit might Rajiv have used besides cities? Why?

2. What other forecast method(s) should Rajiv have used besides the sales force composite moving average? Why?

3. What type of sales quota did Rajiv use? Did he set the appropriate quota level? Why or why not?

Implementation of the Sales Program

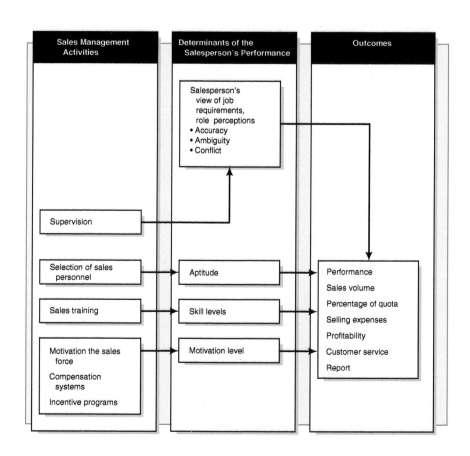

Sales Management Activities	Determinants of the Salesperson's Performance	Outcomes
	Salesperson's view of job requirements, role perceptions • Accuracy • Ambiguity • Conflict	
Supervision		
Selection of sales personnel	Aptitude	Performance Sales volume
Sales training	Skill levels	Percentage of quota Selling expenses
Motivation the sales force Compensation systems Incentive programs	Motivation level	Profitability Customer service Report

CHAPTER 6

Salesperson Performance: Behavior, Role Perceptions, and Satisfaction

LEARNING OBJECTIVES

How a salesperson performs is the result of a complex interaction of many factors. Many of those factors are the result of an individual's personal characteristics, motivation, and perceptions of the job. It is vital that sales managers have a clear understanding of salesperson performance so that they can maximize the performance potential of the salespeople in the organization. This chapter will present a model of salesperson performance and lay the groundwork for the information in Chapters 6 through 11. In addition, this chapter focuses on one of the key elements in the model: the salesperson's role perceptions.

After reading this chapter, you should be able to

- Understand the model of salesperson performance.
- Identify the various components that make up the model.
- Discuss the role perception process.
- Understand why the role of salesperson is susceptible to role issues.
- Discuss how role conflict, role ambiguity, and role accuracy influence a salesperson's role perceptions.

A number of factors can affect a salesperson's performance. When sales managers implement sales programs, they must motivate and direct the behavior of sales representatives toward the company's goals. Sales managers, therefore, must understand why people in the sales force behave the way they do. This chapter offers a model to understand sales force behavior. The model highlights the links between a salesperson's performance and the determinants of that performance. In addition, the chapter examines one of the key elements of the model, a salesperson's role perceptions. Put simply, salespeople operate in a unique environment where the nature of the roles is changing. The second part of the chapter will delineate how a salesperson's role perceptions affect his or her performance. Complete understanding of the model should develop as you study the remainder of this section, which discusses the basic components of the model in detail.

UNDERSTANDING SALESPERSON PERFORMANCE—WHY IS IT IMPORTANT FOR SALES MANAGEMENT?

Understanding the model of salesperson performance—as discussed over the next several chapters and presented in Exhibit 6.1—is extremely important to the sales manager because almost everything he or she does can influence it. For example:

* The way the sales manager organizes and deploys the sales force can affect salespeople's perceptions of the job.

* How the manager selects salespeople and the kind of training they receive can affect the aptitude and skill of sales personnel.

* The compensation program and the way it is administered can influence motivation levels and overall sales performance.

The model offers the sales manager a tool for visualizing the effects of his or her activities and for appreciating the interrelated roles of the options under his or her command. This chapter outlines the model and highlights the various components. In addition, it discusses a critical component of the model—role perceptions—and delineates the evidence supporting its effects and the influences on it.

THE MODEL

Research in industrial and organizational psychology suggests a worker's job performance is a function of five basic factors: (1) role perceptions, (2) aptitude,

EXHIBIT 6.1
Model of the determinants of a salesperson's performance

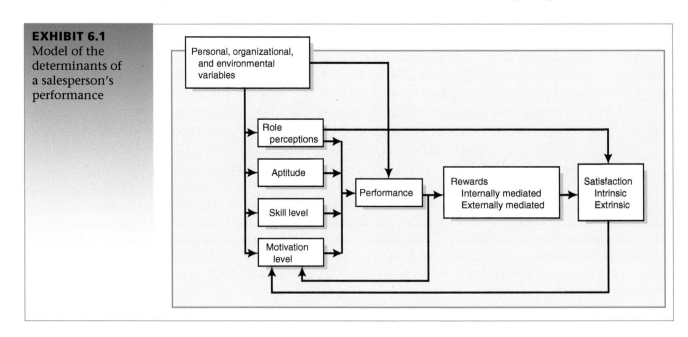

(3) skill level, (4) motivation, and (5) personal, organizational, and environmental variables.[1] Exhibit 6.1 presents an overall model of a salesperson's performance that includes these factors as primary determinants. The success of any salesperson is a complex combination of these forces, which can positively, or negatively, influence his or her performance.

Although not pictured in the model, substantial interaction occurs among the determinants. As a result, if a worker is deficient in any of these factors, he or she could be expected to perform poorly. If the salesperson has innate ability and the motivation to perform but lacks understanding of how the job should be done, for example, he or she could still perform below expectations. Similarly, if the salesperson has the ability and accurately perceives how the job should be performed but lacks motivation, he or she is likely to perform poorly.

One other note: The factors in the model are not independent of each other. It is not clear how the factors interact, and indeed, they almost certainly vary somewhat with each individual. However, it is fairly certain that the determinants are interrelated.

The Role Perceptions Component

The role attached to the position of salesperson represents the set of activities or behaviors to be performed by anyone occupying that position. While discussed in much greater detail later in the chapter, this role is defined largely through the expectations, demands, and pressures communicated to the salesperson by his or her role partners. These partners include people both outside and within the individual's firm who have a vested interest in how the salesperson performs the job— top management, the individual's supervisor, customers, and family members. The salesperson's perceptions of these expectations strongly influence the individual's definition of his or her role in the company and behavior on the job.

The role perceptions component of the model has three dimensions: role accuracy, perceived role conflict, and perceived role ambiguity. The term role accuracy refers to the degree to which the salesperson's perceptions of his or her role partners' demands—particularly those of company superiors—are accurate. Perceived role conflict arises when a salesperson believes the role demands of two or more of his or her role partners are incompatible. Thus, the individual cannot possibly satisfy them all at the same time. A salesperson suffers from role conflict, for example, when a customer demands a delivery schedule or credit terms the sales rep believes will be unacceptable to company superiors. Perceived role ambiguity occurs when salespeople believe they do not have the information necessary to perform the job adequately. The salespeople may be uncertain about what some role partners expect of them in certain situations, how they should satisfy those expectations, or how their performance will be evaluated and rewarded.

The model indicates the three role perception variables have psychological consequences for the individual salesperson. They can produce dissatisfaction with the job. They can also affect the salesperson's motivation.[2] All these effects can increase turnover within the sales force and hurt performance. However, role stress (role conflict and role ambiguity) does not necessarily always imply a negative job outcome (e.g., increased turnover). Indeed, research suggests that a certain degree of role conflict and ambiguity enables salespeople to make creative decisions that can be beneficial to the customer and the organization. Business-to-business salespeople are particularly vulnerable to role inaccuracy, conflict, and ambiguity. Several personal and organizational variables can affect people's role perceptions. Fortunately, many of these variables can be controlled or influenced by sales management policies and methods, thus allowing the sales manager to influence the performance of individual salespeople.[3]

The Aptitude Component

The model of sales performance in Exhibit 6.1 treats an individual's sales aptitude largely as a constraint on the person's ability to perform the sales job. This assumes there is an adequate understanding of the role to be performed, the motivation, and the learned skills. In other words, two people with equal motivation, role perceptions, and skills might perform at very different levels because one has more aptitude or ability than the other.

There has been a lot of research on the effect of aptitude on sales performance. Sales aptitude includes a number of factors, such as verbal intelligence, mathematical ability, and sales expertise. In general, the results of the research have found there is a relationship between aptitude and performance. Unfortunately, broad measures of aptitude by themselves do not explain a very large proportion of the variation in sales performance.[4]

Broad measures of aptitude may not predict sales performance for several reasons. First, motivation refers to the salesperson's desire to expend effort on very specific sales tasks such as calling on new accounts or preparing sales presentations, and it varies by sales position (experienced key account managers need to accomplish different tasks than new-account salespeople). As a result, the appropriate definition of aptitude, and the appropriate measures of the construct, may vary greatly from industry to industry, firm to firm, and product line to product line. For example, selling highly technical products requiring an engineering background (e.g., building construction) might demand math skills that an office supplies salesperson may not need to be successful.

Second, aptitude may affect performance in more ways than by simply moderating an individual's ability to do the job. It may also affect the salesperson's motivation to perform. For example, the salesperson's perceived ability to perform a task and his or her general self-confidence influence the individual's perceptions of whether increased effort will lead to improved performance. Furthermore, salespeople's intelligence and feelings as to whether they largely control their own destiny or whether this destiny is largely controlled by outside forces (internal versus external locus of control) affect whether they believe improved performance will lead to improvement in rewards they desire. All this suggests that objective measures of sales aptitude may be insufficient by themselves. The role of sales aptitude in salesperson performance as well as methods by which sales managers ascertain an individual's sales aptitude are discussed in Chapter 8.

The Skill-Level Component

Skill level refers to the individual's learned proficiency at performing the necessary tasks[5] and include such learned abilities as interpersonal skills, leadership, technical knowledge, and presentation skills. The relative importance of each of these skills, and the necessity of having other skills, depends on the selling situation. Different kinds of skills are needed for different types of selling tasks. Aptitude and skill levels are thus related constructs. Aptitude consists of relatively enduring personal abilities, whereas skills are proficiency levels that can change rapidly with learning and experience. The skill sets of a salesperson for Oracle selling multimillion-dollar network systems are different from someone selling Audi automobiles to consumers.

The salesperson's past selling experience and the extensiveness and content of the firm's sales training programs influence skill level. Although American companies spend large amounts of money on sales training, there is almost no research concerning the effects of these training programs on salespeople's skills, behavior, and performance. We will discuss training the sales force in much greater detail in Chapter 10.

The Motivation Component

Over the years, motivation has meant various, and often inconsistent, things in the literature, although some recent consensus seems to be emerging. For our purposes, motivation is viewed as the amount of effort the salesperson desires to expend on each activity or task associated with the job. These activities include calling on existing and potential new accounts, developing and delivering sales presentations, and filling out orders and reports.

The salesperson's motivation to expend effort on any task seems to be a function of the individual's (1) expectancies and (2) valences for performance. Expectancies are the salesperson's estimates of the probability that expending effort on a specific task will lead to improved performance on some specific dimension. For example, will increasing the number of calls made on potential new accounts lead to increased sales? Valences for performance are the salesperson's perceptions of the desirability of attaining improved performance on some dimension or dimensions. For example, does the salesperson find increased sales attractive?

A salesperson's valence for performance on a specific dimension, in turn, seems to be a function of his or her (1) instrumentalities and (2) valences for rewards. Instrumentalities are the salesperson's estimates of the probability that improved performance on that dimension will lead to increased attainment of particular rewards. For example, will increased sales lead to increased compensation? Valences for rewards are the salesperson's perceptions of the desirability of receiving increased rewards as a result of improved performance. Does the salesperson, say, find an increase in the compensation level attractive? A salesperson's expectancy, instrumentality, and valence perceptions can all affect the person's willingness to expend effort on a specific task or to engage in specific behaviors. Sales managers constantly try to find the right mix of motivation elements to direct salespeople in specific directions. The problem is particularly difficult because rewards that motivate one salesperson may not motivate another. There is the example of the manager at a leading consulting company in Chicago who gave his top performer a new mink coat. The only problem was that the individual did not wear fur. Rewarding the salesperson was a great idea, but the implementation of the reward led to problems for the sales manager. Moreover, what motivates a person at one stage in his or her career may not motivate the rep during some other period, as the Leadership box indicates.

The salesperson's expectancy, instrumentality, and valence perceptions are not directly under the sales manager's control. But they can be influenced by things the sales manager does, such as how he or she supervises the salesperson or rewards the individual.[6] Since the salesperson's motivation strongly influences performance, the sales manager must be sensitive to the impact of various factors. These issues are explored more fully in the next chapter.

The Personal, Organizational, and Environmental Variables Component

The sales performance model in Exhibit 6.1 suggests that personal, organizational, and environmental variables influence sales performance in two ways:

LEADERSHIP   Understanding the Value of Value

Research suggests that successful salespeople have bedrock beliefs in what they sell, why they are selling it, and the value of their products, services. As a sales manager, one must teach salespeople to appreciate what they are selling, to value the essence of being a salesperson and the worth they bring to clients. To do this, a manager needs to get to know team members on an individual level, and learn about personalities so that abilities (and dreams) can be maximized. The essence of developing a successful sales organization is to help team members develop a deeper mission for their work, and an understanding for what makes them tick as individuals. Some keys to keep in mind:

Sales culture of meaning: Embrace the importance of the mission of the organization, and the interrelatedness of sales to other parts of an organization. It shouldn't matter what we are selling—the connection is an important part of making people's lives better.

One-on-one understanding of your people: Every person has a different idea of success and what it means to them within the boundaries of your organization. The goal of a sales manager is to understand talents, self-interests, and dreams of team members.

Recognition and reinforcement: Feed the quest for meaning and achievement in more personal victories both in and out of the sales arena.

A high performing sales team is one who's members are deeply passionate about the work they do, recognize sales as an avenue to achieve their dreams, and have their value and importance within a capitalist enterprise continually reinforced.

(1) by directly facilitating or constraining performance and (2) by influencing and interacting with the other performance determinants, such as role perceptions and motivation.

Organizational Variables

Part One described how these variables can influence sales performance directly. The discussion of the organization of the sales force and the design of sales territories reviewed much of the evidence and logic supporting the relationship between performance and organizational factors. These factors include company marketing communications expenditures, the firm's current market share, and the degree of sales force supervision. There is a relationship between performance and environmental factors like territory potential, concentration of customers, the salesperson's workload, and the intensity of competition. The direct impact of the personal, organizational, and environmental variables on performance is thus rather clear.

Consider sales territory design, for example. Research suggests that as salespeople are more satisfied with their territory's design and structure, their performance increases. Including salespeople in the territory design process may seem intuitive, but managers sometimes find it difficult to balance the needs of the organization with the input of the salesperson. Sales managers have learned, however, that by including salespeople in the decision-making process on key issues such as territory design, the performance of the salesperson in that territory may increase over time.[7] The use of computer territory-mapping software has been helpful in enabling sales managers and salespeople to work together creating the most profitable and efficient territory configurations.[8] In the long term, this can lead to lower levels of role ambiguity and higher levels of job satisfaction as well as performance.

Personal Variables

A few studies have found significant relationships between personal and organizational variables—such as job experience, closeness of supervision, performance feedback, influence in determining standards, and span of control—and the amount of role conflict and ambiguity perceived by salespeople. Other studies related personal characteristics to variations in motivation by showing that salespeople's desires for different job-related rewards (e.g., pay, promotion) differ with such demographic characteristics as age, education, family size, career stage, or organizational climate.[9] Overall, though, many questions concerning the effects of personal, organizational, and environmental variables on the other determinants of sales performance remain unanswered. An important concern in recent years has been the effect of global sales responsibilities on individual salesperson performance. For example, are there unique issues faced by salespeople as they move into new international markets that affect their individual performance? The Innovation box discusses this issue.

INNOVATION Critical Global Sales Skills

Sales success in a global environment requires all the skills found in "local" selling—and more. Increasingly, salespeople are asked to build relationships with customers as they move and expand around the world. It was not that long ago that working with a global customer meant working with a member of the Fortune 1000. Today, however, small- and medium-sized companies are expanding into global markets and salespeople must be able to work with those customers. Four essential skills are needed for sales success in the global environment. They include:

Appreciation of cultural differences. It is natural to feel most comfortable in your own culture, and by extension, generally feel less at ease in foreign cultures. Nevertheless, successful selling in a global environment requires the ability to understand and adapt to different cultures. Looking at the selling process from the customer's perspective can help the salesperson adjust his or her presentation to the customer's unique cultural background.

Creative problem solving. Selling is about listening and responding to customers' concerns; this is magnified with global customers. Learning their business, responding to cultural differences, and making changes to a sales presentation based on feedback from the customer are critical to global sales success. Indeed, global salespeople know that being able to respond quickly to rapidly changing business and cultural conditions is often the difference between making and losing the sale.

Ability to let business relationships develop. In the United States, business relationships develop faster than anywhere else in the world. Decisions are based on the salesperson's ability to deliver an effective value proposition to the customer. However, in other cultures the business relationship develops more slowly and places a greater emphasis on the personal as well as business relationship.

Possess strong technology skills. Smartphones, laptops, and wireless communication are as important to the salesperson as pen and paper were in the twentieth century. Younger salespeople (Gen X and Y as well as younger baby boomers) are the most comfortable using technology. Keep in mind these are not the only global sales skills, but they are important to anyone considering a career in global sales.

Personal Variables—Being a Good Corporate Citizen

As the role of salesperson changes from focusing on single transactions to building and maintaining a relationship with customers, salespeople have been asked to engage in a whole range of activities that can be described as organizational citizenship behaviors (OCBs). These focus on four basic types of behavior: (1) sportsmanship, (2) civic virtue, (3) conscientiousness, and (4) altruism. As Exhibit 6.2 demonstrates, these behaviors are directed at improving the overall effectiveness of the organization. Sportsmanship is an enthusiasm on the salesperson's part to endure suboptimal conditions without complaining to superiors or other salespeople (e.g., slow reimbursement of expenses or reduced administrative support). Civic virtue is a proactive behavior that includes making recommendations to management that will improve the overall performance of the organization (e.g., providing feedback from customers even though it may not be complimentary). Conscientiousness is the willingness to work beyond the "normal" expectations of the job (e.g., working late or on weekends). Altruism refers to helping others in the organization (e.g., mentoring younger salespeople).

There is a growing understanding that salespeople who engage in these kinds of activities perform better on both outcome-based measures (sales volume)

Sportsmanship

1. Consume a lot of time complaining about trivial problems (lack of sportsmanship).
2. Tend to make mountains out of molehills—make problems bigger than they are (lack of sportsmanship).
3. Always focus on what's wrong with my situation rather than the positive side of it (lack of sportsmanship).

Civic Virtue

1. Keep up with developments in the company.
2. Attend functions that are not required but that help the company image.
3. Risk disapproval in order to express my beliefs about what is best for the company.

Conscientiousness

1. Conscientiously follow company regulations and procedures.
2. Turn in budgets, sales projections, expense reports, and so on earlier than required.
3. Return phone calls and respond to other messages and requests for information promptly.

Altruism

1. Help orient new agents even though it is not required.
2. Always ready to help or lend a helping hand to those around me.
3. Willingly give of my time to others.

Adapted from Nigel F. Piercy, David W. Cravens, and Nikala Lane, "Sales Manager Behavior-Based Control and Salesperson Performance: The Effects of Manager Control Competencies and Organizational Citizenship Behavior," *Journal of Marketing Theory and Practice* 20, no. 1 (Winter 2012), pp. 7–22.

EXHIBIT 6.2
Components of organizational citizenship

and behavior-based measures (customer satisfaction). Measuring salesperson performance will be discussed in Part Three. Engaging in activities that enhance the overall organization will most likely play an ever more important role in the salesperson's performance. As we have seen earlier in the text, the responsibilities of the salesperson are changing, and a greater focus on the organization and its relationship to customers is part of that process.

REWARDS

The performance model in Exhibit 6.1 indicates that the salesperson's job performance affects the rewards the representative receives. The relationship between performance and rewards is very complex, however. For one thing, firms often choose to evaluate and reward different dimensions of sales performance. Companies use a variety of performance-based metrics to evaluate their salespeople including total sales volume, quota attainment, selling expenses, profitability of sales, new accounts generated, services provided to customers, performance of administrative duties, or some combination of these. Different firms are likely to use different dimensions. Even firms that use the same performance criteria are likely to have different relative emphases. A company can also bestow a variety of rewards for any given level of performance.

The model distinguishes between two broad types of rewards: extrinsic and intrinsic. Extrinsic rewards are those controlled and offered by people other than the salesperson, such as managers or customers. These include such things as pay, financial incentives, security, recognition, and promotion, rewards that are generally related to low-order human needs. Intrinsic rewards are those that salespeople primarily attain for themselves. They include such things as feelings of accomplishment, personal growth, and self-worth, all of which relate to high-order human needs.

As the model in Exhibit 6.1 suggests, salespeople's perceptions of rewards they will receive in return for various types of job performance, together with the value they place on those rewards, strongly influence their motivation to perform.

SATISFACTION

The job satisfaction of salespeople refers to all the characteristics of the job that representatives find rewarding, fulfilling, and satisfying, or frustrating and unsatisfying. As Exhibit 6.3 indicates, there are seven different dimensions to sales job satisfaction: (1) the job itself, (2) coworkers, (3) supervision, (4) company policies and support, (5) pay, (6) promotion and advancement opportunities, and (7) customers. Salespeople's total satisfaction with their jobs is a reflection of their satisfaction with each of these elements.[10]

How job satisfaction relates to motivation, performance, organizational citizenship behaviors, and turnover is a complicated issue. Individuals who leave an organization often attribute their decision to leave on either supervision or career issues. People that find it difficult to get along with their managers often feel they can't take it any more and "get pushed" from their jobs. On the other hand, individuals dissatisfied because of career issues identify a combination of pay, promotion, and advancement opportunities within the company and "get pulled" to other employers. Thus, although job satisfaction is related to turnover, the relationship is complex and involves variables within the company (supervision and advancement opportunities) as well as those external to the company (alternative jobs).

As Exhibit 6.1 suggests, the rewards received by a salesperson have a major impact on the individual's satisfaction with the job and the total work environment. The seven dimensions of satisfaction can be grouped, like rewards, into two major components: intrinsic and extrinsic. Extrinsic satisfaction is associated with the extrinsic rewards bestowed on the salesperson, such as satisfaction with pay, company policies and support, supervision, coworkers, chances for promotion, and customers. Intrinsic satisfaction is related to the intrinsic rewards the salesperson obtains from the job, such as satisfaction with the work itself and with the opportunities it provides for personal growth and accomplishment.

The amount of satisfaction salespeople obtain from their jobs is also influenced by their role perceptions.[11] Salespeople with high levels of conflict tend to be less satisfied than those who do not. So do those who experience great uncertainty in what is expected from them on the job.

Job Satisfaction Component	Sample Items	
The job itself	My work is challenging.	**EXHIBIT 6.3** Components of job satisfaction
	My work gives me a sense of accomplishment.	
	My job is exciting.	
Coworkers	My coworkers are selfish.	
	My coworkers are intelligent.	
	My coworkers are responsible.	
Supervision	My sales manager is tactful.	
	My sales manager really tries to get our ideas.	
	My sales manager sees we have the things we need to do our job.	
Company policies	Compared with other companies, company benefits are good.	
	The company sales training is not carried out in a well-planned program.	
	Management is progressive.	
Pay	My income provides for luxuries.	
	My compensation does not give me much incentive to increase my sales.	
	My selling ability largely determines my earnings in this company.	
Promotion	My opportunities for advancement are limited.	
	Promotion in this company is based on ability.	
	I have a good chance for a promotion.	
Customers	My customers are fair.	
	My customers blame me for problems over which I have no control.	
	My customers respect my judgment.	

Research supports the complex relationship between various job satisfaction dimensions and a variety of constructs. For example, the salesperson's customer orientation (do they value the customer and focus on meeting their needs) impacts their job satisfaction. Interestingly, salespeople's job satisfaction is also impacted by the customer orientation of their sales manager. Even salespeople who are not customer oriented report even lower job satisfaction if they perceive their manager is not customer oriented. Organizational support also impacts a salesperson's job satisfaction. If salespeople perceive higher levels of organizational support their job satisfaction goes up. It is important to note, however, that too much organizational support has a negative consequence—salespeople become too comfortable and are less willing to engage the customer.[12]

Finally, a salesperson's job satisfaction is likely to affect the individual's motivation to perform, as suggested by the feedback loop in Exhibit 6.1. The relationship between satisfaction and motivation is, however, neither simple nor well understood. It is explored more fully in the next chapter.

As noted previously, the salesperson's role perceptions play a critical role in their overall performance. In the remainder of the chapter we will explore this variable in the model.

THE SALESPERSON'S ROLE PERCEPTIONS

The role component of the model has important implications for sales managers. Role perceptions affect salesperson performance in many ways. For example, feelings of ambiguity, conflict, and inaccurate role perceptions can cause psychological stress and job-related anxiety for salespeople. These, in turn, can lead to lowered performance. Fortunately, there are things the sales manager can do to minimize the negative consequences associated with role perceptions. The kind of salespeople that are hired, the way they are trained, the incentives used to motivate them, the criteria used to evaluate them, and the way they are supervised can all affect perceptions of role. These factors can also determine whether these perceptions are ambiguous, in conflict, or inaccurate. That is why the role components of the salesperson performance model are discussed in this chapter.

What makes understanding and managing role perceptions even more complicated is that not all the consequences of role ambiguity, role conflict, and role accuracy are negative. Eliminating ambiguity and conflict can reduce the challenge for a salesperson and actually limit long-term performance. The task for the sales manager is to create an environment that will stimulate and motivate the salesperson while reducing or at least minimizing the negative effects of role stress that are a natural part of selling.

STAGES IN DEVELOPING THE SALESPERSON'S ROLE

Every employee within the firm occupies a position to which a role is attached. This role represents the activities and behaviors that are to be performed by any person who occupies that position. The salesperson's role is defined through a three-step process.[13]

Stage 1: Role Partners Communicate Expectations

First, expectations and demands concerning how the salesperson should behave, together with pressures to conform, are communicated to the salesperson by members of that person's role set. The salesperson's role set consists of people with a vested interest in how the representative performs the job. These people include the individual's immediate superior, other executives in the firm, purchasing agents and other members of customers' organizations, and the salesperson's family. They all try to influence the person's behavior, either formally through organizational policies, operating procedures, and training programs, or informally through social pressures, rewards, and sanctions.

Stage 2: Salespeople Develop Perceptions

The second part of the role definition process involves the perceived role. This is salespeople's perceptions of the expectations and demands communicated by their role-set members. Salespeople perform according to what they think role-set members expect, even though their perceptions of those expectations may not be accurate. To really understand why salespeople perform the way they do, it is necessary to understand what salespeople think the members of the role set expect. At this stage of the role definition process, three factors can wreak havoc with a salesperson's job performance and mental well-being. As Exhibit 6.4 suggests, the salesperson may suffer from perceptions of role ambiguity, role conflict, or role inaccuracy.

Perceived role ambiguity occurs when representatives do not think they have the necessary information to perform the job adequately. They feel uncertain about how to do a specific task, what the members of the role set expect in a particular situation, or how their performance is evaluated by members of the role set.

Salespeople, indeed everyone, are bombarded with messages and stimuli all the time. As a result, the ability to switch between multiple tasks within the same block of time (called polychronicity) has become more common. Research suggests that salespeople with a higher propensity for polychronicity exhibit higher performance levels and less role ambiguity. In addition, effective time management has also shown to lower role ambiguity and improve performance. The ability to work efficiently and effectively in a dynamic sales environment is a big advantage in managing negative role perceptions.[14]

Perceived role conflict exists when a salesperson believes the role demands of two or more members of the role set are incompatible. A customer, for example, may demand unusually liberal credit terms or delivery schedules that are unacceptable to the salesperson's superiors. The representative's perception that it is not possible to simultaneously satisfy all members of the role set creates conflicting role forces and psychological conflict within the salesperson.

Perceived role inaccuracy arises when the salesperson's perceptions of the role partners' demands are inaccurate. Does the salesperson's idea about what the role partners desire correspond to their actual expectations? Role inaccuracy differs from role ambiguity in that, with role inaccuracy, the salesperson feels fairly certain

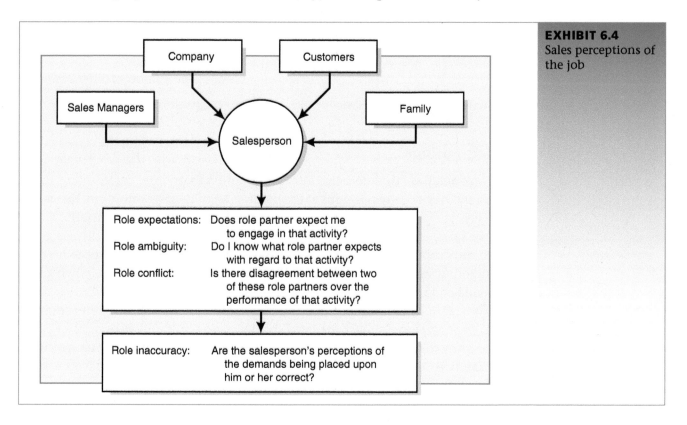

EXHIBIT 6.4
Sales perceptions of the job

about what should be done—except that the sales rep is wrong. It differs from role conflict in that the salesperson does not see any inconsistencies in that it is unrealized. The representative does not know that the perceptions held are inaccurate.

Stage 3: Salespeople Convert Perceptions into Behaviors

The final step in the role definition process involves the salesperson's conversion of these role perceptions into actual behavior. Both the salesperson's job behavior and psychological well-being can be affected if there are perceptions of role ambiguity or conflict or if these perceptions are inaccurate. There is a good deal of evidence, for example, that high levels of both perceived ambiguity and conflict are directly related to high mental anxiety and tension and low job satisfaction. Also, the salesperson's feelings of uncertainty and conflict and the actions taken to resolve them can have a strong impact on ultimate job performance.[15] At a minimum, the salesperson's performance is less likely to be consistent with management's expectations and desires when the representative is uncertain about what those expectations are, believes that the customers or family hold conflicting expectations, or has inaccurate perceptions of those expectations.

THE SALESPERSON'S ROLE IS VULNERABLE

Several characteristics of the salesperson's role make it particularly susceptible to role conflict, role ambiguity, and the development of inaccurate role perceptions:

1. Salespeople operate at the boundary of the firm.
2. A salesperson's performance affects the occupants of a large number of other positions.
3. The salesperson's role changes often, and the role itself is innovative.

Boundary Position

Salespeople are likely to experience more role conflict than other organization members because they occupy positions at the boundaries of their organization. Key members of each salesperson's role set—the customers—are in external organizations. As a result, the salesperson receives demands from organizations that have diverse goals, policies, and problems. Since each role partner (customers and the salesperson's own organization) wants the salesperson's behavior to be consistent with their own goals, the demands on the salesperson are diverse and often incompatible.

A customer, for example, may question the salesperson on the long-term commitment of the company to meet the needs of the customer. Employees of Blackberry, formerly known as Research in Motion, the Canada-based smart phone manufacturer, have been asked about the long term viability of the company given a series of product failures. They have been told to be honest and explain to customers what the company is doing to earn back their trust and business. The issue is to balance the amount of information given to the customer with the customer's legitimate concerns about the future ability of the company to meet existing product and customer service pledges.[16] The salesperson gets caught in the middle. To satisfy the demands of one role partner, the rep must deal with the concerns and demands of the other.

Another problem that arises from the salesperson's boundary position is that the role partners in one organization often don't appreciate the expectations and demands made by role partners in another. A customer, for example, may not know company policies or the constraints under which the salesperson must operate. Or the salesperson's superiors may formulate company policies without understanding the particular needs of some customers. Even a role partner who is aware of another's demands may not understand the reasoning behind them and consider them arbitrary or illegitimate.

A boundary position also increases the likelihood that the salesperson will experience role ambiguity or form inaccurate perceptions. Contact with many of the salesperson's role partners (manager, other salespeople), though regular, is probably infrequent and often brief. Under such conditions, it is easy for the salesperson to feel uncertain about what the company expects and how well he or she is performing.

The "Remote" Sales Force

Increasingly, salespeople operate from remote offices (often their home) and spend very little time in their company's offices. As they operate on the boundary of the organization, role stress can occur leading to lower performance over time. While cost considerations are certainly a factor in the trend toward moving salespeople out of company offices, there are also potential benefits in improved customer relationship management as salespeople seek to get closer to the customer. Not surprisingly, however, being separated from the organization can lead to higher levels of alienation and isolation from the company. The end result of these negative attitudes can be lower levels of satisfaction and performance.

Recent research suggests that managers can play a significant role in mitigating the negative effect of a salesperson being located outside the company office. The key is for the manager to remain in contact with the salesperson, assuring them they are still a vital part of the organization. In addition, salespeople need to get feedback on their performance and how they can continue to improve their selling skills. Many companies, including Google, HP, and others, have salespeople who work remotely from their homes with great results, and there are valid reasons for companies to encourage salespeople to work away from the office.[17]

Large Role Set

The salespeople's role set includes many diverse individuals. The representative may sell to hundreds of customers, and each expects his or her own particular needs and requirements to be satisfied. In addition, people within the firm rely on the salesperson to execute company policies in dealings with customers and for the ultimate success of the firm's revenue-producing efforts. The specific design-performance criterion a product is supposed to satisfy, and the delivery and credit terms the salesperson quotes, can directly influence people in the engineering, production, and credit departments, for example. All these people may hold definite beliefs about how the salesperson should perform the job, and they will all pressure the individual to conform to their expectations.

The large number of people from diverse departments and organizations who depend on the salesperson increases the probability that at least some role demands will be incompatible. It also increases the probability that the salesperson's perceptions of some demands will be inaccurate and that the rep will be uncertain about others.

Selling in a Team

The complex nature of the relationship between company and customer has created a need for salespeople to work in teams that include specialists from many parts of the company (technical, manufacturing, logistics, and others). As a result, the role of salesperson has evolved in many cases from one of selling to the customer to one of managing the relationship between the company and the customer. Companies as diverse as 3M, Siemens, and Apple have created sales teams managed by salespeople. In addition, in-house salespeople and customer service representatives create additional contact with the customer that often requires greater coordination with the salesperson. This can create role conflict for salespeople as they deal with the expectations and demands of many individuals within the sales team and the organization as a whole.

Innovative Role

The salesperson's role is frequently innovative because it is often necessary to produce new solutions to nonroutine problems. This is particularly true when the salesperson is selling highly technical products or engineered systems designed to the customer's

TECHNOLOGY Sales Technology Revolution Can Improve Sales Performance

A wide range of new technologies including social media, cloud-based tools, smart phones, and tablet computers has dramatically effected personal selling. Salespeople are no longer chained to desks or landlines, and customers expect salespeople to be available 24/7. The challenge lies in integrating new technologies into the selling process and identifying the right technologies to enable salespeople to be more efficient and effective. Often salespeople, even high performers, are reluctant to adopt new technology. At the same time customers are demanding immediate access and accurate information.

Many sales executives mention the iPad, iPhone, and apps as the most useful new sales technologies. Salespeople do not want to carry more gadgets than necessary and tablets like the iPad make it easier for those who don't want to waste time learning how to navigate a new format.

Armed with iPhones and iPads, salespeople can input and share data anytime and anywhere. The convergence of mobile, social, and analytics, along with "the simplicity of building apps in the cloud" have greatly improved the salesperson's knowledge level and customer interaction. Managers do not what their salespeople to be overwhelmed with technology; rather, the technology should allow people to spend less time inputting data and more time selling. In the new sales environment, customer responsiveness is critical and using technology effectively is often an essential tool in maintaining and growing the customer relationship.

specifications. The salesperson selling standardized products must also display creativity in matching the company's offerings to the customer's particular needs. With potential new accounts, this is an extremely difficult, but critical, task. The Technology box indicates another way in which salespeople can be caught in the middle between the demands of their customers and the expectations of their employers.

Occupants of innovative roles tend to experience more conflict than other organization members because they must have flexibility to perform their roles well. Such people must have the authority to develop and carry out innovative solutions. This need for flexibility often brings the salesperson into conflict with the company's standard operating procedures and the expectations of organization members who want to maintain the status quo. The production manager, for example, may frown on customized products because of increased production costs and negative effect on schedules, although marketing, and particularly the salespeople, might desire flexible production schedules that allow for greater customer input and more custom-designed products.

Occupants of innovative roles also tend to experience more role ambiguity and inaccurate role perceptions than occupants of noninnovative roles because they frequently face unusual situations where they have no standard procedures or past experience to guide them. Consequently, they are often uncertain about how their role partners expect them to proceed. The perceptions they do have are more likely to be inaccurate because of the nonroutine nature of the task. The flexibility that is needed to fulfill an innovative role can consequently have unforeseen, negative consequences.

Innovation in Communication Affects the Sales Role

The innovative nature of the sales role is changing very quickly. Salespeople interface with customers in a variety of new ways and customers connect with companies using the Internet and other electronic applications. As customers become "wired" to their suppliers, they expect even greater service, placing new demands on salespeople to know not only their own products but all the issues and concerns of their customers.

Cisco Systems, for example, created a B2B direct-order website for customers. Initially, salespeople expressed a great deal of concern about how such a site would affect their responsibilities. They experienced role conflict as their perception of the salesperson's job was changing based on the customer's ability to order directly from the website.

However, once they understood the site actually represented an opportunity to engage in greater problem-solving and value-added activities, performance of the sales force went up dramatically.

ROLE CONFLICT AND AMBIGUITY

In discussing the causes and consequences of the various role perceptions, it is useful to separate the concepts of role conflict and role ambiguity, on the one hand, and inaccurate role perceptions, on the other.

Common Expectations and Key Areas of Conflict and Ambiguity

Different sales jobs require different tasks and place different demands on salespeople. The senior account executive for Zara selling dresses to a head buyer at Macy's Department Stores will likely be most concerned with follow-up service to make sure the reorders for styles, colors, or sizes arrive in time for the current selling season. On the other hand, the salesperson for GE Motors selling oil pumps to a refinery is most concerned with making sure the equipment can handle the load, chemicals, and other harsh conditions to which it will be subjected. Thus, it is next to impossible to develop one set of expectations common to all sales jobs. Even firms within the same industry often place different demands on their salespeople. Nevertheless, the empirical evidence prompts several major conclusions:[18]

1. *Different role partners emphasize different types of expectations.* Salespeople see some role partners as being concerned with what they do—company superiors focus on the functional aspects of the job such as handling back charges and adjustments, expediting orders, and supervising installations. Others are more concerned with how they do it—family members are concerned about the salesperson's hours of work and customers are interested in the ability of the salesperson to get along with them.

2. *Perceived role expectations are consistent among salespeople.* Salespeople are consistent in their company's expectations as communicated by company superiors and sales managers. On the other hand, salespeople do not perceive similar role expectations regarding the demands of family members. These demands are much more likely to differ from salesperson to salesperson. This suggests that no matter what the company expects in hours of work, relations with customers, travel, and the like, a substantial number of its salespeople are likely to be in conflict with their family's expectations.

3. *Most business-to-business salespeople are plagued by ambiguity concerning some aspect of their job.* For example, salespeople indicate they are often uncertain about company policies, how company superiors are evaluating their performance, or what their sales managers expect. In comparison, very few are uncertain about the expectations or evaluations of customers or family members. This suggests customers and family members communicate their role expectations more effectively than company superiors do. Perhaps this is not surprising since a representative faces customers and family members almost daily, whereas company policies are communicated through infrequent sales meetings, e-mails, and other less effective means.

4. *Most salespeople perceive conflicts between some company policies or expectations and their customers' demands.* Customers are usually seen as demanding more from their salesperson—more services, more honesty, more price concessions, and so

forth. Sales managers and other company executives are seen as demanding that the salesperson hold down selling expenses and customer concessions. Most salespeople believe that their company superiors and customers expect them to travel, work flexible hours, and be available to customers in the evenings and on weekends. Unfortunately, they also believe these expectations conflict with the desires of their families. Although work–family conflicts are not unique to salespeople, their pervasiveness in the sales force should be recognized as a major influence on job satisfaction and performance.

Consequences of Conflict and Ambiguity

Most people experience occasional role conflict and ambiguity. In small doses, role conflict and ambiguity may be good for the individual and the organization. When there are no disagreements and no uncertainty associated with a role, people can become so comfortable in the position that they constantly strive to preserve the status quo. Some role stress, therefore, can lead to useful adaptation and change. In sum, there is a level of hostility below which conflict and ambiguity may be benign but above which they will be negative. Excessive role stress can have dysfunctional consequences, both psychological and behavioral, for the individual and the organization, as Exhibit 6.5 indicates. Consider first the psychological consequences.

Psychological Consequences

When a salesperson perceives that role partners have conflicting expectations about how the job should be performed, the salesperson becomes the "person in the middle." How can they satisfy the demands of one role partner without incurring the wrath or disappointment of others? Take, for example, the customer service representatives at Verizon Communications. A new performance evaluation program placed a great deal of emphasis on selling new products and services to customers who called in with questions (and often problems). Salespeople felt they had to put the sales function ahead of helping customers with problems and questions. Ultimately, they saw their role as problem solving and providing service to customers, while the company viewed them as salespeople. This situation can produce psychological conflict, which is uncomfortable for the individual. Job tensions increase, and the salesperson tends to worry more about conditions and events at work than usual. The salesperson's overall feelings of anxiety increase, and the rep is likely to become less satisfied with role partners, the company, and the job.[19]

Perceived role ambiguity can have similar negative consequences. When salespeople feel they lack the information necessary to perform the job adequately, or they don't know what role partners expect of them, they lose confidence in their ability to perform the sales role successfully. Salespeople tend to worry a great deal about whether they are doing the right thing and about how role partners will react

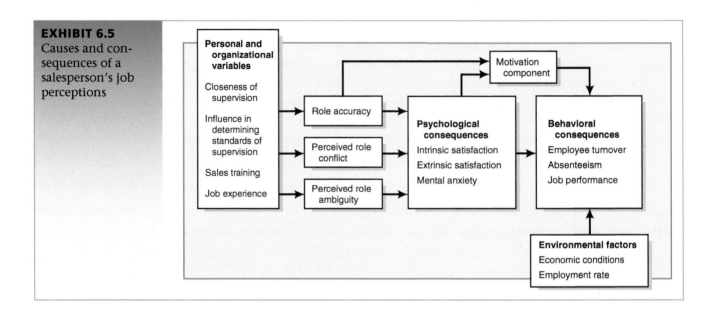

EXHIBIT 6.5
Causes and consequences of a salesperson's job perceptions

to their performance. They may also lose confidence in role partners and blame them for failing to communicate their expectations and evaluations adequately. Like conflict, then, perceived role ambiguity is likely to increase a salesperson's mental anxiety and decrease job satisfaction.[20]

Although both conflict and ambiguity affect job satisfaction negatively, they do so somewhat differently. Perceived role conflict primarily affects extrinsic job satisfaction but has little or no effect on the intrinsic satisfactions salespeople derive from the job. Salespeople's ability to obtain extrinsic rewards, such as more pay, a promotion, praise, and recognition, is influenced by role partners. Therefore, conflicts among the expectations and demands of those role partners not only make it more difficult for salespeople to satisfy their demands but also jeopardize the salesperson's ability to earn desired extrinsic rewards. On the other hand, such conflicts may not restrain their ability to obtain intrinsic satisfactions from the job. Even when two or more role partners cannot agree on how reps should perform, salespeople may still gain a sense of accomplishment from working or improving personal abilities.

Unlike perceived conflict, ambiguity has a negative impact on the intrinsic components of salespeople's job satisfaction as well as the extrinsic components.[21] When salespeople are uncertain about how they should be doing the job, whether they are doing it right, and how others are evaluating their performance, they are likely to lose self-confidence, and their self-esteem suffers. Ambiguity, therefore, reduces the ability to obtain intrinsic rewards and satisfactions from the job. Similarly, if salespeople are uncertain about how role partners are evaluating their performance, they become uncertain about their chances for promotion or pay increases. Finally, salespeople are likely to be dissatisfied with role partners who fail to make clear their expectations and evaluations, thus causing emotional discomfort in the sales force.

ETHICAL MOMENT Role Stress and Ethical Decision Making

Stress in selling is common and managing it effectively is important for the salesperson and the organization. One of the challenges is that some role conflict and ambiguity can actually motivate salespeople and serve to sharpen their sales skills. Unfortunately, too much stress can very quickly have significant negative consequences. This often manifests itself in the salesperson's ethical decision making.

One area where this issue is particularly acute is managing the customer relationship. It is not uncommon for salespeople to be under pressure to meet performance goals. In and of itself that is not a problem and is part of the sales process. However, if the salesperson is experiencing high levels of role conflict or ambiguity, the resulting role stress can create an environment where the salesperson is making decisions from a short-term, narrow-focused perspective. In those situations without a strong ethical decision making process it may seem more reasonable to offer customers gifts, bribes, or other concessions to close the sale. While that may seem like a good idea, it puts both the salesperson and company at great risk and almost certainly leads to dismissal once the activity has been discovered.

Why do salespeople engage in those activities with the real threat of dismissal once discovered? The short answer is because of role stress and its ability to influence decision making. Managing role stress is important for many reasons not the least of which are the ethical implications of experiencing too much role stress at the work place.

Question to Ponder:

- Can you identify other possible examples of how role stress (conflict, ambiguity) could impact a salesperson's ethical decision making?

Behavioral Consequences

Perceived role conflict and ambiguity can produce dysfunctional behavior consequences among the sales force. It is naive to think that a happy worker is invariably a productive worker, but evidence collected from a variety of occupations suggests that a worker's satisfaction influences job behavior. For instance, a negative relationship consistently appears between job satisfaction and absenteeism and employee turnover. Low satisfaction is also related to turnover among salespeople, although the relationship is moderated by economic conditions and the availability of alternative jobs.[22]

Another relationship that appears in studies of other occupations is a positive correlation between satisfaction and performance, although there is controversy over the nature of the relationship. Some argue that high satisfaction leads to good performance; others argue that good performance makes workers more satisfied with their jobs. The available sales management literature seems to suggest a salesperson's job satisfaction is directly related to performance on the job and that conflict and ambiguity are negatively related to sales performance.[23] Role ambiguity and role conflict even affect whether sales managers and salespeople agree on how well the salesperson is doing the job.[24]

Managing Conflict and Ambiguity in a Salesperson

Given that conflict and ambiguity produce dysfunctional psychological and behavioral consequences for salespeople, the next question is: Can sales management do anything to hold conflicts and ambiguities at a reasonable level or help the salesperson deal with them when they occur? Evidence suggests that experienced salespeople perceive less conflict than less-experienced representatives.[25] Perhaps this is because salespeople who experience a great deal of conflict become dissatisfied and quit, whereas those who stay on the job do not perceive much conflict.

On the other hand, salespeople may learn with experience how to deal with conflict. They may learn demands that initially appear to be in conflict turn out to be compatible or they learn how to resolve conflicts so they are no longer stressful. Finally, salespeople may build up psychological defense mechanisms to screen out conflicts and ease the tension. If these hypotheses are correct, sales training programs can prepare new salespeople to deal with conflicts they will encounter on the job.

Perceived role conflict also seems to be affected by how closely salespeople are supervised. When sales managers structure and define their roles, salespeople seem to experience more conflict. Perhaps close supervision decreases flexibility in dealing with diverse role expectations. Another way to reduce role conflict, then, is to give salespeople a greater voice in what they do and how they do it.

There also seem to be things management can do to reduce role ambiguity. It also depends on experience, so sales training can help salespeople cope with it. Perhaps more importantly, it depends on the manager's supervisory style. Less ambiguity is experienced when salespeople are closely supervised and have some influence over the standards used to control and evaluate their performance.[26] Closely supervised salespeople are more aware of the expectations and demands of their supervisors, and inconsistent behaviors can be more quickly brought to their attention.

Similarly, salespeople who have input in determining the standards by which they are evaluated are more familiar with those standards, which tends to reduce role ambiguity. One direct way of affecting the closeness with which salespeople feel supervised is by altering the sales manager's span of control by changing the number of people reporting directly to the manager. An increase in the span of control tends to increase salespeople's perceived role ambiguity. Reducing it tends to allow closer supervision, which tends to make job-related issues clearer to salespeople.[27]

Close supervision can thus be a two-edged sword. While it can reduce ambiguity, supervision that is too close can increase a salesperson's role conflict and job dissatisfaction because the salesperson may no longer feel there is enough latitude to deal effectively with the customer or enough creativity to service the account. The problem is particularly acute when sales managers use coercion and threats to direct the salespeople under them.[28] Sales managers must walk a very fine line in how closely and by what means they supervise the people under them.

ROLE ACCURACY

The role component of the model contains three variables: role conflict, role ambiguity, and role accuracy. It is appropriate to highlight role accuracy separately for two reasons. First, role accuracy can be viewed both generally and from the stand-point of specific linkages. When it is viewed generally, its impact and antecedents are similar to those for role conflict and ambiguity. But additional insight is gained by looking at role accuracy with respect to specific linkages. Second, role accuracy specifically influences the motivation component of the model, and to understand role accuracy, it is necessary to assess its impact on the salesperson's motivation to perform.[29]

Nature of Role Accuracy

A salesperson has accurate role perceptions when he or she correctly understands what role partners expect when performing the job. Role accuracy involves such considerations as whether salespeople correctly think they can negotiate on price, promise shorter delivery times than normal, and handle back charges and adjust-ments for customers.

Activities* 1980s	Now	
1. *Selling* Plan selling activities Qualify prospects Present sales presentation Handle objections	*Selling* Plan selling activities Qualify prospects Present sales presentation Handle objections	**EXHIBIT 6.6** Common activities, performance criteria, and rewards for industrial salespeople
2. *Working with orders* Correct, expedite orders	*Working with orders* Correct, expedite orders	
3. *Servicing the product* Supervise installation Train customers	*Servicing the product* Supervise installation Train customers	
4. *Information management* Receive feedback from clients Provide technical information to clients Provide feedback to superiors	*Information management* Receive feedback from clients Provide technical information to clients Provide feedback to superiors	
5. *Servicing the account* Assist with inventory control Handle local advertising	*Servicing the account* Assist with inventory control Handle local advertising	
6. *Conference/meetings* Attend local/regional/national sales meetings	*Conference/meetings* Attend local/regional/national sales meetings	
7. *Training/recruiting* Identify, recruit, and train new salespeople	*Training/recruiting* Identify, recruit, and train new salespeople	
8. *Entertaining* Entertain clients consistent with company policies	*Entertaining* Entertain clients consistent with company policies	
9. *Travel* Travel as required by customer demand	*Travel* Travel as required by customer demand	
10. *Work with channel members* Maintain relationships with distributors	*Work with channel members* Maintain relationships with distributors	

EXHIBIT 6.6	**Activities* 1980s**	**Now**
Common activities, performance criteria, and rewards for industrial salespeople (continued)	NEW	*Relationship management* Build relationships with customers Maintain relationship with current customers Networking inside customer operations
	NEW	*Team management* Managing team interactions with customers Mentoring new salespeople inside sales team
	NEW	*Technology management* Communication with customers using new technologies Incorporate new communication skills consistent with customer demands

Performance Criteria
Total sales volume and volume increase over last year
Degree of quota attainment
Selling expenses and their decrease versus last year
Profitability of sales and their increase over last year
New accounts generated
Improvement in service provided to customers
Customer satisfaction of sales relationship

Rewards
Pay
   Increased take-home pay
   Increased bonuses and other financial incentives
Promotion
   Higher level job
   Better territory
Nonfinancial incentives (contests, travel, etc.)
Special recognition (clubs, awards, etc.)
Job security
Feeling of self-fulfillment
Feeling of worthwhile accomplishment
Opportunity for personal growth and accomplishment
Opportunity for independent thought and action

Sources: Adapted from William Moncrief, Greg. W. Marshall, and Feliecia G. Lassk, "A Contemporary Taxonomy of Sales Positions," *Journal of Personal Selling & Sales Management* 26, no. 1 (Winter 2006), pp. 56–65; and Greg W. Marshall, William C. Moncrief, and Felicia G. Lassk, "The Current State of Sales Force Activities," *Industrial Marketing Management* 28 (1999), pp. 87–98.

More specifically, role inaccuracy arises when the salesperson incorrectly perceives the relationships between activities and performance dimensions, or between performance dimensions and rewards. In terms of the model in Exhibit 6.1, this type of role inaccuracy relates to the motivation component and, more particularly, to the expectancy and instrumentality estimates. For example, a salesperson who does not accurately perceive how making more calls leads to more sales has linkage role inaccuracy with respect to this expectancy, or activity–performance, linkage. If the rep does not accurately perceive the relationship between more sales and a promotion, the person has linkage role inaccuracy with respect to this instrumentality, or performance–reward, linkage.

There is great potential for this type of specific linkage role inaccuracy among salespeople because all three components—activities, performance dimensions, and rewards—are multidimensional. There are consequently a great many linkages, which increases the chances a salesperson will have inaccurate perceptions about at least some of them. Some common activities in which salespeople are expected to engage, the criteria used to evaluate their performance, and the rewards typically used to motivate them are listed in Exhibit 6.6.[30] Not all salespeople in every firm are expected to engage in all these activities, nor are they evaluated on each performance dimension. Neither do all firms provide the same rewards to the same degree. This makes it very difficult to discuss linkage inaccuracy in a way that is useful to sales managers in general. One has to get down to the level of the individual firm and the linkages operating there to discuss the concept.

In addition, the many roles of the salesperson change over time. As noted in Exhibit 6.6, salespeople are being asked to communicate with customers in new ways, employing new technologies. Equally important is the realization that in many cases the salesperson will no longer be the only person communicating with the customer. Indeed, the salesperson may only be one individual in a complex relationship that consists of technical specialists, customer service representatives, and others who interact with the customer on a regular basis. Salespeople become "relationship managers" in addition to holding the traditional roles associated with selling.

SUMMARY

This chapter, the first on implementing the sales program, presented a model of salesperson performance. In addition, the chapter examined the critical component of the model, the salesperson's role perceptions.

The model suggests that a salesperson's performance is a function of five basic factors: (1) role perceptions, (2) aptitude, (3) skill level, (4) motivation, and (5) personal, organizational, and environmental variables. There is substantial interaction among the components. A salesperson who is deficient with respect to any one could be expected to perform poorly.

The role perceptions of the salesperson are defined largely through the expectations, demands, and pressures communicated by his or her role partners. Role partners are people both within and outside the company who are affected by the way the salesperson performs the job. Three major variables create an individual's role perceptions: role accuracy, perceived role ambiguity, and perceived role conflict. Role accuracy refers to the degree to which the salesperson's perceptions of his or her role partners' demands are accurate. Perceived role ambiguity occurs when the salesperson does not believe he or she has the information to perform the job adequately. Perceived role conflict arises when a salesperson believes that the demands of two or more of his or her role partners are incompatible.

The role of salesperson is particularly susceptible to feelings of ambiguity and conflict and to forming inaccurate perceptions. There are three reasons for this: (1) It is at the boundary of the firm, (2) the salesperson's relevant role set includes many other people both within and outside the firm, and (3) the position of sales rep often requires a good deal of innovativeness.

Aptitude refers to the salesperson's innate ability to do the job and includes such things as physical factors, mental abilities, and personality characteristics. Aptitude is a constraint on the person's ability to perform the sales job given an adequate understanding of the role to be performed, motivation, and learned skills and the absence of other constraints.

Skill level refers to the person's learned proficiency at performing the necessary tasks. It is different from aptitude. Whereas aptitude consists of relatively enduring personal abilities, skills are proficiency levels that can change rapidly with learning and experience.

Motivation refers to the effort the salesperson desires to expend on each activity or task associated with the job such as calling on potential new accounts or developing sales presentations. The motivation to expend effort on any particular task depends on (1) expectancy—the salesperson's estimate of the probability that expending effort on the task will lead to improved performance on some dimension—and (2) valence for performance—the salesperson's perception of the desirability of improving performance on that dimension. The valence for performance on any dimension is, in turn, a function of (1) instrumentality—the salesperson's estimate of the probability that improved performance on that dimension will lead to increased attainment of particular rewards—and (2) valence for rewards—the salesperson's perception of the desirability of receiving increased rewards as a result of improved performance.

The personal, organizational, and environmental variables influence sales performance in two ways: (1) by directly facilitating or constraining performance and (2) by influencing and interacting with other performance determinants, such as role perceptions and motivation.

The performance of the salesperson affects the rewards the individual receives. There are two basic types of rewards: extrinsic rewards, which are controlled and bestowed by people other than the salesperson, and intrinsic rewards, which are those that people primarily attain for themselves.

The rewards received by a salesperson have a major impact on the individual's satisfaction with the job and the total work environment. Satisfaction can also be of two types. Intrinsic satisfaction is related to the intrinsic rewards the salesperson obtains from the job, such as satisfaction with the work and the opportunities it provides for personal growth and sense of accomplishment. Extrinsic satisfaction is associated with the extrinsic rewards bestowed on the salesperson, such as pay, chances for promotion, and supervisory and company policies.

KEY TERMS

role accuracy	valences for performance	extrinsic rewards
perceived role conflict	instrumentalities	intrinsic rewards
perceived role ambiguity	valences for rewards	job satisfaction
motivation	organizational citizenship	
expectancies	behaviors (OCBs)	

BREAKOUT QUESTIONS

1. The president of Part-I-Tyme, manufacturer of salty snack foods, was dismayed over the dismal sales results reported for the first six months. A new product, a deluxe cookie, had been taste tested and consumers' responses were very positive. Part-I-Tyme's sales force consisted of 500 individuals in 25 sales districts around the country. They called on buyers for grocery chains and large restaurant chains. Over the years, the company had developed an excellent reputation with their customers. Part-I-Tyme's president was convinced the product would be well received by the company's customers and ultimately by consumers. However, it was obvious that something was wrong. The sales force had not really been enthusiastic about the product. How would you determine the nature of the problem? Can you use the model of salesperson performance in this situation?

2. Although many different kinds of tests exist, their ability to predict sales performance has been weak. How do you account for this?

3. A sales representative for High Speed Technologies is faced with a demand from an important customer that is in direct conflict with company policies. The customer wants several product modifications with no change in price. What can the sales rep do to handle this conflict?

4. The sales force at Fire Protection Systems, a manufacturer of fire prevention systems for industrial applications, have been told they will now have to sell small fire extinguishers to the retail market. They have never sold in the retail market, and the company is going up against much larger competitors that have sold in that market for many years. What role problems are likely to occur?

5. Maria Gomez-Simpson, a customer service rep with GRA–JUS Associates, spends considerable time traveling to various customer offices. As a result, she often arrives home late. Maria asked her manager if she could rearrange her Thursday work schedule to allow her to attend an evening class at a local college. Which of the following statements best reflects how to manage the conflict created by Maria's request?

    a. "Since we're talking about only one night, go ahead, sign up for the course, and we'll work out the details."
    b. "We need to discuss this first to see if there is some way you can be back most of the Thursdays in time for your course and still get the job done as well."
    c. "We know that you get home late on certain days, but it is part of the job. Maybe you can take the course some other time."

6. Ethical Question. You are the sales manager at Uptick pharmaceuticals and have been reviewing the sales performance of your team. One of your best salespeople, William Bedford, has been performing significantly below expectations for the last six months. His sales are down and he is making few customer calls. You call him in for a meeting and he reports that his wife has been ill and he has been having to take on further responsibilities at home. He indicates she is doing better but expects her to be recovering for the 12–18 months. As a key salesperson in a large territory you know that is too long for the territory to be underrepresented. What should you do about Mr. Bedford? How would you address the needs of the sales territory?

LEADERSHIP CHALLENGE: TOUGH CHOICES

Michael Yardley was worried as he hung up from a phone call with Megan Barnes, the most promising salesperson at Spring Board Technologies (SBT). Michael had hired Megan out of college only four years ago, and already Megan had distinguished herself as one of the best salespeople in the company. This was saying something as SBT had a worldwide sales force of more than 2,000 salespeople. Michael had already promoted Megan to senior sales account manager. In addition, Melissa Hendrix, executive vice president of sales for the company, had made it known to Michael and Megan that she was well aware of her performance and had targeted her for a fast track in the company.

Now Michael had just learned Megan was going to have her first baby, and he was having serious doubts about her future. Megan had married her college sweetheart soon after graduation. He was an engineer, and they had both come to enjoy the benefits of two incomes. Megan's sales success had surprised her. Her natural ability coupled with a focus on contemporary selling had given her the opportunity to build significant partnerships with some of SBT's largest customers. At the same time, Megan had communicated to Michael that, at some point, she wanted to have a family. Megan was experiencing a great deal of role conflict. She wanted to take the time to start a family (she had thought she would take five years off while the baby was getting ready to start school) but also wanted to continue her career at SBT. At the same time, Michael was concerned about losing his star salesperson, dealing with customer disappointment, and having to tell Melissa that a person she had felt was on the fast track at the company may be leaving to start a family. He knew there were no easy answers and was considering the options for Megan as well as SBT.

Questions

1. If you were Megan, what would you do and why? What factors should most influence her decision? Is this an either/or choice?

2. If you were Michael, how would you handle this situation? What advice would you offer to Megan?

3. If you were Melissa, would you get involved in Megan's decision? Why or why not?

ROLE-PLAY: QUEENS PARK SOLDIERS

Situation

Jerry Momper loves sports. He has just finished up a degree in sports marketing at Pinnacle University in London and to his great pleasure, he is in the first month of his dream job, a sales person (the title is account manager) for small- and medium-sized accounts for the Queens Park Soldiers (his favorite soccer team). In general, he will be responsible for developing new customer relationships with companies in London and the surrounding area, as well as working on enhancing relationships with firms that are already loyal customers of the Soldiers. His "product" is blocks of seats, special boxes and events at historic Loftus Road Stadium, as well as Soldiers promotions that can be held at various places of businesses as a marketing campaign for the customer's business

The problem (actually its more of an opportunity) is this is a brand new position. Over the years the team has had a major account position, similar to the one Jerry now has, but more focused on big companies that might want to send a lot of people to games. The major account manager had also worked with smaller firms as needed, but Jerry's position allows the team to better tap into a lucrative market in the area. The person who continues to hold the major account manager position is Rex Wicke, a great guy about 40 years old who has been with the team in one administrative job or another for 19 years. Rex is something of an icon in sports marketing in the London area, and Jerry knows he can learn a lot from him.

Jerry has decided to set up a meeting to get a better feel for some important aspects of his new role at the Soldiers and more specifically some of the activities he may be asked to perform. Having a sales management course at Pinnacle University, Jerry knows a lot about salesperson performance from the class but has never worked as a salesperson before.

Characters in the Role-Play

Jerry Momper, small- and medium-sized account manager, Queens Park Soldiers
Rex Wicke, major account manager, Queens Park Soldiers

Assignment

Break into pairs, with one student playing each character. It doesn't matter what the actual gender mix of your pair is. Before you stage the meeting between Jerry and Rex, work separately to come up with a set of role issues you each believe will be important to discuss for Jerry's benefit in the new job. Also, jot down some of the more important sales activities you anticipate will be part of the new position. Then get together and role-play the meeting between Jerry and Rex. Share your ideas—especially pay attention to potential sources of role problems. To the extent possible, come to agreement between the two of you about some performance criteria and rewards that might be appropriate for this new position.

MINICASE: VAUGHN MANUFACTURING COMPANY

Vaughn Manufacturing is a London-based automobile parts manufacturer. Specifically, it manufactures crankshafts, a key component of the engine, and sells directly to automobile manufacturers (also known as original equipment manufacturers, or OEMs) like General Motors, as opposed to selling to engine manufacturers. While selling directly to OEMs grants Vaughn a higher "Tier 1" status in the automobile business and direct access to the biggest players, it also means Vaughn has very little leverage in negotiating with the much larger OEMs.

England is by far the largest and most important sales territory for Vaughn, and its district sales manager is Keith Horton, a 26-year company veteran. Horton personally recruited several members of his team, who he calls "young guns," and takes great pride that the team's sales volume is consistently the highest in the company. Horton's managerial style can best be described as aggressive, and he often insults or pressures his salespeople in order to increase their performance. In his words, "auto-manufacturing is a cut-throat business, and I want my salespeople to be tough. I want to be the toughest thing that my salespeople ever face, so that customers will seem like pussycats by comparison." Although he closely watches the performance of the salespeople, the company provides little training or specific sales guidance. He feels that salespeople learn toughness by figuring things out for themselves.

The newest salesperson on the team is Raul Sajak, a 23-year-old recent college graduate. Raul is highly intelligent, graduating at the top of his class, sensitive, and extraordinarily good with relating to people. Although he could have worked in nearly any business, he wanted to join Vaughn, in part because he was a successful retail automobile salesperson throughout college and loved doing it. He is married and is preparing for the arrival of a new baby.

Although Raul started strong in his first year at Vaughn, he has struggled recently, being well below quota in nearly every sales category for the last quarter of the fiscal year. As the automobile market becomes more competitive, customers have been more difficult, making sales negotiations more complex, and creating further challenges for Raul. Vaughn's attorneys require that Raul and the other salespeople negotiate specific contract terms with respect to legal liability, but OEMs now require that suppliers sign their standard purchase agreement without negotiation if the supplier wants to sell at a given price. Furthermore, OEMs have very specific product specification requirements that Vaughn engineers tell Raul they will have trouble meeting. Raul often feels caught in the middle between the various interests inside the company. Compounding the problem is the feeling that he cannot go to Horton for guidance.

In addition, Raul is uncomfortable with the intimidation tactics of Horton and the OEMs. Horton has encouraged his sales team to bluff when asked about the wholesale cost of the crankshafts in order to make a sale and threaten to walk out of the sales negotiation with a "take it or leave it" approach. Raul is concerned that he cannot use the friendly, open, and intelligent sales approach to which he is accustomed.

Horton does not understand Raul's falling performance: "I don't get it. Raul is compensated on a 100 percent commission basis, so he has the incentive to sell more and make a great deal of money. I even offer free tickets to local professional sporting events like soccer games and cricket matches when my salespeople meet or exceed sales goals. If he works as long as I have, he can be promoted to sales manager too."

Questions

1. Based on the model for salesperson performance, what are the possible causes for the diminished performance of Raul?
2. What can Horton do to improve the sales performance of Raul?

CHAPTER 7

Salesperson Performance: Motivating the Sales Force

LEARNING OBJECTIVES

Salespeople operate in a highly dynamic, stressful environment outside of the company. As we have already seen in Chapter 6, there are many factors that influence the salesperson's ability to perform. One of the most critical factors is motivation. It is very important that sales managers understand the process of motivation and be able to apply it to each individual in the sales force in such a manner as to maximize his or her performance potential.

After reading this chapter, you should be able to

- Understand the process of motivation.
- Discuss the effect of personal characteristics on salesperson motivation.
- Understand how an individual's career stage influences motivation.
- Discuss the effect of environmental factors on motivation.
- Discuss the effect of factors inside the company on motivation.

Unfortunately, many firms are not successful in developing systems or programs that are appropriate for the marketing challenges they face and the kinds of people they employ. Consequently, their salespeople are either undermotivated or stimulated to expend too much time and effort on the wrong tasks and activities. In either case, sales effectiveness and productivity suffer.

In view of the complicated nature of motivation and its critical role in sales management, the rest of this chapter as well as Chapter 11 (on compensation) are devoted to the subject. This chapter examines what is known about motivation as a psychological process and how a person's motivation to perform a given job is affected by environmental, organizational, and personal variables. Chapter 11 discusses compensation plans and incentive programs sales managers use to stimulate and direct salespeople's efforts.

THE PSYCHOLOGICAL PROCESS OF MOTIVATION

Most industrial and organizational psychologists view motivation as an individual's choice to (1) initiate action on a certain task, (2) expend a certain amount of effort on that task, and (3) persist in expending effort over a period of time.[1] For our purposes, motivation is viewed as the amount of effort the salesperson desires to expend on each activity or task associated with the job. This may include calling on potential new accounts, developing sales presentations, and managing technology. The psychological process involved in determining how much effort a salesperson will want to expend and some variables that influence the process are shown in Exhibit 7.1.

The conceptual framework outlined in Exhibit 7.1 is based on a view of motivation known as *expectancy theory*. A number of other theories of motivation exist,[2] and many of them are useful for explaining at least a part of the motivation process. However, expectancy theory incorporates and ties together, at least implicitly, important aspects of many of those theories. It has been the subject of much empirical research in sales management, and it also provides a useful framework for guiding the many decisions managers must make when designing effective motivational programs for a sales force. Consequently, the remainder of this discussion focuses primarily on expectancy theory, although several other theories are mentioned later when we examine how personal characteristics affect the motivation of different individuals.

Major Components of the Model

The model in Exhibit 7.1 suggests that the *level of effort expended* by a salesperson on each *job-related task* will lead to *some level of performance on some performance dimension*. These dimensions include, for example, total sales volume, profitability of sales, and new accounts generated. It is assumed the salesperson's performance

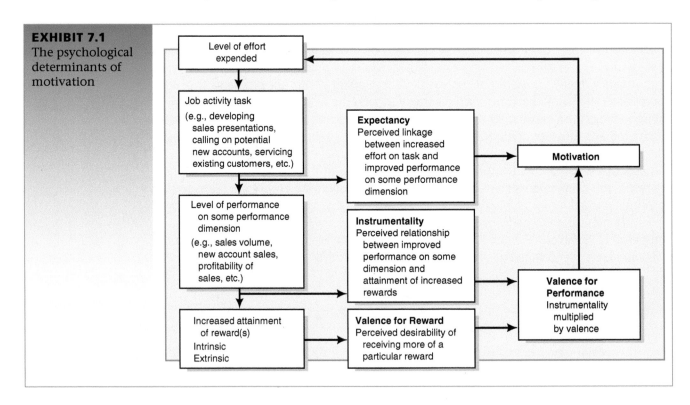

EXHIBIT 7.1
The psychological determinants of motivation

on some of these dimensions will be evaluated by superiors and *compensated with one or more rewards*. These might be externally mediated rewards, like a promotion, or internally mediated rewards, such as feelings of accomplishment or personal growth.

A salesperson's *motivation* to expend effort on a given task is determined by three sets of perceptions: (1) expectancies—the perceived linkages between expending more effort on a particular task and achieving improved performance; (2) *instrumentalities*—the perceived relationship between improved performance and the attainment of increased rewards; and (3) *valence for rewards*—the perceived attractiveness of the various rewards the salesperson might receive.

Expectancies—Perceived Links between Effort and Performance

Expectancies are the salesperson's perceptions of the link between job effort and performance. Specifically, expectancy is the person's probability estimate that expending effort on some task will lead to improved performance on a dimension. Sales managers are concerned with two aspects of their subordinates' expectancy perceptions: magnitude and accuracy. The following statement illustrates an expectancy perception: "If I increase my calls on potential new accounts by 10 percent [effort], then there is a 50 percent chance [expectancy] that my volume of new account sales will increase by 10 percent during the next six months [performance level]." Key questions that arise from a salesperson's expectancies and their implications for sales managers are identified in Exhibit 7.2.

Accuracy of Expectancies

The accuracy of expectancy estimates refers to how clearly the salesperson understands the relationship between effort expended on a task and the resulting achievement on some performance dimension. When salespeople's expectancies are inaccurate, they are likely to misallocate job efforts. They spend too much time and energy on activities that have little impact on performance and not enough on activities with a greater impact. Consequently, some authorities refer to attempts to improve the accuracy of expectancy estimates as "trying to get salespeople to work smarter rather than harder."[3]

Working smarter requires that the salesperson have an accurate understanding of what activities are most critical—and therefore should receive the greatest effort—for concluding a sale. Of course, a single activity might be carried out in a number of ways. For instance, a salesperson might employ any of several different sales techniques or strategies when making a sales presentation. Therefore, working smarter also requires an ability to adapt the techniques used to the needs and preferences of a given buyer.

As a result of the war on terrorism and events in the Middle East, salespeople have learned to adapt to a new selling environment. For example, due to security concerns as well as higher travel costs customers and salespeople are considering

EXHIBIT 7.2 Important questions and management implications of salespeople's expectancy estimates	**Question**	**Management Implications**
	Accuracy of Expectancy Estimates	• If substantial variation exists, salespeople may devote too much effort to activities considered unimportant by management, and vice versa. This might indicate a need for the following: —More extensive/explicit sales training. —Closer supervision. —Evaluation of salesperson's effort and time allocation as well as performance.
	• Are salespeople's views of the linkage between activities and performance outcomes consistent with those of sales managers?	
	• Are there large variations in expectancy perceptions between high performers and low performers in the sales force?	• If high-performing salespeople hold reasonably consistent views concerning which activities are most important in producing good performance, those views might be used as a model for sales training/professional development programs.
	Magnitude of Expectancy Estimates	
	• All other things equal, the higher the salesperson's expectancy estimates, the greater the individual's motivation to expend effort. —Do personal characteristics of salespeople influence the size of their expectancies? Overall self-esteem? Perceived competence? Mental ability (Intelligence)? Previous sales experience?	• If such relationships are found, they may suggest additional criteria for recruitment/selection.
	—Do perceptions of uncertainty or constraints in the environment (e.g., materials shortages, recession, etc.) reduce salespeople's expectancy estimates?	• During periods of economic uncertainty, management may have to change performance criteria, evaluation methods, or compensation systems to maintain desired levels of effort from the sales force (e.g., lower quotas, reward servicing rather than selling activities).

other ways of communicating with one another. As a result, presentation skills are more important than ever as Web-conferencing and teleconferencing are replacing the one-on-one presentation. As one management consultant put it, "If I do a teleconference, I'll have to prepare much more of a presentation." These kinds of changes have led to new skills and the reinforcement of existing ones. It is important that management motivate salespeople to expend effort on appropriate activities or approaches that can increase performance and lead to greater satisfaction within the sales force.

Unfortunately, it is possible for a salesperson to misjudge the true relationship between the effort expended on a particular task and resulting performance. When this happens, the salesperson misallocates efforts. The rep spends too much time and energy on activities that have relatively little impact on performance and not enough on activities with greater impact. Making matters even more complex, research suggests that successful salespeople can overestimate their abilities and expend too much effort attempting to close the sale. In these situations salespeople believe that with a little more effort (and resources) they will be successful.[4]

Research suggests that a salesperson's immediate superior, with presumably greater knowledge and experience, will more accurately perceive the linkages between effort and performance. If this is true, then inaccurate expectancy perceptions can be improved through closer contact between salespeople and their supervisors. Expanded sales training programs, closer day-to-day supervision of the sales force, and periodic review of each salesperson's time and effort by the supervisor should improve the accuracy of expectancy estimates.

Salespeople often complain that supervisors have an unrealistic view of conditions in the field. In addition, they do not realize what it takes to make a sale.[5] If these complaints are valid, managers' perceptions of the linkages between effort and performance may not be appropriate criteria for judging the accuracy of salespeople's expectancies. It may be better to use the expectancy estimates of the highest performing salesperson in the company as a model for sales training and supervision.

Magnitude of Expectancies

The magnitude of expectancy estimates reflects the salesperson's perceptions of his or her ability to control or influence his or her own job performance.

Several individual characteristics are likely to affect these expectancies. Some psychologists suggest that a salesperson's overall level of self-esteem and perceived ability to perform necessary tasks are positively related to the magnitude of the person's expectancy estimates.[6] Similarly, the salesperson's general intelligence and previous sales experience may influence the individual's perceived ability to improve performance through personal efforts. If these relationships are true, they may be useful supplementary criteria for the recruitment and selection of salespeople.

Environmental characteristics also influence a salesperson's perceptions of the linkages between effort and performance. How the salesperson perceives general economic conditions, territory potential, the strength of competition, restrictions on product availability, and so forth are all likely to affect his or her thoughts on how much sales performance can be improved by simply increasing efforts. The greater the environmental constraints a salesperson sees as restricting performance, the lower the rep's expectancy estimates will be. Turbulence in financial markets, and fluctuations in leading global economies have created a great deal of economic uncertainty in many global markets. This has led companies to reevaluate their purchases, and consequently, salespeople are faced with a much more complex and difficult selling environment. Therefore, managers may find it desirable to change performance criteria or evaluation methods during periods of economic uncertainty to maintain desired levels of effort from the sales force.

EXHIBIT 7.3
Factors influencing the motivation process

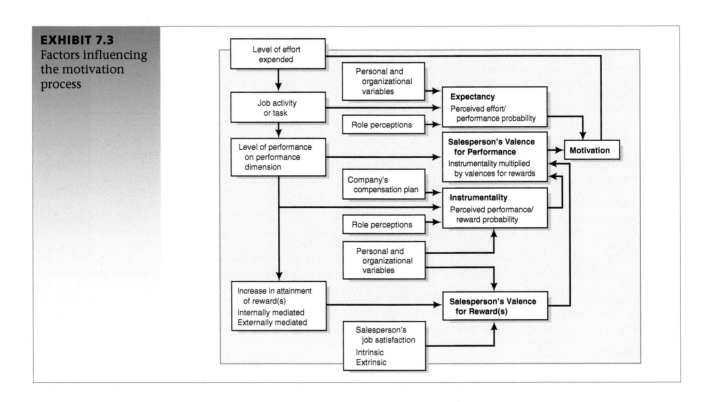

As Exhibit 7.3 indicates, personal and organizational characteristics affect the magnitude and accuracy of salespeople's expectancy perceptions. Managers must consider these factors when deciding on supervisory policies, compensation, and incentive plans so their subordinates' expectancies will be as accurate as possible. The factors that affect salespeople's expectancy estimates, along with their managerial implications, are discussed later in this chapter.

Instrumentalities—Perceived Links between Performance and Rewards

Like expectancies, instrumentalities are probability estimates made by the salesperson. They are the individual's perceptions of the link between job performance and various rewards. Specifically, an instrumentality is a salesperson's estimate of the probability that an improvement in performance on some dimension will lead to a specific increase in a particular reward. The reward may be more pay, winning a sales contest, or promotion. As with expectancies, sales managers should be concerned with both the magnitude and the accuracy of their subordinates' instrumentalities.

Accuracy of Instrumentalities

The accuracy of instrumentality estimates refers to the true linkages between performance on various dimensions and the attainment of rewards as determined by management practices and policies on sales performance evaluation and rewards for levels of performance.[7] Exhibit 7.4 identifies some important questions for sales management regarding a salesperson's instrumentality estimates and their implications. These policies and practices may be misperceived by the salesperson leading the individual to concentrate on improving performance in areas that are less important to management and ultimately become disillusioned with his or her ability to attain rewards.

Thus, it is important to compare salespeople's instrumentality perceptions with stated company policies and management perceptions of the true or desired linkages between performance and rewards. If salespeople do not accurately perceive how performance is rewarded in the firm, management must improve the accuracy of those perceptions. This is done through closer supervision and more direct feedback about evaluation and the determination of rewards.

Magnitude of Instrumentalities

One variable that has a notable impact on the magnitude of instrumentality estimates is the firm's compensation plan. For example, a salesperson compensated

Question	Management Implications	EXHIBIT 7.4
Accuracy of Instrumentality Estimates • Are salespeople's views of the linkage between performance on various dimensions and the rewards they will receive consistent with those of sales managers?	• If substantial variation exists, salespeople may concentrate on aspects of performance considered relatively unimportant by management, and vice versa. This might indicate the need for the following: —More extensive/explicit sales training. —Closer supervision. —More direct feedback to salespeople concerning how performance is evaluated and how rewards are determined.	Important questions and management implications of salespeople's instrumentality estimates
Magnitude of Instrumentality Estimates • How are salespeople's instrumentality estimates influenced by their compensation system (salary versus commission)? —Do salespeople on commission have higher instrumentality estimates for performance dimensions related to short-term sales volume? —Do salaried salespeople have higher instrumentalities for performance dimensions not directly related to short-term sales volume?	• If such relationships are found, managers should select the type of compensation plan that maximizes instrumentality estimates for those performance dimensions considered most crucial.	
• Do personal characteristics of salespeople influence the size of their instrumentality estimates? —Feelings of internal control? —Mental ability? —Sales experience?	• If such relationships are found, they may suggest additional criteria for recruitment/selection.	

largely or entirely by commission is likely to perceive a greater probability of attaining more pay by improving performance on the dimensions directly related to total sales volume (increase in total sales dollars or percentage of quota). On the other hand, the salaried salesperson is more likely to perceive a greater probability of receiving increased pay for improving performance on dimensions not directly related to short-term sales volume (new-account generation, reduction of selling expenses, or higher customer satisfaction).

The salesperson may also be rewarded with promotion, recognition, and feelings of accomplishment and may value these other rewards more highly than an increase in pay. In any case, the company's compensation plan is unlikely to affect the salesperson's perceptions of the linkages between performance and these nonfinancial rewards. Therefore, a compensation plan by itself is inadequate for explaining differences in motivation among salespeople.

The salesperson's personal characteristics also influence the magnitude of instrumentality estimates. For example, the individual's perception of whether he or she controls life's events or whether these events are determined by external forces beyond the individual's control. Specifically, the more salespeople believe they have internal control over their lives, the more likely they are to believe improved performance will result in the attainment of rewards.

Besides the firm's compensation policies, other organizational factors and the personal characteristics of the salespeople can influence both the magnitude and the accuracy of their instrumentality estimates and are explored in a later section of this chapter and in Chapter 11.

Valences for Rewards

Valences for rewards are salespeople's perceptions of the desirability of receiving increased rewards from improved performance. One question about valences that has always interested sales managers is whether there are consistent preferences among salespeople for specific kinds of rewards. Are some rewards consistently valued more highly than others?

Historically, many sales managers assume monetary rewards are the most highly valued and motivating rewards. They believe recognition and other psychological rewards are less valued and spur additional sales effort only under certain circumstances. Very little research has tested whether salespeople typically desire more pay than other rewards. Thus, the assumption is based largely on the perceptions of sales managers rather than on any evidence obtained from salespeople themselves.

There is evidence to suggest that other rewards are at least as important as financial compensation. One vice president of manufacturing for a large British based company puts it this way, "You can throw money at people—bonuses, incentives, rewards, additional skills training—and they're all important parts of what the manager offers. But praise is number one. It goes a long way when you give them that pat on the back." Recent research suggests that more and more companies consider other factors as or even more important than compensation. According to one

TECHNOLOGY   New Technology Is a Great Motivator

One of the challenges for sales managers is to find tools that will motivate the sales force. While money is certainly the primary motivator it is by no means the only one and, in many situations, there are other motivators that work as well or better.

Among the many different types of incentives available to managers, research suggests that one of the most effective is technology and more specifically the iPad. While millions of people enjoy using the iPad it remains, years after its introduction, a popular product with consumers and business. Research also confirms that it is a very popular incentive for both consumers and employees. Recently a health care system was looking to increase employee participation in workplace surveys. Historically, the company had about 65 percent participation but when they decided to offer an iPad as an incentive participation in the survey was over 80 percent.

In selling, a number of companies have used iPads in their incentive programs with positive affects. Sales professionals indicate that new technologies like the iPad generate more interest and raise awareness of the sales programs they are designed to promote. They note that technology provides a tangible incentive for the salesperson that lasts beyond money handed out in a check. Not surprisingly, new technology is particularly effective with younger salespeople who, as a group, are less motivated by money than their older, baby boomer colleagues.

sales executive, "Good management equals better performance and better motivation." The use of cash as an incentive has actually been declining. Companies are incorporating other forms of incentives such as debit/gift cards and leisure trips.[8]

An even more extreme view of financial rewards argues that linking pay to performance can have a negative effect on employees' motivation over time.[9] In this view, when pay is tied to performance, employees become less interested in what they are doing and more interested in simply capturing the reward. Intrinsic motivation is eaten away by extrinsic motivators like commissions and incentive contests, and employee creativity and quality of work may suffer as a result.

In light of these contradictory arguments and research results, is the conventional wisdom that salespeople desire money more than other rewards wrong? Or do salespeople simply desire a greater variety of rewards and work-related options than individuals in other kinds of jobs? Several studies focused on business-to-business salespeople generally support the conventional view. Their findings suggest that, on average, salespeople place a higher value on receiving more pay than any other reward, including intrinsic rewards like feelings of accomplishment or opportunities for personal growth. More recently, research in a nonsales setting confirms the importance of financial incentives as the primary reward, although recognition among peers was also found to be a significant motivator.[10] Informal surveys affirm that, while there are many different ways to motivate salespeople, compensation is still dominant. Overall, sales executives favor money, but offering other incentives makes sense in some cases. One high ranking sales executive summarized the view of many executives, "I'll go with cash [as the best incentive]. People can't always get away for trips. Besides, cash gives them a choice."[11]

No universal statements can be made about what kinds of rewards are most desired by salespeople and most effective for motivating them. Salespeople's valences for rewards are likely to be influenced by their satisfaction with the rewards they are currently receiving. Their satisfaction with current rewards, in turn, is influenced by their personal characteristics and by the compensation policies and management practices of their firm.

CAN THE MOTIVATION MODEL PREDICT SALESPERSON EFFORT AND PERFORMANCE?

Several studies have tested the ability of motivation models such as the ones outlined in Exhibits 7.1 and 7.3 to predict the amount of effort workers will expend on various job activities. The findings support the validity of such expectancy models of motivation.[12]

The salesperson model of performance suggests motivation is only one determinant of job performance. Thus, it seems inappropriate to use only motivation to predict differences in job performance. However, several studies have attempted to do just that, with surprising success reporting that an individual's motivation to expend effort can explain up to 40 percent of the variation in the overall job performance.[13]

It is nice to know that models like Exhibit 7.1 are valid descriptions of the psychological processes that determine a salesperson's motivation. However, there is a question of even greater relevance to sales managers as they struggle to design effective compensation and incentive programs: How are the three determinants of motivation—expectancy perceptions, instrumentality perceptions, and valences for rewards—affected by (1) differences in the personal characteristics of individuals, (2) environmental conditions, and (3) the organization's policies and procedures? The impact of each of these variables on the determinants of motivation is now examined in greater detail.

THE IMPACT OF A SALESPERSON'S PERSONAL CHARACTERISTICS ON MOTIVATION

When placed in the same job with the same compensation and incentive programs, different salespeople are likely to be motivated to expend widely differing amounts of effort. People with different personal characteristics have divergent perceptions of the links between effort and performance (expectancies) and between performance and rewards (instrumentalities). They are also likely to have different valences for the rewards they might obtain through improved job performance. The personal characteristics that affect motivation include (1) the individual's satisfaction with current rewards, (2) demographic variables, (3) job experience, and (4) psychological variables, particularly the salesperson's personality traits and attributions about why performance has been good or bad. Let's examine the impact of each of these sets of variables on salespeople's expectancies, instrumentalities, and valences.

It should also be noted that many of these personal characteristics change and interact with one another as a salesperson moves through various career stages. For instance, when people begin their first sales job, they are likely to be relatively young and have few family responsibilities, little job experience, and low task-specific self-esteem. Later in their careers, those salespeople will be older and have more family obligations, more experience, and more self-esteem. As a result, their valences for various rewards and their expectancy and instrumentality estimates are all likely to change as their careers progress. Consequently, a later section of this chapter examines how salespeople's motivation is likely to change during their careers and addresses some managerial implications of such changes.

Satisfaction

Is it possible to pay a salesperson too much? After a salesperson reaches a certain satisfactory level of compensation, does he or she lose interest in working to obtain still more money? Does the attainment of nonfinancial rewards similarly affect the salesperson's desire to earn more of those rewards? The basic issues underlying these questions are whether a salesperson's satisfaction with current rewards has any impact on the desire for more of those rewards or on different kinds of rewards. The relationship between satisfaction and the valence for rewards is different for rewards that satisfy lower-order needs (e.g., pay and job security) than for those that satisfy higher-order needs (e.g., promotions, recognition, opportunities for personal growth, self-fulfillment). Maslow's theory of needs hierarchy,[14] Herzberg's theory of motivation,[15] and Alderfer's existence, relatedness, and growth theory[16] all suggest that lower-order rewards are valued most highly by workers currently dissatisfied with their attainment of those rewards. In other words, the more dissatisfied a salesperson is with current pay, job security, and other rewards related to lower-order needs, the higher the desire to increase those rewards. In contrast, as salespeople become more satisfied with their attainment of lower-order rewards, the value of further increases in those rewards declines.

The theories of Maslow, Herzberg, and Alderfer further suggest that high-order rewards are not valued highly by salespeople until they are relatively satisfied with their low-order rewards. The greater the salesperson's satisfaction with low-order rewards, the higher the desire for high-order rewards.

Perhaps the most controversial aspect of Maslow's and Alderfer's theories is the proposition that high-order rewards have increasing marginal utility. The more satisfied a salesperson is with the high-order rewards received from the job, the higher the value he or she places on further increases in those rewards.

Research in industrial psychology provides at least partial support for these suggested relationships between satisfaction and the valence of low-order and high-order rewards. Some of the evidence is equivocal, though, and some propositions—particularly the idea that high-order rewards have increasing marginal utility—have not been tested adequately.

In general, research suggests that salespeople who are relatively satisfied with their current income (a lower-order reward) have lower valences for more pay than those who are less satisfied. Most of these studies also report salespeople who are relatively satisfied with their current attainment of higher-order rewards, such as recognition and personal growth, tend to have higher valences for more of those rewards than those who are less satisfied. However, the evidence is mixed concerning whether salespeople who are relatively satisfied with their lower-order rewards have significantly higher valences for higher-order rewards than those who are less satisfied, as the theories would predict.[17]

Demographic Characteristics

Demographic characteristics, such as age, family size, and education, also affect a salesperson's valence for rewards. At least part of the reason for this is that people with different characteristics tend to attain different levels of rewards and are therefore likely to have different levels of satisfaction with their current rewards. Although there is only limited empirical evidence regarding salespeople, some conclusions can be drawn from studies in other occupations.[18] These conclusions are summarized in Exhibit 7.5.

Generally, older, more experienced salespeople obtain higher levels of low-order rewards (e.g., higher pay, a better territory) than newer members of the sales force. Thus, it could be expected that more experienced salespeople are more satisfied with their lower-order rewards. Consequently, they should have lower valences for lower-order rewards and higher valences for higher-order rewards than younger and less experienced salespeople.

A salesperson's satisfaction with their current level of lower-order rewards may also be influenced by the demands and responsibilities he or she must satisfy with those rewards. A salesperson with a large family to support, for instance, is less likely to be satisfied with a given level of financial compensation than a single salesperson. Consequently, the more family members a salesperson must support, the higher the valence for more lower-order rewards.

Finally, individuals with more formal education are more likely to desire opportunities for personal growth, career advancement, and self-fulfillment than those with less education. Consequently, highly educated salespeople are likely to have higher valences for higher-order rewards.

Job Experience

As people gain experience on a job, they are likely to gain a clearer idea of how expending effort on particular tasks affects performance. Experienced salespeople are also more likely to understand how their superiors evaluate performance and how particular types of performance are rewarded in the company than their inexperienced counterparts. Consequently, a positive relationship is likely between the years a salesperson has spent on the job and the accuracy of his or her expectancy and instrumentality perceptions.

Demographic Variable	Valence for Higher-Order Rewards	Valence for Lower-Order Rewards	
Age	+	−	**EXHIBIT 7.5** The influence of demographic characteristics on valence for rewards
Family size		+	
Education	+	+	

In addition, the magnitude of a salesperson's expectancy perceptions may be affected by experience. As they gain experience, salespeople have opportunities to sharpen their selling skills; and they gain confidence in their ability to perform successfully. As a result, experienced salespeople are likely to have larger expectancy estimates than inexperienced ones.[19]

Psychological Traits

An individual's motivation also seems to be affected by psychological traits. Various traits can influence the magnitude and accuracy of a person's expectancy and instrumentality estimates, as well as valences for various rewards, as summarized in Exhibit 7.6. People with strong achievement needs are likely to have higher valences for such higher-order rewards as recognition, personal growth, and feeling of accomplishment. This is particularly true when they see their jobs as being relatively difficult to perform successfully.[20]

The degree to which individuals believe they have internal control over the events in their lives or whether those events are determined by external forces beyond their control also affects their motivation. Specifically, the more salespeople believe they have internal control over events, the more likely they are to think they can improve their performance by expending more effort. They also believe improved performance will be appropriately rewarded. Therefore, salespeople with a high *internal locus of control* are likely to have relatively high expectancy and instrumentality estimates.[21]

There is evidence that intelligence is positively related to feelings of internal control.[22] Those with higher levels of intelligence—particularly, verbal intelligence—are more likely to understand their jobs and their companies' reward policies quickly and accurately. Thus, their instrumentality and expectancy estimates are likely to be more accurate.

Finally, a worker's general feeling of self-esteem and perceived competence and ability to perform job activities (task-specific self-esteem) are both positively related to the magnitude of expectancy estimates.[23] Since such people believe they have the talents and abilities to be successful, they are likely to see a strong relationship between effort expended and good performance. Also, people with high levels of self-esteem are especially likely to attach importance to, and receive satisfaction from, good performance. Consequently, such people probably have higher valences for the higher-order, intrinsic rewards attained from successful job

EXHIBIT 7.6
The influence of psychological traits on the determinants of motivation

Personality Trait	Motivational Variables					
	Expectancies		Instrumentalities		Valences	
	Magnitude	Accuracy	Magnitude	Accuracy	Higher Order	Lower Order
High need achievement					+	
Internal locus of control	+		+			
Verbal intelligence	+	+	+	+		
General self-esteem	+				+	
Task-specific self-esteem	+				+	

performance, although the lone study to examine the impact of self-esteem on salespeople's reward valences failed to support this proposition.[24]

Performance Attributions

People try to identify and understand the causes of major events and outcomes in their lives. These are called performance attributions. A given individual might attribute the cause of a particular event—such as good sales performance last quarter—to the following:

1. Stable internal factors that are unlikely to change much in the near future, such as personal skills and abilities.

2. Unstable internal factors that may vary from time to time, such as the amount of effort expended or mood at the time.

3. Stable external factors, such as the nature of the task or the competitive situation in a particular territory.

4. Unstable external factors that might change next time, such as assistance from an unusually aggressive advertising campaign or good luck.

The nature of a salesperson's recent job performance, together with the kind of causes to which the rep attributes that performance, can affect the individual's expectancy estimates concerning the likelihood that increased effort will lead to improved performance in the future.[25] Various attributions' likely effects on the magnitude of a salesperson's expectancy estimates are summarized in Exhibit 7.7.

As Exhibit 7.7 indicates, expectancy estimates are likely to increase if recent successful sales performance is attributed to either stable or unstable internal causes or to stable external causes. For instance, salespeople are likely to attach even higher expectancies to future performance where they take credit for past success, as the result of either superior skill (stable internal cause) or personal effort (unstable internal cause). Salespeople's expectancies are also likely to increase where past success is attributed to a perception that the task is relatively easy (stable external cause). However, if past successful performance is attributed to an unstable external cause that could change in the next performance period—such as good

Performance Attribution	Impact on Magnitude of Salesperson's Expectancy Estimates	EXHIBIT 7.7
Good Performance Attributed to:		The influence of performance attributions on the magnitude of a Salesperson's Expectancy estimates
Stable internal cause	+	
Unstable internal cause	+	
Stable external cause	+	
Unstable external cause	0	
Poor Performance Attributed to:		
Stable internal cause	–	
Unstable internal cause	+	
Stable external cause	–	
Unstable external cause	0	

luck—there is no basis for salespeople to revise their expectancy estimates in any systematic way.

Suppose a salesperson performed poorly last quarter. Exhibit 7.7 indicates the impact of that poor performance on the individual's expectancy estimates is influenced by the causal attributions of the person. If the salesperson attributes poor past performance to stable causes that cannot be changed in the foreseeable future, such as low ability (stable internal cause) or a difficult competitive environment (stable external cause), his or her expectancy estimates are likely to be lower. Interestingly, research suggests that when salespeople attribute poor performance to stable internal causes (such as low ability), they blame themselves for the failure and may seek help from others in order to improve their performance next time. However, if the poor performance is attributed to an unstable internal cause— such as not expending sufficient effort to be successful—the person's expectancies may actually increase. The person may believe performance can be improved simply by changing the internal factor that caused the problem last time—by expending more effort.

A key to the application of attributions to performance is the accurate analysis of the salesperson's behavior and attitudes. If, for example, the salesperson consistently blames the customer, the competition, or the economic situation for poor performance when, in fact, the poor performance is due to internal factors (lack of effort or ability), then it is unlikely the problem can be easily corrected. Fortunately, research suggests that in most cases salespeople are realistic of their assessment of the attributing success or failure to specific external and internal factors.

Management Implications

The relationships between salespeople's personal characteristics and motivation has two broad implications for sales managers. First, people with certain characteristics are likely to understand their jobs and their companies' policies especially well. They also perceive higher expectancy and instrumentality links. Such people should be easier to train and be motivated to expend greater effort and achieve better performance. Therefore, as researchers and managers gain a better understanding of these relationships, it may be possible to develop improved selection criteria for hiring salespeople who are easy to train and motivate.

Second, and more important, some personal characteristics are related to the kinds of rewards salespeople value. This suggests sales managers should examine the characteristics of their salespeople and attempt to determine their relative valences for various rewards when designing compensation and incentive programs. Also, as the demographic characteristics of the sales force change, a manager should be aware that salespeople's satisfaction with rewards and their valences for future rewards might also change. There is little doubt that understanding the nature of the relationship between the salesperson's personal characteristics and motivation is difficult and requires a unique understanding of each individual. The Leadership box highlights how important it is to understand each individual in order to maximize their motivation.

CAREER STAGES AND SALESPERSON MOTIVATION

The previous discussion of the personal factors affecting motivation also suggests that salespeople's expectancy estimates and reward valences are likely to change as they move through different stages in their careers. As a person grows older and gains experience, demographic characteristics and financial obligations change, skills and confidence tend to improve, and the rewards he or she receives—as well as satisfaction with those rewards—are likely to change. We have seen that all of these factors can affect an individual's expectancies and reward valences.

LEADERSHIP   **How to Lead a Pack of Alpha Dogs**

In the case of younger generations of great employees, managers may have to learn to manage a team of aggressive, talented people who do not have automatic respect for their seniors. Dealing with this type of team can be a challenge, as subordinates will constantly be asking and expecting managers to prove that their approach is the right one. It might be easy to get caught on the defensive. Two options that generally present themselves in this scenario is to squelch the interferences and risk losing high potential employees to competitors; hear them out, be ready to make your own case and risk feeling resentful for being put on the spot.

Suggestions for managers of alpha dogs include:

1. Look for ways to have authentic, one-on-one conversations with your people. Generally, alphas are more likely to listen to you when they know their voices are being heard as well.

2. Remember that it's about serving your company and its people. Don't make customers pay for a misguided attempt at making things easier for you. Look for efficiencies to free you up to add value to the role.

3. Be an "A player" yourself. Talented, alpha employees pride themselves on being passionate and innovative. Make sure you bring this same passion to the table; look for areas to explore and add a level of personal challenge to the job in the same manner you expect from your employees.

Career Stages

Research has identified four career stages through which salespeople go: exploration, establishment, maintenance, and disengagement.[26] Typical paths of progression through these four career stages are diagrammed in Exhibit 7.8.

Exploration Stage

People in the earliest stage of their careers (typically individuals in their 20s) are often unsure about whether selling is the most appropriate occupation for them and whether they can be successful salespeople. To make matters worse, underdeveloped skills and a lack of knowledge tends to make people at this early stage among the poorest performers in the sales force. Consequently, people in the exploration stage tend to have low psychological involvement with their job and low job satisfaction. As Exhibit 7.8 indicates, this can cause some people to become discouraged and quit and others to be terminated if their performance does not improve.

Because salespeople in the exploration career stage are uncertain about their own skills and the requirements of their new jobs, they tend to have the lowest expectancy and instrumentality perceptions in a firm's sales force. They have little confidence that expending more effort will lead to better performance or that improved performance will produce increased rewards. But they do have relatively high valences for high-order rewards, particularly for personal growth and recognition. They seek reassurance that they are making progress and will eventually be successful in their new career. Consequently, good training programs, supportive supervision, and a great deal of recognition and encouragement are useful for motivating and improving the performance of salespeople at this formative stage of their careers.

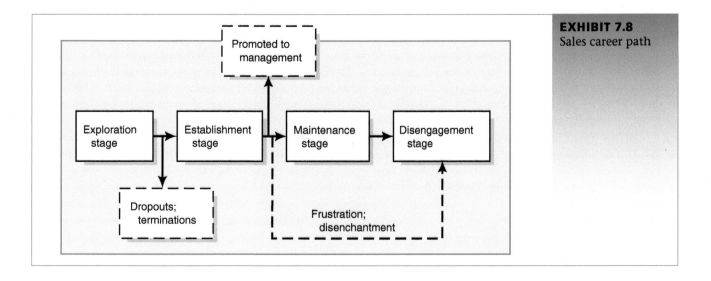

EXHIBIT 7.8
Sales career path

Establishment Stage

Those in the establishment stage—usually in their late 20s or early 30s—have settled on an occupation and desire to build it into a successful career. Thus, the major concerns of salespeople at this stage involve improving their skills and their sales performance. As they gain confidence, these people's expectancy and instrumentality perceptions reach their highest level. People at this stage believe they will be successful if they devote sufficient effort to the job and their success will be rewarded.

Because people at this career stage are often making other important commitments in their lives—such as buying homes, marrying, and having children—their valences for increased financial rewards tend to be relatively high. However, their strong desire to be successful—and in many cases the desire to move into management—makes their valences for promotion higher at this stage than at any other. They also have very high valences for recognition and other indications that management approves of their performance and considers them worthy of promotion.

However, the strong desire for promotion at this stage can have negative consequences. As shown in Exhibit 7.8, some successful people may win promotions into sales or marketing management, but many others will not, at least not as soon as they hoped. Some of these individuals become frustrated by what they consider to be slow progress and quit for jobs in other companies that promise faster advancement or they move prematurely into a disengagement stage. To help prevent this,

---

ETHICAL MOMENT **When Job and Family Collide**

The sales profession offers many advantages and opportunities but also presents challenges. Nowhere is this more apparent than the conflict between job and family. Salespeople by the nature of their position often operate externally to a company office. Indeed, increasingly we see companies have salespeople work from their homes. Your first reaction might be that this type of arrangement would reduce the conflict between job and family, as the salesperson should be home more often.

However, if the office is at home then the salesperson is always at work (even when they are home). This has been exacerbated by the "always on" technology that creates a "respond now" mentality for many customers. As a result, salespeople can find it difficult to separate their work and family lives. How does a salesperson respond to his or her children when they run into the home office to play after coming home from school? How easy is it to go back in the office in the evenings to check email, complete a report, or perform some other work activity?

These challenges create conflict for salespeople and serve to diminish their motivation over time. This is particularly true for younger salespeople who are motivated to work hard but also face the challenge of raising a family with young children. It takes a lot of thoughtful planning for salespeople to find the balance between work and family and accept the realization there will be trade-offs between the two.

Question to Ponder:

- How much travel or time away from home would you be willing to spend when you are married with children?

managers should guard against building unrealistic expectations concerning the likelihood and speed of future promotions among their establishment-stage salespeople. Research interviewing people who have left a company finds one of the most common reasons cited is dissatisfaction with career opportunities such as pay, promotion, and advancement opportunities.

Maintenance Stage

This stage normally begins in a salesperson's late 30s or early 40s. The individual's primary concern at the maintenance stage is with retaining the present position, status, and performance level within the sales force, all of which are likely to be quite high. For this reason, people in the maintenance stage continue to have high valences for rewards that reflect high status and good performance, such as formal recognition and the respect of their peers and superiors.

By this stage, though, both the opportunity and desire for promotion diminish. Consequently, instrumentality estimates and valences concerning promotion fall to lower levels. But salespeople at this stage often have the highest valences for increased pay and financial incentives of anyone in the sales force. Even though such people are among the highest-paid salespeople, they tend to want more money due to both increased financial obligations (e.g., children getting ready for college, large mortgages) and a desire for a symbol of success in lieu of promotion.

Disengagement Stage

At some point, everyone must begin to prepare for retirement and the possible loss of self-identity that can accompany separation from one's job. This usually begins to happen when people reach their late 50s or early 60s. During this disengagement stage, people psychologically withdraw from their job, often seeking to maintain just an "acceptable" level of performance with a minimum amount of effort in order to spend more time developing interests outside of work. As a result, such people have little interest in attaining more high-order rewards—such as recognition, personal development, or a promotion—from their jobs. Because they tend to have fewer financial obligations at this stage, they are also relatively satisfied with their low-order rewards and have low valences for attaining more pay or other financial incentives. Not surprisingly, then, salespeople at this career stage have average performance levels lower than any others except new recruits in the exploratory stage. And their low valences for either high- or low-order rewards make it difficult to motivate them.

What is most disconcerting about disengagement, however, is that it does not occur only among salespeople at the end of their careers. As mentioned earlier, long before they approach retirement age, people may become bored with their jobs and frustrated by a failure to win promotion. Such people may psychologically withdraw from their jobs rather than search for a new position or occupation. They are commonly referred to as *plateaued salespeople*—people who have stopped developing, stopped improving, and often stopped showing an interest. In summary, the individual concerns, challenges, and needs associated with each career stage—together with the implications for motivating a salesperson at that stage—are presented in Exhibit 7.9.

The Problem of the Plateaued Salesperson

Plateauing, or early disengagement, is not an isolated phenomenon among salespeople. Indeed, it has been suggested that 96 percent of all companies have a problem with plateaued salespeople.[27] Moreover, as many as 25 percent of all salespeople operate in a comfort zone that reduces or eliminates the motivation to be a high performer.

Causes of Plateauing

The primary causes of early disengagement are the boredom and frustration that arise when a relatively young person is kept in the same job too long and sees little likelihood of a promotion or other expansion in job responsibilities in the near future. Among the reasons frequently cited for plateauing are (1) lack of a clear career path, (2) boredom, and (3) failure to manage the person effectively. It appears that the same factors hold for both men and women.

One factor, however, may be a more important cause of plateauing among saleswomen than salesmen, burnout. Although the reasons are not fully understood, it could be due to the demands of their multiple roles (mother, wife) in addition to those of their jobs. It has also been suggested the opportunity to earn high levels of pay provided by commission-based compensation systems can increase the rate of plateauing in a sales force. Managers indicate salespeople compensated by commission may more easily earn sufficient pay to meet their economic needs and thereby become less motivated by the chance to earn still higher financial compensation. We explore this issue in more detail in Chapter 11.

Possible Solutions

All of this suggests that one way of reducing the plateauing problem in a sales force—and of remotivating salespeople who have reached a plateau—is to develop clearly defined career paths for salespeople who are good performers but are not promoted into management early in their careers. Such alternative career paths typically involve promotions to positions within the sales force that involve additional responsibility and more demanding challenges.

For instance, a firm might develop a career path involving frequent promotions to increasingly lucrative and challenging territories or assignments to larger and more high-profile accounts or promote high-performing salespeople into key account management positions. The idea is to provide opportunities for frequent changes in job duties and responsibilities to increase job variety. Simultaneously, job changes can be used as rewards for good performance to motivate

	Exploration	Establishment	Maintenance	Disengagement	EXHIBIT 7.9
Career concerns	Finding an appropriate occupational field	Successfully establishing a career in a certain occupation	Holding on to what has been achieved Reassessing career, with possible redirection	Completing one's career	Characteristics of different stages in a salesperson's career
Developmental tasks	Learning the skills required to do the job well Becoming a contributing member of an organization	Using skills to produce results Adjusting to working with greater autonomy Developing creativity and innovativeness	Developing broader view of work and organization	Establishing a stronger self-identity outside of work Maintaining a high performance level	
Personal challenges	Must establish a good initial professional self-concept	Producing superior results on the job in order to be promoted Balancing the conflicting demands of career and family	Maintaining a high performance level Maintaining motivation though possible rewards have changed Facing concerns about aging and disappointment over what one has accomplished Maintaining motivation and productivity	Acceptance of career accomplishments Adjusting self-image	
Psychosocial needs	Support Peer acceptance Challenging position	Achievement Esteem Autonomy Competition	Reduced competitiveness Security Helping younger colleagues	Detachment from organization and organizational life	
Impact on motivation	Low expectancy and instrumentality perceptions High valences for higher-order rewards, such as personal growth and recognition Supportive supervision is critical	Highest expectancy and instrumentality perceptions High valences for pay, but highest valences for promotion and recognition Must avoid generating unrealistic expectations	Instrumentality and valences for promotion fall Valences for recognition and respect remain high Highest valences for increased pay	Lowest instrumentality perceptions and valences for both higher-order and lower-order rewards Still desires respect, but that is unlikely to motivate additional effort	

Source: Adapted from William L. Cron, "Industrial Salesperson Development: A Career Stages Perspective," *Journal of Marketing* (Fall 1984), p. 40; William L. Cron, Alan J. Dubinsky, and Ronald E. Michaels, "The Influence of Career Stages on Components of Salesperson Motivation," *Journal of Marketing* (January 1988), pp. 78–92.

INNOVATION **Money Isn't Everything**

New research from thought leaders such as McKinsey, Harvard Business Review, PricewaterhouseCoopers and Aberdeen suggests that organizations that outperform rivals in financial categories are twice as likely to provide non-cash incentives. According to the Incentive Research Foundation (irf.org), studies show that organizations that have reward systems in place—to reinforce stellar performance and sustain cultures that support collaboration and openness—outperform those organizations that don't have reward systems. Of course, non-cash incentive programs don't work alone. Offering more meaningful and challenging work, along with a performance management process that's transparent and trustworthy, are essential to attracting and retaining talent.

Unfortunately, the McKinsey report suggests businesses have not only reduced their focus on financial incentives, they have cut back the use of non-financial ones as well. Thirteen percent of respondents to a survey report that managers praise their subordinates less often; 20 percent say opportunities to lead projects or task forces are scarcer; and 26 percent report that leadership attention to motivate talent is less forthcoming. The report also suggests that managers hesitate to challenge traditional managerial wisdom and continue to see motivation in terms of the size of compensation.

More and more companies are working to understand what motivates employees beyond financial compensation, especially when times are tough. Many have decided to emphasize recognition rather than "reward" by making people feel more valued during difficult times. Smart managers understand that a talent strategy that accentuates the frequent use of appropriate non-financial motivators will benefit their companies in both good and bad times.

salespeople and show they are valued employees even though they do not move into management.

To be effective, however, promotions along the sales career path must be real and not simply changes in title. They must involve actual changes in duties and responsibilities, and be offered on the basis of good past performance.

Another closely related approach to revitalizing plateaued salespeople is to enrich their current jobs by finding ways to add variety and responsibility without developing a complicated system of hierarchical positions and promotion criteria. This is a more viable approach in smaller firms, and will probably become more popular as firms reduce the number of sales managers and adopt flatter sales force structures. For example, plateaued salespeople might be asked to devote time to training and mentoring new recruits, gathering competitive intelligence, or becoming members of cross-functional account management or product development teams. Money is often used to motivate salespeople but as the Innovation box notes, it is not always effective.

THE IMPACT OF ENVIRONMENTAL CONDITIONS ON MOTIVATION

Environmental factors such as variations in territory potential and strength of competition can constrain a salesperson's ability to achieve high levels of performance. Such environmental constraints can cause substantial variations in performance across salespeople. In addition to placing actual constraints on performance, however, environmental conditions can affect salespeople's perceptions of their likelihood of succeeding and thus their willingness to expend effort.

Although management can do little to change the environment faced by its salespeople (with the possible exception of rearranging sales territories), an understanding of how and why salespeople perform differently under varying environmental circumstances is useful to sales managers. Such an understanding provides clues about the compensation methods and management policies that will have the greatest impact on sales performance under specific environmental conditions.

In some industries, the pace of technological change is very rapid, and salespeople must deal with a constant flow of product innovations, modifications, and applications. Salespeople often appreciate a constantly changing product line because it adds variety to their jobs, and markets never have a chance to become saturated and stagnant. For example, it is common in the laptop computer industry to speak of product life cycles in months, not years. One leading manufacturer replaces its entire line of laptop computers every nine months. However, a rapidly changing product line can also cause problems for the salesperson. New products and services can require new selling methods and result in new expectations and demands from role partners. Consequently, an unstable product line may lead to less accurate expectancy estimates among the sales force.

In some firms, salespeople must perform in the face of output constraints, which can result from short supplies of production factors, including shortages of raw materials, plant capacity, or labor. Such constraints can cause severe problems for the salesperson. In one paper-products firm a few years ago, salespeople were penalized for exceeding quotas. In general, salespeople operating in the face of uncertain or limited product supplies are likely to feel relatively powerless to improve their performance or rewards through their own efforts. After all, their ultimate effectiveness is constrained by factors beyond their control. Therefore, their expectancy and instrumentality estimates are likely to be low.

There are many ways of assessing the strength of a firm's competitive position in the marketplace. One might look at its market share, the quality of its products and services as perceived by customers, or its prices. Regardless of how competitive superiority is defined, though, when salespeople believe they work for a strongly competitive firm, they are more likely to think selling effort will result in successful performance. In other words, the stronger a firm's competitive position, the higher its salespeople's expectancy estimates are likely to be.

Sales territories often have very different potentials for future sales. These potentials are affected by many environmental factors, including economic conditions, competitors' activities, and customer concentrations. Again, though, the salesperson's perception of the unrealized potential of the territory can influence his or her motivation to expend selling effort. Specifically, the greater the perceived potential of a territory, the higher the salesperson's expectancy estimates are likely to be.

THE IMPACT OF ORGANIZATIONAL VARIABLES ON MOTIVATION

Company policies and characteristics can directly facilitate or hinder a salesperson's effectiveness. Such organizational variables may also influence salespeople's performance indirectly, however, by affecting their valences for company rewards and the size and accuracy of their expectancy and instrumentality estimates. Companies continue to seek new ways to connect the salesperson (or any employee) with the organization. Some such as Deloitte have asked employees to consider a spiritual connection to their work and connecting their work to the community. The goal is to create a more motivated, connected individual to the organization.[28] These relationships between organizational variables and the determinants of motivation are summarized in Exhibit 7.10.

Increasingly, companies are looking for ways to increase the efficiency and effectiveness of their marketing efforts. In that regard they seek to identify synergies between their brand, advertising, sales efforts, and other marketing communications. Research indicates that salespeople who identify with their company's brand perform better; put simply, it's helpful if the salesperson really believes in the brand. In the much the same way, salespeople who identify with a company's advertising also are more motivated and perform better. This certainly highlights the important of creating a connection between sales and marketing.[29, 30]

Supervisory Variables and Leadership

According to one highly regarded theory of leadership, a leader attains good performance by increasing subordinates' personal rewards from goal attainment and by making the path to those rewards easier to follow—through instructions and training, by reducing roadblocks and pitfalls, and by increasing the opportunities for personal satisfaction.[31]

This theory suggests that effective leaders tailor their style and approach to the needs of their subordinates and the kinds of tasks they must perform. When the subordinates' task is well defined, routine, and repetitive, the leader should seek ways to increase the intrinsic rewards of the task. This might be accomplished by assigning subordinates a broader range of activities or by giving them more flexibility to perform tasks. When the subordinate's job is complex and ambiguous, that person is likely to be happier and more productive when the leader provides relatively high levels of guidance and structure.

In most occupations, workers perform relatively well-defined and routine jobs, and they prefer to be relatively free from supervision. They do not like to feel their superiors "breathing down their necks." Business-to-business salespeople, however, are different. They occupy a position at the boundary of their companies, dealing with customers and other nonorganization people who may make conflicting demands. Salespeople frequently face new, nonroutine problems. Consequently, evidence shows B2B salespeople are happier when they feel relatively closely

EXHIBIT 7.10		Motivational Variables					
Influence of organizational variables on the determinants of motivation		Expectancies		Instrumentalities		Valences	
	Organizational Variables	**Magnitude**	**Accuracy**	**Magnitude**	**Accuracy**	**Higher Order**	**Lower Order**
	Closeness of supervision		+		+		
	Span of control		−		−		
	Influence over standards				+		
	Frequency of communication		+		+		
	Opportunity rate					Curvilinear	
	Recognition rate					Curvilinear	
	Compensation rate						−
	Earnings opportunity ratio						+

supervised, and supportive supervision can increase their expectancy and instrumentality estimates for attaining extrinsic rewards. Closely supervised salespeople can learn more quickly what is expected of them and how they should perform their job. Consequently, such individuals should have more accurate expectancies and instrumentalities than less closely supervised salespeople. But, as we discussed, close supervision can increase role conflict since it can reduce flexibility in accommodating and adapting to customers' demands.

Another organization variable related to the closeness of supervision is the firm's first-level sales managers' span of control. The more salespeople each manager must supervise (the larger the span of control), the less closely the manager can supervise each person. Therefore, the impact of span of control on role perceptions and motivation variables should be the opposite of the expected impact of close supervision, although this is changing as the result of technology.

Another related supervisory variable is the frequency with which salespeople communicate with their superiors. The greater the frequency of communication, the less role ambiguity salespeople are likely to experience and the more accurate their expectancy and instrumentality estimates should be. Again, however, frequent contact with superiors may increase the individual's feelings of role conflict. At the same time, research suggests that salespeople who have a strong identification with their manager exhibit higher performance levels; however, over identification (the relationship between manager and salesperson becomes too close) can have a negative impact.[32]

Incentive and Compensation Policies

Management policies and programs concerning higher-order rewards, such as recognition and promotion, can influence the desirability of such rewards in the salesperson's mind. For these rewards, there is likely to be a curvilinear relationship between the perceived likelihood of receiving them and the salesperson's valence for them. For example, if a large proportion of the sales force receives some formal recognition each year, salespeople may think such recognition is too common, too easy to obtain, and not worth much. If very few members receive formal recognition, however, salespeople may believe it is not a very attractive or motivating reward simply because the odds of attaining it are so low. The same curvilinear relationship is likely to exist between the proportion of salespeople promoted into management each year (the opportunity rate) and salespeople's desire for promotion.[33]

Another issue is preferential treatment for "stars." The goal of recognition and other forms of incentives is to motivate people to do better, but what happens when one star demands and receives much more than the average or even much more than the company's other top performers?

A company's policies on the kinds and amounts of financial compensation paid to its salespeople are also likely to affect their motivation. As seen, when a person's lower-order needs are satisfied, they become less important and the individual's valence for rewards that satisfy such needs, such as pay and job security, is reduced. This suggests that in firms where the current financial compensation is relatively high, salespeople will be satisfied with their attainment of lower-order rewards. They will have lower valences for more of these rewards than people in firms where compensation is lower.

The range of financial rewards currently received by members of a sales force also might affect their valences for more financial rewards. If some salespeople receive much more money than the average, many others may feel underpaid and have high valences for more money. The ratio of the total financial compensation of the highest-paid salesperson to that of the average in a sales force is the earnings opportunity ratio. The higher this ratio is within a company, the higher the average salesperson's valence for pay is likely to be.

Finally, the kind of reward mix offered by the firm is a factor. Reward mix is the relative emphasis placed on salary versus commissions or other incentive pay and nonfinancial rewards. It is likely to influence the salesperson's instrumentality estimates and help determine which job activities and types of performance will receive the greatest effort from that salesperson. The question from a manager's viewpoint is how to design an effective reward mix for directing the sales force's efforts toward the activities believed to be most important to the overall success of the firm's sales program. This leads to a discussion of the relative advantages and weaknesses of alternative compensation and incentive programs, the topic of Chapter 11.

SUMMARY

The amount of effort the salesperson desires to expend on each activity or task associated with the job—the individual's motivation—can strongly influence job performance. This chapter reviewed the factors that affect an individual's motivation level. The chapter suggested an individual's motivation to expend effort on any particular task is a function of that person's (1) expectancy, (2) instrumentality, and (3) valence perceptions.

Expectancy refers to the salesperson's estimate of the probability that expending a given amount of effort on some task will lead to improved performance on some dimension. Expectancies have two dimensions that are important to sales managers—magnitude and accuracy. The magnitude of a salesperson's expectancy perceptions indicates the degree to which the individual believes that expending effort on job activities will directly influence job performance. The accuracy of expectancy perceptions refers to how clearly the individual understands the relationship between the effort expended on a task and the performance on some specific dimension that is likely to result.

Instrumentalities are the person's perceptions of links between job performance and various rewards. Specifically, an instrumentality is a salesperson's estimate of the probability that a given improvement in performance on some dimension will lead to a specific increase in the amount of a particular reward. A reward can be more pay, winning a sales contest, or promotion to a better territory. As with expectancies, sales managers need to be concerned with both the magnitude and accuracy of their subordinates' instrumentalities.

The salesperson's valence for a specific reward is the individual's perception of the desirability of receiving increased amounts of that reward. This valence, along with the individual's valence for all other attractive rewards and the person's instrumentality perceptions, determines how attractive it is to perform well on some specific dimension.

Several factors influence salespeople's expectancy, instrumentality, and valence perceptions. Three major forces are (1) the personal characteristics of the individuals in the sales force, (2) the environmental conditions they face, and (3) the company's own policies and procedures. The chapter reviewed some major influences and their likely impacts on each of the three categories.

KEY TERMS

motivation
expectancies
   accuracy of expectancy
     estimates
   magnitude of expectancy
     estimates
   instrumentalities
   accuracy of
     instrumentality estimates

magnitude of
instrumentality estimates
valences for rewards
performance attributions
   (stable, unstable, internal,
   external)
career stages (exploration,
   establishment, maintenance,
   disengagement)

plateauing
earnings opportunity
   ratio

BREAKOUT QUESTIONS

1. Sales support personnel include customer service reps, account coordinators, sales assistants, and others whose efforts have a critical impact on a sales force's success. The chapter discusses motivation from the perspective of the sales force. How would you

apply the concepts discussed in the chapter to sales support personnel? What can a company do to motivate sales support personnel?

2. "What's all this stuff about different pay packages and different incentive plans based on how long a sales rep has been with the company?" demanded the irate sales manager. "Around here, everybody gets the same treatment. We're not offering customized compensation packages." What are the problems associated with motivating sales reps on the basis of their stage in the career cycle?

3. How do you motivate sales representatives when money is not effective? What can a sales manager do to motivate the successful salesperson?

4. Most sales reps dislike inputting data into the company's CRM system. They think their time could be spent more profitably, such as calling on accounts. Using Exhibit 7.3, trace the thought process sales reps go through as they consider applying more effort to putting customer data into the computer. Do the same for applying more effort to calling on accounts.

5. How would you respond to a salesperson who says the following? "You are asking me to spend more time calling on new accounts, but I do not see the point in doing so; most of my business comes from my existing accounts."

6. Ethical Question. You are Vice President of Sales for a global chemical company. How would you address the concerns of Emma Smith who has asked to go to part time for the next 3 years while she takes care of new newborn child? Emma has been one of your best salespeople but would now like to work less, at least for the next few years, so she could focus on her family.

LEADERSHIP CHALLENGE: WHAT HAVE YOU DONE FOR ME LATELY?

Terri Ann Masters, Vice President of Sales for Startech Corporation, was wrestling with a critical issue related to one of her longtime and, until recently, most talented salespeople, Jason Benjamin. Startech was a French high-tech manufacturer with its corporate offices in Paris and manufacturing operation in France and China. Jason, whose territory included Silicon Valley in California, had been one of Startech's top salespeople for 11 of his 15 years with the company. At first, Terri Ann thought it was just "bad luck" and Jason would be able to turn it around. Now, however, after four years of seeing Jason miss sales targets and hearing increasing complaints from customers, Terri Ann knew something was wrong.

This was especially critical for Startech because Jason called on some of the company's biggest clients. Jason had worked his way up in the company and been given these accounts seven years ago. During his first three years with the accounts, Jason generated substantial new business from his clients. Management with the customers had actually gone to the trouble of calling Terri Ann and complimenting Startech on the relationship Jason had established. The end result was that Jason frequently exceeded his sales quotas and received healthy bonuses.

In the last few years, however, there was very little new business coming from Jason's accounts. At the same time, Terri Ann knew these companies were growing and were taking business to other competitors. It was not that Jason had lost the accounts; they were still doing a reasonable business with Startech. Rather, Terri Ann recognized there was additional business the company was not getting for some reason.

Of even greater concern was the number of complaints about Jason that had been coming in to Terri Ann. Jason certainly did not have the greatest number of complaints, but given his history, they were high. In addition, Jason seemed to be less motivated. When Terri Ann would call his office on Friday afternoons, she would find that he had already left for the weekend. The "old" Jason was one of the hardest-working salespeople in the company. In addition, EU and French employment law limited Terri Ann's flexibility in dealing with employment performance issues.

The problem was coming to a head. Management had a big push inside the company to increase productivity. Terri Ann also had several younger salespeople who were eager to move into larger, more demanding, and higher potential accounts.

Questions

1. You are Terri Ann Masters. What would you do about Jason Benjamin?

2. What would you do with these younger salespeople who are looking for new opportunities inside the company?

3. Offer ideas on why Jason's performance might have slipped after all these years with the company.

ROLE-PLAY: MAVEN SOFTWARE

Situation

Maven Software provides unique solutions for dental offices that want to fully integrate their patient records, billing, insurance filing, and outbound patient correspondence. Maven started out in 1984 in St. Louis as a local provider of forms utilized by doctors and dentists for record-keeping. Bob Perkins (Bob Sr.) started the firm, and when he retired in 2008 Bobby (Bob Jr.) took over as CEO. In an amazing evolution, the company has become a leading provider in the United States of integrated software solutions for dentists (they made the decision in 2002 to fully devote their efforts to that one market).

Arthur Grabber is one of the three original employees hired by Bob Sr. Arthur was the original salesperson for Maven and for years devoted his time and energy to "beating the bushes" for business—originally largely by phone and, where possible, by face-to-face sales calls. The transition to a technology product focus was a little rough for Arthur, but his relationships with key clients he developed and nurtured over many years helped him overcome the product transition. Arthur is 55 and plans to retire at age 60. Instead of being "the" salesperson for Maven, he is now one of 23 client executives who live in geographically dispersed locations throughout the United States. The sales director is a very competent woman named Leona Jones, who came to Maven in 2012 after a ten year career in sales management with Merck.

Lately, Leona has been thinking a lot about Arthur, his history with the company, and his enormous contributions to its success over 30 years. In a way, she is in awe of his accomplishments. On the other hand, he has been rather slow to adopt technological aids to the sales process (he is reluctant to use social media as a source of client communication, for example). And she is cognizant of the fact that at this stage in Arthur's career, piling more salary and incentive pay onto him is very unlikely to motivate him to change his basic sales approach. Don't misunderstand—it's not that Arthur is a "problem" salesperson; he brings in slightly better sales results annually than the average. But she would like to find a way to address his impending move from the maintenance stage to the disengagement stage of the career cycle.

She picks up the phone and calls Arthur, who is working in his in-home office in a suburb of St. Louis. She asks him to schedule a meeting to catch up on a few things related to planning business for the remainder of the year. During that meeting, she also plans to open up a nonthreatening, friendly dialogue about how Arthur would like to see his last five years with Maven unfold.

Characters in the Role-Play

Arthur Grabber, client executive for Maven Software, based in St. Louis
Leona Jones, sales director for Maven Software, based in St. Louis

Assignment

Break into pairs, with one student playing each character. The student playing Arthur simply needs to get into the character of a salesperson at his stage of the career cycle. The student playing Leona needs to develop a set of issues to bring up with Arthur about important aspects of how to enhance his productivity and satisfaction as he moves into the last few years of employment with the company. The dialogue should be positive, with the goal to come out of the meeting with some specific items for follow-up and implementation.

MINICASE: LAND ESCAPE VACATION CLUB

Land Escape Vacation Club sells fractional interests in time-share vacation properties at various beach locations. For example, an owner will purchase an interest of four weeks a year at a Land Escape property in a place like Hilton Head, South Carolina. Prospective buyers are offered a free weekend stay at a Land Escape resort if they listen to a sales presentation while they are there.

Sales at the La Jolla, California, location have been inconsistent over the past two years, and the sales manager, Denise London, has been asked by Land Escape's vice president of sales to review the profiles of her three salespeople in order to come up with a plan to improve sales.

Catalina Curtis

Catalina is a woman in her 30s with a husband and two small children at home. She was once a television weather forecaster (she would say "meteorologist") but got fired and was forced to do something else. She thought that working in sales would be for the short term until another television opportunity came about, but she has now been in Land Escape sales for about three years. Trying to make the best of a bad situation, she was very enthusiastic when she first began selling, but her enthusiasm and energy level have been waning as she has realized that she will probably continue doing sales for the long term. She and her husband feel some financial pressure because of their decision to put their children in private school, which is very costly. The economy has been difficult, and Catalina is beginning to believe she cannot succeed no matter what she does.

She is somewhat insecure and sensitive but conscientious and a team player. She likes people and seeks personal relationships with customers and takes a long-term approach. Her philosophy is "if potential customers don't want to buy right away, I don't pressure them. I will keep in contact with them and eventually they will come back and buy." Denise does not care for Catalina's style and tends to let her operate without supervision, because, frankly, she doesn't know what to tell her to do better.

Zach Jones

Zach is 25 years old, just two years out of college. He has been with Land Escape for approximately eight months now. He is a perfectionist and highly competitive. Before he came to Land Escape, he had no previous sales experience, but he does have a natural selling skill. He is a little bit of a loose cannon and is not afraid to bend or even break the rules. Needless to say, he is not the least bit self-conscious. Some find him friendly and like his engaging style; however, some are turned off by it and see him as a stereotypical "slick" salesperson.

His goal is to make as much money as possible in a short amount of time. He will decide later whether he wants to stay in sales for the long term; right now he just wants to be young and have fun. He is favored by the sales manager, Denise, who sees him as a potential star because of his early success. As a result, she gives him closer supervision and guidance.

John Sargent

John is the dean of the group at age 53. He has been in Land Escape sales since its inception 12 years ago and was in sales for ten years before that time. He is good at what he does. He says, "I've pretty much mastered the art of time-share selling, and I'm cruising along. I know exactly how much effort to make to get the sale, so why should I do any more than that?"

His art-collecting hobby now interests him more than selling, and he has no desire to be promoted to sales manager or move to a different location. John is somewhat resentful that he has a female manager who has less experience than he does and has made it known that he needs no supervision from her. He does well enough that Denise complies and just lets him sell without a close watch.

Denise knows she needs to make some changes, but is not sure what to do. She feels the current compensation plan of 70 percent commission and 30 percent salary is fairly generous, and she even runs the occasional sales contest to boost numbers during the slower months. She had better think of something quickly before the VP gives her a "permanent vacation."

Questions

1. In what career stage would you place each of the three salespeople?

2. If you were the sales manager, how would you motivate each salesperson? Explain your recommendations.

3. What measures might you use to motivate them as a group?

CHAPTER 8

Personal Characteristics and Sales Aptitude: Criteria for Selecting Salespeople

LEARNING OBJECTIVES

What makes a good salesperson? This question is the focus of Chapter 8. Perhaps no other question faced by sales managers is more important because it has such a profound effect on every aspect of a manager's job. From recruiting and selecting to motivating and evaluating a sales force, one of the important questions—if not the most important—is, What makes that person successful (or not successful)? Sales managers are constantly looking for those characteristics that consistently define success or failure.

After reading this chapter, you should be able to

- Understand the answer to the question, "Are good salespeople born or made?"
- Define the characteristics of successful salespeople.
- Explain the role of sales aptitude in sales performance.
- Understand the different success characteristics for different sales positions.

ARE GOOD SALESPEOPLE BORN OR MADE? THE DETERMINANTS OF SUCCESSFUL SALES PERFORMANCE

Stable, self-sufficient, self-confident, goal-directed, decisive, intellectually curious, accurate—these are personal traits one major personnel testing company says an individual should have to be a successful salesperson. A crucial question, though, is whether the presence or absence of such traits is determined by a person's genetic makeup and early life experiences, or whether they can be developed through training, supervision, and experience after the person is hired for a sales position. In other words, are good salespeople born or made?

Many companies in the pharmaceutical industry believe that successful salespeople are both born and made. They spend a great deal of time and energy identifying characteristics and selection criteria for success in a sales position at the company. Firms gather information about potential new hires through interviews, references, and tests to determine which candidates have the traits and characteristics they believe are important determinants of future sales success. But these same companies also devote substantial resources to training and supervisory programs aimed at further developing each new salesperson's skills, knowledge, and motivation.

Many sales executives have somewhat mixed feelings concerning what it takes to become a successful salesperson. In a study several years ago, a majority of managers indicated they believe good salespeople are made rather than born. Sales and marketing executives said training and supervision are more critical determinants of selling success than the inherent personal characteristics of the individual.[1] However, these same executives also described men and women they knew as being "a born salesperson." And a minority argued that personal traits were critical determinants of good sales performance. For example, one executive asked, "Can they teach ego, train it into an individual? Can they teach personal drive or persistence that gets the sale?"[2]

Thus, while most managers believe that the things a firm does to train and develop its salespeople are the most critical determinants of their future success, many also believe that a firm cannot put in the salesperson all the elements of success and that certain basic personal traits—such as a strong ego, self-confidence, decisiveness, and a need for achievement—are necessary requirements. Is it possible that both sets of factors play crucial roles in shaping a salesperson's performance? A review of past empirical research on this issue can help provide a more definitive answer.

ETHICAL MOMENT   The Ethics of Stereotyping

Despite its negative connotation, everyone draws conclusions about people with very little actual knowledge about that person based on their looks, gender, clothes, and other factors. Stereotyping is a way for people to draw conclusions about people quickly. Of course, we can all remember situations where our conclusions were wrong but, in general, most people still do it, at least in certain situations.

In sales, stereotyping can be particularly ineffective and even harmful to identifying successful salespeople. Dismissing a potential candidate because of the way they look or talk without considering established job criteria misses the opportunity to diversify the sales force. Companies train sales managers to look beyond superficial criteria (looks, gender, speech patterns) because, one, many of those criteria are illegal in the United States and other counties but, two, they distort the hiring process. A successful organization realizes the need to clearly identify the critical success factors for a particular position and hire individuals with those characteristics.

Unfortunately, far too many sales managers still trust their "instinct" rather than defined job-related personal characteristics. In addition, while this is certainly less true today than ever before, some managers find it difficult to manage a diverse sales force. As you might expect, these sales managers perpetuate stereotypes. At the same time, as these managers retire or are asked to leave a company, they are replaced with sales managers who want to hire the best people for the job without regard to unimportant criteria.

Question to Ponder:

- What stereotypes do you think exist in sales? Are those stereotypes valid? As a sales manager how would you address stereotyping in your organization?

A Review of Past Research

A research technique known as meta-analysis has been used to integrate and evaluate the findings of a large number of past research studies examining relationships between the performance of individual salespeople and a variety of personal and organizational factors that might influence that performance.[3] Based on summary of the analysis, variables were grouped into the six categories shown in Exhibit 8.1. The exhibit also shows the actions a sales manager or top executive might take to influence or control each group of determinant variables. Note that two of the categories—aptitude and personal characteristics—contain enduring personal traits and past experiences of the salesperson. These variables are impossible for the manager to influence or change, except by choosing salespeople with desirable traits. A third category—skill levels—includes personal abilities that can change and improve as the salesperson gains knowledge and experience. Thus, skill variables can be influenced by management through effective training programs and supervision. The remaining three categories of determinant variables—role perceptions, motivation, and organizational characteristics—are also directly influenced by management through such means as supervision, compensation and reward systems, and other company policies and programs.

Due to the nature of the analysis, it is important to remember that specific conclusions should be drawn carefully. With this in mind, however, the following can be implied from the analysis of the determinants of sales performance:

- While all six categories of personal and organizational variables account for some of the variance in performance across salespeople, no single category accounts for more than about 8.5 percent of the variance in performance. This means that no single category does a very good job of explaining performance and suggests the performance of a given salesperson is a function of a variety of influences, including both personal traits and organizational factors.

- The strengths of the relationships between some categories and sales performance vary according to the type of customer and the kind of product or service being sold. This suggests that different personal traits, aptitudes, and skills are required for success in different kinds of sales jobs.

- On average, factors that sales managers can control or influence—such as role perceptions, skills, and motivation—account for the largest proportion of the variance in performance across salespeople. But enduring personal characteristics—such as aptitude, personal background, and personality traits—are also related to individual differences in performance.

These conclusions suggest that successful salespeople are both born and made. Selecting recruits with personal traits and abilities appropriate for specific selling tasks is an important determinant of their ultimate sales performance, but how those salespeople are managed is even more crucial to their success.

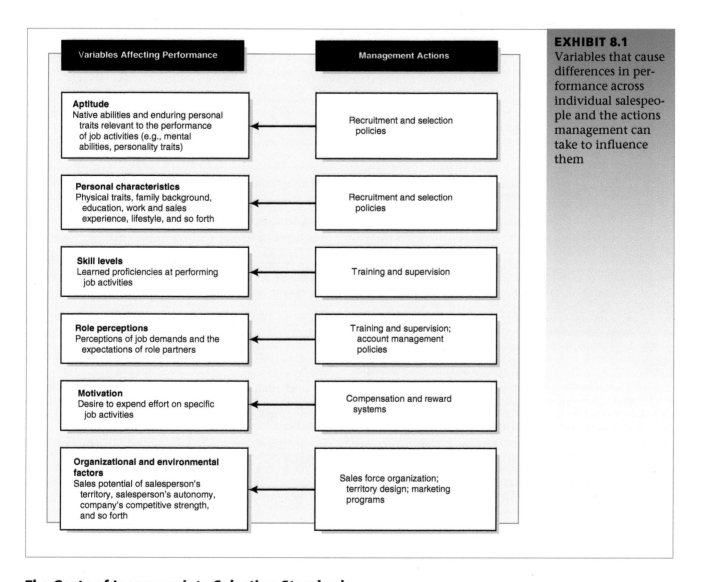

EXHIBIT 8.1
Variables that cause differences in performance across individual salespeople and the actions management can take to influence them

The Costs of Inappropriate Selection Standards

Although personal characteristics may have less influence on a salesperson's long-term performance than company policies and management actions, firms should pay close attention to hiring the right kinds of people for their sales forces for another reason. People lacking the appropriate personal traits and abilities are more likely to become frustrated and quit—or be fired—before training and experience can turn them into productive employees. It has been estimated that as much as 65 percent of unwanted turnover is a result of job dissatisfaction stemming from frustrated employees hired into poorly fitting jobs. Reducing the cost of turnover can have huge benefits for a large company. Global Imaging Systems (GIS), a subsidiary of Xerox, is a provider of copiers, video conferencing, network integration, and other imaging solutions to middle market companies. It was estimated that Global Imaging's turnover costs them $11.25 million per year. By changing the selection process, GIS experienced a 25 percent reduction in turnover which translated into savings of $2.8 million. Reducing turnover also benefits small companies. Connecticut Business Systems, also a subsidiary of Xerox, lowered its turnover from 89 percent a year to 13 percent, which translates into substantial savings in a company of only 200 employees.

Research suggests that on average, about 15 percent of a firm's sales force will quit or be terminated in a given year[4] and the odds that a given salesperson will either quit or be fired during his or her first five years of employment approach 50–50. From this one may conclude that companies are not always successful in identifying and hiring people with the necessary personal characteristics and abilities for success.[5]

Because firms spend a great deal of money and time training new salespeople, mistakes in recruitment and selection that lead to high early turnover rates can be very costly. Firms with high-tech products or broad and complex product lines can spend more than $100,000 a year training a salesperson. Across a broader range of consumer and industrial goods and service industries, firms spend an average of four months and more than $7,000 training each new sales rep.[6] In addition, it takes from three months to a year before new sales reps generate enough sales to cover their compensation and expenses.[7] Thus, when a frustrated salesperson quits in the first year or two of employment, the firm never recoups the cost of recruiting and training that individual.

Because mistakes in recruitment and selection can be costly in the short term and lead to lower productivity in the long term, many sales managers consider the evaluation and selection of new recruits to be among the most important aspects of their jobs. As a result, the remainder of this chapter examines some of the personal and psychological characteristics related to a person's ability to carry out different types of sales jobs.

CHARACTERISTICS OF SUCCESSFUL SALESPEOPLE

Aptitude and personal characteristics are typically thought to place an upper limit on an individual's ability to perform a given sales job. Two people with equal motivation, role perceptions, and training might perform at different levels because one does not have the personal traits or abilities necessary to do the job as well as the other. The questions to consider are these: What specific personal traits and abilities enable a person to achieve good sales performance? What are the determinants of sales aptitude?

Characteristics Sales Managers Look For

One way to answer these questions is to identify the personal characteristics that sales managers look for when selecting new salespeople. Research indicates that enthusiasm consistently ranks among the personal attributes sales managers consider most important in recruiting. Other characteristics considered relatively important are good organizational abilities, ambition, and the two related attributes of persuasiveness and communication skill. Although many executives consider previous sales experience to be important in indicating the sales aptitude of new employees, general experience in selling is typically viewed as more relevant than specific product or industry experience.[8]

Surveys asking executives what they look for when hiring new salespeople are instructive, but they do not provide a definitive answer to the question of what personal characteristics make some individuals better salespeople than others. For one thing, the studies cited above reflect only the opinions of American managers concerning what characteristics are related to selling success in the U.S. market. As firms become strong global competitors, managers wrestle with the question of whether different characteristics are related to successful sales performance in different countries. The question of cross-cultural characteristics is examined in the Leadership box.

Also, manager surveys merely reflect the opinions and perceptions of those sales executives who responded. Although those perceptions may be based on years of practical experience, they can still be inaccurate, biased, or based on knowledge of only a limited range of industries or types of selling jobs. A more objective way to determine what specific personal characteristics are most strongly related to selling success is to study a large cross section of salespeople. To this end, it would be very

---

LEADERSHIP German–American Cross-Cultural Business Differences

As we will see in the next chapter, many companies have identified specific criteria for evaluating and hiring potential new salespeople. In some cases, those criteria have been validated by comparing the characteristics of high-performing salespeople with low performers who have quit or been dismissed. When those same companies expand operations into other countries, however, it is often more difficult to find sales recruits who fit the established criteria. In addition, those criteria can change as companies move into new areas of the world. Cultural differences cause some personal traits and characteristics to be more critical for success in certain countries than others. Consequently, many global companies have had to adapt their salesperson selection criteria to the cultural and social conditions that exist in different countries.

Consider the cross-cultural differences between Germany and the United States. Germans, in general, have more respect for authority; as a result, the more casual management style found in many American companies makes them uncomfortable. At the same time, Americans are less concerned with job titles, which creates some awkward moments in the more formal German business environment.

Germans are also less likely to mix business with social events, making it much less likely to see German salespeople having dinner with their customers. In addition, most Germans learn English as a second language and they are much more comfortable doing business internationally than Americans who, historically, take a more U.S.-centric perspective. Finally, Americans dress more informally than their German counterparts. For example, it is unlikely you would find a German executive wearing short sleeve shirts.

These and other cultural differences encourage companies to adapt their selection criteria to meet the needs of local customers as they move into new markets around the world. They also make changes in their training to support the skill sets required in individual countries. While identifying individuals with appropriate cultural sensitivities is difficult, companies understand the importance of finding salespeople with the ability to adapt their personal style to fit unique selling situations in front of any customer, whether that customer is in the United States, Germany, or anywhere else.

useful to examine in more detail the specific variables included in the aptitude, skill levels, and personal characteristics categories of the meta-analysis of past research that we discussed earlier. Fortunately, there is research that has done exactly that.[9]

Research Concerning the Personal Characteristics of Successful Salespeople

One limitation of the meta-analysis of factors related to differences in sales performance discussed earlier was that the six categories of variables were very broadly defined. Each category contained a large number of more specific items, some of which may be much more strongly related to differences in sales performance than the average for the whole category. Consequently, a second analysis was done after breaking up the broad aptitude, skill levels, and personal characteristics categories into more narrowly defined subcategories of closely related variables.

It is important to note, though, that some of the variables reported in Exhibit 8.2 can no longer be legally collected for use in the selection process. For example, potentially discriminatory information about such physical characteristics as age, sex, and race cannot be included on applications. These and other legal and social concerns related to cultural diversity in the workforce are discussed later in this chapter and in Chapter 9.

A number of variables are related to salespeople's psychological traits and abilities. The exhibit defines seven subcategories of personality traits, five groups of other enduring aptitude factors or mental abilities, and five groups of skills. Note that the aptitude, personality, and skill variables must be measured explicitly during the selection process through the use of formal, scored tests or assessment techniques.[10]

Overview of Findings

As expected, this detailed analysis uncovered specific personal characteristics and traits that can better distinguish between high- and low-performing salespeople—and some that are even worse predictors of performance—than the broad categories of variables examined earlier. Although no single trait could account for a majority of the variance in performance across salespeople, Exhibit 8.2 shows that some personal variables (such as an individual's personal history and family background, current marital and family status, and vocational skills) can account for as much as 20 percent of the variance in selling success. Some traits on which sales managers commonly rely to evaluate new recruits (such as educational attainment, intelligence test scores, or sociability) have not proven effective in accounting for difference in sales performance. Thus, the following sections discuss these widely varying relationships between personal variables and sales performance in depth.

One finding was consistent, however, across all the research. Different types of selling situations appear to require salespeople with different personal traits and abilities. Consequently, the last section of this chapter examines the evidence concerning what personal traits and abilities are best suited to different types of sales jobs.

Demographic and Physical Variables

The meta-analysis results in Exhibit 8.2 indicate those demographic factors, such as sex and age, and physical characteristics, such as height and appearance, account for much less than 5 percent of the difference in performance across salespeople. The lack of any strong relationships between these variables and sales performance is a very important finding. It has implications for public policy regarding equal employment opportunities for women and minorities, and it refutes the conventional wisdom espoused by some sales managers in the past.

Gender and Race Like many other job categories, business-to-business selling was predominantly a white male occupation for many decades and employment opportunities for women and racial minorities were severely limited. Recent U.S. census data indicate that while blacks accounted for about 12 percent of the population, less than 9 percent of all sales jobs were held by black workers. Similarly, women accounted for less than 25 percent of people selling manufactured goods.

Variable	Percentage of Variance in Performance Explained	
Demographic and physical characteristics—physical traits		**EXHIBIT 8.2** Summary of the effect of variables on salesperson performance
Age*	Less than 5%	
Gender*	Less than 5%	
Physical appearance	Less than 5%	
Height, weight, neatness, and general appearance		
Background and experience—developmental education and work experience		
Personal history and family background*	Almost 21%	
Father/mother occupation, number of siblings, family responsibilities		
Level of educational attainment	Less than 5%	
Years of school, degrees earned, grade average		
Educational content	Less than 5%	
College major, number of business courses		
Sales experience	Less than 5%	
Years of sales experience, number and types of sales jobs, promotions		
Nonsales work experience	Less than 5%	
Work history, including military service, length of time in past jobs		
Current status and lifestyle—present marital, family, and financial status		
Marital/family status*	Almost 12%	
Current marital status, number and ages of dependents		
Financial status	Approximately 6%	
Past and current income levels, family income, home ownership		
Activities/lifestyle*	Less than 5%	
Church attendance, club memberships, hobbies, interests		
Aptitude—enduring personal characteristics that determine an individual's overall ability to perform a sales job		
Intelligence	Less than 5%	
Measure of mental abilities, score on intelligence tests		

EXHIBIT 8.2 Summary of the effect of variables on salesperson performance (continued)	**Variable**	**Percentage of Variance in Performance Explained**
	Cognitive ability	Almost 7%
	Mental flexibility, ideational fluency, spatial visualization, inductive and logical reasoning, associative and visual memory	
	Verbal intelligence	Less than 5%
	Comprehension and manipulation of words, verbal skills	
	Math ability	Less than 5%
	Comprehension of quantitative relationships	
	Sales aptitude	Less than 5%
	Enduring personal characteristics and abilities thought to be related to the performance of specific sales tasks	
	Personality—enduring personal traits that reflect an individual's consistent reactions to situations encountered in the environment	
	Responsibility	Less than 5%
	Dependability, emotionally stable, punctual, adjusts well to frustration, keeps promises, and follows plans	
	Dominance	
	Takes command, exerts leadership, pushes own ideas, wants power versus being submissive	
	Sociability	Less than 5%
	Enjoys social activities and interaction, likes to be around other people, and is talkative and gregarious	
	Self-esteem	Less than 5%
	Physically, personally confident and can stand criticism, believes others have a positive attitude toward him or her	
	Creativity/flexibility	Less than 5%
	Innovative, flexible, ready to entertain new ideas and ways of doing things, individualistic	
	Needs for achievement/intrinsic reward	Less than 5%
	Wants to do his or her best, seeks success in competition, gains satisfaction from accomplishment and personal development	
	Need for power/extrinsic reward	Less than 5%
	Motivated primarily by desires for money or advancement, has strong need for security, desires increased power and authority	
	Skills—learned proficiencies and attitudes necessary for effective performance of specific job tasks (these can change with training and experience)	
	Vocational skills	Almost 9.5%
	Job- and company-specific skills, technical knowledge, knowledge of the company and its policies	
	Sales presentation	Almost 5%
	Skills related to identifying and evaluating customer needs, presentation style, ability to handle objections, close the sale	
	Interpersonal	Less than 5%
	Skills related to understanding, persuading, and getting along with other people	
	General management	A little over 9%
	Skills related to organizing, directing, and leading other people	
	Vocational esteem	Less than 5%
	Degree of preference for the tasks and activities associated with the sales job	

* These areas are considered inappropriate or illegal in selecting a job candidate.

One major reason for this unequal employment was the widely held misperception that some customers would be reluctant to deal with or buy from minority salespeople. Similarly, many sales managers thought women were too emotional and lacking in aggressiveness and self-confidence to be effective salespeople. Some managers thought turnover rates would be higher for women due to marriage and childbirth. The view of many older sales managers could be summarized by the following quote, "I'm not sure exactly how I'd manage a woman if I did hire one."[11] Fortunately, these managers have, for most part, retired or been replaced over the last several years.

Social Changes Have Improved Employment Opportunities Women and minorities are moving into senior positions and are demonstrating tremendous skill and ability in business-to-business selling, but there is still work to be done. Recent data suggest women account for approximately 25 percent of sales reps and hold less than 20 percent of the sales management positions. It is important to note, however, that women have achieved greater acceptance in some industries, such as communications, publishing, insurance, and business services, than in more traditionally male-dominated industries such as construction, machinery, and primary metals.

Another issue women face in many professions, including sales, is compensation relative to their male counterparts. Again, while progress has been made, there is still a gap between compensation levels for men and women in the same positions. While the discrepancies in income vary throughout an individual's career, there is a consistent gap between the income levels of men and women in sales. Historical trends suggest the gap is closing, but clearly it is still present in sales.

Until recently, there has been a perception that older salespeople lack the energy and are too inflexible to be successful in the highly competitive world of sales. Researchers suggest that this may not be true and that older salespeople work at least as hard and are just as committed to their jobs as younger salespeople. As one sales consultant put it, "Stereotypes of older salespeople have definitely lost their thunder." The issue of age has become much more important as baby boomers (born between 1946–1964) retire in large numbers.

The positive trends in the employment of women and minorities in recent years have resulted from a variety of social changes, including pressures exerted by the civil rights movement, changing attitudes concerning women's roles, increasing career orientation among women, and legal requirements. The rights of women and minorities to equal employment opportunities in selling, as well as in other occupations, are protected by federal laws. Title VII of the Civil Rights Act prohibits discrimination in hiring, promotions, and compensation. It covers all private employers of 15 or more persons.

The Equal Employment Opportunity Commission administers Title VII and has had broad enforcement powers. While enforcement policies have fluctuated with political changes in the executive branch of the federal government over the years, the commission's guidelines prohibit withholding jobs or promotions because of either customer preferences for salespeople of a particular race or sex or presumed differences in turnover rates. They also prohibit separate promotional paths or seniority lists. Additional legislation has outlawed discrimination on the basis of age and physical disabilities. These important pieces of employment legislation and their implications for sales force recruitment and hiring decisions are examined in more detail in Chapter 11.[12]

Cultural Diversity and Changing Attitudes Have sales managers' attitudes changed as more women and minorities have been added to their sales forces? Unfortunately, there has been little relevant empirical research comparing the job performance of minority salespeople with that of other ethnic groups; however, the growing number of successful minority salespeople and sales managers provides strong anecdotal evidence of their performance capabilities. In addition, many leading firms such as IBM and Procter & Gamble are extremely active in recruiting minorities for their sales forces.

The experiences of these companies suggest that, given adequate training and solid company support, minority salespeople have no major difficulties gaining access to customers. Also, their job performance is not systematically different from that of the rest of the sales force. Furthermore, increasingly, minority salespeople are the sales leaders.

As for saleswomen, there is no evidence of consistent differences in the productivity of men and women in business-to-business sales. While men and women are seen as sharing the potential for sales success, both groups are still often perceived to have unique job requirements and concerns and special strengths that enable them to perform better on different aspects of the sales job. For instance, the etiquette involved in traveling with male colleagues or entertaining male clients can still pose uncertainties for some saleswomen, and while attitudes have changed, it is still more common to see men "on the road" than women. However, college sales programs around the world have seen huge increases in women so that may be changing over the next few years. Similarly, surveys suggest some sales managers and purchasing agents judge salesmen as being better than saleswomen on some dimensions of job performance, such as technical assistance, but perceive saleswomen to be superior on other attributes, including preparation for sales presentations and follow-through.[13]

One must question such generalizations concerning the comparative strengths and weaknesses of salesmen and saleswomen, however. Research suggests variations in sales performance are probably much greater within each group than between them.[14] Thus, there is little that is inherently and unalterably either "male" or "female" about any aspect of good sales performance.

Physical Characteristics and Customer Similarity While demographic and physical attributes are not strongly related to sales performance in general, particular characteristics may enable a salesperson to deal more effectively with some types of customers than with others. Consequently, some research studies have taken a *dyadic* approach to try to explain variations in performance among salespeople.

Most of the studies test a very simple hypothesis: Salespeople are more likely to be successful when they are dealing with prospects similar to themselves in demographic characteristics, personality traits, and attitudes than when their prospects have characteristics different from their own. It is a natural tendency to understand, have empathy for,

TECHNOLOGY   Personal Image and Apps

While it may seem superficial, it is a fact of human nature that people's looks and how they present themselves do matter. Humans are visual and respond to people's appearances and demeanor. The problem is many sales managers don't feel comfortable giving salespeople feedback about personal issues such as dress. While not everyone agrees on the most appropriate dress, the consensus is it is better to be slightly overdressed relative to the customer than underdressed.

Image is important both in relationships with the customer and in the hiring process. Customers respond to the salesperson's physical appearance. For example, research suggests that salespeople with an unkempt or sloppy look (hair too long, shirt not tucked in) have a harder time making the sale.

This problem has been solved, in part, by a growing number of personal image apps (many directed at the business environment). For example, there are more than a dozen apps on how to tie a tie and there are various apps that present proper business etiquette and dress in a variety of countries (from China to Italy), even apps that make your smart phone a mirror for the last minute checkup.

At the same time, a number of websites offer advice on any personal image topic imaginable. From monster.com to YouTube, there is no shortage of advice on the Internet for presenting a positive image. Interestingly, much of the advice has not changed over the years, particularly for the job interview. However, it is clear that personal image is important and technology is there to help.

and be attracted to other people more like us. Therefore, a salesperson may be better able to understand a customer's problems and needs, communicate a sales message, and persuade the prospect to make a purchase when the rep has physical characteristics, personality traits, and attitudes similar to those of the prospect.[15]

The implications of this hypothesis seem simple and straightforward: Managers should hire salespeople with demographic and personality characteristics as similar as possible to those of the prospects upon whom they will be calling. However, there are two fundamental problems with this prescription. For one thing, it is often impossible to implement. Because buyers and purchasing agents come in all shapes and sizes and vary widely in characteristics, it can be difficult to match a salesperson's attributes with those of all or even most potential customers. A second much more fundamental problem is that research does not support the validity of the similarity hypothesis. For example, one study found that a very small percentage of the differences (less than 2 percent of the variance) in the amount purchased by different customers could be explained by salesperson–customer similarity.[16]

While it may be difficult, at best, to find salespeople with demographic and personality characteristics similar to their customers, this does not mean that physical appearance and image are not important. Image is important in maintaining a successful relationship with customers and plays a critical role in the hiring process, as managers are not as likely to hire someone who is sloppily dressed or presents a less than professional image. This is one reason why it is important to be careful about the photos posted to Facebook or other social media as recruiters look at the image an individual presents to the public.

Background and Experience

One of the surprises in the findings presented in Exhibit 8.2 is that personal history and family background variables are among the best predictors of sales success, accounting for an average of about 20 percent of the variance in performance across salespeople.

INNOVATION   The Educated Sales Force

The level of education among salespeople today has never been higher. Almost two-thirds of all salespeople have a college degree and the number of salespeople with advanced degrees is also increasing. While there is a great deal of variance in educational levels across industries, overall, education is an important characteristic of today's salesperson despite the fact that it has not been shown to be a significant predictor of performance.

Some industries, such as pharmaceuticals, recruit only college graduates while others such as retail recruit from a broader range of educational backgrounds. Not surprisingly, sales managers have a variety of opinions on the importance of education in selling. These generally fall into one of two broad camps. On one hand are managers who believe a college education demonstrates knowledge and motivation. On the other hand, some managers believe that the best educational experience is the "school of hard knocks" or life experiences. In reality, it is likely both are right; certainly a college education does a great job of preparing people for a professional career in selling. At the same time, life experiences provide a terrific context for people in dealing with customers and business situations.

Source: Authors

This suggests that information about such things as whether a person held part-time jobs or had substantial family responsibilities as a youngster provides a good indication of likely emotional maturity and motivation. These traits, in turn, are important determinants of sales performance, particularly for young recruits. Increasingly, it is also beneficial, if not essential, for salespeople to be multilingual, especially in some professions and in certain geographic areas. For example, Spanish is spoken widely in parts of Texas, California, Florida, and many urban areas in the Northeast and Midwest. Salespeople who have mastered Spanish can find greater opportunities in many sales careers such as real estate.

More surprising, perhaps, is that some of the background factors on which sales managers most commonly rely when evaluating potential recruits—such as the person's educational attainment, course of study, and general work experience—do not show much relationship with sales performance. Companies still seek individuals with a college education. The Innovation box speaks to the issue of education and its importance in sales success.

Even a person's past sales experience—a factor that receives primary emphasis in some firms' recruitment and selection—does not do a good job of explaining differences in performance across salespeople. Surprisingly, companies continue to focus on hiring sales representatives with prior experience. One study reported that nearly half of the companies preferred hiring individuals with one to three years experience, and 40 percent wanted even more experience (more than three years). Only 10 percent indicated they hire new salespeople with less than one year of experience. More recently, high-tech companies have looked to recruit sales professionals with proven track records that can make a difference immediately. In light of the rapidly changing technology landscape, many companies feel they do not have the time to train a salesperson to be successful.[17]

Current Status and Lifestyle Variables

As was the case with personal history and family background, a person's current marital and family status, income level, and financial obligations (e.g., a large mortgage) are relatively good predictors of sales performance. Variables related to marital and family status account for about 12 percent of the variance in performance across salespeople (Exhibit 8.2). However, be aware that it is not appropriate for interviewers to ask about marital status or specific issues related to family status (number of kids). As we see later, though, these relationships are much stronger for some kinds of sales jobs than for others. At the same time, a person's lifestyle does not appear to be closely related to sales performance, accounting for less than 5 percent of individual differences in sales performance.

Aptitude Variables

Despite the variety of tests of sales aptitude developed specifically for selecting salespeople, such measures explain less than 5 percent of differences in sales performance. Once again, however, the ability of sales aptitude to predict performance varies greatly across different types of sales jobs. We explore this in more detail in the next section of this chapter.

Most tests of general mental aptitude or abilities—such as general intelligence tests, measures of verbal ability and fluency, and tests of math ability—are all relatively uncorrelated with sales performance. But a person's ability to think logically and display flexibility in solving problems—an ability measured by tests of cognitive ability—is a relatively good indicator of likely success in selling. Cognitive ability measures explain nearly 7 percent of the variance in performance across salespeople.

Personality Variables

More studies have attempted to explain individual variations in sales performance by examining personality trait differences than any other personal characteristic. Also, much of the conventional wisdom to which sales managers and consultants have adhered over the years has stressed the importance of such personality traits as self-esteem, extraversion, sociability, dominance, and a strong need for achievement as determinants of sales success. It is rather disappointing, then, to discover that individual personality traits explain a very small percentage of the differences in salespeople's performance (less than 5 percent of the variance).

Recent research has found the type of sales job must be considered. For example, extraversion is measured using items like "I am the life of the party." For years conventional wisdom believed that an extravert would perform well in all sales roles. However, recent research suggests extraversion is positively related to sales roles such as retail and call centers (inside sales), but negatively related to performance in business-to-business sales roles. Potential B2B customers felt that extraverts did a poor job of relating a product to their business needs. As good B2B salespeople say, "It isn't about talking, it's about listening." The research concluded that using a personality test to predict sales success is best achieved when the test is designed for a specific sales role.

More recent research suggests that cooperative behavior is a key characteristic for success. At this point, the best predictors of a person's willingness to be cooperative are past tendencies of cooperativeness or specific personality tests that focus on measuring cooperative attitudes and behavior. However, some personality tests that focus on only a few broad, stable traits—such as extroversion, openness to experience, and conscientiousness—may be more strongly related to sales success.[18] Other personality factors may also need to be considered, for example, the individual's competitiveness and "coachability" (their willingness to work with a sales mentor). Research indicates these traits can positively impact sales success. In addition, other traits such as emotional intelligence, which may serve to mitigate job stress, as well as empathy for the customer may have a role in improving sales performance and should be evaluated as criteria for selection.[19-22]

Skill Variables

Vocational skills encompass a salesperson's acquired knowledge and abilities directly related to the company, its products, and customers. Not surprising, the more skill a salesperson has, the better the performance is likely to be. Vocational skills account on average for more than 9 percent of the variance in sales performance. It is also no surprise that differences in salespeople's skill at preparing and delivering good sales presentations can explain as much as 5 percent of the differences in their performance. Sales managers also evaluate how well individuals use technology in their presentations. As the technology and customers become more sophisticated, the quality of the presentation must get better. Consequently, the ability to deliver quality presentation becomes more important.

General management skills, such as organizational and leadership abilities, account for approximately 9 percent of the variance in performance across salespeople. This is to be expected since most salespeople have the freedom to manage their own time and to organize their efforts within their territories. Also, some salespeople

EXHIBIT 8.3 The characteristics of salespeople who win customer trust[23]	Customers and salespeople were asked, What kind of rep is most trustworthy? Salespeople indicated listening skills were most important in building trust with the customer while customers believed product knowledge was the key in winning trust.	
Characteristic	**Percentage of Customers Responding**	**Percentage of Salespeople Responding**
Product knowledge	79.5%	79.6%
Understands business	63.9	73.1
Reliable	63.1	75.9
Understands needs of customer	63.1	85.3
Confidence in product	54.1	63.8
Likable	53.3	55.6
Positive attitude	50.8	71.2
Good listening skills	44.3	87.2
Intelligent	41.8	40.3
Asks good questions	39.3	65.9
Self-confident	22.1	45.6
Well-dressed	14.8	29.1

must work closely and coordinate their efforts with a customer's personnel to carry out such tasks as sales engineering, installation of equipment, and training of the customer's employees. Interestingly, interpersonal skills related to understanding and getting along with people are not strongly related to ultimate sales performance. This runs counter to the conventional wisdom offered by many authorities. Organizations are asking salespeople, indeed everyone in the organization, to do more with fewer resources. Research suggests that resourceful salespeople are able to drive greater value to the company making this an important sales skill.[24]

Finally, the lack of significant sales performance predictors is not surprising. Customers and salespeople cannot even agree on which skills are critical for sales success. Exhibit 8.3 highlights the problems in identifying characteristics that build trust between customer and salespeople. While salespeople indicate listening skills are most critical in building trust with the customer, customers themselves rank product knowledge number one.[25]

JOB-SPECIFIC DETERMINANTS OF GOOD SALES PERFORMANCE

It is clear that different types of sales jobs require salespeople to perform different tasks and activities under different circumstances. It would seem to make sense, then, to develop task-specific definitions of sales aptitude and ability, since the traits and skills needed to be successful in one type of sales job may be irrelevant to another. As discussed in Chapter 9, this kind of task-specific, or *contingency*, approach is the one sales managers should use when determining what traits and abilities to look for in new sales recruits. Unfortunately, little published research is available to guide sales managers in deciding what personal characteristics are most important in enabling salespeople to perform well in specific types of sales jobs.[26] The findings of research to date are examined below.

Selling Different Types of Products and Services

The previous research discussed earlier found that the strength of the relationships between some personal characteristics and sales performance varied widely across studies. Some of the variation was because different studies examined samples of salespeople engaged in selling different types of products. Thus, a given trait might bear a strong relationship with performance in studies where the respondents were selling business-to-business goods to organizational customers, but the same trait might have only a weak relationship to performance in studies focused on people selling consumer goods or services.

Overall, the following variables have been shown to be different across different kinds of selling environment:

- Personal history and family background
- Marital and family status

- Sales aptitude
- Dominance
- Self-esteem
- Sales presentation skills
- Interpersonal skills

The findings suggest that for people selling business-to-business products to institutional customers, "professional" skills and traits—such as sales aptitude, sales presentation skills, interpersonal skills, and self-esteem—are relatively good predictors of successful performance.

However, for jobs involving the sale of services, such job-related skills appear to be relatively less important. Traits related to aggressiveness and motivation, such as a dominant personality and family obligations, are better indicators of success in selling services than they are for jobs involving either consumer or business-to-business goods.

Different Types of Sales Jobs

Chally Group Worldwide, a world leader in sales consulting, has studied the characteristics of successful and unsuccessful salespeople in specific jobs across a large number of organizations. They identified four categories of business-to-business sales jobs: 1) the closer, 2) the consultant, 3) the relationship builder, and 4) the order taker. A summary of their research is provided in Exhibit 8.4.[27] While it is not appropriate to draw specific conclusions about each type of sales job, it is clear that different types of sales positions require different kinds of sales skills and abilities.

EXHIBIT 8.4 Types of sales jobs	**SALES PROFESSIONAL**	**CHARACTERISTICS**
	Closer	• Does not have a high fear of personal rejection.
		• Thrives in a sales environment that requires salespeople to quickly establish a prospect's emotional desire and need for their product.
	Consultant	• Identified as patient with excellent interpersonal contact and a certain amount of aggressiveness.
		• Typically more career-oriented and academically inclined.
		• Able to handle personal rejection and the fear of failure.
		• They exhibit self-confidence, patience, and the ability to quickly develop interpersonal relationships with all business prospects.
	Relationship Builder	• This salesperson likes independence and the freedom of sales, the feeling that they are their own boss.
		• They exercise discipline and take responsibility for their actions.
	The Order Taker	• Requires little personal involvement.
		• Relatively little risk of personal rejection.

IMPLICATIONS FOR SALES MANAGEMENT

What has this review of the knowledge accumulated through experience and published research taught us about the personal characteristics related to sales aptitude and the potential for selling success? For one thing, no general physical characteristics, mental abilities, or personality traits appear to be consistently related to sales aptitude and performance in all companies and selling situations. Also, the evidence suggests it is probably neither wise nor practical for a sales manager to try to select salespeople with characteristics that match those of their potential customers. The possible exception is in selling to consumers. Instead, the most potentially useful approach to defining sales aptitude and evaluating a person's potential is first to determine the kinds of tasks involved in a specific sales job. Then, one can evaluate the relevance of particular characteristics and abilities for enabling a person to carry out those tasks successfully.

Unfortunately, very little research has either analyzed the tasks and activities unique to particular types of selling or identified the personal traits and abilities important for success in different sales jobs. For the time being, then, sales executives must develop their own specifications concerning what to look for in new sales recruits. Those specifications should be developed after a careful analysis and description of the tasks and activities involved in selling the firm's products to its target market. There should also be an evaluation of the characteristics and qualifications that new salespeople must have to perform those tasks and activities. Therefore, Chapter 9 examines the methods and procedures involved in sales force recruitment and selection. It begins with a discussion of how to carry out a job analysis and develop a list of qualifications to use in evaluating recruits.

SUMMARY

This chapter, the first of two dealing with salesperson selection, sought to review the evidence regarding what personal and psychological characteristics are related to an individual's likely performance as a salesperson. Personal traits and aptitude are typically thought to place an upper limit on an individual's ability to perform a given sales job.

Several sets of personal factors are thought to affect a salesperson's ability to perform, including the following:

1. Demographic and physical characteristics—such as age, sex, and physical appearance.
2. Background and experience factors—such as a person's personal history and family background, educational attainment, and sales experience.
3. Current status and lifestyle variables—including a person's marital and financial status and activities outside of the job.

4. Aptitude variables—enduring mental characteristics such as intelligence, cognitive abilities, and sales aptitude.
5. Personality traits—including such characteristics as sociability, dominance, and self-esteem.
6. Skill levels—learned proficiencies, such as vocational skills (e.g., product knowledge), interpersonal skills, sales presentation skills, and general management skills.

Although a number of reasons can be advanced as to why these factors might be related to sales performance, the available evidence suggests that none is consistently related to performance when examined across industries and job settings.

One of the more persuasive reasons for these inconsistent relationships is that particular characteristics of salespeople enable them to deal more effectively with some kinds of customers than with others. Consequently, some studies have used a dyadic approach to explain variations in performance among salespeople. The basic hypothesis is that salespeople are more likely to be successful when they deal with prospects who are similar to themselves in terms of demographic characteristics, personality traits, and attitudes. The implication of the dyadic perspective for sales managers is that they should hire salespeople with characteristics similar to the customers on whom they will call. But such a strategy can be hard to implement in business-to-business selling, and it is likely to become even more difficult as both sales recruits and customer organizations become more culturally diverse. Also, the existing research evidence does not consistently support the proposition.

The most important conclusion regarding salespeople selection is that there are many different types of selling jobs. Each type requires the salesperson to perform a variety of different tasks and activities under different circumstances. Consequently, the most useful approach to defining sales aptitude and evaluating a person's potential for future success is, first, to determine the kinds of tasks involved in a specific sales job. Then one can evaluate the relevance of particular characteristics and abilities for enabling a person to carry out those tasks successfully.

KEY TERMS

selection criteria	psychological traits
physical characteristics	skill variables

BREAKOUT QUESTIONS

1. Mark and Cynthia have just finished a long session that produced a heated discussion concerning hiring people who are overweight. Mark stressed that overweight people are considered lazy, sloppy, and lacking in self-esteem. He insisted that no sales manager would overlook these features and hire such a person. "What a waste of money, since customers don't want to do business with a tubbo," argued Mark. Cynthia countered with equal conviction, accusing Mark of stereotyping all people who are overweight. She asked Mark if he knew that for some people the problem was genetic

and not overindulgence. "Besides," she stressed, "not hiring someone because of his or her weight just happens to be illegal." Is it legal not to hire a person because of his or her weight?

2. As we saw in the chapter, women are playing an increasingly important role in selling both as salespeople and as sales managers. What are the challenges facing women and other minorities as they become involved in a sales career?

3. Enthusiasm is one of the more important attributes sales executives look for in new salespeople. How would you measure or determine whether an applicant possessed enthusiasm? If an applicant lacks enthusiasm but shows a positive interest in sales, would it be possible to teach enthusiasm?

4. The sales manager of a company manufacturing orthopedic medical equipment attempts to hire salespeople based on the personalities of the customers. The sales manager uses the same process when assigning salespeople to customers. In other words, the similarity hypothesis discussed earlier is being applied. Does this process make sense? As a sales manager, would you use the similarity theory in hiring salespeople or assigning salespeople to customers? Why or why not?

5. Ethical Question. You are the sales director for a company with operations around the world and have been asked by the vice president of sales to identify a candidate to open up a new territory in the Middle East. The VP has noted that it is difficult for women to be accepted in business and suggests you choose a man; however, the most qualified individual on your sales force is a women. What do you do?

LEADERSHIP CHALLENGE: CHARACTERISTICS OF THE GREAT SALESPERSON

Thad Williams had the kind of problem many sales managers wish they could experience more often. He just came out of a strategic planning meeting with senior management at his company, Logistics Logic (a leading supplier of logistics solutions for manufacturing companies). The emphasis in many organizations on supply chain management had created huge demand for the products and services offered by Logistics Logic. Started by Eric Lemaster in 1985 and originally based in London, the company had developed an excellent reputation by helping companies become more efficient and effective in managing the flow of goods in and out of the organizations. Logistics Logic worked with key players in the supply chain management industry (FedEx, UPS, DHL, and others) to develop custom-designed hardware and software for unique logistics solutions. The company had found a great niche for its products by focusing on medium-sized companies around the world.

Thad had been with the company for 10 years and worked his way up to vice president of sales. In the last 15 years the company had experienced huge growth in Asia. As result, while maintaining offices in London, Mr. Lemaster decided to move Logistics Logic's senior management and operations to Hong Kong in 2001. Revenue exceeded $350 million last year, and the company had a worldwide sales force of 150. At this meeting, Thad had been given the go-ahead to hire 20 new salespeople, primarily in Asia. This would represent one of the largest increases of salespeople in the company's history and was based on the goal of taking the company to $400 million in the next two years.

The typical salesperson was a male in his early 40s with a technical background in logistics. Interestingly, however, Thad had noticed that most of the new salespeople (those hired in the last three years) were women (7 out of 10). Salespeople needed a very good knowledge of logistics and the fundamentals of contemporary selling. The compensation system allowed salespeople to earn a good living, with many earning in excess of $125,000 per year.

Thad had also noticed the typical customer had changed in recent years. When he started, customers were often men in their 50s who had little formal education in logistics. Now customers were most often experienced men and women with formal training in supply chain management.

Logistics Logic, and more specifically Thad Williams, knew the company's new salespeople were critical to the organization's continued success. The question was, what would make a successful Logistics Logic salesperson now?

Questions

1. What qualities and characteristics do you think are important for a new salesperson at Logistics Logic? Why?

2. What kind of person would you recruit (experienced versus less experienced, age, education, background, etc.)?

ROLE-PLAY: BASS BROKERS, INC.— PART A

Situation

Sales vice president Roscoe Lee slammed his fist down on the desk in his office, startling human resources manager Pat Tollford. "Sales District 5 has got to get control of their turnover," Roscoe exclaimed. "Why is the turnover rate among salespeople in that district running 20 percent annually when the company average is less than 3 percent per year?"

Roscoe and Pat work at the home office of Bass Brokers, Inc., a sales brokerage firm that represents lines of fishing equipment sold in a variety of retail outlets across the United States and Canada. Bass Brokers was started in 1987 by avid fisherman Pug Pike, who literally sold fishing lures out of the trunk of his car to mom-and-pop tackle shops in Louisiana and Mississippi. Bass Brokers now represents some of the top lines of lures and other fishing equipment supplies and has grown to a sales force of 60 spread across six sales districts in the United States and Canada. Each district is led by a district sales manager who reports directly to Roscoe.

The fact that one of Bass Brokers' sales districts is experiencing high turnover is quite troubling, as the firm prides itself on really understanding the selection criteria necessary to ensure that the salespeople it hires will have a high likelihood of success with the company. Among the core values of Bass Brokers are building customer relationships, fair and civil treatment of all employees, and involvement of all employees in the process of company planning and decision making. Bass Brokers salespeople are compensated by a combination of base salary and commission on products sold. Because the firm has such a positive culture and tries hard to use selection criteria that are a good match to the firm, turnover has never been a problem—in fact, historically nearly all of the company's new salespeople have been hired to fill openings created in three ways: retirements, promotions, or salespeople leaving Bass Brokers on good terms to take a more lucrative sales position elsewhere. Over the past two years, District 5 has lost four salespeople, each of whom had left the company within a short time of being hired, and each of whom seemed to never really fit in well with the needs of Bass Brokers.

This history has led Roscoe and Pat to conclude that a problem exists with the selection criteria used in District 5. The district manager there, Jason Queen, is the newest district manager at Bass Brokers, having been promoted from a sales job in another district of the firm three years ago. The district has ten sales positions reporting to Jason. Six of these are long-term Bass Brokers salespeople who continue to do well and enjoy working for Jason. The other four were new people who have turned over during the past 24 months. In Jason's estimation, and Roscoe and Pat concur, these four individuals never really caught on to the Bass Brokers way of doing business.

Despite its success in the sales area, Bass Brokers has never formalized selection criteria for its salespeople. Nowhere in either the HR department or the sales department does any documentation of the specific personal characteristics and sales aptitude criteria for selecting salespeople exist. Because of the turnover problem in District 5, before any more new salespeople are hired, Roscoe and Pat must brainstorm and develop a list of these criteria.

Characters in the Role-Play

Roscoe Lee, vice president of sales for Bass Brokers, Inc.
Pat Tollford, human resource manager for Bass Brokers, Inc.

Assignment

Break into pairs, with one student playing each character. It doesn't matter what the actual gender mix of your pair is. Before you stage the continuation of the above-mentioned meeting between Roscoe and Pat, work separately using the material in your chapter to come up with a logical set of selection criteria you each believe will be important to discuss in the meeting. Then get together and role-play the meeting between Roscoe and Pat. Think about the various types of clients Bass Brokers is likely to sell fishing products to—essentially, any type of retail outlet that carries such products. Also consider what you learned above about the culture and values of the company. Roscoe and Pat's goal is to compare their ideas and come up with a list of selection criteria that are most important to apply in hiring Bass Brokers salespeople. For the criteria that make your final list, be sure to note why you two agree each is important.

MINICASE: J.P. REYNOLDS INVESTMENTS

Raymond Baker is J.P. Reynolds Investments' district sales manager for the Southeastern Region (covering Florida, Georgia, South Carolina, Tennessee, and Alabama). J.P. Reynolds sells a variety of mutual funds and other investment products to financial services companies that are retailer sellers of such products. It generally offers its investment products to small- and medium-sized customers, such as regional banks, as opposed to large financial services companies.

Raymond recently lost his best salesperson and must replace him immediately. This morning he interviewed two job candidates, Dag Wicklo and Katharine Bryant, for the position of sales representative, level II (three to six years of experience), for about 45 minutes each. Dag is 26, tall, athletic, enjoys outdoor activities, is not married, has no children, and is clearly from the South. He came to the interview with very short-cropped hair and a slightly wrinkled suit. He scored slightly below average on the test of general mental aptitude administered by the HR department. Katharine is 36, shorter than average, not athletic, is married to a wealthy financier, has two children, and is originally from New York. She is wearing a very formal black suit and expensive-looking shoes. She scored well on the test of general mental aptitude.

Here are a few excerpts from the respective interviews:

RB: How would you describe your selling style?

DW: Ray, I'm a go-getter. I'm young, enthusiastic, and I love selling. I also love money, so I love working with investment products and love the commission-based nature of the business. Most of all I love people, and they respond well to me. By the end of a meeting, I feel like I'm with a friend, and the sale happens so naturally, it doesn't even feel like selling.

KB: Mr. Baker, I try to know my product inside and out and present a clear, logical case as to why my customer should purchase it. However, I don't get down and beg for the sale. If the customer does not want to buy, I simply go to the next prospect. Also, I try to stay as professional as possible and not get too close to the customers.

RB: What strengths and weaknesses would you bring to this position?

DW: My number-one strength is that I'm very likable. I speak Spanish, Portuguese, and English, so I can talk to almost anyone. Also, despite my young age, I have five years of sales experience in the investment field and have received high performance evaluations. I'm confident, resilient, and creative. I find a way to solve a problem. Finally, I'm a good presenter and like to speak without any prepared speech or remarks.

   My biggest weakness is that I can be less than organized. I sometimes let my creative energy get the better of me, and I'm not always the most professional or polished guy. I get the job done in my own way, I guess. Also, I don't have much formal college education and don't understand the technology as well as I would like. I'm sure I can learn it, though.

KB: I take command of a room or a situation well and don't let anyone intimidate me. I have a master's degree in art history and have the intelligence to handle myself well and understand the products. Also, I am extremely organized. If you asked them, my children can verify what a tight ship I run at home. Although I do not have sales experience in selling investment products, my husband is an investment banker, as was my father, so I can speak the language.

   My main weakness is that I have only two years of sales experience, but I have owned and managed my own business before. Also, I don't need the money, so I'm not as aggressive as some of these young bucks in terms of sales volume. However, I feel that I can relate well to the customer and will understand them better because of my other business experience.

Joanna Baer, the vice president of sales and Raymond's immediate boss, just interviewed each applicant this afternoon and has called Raymond into her office to discuss the situation. Because of the pressing need, the company needs to make an offer to one of the two candidates. Raymond knows he must evaluate the applicants quickly and make a recommendation to Joanna.

Questions

1. What categories of variables affecting performance can you identify?

2. Within each category, which variables do you think are relevant to a salesperson's performance at J.P. Reynolds? Why?

3. If you were Raymond, which applicant would you recommend to Joanna to hire? Why?

CHAPTER 9

Sales Force Recruitment and Selection

LEARNING OBJECTIVES

Perhaps more than any other function of the sales manager, successfully recruiting new salespeople into the company is critical to the long-term success of the organization. As markets expand both domestically and internationally, companies continue to seek qualified new candidates to fill sales positions. At the same time, it is likely that talented people in the organization are being recruited, often by competitors, and leaving for other opportunities. Finally, competition for talented candidates is fierce and the cost of poor recruiting is high, in both direct and indirect costs. For all these reasons, recruiting and selecting salespeople has become a very important part of the sales manager's job. This chapter will outline the process of recruiting new salespeople into the organizations.

   After reading this chapter, you should be able to

- Understand the key issues that drive the recruitment and selection of salespeople.
- Identify who is responsible for the recruitment and selection process.
- Understand a job analysis and how selection criteria are determined.
- Define the sources for new sales recruits.
- Explain the selection procedures.
- Understand the equal opportunity requirements for selecting salespeople.

RECRUITMENT AND SELECTION ISSUES

Hiring the best employee is a difficult and complex task and there are a variety of important issues that must be resolved when recruiting and selecting new salespeople. These issues are diagrammed in Exhibit 9.1.

   The first decision to be made concerns who in the company will have the responsibility for hiring new salespeople. While it is common to assign this responsibility to field sales managers, top sales executives or personnel departments play a more active role and bear more of the burden for this important function in some firms.

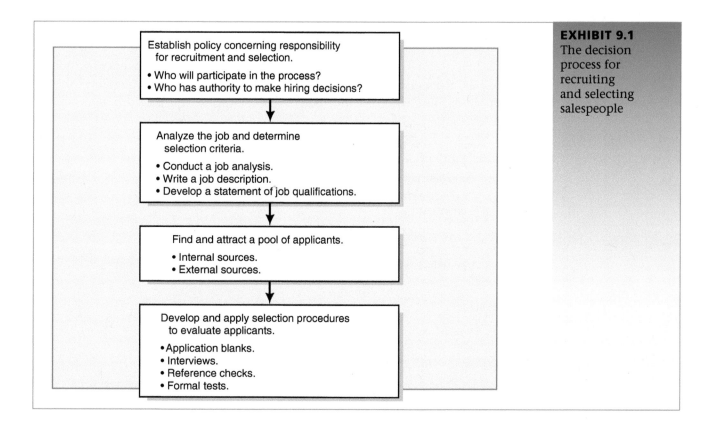

EXHIBIT 9.1
The decision
process for
recruiting
and selecting
salespeople

Regardless of who has the responsibility for recruiting new sales reps, certain procedures should be followed to ensure that new recruits have the aptitude for the job and the potential to be successful. As discussed in Chapter 8, there do not seem to be any general characteristics that make some people better performers across all types of sales jobs. Therefore, a thoughtful recruitment process includes a thorough analysis of the job and a description of the qualifications that a new hire should have. The company then seeks to find and attract a pool of job applicants with the proper qualifications. The objective, in other words, is not to maximize the number of job applicants but to attract a few good applicants. This is because of the high costs involved in attracting and evaluating candidates. For instance, a large industrial services firm estimates that it spent more than $1 million to hire and evaluate candidates in order to hire 50 new salespeople. And it cost another $1 million to train those new recruits. The final stage in the hiring process is to evaluate each applicant using personal history information, interviews, reference checks, and formal tests. The purpose is to determine which applicants have the characteristics and abilities for success. During this stage of the evaluation and selection process, managers must be especially careful not to violate equal employment opportunity laws and regulations.

The remaining sections of this chapter discuss the specific methods and procedures managers might use at each stage of the recruitment and selection process. The recruiting process is complex, and the selection of the right candidate is a function of many different criteria. As demonstrated in Exhibit 9.2, companies use a variety of tools to help them identify the right candidates. Although the primary focus is on "how to do it" from a manager's point of view, some material in this chapter should be useful for learning what is expected if you ever apply for a sales job.

EXHIBIT 9.2
The hiring quiz
	Managers are always searching for tools that will enable them to make better hiring decisions. Here is a quiz for managers to help in defining the right candidate.
	The right candidate is a function of the score to the quiz.
	
	1. Are you in an industry with
	
	  a. Relatively few well-known competitors and few changes in relation to new products and service? (1 point)
	  b. New competition entering the market and rapid changes to products and services introduced? (2 points)
	
	2. What category fits your product?
	
	  a. Capital equipment (1 point)
	  b. Consumer (2 points)
	  c. Service (3 points)
	
	3. If your product is technical in nature, what is your level of technical sales support?
	
	  a. Strong (1 point)
	  b. Average (2 points)
	  c. Weak (3 points)
	
	4. How do you market your product?
	
	  a. Heavily (1 point)
	  b. Very little (2 points)
	  c. Rely on sales staff to do it (3 points)
	
	5. Are you interested in
	
	  a. The development of additional business within existing accounts? (1 point)
	  b. The management of an existing line of business within mature accounts? (2 points)
	  c. The promotion of a new product to prospective customers? (3 points)
	
	6. How much time can you afford to hire and train new sales staff before receiving a return on your investment?
	
	  a. 30–90 days (1 point)
	  b. 91–180 days (2 points)
	  c. 181 days or more (3 points)
	
	7. Will your sales staff work in an office where
	
	  a. Direct supervisor is present? (1 point)
	  b. No direct supervisor is present? (3 points)
	
	8. Will your sales staff
	
	  a. Rely on other sales personnel to prospect and qualify potential customers? (2 points)
	  b. Qualify prospects themselves? (0 points)

9. How much time will you spend training your new hire?

   a. 81 hours or more (1 point)
   b. 41–80 hours (2 points)
   c. 0–40 hours (3 points)

10. How much time will you spend coaching and counseling your new sales staff?

   a. 21 hours or more per week (1 point)
   b. 11–20 hours per week (2 points)
   c. 0–10 hours per week (3 points)

EXHIBIT 9.2
The hiring quiz
(continued)

Add your total points and then refer to the description below to determine the best type of individual for your sales efforts.

HOW TO SCORE

1. Add your total points from questions 1–10.
2. Match your point total to the corresponding point totals below.
3. Your ideal candidate will possess the characteristics indicated for the point total.

PRIMARY CHARACTERISTIC OF SALESPERSON

13 points or less: Tenacity, rapport building, work standards, oral communication, ability to learn
14–18 points: Leadership, planning and organization, job motivation, presence
19–28 points: Persuasiveness, negotiation, analysis, initiative, written communication

SECONDARY CHARACTERISTIC OF SALESPERSON

13 points or less: Planning and organization, listening, job motivation, initiative, written communication
14–18 points: Analysis, tenacity, oral communication, written communication, rapport building
19–28 points: Independence, listening, oral communication, presence, planning

SOURCE OF SALES RECRUITS

13 points or less: New college graduate or hire from within
14–18 points: Hire from within or competitive hire
19–28 points: Competitive hire

Source: Adapted from Walt Shedd, "Ten Steps to Top Sales Professionals," www.sellingpower.com, July 2015.

WHO IS RESPONSIBLE FOR RECRUITING AND SELECTING SALESPEOPLE?

Several years ago, an MBA student at the authors' school was recruited for a sales job with a major manufacturer of outdoor and garden equipment. She was interviewed extensively and wined and dined, not only by the sales manager, who was her prospective supervisor, but also by higher-level executives in the firm, including the vice president of marketing. All this attention from top-level managers surprised the candidate. "After all," she said, "it's only a sales job. Is it common for so many executives to be involved in recruiting new salespeople?"

The student's question raises the issue of who should have the primary responsibility for recruiting and selecting new salespeople. The way in which a company answers this question typically depends on the size of the sales force and the kind of selling involved. In firms with small sales forces, the top-level sales manager commonly views the recruitment and selection of new people as a primary responsibility. In larger, multilevel sales forces, however, the job of attracting and choosing new recruits is usually too extensive and time-consuming for a single executive. In such firms, authority for recruitment and selection is commonly delegated to lower-level sales managers or staff specialists.

In companies where the sales job is not very difficult or complex, new recruits do not need any special qualifications, and turnover rates in the sales force are high—as in firms that sell retail consumer goods—first-level sales managers often have sole responsibility for hiring. When a firm must be more selective in choosing new recruits with certain qualifications and abilities, however, a recruiting specialist may assist first-level managers in evaluating candidates and making hiring decisions. These staff positions are usually filled by sales managers who are being groomed for higher-level executive positions.

In some firms, members of the personnel department—or outside personnel specialists—assist and advise sales managers in hiring new salespeople instead of assigning such duties to a member of the sales management staff. Companies like Ritz-Carlton use outside consultants to help them screen and isolate certain individuals with the specific skill sets needed for success. This approach helps reduce duplication of effort and avoids friction between the sales and personnel departments. One disadvantage is that personnel specialists may not be as knowledgeable about the job to be filled and the qualifications necessary as a member of the sales management staff. When the personnel department or outside specialist is involved in sales recruiting and hiring, they usually help attract applicants and aid in evaluating them. The sales manager, however, typically has the final responsibility for deciding whom to hire.

Finally, when the firm considers the sales force a training ground for sales and marketing managers, human resource executives or other top-level managers may participate in recruiting to ensure new salespeople have management potential. This was the situation in the firm that interviewed our MBA student. Although it wanted to hire her for "just a sales job," company executives saw that job as a stepping-stone to management responsibilities.

JOB ANALYSIS AND DETERMINATION OF SELECTION CRITERIA

Research relating salespeople's personal characteristics to sales aptitude and job performance suggests there is no single set of traits and abilities sales managers can use as criteria in deciding what kind of recruits to hire. Different sales jobs require different skill sets, and this suggests people with different personality traits and abilities should be hired to fill them. The first activities in the recruitment and selection process thus should be the following:

1. Conduct a job analysis to determine what activities, tasks, responsibilities, and environmental influences are involved in the job to be filled.

2. Write a job description that details the findings of the job analysis.

3. Develop a statement of job qualifications that determine and describe the personal traits and abilities a person should have to perform the tasks and responsibilities involved in the job.

Most companies, particularly larger ones, have written job descriptions for sales force positions. Unfortunately, those job descriptions are often out of date and do not accurately reflect the current scope and content of the positions. The responsibilities of a given sales job change as the customers, the firm's account management policies, the competition, and other environmental factors change. Unfortunately firms often do not conduct new analyses and prepare updated descriptions to reflect those changes. Also, firms create new sales positions, and the tasks to be accomplished by people in these jobs may not be spelled out.

Consequently, a critical first step in the hiring process is for management to make sure the job to be filled has been analyzed recently and the findings have been written out in great detail. Without such a detailed and up-to-date description, the sales manager will have more difficulty deciding what kind of person is needed. In addition, prospective recruits will not really know for what position they are applying.

Who Conducts the Analysis and Prepares the Description?

In some firms, analyzing and describing sales jobs are assigned to someone in sales management. In other firms, the task is assigned to a job analysis specialist, who is either someone from the company's personnel department or an outside consultant. Regardless of who is responsible for analyzing and describing the various selling positions within a company, however, it is important that the person collect information about the job's content from two sources: (1) the current occupants of the job and (2) the sales managers who supervise the people in the job.

Current job occupants should be observed or interviewed, or both, to determine what they actually do. Sales managers at various levels should be asked what they think the job occupant should be doing in view of the firm's strategic sales program and account management policies. It is not uncommon for the results of the job analysis to discover salespeople doing things management does not know and not performing activities management believes are important. Such misunderstandings and inaccurate role perceptions illustrate the need for accurate and detailed job descriptions.[1]

Job descriptions written to reflect a consensus between salespeople and their managers can serve several useful functions in addition to guiding the firm's recruiting efforts. They can guide the design of a sales training program to provide new salespeople with the skills to do their job more effectively. Similarly, detailed job descriptions can serve as standards for evaluating each salesperson's job performance, as discussed in Chapter 13.

In many companies, there are a variety of sales positions. In some cases, the job title may not even include the word sales, even though the responsibilities are primarily those of a sales representative. Exhibit 9.3 presents the job descriptions for several different types of sales positions at Dell Corporation. Note that in each description, the company seeks to delineate many of the items covered in the next section. It is also important to be aware that, while both positions are sales related, they require different skills and experience levels. While not all companies provide this kind of detailed job description, it is extremely beneficial to the probability of long-term success for the candidate if both the company and potential salesperson know exactly what the expectations are before employment.

Content of the Job Description

Good job descriptions of sales jobs typically cover the following dimensions and requirements:

1. The nature of product(s) or service(s) to be sold.

2. The types of customers to be called on, including the policies concerning the frequency with which calls are to be made and the types of personnel within customer organizations who should be contacted (e.g., buyers, purchasing agents, plant supervisors).

3. The specific tasks and responsibilities to be carried out, including planning tasks, research and information collection activities, specific selling tasks, other promotional duties, customer servicing activities, and clerical and reporting duties.

4. The relationships between the job occupant and other positions within the organization. To whom does the job occupant report? What are the salesperson's responsibilities to the immediate superior? How and under what circumstances does the salesperson interact with members of other departments, such as production or engineering?

5. The mental and physical demands of the job, including the amount of technical knowledge the salesperson should have concerning the company's products, other necessary skills, and the amount of travel involved.

6. The environmental pressures and constraints that might influence performance of the job, such as market trends, the strengths and weaknesses of the competition, the company's reputation among customers, and resource and supply problems.

ACCOUNT EXECUTIVE IV GLOBAL ALLIANCES

EXHIBIT 9.3
Job descriptions—
Dell Corporation

Description

Identifies and pursues strategic business opportunities through partnerships and/or strategic alliances.

- Responsible for selling Dell's products and services through large application and outsourcing vendors.
- May be responsible for special programs and/or solutions.
- Sells Dell Managed Service (DMS) and Dell Professional Service (DPS) lines.
- Teams with internal Dell resources and leads the cross-functional team in making the best business decisions.
- Focuses on delivering a positive customer experience according to Dell standards.

Responsible for building strong, complex alliances with global System Integrators (SIs).

- SIs who take advantage of the Dell direct model and help create new innovative approaches to the outsourcing marketplace.

- Responsible for global, strategic, coordination of "go-to-market" strategies that help drive exponential sales growth into the outsourcing marketplace.

Qualifications

Sales thought leader, influencing how segment functions/engages client set.

- Leveraged to serve as coach/mentor.

- Creates superior relationships with senior level executives and influential stakeholders to sustain a long-term relationship.
- Has boardroom/executive presence.
- Significant complexity through both SI relationships and Enterprise product/service solutions.

Strong history of complex relationship building.

- Sales history showing ability to sell solutions in complex environments.
- Strong understanding of operational issues and solutions.
- Proven strength in outsourcing and complex service environments.
- Ability to build solid virtual teams.
- Very strong negotiation skills and financial strength.
- Establishes organizational initiatives that enable greater focus on customers.
- Organizes Dell-wide teams in response to SI / customer needs / opportunities 15 years of sales experience or related, industry or segment experience.

- Five years or more specialty sales (System Integrator, Alliance Experience).

ESL (EDUCATION, STATE, AND LOCAL GOVERNMENT) LARGE BUSINESS—ACCOUNT EXECUTIVE

Description

Principal Duties and Responsibilities:

EXHIBIT 9.3
Job descriptions—
Dell Corporation
(continued)

Responsible for Education, State, and Local Government Middle Market account penetration, customer satisfaction and sales growth for long-term results.

1. Ability to act as a Territory Manager by organizing and leveraging all Dell resources to meet territory needs.
2. Develops and plans territory strategies and activities for education accounts such as, selecting accounts, selecting products for calls, identifying buyer influences, overcoming objections, introducing new products, selling all lines of business, making sales presentations and negotiating.
3. Provide customer and competitor feedback to management.
4. Attend and participate in industry sales conferences and trade shows.
5. Requires complex selling skills and responsibility.

Qualifications

Knowledge, Skills, Education, and Abilities:
- Strong knowledge of industry, service, and enterprise products, and proactive selling skills.
- Experience dealing with objections.
- Strong organizational and planning skills.
- Strong verbal and written communication skills.
- Ability to operate remotely and travel.
- Bachelor's degree desired, with a minimum of seven years of related experience.
- Requires proven selling ability in previous positions.
- 8–10 years of sales experience.
- 5–7 years of related industry or segment experience.

Source: Adapted from the Dell website, www.dell.com, July 2015.

Determining Job Qualifications and Selection Criteria

Determining the qualifications a prospective employee should have to perform a given sales job is the most difficult part of the recruitment and selection process. The sales manager—perhaps with assistance from a workforce planning specialist or a vocational psychologist—should consider the relative importance of all the personal traits and characteristics discussed previously. These include physical attributes, mental abilities and experience, and personality traits.

The problem is that nearly all these characteristics are at least somewhat important in choosing new salespeople. No firm, for instance, would actively seek sales recruits who are unintelligent or lacking in self-confidence. At the same time, it is unlikely that many job candidates possess high levels of all the desirable characteristics. The task, then, is to decide which traits and abilities are most important in qualifying an individual for a particular job and which are less critical. Also, consideration should be given to trade-offs among the qualification criteria. Will a person with a deficiency in one important attribute still be considered acceptable if he or she has outstanding qualities in other areas? For example, will the firm be willing to hire someone with only average verbal ability and persuasiveness if that person has an extremely high degree of ambition and persistence?

Methods for Deciding on Selection Criteria

Simply examining the job description can assist decision makers making choices about the key qualifications in new salespeople. If the job requires extensive travel, for instance, management might look for applicants who are younger, have few family responsibilities, and want to travel. Similarly, statements in the job description concerning technical knowledge and skill can help management determine the educational background and previous job experience to look for when selecting from a pool of candidates. For example, in the Dell Corporation job descriptions in Exhibit 9.3, one of the positions (ESL Large Business Account Executive) required extensive travel and work experience. Criteria like these will often serve to limit the number of candidates.

Larger firms go one step further and evaluate the personal histories of their existing salespeople to determine what characteristics differentiate between good and poor performers. As seen in Chapter 8, this analysis seldom produces consistent results across different jobs and different companies. It can produce useful insight, however, when applied to a single type of sales job within a single firm.

Current salespeople might be divided into two groups according to their level of performance on the job: one group of high performers and one of low performers. The characteristics of the two groups are then compared on the basis of information from job application forms, records of personal interviews, and intelligence, aptitude, and personality test scores. Alternatively, statistical techniques might be used to look for significant correlations between variations in the personal characteristics of current salespeople and variations in their job performance. In either case, management attempts to identify personal attributes that differ significantly between high-performing and low-performing salespeople. The assumption is that there may be a cause-and-effect relationship between such attributes and job performance. If new employees are selected who have attributes similar to those of people who are currently performing the job successfully, they also may be successful.[2]

In addition to improving management's ability to specify relevant selection criteria for new salespeople, a firm should conduct a personnel history analysis for another compelling reason. Such analyses are necessary to validate the selection criteria the firm is using, as required by government regulations on equal employment opportunity in hiring. This issue is discussed later in this chapter. Besides comparing the characteristics of good and poor performers in a particular job, management might also try to analyze the unique characteristics of employees who have failed—people who either quit or were fired. One consulting firm, the Klein Institute for Aptitude Testing, suggests that the following characteristics are frequently found among salespeople who fail:

1. Instability of residence.
2. Failure in business within the past two years.

3. Unexplained gaps in the person's employment record.

4. Recent divorce or marital problems.

5. Excessive personal indebtedness; for example, bills could not be paid within two years from earnings on the new job.

The firm might attempt to identify such characteristics by conducting exit interviews with all salespeople who quit or are fired. However, although this sounds like a good idea, it seldom works well in practice. Salespeople who quit are often reluctant to discuss the real reasons for leaving a job, and people who are fired are not likely to cooperate in any research that will be of value to their former employer. However, some useful information about ex-salespeople can often be obtained from the application forms and test scores recorded when they were hired. They may also have spoken with the managers who were their supervisors at the time they left the company.

On the basis of these kinds of information, a written statement of job qualifications should be prepared that is specific enough to guide the selection of new salespeople. These qualifications can then be reflected in the forms and tests used in the selection process, such as the interview form in Exhibit 9.4.[3]

RECRUITING APPLICANTS

Some firms do not actively recruit salespeople. They simply choose new employees from applicants who come to them and ask for work. Although this may be a satisfactory policy for a few well-known firms with good products, strong positions in the market, and attractive compensation policies, today's labor market makes such an approach unworkable for most companies.

Firms that seek well-educated people for sales jobs must compete with many other occupations in attracting such individuals. To make matters worse, people with no selling experience frequently tend to have negative attitudes toward sales jobs. Also, the kinds of people who do seek employment in sales often do not have the qualifications a firm is looking for, particularly when the job involves relatively sophisticated selling, such as technical or new-business sales. Consequently, the company may have to evaluate many applicants to find one qualified person.

This is one area in which some firms try to be efficient but end up being inefficient and often ineffective. They attempt to hold down recruiting costs on the assumption that a good training program can convert marginal recruits into solid sales performers. As we saw in the last chapter, however, some of the determinants of sales success, such as aptitude and personal characteristics, are difficult or impossible to change through training or experience. Therefore, spending the money and effort to find well-qualified candidates is a profitable investment. In certain

Business Division Applicant Interview Form

EXHIBIT 9.4
Applicant interview form

Applicant name: _____   Date: _____

Interview with: Time:

1. _____   _____
2. _____   _____
3. _____   _____
4. _____   _____

Rating:
5—Excellent
4—Above average
3—Average
2—Fair
1—Poor

Directions: Check square that most correctly reflects characteristics applicable to candidate. An outstanding candidate would score 95 to 100.

	1	2	3	4	5

General appearance
  1. Neatness, dress
  2. Business image

Impressions
  3. Positive mannerisms
  4. Speech, expressions
  5. Outgoing personality
  6. Positive attitude

Potential sales ability
  7. Persuasive communication
  8. Aggressiveness
  9. Sell and manage large accounts
  10. Make executive calls
  11. Organize and manage a territory
  12. Work with others
  13. Successful prior experience
  14. Potential for career growth

Maturity
  15. General intelligence, common sense
  16. Self-confidence
  17. Self-motivation, ambition
  18. Composure, stability
  19. Adaptability
  20. Sense of ethics

General comments: _____

Overall rating (total score): _____

Would you recommend this candidate for the position? _____

Why or why not?

industries, and when environmental conditions make the job market tight for recruiting companies, even finding sufficient numbers of qualified individuals can be a challenge. For example, the life insurance industry reports that it must interview between 60 and 120 people to find one hire.[4]

In view of the difficulties in attracting qualified people to fill sales positions, a well-planned and effectively implemented recruiting effort is usually a crucial part of the firm's hiring program. The primary objective of the recruiting process should not be to maximize the total number of job applicants. Too many recruits can overload the selection process, forcing the manager to use less thorough screening and evaluation procedures. Intel, for example, receives thousands of applications every day. Besides, numbers do not ensure quality. The focus should not be on how many recruits can be found but on finding a few good ones.

Therefore, the recruiting process should be designed to be the first step in the selection process. Self-selection by the prospective employees is the most efficient means of selection. The recruiting effort should be implemented in a way that discourages unqualified people from applying. For example, many companies have adopted the Internet as a recruiting source for potential candidates. Often companies like IBM have a screening procedure by which candidates can provide certain key pieces of data about themselves, and the company will search its job openings to look for a match. It is important that recruiting communications point out both the attractive and unattractive aspects of the job to be filled, specify the job qualifications, and state the likely compensation. This will help ensure that only qualified and interested people apply for the job. Also, recruiting efforts should be focused only on sources of potential applicants where fully qualified people are most likely to be found.

Sales managers can go to a number of places to find recruits or leads concerning potential recruits. Internal sources consist of other people already employed in other departments within the firm, whereas external sources include people in other firms (who are often identified and referred by current members of the sales force), educational institutions, advertisements, and employment agencies.

Each source is likely to produce candidates with somewhat different backgrounds and characteristics. Therefore, while most firms seek recruits from more than one source, a company's recruiting efforts should be concentrated on sources that are most likely to produce the kinds of people needed. Research suggests that firms use many different sources for finding recruits, depending on the type of sales job they are trying to fill. When the job involves missionary or trade selling, firms rely most heavily on a variety of external sources, such as advertisements, employment agencies, and educational institutions. When the job involves technical selling requiring substantial product knowledge and industry experience, firms focus more heavily on employees in other departments within the company and on personal referrals of people working for other firms in the industry.[5] The relative advantages and limitations of each of these sources of new recruits are discussed in more depth in the following sections.

LEADERSHIP The Challenge of Recruiting a Global Sales Force

What makes one salesperson successful and another a failure? This is a question sales professionals have been trying to answer for years. Indeed, as we have been discussing in earlier chapters, the characteristics of sales success are difficult, if not impossible, to identify. Consider then the challenge of a company recruiting a global sales force. Not only is it faced with the significant challenge of trying to determine the qualities to look for in a salesperson, but it must also deal with social and cultural differences.

Sales experts suggest that rather than focus on differences, firms should focus on the similarities. This is not to say that all salespeople should be the same, but rather, the focus should be on the sales tasks. Specifically, as companies seek to build long-term customer relationships, the basic qualities needed by the salesperson are the same whether they are selling in Orlando or Osaka, New York or New Delhi.

Empathy, communication, and the ability to be self-motivating are characteristics that salespeople need in today's selling environment, no matter where they work. In addition, the ability to understand, work with, and feel comfortable using technology is becoming a critical success factor in selling. Since salespeople are equipped with cell phones and laptops, they need to be able to use the technology to maximize the customer relationship.

Focusing on the fundamental qualities needed to build a successful customer relationship rather than social and cultural differences enables companies to develop a more consistent pool of potential salespeople around the world. Coupled with effective ways of measuring the individual's abilities, this approach can give global sales managers a useful strategy in sales force recruitment.

All of the recruiting issues faced by sales managers are magnified as companies expand globally and seek to hire salespeople in new international markets. Cultural differences, language barriers, and legal restrictions create additional concerns about hiring the right people for the sales position. The key is for a company to have done its homework and research each new market before making the decision to enter it. For example, in many European countries it is much more difficult to terminate an employee than in the United States. This makes the hiring decision much more difficult. It is important for a company to understand the legal requirements of hiring new salespeople before hiring them. The Leadership box discusses the challenges of recruiting a global sales force.

People in nonsales departments within the firm, such as manufacturing, maintenance, engineering, or the office staff, sometimes have latent sales talent and are a common source of sales recruits. Past surveys suggest that more than half of U.S. industrial goods producers hire at least some of their salespeople from other internal departments.

Recruiting current company employees for the sales force has distinct advantages:

1. Company employees have established performance records, and they are more of a known quantity than outsiders.

2. Recruits from inside the firm should require less orientation and training because they are already familiar with the company's products, policies, and operations.

3. Recruiting from within can bolster company morale, as employees become aware that opportunities for advancement are available outside of their own departments or divisions.

To facilitate successful internal recruiting, the company's personnel department should always be kept abreast of sales staff needs. Because the personnel staff is familiar with the qualifications of all employees and continuously evaluates their performance, they are in the best position to identify people with the attributes necessary to fill available sales jobs.

Internal recruiting has some limitations. People in nonsales departments seldom have much previous selling experience. Also, internal recruiting can cause some animosity within the firm if supervisors of other departments think their best employees are being pirated by the sales force.

External Sources

Although it is often a good idea to start with internal sources when recruiting new salespeople, most of the time there will not be enough qualified internal candidates to meet the human resource needs of a firm's sales force. As a result, the vast majority of companies must expand the search to cover external sources.

Referral of People from Other Firms

In addition to being potential sales employees themselves, company personnel can provide management with leads to potential recruits from outside the firm. Current salespeople are in a good position to provide their superiors with leads to new recruits. They know the requirements of the job, they often have contacts with other salespeople who may be willing to change jobs, and they can do much to help "sell" an available job to potential recruits. Consequently, many sales managers make sure their salespeople are aware of the company's recruiting needs. Some companies offer bonuses as incentives for their salespeople to recruit new prospects. Such referrals from current employees must be handled tactfully so as not to cause hard feelings if the applicant is rejected later.

Customers can also be a source of sales recruits. Sometimes a customer's employees have the kinds of knowledge that make them attractive as prospective salespeople. For instance, department store employees can make good salespeople for the wholesalers or manufacturers that supply the store because they are familiar with the product and the procedures of store buyers. Cosmetics companies such as Estée Lauder and L'Oréal recruit from the ranks of department store personnel.

Customers with whom a firm has good relations may also provide leads concerning potential recruits who are working for other firms, particularly competitors. Purchasing agents know what impresses them in a salesperson, they are familiar with the abilities of the sales reps who call on them, and they are sometimes aware when a sales rep is interested in changing jobs.

The question of whether a firm should recruit salespeople from its competitors, however, is controversial. Such people are knowledgeable about the industry from their experience. They also might be expected to "bring along" some of their current customers when they switch companies. This does not happen frequently, however, since customers are usually more loyal to a supplier than to the individual who represents that supplier.

On the other side of the argument, it is sometimes difficult to get salespeople who have worked for a competing firm to unlearn old practices and to conform to their new employer's account management policies. Also, some managers think recruiting a competitor's personnel is unethical. They believe it is unfair for firm B to recruit actively someone from firm A after A has spent the money to hire and train that person. Such people may be in a position to divulge A's company secrets to B. Consequently, some firms refuse to recruit their competitor's salespeople, although whether such policies are due to high ethical standards, the expense of retraining, or fear of possible retaliation is open to question.

Advertisements

A less selective means of attracting job applicants is to advertise the available position. When a technically qualified or experienced person is needed, an ad might be placed on an industry trade or technical website. More commonly, advertisements are placed on general job websites such as Monster to attract applicants for relatively less demanding sales jobs that don't require special qualifications. A well-written ad can be very effective for attracting applicants. As suggested, however, this is not necessarily a good thing. When a firm's advertisements attract large numbers of applicants who are unqualified or only marginally interested, the firm must engage in costly screening to identify legitimate candidates.[6] If a firm does use ads in recruiting, it must decide how much information about the job it should include in the ads. Many sales managers argue that *open ads*, which disclose the firm's name, product to be sold, compensation, and specific job duties, generate a more select pool of high-quality applicants, lower selection costs, and decreased turnover rates than ads without such information. Open ads also avoid any ethical questions concerning possible deception.

However, for less attractive, high-turnover sales jobs, some sales managers prefer *blind ads*, which carry only minimal information, sometimes only a phone number. These maximize the number of applicants and give the manager an opportunity to explain the attractive features of the job in a personal meeting with the applicant.[7] The use of blind ads is declining as candidates demand more information about the position and company they are considering.

Employment Agencies

Employment agencies are sometimes used to find recruits, usually for more routine sales jobs such as retail sales. However, executive search firms such as

Heidrick and Struggles specialize in finding applicants for more demanding sales jobs. Some sales managers have had unsatisfactory experiences with employment agencies. They charge that agencies are sometimes overzealous in attempting to earn their fees, and send applicants that do not meet the job qualifications. Others argue, however, that when a firm has problems with an employment agency, it is often the fault of the company for not understanding the agency's role and not providing sufficient information about the kinds of recruits it is seeking. When a firm carefully selects an agency with a good reputation, establishes a long-term relationship, and provides detailed descriptions of job qualifications, the agency can perform a valuable service. It locates and screens job applicants and reduces the amount of time and effort the company's sales managers must devote to recruiting.

In recent years, new online companies such as monster.com have taken the concept of the employment agency in a new direction. Increasingly, employment websites provide a valuable service, enabling employers to learn about potential candidates over the Internet. At the same time, individuals can learn about thousands of positions efficiently and effectively online.

Educational Institutions

College and university placement offices are a common source of recruits for firms that require salespeople with proven intellectual ability or technical backgrounds. Most educational institutions in fact allocate resources to "career management" departments that enhance the development of careers for their graduates. Educational institutions are a particularly effective source when the sales job is viewed as a first step toward a career in management. College graduates are often more socially poised than people of the same age without college training, and good grades provide evidence the person can think logically, budget time efficiently, and communicate reasonably well.

But younger college graduates seldom have much selling experience, and are likely to require more extensive orientation and training in selling fundamentals. Also, college-educated sales recruits have a reputation for "job hopping," unless the jobs are challenging and promotions are rapid. One insurance company, for instance, stopped recruiting college graduates when it found that such recruits did not stay with their jobs very long. Such early turnover is sometimes more the fault of the company than of the recruits. When recruiters paint an unrealistic picture of the job demands and rewards of the position to be filled, or when they recruit people who are overqualified for the job, high turnover is often the result.[8]

There is, however, a growing movement to professionalize the sales career, with a number of colleges and universities creating comprehensive sales programs, led by a group of schools in the University Sales Center Alliance. Currently there are more than thirty schools offering a four-year degree in sales and many more that give students the opportunity to earn a certificate or minor in sales. These programs often require an internship to acquire real-world sales experience and provide valuable insight into various sales career options. Graduates of these programs are highly sought after by companies, as the time it takes for a graduate to become productive is reduced by 50 percent over other graduates. Moreover, they are 35 percent less likely to leave their employer. Although professional sales programs are valued by employers, universities are just now embracing them, primarily due to the outdated and incorrect belief that personal selling is not a true academic discipline.

Junior colleges and vocational schools are another source of sales recruits that has expanded rapidly in recent years. Many such schools have programs explicitly designed to prepare people for selling careers. Thus, companies do not have to contend with the negative attitudes toward selling they sometimes encounter in four-year college graduates. Junior colleges and vocational schools are particularly good sources of recruits for sales jobs that require reasonably well-developed mental and communications abilities, but where advanced technical knowledge or a four-year degree is not essential.

Internet

Increasingly, companies are seeking applications over the Internet. Indeed, as seen in Exhibit 9.3, companies such as Dell Corporation are posting jobs and requesting that candidates submit their applications over the Internet and appropriate action is taken. In many cases, younger candidates are as comfortable submitting Internet applications as they are filling them out on paper. In addition, by targeting the Internet application to specific job postings, the company can direct the information to the right people very efficiently. For example, Internet applications to Dell include a unique job reference so that the information can be sent to the right people at a specific geographic location.

While the use of the Internet to recruit salespeople is clearly increasing, the unique aspects of the sales position coupled with the need to meet and interview individuals in person make it a difficult tool for recruiting purposes. However, as a screening device it is effective since a large number of applications can be processed easily. Some companies, such as Google, receive thousands of applications per day for positions throughout the company. By using the Internet, they can process these applications to the right people efficiently and effectively.

Increasingly one of the most useful recruiting tools for companies is social media, the Technology box highlights the primary social tools used by business.

TECHNOLOGY   **Social Media as a Recruiting Tool**

Social media is the new source for company recruiters looking to external sources for new employee. Social recruiting uses tools like LinkedIn, Facebook, and Twitter to position a company in front of the most qualified, talented, and largest pool of applicants. The challenge for the company is using the tools to find the right person for the job.

LinkedIn is a network of global professionals, each with their own personal network. In this forum, you can find, be introduced to, and collaborate with other professionals. The site includes multiple job boards and allows you to connect with individuals and companies. The typical way to use LinkedIn is to post available jobs and search for candidates. If the budget allows, you can also sign up for LinkedIn Talent Advantage, an exclusive suite of resources for recruiters. LinkedIn also allows for users to join groups that are relevant to their experience or field. In this manner, recruiters can build a network for connections that includes friends, family, employers, coworkers, clients, or local entrepreneurs. Connections are important since you never know when good talent will emerge. Even without posting a job, you can advertise via your network activity box to let everyone you are connected to know you are hiring.

Facebook provides a searchable directory that lists users and groups and offers three different tools for recruiters. One option is to post a job ad on Facebook Marketplace. This requires basic information such as location, job category, subcategory, title, why you need to fill this position, description, and if you want to post an image with the job posting. One downside to this is that you can't target it to a specific group of people. Facebook pages are also free and can be used to share your business and products with users. Sometimes these business pages are used as recruiting tools directed at people who are already passionate about your company. The third option is the Facebook Ad, which allows you to choose the exact audience that you are looking to target. You'll have to answer a series of questions about the job description and people characteristics and then Facebook tells you how many people fit that criterion. There is a fee either per click or per impression.

Twitter is a micro blogging site that allows recruiters to advertise jobs in fewer than 140 characters. If the company doesn't have a large network of followers, you can use the search function to search for people you know, by location, by industry or interest and by popularity etc. The company's Twitter account is also an opportunity to inform potential hires. Tweets say a lot about the company and how it communicates.

SELECTION PROCEDURES

After the qualifications necessary to fill a job have been determined and some applicants have been recruited, the final task is to determine which applicants best meet the qualifications and have the greatest aptitude for the job. To gain the information needed to evaluate each prospective employee, firms typically use some combination of the following selection tools and procedures:[9]

1. Application blanks

2. Personal interviews

3. Reference checks

4. Physical examinations

5. Psychological tests

   a. Intelligence

   b. Personality

   c. Aptitude/skills

Past research studies suggest that, on average across all occupations, composites of psychological test scores have the greatest predictive validity for evaluating a potential employee's future job performance, whereas evaluations based on personal interviews have the lowest. In other words, test scores have the highest correlations with candidates' subsequent performance on the job and account for about 28 percent of the variance in subsequent performance across new hires. Ratings based on personal interviews, on the other hand, account for only about 2 percent of variance in subsequent performance.[10] Given the ability of psychological tests to do a better job of predicting sales performance, it is surprising that firms actually use personal interviews much more frequently. A survey of selection procedures followed by 121 industrial firms suggests personal interviews are almost universally employed, while psychological tests are the least-used selection tool, although their use is increasing again. However, large firms are somewhat more thorough in their use of psychological tests—and the development of detailed job descriptions—than smaller firms.

Application Blanks

Although professional salespeople often have résumés to submit to prospective employers, many personnel experts believe a standard company application form makes it easier to assess applicants. A well-designed application blank helps ensure that the same information is obtained in the same form from all candidates.

The primary purpose of the application form is to collect basic information about the recruit's personal history. Forms typically ask for facts about the candidate's physical condition, education, business experience, military service, and outside interests/activities and can be used to screen for basic qualifications such as educational experience.

A second function of the application form is to help managers prepare for personal interviews with job candidates. Often a recruit's responses to items on the application raise questions that should be explored during an interview. If the application shows that a person has held several jobs within the past few years, for example, the interviewer should attempt to find out the reasons for these changes. Perhaps the interviewer can determine whether the applicant is a "job hopper" who is unlikely to stay with the company very long. Indeed, a study conducted at one pharmaceutical firm found that common application information—such as candidates' tenure in their previous jobs and their amount of sales experience—was able to distinguish salespeople more likely to stay with the hiring company over time from those who were more likely to quit.[11]

Personal Interviews

In addition to probing into the applicant's history, personal interviews enable managers to gain insight into the applicant's mental abilities and personality. An interview provides a manager with the opportunity to assess a candidate's communication skills, intelligence, sociability, aggressiveness, empathy, ambition, and other traits related to the qualifications necessary for the job. Different managers use many different interviewing approaches to accomplish these objectives. These methods of conducting personal interviews, however, can all be classified as either structured or unstructured.

In structured interviews, each applicant is asked the same predetermined questions. This approach is particularly good when the interviewer is inexperienced at evaluating candidates. The standard questions help guide the interview and ensure that all factors relevant to the candidate's qualifications are covered. Also, asking the same questions of all candidates makes it easier to compare their strengths and weaknesses. To facilitate such comparisons, many firms use a standard interview evaluation form on which interviewers rate each applicant's response to each question together with their overall impressions of the candidate.

One potential weakness of structured interviews is that the interviewer may rigidly stick to the prepared questions and fail to identify or probe the unique qualities of each candidate. In practice, though, structured interviews are often not as inflexible as the criticism implies. As a manager gains interviewing experience, he or she often learns to ask additional questions when an applicant's response is inadequate without disturbing the flow of the interview.[12]

At the other end of interviewing techniques is the unstructured interview. Such interviews seek to get the applicant talking freely on a variety of subjects. The interviewer asks only a few questions to direct the conversation to topics of interest, such as the applicant's work experiences, career objectives, and outside activities. The rationale for this approach is that significant insight into the applicant's character and motivations can be gained by allowing the applicant to talk freely with a minimum of direction. Also, the interviewer is free to spend more time on topics where the applicant's responses are interesting or unusual.

Successful, unstructured interviewing requires interviewers with experience and interpretive skills. Because there is no predetermined set of questions, there is always a danger that the interviewer will neglect some relevant topics. It is also more difficult to compare the responses of two or more applicants. Consequently, since most firms' sales managers have relatively little experience as interviewers, structured interviews are much more common in selecting new salespeople than unstructured approaches.

Within the interview itself, particularly those that are relatively unstructured, some sales managers use additional techniques to learn as much as possible about the applicant's character and aptitude. One such technique is the stress interview. The interviewer puts the applicant under stress in one of many ways, ranging from silence to constant, aggressive probing and questioning. The rationale for this technique is that the interviewer may learn how the applicant will respond to the stress encountered in selling situations.

Another approach is for the interviewer to ask the applicant to sell something. "Hand the prospect a stapler, a laptop computer, or any other object that's handy and ask him to 'sell' it. . . . A pro should be able to sell anything," says one sales manager. "The one thing he's got to do is to ask for the order. Seven of ten fail to do so."[13]

Techniques like these can be useful to assess a candidate's character and selling skills, but they should be used as only one part of the interview. Sometimes sales managers become so obsessed with finding the "one best way" to assess candidates that they allow interviewing gimmicks to get in the way of real communication. After all, another purpose of job interviews is to provide candidates with information about the job and company so they will be interested in taking the job. One real danger with gimmicky interviewing techniques is that the applicant will be turned off and lose interest in working for the firm. Regardless of the interviewing technique, more managers rely on interviews to evaluate sales candidates than any other selection tool. Yet as we saw earlier, there is some evidence that evaluations based on personal interviews are among the least-valid predictors of job performance.

If an applicant makes it past the face-to-face interviews, a reference check is often the next step. Some sales managers question the value of references because "they always say nice things." However, with a little resourcefulness, reference checks can be a valuable selection tool.

Checking references can ensure the accuracy of factual data about the applicant. It is naive to assume that everything a candidate has written on a résumé or application form is true. Facts about previous job experiences and college degrees should be checked. As we have seen, individuals do not always tell the truth on their résumés (before becoming vice president, Joe Biden was caught providing false information on his résumé).

The discovery of false data on a candidate's application raises a question about basic honesty as well as about what the candidate is trying to hide. References can supply additional information and opinions about a prospect's aptitude and past job performance. Calling a number of references and probing them in depth can be time-consuming and costly, but it can also produce worthwhile information and protect against making expensive hiring mistakes.[14]

ETHICAL MOMENT   Personal Interview Ethics

Personal interviews are one of the most widely used selection tools for all employees, but especially sales. The reasons are obvious: It gives the recruiter first hand information about the job applicant, allows the recruiter to assess first hand the applicants communications skills as well as other benefits. However, it is also one of the least accurate tools for selecting potential employees, which is why companies generally employ multiple selection tools.

One of the primary ethical challenges is overcoming the personal bias that recruiters bring to the interview. Almost anything can influence the recruiter, from stereotyping (which we discussed earlier) to the time of day (late in the day versus early morning), personal life (problems at home), and a variety of factors. Experienced recruiters can overcome these issues to focus on the interview but many recruiters allow personal bias to influence the process. The influence can take many forms from the questions asked to how particular answers are interpreted. In most cases the interviewee may not even be aware of the problem.

Recruiters must be trained to leave any issue, problem, or personal concern at the interview door. Many if not most organizations use multiple interviews across several individuals to help alleviate the challenge of having a single person conduct the interview. Ultimately, because the personal interview is such an important selection tool, companies realize the importance of "getting it right".

Question to Ponder:

- Can you identify any issues or problems that might affect an interviewer during the interview process? What would you do if you encountered interview bias during an interview?

Physical Examinations

One typically does not think of selling as physically demanding, yet sales jobs often require a great deal of stamina and the physical ability to withstand lots of stress. Consequently, even though physical examinations are relatively expensive compared with other selection tools, many sales managers see them as valuable aids for evaluating candidates.

However, managers should be very cautious in requiring medical examinations, including specific tests for such things as drug use or the HIV virus, for prospective employees. Under the Americans with Disabilities Act (discussed in more detail later in this chapter), it is no longer advisable to use a standard physical examination for all positions. If used, the physical exam should focus only on attributes directly related to the requirements of the job to be filled. For example, in many sales positions, conditions such as diabetes or epilepsy would have little or no impact on the candidate's ability to perform. Therefore, questions concerning such conditions should be avoided, and any information collected for emergency situations should be kept confidential. Under the law's guidelines, a physical examination should be performed only after a job offer has been extended. And the job offer cannot be made conditional on the results of the physical exam unless all new hires for a position are subjected to the same physical exam and the results of those exams are treated as confidential medical records.[15]

Tests

A final set of selection tools used by many firms consists of tests aimed at measuring an applicant's mental abilities and personality traits. The most commonly used tests can be grouped into three types: (1) intelligence, (2) aptitude, and (3) personality tests. Within each category exist a variety of different tests used by different companies. The Innovation box highlights how psychometric testing can be used in the sales hiring process.

Intelligence Tests

Intelligence tests are useful for determining whether an applicant has sufficient mental ability to perform a job successfully. Sales managers tend to believe these are the most useful of all the tests commonly used in selecting salespeople. General intelligence tests are designed to measure an applicant's overall mental abilities by examining how well the applicant comprehends, reasons, and learns. The Wonderlic Personnel Test is one common general intelligence test. It is popular because it is short; it consists of 50 items and requires only about 12 minutes to complete. The WPT can be administered using paper, a computer, or over the Internet. Finally, it is available in more than 15 languages, including Chinese and Russian.

When the job to be filled requires special competence in one or a few areas of mental ability, a specialized intelligence test might be used to evaluate candidates. Tests are available for measuring such things as speed of learning, number facility, memory, logical reasoning, and verbal ability.

INNOVATION   Psychometric Testing in the Sales Hiring Process

Research suggests that newly hired sales professionals do not possess job-specific traits one third of the time even though they successfully complete the job interview process and initial training. As a result companies look for options to help improve the recruiting process. One solution is to test candidates using a psychometric instrument that is directly connected to a specific job profile and must be integrated into a strategic approach for recruitment and selection. When executed properly the test can be an objective decision-making tool that is tied directly to a specific hiring decision. The goal is to determine a candidate's fitness for a particular role.

While companies generally contract out testing to full-service sales training providers, it is important that the hiring manager first identify the specific traits needed for success. Traits are specific, innate capabilities possessed by a candidate to one degree or another. So the question becomes not whether or not the candidate can fulfill a job profile (or description) but whether he or she can execute the specific company strategies. As a result, the psychometric test measures the traits identified in the job profile that reflect the company's defined strategy to serve customers, win market share, or outperform the competition.

Recruiting professionals believe in the old adage—hire slowly, fire quickly. Companies often learn the hard way that it is good strategy to spend the money up front on the hiring process to avoid spending additional resources in the long run to train a person who lacks the necessary traits for the role.

Aptitude Tests

Aptitude tests are designed to determine whether an applicant has an interest in, or the ability to perform, certain tasks and activities. For example, the Strong Interest Inventory asks respondents to indicate whether they like or dislike a variety of situations and activities. This can determine whether applicants' interests are similar to those of people who are successful in a variety of different occupations, including selling. Other tests measure skills or abilities, such as mechanical or mathematical aptitude, that might be related to success in particular selling jobs.

One problem with at least some aptitude tests is that instead of measuring a person's innate abilities, they measure current level of skill at certain tasks. At least some skills necessary for successful selling can be taught, or improved, through a well-designed training program. Therefore, rejecting applicants because they currently do not have the necessary skills can mean losing people who could be trained to be successful salespeople.

Personality Tests

Many general personality tests evaluate an individual on numerous traits. For example, the Edwards Personal Preference Schedule—offered by many testing organizations—measures 24 traits such as sociability, aggressiveness, and independence. Such tests, however, contain many questions, require substantial time to complete, and gather information about some traits that may be irrelevant for evaluating future salespeople. Consequently, more limited personality tests have been developed in recent years that concentrate on only a few traits thought to be directly relevant to a person's future success in sales.[16] These are often designed and administered by individual testing services. For example, Walden Testing has a specific test to assess an individual's selling skills.

Concerns about the Use of Tests

During the 1950s and early 1960s, tests—particularly general intelligence and sales aptitude tests—were widely used as selection tools for evaluating potential sales-people. However, due to a number of legal concerns and restrictions posed by civil rights legislation and equal opportunity hiring practices, companies had cut back the use of these tests until recently. Now, current evidence suggests that properly designed and administered tests are valid selection tools, which has spurred an increase in their popularity, although they are somewhat more widely used in large firms than in smaller ones.[17]

Despite the empirical evidence, however, managers continue to be leery of tests, and many firms do not use them as part of their evaluation of sales recruits. There are a number of reasons for these negative attitudes.

For one thing, despite the evidence that tests have relatively high predic-tive validity on average, some managers continue to doubt that tests are valid for predicting the future success of salespeople in their specific firm. As discussed in Chapter 8, no personality traits have been found to positively affect performance across a variety of selling jobs in different firms. Thus, specific tests that meas-ure such abilities and traits may be valid for selecting salespeople for some jobs but invalid for others. Also, tests for measuring specific abilities and characteris-tics of applicants do not always produce consistent scores. Some commercially available tests have not been developed using established scientific measurement procedures; as a result, their reliability and validity are questionable. Even when a firm believes a particular trait, such as empathy or sociability, is related to job perfor-mance, there is still a question about which test should be used to measure that trait.

A related concern, particularly in the case of personality tests, is that some creative and talented people may be rejected simply because their personalities do not conform to test norms. Many sales jobs require creative people, particularly when those people are being groomed for future management responsibilities. Yet these people seldom fit an average personality profile because the "average" person is not particularly creative.

Another concern about testing involves the possible reactions of the people who are tested. A reasonably intelligent, "test-wise" person can "fudge" the results of many tests by selecting answers he or she thinks management will want. These answers may not accurately reflect that person's feelings or behavior. Also, many prospective employees view extensive testing as a burden and perhaps an inva-sion of privacy. Therefore, some managers fear that requiring a large battery of tests may turn off a candidate and reduce the likelihood of accepting a job with the firm.

Finally, a given test may discriminate between people of different races or sexes, and the use of such tests is illegal. Consequently, some firms have abandoned the use of tests rather than risk a legal challenge.

Guidelines for the Appropriate Use of Tests

To avoid, or at least minimize, the preceding testing problems, managers should keep the following guidelines in mind:

1. Test scores should be considered as a single input in the selection decision. Managers should not rely on them to do the work of other parts of the selection process, such as interviewing and checking references. Candidates should not be eliminated solely on the basis of test scores. The best approach is to incorporate information from multiple sources (such as a test, interview, and selection process). The different types of data increase confidence by using multiple sources to corroborate the decision. Chally's "How to Select a Sales Force that Sells" (2005) provides a lot of guidance on how information from a written test, interview, and reference check can be integrated to select a salesperson.

2. Applicants should be tested on only those abilities and traits that management, on the basis of a thorough job analysis, has determined to be relevant for the specific job. Broad tests that evaluate a large number of traits not relevant to a specific job are probably inappropriate.

3. When possible, tests with built-in internal consistency checks should be used. Then the person who analyzes the test results can determine whether the applicant responded honestly or was faking some answers. Many recently designed tests ask similar questions with slightly different wording several times throughout the test. If respondents are answering honestly, they should always give the same response to similar questions.

4. A firm should conduct empirical studies to ensure the tests are valid for predicting an applicant's future performance in the job. This kind of hard evidence of test validity is particularly important in view of the government's equal employment opportunity requirements. Often this requires hiring an expert consultant in employment testing such as an industrial-organizational psychologist or using a testing firm that has such expertise on staff.

5. It is important to include both high and low performers in a validation study. Simply benchmarking and identifying top employees will not identify the traits and skills that differentiate good from poor performers.

EQUAL EMPLOYMENT OPPORTUNITY REQUIREMENTS IN SELECTING SALESPEOPLE

The number of federal lawsuits alleging workplace discrimination is large and growing.[18] The primary basis for these suits is Title VII of the 1964 Civil Rights Act, which forbids discrimination in employment on the basis of race, sex, religion, color, or national origin. A number of federal laws have extended this protection against job discrimination to include such factors as age and physical and mental disabilities, as summarized in Exhibit 9.5. Consequently, extreme care should be taken to ensure the selection tools a firm uses in hiring salespeople—especially its interviewing and testing procedures—are not biased against any subgroup of the labor force. Exhibit 9.6 offers guidelines concerning the kinds of illegal or sensitive questions managers should avoid when conducting employment interviews or designing application forms.

Requirements for Tests

Section 703(h) of the 1964 Civil Rights Act approves the use of "professionally developed ability tests," provided such tests are not "designed, intended, or used to discriminate because of race, color, religion, sex, or national origin." Suppose, however, an employer innocently uses a test that does discriminate by having a larger proportion of men than women, or a larger percentage of whites than blacks, receive passing scores. Has the employer violated the law? Not necessarily.

In such cases, the employer must prove the test scores are valid predictors of successful performance on the job in question. In other words, it is legal for a firm to hire more men than women for a job if it can be proven that men possess more of some trait or ability that will enable them to do the job better. This requires that the employer have empirical evidence showing a significant relationship between scores on the test and actual job performance. The procedures a firm might use to produce this kind of evidence were described earlier in this chapter when discussing how to determine whether particular job qualifications are valid.[19]

EXHIBIT 9.5 Legislation affecting recruitment and selection	**Legislative Act**	**Purpose**
	Civil Rights Act of 1866	Gives blacks the same rights as whites and has since been extended by the courts to include all ethnic groups.
	Civil Rights Act of 1964 (Title VII)	Prohibits discrimination in employment based on race, color, religion, national origin, or sex.
	Age Discrimination in Employment Act (1967)	Prohibits discrimination against people ages 40 to 70.
	Fair Employment Opportunity Act (1972)	Founded the Equal Employment Opportunity Commission to ensure compliance with the Civil Rights Act.
	Rehabilitation Act of 1973	Requires affirmative action to hire and promote handicapped persons if the firm employs 50 or more workers and is seeking a federal contract in excess of $50,000.
	Vietnam Era Veterans Readjustment Act (1974)	Requires affirmative action to hire Vietnam veterans and disabled veterans of any war by firms holding federal contracts in excess of $10,000.
	Americans with Disabilities Act (1990)	Prohibits discrimination based on handicaps or disabilities—either physical or mental. Applied to all employers with 25 or more employees beginning July 26, 1992, and extended to employers with 15 or more workers on July 26, 1994.

EXHIBIT 9.6
Illegal or sensitive
questions that
should be
eliminated from
employment
applications and
interviews

Category	Illegal or Sensitive Topics
Nationality or race	It is not permissible to make comments or ask questions related to the race, color, national origin, or descent of an applicant (or even his or her spouse). An applicant should not be asked to provide a photograph. An applicant can be asked to demonstrate proficiency in another language if that is a requirement of the job, but he or she cannot be asked if that is his or her native language. An applicant may be asked if he or she is a U.S. citizen but not whether he or she is a native or naturalized citizen. It is permissible to ask if the individual has the legal right to remain and work in the United States.
Religion	It is not permissible to ask about an individual's religious beliefs. In addition, do not ask whether the company's schedule would interfere with the individual's religion.
Sex and marital status	An applicant's gender should not be a part of the hiring discussion, unless it is directly related to the job itself. In addition, questions about the spouse (for example, spouse's employment status) are not permitted. Finally, no questions regarding family size (currently or planned in the future) are permitted.
Age	It is permitted to ask if the individual is a minor or over the age of 70; however, the applicant should not be asked specific questions about his or her age or date of birth.
Physical characteristics, disabilities, health problems	Avoid all questions related to an individual's personal health situation. However, once a description of the job has been provided, the applicant may be asked whether or not he or she has any physical or mental condition that would limit his or her ability to perform the job.
Height and weight	It is important to be sensitive to questions about height and weight because, while they are not illegal, they could provide the basis for discrimination on certain demographic and or ethnic groups (women, Asians, and others).
Financial situation (bankruptcy)	Questions about an individual's financial situation should be avoided as it is illegal to deny employment to someone solely on the basis of whether or not he or she has filed for bankruptcy.
Arrests and convictions	It is illegal to ask about prior arrests; however, it is permissible to ask about convictions provided the employer provides a statement about how the information will be used in the selection process.

Requirements for Interviews and Application Blanks

Because it is illegal to discriminate in hiring on the basis of race, sex, religion, age, and national origin, there is no reason for a firm to ask for such information on its job application forms or during personal interviews. It is wise to avoid all questions in any way related to such factors. Then there will be no question in the applicant's mind about whether the hiring decision was biased or unfair. This is easier said than done, however, because some seemingly innocent questions can be viewed as attempts to gain information that might be used to discriminate against a candidate.

SUMMARY

This chapter reviewed the issues that surround the recruitment and selection of new salespeople. The issues discussed ranged from who is responsible for these tasks to the impact of federal legislation barring job discrimination on selection procedures.

Two factors are primary in determining who has the responsibility for recruiting and selecting salespeople: (1) the size of the sales force and (2) the kind of selling involved. In general, the smaller the sales force, the more sophisticated the selling task; and the more the sales force is used as a training ground for marketing and sales managers, the more likely it is that higher-level people, including the sales manager, will be directly involved in the recruitment and selection effort. To ensure that recruits have the aptitude for the job, it is useful to look at the recruitment and selection procedures as a three-step process. The steps are (1) a job analysis and description, (2) the recruitment of a pool of applicants, and (3) the selection of the best applicants from the available pool.

The job analysis and description phase includes a detailed examination of the job to determine what activities, tasks, responsibilities, and environmental influences are involved. This analysis may be conducted by someone in the sales management ranks or by a job analysis specialist. Regardless of who does it, it is important for that person to prepare a job description that details the findings of the job analysis. Finally, the job description is used to develop a statement of job qualifications, which lists and describes the personal traits and abilities a person should have to perform the tasks and responsibilities involved.

The pool of recruits from which the firm finally selects can be generated from a number of sources, including (1) people within the company, (2) people in other firms, (3) educational institutions, (4) advertisements, and (5) employment agencies. Each source has its own advantages and disadvantages. Some, such as advertisements, typically produce a large pool. The key question the sales manager needs to address is which source or combination of sources is likely to produce the largest pool of good, qualified recruits.

Once the qualifications necessary to fill a job have been determined and applicants have been recruited, the final task is to determine which applicant best meets the qualifications and has the greatest aptitude for the job. To make this determination, firms often use most, and in some cases all, of the following tools and procedures: (1) application blanks, (2) face-to-face interviews, (3) reference checks, (4) physical examinations, and (5) intelligence, aptitude, and personality tests. Although most employers find the interview and then the application blank most helpful, each device seems to perform some functions better than the other alternatives. This may explain why most firms use a combination of selection tools.

Title VII of the 1964 Civil Rights Act forbids discrimination in employment on the basis of race, sex, color, religion, or national origin. A firm must be careful, therefore, about how it uses tests, how it structures its application form, and the questions it asks during personal interviews so as not to be charged with noncompliance with the act. A firm that uses tests, for example, must be able to demonstrate empirically that the attributes measured are related to the salesperson's performance on the job.

KEY TERMS

job description	selection tools and	unstructured interview
internal sources	procedures	
external sources	structured interview	

BREAKOUT QUESTIONS

1. The sales manager for one of the nation's largest producers of consumer goods has identified eight factors that appear to be positively related to effective performance. The manager of human resources, who is concerned about high turnover rates among the sales force, would like to use this information to improve the company's recruiting and hiring process. The key factors are: (*a*) priority setting, (*b*) initiative and follow-through, (*c*) working effectively with others, (*d*) creativity and innovation, (*e*) thinking and problem solving, (*f*) leadership, (*g*) communication, and (*h*) technical mastery.

   How could these factors become part of the company's recruiting and hiring process? How would you define these factors and determine if applicants for sales positions possess these factors?

2. In a recent discussion on the use of the Internet to generate applications, the following quote was made and illustrates the application of the Internet to the recruiting and selection process:

   It doesn't care whom you know, what kind of suit you're wearing, or whether you have a firm handshake. Salespeople looking for a job may soon have to face their toughest interview yet—with a computer.

   What are the advantages of using the Internet to conduct preliminary job interviews? What problems is a company that uses computer-aided interviewing likely to encounter?

3. College recruiters were discussing some of the students they had interviewed that day. One interviewer described a female applicant with excellent credentials as follows: "She looked too feminine, like she would need someone to take care of her, and she was not all that serious about a sales job with us." When asked to explain her comments, the interviewer said, "Under her jacket she wore a flowery blouse with little flowing sleeves and a lace collar." The other recruiter countered and asked, "What do a flowery blouse, flowing sleeves, and a lace collar have to do with performance?" Comment.

4. One potential source of applicants for sales positions are sales representatives who work for competitors. One sales manager indicated, "Pirating sales representatives from other companies makes sense. Let them do the training, then we'll hire them." Is this ethical? Is this legal? Does this practice make good business sense?

5. Ethical Question. The vice president of human resources has called you and asked you to consider using a new personality test for recruiting salespeople. The test measures skills that you don't believe are relevant for the sales position. How should you respond to the vice president of human resources?

LEADERSHIP CHALLENGE: INTERNET OR INTERVIEW

Ron Deaple considered all his options. As key account sales manager for Cutting Edge Technology (CET), a London-based manufacturer of special purpose computer circuits, he was responsible for sales and support of the company's most important customers. The company's most important business was to manufacturers such as Dell and Lenovo as well as other product companies such as Samsung. Ron's position made him ultimately responsible for the relationship with these customers.

Key account managers at CET were often younger, highly motivated individuals. While a technology background was helpful, Ron found it was even more important for these individuals to have an understanding of contemporary selling. He believed if an individual knew about relationship building he could train them on the technical aspects of the job. Ron had personally recruited nearly all of the 50 key account managers. Up to now, Ron had recruited from other companies, hiring individuals with at least five years experience. In addition, Ron believed that it was critical for applicants to go through at least three interviews including one with himself, the executive vice president of marketing, and at least one other key account manager.

Recently, senior management had targeted Central Europe for expansion. Many technology companies are locating facilities in the area, leading to significant opportunities for market growth. CET has decided to open a regional office in Prague, Czech Republic, and Ron is tasked with hiring three new key account managers to be based there. The question was how to identify and recruit individuals for this new office.

It had become clear to Ron and others at CET that the old methods of relying on word of mouth and industry contacts were not going to be sufficient sources of new applicants in the future. Ron knew a logical source of new applicants would be the Internet. They were a technology company, and looking for potential new salespeople on the Internet would expand the list of possible candidates. His concern was the lack of direct contact with the person applying for the position. Sure he could generate a lot of applicants, but how could he be sure to get the *right* applicants. In addition, he believed the interview process was essential to identifying good candidates and that was not possible over the Internet. However, being based in London made personal interviews with all the candidates difficult at best.

Questions

1. What are the strengths and weaknesses of recruiting on the Internet? What are the strengths and weaknesses of face-to-face interviews in the recruiting process?

2. How would you address Ron Deaple's concerns of using the Internet in his recruiting process?

3. Design a program that would enable you to incorporate both the Internet and personal interviews in the recruiting process.

ROLE-PLAY: BASS BROKERS, INC.— PART B

Situation

This situation is a continuation of the situation presented in the Chapter 8 role-play. Go back and read that role-play and your notes from it to refamiliarize yourself with the scenario.

Now that Roscoe Lee and Pat Tollford have agreed on the key selection criteria Bass Brokers, Inc., should use when selecting new salespeople, they have decided that they can further help the district sales managers, and especially District 5 sales manager Jason Queen, by developing some guidelines for recruiting sales position applicants and by developing a more formalized selection procedure for salespeople. As Bass Brokers' newest district manager, Jason is delighted that he will benefit from these new guidelines and procedures as he works to hire replacement salespeople and reduce his district's turnover. Roscoe and Pat have invited Jason into the home office to secure his input on these issues.

Characters in the Role-Play

Roscoe Lee, vice president of sales for Bass Brokers, Inc.
Pat Tollford, human resource manager for Bass Brokers, Inc.
Jason Queen, District 5 sales manager for Bass Brokers, Inc.

Assignment

Break into groups of three, with one student playing each character. It doesn't matter what the actual gender mix of your group is. Before you stage the meeting, work separately using the material in your chapter to come up with your recommendations for (1) a logical plan for recruiting Bass Brokers salespeople, especially focused on the right *sources* of recruits, and (2) a selection process, especially focused on the right *selection tools and procedures*. You will need to be prepared to justify your recommendations in the meeting. Then, get together and role-play the meeting with Roscoe, Pat, and Jason. The group should first discuss approaches to recruiting and come to a consensus. Then the group should discuss selection tools and procedures and come to a consensus. Be sure everyone shares their own recommendations and justifies them. In the end, you want to come out of the meeting with a unified plan so that Jason and the other district sales managers at Bass Brokers can implement the ideas with their next hiring process.

MINICASE: DIGITAL AGE GAMES

Digital Age Games is a video game publisher that took gaming to a new level in the early 1990s with its well-known "Sack Attack—Extreme Football" game. Unfortunately, it has not had a popular game title since that time and is attempting to make a comeback with its new game "Drop-Kick—Extreme Wrestling." However, Digital Age has found that there is "extreme" competition for space on retailer shelves, as the top three game publishers (Digital Age is not one of them) have a 90 percent share of the market and a corresponding share of shelf space. Therefore, Digital Age's sales group is an area of key concern.

To address this concern, Digital Age's management has hired Shirley Hill, job analysis consultant, to conduct a job analysis of the company's sales positions and give overall advice on how to improve the recruitment process for those positions.

Shirley began her analysis by doing research on the gaming industry as a whole, reviewing the sales structure and job descriptions of Digital Age's major competitors and determining goals and objectives of Digital Age's management. Management told her that it wants to focus on customer prospecting and product demonstration by increasing in-person sales-person attention (and therefore, salesperson travel). It also wants employees with gaming knowledge who will better understand product detail and be able to communicate it to customers.

She spoke at length with the sales managers to determine what the salespeople actually *do*, as well as which are high performers and which are low performers. On her office visits with management, she perceived the tension her presence brought to the sales representatives, who were concerned that their jobs may be at stake, so she spared them and herself by not talking with them directly.

Because the job descriptions had not been updated since 1997, her next order of business was to create a new description for the sales representative position. Her draft job description is as follows:

Sales Representative

The Digital Age Games North American sales organization drives the placement, retail marketing, and retail advertising support for consumer goods in its established retail and distribution channels.

The sales representative must:

- Manage U.S. video game distributors and other regional accounts for both video game and PC game products.
- Achieve quarterly sell-in objectives and revenue targets.
- Maintain established accounts through regular customer contact in pursuit of follow-on sales.
- Provide crisp and consistent feedback/communication to managers and others as required.

Selection criteria:

- 2–3 years of experience in sales of entertainment products.
- Bachelor's degree.
- Team player who can deal with ambiguity.
- Customer service–oriented.
- Strong presentation and communication skills.
- Excellent organizational skills and attention to detail.

Finally, Shirley made recommendations as to sources for new sales recruits. Because knowledge of gaming and the product is central to the position, she recommended that the company primarily look to applicants who are existing employees in the company. Similarly, Shirley reasoned, by advertising positions on the Internet, both on Digital Age's website and other third-party job sites, Digital Age would attract tech-savvy applicants. Shirley insisted that these two sources would provide more than enough quality applicants.

Shirley was quite satisfied with her analysis and recommendations, but management has some concerns and has scheduled a feedback meeting with her.

Questions

1. From the facts given, did Shirley do a proper job analysis? What else could she have done to evaluate the current positions? Explain.

2. Evaluate the job description. Is there anything you would have added, deleted, or changed?

3. Besides those recommended by Shirley, what other source(s) of applicants might Digital Age use for recruiting new salespeople? Why?

CHAPTER 10

Sales Training: Objectives, Techniques, and Evaluation

LEARNING OBJECTIVES

Salespeople operate in a highly competitive and dynamic environment. In addition, new salespeople must assimilate a great deal of information about the company, products, and customers. A key element in enhancing the success of current salespeople and preparing new salespeople is training. Companies in the twenty-first century realize that good training is an essential component of success for the sales force. This chapter will examine the objectives, techniques, and methods of evaluating training in the sales force.

After reading this chapter, you should be able to

- Identify the key issues in sales training.
- Understand the objectives of sales training.
- Discuss the development of sales training programs.
- Understand the training of new sales recruits and experienced salespeople.
- Define the topics covered in a sales training program.
- Understand the various methods for conducting sales training.
- Discuss how to measure the costs and benefits of sales training.

ISSUES IN SALES TRAINING

Training salespeople is a huge industry; American companies spend more than $50 billion annually on training. Exhibit 10.1 lists the top ten training organizations as determined by *Training* magazine. It is not surprising then that the subject of sales training usually produces considerable interest among managers at all levels of the company. Sales managers at all levels have a variety of objectives for training. Chief sales officers want the sales training to provide specific details about certain industries and teach the sales reps to develop close relationships with customers—a critical issue, especially with large major or key accounts. Market managers are interested in how much training sales representatives receive in dealing with the complex customer problems. Product managers, of course, hope the salespeople have been well schooled in product knowledge, specifications, and applications. Even managers external to the marketing function, such as human resource managers, have a stake in the sales training process. Recruiters know that highly regarded sales training programs enhance the firm's ability to recruit and retain salespeople. A few firms have developed such strong sales training programs that participants who complete the program liken the process to having earned a second degree or an MBA.

When determining sales training needs, three issues must be considered:[1]

- *Who should be trained?* In most organizations new sales recruits receive a combination of training and orientation to company policies and procedures. But this raises the issues of training for different types of salespeople and, depending upon how market or competitive changes may have altered the nature of sales tasks, training for different stages of the same salesperson's career.

- *What should be the primary emphasis in the training program?* Sales training can encompass the following: product knowledge, company knowledge, customer knowledge, or selling skills (e.g., time management or presentation skills). All of these may be important, but the relative importance of each type of training differs depending upon the selling situation, the feasible scope and costs of sales training, and the nature of the company's marketing strategy.

- *How should the training process be structured?* The following methods are options: On-the-job training and experience versus a formal and more consistent centralized program; Web-based or instructor-based, and in-house training versus outside expertise.

The points raised earlier clearly indicate that sales training is ongoing and not likely completed in a onetime event. Ideally, sales training for new recruits will instill, in a relatively short period of time, a vast amount of knowledge that has taken skilled sales representatives years to acquire. Sales training for experienced salespeople,

Organization	EXHIBIT 10.1
1. Keller Williams Realty, Inc.	*Training* magazine's top training companies
2. Jiffy Lube International	
3. Capital BlueCross	
4. CHG Healthcare Services	
5. Blue Cross Blue Shield of Michigan	
6. ABF Freight	
7. McCarthy Building Companies, Inc.	
8. Wequassett Resort and Golf Club	
9. Capital One	
10. Nationwide Mutual Life Insurance Co.	

Source: Adapted from Training Management online, www.trainingmag.com, July 2015.

on the other hand, may be the result of new product offerings, changes in market structure, new technologies, competitive activities, and so on, plus a desire to reinforce and upgrade critical selling skills. Although some sales managers have a narrow view about the objectives of sales training—for example, to increase motivation—others identify a variety of objectives.

OBJECTIVES OF SALES TRAINING

Although the specific objectives of sales training may vary from firm to firm, there is some agreement on the broad objectives. Sales training is undertaken to increase productivity, improve morale, lower turnover, improve customer relations, and produce better management of time and territory.

Increase Productivity

One objective of sales training is to provide valuable skills that will have a positive effect on selling performance. In a relatively short time, sales training attempts to teach and enhance critical selling skills. The time it takes for a new member of the sales force to achieve satisfactory levels of productivity is thus shortened considerably. Alcatel-Lucent for example, credits much of its success in the industry to having a well-trained sales force. Over the last several years, the telecommunications industry has experienced significant decline globally; however, Alcatel-Lucent has done better than the industry average due in part to its additional sales force training.[2]

Improve Morale

How does sales training lead to better morale? One of its objectives is to prepare trainees to improve their productivity as quickly as possible. If sales trainees know what is expected of them, they will be less likely to experience the frustration that arises from trying to carry out a job without adequate preparation. Without sales training, sales representatives may not be able to answer questions that customers have, increasing the salesperson's aggravation and lowering morale. Evidence indicates salespeople who are uncertain about their job requirements tend to be less satisfied with their jobs. Conversely, this same evidence shows salespeople who are well aware of the job requirements are also more satisfied with their company's sales training activities. Finally, research indicates that when training seeks to connect salespeople with other salespeople and employees the salesperson's overall morale and performance increases.[3]

Creating the right format for sales training is a challenging task. Competent sales training is not a function of motivational hype but rather delivering specific skills and techniques designed to enhance the salesperson's ability to be successful in the field.

Lower Turnover

If sales training can lead to improved morale and greater job satisfaction, then the result should be lower turnover in the sales force. Young, inexperienced salespeople are more likely to get discouraged and quit as a result of not being prepared for the job. Turnover can also lead to customer problems, since many customers prefer continuity with their sales representative. A customer called on by a salesperson who suddenly quits may transfer business to other suppliers rather than wait for a new representative. Sales training, by leading to lower turnover, alleviates such problems. Young, inexperienced salespeople are particularly prone to making mistakes and getting discouraged, which can lead to a decision to leave the company. However, research asserts that sales managers who ensure that new hires understand that mistakes are part of the learning process and encourage trainees to accept the possibility of error or even failure to meet early goals so long as they continue to develop the skills necessary for success in their position.[4]

Improve Customer Relations

One benefit of sales training that accompanies lower turnover is continuity in customer relationships. Having the same sales representative call on customers on a regular basis promotes customer loyalty, especially when the salesperson can handle customer questions, objections, and complaints. Customers place orders for their own benefits. Inadequately trained salespeople are usually not able to provide these benefits, and customer relations suffer.

Improve Selling Skills

Many companies believe that improving basic selling skills can lead to improved performance in the field. For example, time and territory management is a subject in many sales training programs. How much time should be devoted to existing accounts versus how much to call on potential new accounts? How often should each class of account be called on? What is the most effective way of covering the territory with respect to miles driven and time spent? Many sales training programs provide salespeople with answers to these questions.

In addition, over time, research on the relationship between salesperson and customer can lead to new approaches in sales training. For example, recent research suggests that it can be beneficial for salespeople to provide more structure to the sales presentation in dealing with inexperienced customers. A focused selling strategy designed to create an "agenda" for the customer as they move through the decision-making process can be helpful for new customers who are unaware of the product/services performance characteristics or benefits. This kind of information can be conveyed to salespeople very effectively in a sales training program.[5]

THE DEVELOPMENT OF SALES TRAINING PROGRAMS

There is no question that sales training is an important function. However, numerous problems arise when trying to implement sales training programs. Recently, senior training managers from more than 30,000 organizations were asked to identify their most important training issues and priorities. They identified linking training programs with business strategy as the top priority over the next several years. This means training salespeople to be customer-focused and providing them with tools necessary to build strong customer relationships by adding value to the customer's business. These senior managers, however, cited some very significant obstacles in achieving their training goals. These obstacles included,

- Top management not dedicated to sales training.

- Lack of buy-in from frontline sales managers and salespeople.

- Salespeople's lack of understanding of what the training is supposed to accomplish (objectives).

- Salespeople's lack of understanding regarding the application of the training to their everyday tasks (lack of connection between training and specific sales tasks).[6]

These issues raise an important question. What is management doing that allows some of these problems to occur? Two problems exist. First, management too often expects sales training to solve all the company's sales problems when, in fact, the problem with sales might not even be connected with the sales force (for example, poor product quality or an inefficient supply chain that is unable to deliver products on time). Providing more training to the sales force will not help the company's sales if the product or service does not add value for the customer. If the sales problems are not resolved, budget-cutting activities often start with the sales training program. In addition, too often management fails to understand sales training. Sales training is viewed as a cost of doing business rather than as an investment that pays future dividends. Why are only costs evaluated and not the other half of the operating statement (additional revenue generated from effective training)?[7] The second problem rests within the sales training function: namely, the evaluation of sales training programs. Historically, too many sales training programs have been conducted without measuring the benefits. Although companies are spending more time and effort on measuring the results of training, the problem of measurement persists. Evaluation is difficult, but considering the millions of dollars devoted to sales training, it is not unreasonable to expect some attempt to measure the benefits.

We will discuss in greater detail how to evaluate sales training programs later in the chapter. The Innovation box discusses the failure of sales training programs and a phased approach to enhancing their success.

INNOVATION Effective Sales Training on a Budget

Budget concerns drive many managers to cut sales training programs. However, effective sales training doesn't have to involve hiring expensive external trainers or using limited internal resources. Generally, continuous learning is the key to success. After businesses determine the essential sales training topics (account planning, prospecting skills and strategy, public speaking and pitching skills, business acumen, proposal writing and resilience) careful planning can ensure that the training is efficient and effective. Six of the most useful sales training tips include:

1. **Time Allocation**—Identify those skills and attributes that require the longest learning time.

2. **Prioritize your training**—Concentrate on training topics you can do in-house.

3. **Seek external training only when necessary**—Use external training only for those skill sets not available from internal resources and just invest in the training that is essential to seek professional help for.

4. **Reading material in abundance**—Blogs and other online sources can be a great resource and allow salespeople to gain knowledge continuously.

5. **Open communication**—Encourage open communication with salespeople to discuss their issues and concerns.

6. **Invest in seminars**—Seminars are a low cost way of putting salespeople in contact with highly experienced and knowledgeable experts in their field.

Creating Credibility in Sales Training

Many sales trainers believe their programs lack credibility. Budget-cutting efforts are too often directed at existing sales training programs.[8] This may reflect management's feelings that these programs are accomplishing little and are expendable. Sales training programs have to fit the long-term goals and objectives of the organization, and just like the company's own products and services, they must deliver value to the organization.

Analyze Needs

The starting point in creating credibility is to conduct a sales training analysis that analyzes the training needs of the sales force (see Exhibit 10.2). One way to do this is to travel with sales reps and observe and ask them what they need to know to perform their jobs more effectively. Field sales managers are an excellent source of information because they are closest to salespeople. Interviews with key members of management can also identify training needs. One expert advocates sending anonymous questionnaires to customers asking, What do you expect of a salesperson in the industry? How do salespeople disappoint you? Which company in the industry does the best selling job? In what ways are its salespeople better? Other sources include company records showing turnover data, performance evaluations, and sales and cost analyses. Attitudinal studies conducted with the sales force provide additional insights. This analysis of needs answers three basic questions: Where in the organization is training needed? What should be the content of the training program? Who needs the training? Experts recommend that to get the most out of their training dollar managers should (1) train the right personnel for the right jobs, (2) focus on the highest potential personnel, (3) identify those that can benefit most from training, and (4) realize skills training that maximizes strengths can be more effective than training aimed at overcoming weaknesses.

Determine Objectives

It is important to set realistic objectives. Research estimates that even effective training cannot improve a person's skills by more than 20 percent. Thus, people in the wrong

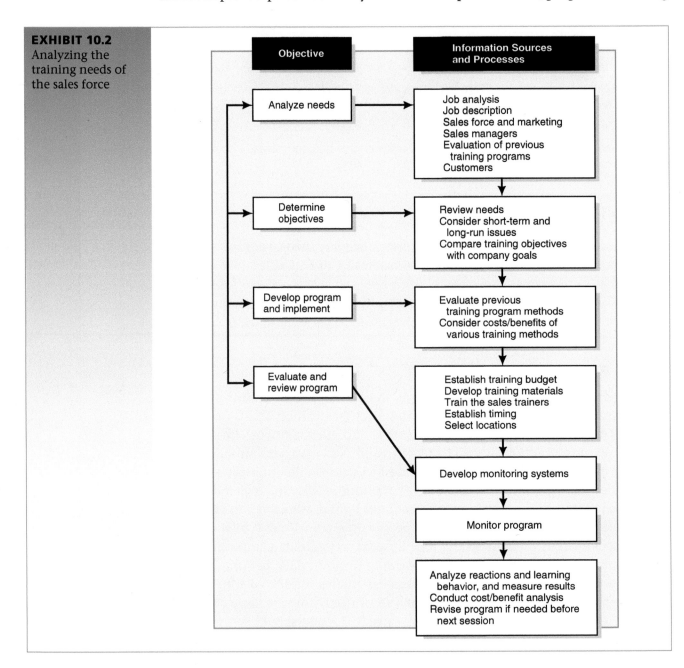

EXHIBIT 10.2
Analyzing the training needs of the sales force

positions cannot be trained to become top performers, only their "bad" skills can be improved to "not quite as bad." As a result setting specific, realistic, and measurable objectives for the sales training program is critical. The objectives may include learning about new products, sales techniques, or company procedures. Keep the objectives simple; for example, management may want a 10 percent sales increase, which then becomes the broad objective of the training program. The specific objective might be to teach sales reps how to call on new accounts, which will help lead to the broad objective. Measurability is critical in sales training. More will be said about this later.

Develop and Implement Program

At this point, a decision has to be made concerning developing the training program or hiring an outside organization to conduct it. Many companies, both large and small, outsource at least a part of their sales training. Small companies often outsource most of their training. Large companies usually develop most of their own programs and use outside agencies to handle specific or special training needs. When considering an outside training supplier, it is critical to conduct a careful investigation. One sales manager mentioned how embarrassed he was by retaining a company that put on an "entertaining song-and-dance routine" that cost $65,000 but failed to have any lasting effect. Use of outside sources is encouraged only if they meet the objectives of the company.

Evaluate and Review Program

Designing a measurement system is the next step. Here are some questions that need to be asked:

- What do we want to measure?

- When do we want to measure?

- How do we do it? What measuring tools are available?

Using tests to measure learning is not difficult; however, measuring the application of training in the field is very difficult. Whether a salesperson can demonstrate a product can be evaluated during a training session. But whether that same individual demonstrates the product effectively in front of a customer is harder to assess. This is why field sales managers are an important link: They can provide follow-up and feedback information on the salesperson's ability to retain and use sales training takeaways in the field. The field sales managers can also coach the salesperson if there is a need for follow-up.

Finally, evaluations of sales performance provide additional evidence on the value of training, although such information must be used carefully. Changes in performance, like sales increases, may be due to factors not related to sales training; and when training managers claim they are, it casts doubts on the sales training efforts.

Larger companies must decide which group to train. Most of the time some groups are targeted for training before others. It is also important to remember that not everyone in the sales force needs training. Certainly, newly hired recruits need training, whether it's on the job at first, more centralized, or some other arrangement. When procedures or products change, everyone needs training. If certain salespeople are having specific problems related to performance or attitude, the training needs to be directed at them individually. To include the entire force wastes resources and creates problems, especially among those not experiencing the same issues. When a new training method is being tested, it is wise to use a group that will be receptive. This increases credibility, creating a favorable climate for continuation.

Since measurement is crucial, the sales trainer needs to collect data before training starts. The needs analysis discussed earlier provides relevant information pertaining to program content. For example, if management knew some salespeople had difficulty managing their sales calls, observation by the trainer or the field sales manager after the program should provide data indicating the value of the training. Call reports would be another source of information. Follow-up must continue beyond the initial check because the use of new skills may drop off.

The data collection process should provide sales trainers with information that will justify the program. Top management wants to know if the benefits exceed or equal the costs. Keeping top management informed about the success of training programs contributes to the overall credibility.

Sales training programs, whether being sold to the sales manager or top management, must be credible. Management can always find other alternatives for spending resources.

TRAINING NEW SALES RECRUITS

Larger companies have specific programs for training new sales recruits. These programs differ considerably in length and content, however. The differences often reflect variations in company policies, the nature of the selling job, and types of products and services. Even within the same industry, sales training programs vary in length, content, and technique.

Although a few companies have no set time for training sales recruits, most firms have embraced the notion of a fixed period for formal training. The time varies from just a couple of days in the office, followed by actual selling combined with on-the-job coaching, to as long as two or three years of intensive training in a number of fields and skills.

What accounts for this variation? First, training needs vary from firm to firm and even within a firm. For example, one manufacturer of drugs has a seven-week program for new recruits who will sell conventional consumer products. For those recruits destined to sell more technical products, the training lasts two years.

Second, training needs vary because of differences in the needs and aptitudes of the recruits. Experienced recruits have less need for training than inexperienced recruits, although most large firms require everyone to go through some formal training. One B2B firm requires a one-week program for experienced recruits, but inexperienced recruits may require a two- to three-year program.

A final reason for variation in the length of training programs is company philosophy. Some sales managers believe training for new recruits should be concentrated at the beginning of a sales career, but others think it should be spread over a longer time, including a large dose of learning by doing.[9]

TRAINING EXPERIENCED SALES PERSONNEL

After new salespeople are assigned to a field position, they quickly become involved in customer relationships, competitive developments, and other related matters. Over time, their knowledge of competitors and market conditions becomes dated. Even their personal selling styles may become stereotyped and less effective. Also, because of changes in company policies and product line, salespeople require refresher or advanced training programs. Almost without exception managers believe the need to learn is a never-ending process and even the most successful salespeople can benefit from additional training.

Additional training often occurs when a sales representative is being considered for promotion. In many companies, a promotion is more than moving from sales to district sales manager. A promotion can include being assigned better customers, transferring to a better territory, moving to a staff position, or being promoted to sales management. Whenever salespeople are assigned better customers or better territories, additional sales training acquaints them with their increased responsibilities.

Many companies decentralize the training for experienced salespeople. Lucent, IBM, and Apple are among those that get training into the field using Internet-based programs.

Training experienced salespeople is viewed as providing insurance for a company's major asset. Debbie Brady, director of learning and organizational effectiveness at Edward Jones, a financial services company, notes that the company's focus on training allows it to "thrive in the chaos." She states, "By cultivating our next generation of leaders and preserving the company culture, we are allowing our employees to truly learn and grow."[10]

SALES TRAINING TOPICS

For new salespeople, the content of sales training tends to remain relatively constant over time. Product or service knowledge appears in the majority of programs as well as an orientation on the market/industry, company, and basic selling skills. Beyond these standard topics, there exists a vast array of different subjects that range from the logical, such as training sales reps in how to build successful customer relationships, and team selling, to some questionable topics, such as training the sales force to modify their sales presentation based on whether the customer is "left-brained" or "right-brained."

Product Knowledge

Although product knowledge is one of the most important topics, knowing when and how to discuss the subject in a sales call is probably even more important. More time is typically spent on product knowledge than any other subject, although the time spent varies with the product sold.

Companies that produce technical products, such as technology companies, spend more time on this subject than manufacturers of nontechnical products. Hewlett-Packard, Microsoft, and others allocate a great deal of time educating salespeople on their products and services to better service customers. It is critical that the right product or service be applied to each customer's unique application.

Product knowledge involves knowing not only product specifications but also how the product is used and, in some cases, how it should not be used. One producer of network computer servers gives newly hired sales engineers extensive in-plant exposure to technical and engineering matters. Before field assignment, they spend time in a customer's operations, where they learn about the customer's business processes and operations under realistic conditions.

Product knowledge is not limited to the company's products. Customers often want to know how competitive products compare on price, construction, performance, and compatibility with each other. Customers expect reps to show them how the seller's products can be coordinated with competitive products, such as in a computer installation that involves a number of products by different manufacturers. One manufacturer of power tools that supplies tools to the construction industry exposes sales trainees to competitors' tools so they will know which best handles the customer's demands.

A major objective in product knowledge training is to enable a salesperson to provide potential customers with the information needed for rational decision making. Some benefits that accrue to salespeople as they acquire product knowledge include

1. Pride and confidence in product quality.

2. Self-assurance emanating from technical knowledge of product makeup.

3. Communication with customers through the use of the operational vocabulary peculiar to the industry.

4. Understanding of product functioning that allows effective diagnosis of customer problems.[11]

All these benefits contribute to improved salesperson–customer interaction.

Market/Industry Orientation

Sales training in the market/industry orientation covers both broad and specific factors. From a broad viewpoint, salespeople need to know how their particular industry fits into the overall economy. Economic fluctuations affect buying behavior, which affects selling techniques. Information about inflationary pressure, for example, may be used to persuade prospective buyers to move their decision dates ahead. If the sales force is involved in forecasting sales and setting quotas, knowledge of the industry and the economy is essential.

From a narrower viewpoint, salespeople must have detailed knowledge about present customers. They need to know their customers' buying policies, patterns, and preferences and the products or services these companies produce. In some cases, sales reps need to be knowledgeable about their customers' customers. This is especially true when sales representatives sell through wholesalers or distributors that often want salespeople to assist them with their customers' problems. These salespeople are expected to know the needs of both wholesalers and retailers, even though the retailers buy from the wholesalers.

Company Orientation

New salespeople need to learn company policies that affect their selling activities. Like all new employees, they are made aware of personnel policies on a variety of items such as salary structure and company benefits.

Salespeople expect customers to request price adjustments, product modifications, faster delivery, and different credit terms. Most companies have policies on such matters arising from legal requirements or industry practices. Too often, however, avoidable delays and lost sales result when salespeople are not made aware of important company policies.

Two different learning environments provide salespeople with knowledge of company policies. The first places sales trainees inside the home office working in various departments, such as credit, order processing, advertising, sales promotion, or shipping. The second method has the new salesperson working as an inside sales coordinator or customer service representative processing customer orders, maintaining e-mail and telephone contact with customers, and sometimes serving as the company contact for a group of customers.

Major corporations provide the sales force with online manuals or tablet computers that cover product line information and company policies. A well-prepared sales manual can give a sales representative a quick answer to a customer's question.

Time and Territory Management

New salespeople frequently need assistance in managing their time and territories. A survey by Learning International suggests that salespeople perceive this as an important problem. Management also considers time management a critical issue. Blue Cross and Blue Shield instituted Internet-based learning for the salespeople to provide more time for them to spend with their customers. Dan Goettsch, sales training manager, states, "One of the big issues here is the notion that selling time is a very precious commodity. Any time [out of the field] is costly for sales folks."[12]

The familiar 80–20 ratio, where 20 percent of a company's customers account for 80 percent of the business, applies to time and territory management in the reverse direction. It is not unusual to find sales representatives who are skilled in all areas except efficient time management spending 80 percent of their time with customers who account for only 20 percent of sales. In addition, assigning a salesperson too many accounts or a territory that is too large leads to time and territory management problems.

A manufacturer of micrographic equipment trains salespeople to "plan your work—work your plan." Although some instruction in time management is provided by this company during classroom training, the major responsibility rests with the district sales managers. Sales representatives turn in their projected activities every two weeks and review their district sales manager's past plans and performance. The district sales manager helps them modify the projected plans for greater efficiency. The desire for more effective time and territory management has led to greater telephone and e-mail usage.

Legal/Ethical Issues

Lapses in ethical conduct have been known to lead to legal problems. Statements—or, rather, misstatements—made by salespeople have legal and ethical implications. Companies today have made ethics a focus of their training and expend a great deal of resources to be sure that everyone in the organization understands the company's ethical values. Read the Ethical Moment in this chapter for more information on the ethical issues in sales training.

Technology

Today companies issue salespeople laptop or tablet computers. In addition, many companies, such as IBM, also create "home offices" for their sales force that eliminate the need to go into an office at all. With a high-speed network connection, laptop or desktop computer, printer, and cell phone, a salesperson is almost totally self-sufficient. Salespeople use PCs to plan their call activities, submit orders, send reports, check on inventory and price levels, receive messages, and present product and service demonstrations. In some cases, the sales rep can access the company's

---

ETHICAL MOMENT   Training Ethics

The importance of ethics in business continues to be a focus on companies around the world. The unfortunate and all-too-frequent examples of ethical lapses by individuals in many different organizations continue to be in the headlines almost every week. Among the challenges is the difficult problem of hiring individuals with sufficient ethical judgment that aligns with company ethical values. However, once an individual is hired what happens next?

Companies today are spending more resources (time and money) on ethical training than ever before. They realize that while it is almost impossible to fundamentally change someone's ethical value system, it is possible; indeed, it is essential that everyone in the organization understand the company's ethical values, the code of conduct expected of employees, and the consequences of violating the code.

Perhaps it is not surprising to know that one of the areas in an organization that experiences the greatest number of ethical challenges is personal selling. The ethical pressure on salespeople is profound and, as a result, companies understand the need to offer salespeople a great deal of ethical training. Almost every sales organization spends time working through the ethical challenges and scenarios with their salesforce to help prepare them for the difficult ethical decisions they face every day.

Question to Ponder:

- Can you identify one ethical challenge a salesperson might face and then create a sales training exercise to help the salesperson deal with the issue more effectively?

TECHNOLOGY Training—There's an App for That

The dramatic growth of mobile technology is improving training across a broad range of groups from customers to salespeople. Retailers, for example, use apps to demonstrate products and services to their customers. A wide range of companies and organizations use apps to pass along core values, institutional knowledge, and best practices to employees. This kind of information is quite helpful to new employees who lack the institutional knowledge about a company.

Organizations also use mobile apps to track or manage the path or sequence of training as well as verify what kind of training has occurred. The information from these apps is analyzed to identify future training needs and allow employees to track their own personal development.

Training professionals realize the future of training includes designing tools for mobile audiences. At the enterprise level, apps must be able to respond to changing conditions, regulations, new products/services, markets, or new customers. They are moving from supplementary training to primary training, making training truly an any-time, anywhere activity.

decision support system (DSS) to learn what products have been selling in an area or for a specific customer.

Companies have found that proper use of technology allows their salespeople more face-to-face customer contact time. It also enables salespeople to respond much faster to the customer. The cell phone puts the customer in contact with the salesperson almost all the time. Coupled with direct network connections that companies such as General Motors and Ford have with their suppliers, it is no wonder that many customers report much better communication between themselves and the salespeople who call on them. The Technology box talks about the use of Internet technology in training. One of the challenges that salespeople face in using technology is something called "technostress." This is the stress caused by the use of sales force information systems in the work place and their negative impact on sales performance. Research indicates that one way to mitigate technostress is by providing adequate training on how to use the technology as well as the benefits so salespeople understand the reasons for using it. After the training is completed managers should continue to coach salespeople on the continued use of any new technology.[13]

Specialized Training Topics

Companies are frequently coming to the conclusion that training is most effective when it is specialized and tailored to individual job functions.[14] For example, price objections are common in sales transactions, and sales managers are not pleased if they feel that sales reps offer discounts too quickly. Recently, Johnson Controls Inc., a manufacturer of automated control systems based in Atlanta, instituted a six-month training program to address the issue of price negotiations. One solution adopted by Johnson Controls was to provide salespeople with detailed financial information to help them make more profitable decisions.

Many companies, like Caterpillar Inc., spend substantial sums of money each year on trade shows. Increasing cost pressures have forced management to be more concerned about the return from trade shows and other similar expenditures. As a result, Caterpillar personnel selected to staff trade show exhibits undergo a training program to increase their effectiveness in the unique trade show environment. Most salespeople selected have the training and experience to make in-depth presentations in their specialties. But even though they're very good, they are not necessarily skilled at working a trade show. They don't always know how to engage and qualify new prospects, handle big crowds, or weed out the buyers from the "tire kickers."[15]

Other subjects addressed in training programs include body language, eye movement, and even attempts to determine if the prospect is right-brained or left-brained. Indicators of left- or right-brained people might be whether or not a customer wears a watch or carries a calculator.[16] It should be noted, however, that there is no evidence to support this concept in a sales context.

Sales training is also effective in helping salespeople work through problems or issues that may limit their performance. Recently, researchers have reported that sales call anxiety (SCA) can lead to real problems in both a salesperson's effectiveness and efficiency. One of the results of the research is a focus on better training methods to reduce SCA before it becomes a problem for salespeople.[17]

SALES TRAINING METHODS

The most commonly used methods of sales training are on-the-job training, individual instruction, in-house classes, and external seminars. Companies use a variety of techniques, recognizing that different subjects require different methods (Exhibit 10.3). Overlap exists within a given method. On-the-job training includes individual instruction (coaching) and in-house classes held at district sales offices. In addition, companies currently seem more willing than in the past to seek outside help when it comes to solving their training/motivation problems.[18] Finally, companies are realizing that sales training does not need to be boring. The Innovation box on p. 317 illustrates how companies use creative ideas to help train their salespeople.

As has been noted, companies continue to use external sources for a lot of their sales training needs. However, the use of outside sources is not without some controversy. Companies question if they should spend money on outside sales training sources.

EXHIBIT 10.3 Common instruction methods	Classroom with instructor
	Workbooks/manuals
	Public seminars
	Self-assessment
	Role-play
	Case studies
	Computer simulations
	Teleconferencing
	Podcasts

Dr Pepper/Seven Up, like many other companies, has established outsourcing partnerships that provide training programs for all types and levels of employees. The company hired an outside training company, Acclivus, to help improve the customer problem-solving skills of its sales and customer service staff. However, the outsourcing partnership did not eliminate the training function at Dr Pepper/ Seven Up. The net effect was to enhance the training capabilities of the company.[19]

On-the-Job Training

The mere mention of on-the-job training (OJT) sometimes scares new sales recruits. The thought of "learning by doing" is psychologically discomforting to many. Often, this is due to their incorrect perceptions of what is involved in OJT. On-the-job training is not a sink-or-swim approach in which the new salesperson is handed a sales manual and told to "go out and sell." OJT should be a carefully planned process in which the new recruit learns by doing and, at the same time, is productively employed. Furthermore, a good OJT program contains established procedures for evaluating and reviewing a salesperson's progress. Critiques should be held after each sales call and summarized daily. The critiques cover effectiveness, selling skills, communication of information in a persuasive manner, and other criteria.

Research over the last few years suggests that informal on-the-job training is an effective way of learning for salespeople. Indeed, it is suggested that the majority of all learning at work takes place informally. The Education Development Center identified five keys for effective on-the-job informal training:

1. *Teaming*. Bringing together people with different skills to address issues.

2. *Meetings*. Setting aside times when employees at different levels and positions can get together and share thoughts on various topics.

3. *Customer interaction*. Including customer feedback as part of the learning process.

4. *Mentoring*. Providing an informal mechanism for new salespeople to interact and learn from more experienced ones.[20]

5. *Peer-to-peer communication*. Creating opportunities for salespeople to interact together for mutual learning.[21]

A key aspect of on-the-job training is the coaching salespeople receive from trainers, who may be experienced sales personnel, sales managers, or personnel specifically assigned to do sales training. On-the-job training and coaching often occur together; this is referred to as *one-on-one training*. Observation is an integral part of the process. Managers are aware that helping a salesperson reach his or her full potential means spending time with the person one on one. One consultant specializing in sales performance states, "Managers play an essential role in cultivating talent. They need to take on a coaching role." In addition, providing individual feedback can lead to greater salesperson satisfaction. OJT often involves job rotation—assigning trainees to different departments where they learn about such things as manufacturing, marketing, shipping, credits and collections, and servicing procedures. After on-the-job training, many sales trainees proceed to formal classroom training.

Classroom Training

For most companies, formal classroom training is an indispensable part of sales training, although very few of them rely solely on it. Classroom training has several advantages. First, each salesperson receives standard briefings on such subjects as product knowledge, company policies, customer and market characteristics, and selling skills. Second, formal training sessions often save substantial amounts of executive time because executives can meet an entire group of salespeople at once. Third, lectures, presentations, and case discussions can be programmed into a classroom setting. The opportunity for interaction between salespeople is a fourth advantage.

Such interaction is beneficial, since reinforcement and ideas for improvement can come from other salespeople. Interaction is so important that many companies divide salespeople into teams for case presentations, which results in interaction and forces salespeople to become actively involved.

Classroom training also has its disadvantages. It is expensive and time-consuming. It requires recruits to be brought together and facilities, meals, transportation, recreation, and lodging to be provided for them. Sales managers, who are cognizant of these costs and time demands, sometimes attempt to cover too much material in too short a time. This results in less retention of information. Many sessions become mere cram sessions. Sales managers must avoid the natural tendency to add more and more material, because the additional exposure is often gained at the expense of retention and opportunity for interaction.

Role-Playing

A popular technique used in many companies has the salesperson act out the part of a sales rep in a simulated buying session. The buyer may be either a sales instructor or another trainee. Role-playing is widely used to develop selling skills, but it can also be used to determine whether the trainee can apply knowledge taught via other methods of instruction. The salesperson, trainer, and other salespeople critique the trainee's performance immediately following the role-playing session.

Role-playing where a sales trainee performs in front of others and where that performance is subsequently critiqued can be harsh. Some of these problems disappear if the critique is conducted only in the presence of the sales trainee and then only by the sales instructor. When role-playing is handled well, most trainees can still identify their own strengths and weaknesses.

LEADERSHIP   The Value of Just-in-Time Training

From the orientation of new hires to annual training events for the rest of the sales team, billions of dollars are spent each year to improve the skills of salespeople. In many organizations, training represents the single largest investment in sales performance improvement. Unfortunately, this investment is also the most perishable because research suggests that 60–90 percent of skills learned during a training event are lost within 30 days. The rapid loss of information recall strengthens the importance of consistently reinforcing critical information. Let's consider why the problem occurs and a solution.

Problem—Pushing an elephant through a straw

The sheer volume of information included in many training sessions can be overwhelming to most salespeople. Since personal sales training is so expensive, managers frequently make the mistake of compressing a year's worth of learning into a single event. This makes it impossible to reinforce all the content when the event is over. Secondly, since training is typically done when it is convenient for the calendar, information is often not immediately relevant. If a new skill is not immediately reinforced, it will erode very quickly. Ideally, training would be held in close proximity to the need.

Solution—Information when it is needed (just in time)

Rather than having a comprehensive training event with a year's worth of content, industry leaders are opting for smaller, more focused sessions to teach specific skills. This allows for the salespeople to focus on mastering a single skill before moving on. In addition to less content, these training events also take place much closer to when they are needed by the salesperson. This way salespeople are required to demonstrate the skills and retained knowledge almost immediately, thus improving the likelihood that they would stick.

Electronic Training Methods

Electronic training methods, and more specifically the Internet, have revolutionized the delivery of training, not just in sales but across the entire organization. Companies find the Internet to be not only effective in delivering just-in-time information but also very efficient.[22]

Perhaps not surprising, IBM is investing a great deal of time and resources into the delivery of online training to its sales force of more than 100,000 worldwide. Its Internet-based training strategy involves delivering small incremental packets of information on products and customers just in time to complete specific projects currently on the salesperson's activity list. In addition, online chat groups enable the salesperson to gather even more information or provide feedback on current activities.

IBM believes this has led to greater effectiveness in the sales efforts and seeks to make online training a vital part of its overall sales training program. Plans call for 35 percent of IBM sales training to be done over the Internet. The key is to deliver the information when and where the salesperson can use it most. One other significant benefit of the program is the cost saving. IBM estimates it will save $200 million in reduced travel and hotel costs alone.[23]

The most common delivery method is a blended format that includes a combination of online tools and personal instruction. Companies are using a variety of online tools including Learning Management Systems (LMS) and Podcasting. However, the most common online learning technology is the virtual classroom/webcasting/video broadcasting.[24] In addition, while many companies are using open delivery systems directly over the Internet, the most dominant form of online training is the internal company network, with 30 percent of training coming through internal networks.

Do these programs work? Can they train salespeople to effectively interact with customers? Answers to these questions have not been well documented. As with all methods, be it understanding body language or eye movements, there is a great deal of information salespeople need in order to be effective. Online training can be very effective in delivering certain kinds of information but will not likely eliminate the need for one-on-one training for salespeople.[25]

MEASURING THE COSTS AND BENEFITS OF SALES TRAINING

Sales training is a time-consuming and very costly activity. Is all this effort worth the cost? Are sales training costs justified by the benefits produced? If done properly, sales training can be one of the most helpful tools used to increase the satisfaction and performance of salespeople. However, as discussed in the Leadership box, there are many obstacles in the way of a successful training strategy.

Sales training and increased profits have an obscure relationship at best. In the beginning of this chapter, we identified some broad objectives of sales training: improved selling skills, increased productivity, improved morale, lower sales force turnover, better customer relations, and better time and territory management. Unfortunately, pinning down the relationship between sales training and these broad objectives is not easy. Very little research has been done to determine what effect, if any, sales training has on the sales force. Most sales organizations simply assume on blind faith that their sales training programs are successful. After all, if a company has high sales and high profits, why should a sales manager assume sales training is anything but effective?

Sales Training Costs

Business firms spend millions of dollars each year on sales training in hopes of improving overall productivity. The statistics suggest that business has a relatively generous attitude toward sales training. It allocates funds for training with minimal regard for the results. Clearly, measuring the benefits of sales training needs some attention.

Is the measurement process that difficult? After all, if sales training is supposed to lead to better productivity, improved morale, and lower turnover, then why not measure changes in these variables after training has occurred? Some sales managers have done just that. They have assumed: We instituted sales training and shortly afterward sales increased. Therefore, sales training was the reason. Right? Wrong! Unless appropriate procedures are used to design the research by which the benefits are assessed, it is hard to say what caused the sales increase. Sales may have increased as a result of improved economic conditions, competitive activity, environmental changes, seasonal trends, or other reasons. Consequently, research must be carefully designed to isolate these contaminating effects to identify the benefits directly attributable to training.

Measurement Criteria

Even though intervening variables such as changes in competitive activities make evaluation of sales training programs difficult, it is still important to measure training effectiveness. This raises the question: What characteristics of sales training should be assessed? Exhibit 10.4 illustrates an evaluation options matrix. Often companies choose one of the criteria shown in Exhibit 10.4 to measure effectiveness; however a strong argument can be made that several criteria should be used in assessing the results of any sales training program. Measuring what was learned, for example, does not mean much if the company does not also measure changes in behavior. However, it is important to assess sales training programs, because the program should deliver value to the salesperson and organization. The solution rests in properly specifying the objectives and content of the sales training program, the criteria used to evaluate the program, and the proper design of the research so benefits can be unambiguously determined.

Evaluation Level: What Is the Question?	Information Required: What Information to Collect?	Method: How to Collect?	**EXHIBIT 10.4** Evaluation options matrix
Reaction Did participants respond favorably to the program?	Attitudinal	Evaluation Questionnaires Comments Anecdotes Interviews with participants	
Learning Did participants learn concepts or skills?	Understanding of concepts, ability to use skills	Before-and-after test	
Behavior Did participants change their on-the-job behavior?	On-the-job behavior	Behavior ratings, before and after Critical incident technique Time-series analysis	
Results What personal or organizational results occurred?	Changes in sales, productivity, or other performance	Cost–benefit methods	

Measuring Broad Benefits

Broad benefits of sales training include improved morale and lower turnover. Morale can be partially measured by studies of job satisfaction. Suppose, for instance, a company measured job satisfaction as part of a needs analysis and found evidence of problems. A follow-up job satisfaction study after the corrective sales training program would determine if morale changed noticeably.

Measuring reactions and learning is important in sales training for both new and experienced personnel. Most companies measure reactions by asking those attending the training to complete an evaluation form either immediately after the session or several weeks later. Emotions and enthusiasm may be high right after a session, but sales training effectiveness is much more than a "warm feeling." Measuring what was learned requires tests. To what extent did salespeople learn the facts, concepts, and techniques included in the training session? Objective examinations are appropriate.

Measuring Specific Benefits

Liking the program and learning something are not enough. Specific measures to examine behavior changes and results are needed to assess effectiveness. The effectiveness of a sales training program aimed at securing more new customers, for example, is assessed, in part by examining call reports to see whether there are more new customers. Results are measured by tracking new-account sales to see whether they have increased. If the specific objective of sales training is to increase the sales of more profitable items, evidence that this has been accomplished provides a partial measure of training effectiveness. Finally, if reducing customer complaints was the objective, then the appropriate specific measure is whether customer complaints decreased.

The measurement of specific and broad benefits is predicated on the assumption that the sales training program is designed to achieve certain goals. The goals should be established before sales training begins. When specific objectives have been determined, the best training program is developed to achieve these objectives. Most training programs have several objectives. Multiple measurements of the effectiveness of the training program are then a necessary part of evaluating the benefits.

Recent studies reveal that most sales training evaluation measures are simple, consisting primarily of reactions to the program. Meaningful evaluation measures, such as learning, behavior, and results, are used much less frequently. Often, the easiest-to-collect measures—staff comments and feedback from supervisors and trainees—are used the most. Bottom-line evaluation (e.g., changes in sales volume) is used less frequently or not at all.

Exhibit 10.5 shows how sales managers rank the various measures by both importance and frequency of use.[26] Interestingly, the most frequently used measure is course evaluation, but it is only ranked ninth on importance. Course evaluation is a reaction measure that fails to reveal learning, behavioral, and results changes associated with the sales training.

Evaluating the benefits of sales training is difficult. One study asked sales managers to identify the most important restrictions against sales training evaluation. The most common restrictions were time and money and difficulty in gathering the data or gaining access to data.[27]

Recent Trends in Sales Training Evaluation

In recent years there has been a surge of interest in sales training evaluation. Managers are no longer willing to rest on the assumption that sales training must be effective since sales are rising. Managers are now being asked to provide concrete evidence that sales training makes a difference. Evidence based on salesperson reactions or testing what was learned is useful but no longer sufficient proof. If sales training is to be viewed as an investment rather than a cost, then managers must be able to document the benefits in order to calculate a return on investment.

What's behind this movement toward more accountability? A dilemma facing many sales training managers is that while management wants evidence that supports the value of training, funds needed for evaluation, especially measuring actual changes in sales levels, have not been budgeted. This kind of measurement usually requires using a control group, a rare activity in most companies.

There are problems, of course, in equating sales increases with sales training. There are too many variables that could have had a positive effect on sales: introduction of a new product, failure of a competitor, increase in advertising, or improvement in price competitiveness. Regardless of the evaluation method employed, sales training managers face increasing demands as to the value of their programs.

Approach	Type	Importance	Frequency	
Trainee feedback	Reaction	1	2	**EXHIBIT 10.5** Overall ranking of evaluation measures
Supervisory appraisal	Behavior	2	6	
Self-appraisal	Behavior	3	7	
Bottom-line measurement	Results	4	9	
Customer appraisal	Behavior	5	10	
Supervisory feedback	Reaction	6	4	
Performance tests	Learning	7	5	
Training staff comments	Reaction	8	3	
Course evaluations	Reaction	9	1	
Subordinate appraisal	Behavior	10	12	
Pre- vs. post-training measurements	Learning	11	11	
Coworker appraisal	Behavior	12	13	
Knowledge tests	Learning	13	8	
Control group	Learning	14	14	

SUMMARY

Sales training is a varied and ongoing activity that is time-consuming and expensive. Most companies engage in some type of sales training. In fact, most sales managers feel that sales training is such an important activity that they require it for everybody, regardless of their experience. Some common objectives of sales training are to teach selling skills, increase productivity, improve morale, lower turnover, improve customer relations, and improve time and territory management.

Considerable variability exists in the length of sales training programs. Industry differences account not only for variations in length but also for variations in program content. Company policies, the nature of the selling job, and the types of products and services offered also contribute to differences in time spent and on topics covered.

Product knowledge receives the most attention, followed by selling techniques, market/industry orientation, and company orientation. This allocation is the subject of considerable criticism.

As a result of various environmental changes, the content and method of sales training has changed. Standard issue for salespeople today is a cell phone and laptop computer. In addition, they are as likely to receive training via the Internet as they are by another person.

Sales training is very expensive and generally considered beneficial. Accurate measurement of the benefits is difficult. It is hard to isolate the effects produced solely by sales training from those that might have been produced by other factors, such as changes in the economy or the nature of competition. Sales training provides managers with the opportunity to convey their expectations to the sales force. A well-designed training program shows the sales force how to sell. Sales managers can communicate high performance expectations through training and equip the force with the skills needed to reach high-performance levels.

KEY TERMS

sales training analysis	role-playing	sales training costs
on-the-job training (OJT)	electronic training methods	

BREAKOUT QUESTIONS

1. The response from a few of the sales reps from Marlow Technologies toward the new sales training topic was not encouraging. Geoff Marlow, vice president of sales, was dismayed at what he perceived to be a total lack of social graces on the part of the 15-person sales force. To rectify this situation, he retained a consulting firm that specializes in etiquette training to provide a day-long session on the subject. Frank Casey, one of Marlow's sales trainees, was not pleased and said, "What's this? Now we have to go to charm school too! Next thing you know, they'll want to teach us how to dress."

Are such topics as etiquette and dress appropriate for sales training? How would you evaluate the effectiveness of this kind of training?

2. The newly assigned sales representative was perplexed about her inability to learn about consumers' needs. She contends her customers are not willing to tell her what problems they are experiencing. After making several joint calls with her, the district sales manager agreed she was not receiving informative responses to her questions. What are the characteristics of good questions? How can sales reps be trained to ask better questions?

3. One expert contends that sales training is not at all as complicated as some would claim. He predicts that regardless of the advances in communication, resources, technology, and training tools, the basic selling skills that trainers teach salespeople will change very little from those that have been successful during the past 50 years. What will change, according to the expert, is how salespeople are trained to use these skills effectively. Do you agree with this prediction?

4. Ethical Question. One of the challenges in evaluating sales training is developing effective assessment measures. What are some of the ethical challenges sales leaders face in creating unbiased effective training measures?

LEADERSHIP CHALLENGE: TRAIN WHAT?

As Susan Jamison, director of sales training at O&F Products, a world leader in consumer packaged products based in Munich Germany, leaned back in her chair, she was thinking about the upcoming semiannual sales training sessions for the European sales force at O&F. These sessions took place over three days, and while regional directors around the world could alter some of the content to fit local needs, Susan was responsible for putting together the overall outline and content of the training. O&F placed a lot of emphasis on training, and these training sessions were a major element in the company's ongoing commitment to having the best sales force in the industry.

After a series of meetings with senior sales managers as well as input from senior regional management in the company, she was unclear regarding the content of the training this year. Senior sales managers were calling for a focus on new-product information. The company had introduced a number of new products in the last several years, and sales for some of them had not met the company's projections. Senior sales personnel felt it was due, in large part, to a lack of training. In addition, these same individuals felt salespeople would benefit from additional training on some of the existing products, particularly those in which O&F did not enjoy a market leadership position. At the same time, senior management, particularly the General Counsel for the company, wanted the focus to be on sales ethics. Recently, the European Union had been investigating the consumer packaged products industry for unfair and perhaps illegal sales practices to retailers. Given the aggressive nature of the EU's regulatory agencies, the General Counsel and several senior executives wanted the three-day training session to provide salespeople with a better understanding of O&F's ethical practices as well as EU regulations on dealing with retailers.

Susan was in a tough position. She felt both groups had legitimate information to be presented during the training seminar. Unfortunately, there was only sufficient time to focus on one of the areas: ethics or product knowledge.

Questions

1. What are the benefits and limitations of focusing on only product knowledge in training?

2. Do you think you can really train sales ethics?

3. You are Susan Jamison. What would you choose to do in this situation and why?

ROLE-PLAY: BASS BROKERS, INC.— PART C

Situation

This situation is a continuation of that presented in the Chapters 8 and 9 role-plays. Go back and read those and your notes from them to refamiliarize yourself with the scenario.

It is now six months later, and Jason Queen has made two outstanding hires of new salespeople in District 5. The emphasis on proper selection criteria, recruiting sources, and selection tools and procedures seems to have paid off. Bass Brokers' director of sales training, Gloria Long, has just returned from a full week working with Jason and several of his salespeople, including the two new hires. She has scheduled an appointment with Roscoe Lee, her boss and national sales manager, to debrief her "work-with" in District 5.

"I'm pleased with the new hires out in District 5," she tells Roscoe as she sits down across the desk from him. "We've made great progress on institutionalizing our recruiting and selection. Now, what about taking a closer look at our training?" Gloria goes on to explain that, while the typical on-the-job training new Bass Brokers salespeople receive obviously serves its purpose, perhaps it is time to provide some additional companywide training opportunities beyond just the hands-on approach used by the district managers. Roscoe is well aware that Bass Brokers has always relied on district managers to do most of the training and that it usually takes the form of periodically riding with salespeople on client calls and providing constructive feedback for improvement. This approach has been augmented by visits from Gloria, who focuses on riding with each salesperson at least once a year and visiting each district manager quarterly.

"I've thought about this too," Roscoe says. "I agree with you that we should step back and evaluate whether we could do a better job of training our salespeople by using more varied approaches. Especially, I would like us to focus on preparing new salespeople and on providing career enhancing professional development opportunities for all our salespeople. Let's you and I talk now about what the options might be, then we will throw some suggestions out to the district managers for their input."

Characters in the Role-Play

Roscoe Lee, vice president of sales for Bass Brokers, Inc.
Gloria Long, director of training for Bass Brokers, Inc.

Assignment

Break into pairs, with one student playing each character. It doesn't matter what the actual gender mix of your pair is. Before you stage the continuation of the meeting, work separately using the material in your chapter to come up with your recommendations for a mix of sales training methods that you believe would be best for Bass Brokers. You will need to be prepared to justify your recommendations in the meeting. Then get together and role-play the continuation of the meeting between Roscoe and Gloria. Be sure each of you share your ideas and justify them. In the end, you want to come out of the meeting with a unified proposal for sales training at Bass Brokers that could be forwarded to the district managers for their input.

MINICASE: FLETCHER BALL BEARINGS

Fletcher Ball Bearings, based in Lewiston, Maine, is one of the world's leading manufacturers of precision bearings and bearing products. Fletcher sells its products to many industries, including aerospace, communications, health care, and defense. Ball bearings have many uses within these industries, such as gas turbine engines, fuel pumps, aircraft instruments, gyros, dental and surgical hand pieces, and electric motors. As one might expect, these are very complicated products and require a technical knowledge not only of the bearings themselves but also of the products of which they are an integral part.

The company is divided into several divisions, each with its own specialized sales force. The Aero division manufactures and sells bearings for use in end products such as rotary-wing aircraft (helicopters), fixed-wing aircraft, jet engines, missiles, actuators, landing gear, starters, and satellites. The Aero division attempts to hire salespeople with an aerospace or engineering education and relevant work experience. However, the level of expertise varies drastically among its 150 salespeople, and even those with the highest expertise do not know everything because the technology changes so quickly.

A new director of sales, Gordon Chase, joined the company a year ago, and immediately began preaching the need for training in order for salespeople to stay up to date with product knowledge. However, the senior board of the company voted down his one-year training budget request of $8,000 per salesperson and instead reduced it to $2,000 per salesperson. The board's complaint was that the company had spent a great deal of money on training in the past but could not identify any tangible benefits.

So Chase proceeded as best he could under the approved budget and set up a training program that provided five hours of classroom training per month for each salesperson. This included company orientation information, information on specifications of the ball bearings sold by the Aero division, and some information about the prime industry players and their products. The training was administered by internal company managers who were very knowledgeable as to the bearing products and specifications. They also were members of industry associations and had a good working knowledge of aerospace manufacturing operations at key account customers like Lockheed Martin, Boeing, and NASA. The classes were designed to have "something for everyone," so each contained both basic and advanced information.

Chase was pleased that he was able to squeeze so many hours of training from his limited budget. However, not everyone shared his positive assessment. Joe Rodgers, one of the more senior salespeople, commented, "This one-size-fits-all approach of the training frustrates me to no end because in order to get a few nuggets of new, worthwhile information I have to sit through two hours of things I already know!" He and others began to rebel and stopped going to training altogether. Conversely, the new salespeople felt like they were not getting enough introductory training and could not understand some of the more advanced technology updates because they were still trying to master the basics of being a salesperson. Also, the information on the customers and the end products was helpful but not nearly as detailed as the salespeople would have liked it to be.

Chase started a feedback program of collecting anonymous written evaluations after each classroom training session and began to see a trend of negative feelings from the employees. He was concerned that these negative assessments would be the death knell for his fledgling training program and knew he had to make some improvements before the next budget year.

Questions

1. What should Chase have said to the senior board to have received a higher training budget? How can Fletcher measure the benefits of a training program to justify its costs?

2. What additional topics should the training cover?

3. What training methods or trainers other than classroom instruction by internal trainers might Chase consider using to improve the training? Why?

4. What changes would you recommend to help Aero division better satisfy the needs of new personnel versus experienced ones? Why?

CHAPTER 11

Salesperson Compensation and Incentives

LEARNING OBJECTIVES

This chapter provides an overview of key issues related to compensating salespeople. The key issues to understand involve the types of compensation available (especially incentive forms of compensation), and when each might be most effectively offered.

After reading this chapter, you should be able to

- Discuss the advantages and limitations of straight salary, straight commission, and combination plans.
- Explain how and why a bonus component to compensation might be used as an incentive.
- Understand the effective use of sales contests, as well as the potential pitfalls of their use.
- Identify key nonfinancial rewards, and how and why they might be important.
- Recognize key issues surrounding expense accounts in relationship selling.
- Discuss making decisions on the mix and level of compensation.

OVERVIEW OF COMPENSATION AND INCENTIVES

Chapter 11 introduces the concept of rewards. The way the reward structure is implemented in a sales organization is through the compensation plan afforded to salespeople. Three basic questions drive successful compensation programs:

1. Which compensation method is most appropriate for motivating specific kinds of selling activities in specific selling situations?

2. How much of a salesperson's total compensation should be earned through incentive programs?

3. What is the appropriate mix of financial and nonfinancial compensation and incentives for motivating the sales force?

In most firms, the total financial compensation paid to salespeople comprises several components, each of which may be designed to achieve different objectives. The core of sales compensation plans consists of a salary and incentive payments. A salary is a fixed sum of money paid at regular intervals. The amount of salary paid to a given salesperson is usually a function of that person's experience, competence, and time on the job, as well as the sales manager's judgments about the quality of the individual's performance. Salary adjustments are useful for rewarding salespeople for performing customer relationship building activities that may not directly result in sales in the short term, such as prospecting for new customers or providing postsale service. They can also help adjust for differences in sales potential across territories.

Many firms that pay their salespeople a salary also offer additional incentive payments to encourage good performance. Those incentives may take the form of commissions tied to sales volume or profitability, or bonuses for meeting or exceeding specific performance targets (e.g., meeting quotas for particular products within the company's line or for particular types of customers). Such incentives are useful for directing salespeople's efforts toward specific strategic objectives during the year, as well as providing additional rewards for the top performers within the sales force. A commission is a payment based on short-term results, usually a salesperson's dollar or unit sales volume. Since a direct link exists between sales volume and the amount of commission received, commission payments are particularly useful for motivating a high level of selling effort.

A bonus is a payment made at the discretion of management for achieving or surpassing some set level of performance. Whereas commissions are typically paid for

INNOVATION   Outsourcing Incentives

Normally, small to medium-size companies with few salespeople are able to handle their own incentive program. For other, large sales organizations, outsourcing a sales incentive program might be a great business decision. A few indicators that can help determine if your incentive program should be run by an outside firm are:

- There are multiple individuals maintaining the incentive system at moderate salary budgets.
- Your company invests heavily on incentives but your program lacks accountability, reporting tools, and cost/benefit outcomes.
- Your employees complain about inconsistent practices and/or a lack of meaningful rewards.

The modern-day sales process is very complicated and some companies might find it hard to keep their sales force motivated. Many organizations need complex structures and tracking mechanisms for a program's goals. Full-service incentive companies, such as Incentive Intelligence and Impact Incentives, can help consolidate important data sources and information to provide a good view of what is happening with the program. Organizations with lesser needs can use lower-service providers. These companies usually just handle award fulfillment, such as online catalog merchandise or travel rewards.

The most common objection to outsourcing an incentive program involves cost. Executives believe that they can do everything cheaper in-house. However, they may fail to realize hidden costs. The cost of the internal teams that support the program could be very expensive or require an above normal work load. There is also the "cost" of doing a program incorrectly, such as overpaying in-house for an "amateur" design. Innovative ideas and new directions are a couple of benefits that outsourced incentive providers can offer due to their experience in working with previous clients that may have faced the same motivational challenges affecting your company.[1]

each sale that is made, a bonus is typically not paid until the salesperson surpasses some level of total sales or other aspect of performance. When the salesperson reaches the minimum level of performance required to earn a bonus, however, the size of the bonus might be determined by the degree to which the salesperson exceeds that minimum. Thus, bonuses are usually *additional incentives* to motivate salespeople to reach high levels of performance rather than part of the basic compensation plan. Bonuses are almost never used alone as a form of compensation; rather, they are combined with one or more other compensation elements. Attaining quota is often the minimum requirement for a salesperson to earn a bonus. Quotas can be based on goals for sales volume, profitability of sales, or various account-servicing activities. To be effective, quotas (like goals) should be specific, measurable, and realistically attainable. Therefore, bonuses can be offered as a reward for attaining or surpassing a predetermined level of performance on any dimensions for which quotas are set.

In addition to the incentives mentioned here, many firms conduct sales contests to encourage extra effort aimed at specific short-term objectives. For example, a contest might offer additional rewards for salespeople who obtain a specified volume of orders from new customers or who exceed their quotas for a new product during a three-month period. Contest winners might be given additional cash, merchandise, or travel awards.

Finally, a foundation of most compensation plans is a package of benefits. These are designed to satisfy the salesperson's basic needs for security. They typically include such things as medical and disability insurance, life insurance, and a retirement plan. The types and amount of benefits included in a compensation plan are usually a matter of company policy and apply to all employees. However, the benefit package a firm offers its salespeople should be reasonably comparable to those offered by competitors to avoid being at a disadvantage when recruiting new sales talent.

The key forms of financial compensation of salespeople are summarized in Exhibit 11.1. It is important to know that beyond financial compensation, a variety of forms of nonfinancial incentives exist. These might take the form of opportunities for promotion or various types of recognition for performance such as special awards and publications in company newsletters. Nonfinancial incentives will be discussed in more detail later in the chapter.

Sometimes sales organizations may choose to outsource their incentive programs. The Innovation box provides ideas and issues related to incentive program outsourcing.

STRAIGHT SALARY, STRAIGHT COMMISSION, AND COMBINATION PLANS

The three primary methods of compensating salespeople are (1) straight salary, (2) straight commission, and (3) a combination of base salary plus incentive pay in the form of commissions, bonuses, or both. In recent years, a steady trend has

EXHIBIT 11.1
Components and objectives of financial compensation plans

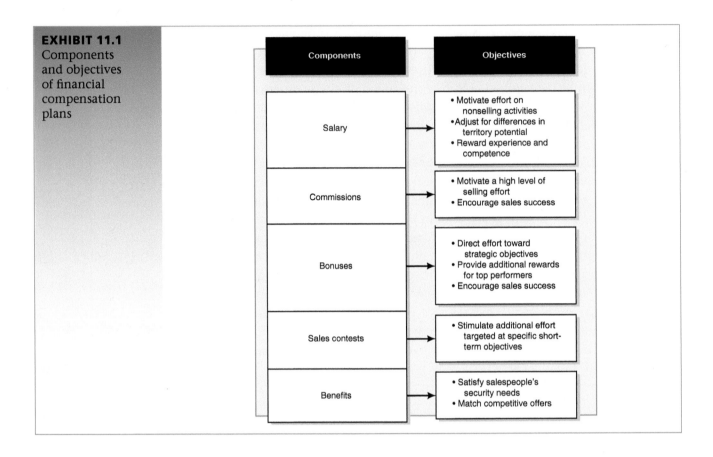

developed away from both straight salary and straight commission plans toward combination plans. Today, combination plans are by far the most common form of compensation.

In essence, managers seek to create a "pay for performance" plan that rewards people using both salary and incentive programs to maximize the salesperson's performance. Unfortunately, creating such programs is very complex, and companies often choose a program based on convenience or cost effectiveness rather than actual benefits to the company.[2] And, much variety exists of preferences of rewards among salespeople.

The following sections highlight the three principal compensation approaches. Exhibit 11.2 summarizes this discussion.

Straight Salary

Two sets of conditions favor the use of a straight salary compensation plan: (1) when management wishes to motivate salespeople to achieve objectives other than short-run sales volume and (2) when the individual salesperson's impact on sales volume is difficult to measure in a reasonable time. Because relationship selling may involve both of these conditions, it is not uncommon for sales jobs with heavy customer care to be compensated by straight salary.

Compensation Method	Especially Useful	Advantages	Disadvantages	**EXHIBIT 11.2** Characteristics of compensation methods for salespeople
Straight Salary	When compensating new sales reps; when firm moves into new sales territories that require developmental work; when sales reps must perform many nonselling activities	Provides sales rep with maximum security; gives sales manager more control over sales reps; is easy to administer; yields more predictable selling expenses	Provides no incentive; necessitates closer supervision of sales reps' activities; during sales declines, selling expenses remain at same level	
Straight Commission	When highly aggressive selling is required; when nonselling tasks are minimized; when company cannot closely control sales force activities	Provides maximum incentive; by increasing commission rate, sales managers can encourage reps to sell certain items; selling expenses relate directly to selling resources	Sales reps have little financial security; sales manager has minimum control over sales force; may cause reps to provide inadequate service to smaller accounts; selling costs are less predictable	
Combination	When sales territories have relatively similar sales potential; when firm wishes to provide incentive but still control sales force activities	Provides certain level of financial security; provides some incentive; selling expenses fluctuate with sales revenue; sales manager has some control over reps' nonselling activities	Selling expenses are less predictable; may be difficult to administer	

Advantages

The primary advantage of a straight salary is that management can require salespeople to spend their time on activities that may not result in immediate sales. Therefore, a salary plan or a plan offering a large proportion of fixed salary is appropriate when the salesperson is expected to perform many customer service or other nonselling activities. These may include market research, customer problem analysis, product stocking, customer education, or sales promotion. Straight salary plans are also common in industries where many engineering and design services are required as part of the selling function, such as in high-technology industries.

Straight salary compensation plans are also desirable when it is difficult for management to measure the individual salesperson's actual impact on sales volume or other aspects of performance. Thus, firms tend to pay salaries to their sales force when (1) their salespeople are engaged in missionary selling, as in the pharmaceutical industry; (2) other parts of the marketing program, such as advertising or dealer promotions, are the primary determinants of sales success, as in some consumer packaged goods businesses; or (3) the selling process is complex and involves a team or multilevel selling effort, as in the case of computers. Career counselors often advise college students interested in taking a first job in relationship selling to try to make that first experience heavier in salary component versus incentive pay. This gives the new salesperson some time to learn the ropes and hone his or her skills while earning a steady income. Because straight salary plans provide salespeople with a steady, guaranteed income, they are often used when the salesperson's ability to generate immediate sales is uncertain, as in the case of new recruits in a field-training program or when a firm is introducing a new product line or opening new territories.

Finally, salary plans are easy for management to compute and administer. They also give management more flexibility. It is easy to reassign salespeople to new territories or product lines because they do not have to worry about how such changes will affect their sales volumes. Also, since salaries are fixed costs, the compensation cost per unit sold is lower at relatively high levels of sales volume.

Limitations

The major limitation of straight salary compensation is that financial rewards are not tied directly to any specific aspect of job performance. Management should attempt to give bigger salary increases each year to the good performers than those given to the poor ones. However, the amount of those increases and the way performance is evaluated are subject to the whims of the manager who makes the decision. Also, salaries do not provide any direct financial incentive for improving sales-related aspects of performance. Consequently, over the long run salary plans appeal more to security-oriented rather than achievement-oriented salespeople.

Straight Commission

A commission is payment for achieving a given level of performance. Salespeople are paid for results. Usually, commission payments are based on the salesperson's dollar or unit sales volume. However, it is becoming more popular for firms to base commissions on the *profitability* of sales to motivate the sales force to expend effort on the most profitable products or customers. The most common way is to offer salespeople variable commissions, where relatively high commissions are paid for sales of the most profitable products or sales to the most profitable accounts. Such a variable commission rate can also be used to direct the sales force's efforts toward other straight sales objectives, such as paying a higher commission on a new product line being introduced.

Advantages

Direct motivation is the key advantage of a commission compensation plan, as a clear and direct link exists between sales performance and the financial compensation the salesperson earns. Consequently, salespeople are strongly motivated to improve their sales productivity to increase their compensation, at least until they reach such high pay that further incremental increases become less attractive. Commission plans also have a built-in element of fairness (assuming that sales territories are properly defined, with about equal potential), because good performers are automatically rewarded, whereas poor performers are discouraged from continuing their low productivity.

Commission plans have some advantages from a sales management viewpoint. Commissions are usually easy to compute and administer. Also, compensation costs vary directly with sales volume. This is an advantage for firms that are short of working capital because they do not need to worry about paying high wages to the sales force unless it generates high sales revenues.

Limitations

Straight commission compensation plans have some important limitations that have caused many firms, especially those engaged in relationship selling, to abandon them. Perhaps the most critical weakness is that management has little control over the sales force. When all their financial rewards are tied directly to sales volume, it often can be difficult to motivate salespeople to engage in relationship building activities that do not lead directly to short-term sales. Consequently, salespeople on commission are likely to "milk" existing customers rather than work to develop new accounts and sustain long-term relationships. For example, they may overstock their customers and neglect service after the sale. Finally, they have little motivation to engage in market analysis and other similar functions that take time away from actual selling activities.

Straight commission plans also have a disadvantage for many salespeople. Such plans make a salesperson's earnings unstable and hard to predict. When business conditions are poor, turnover rates in the sales force are likely to be high because salespeople find it hard to live on the low earnings produced by poor sales. To combat the inherent instability of commission plans, some firms provide their salespeople with a draw, or drawing account. In a draw, money is advanced to a salesperson in months when commissions are low to ensure he or she will always take home a specified minimum amount of pay. The amount of the salesperson's draw in poor months is deducted from earned commissions when sales improve. This gives salespeople some secure salary, and it allows management more control over their activities. A problem arises, however, when a salesperson fails to earn enough commissions to repay the draw. Then the person may quit or be fired, and the company must absorb the loss.[3]

The Technology box provides some examples of how various readily available software packages can calculate and keep track of commission payments.

Combination Plans

Compensation plans that offer a base salary plus some proportion of incentive pay are the most popular because they have many of the advantages but avoid most of the limitations of both straight salary and straight commission plans. The base salary provides the salesperson with a stable income and gives management some capability to reward salespeople for performing customer service and administrative tasks that are not directly related to short-term sales. At the same time, the incentive portion of such compensation plans provides direct rewards to motivate the salesperson to expend effort to improve sales volume and profitability.

TECHNOLOGY   Compensation Software

Keeping track of your sales staff's commissions can be a difficult task, especially if you are operating a small or medium-sized business. With new software, your company can keep track of sales figures and easily calculate commissions. Also, this software is much less costly than if you were to hire administrative personnel. Many of these solutions are cloud-based, which means the company does not have to buy expensive server equipment to run the software.

Many small to medium-sized business may calculate commissions the old fashioned way, by hand or using spreadsheets. These methods can easily lead to mistakes and be very time consuming. If mistakes are made, it could hurt the business's bottom line or even decrease salesperson morale. Compensation software will eliminate this problem and will free up your time to focus on running the business.

There are many solutions and companies to choose from today, which is why it is important to research which one is the right fit for your business. Synygy is currently among one of the favorites for businesses, but there are more, like Xactly Corporation, Callidus, and QCommission. One thing you want to consider for this decision is whether the software is compatible with your other in-house applications, such as QuickBooks. Also, consider whether you want a solution that will operate on your existing servers or in the cloud. Compensation software is great technology that can be very beneficial to your company. It can help you retain good sales staff and help your company figure out how to make a decent profit.[4]

Combination plans bring together a base salary with commissions, bonuses, or both. When salary plus commission is used, the commissions are tied to sales volume or profitability, or both, just as with a straight commission plan. The only difference is that the commissions are smaller in a combination plan than when the salesperson is compensated solely by commission. As described earlier, adding a bonus component typically recognizes the achievement of some specific performance goal.

Whether base salary is combined with commission payments or bonuses, managers must answer several other questions when designing effective combination compensation plans. These include, (1) What is the appropriate size of the incentive relative to the base salary? (2) Should a ceiling be imposed on incentive earnings? (3) When should the salesperson be credited with a sale? (4) Should team incentives be used, and if so, how should they be allocated across members of a sales team? and (5) How often should the salesperson receive incentive payments?

Proportion of Incentive Pay to Total Compensation

What proportion of total compensation should be incentive pay? A sales manager's decision concerning what proportion of the overall compensation package is represented by incentive pay should be based on the degree of relationship selling involved in the job. When the firm's primary selling approaches are directly related to short-term sales (such as increasing sales volume, profitability, or new customers), a large incentive component should be offered. When customer service and other nonsales objectives are deemed more important, the major emphasis should be on the base salary component of the plan. This gives management more control over rewarding the sales force's relationship selling activities.

When the salesperson's selling skill is the key to sales success, the incentive portion of compensation generally should be relatively large. However, when the product has been presold through advertising and the salesperson is largely an order taker, or when the salesperson's job involves a large proportion of missionary or customer service work, the incentive component should be relatively small.

If a particular combination plan is not very effective at motivating salespeople, one of the most common reasons is that the incentive portion is too small to generate much interest. Companies are always challenged to hire and retain the best salespeople. One approach is to open up the incentive component to negotiation on a salesperson-to-salesperson basis, thus creating a very individualized combination plan. In this way, salespeople who seek greater compensation security can focus on more fixed compensation (salary), while others can opt for the potential to earn even higher total compensation by taking greater risks through placing more of their compensation on incentive-based rewards.[5] Such individualized approaches must allow a salesperson to change his or her compensation allocation periodically, perhaps annually.

Incentive Ceilings

Should there be a ceiling or cap on incentive earnings to ensure top salespeople do not earn substantially more money than other employees? This is an issue that is dealt with in very different ways across companies and industries, and for which strong arguments can be made on both sides. Part of the differences in how different firms handle this issue seems to reflect the variation in average compensation levels, with firms in relatively low-paying industries being more likely to impose caps than those in higher-paying lines of trade.

Arguments in favor of using ceilings include that they ensure top salespeople will not make such high earnings that other employees in the firm, sometimes even managers, suffer resentment and low morale. Ceilings also protect against windfalls, such as increased sales due to the introduction of successful new products, where a salesperson's earnings might become very large without corresponding effort. Finally, ceilings make a firm's maximum potential sales compensation expense more predictable and controllable.

A strong counterargument can be made, however, that such ceilings ultimately have a bad effect on motivation and dampen the sales force's enthusiasm. Also, when ceilings are in place, some salespeople may reach the earnings maximum early in the year and be inclined to take it easy for the rest of the year.

The issue of incentive ceilings has become a growing problem in relationship selling, and in particular when compensating a salesperson in a team-selling environment. As team selling brings individuals from around the company to help with a customer, the question becomes how much the sales representative should make in a sale that is the result of the efforts of many individuals inside his or her firm. This problem is made worse as the size of each sale grows larger and larger and is especially relevant when dealing with key accounts. Another problem with incentive ceilings occurs as customers move around the world. How much should the sales representative be compensated for a sale in another part of the world even though that person is servicing the customer's headquarters in his or her territory? The solution to these problems that many companies have chosen is limiting or capping a salesperson's incentive compensation.[6]

Some desired effects of ceilings can be accomplished without arbitrarily limiting the motivation of the sales force by having management pretest any new or revised compensation plan before it is implemented. Sales managers can do this by analyzing the historical records of sales performance by selected salespeople to see how they would have come out under the proposed compensation system. In this test, particular attention should be given to the amount of compensation that would have been earned by the best and poorest performers to ensure that the compensation provided by the plan is both fair and reasonable.

When Is a Sale a Sale?

When incentives are based on sales volume or other sales-related aspects of performance, the precise meaning of a sale should be defined to avoid confusion and irritation. Most incentive plans credit a salesperson with a sale when the order is accepted by the company, less any returns and allowances. Occasionally, though, it makes good sense to credit the salesperson with a sale only after the goods have been shipped or payment has been received from the customer. This is particularly true when the time between receipt of an order and shipment of the goods is long and the company wants its salespeople to maintain close contact with the customer to prevent cancellations and other problems. As a compromise, some plans credit salespeople with half a sale when the order is received and the other half when payment is made.

Team versus Individual Incentives

The increasing use of sales or cross-functional teams to win new customers and service major accounts raises some important questions about the kinds of incentives to include in a combination compensation plan. Should incentives be tied to the overall performance of the entire team, should separate incentives be keyed to the individual performance of each team member, or both? If both group and individual incentives are used, which should be given the greatest weight? These questions have to be addressed successfully by sales managers when designing team-based incentives.[7]

When Should the Salesperson Receive Incentive Payments?

A survey of more than 500 compensation plans found that 21 percent paid salespeople incentive earnings on an annual basis, 3 percent paid semiannually, 24 percent paid quarterly, and 52 percent made monthly payments. In general, plans offering salary plus commission are more likely to involve monthly incentive payments, whereas salary plus bonus plans more often make incentive payments on a quarterly or annual schedule.

ETHICAL MOMENT   **The Ethics of Timing a Sale**

When is a sale a sale? Is it when the contract is signed, the product delivered, payment is received, or . . . perhaps something else? On the surface this may sound like a trivial question, but for sales organizations it is a big deal. The reason is that salesperson performance and rewards are linked to the sale and when the sale is credited to the salesperson can make a big difference in performance evaluations and ultimately compensation, as well as a firm's financial statements. Remember that a sale to a salesperson is revenue to a firm!

An interesting twist to the question "When is a sale a sale?" relates to periodic promotions or sales contests. That is, it is common for B2B firms to run cost-reduction promotions to their customers from time to time. This is done for a variety of reasons from new product introductions to beating competitors to reducing overstocks. Along with the temporary promotional prices, a sales contest might also be included that provides attractive prizes for salespeople who achieve different levels of sales performance during the contest. Now salespeople, being smart and highly competitive, will often be tempted in such cases to go to their buyers and ask them to "load up" during the promotion or contest so that the salesperson can "win," which brings up an ethical dilemma: If I'm simply borrowing business from the future with a customer in order to win a sales contest, have I really done a service to the firm or to my customer? Yes, I might gain some benefit temporarily from this behavior but in many cases I won't see another order on the promoted products for a very long time. And from the customer's side, while they may agree to load up to try to help you out, the truth is customers don't want to have extra inventory sitting around and their doing you a favor this time may create ill will in the long term.

Bottom line, a salesperson must think seriously about the potential for damaging a relationship with a customer and also about whether loading up customers this quarter just creates difficulties in making quota in subsequent quarters. Then too, from a sales organizational perspective, changes in accounting reporting standards (FASB) and legislation such as Sarbanes-Oxley have mandated companies present a more realistic picture of their financial performance, heightening the issue of when a sale is a sale. Companies train sales managers who in turn are expected to make it clear to the salespeople the policies and procedures for accurately reporting a sale.

Question to Ponder:

- What is your viewpoint on loading up customers during product promotions and sales contests? Consider the pros and cons and come to a conclusion on how this issue is best handled.

Shorter intervals between performance and the receipt of rewards increase the motivating power of the plan. However, short intervals add to the computation required, increase administrative expenses, and may make the absolute amount of money received by salespeople appear so small they may not be very impressed with their rewards. Consequently, quarterly incentive payments are an effective compromise.

It is important to note that there's no "one size fits all" magic formula for developing compensation plans.

Steps to Executing the Compensation Plan

There is no "one size fits all" pay plan solution. Depending on the type of product to be sold, the nature of the sales force, and the required outcome, the correct pay plan will be different.

Below is a five-step plan that can be used to tailor compensation packages to specific company needs:

1. Research—Look at past sales and relationships to compensation structures.

2. Define objectives—What are the goals? Increase profit, increase productivity, etc.?

3. Develop plan—Choose pay plan type, target pay, results to be rewarded, and pay formula. The pay formula will involve the mix of base pay and commission. The decision to vary by product should also be made.

4. Test—Test the plan on a spreadsheet using realistic sales results. Analyze different scenarios.

5. Document—This should be easily read and understood by your sales force.

Effective communication of the pay plan and clear definition of the levels of performance required to obtain the different compensation levels are essential.

SALES CONTESTS

Sales contests are short-term incentive programs designed to motivate sales personnel to accomplish specific sales objectives. Although contests should not be considered part of a firm's ongoing compensation plan, they offer salespeople the opportunity to gain financial, as well as nonfinancial, rewards. Contest winners often receive prizes in cash, merchandise, or travel. Winners also receive nonfinancial rewards in the form of recognition and a sense of accomplishment.

Successful contests require the following:

- Clearly defined, specific objectives.
- An exciting theme.
- Reasonable probability of rewards for all salespeople.
- Attractive rewards.
- Promotion and follow-through.[8]

Contest Objectives

Because contests *supplement* the firm's compensation program and are designed to motivate extra effort toward some short-term goal, their objectives should be very specific and clearly defined. Equally important, incentive compensation needs to be consistent with stated corporate objectives. Unfortunately, although companies may believe an objective is important, they do not always create incentives for salespeople that reflect those objectives.

The time frame within which the contest's objectives are to be achieved should be relatively short. This ensures that salespeople will maintain their enthusiasm and effort throughout the contest. But the contest should be long enough to allow all members of the sales force to cover their territories at least once and to have a reasonable chance of generating the performance necessary to win. Therefore, the average duration of sales contests is about three months.

Contest Themes

A sales contest should have an exciting theme to help build enthusiasm among the participants and promote the event. The theme should also be designed to stress the contest's objectives and appeal to all participants. Companies are getting more and more creative in creating themes for contests.

Probability of Winning

Three popular contest formats are available. In the first, salespeople compete with themselves by trying to attain individual quotas. Everyone who reaches or exceeds quota during the contest period wins. A second form requires that all members of the sales force compete with each other. The people who achieve the highest overall performance on some dimension are the winners, and everyone else loses. A third format organizes the sales force into teams, which compete for group and individual prizes.

Historically, individual sales quotas have been the most popular of the three formats. This reliance on individual quotas allows firms to design contests that focus salespeople's effort on specific objectives, do not put representatives in low-potential territories at a disadvantage, and do not undermine cooperation in the sales force by forcing salespeople to compete against each other.

Whichever format is used, it is essential that every member of the sales force have a reasonable chance of winning an award. If there are to be only one or a few winners, many salespeople may think their chances of coming out on top are remote and thus completely give up on the contest. In addition, average or below-average performers may automatically assume the top performers will win the award and not try as hard to hit sales goals. In this respect, contests that provide rewards to everyone who meets quotas during the contest period are desirable. Increasingly, companies are focusing on incentive programs, including contests, that seek to reward more rather than fewer salespeople.

Types of Contest Rewards

Contest rewards can take the form of cash, merchandise, or travel. All three types of rewards are commonly used, and a company may vary the kinds of rewards offered from contest to contest. Companies are also realizing that one size does not fit all.

More and more rewards are being tailored to individual salesperson "hot buttons." Once the dollar value of the reward is established, the winner may choose from several rewards. Or the manager may simply ask what kind of reward the salesperson wants to receive from the company. The idea is to find rewards that motivate each salesperson within the constraints of the budget. As one consultant states, "Tom, your top salesperson, learns that the reward for achieving success in the new sales contest is a set of MacGregor golf clubs. However, Tom's wife just bought him a new set of Callaways complete with the new Big Bertha driver. Chances are that Tom will not be motivated to win another set of clubs."[9]

An Incentive Federation survey found that on average 79 percent of respondents found noncash reward programs to be extremely effective in motivating participants to achieve sales goals.[10] "Cash is great," says a sales and marketing manager for a major insurance company. "But we like to give merchandise so the winner has some boasting rights when they win. And, if we award money, the rep generally won't spend the money on something for themselves—even if it's something they really want." One of the company's salespeople was awarded a suede jacket for a contest he won. "I wear it all the time, and every time I get a compliment, I tell them I won it," he says.

Merchandise also gives management an opportunity to make the reward presentation as part of a ceremony celebrating success. "When you present someone with a watch with all their colleagues around, they can congratulate the winner and, at the same time, see what they can win if they hit their next target," the manager says. And the salesperson agrees: "Merchandise gets me going. A check isn't as tangible as merchandise. You can't really show someone a check—it's not interesting. When you get money, you just mentally lump it in with your paycheck."[11]

Lexington, Kentucky–based printer manufacturer Lexmark International adjusted its incentive program to allow for changing preferences among salespeople. Rather than offering a one-size-fits-all reward, Lexmark adopted a points-based program in which salespeople can select gifts from a catalog. So far, the most popular items have been useful products for the home.[12]

Whatever form of reward is used, the monetary value must be large enough to be attractive to the participants, given their level of compensation. An iPad for example, may be more attractive when the average salesperson makes $40,000 per year than when the average compensation is $100,000.

Contest Promotion and Follow-through

To generate interest and enthusiasm, contests should be launched with fanfare. Where possible, firms should announce contests at national or regional sales meetings. Follow-up promotion is also necessary to maintain interest throughout the contest period. Special websites where salespeople can enter password-protected personal pages facilitate this. As the contest proceeds, salespeople should be given frequent feedback concerning their progress so they know how much more they must do to win an award. Finally, winners should be recognized within the company, and prizes should be awarded promptly.

Criticism of Sales Contests

Although many sales managers believe contests are effective for motivating special efforts from salespeople, contests can potentially cause a few problems, particularly if they are poorly designed or implemented.

Some critics argue that contests designed to stimulate sales volume may produce results that are largely fleeting, with no lasting improvement in market share. Salespeople may "borrow" sales from before or after the contest to increase their volume during the contest. They may hold back orders before the start of the contest and rush orders that would normally not be placed until after the contest. As a result, customers may be overstocked, causing sales volume to fall off for some time after the contest is over.

Contests may also hurt the cohesiveness and morale of the company's salespeople. This is particularly true when contests force individual salespeople to compete with one another for rewards and when the number of rewards is limited.

Finally, some firms tend to use sales contests to cover up faulty compensation plans. That is, salespeople should not have to be compensated a second time for what they are already being paid to do. Thus, contests should be used only on a short-term basis to motivate special efforts beyond the normal performance expected of the sales force. If a firm finds itself conducting frequent contests to maintain an acceptable level of sales performance, it should reexamine its entire compensation and incentive program.

NONFINANCIAL REWARDS

Most sales managers consider opportunities for promotion and advancement second only to financial incentives as an effective sales force motivator. This is particularly true for young, well-educated salespeople who tend to view their jobs as stepping-stones to top management. One common career path is from salesperson to district sales manager to top sales management. Thus, if a person has been with a firm for several years without making it into sales management, the individual may start to believe such a promotion will never happen. Consequently, veteran salespeople may begin to concentrate solely on financial rewards, or they may lose motivation and not work as hard at their jobs.

To overcome this problem, some firms have instituted two different career paths for salespeople. One leads to management positions, while the other leads to more advanced positions within the sales force. The latter usually involves responsibility for dealing with key accounts or leading sales teams. In this system, even though a salesperson may not make it into management, he or she can still work toward a more prestigious and lucrative position within the sales force. To make advanced sales positions more attractive as promotions, many firms provide people in those positions with additional perquisites, or perks, including higher compensation, a better automobile, and better office facilities.

RECOGNITION PROGRAMS

Contest awards and promotions to positions with more responsibility provide recognition for good performance, but many firms also have separate recognition programs to provide nonmonetary rewards. As with contests, effective recognition programs should offer a reasonable chance of winning for everyone in the sales force. But if a very large proportion of the sales force achieves recognition, the program is likely to lose some of its appeal because the winners feel no special sense of accomplishment.

Consequently, effective recognition programs often recognize the best performers across several different performance dimensions. For example, winners might include persons with the highest sales volume for the year, the biggest percentage increase in sales, the biggest dollar increase, the highest number of new customers, the largest sales per account, and the best customer retention record. Recognition is an attractive reward because it makes a salesperson's peers and superiors aware of the outstanding performance. Communicating the winner's achievements, through recognition at a sales meeting, publicity in the local press, announcements in the company's internal newsletter, or other ways, is an essential part of a good recognition program. Also, firms typically give special awards as part of their recognition program, and these are often awards with low monetary but high symbolic value, such as trophies, plaques, or rings. Finally, as Exhibit 11.3 points out, objectivity and good taste are also important ingredients of effective recognition programs, as they are for contests and other incentives.

EXPENSE ACCOUNTS

Expense items incurred by sales reps in the field—travel, lodging, meals, and entertaining customers—can be substantial. Depending on the industry and type of sales job, it is not unusual for field selling expenses to approach $25,000 or more per salesperson, and in some cases they are much higher. The growing trend of creating home offices for salespeople has increased expenses related to technology. Many firms have experimented with a variety of expense reimbursement plans. Such plans range from unlimited reimbursement for all "reasonable and allowable" expenses to plans where salespeople must pay all expenses out of their total compensation. Obviously, access to an expense account represents an enhancement to a salesperson's compensation.

Regardless of its size or cost, any recognition program should incorporate the following features:

EXHIBIT 11.3
Guidelines for effective formal recognition programs

- *The program must be strictly performance-based*, with no room for subjective judgments. If people suspect that it is in any way a personality contest, the program will not work. The winners should be clear to anyone looking at the data.
- *It should be balanced*. The program should not be so difficult that only a few can hope to win or so easy that just about everyone does. In the first case, people will not try; in the second, the program will be meaningless.
- *A ceremony should be involved*. If rings are casually passed out or plaques sent through the mail, a lot of the glamour of the program will be lost.

- *The program must be in good taste*. If not, it will be subject to ridicule and, rather than motivate people, it will leave them uninspired. No one wants to be part of a recognition program that is condescending or tacky. The program should make people feel good about being part of the company.
- *There must be adequate publicity*. In some cases, sales managers do such a poor job of explaining a program or promoting it to their own salespeople that no one seems to understand or care about it. Prominent mention of the program in company publications is the first step to overcoming this handicap.

When deciding which form of expense reimbursement to use, sales managers must make trade-offs between tight control aimed at holding down total expenses and the financial well-being—and the subsequent motivation level—of salespeople. Some expense items—such as entertainment expenses, club dues, and the costs of personal services while the salesperson is away from home—can be considered either legitimate business expenses that should be reimbursed by the company or personal expenses that the salesperson should pay. Obviously, company policies and reimbursement plans that treat such costs as business expenses increase the salesperson's total financial compensation but also increase the firm's total selling costs. Different reimbursement plans have an impact on the effective financial compensation received by, and the motivation level of, a firm's salespeople. Three key types of plans are direct reimbursement, limited reimbursement, and no reimbursement.

Direct Reimbursement Plans

One popular type of expense reimbursement plan involves direct and unlimited reimbursement of all "allowable and reasonable" expenses. The primary advantage is that direct reimbursement plans give the sales manager some control over both the total magnitude of sales expenses and the kinds of activities in which salespeople will be motivated to engage. If a particular activity, such as entertaining potential new accounts, is thought to be an important ingredient of the firm's account management policies, salespeople can be encouraged to engage in that activity by being informed that all related expenses will be reimbursed. On the other hand, managers can discourage their subordinates from spending time on unimportant tasks by refusing to reimburse expenditures for such activities.

Thus, company policies concerning reimbursable expenses can be a useful tool for motivating and directing sales effort. Some firms report they adjusted their expense reimbursement policies according to the differences in the territories covered or the job activities required of different members of their sales forces. For example, some firms reimburse a broader range and higher levels of expenses for their key account managers than for members of their regular field sales force.

Reimbursement under such plans is contingent on the salesperson submitting receipts or detailed records justifying expense claims, so the processing and evaluation of expense claims add to the firm's sales administration costs.

Limited Reimbursement Plans

Some firms limit the total amount of expense reimbursement, either by setting maximum limits for each expense item (such as a policy that limits reimbursement for restaurant meals to $50 per person) or by providing each salesperson with a predetermined lump-sum payment to cover total expenses. This approach keeps total selling expenses within planned limits—limits that are often determined by the sales expense budget set at the beginning of the year. In some cases, budgeted expense amounts may vary across members of the sales force, depending on the past or forecasted sales volume or the requirements of the territories.

Unless the budgeted limits are based on an accurate understanding of the costs associated with successful sales performance in each territory, however, limited reimbursement plans can hurt motivation and sales performance. Individual salespeople may believe their ability to do a good job is constrained by tightfisted company expense reimbursement policies. Rather than pay for necessary activities out of their own pockets, salespeople are likely to avoid or cut back on certain expense activities to keep their costs within their budgets.

No Reimbursement Plans

Some firms require salespeople to cover all of their own expenses. Such plans usually involve paying the salesperson a relatively higher total financial compensation to help cover necessary expenses and thus represent a variation of the predetermined lump-sum approach. Such plans are most commonly associated with straight commission compensation plans involving high-percentage commissions. The rationale is that salespeople will be motivated to spend both the effort and money necessary to increase sales volume so long as the resulting financial rewards are big enough to be worthwhile.

As with limited reimbursement plans, such approaches help the firm limit sales expenses or, in the case of commission plans, make them a totally variable cost that moves up and down with changes in sales volume. However, they also sacrifice management control over the motivation and types of activities engaged in by members of the sales force.

MAKING COMPENSATION AND INCENTIVE PROGRAMS WORK

The many complex issues involved make designing and implementing an effective compensation and incentive program difficult. Many managers wonder whether their company's program is as effective as possible in motivating the kinds and amounts of effort they desire from salespeople. And sometimes compensation plans just get so complicated that they have to be retooled to make them understandable to the sales force.

To make matters worse, even well-designed motivational programs can lose their effectiveness over time. As we discussed earlier in the book, the characteristics of relationship selling are different from other approaches to selling, and this fact along with the changing nature of the market environment can cause motivation programs to lose their effectiveness. As salespeople become satisfied with the rewards offered by a particular incentive plan, for instance, the requirements of the job or the customer may change. The Leadership box describes a possible result when reward systems do not match current job needs.

Recognizing such problems, an increasing number of firms frequently review their compensation and incentive policies. Many firms adjust their total compensation levels at least annually, and they are increasingly willing to make more substantial adjustments in their programs when circumstances demand. Some firms have established compensation and incentive committees to regularly monitor sales motivation programs for fairness and effectiveness. Two major issues involve (1) assessing the firm's relationship selling objectives and (2) determining which aspects of job performance to reward.

Assessing the Relationship Selling Objectives

A major purpose of any sales compensation program is to stimulate and influence the sales force to work toward accomplishing the objectives of securing, building, and maintaining long-term relationships with profitable customers. As a first step in deciding what job activities and performance dimensions a new or improved motivation program should stimulate, a manager should evaluate how salespeople are allocating their time. On what job activities do they focus, and how much time do they devote to each? How good are their current outcomes on various dimensions of performance, such as total sales volume, sales to new customers, or retention of existing customers? Much of this information can be obtained from job analyses the firm conducts as part of its recruitment and selection procedures, as well as from performance evaluations and company records.

LEADERSHIP   The Perils of Rewarding A While Hoping for B

Steven Kerr coined the phrase "Rewarding A while Hoping for B" way back in 1975 in an article in the *Academy of Management Review*. His premise was this: Very frequently, organizations establish reward systems that pay off one behavior even though the rewarder hopes dearly for some other behavior." This concept has strong application in sales force compensation plans, especially in today's complex environment of relationship selling.

Sales managers who wonder why their salespeople's behaviors do not seem to match their organization's goals might do well to consider that their reward systems pay off salespeople for behaviors other than those sought by the firm. In the past, rewarding salespeople was easier. Then, the focus was on individual salespeople approaching customers on a transaction-to-transaction basis. The focus today is on not just the salesperson but the whole organization working together toward developing long-term customer relationships. Do straight commission plans make sense in this environment? Not likely, as such approaches are the epitome of motivating individual sales efforts and not teamwork.

As an example, take hypothetical salesperson Chris. To achieve goals that yield desired results, Chris often has to rely in part on the performance of teammates who represent other functional areas of the firm. Unlike many salespeople of the past, Chris cannot individually and directly control much of the relationship selling process. Chris can marshal internal resources and apply them to the relationship-building process and can certainly serve as a point person for managing the relationship, but he cannot directly control the actions of the whole team. Clearly, in such a situation standard compensation and incentive systems are inadequate.

Firms cannot expect salespeople to focus on operating effectively within a team or on securing, building, and maintaining long-term relationships with profitable customers if the reward system doesn't recognize and compensate them for these behaviors. That is, the "Hoping for B" should be matched by "Rewarding B." In the relationship selling environment, incentives must be rethought and performance appraisal instruments must be refashioned to reflect the goals and behavior required for success today.

Steven Kerr had it right in 1975: "For an organization to act upon its members, the formal reward system should positively reinforce desired behaviors, not constitute an obstacle to be overcome."[13]

This assessment of the sales force's current allocation of effort and levels of performance can then be compared to the firm's specific objectives for relationship selling. Such comparisons often reveal that some selling activities and dimensions of performance are receiving too much emphasis from the sales force, while others are not receiving enough. This situation necessitates an adjustment in the incentive plan; in particular, it requires an immediate look at the quotas salespeople are working against. An important sales management function is monitoring whether the compensation and incentive plan, as well as associated quotas, continue to be effective over time in motivating the sales force. Remember, to be effective, quotas (which are goals for attaining some aspect of the sales job) must be specific, measurable, and realistically attainable. Overall, changing compensation plans successfully can be tricky.

Determining Which Aspects of Job Performance to Reward

When the firm's relationship selling objectives are misaligned with its sales force's allocation of time, the compensation and incentive program can be redesigned to more strongly reward desired activities or performance outcomes, thus motivating the sales reps to redirect their efforts.

Exhibit 11.4 lists specific activities and performance dimensions that can be stimulated by a properly designed compensation and incentive program. Of course, managers would like their salespeople to perform well on all of these dimensions, and as we saw earlier in the chapter, different components of a compensation program can be designed to reward different activities and achieve multiple objectives.

It is a mistake to try to motivate salespeople to do too many things at once. When rewards are tied to numerous aspects of performance, (1) it becomes difficult for a salesperson to focus on improving performance dramatically in any one area, and (2) the salesperson is more likely to be uncertain about how total performance will be evaluated and about what rewards can be obtained as a result of that performance. In short, complex compensation and incentive programs may lead to great confusion by salespeople. Thus, it is better for compensation and incentive plans to link rewards to only the key aspects of job performance. They should be linked to those aspects consistent with the firm's highest-priority relationship selling objectives.

• Sell a greater overall dollar volume. • Increase sales of more profitable products. • Push new products. • Push selected items at designated seasons. • Achieve a higher degree of market penetration by products, kinds of customers, or territories. • Secure large average orders.	• Secure new customers. • Service and maintain existing business. • Reduce turnover of customers. • Encourage cooperation among members of sales or account management teams. • Achieve full-line (balanced) selling. • Reduce direct selling costs. • Increase the number of calls made. • Submit reports and other data promptly.	**EXHIBIT 11.4** Sales activities and performance outcomes that might be encouraged by compensation and incentive programs

The complex relationship between today's customers and their suppliers has created the need for salespeople to cooperate and work with many individuals within their own firm as well as within the customer's business. Many of the performance outcomes identified in Exhibit 11.4 will not be achieved unless salespeople cooperate with others. Linking financial compensation programs with the need for salesperson cooperation is critical in building long-term relationships with customers.[14] Oracle's Siebel CRM applications, for example, and others link sales force compensation with customer-oriented metrics such as customer satisfaction. One reason for the reluctance of many firms to base rewards on customer satisfaction is the difficulty of measuring changes in satisfaction over time. Also, while there is some evidence that strong satisfaction-based incentives improve customer service by salespeople, some managers worry that such incentives may distract sales reps from the tasks necessary to capture additional sales volume in the short term. To offset this problem, some firms combine customer-satisfaction–based incentives with bonus or commission payments tied to sales quotas or revenue. Unfortunately, such mixed-incentive plans can sometimes add additional confusion in the sales force and even lead to reductions in customer service levels.[15] The bottom line, then, is that although rewarding customer service is an attractive goal, it can present some thorny measurement and design issues for the sales manager that will have to be worked out.[16]

Adding rewards for good customer service, although an important step, means that compensation of consultative selling approaches will likely be even more challenging. Sixty-five percent of sales managers believe that building consulting competencies in their sales force is a key to driving their company's growth. As such, managers cannot reward their sales force merely for what products they want pushed, but rather for how well they build a profitable relationship for both parties. This approach is value management, which is about understanding what the customer needs, providing the benefits the customer is looking for, and having that customer understand how those benefits translate into a better top-line or a better bottom-line. The key is determining what fulfills the customer need and what will do that profitably for both the sales organization and the customer. It may not yet be clear how to best compensate salespeople for consulting skills, but without doubt the issue is a top priority for sales organizations today.[17]

As we learned in Chapter 3, many firms have turned to CRM systems to help manage their overall customer relationship activities. A critical issue arises as to how the CRM system, which as we know is an important tool for the sales force, fits in with the firm's compensation plan.

DECIDING ON THE MOST APPROPRIATE MIX AND LEVEL OF COMPENSATION

All salespeople do not find the same kinds of rewards equally attractive. Needs and preferences for a particular reward vary, depending on personalities, demographic characteristics, and lifestyles of different salespeople. Consequently, no single reward—including money—is likely to be effective for motivating all of a firm's salespeople. Similarly, a mix of rewards that is effective for motivating a sales force at one time may lose its appeal as the members' personal circumstances and needs change and as new salespeople are hired. In view of this, a wise preliminary step in designing a sales compensation and incentive package is for a firm to determine its salespeople's current preferences for various rewards.[18]

The decision about how much total compensation (base pay plus any commissions or bonuses) a salesperson may earn is crucial in designing an effective motivation program. The starting point for making this decision is to determine the gross amount of compensation necessary to attract, retain, and motivate salespeople who can manage the firm's customer relationships. This also depends on the specific type of sales job in question, the size of the firm and the sales force, and the resources available to the firm.

In Chapter 2 we introduced several different types of sales jobs, and it is important to note that average compensation varies substantially across these. In general, more complex and demanding sales jobs, which require salespeople with special qualifications, offer higher pay than more routine sales jobs. To compete for the best talent, a firm should determine how much total compensation other firms in its industry or related ones pay people in similar jobs. Then the firm can decide whether to pay its salespeople an amount that is average in relation to what others are paying or above average. Few companies consciously pay below average (although some do so without realizing it) because below-average compensation generally cannot attract the right level of selling talent.

The decision about whether to offer total compensation at an average or premium level depends in part on the size of the firm and its sales force. Large firms with good reputations in their industries and large sales forces generally offer only average compensation. Such firms, such as Intel or Cisco, can attract sales talent because of their reputation in the marketplace and because they are big enough to offer advancement into management. Also, such firms can hire younger people, often just out of school, as sales trainees and put them through an extensive training program. This allows them to pay relatively low gross compensation because they do not have to pay a market premium to attract older, more experienced salespeople. In contrast, smaller firms often cannot afford extensive training programs. Consequently, they must often offer above-average compensation to attract experienced sales reps from other firms.

Dangers of Paying Salespeople Too Much

Some firms, regardless of their size or position in their industries, offer their salespeople opportunities to make very large amounts of financial compensation. The rationale for such high incomes is that opportunities for high pay will attract the best talent and motivate members of the sales force to continue working for higher and higher sales volumes. This leads some sales managers to be ambivalent about the potential for paying their salespeople too much, since in their view salesperson compensation relates directly to their volume of sales.

Unfortunately, overpaying salespeople relative to what other firms pay for similar jobs and relative to what other employees in the same firm are paid for nonsales jobs can cause major problems. For one thing, compensation is usually the largest element of a firm's selling costs. Therefore, overpaying salespeople unnecessarily increases selling costs and reduces profits. Also, it can cause resentment and low morale among the firm's other employees and executives when salespeople earn more money than even top management. It then becomes virtually impossible to promote good salespeople into managerial positions because of the financial sacrifice they would have to make. Finally, it is not clear that offering unlimited opportunities to earn higher pay is always an effective way to motivate salespeople to continually increase the selling effort—that is, at some compensation level, the next dollar earned would almost have to begin to show diminishing returns in terms of salesperson motivation.

Dangers of Paying Salespeople Too Little

Overpaying salespeople can cause problems, but it is critically important not to underpay them. Holding down sales compensation may appear to be a convenient way to hold down selling costs and enhance profits, but this is usually not true in the long run. When buying talent in the labor market, a company tends to get what it pays for. If poor salespeople are hired at low pay, poor performance will almost surely result. If good salespeople are hired at low pay, the firm is likely to have high turnover, with higher costs for recruiting and training replacements and lost sales.

In the high-flying days of the original e-commerce boom, many technology companies offered low salaries but stock options that offered salespeople (and everyone else in the firm) the promise of great wealth when the options were cashed in later. However, as the technology sector fell on more difficult economic times, the ability of these companies to reward salespeople with stock options diminished to the point where many technology companies have gone back to financial compensation as the primary motivator.[19] This raises a question of cause and effect. Do firms perform well because they create the opportunity for the big payday, which does not always happen, or are they more successful if they pay people what they are worth plus an incentive for outstanding performance? In either case, paying what it takes to attract and keep a competent sales force seems a more likely path to high performance in relationship selling than being overly creative with the latest financial gimmicks designed to recruit but not necessarily retain the best people.

During the so-called "great recession" that began about 2007, it was very tempting for sales organizations to cut compensation (and many other) budgets in order to save money. However, such cutbacks can result in short-term cost savings at the expense of long-term market opportunity. When the tough economic times end and jobs become more plentiful again, disgruntled salespeople may easily "jump ship" for a better compensation model—taking with them a great deal of experience and possibly many important customer relationships.[20]

Changing the Compensation Plan

It has been shown that changing the compensation mix can have a detrimental effect on employee performance. This change may come in two main forms:

1. Changing from a performance-sensitive scheme to a less performance-sensitive scheme—This can lead to poorer performance and, perhaps more importantly, the loss of higher-performing salespeople from the company.

2. Frequent changes, regardless of the type—Many companies, when underperforming, look to the compensation program and change it, hoping it can act as a driver for better performance. However, the compensation program is a tool and paying staff to do more or different tasks will not ultimately fix the underlying problems within the firm.

Changing the compensation scheme should not be discouraged altogether. In some instances, changes should be made, especially if the scheme is in contradiction to the company objectives. However, any changes should be more than surface level, and should undoubtedly add value to the compensation plan.

SUMMARY

To effectively manage the relationship selling function, sales managers must be concerned with the firm's compensation system. Which rewards do salespeople value? How much of each is optimum? How should the rewards be integrated in a total compensation system? This chapter provides insights to these issues.

In determining the most effective form of financial compensation, the firm must decide whether it should use (1) straight salary, (2) straight commission, or (3) a combination of base salary and incentive pay such as commissions, bonuses, or both. Most companies today use a combination approach. The base salary provides the salesperson with a stable income while allowing the company to reward its salespeople for performing tasks not directly related to short-term sales. The incentive portion of combination plans provides direct rewards to motivate salespeople to expend effort to improve their sales volume or profitability. To be effective, the incentive pay portion of the combination plan has to be large enough to generate the necessary interest among salespeople. Sales contests are often part of the incentive portion of compensation systems. To be successful, a sales contest needs to have (1) clearly defined, specific objectives, (2) an exciting theme, (3) a reasonable probability of rewards for all salespeople, (4) attractive rewards, and (5) effective promotion and follow-through.

Nonfinancial incentives can play an important role in a firm's compensation system. Opportunities for salesperson promotion and advancement, recognition programs, and other forms of nonfinancial incentives can be effective sales motivators. For recognition programs to be effective, the salesperson's peers and superiors must be made aware of his or her outstanding performance. This can be done through recognition at a sales meeting, publicity in the local press, announcements in the company's internal newsletter, or other ways. Because all salespeople cannot possibly move into sales management positions, some companies have dual career paths to maintain the motivating potential of promotion and advancement. One path leads to positions in the sales management hierarchy; the other leads to greater responsibilities in sales positions such as a larger territory or key account position.

Expense accounts can enhance a salesperson's overall compensation. Three common means of handling salesperson expenses are direct reimbursement, limited reimbursement, and no reimbursement. When everything else is said and done, the sales manager must determine an appropriate mix and level of compensation for salespeople that maximizes the compensation plan's motivational value, is fair, and also is consistent with the firm's resource capabilities.

KEY TERMS

compensation plan	quota	draw
salary	sales contests	perquisites (perks)
incentive payment	benefits	expense account
commission	nonfinancial incentives	
bonus	variable commission rate	

BREAKOUT QUESTIONS

1. We know that the use of selling teams, sometimes including both salespeople and others from the firm, to accomplish relationship selling is common practice today. As with individual salespeople, the success of these teams depends, in part, on the reward systems used to motivate and recognize performance. How would you develop a compensation plan that motivates members of a selling team? How can you ensure the plan is fair for everybody involved?

2. The Ruppert Company needed to build market share quickly. To motivate sales growth, Ruppert installed a straight commission compensation plan: The more the sales reps sold, the more they made. This strategy seemed to work—sales volume climbed and the Ruppert Company captured more market share. After two years on this program, sales growth flattened out and Ruppert began to lose market share. Sales reps continued to earn $85,000 to $90,000 on average in commissions through developing and penetrating current key accounts in their territories. Studies showed the sales force was not overworked and further territory penetration was clearly possible. What do you think was happening?

3. When OfficeSolutions, a software producer, went into business, it needed to establish market share quickly. To accomplish this, it decided to pay the sales force on a commission basis. After two years, however, the company had a large base business and customers began to complain that salespeople were not spending enough time with them on postsale service and problem solving, important relationship selling activities. The salespeople said they did not make any money on problem solving and they would rather spend their time finding new customers. What's more, salespeople spent little or no time selling the new products on which OfficeSolutions was staking its future. The salespeople said they could sell the old products more easily and earn more money for both themselves and the company. How might the company rework its compensation plan to begin to resolve this issue?

4. When designing sales compensation plans, it is important to meet the relationship selling objectives and at the same time appropriately reward the person who has to meet those objectives. How would you design sales compensation plans to match the following different company objectives and sales environmental situations?

   a. Company has a high revenue growth objective in a sales environment characterized by frequent product introductions, boom markets, and a loose competitive structure.

   b. Company has a protect-and-grow revenue objective in a sales environment characterized by slow growth, many competitors, and few product introductions. The firm's primary source of differentiation is its excellent sales force.

   c. Company's objectives are to have an overall revenue growth and balanced product mix sales. The sales environment has multiple customer markets, many product groups, high-growth and low-growth products, and high and low sales intensity.

   d. Company's objective is to maintain revenue and have new account sales growth (that is, conversion selling by taking customers from the competition). The sales environment is a moderate-to-slow–growth marketplace.

5. Sales contests, although very popular, raise questions concerning their value. Questions asked include: Don't they simply shift into the contest period sales volume that

would have occurred anyway? How can everyone be equally motivated when certain territories have a built-in edge because of customer and market characteristics? Won't the contest backfire if people feel they haven't had a fair chance to win? Will all sales reps participate with equal enthusiasm when there can be only a few winners? Respond to each of these objections.

6. A sales manager says, "You can never hold enough sales contests for your salespeople. The more the merrier. . . . They are guaranteed to increase your business." Evaluate this statement.

7. Things are tough at Morgan, Inc. For the last several months, sales reps, who are paid on a commission basis, have barely covered their monthly personal expenses. To help the sales force through these tough times, Morgan executives decided to introduce monthly draws. Sales reps whose commission earnings fall below a specified monthly amount receive a special loan, or draw, against commissions. When sales and commissions improve, the sales reps will repay the cash advance from future earnings. Under what conditions will this plan help Morgan achieve its sales strategy? Under what conditions is it likely to fail? (Hint: Think about what might happen in the future in terms of sales volume.)

8. Assume you are taking a job in relationship selling right out of college. What would be your own ideal compensation mix? Why do you prefer the one you propose?

9. What are the pros and cons of placing ceilings on salesperson incentives? If you were a sales manager, would there ever be a situation where you would advocate the use of incentive ceilings? If so, in what situation and why?

10. Veteran salespeople can pose unique challenges in terms of compensation. Why? What would you suggest in terms of designing a compensation plan that would motivate a veteran sales rep?

11. Ethical Question. You are the VP of sales for a large, global technology company. Each of your 15 key accounts is handled by a separate team of between four and seven specialists (depending on the size of the account) and each team is headed by a key account manager. He or she is ultimately held responsible for the success of the account including quota achievement and other goals. Recently, senior management has been pushing to restructure the compensation system to allocate more rewards to the other members of the key account sales teams in order to better recognize their contributions. Currently, the key account manager receives about 60 percent of the incentive rewards (in the form of bonuses), while the other team members split the remaining 40 percent. The proposed new plan changes the bonus split to 50–50. As VP of sales, what do you think about this proposed change? Do you support it, and if not do you have a better idea? Assuming upper management pushes the change through, how would you go about implementing it in your organization?

LEADERSHIP CHALLENGE: ONE FOR ALL, ALL FOR ONE

Danielle Drexel was getting ready to make some important decisions for her company, Dynamic Printing. She had started the company in Chicago and in a little more than 12 years it had become one of the area's largest printers. With more than 50 salespeople in the Chicago area, the company had built a reputation for quality printing, great service, and fair prices.

Over the years the printing business had changed. When Danielle started the company, salespeople called on customers. Once a relationship had been established, customers would send the work to the shop. Often the salespeople would handle the pickup and delivery or the customers would have a courier do the job. Salespeople oversaw the job and the customer had little contact with anyone other than the salesperson.

As customers demanded more and better service, Dynamic Printing had created customer service representatives (CSRs) who handled problems and inquiries over the phone. These CSRs were responsible for a group of customers and worked closely with salespeople to enhance the customer's relationship with the company. In the last few years, Dynamic had seen the need for a third group, Inside Support Personnel (ISP), to help with the flow of orders and other issues that came up inside the company. ISPs worked for the CSRs and helped support the overall customer service experience.

As a result of these changes, each customer (particularly those who were regular customers of Dynamic Printing) had a sales team. Unfortunately, the compensation system at Dynamic Printing had not changed in 10 years. Specifically, salespeople received a 10 percent commission on gross sales for each of their customers. It made no difference how the sales were generated (by the salesperson or by calling into the store and talking with a CSR). CSRs and ISPs were paid a straight salary (with the CSRs making about 30 percent more, on average, than the ISP employees).

As Danielle sat in her office, she came to realize that this system was no longer valid. Over the last five years the sales mix had changed and sales generated in house now accounted for 50 percent of all sales for many customers. The CSRs and ISPs had expressed frustration that they were responsible for a lot of business and they received no credit. Indeed, they argued, the salespeople were receiving money for work they did with the customer. Danielle knew something had to change, but what?

Questions

1. As a CSR, what do you think is a fair solution to the compensation problem?

2. As a salesperson, what do you think is a fair solution to the compensation problem?

3. You are Danielle. What would you do about the compensation system at Dynamic Printing and why?

ROLE-PLAY: CANNONBALL EXPRESS

Situation

"Lordy, lordy, Big Jim's forty" the e-mail birthday card screamed out from the monitor on the computer stand in his office in the Buckhead district of Atlanta. Well, Cannonball Express VP of sales (and birthday boy) Jimmy "Big Jim" Cooley didn't need to be reminded. In fact, he has been thinking a lot lately not so much about his own trek into middle age, but more about the fact that most of his sales force are, to put it delicately, no longer spring chickens. In fact, at 40 Big Jim is 7 years younger than the average age of his sales force!

Cannonball Express, based in Atlanta, operates an intracity fast delivery small package and parcel service network throughout the southern United States. In Big Jim's business, "intracity" means that he doesn't try to compete directly with UPS, FedEx, DHL, or Express Mail, who focus on intercity (between-city) delivery. To the contrary, Cannonball Express's business is totally focused on getting packages from point A to point B *within a metropolitan area*, so that the item is received the same day it is shipped. Attorneys, physicians, bankers, real estate professionals, and insurance agents are typical users. However, any person or business can call Cannonball Express's toll-free number for a pickup guaranteed to be within two hours of the phone call. The firm operates in 14 separate metropolitan areas and has been in business since 1990. Big Jim started as a delivery driver in Charlotte and worked his way up the company ladder to regional sales manager and then VP of sales in 2000, a position in which he has had a phenomenally successful run. Under his leadership, sales have grown an average of 9 percent per year, although lately the growth has been more in the 3–4 percent range.

Across the company, Cannonball Express has 34 salespeople and three sales managers. The sales force focuses exclusively on the B2B market, both in securing new customers and in nurturing existing customers. An astounding 87 percent of this team has been with the company 10+ years, and the average age of the group is 47. Big Jim has always been a believer in providing a strong mix of compensation and incentives, including a salary component, commission, and financial bonuses for achieving specific goals, which might vary over time depending on business trends. Given the very low turnover, it is not surprising that the salespeople are generally quite satisfied with all aspects of their job and very dedicated to the firm and its success. However, this past year Big Jim has for the first time begun to hear some grumbling in the ranks about the compensation plan. Between this and the declining sales increases, Big Jim has decided it is time to act.

Two weeks ago, Big Jim pulled in the three regional sales managers for a meeting about this topic in Atlanta. Carlos Rivera came up from Florida, Judy Bentley flew down from Arlington, Virginia, and Max Moncrief hopped on the MARTA train for the short ride over to Buckhead from the other side of Atlanta. From this day-long meeting, it was decided that a new compensation plan needs to be developed that takes into account (a) the changing preferences for incentives of an older sales force and (b) the need for rejuvenating the annual growth rate percentage. Big Jim has charged each of the three regional managers to come up with their own ideas with justifications. He has scheduled another meeting at headquarters in two weeks to go over the options and make a decision.

Characters in the Role-Play

Jimmy "Big Jim" Cooley, VP of sales
Carlos Rivera, regional sales manager for Florida, Alabama, Mississippi, and Louisiana
Judy Bentley, regional sales manager for Virginia, the District of Columbia, Kentucky, and Tennessee
Max Moncrief, regional sales manager for Georgia and the Carolinas

Assignment

Break into groups of four, with one student playing each character. It doesn't matter what the actual gender mix of your group is. Before you stage the meeting, work separately using the material in your chapter to come up with your own recommendation for a new compensation and incentive plan for Cannonball Express that you believe will best address the issues identified in the story. Be prepared to justify why you believe each element in your plan is appropriate. Then get together and role-play the meeting among Big Jim, Carlos, Judy, and Max. In the end, you want to come out of the meeting with agreement on a new incentive and compensation plan.

MINICASE: FRANCESCO'S BIKE WORLD

Francesco Rizzo established Francesco's Bike World, a retailer of bicycles and related parts and gear, in 2010 in Milan, Italy. The company saw steady growth in its first few years and had opened eight stores throughout Italy by the beginning of 2016. Francesco is the owner and acts as the general manager for all stores. Each store has one manager and four to six salespeople, with two to three working on the sales floor at any given time. Francesco himself is a bike enthusiast and rides more than 200 kilometers per week. He encourages his sales staff to do the same and looks for fellow bike enthusiasts when hiring. As a result, the sales staff generally loves to buy equipment from the store, especially since Francesco gives an employee discount of 10 percent.

Francesco's sales revenues increased by almost 15 percent each year for the first five years of the company's existence. But since that time, sales revenues and profits have declined at approximately the same rate. According to Francesco's analysis, the decline did not seem to have a single cause: a down economy, opening too many stores too quickly, rise of price from suppliers. He has tried to reduce costs to maintain consistent profits but has cut them to the point where the only remaining reductions would be to begin closing stores, which he does not want to do.

Francesco has always prided himself on having a top-notch sales staff. Although the staff shares a common bond of love for cycling, they are a heterogeneous group in other ways. About one-half are in their 20s, one-quarter in their 30s, and one-quarter in their 40s. Some have families, some do not. Some are married, some are single. Some rely solely on the job income to live, some do not. For the first six years, Francesco paid his staff a straight salary in the range of €22,000 to €34,000, depending on sales experience, with an annual bonus of €500 if the salesperson met the standard sales quota for the year. Francesco liked the stability the salary provided his staff, especially those with families. However, after the sales began to drop with the onset of the recession in 2008. Francesco decided that the staff would sell more if they were better motivated. So he instituted a new compensation plan that paid the sales staff on 100 percent commission. To allow for some stability, there was a system of a "draw" where employees could borrow against future commissions. This plan has now been in place for almost four years, but sales are still declining. Francesco recently sat down with his best store manager, Luca Moretti, to assess the commission-based compensation plan.

They started with Francesco's business goals in order of importance: (1) increase sales revenues relative to quota, (2) increase customer satisfaction and customer loyalty, (3) increase sales for certain product lines, (4) take advantage of bike knowledge of the sales staff, and (5) encourage bicycle riding in local events.

Then they examined the staff. Luca's first observation was that the sales skills of his staff vary greatly. For example, top performer Leonora Rossi has no trouble meeting her monthly quota; she even makes it so early in the month that she can relax for the remaining time. However, other salespeople like Ruggiero Giordano do not sell as easily and feel pressure because they support big families. Moreover, Ruggiero and others have taken money from the draw but then felt even more pressure for being far behind. Several have even quit to eliminate their debt, leaving Francesco with a loss and having to incur the added expense of training new hires. In addition, the sales approach has evolved into one of pressuring the customer to buy rather than building a relationship and taking the true needs of the customer into account. Also, there has been little effort to follow up with customers after a sale, assist with bike maintenance, or even clean up the store. As a result, customer loyalty and retention have been down. Furthermore, the old team environment, where a salesperson with a customer would call over a more knowledgeable salesperson to answer a customer question, has been replaced with an "every person for her- or himself" mentality.

Francesco and Luca decided that things must change, and the compensation plan was the place to start.

Questions

1. Did Francesco and Luca do a good job of assessing the situation with respect to the compensation plan? What other information would you like to have that is not given?

2. What were the advantages and disadvantages of Francesco's straight salary compensation plan? What were the advantages and disadvantages of his straight commission plan?

3. Given the preceding facts, recommend to Francesco a combination compensation plan that would best suit his situation. What other compensation devices might you use in addition to bonus, salary, and commission? Explain your recommendation.

PART 3

Evaluation and Control of the Sales Program

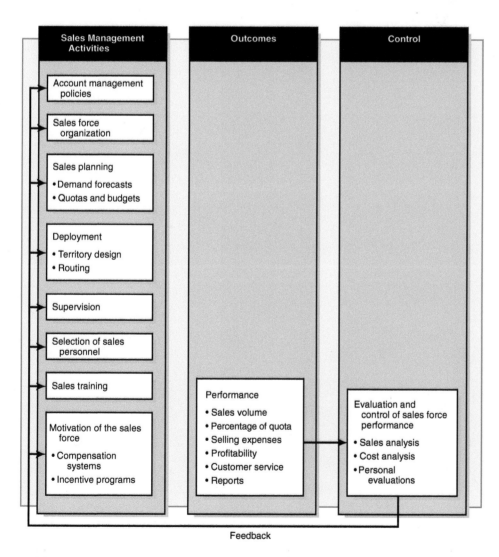

CHAPTER 12

Cost Analysis

LEARNING OBJECTIVES

Many students of sales and marketing like to focus on the revenue side. They migrate to sales positions because making things happen is an essential function of creating business. But costs are important, too, and managing costs carefully is often the difference between a thriving business and one that struggles to exist.

After completing this chapter, you should be able to

- Select the appropriate cost allocation method for various sales management situations.
- Describe how such methods would be implemented.
- Discuss the importance of return on assets managed (ROAM) and be able to calculate ROAM.
- Apply financial cost analysis to sales management situations in order to make decisions.

Not too long ago, a company (which asked to remain nameless) set a sales goal for a particular product of 100,000 new units. It dropped two products that were similar and increased sales for the preferred product from 70,000 units to three times the goal, or 300,000 units. The sales force had their best year ever, making more money per salesperson than ever before. Yet, every unit they sold cost an average $2.00 in losses. How could this happen?

Over a half-million dollars were lost because information concerning performance wasn't gathered and shared on a timely basis. Increasing competition in a global marketplace makes avoiding such mistakes all the more imperative. More than half of top sales executives see operational excellence, quality, and cost control as the most valuable strength a company will need to have in order to compete.[1] Costs were higher than expected, prices were lower than expected as more buyers took advantage of quantity discounts, and, worse, the information didn't reach decision makers in time.

Cost analysis is complementary to sales analysis in sales force management. While sales analysis focuses on the results achieved, cost analysis looks at the costs incurred in producing those results and whether the returns justify the expenditures. Companies sometimes implement systems and procedures that are intended to increase sales but do not always produce profit increases. To determine whether the returns justify the expenditures, it is necessary to gather, classify, compare, and study marketing cost data, which is the essence of marketing cost analysis. (See how companies

INNOVATION   **Learning about the Lifetime Value of the Customer**

Putting together and maintaining a sales force is expensive. Successful companies know they need to assess how best to use such a valuable resource. One tool being used by more and more companies is a measure of the Lifetime Value of the Customer. This is a measure of each customer's long-term value, or profitability. Companies have come to realize that not all customers are created equal. Some customers thought to be very profitable turn out to be a lot less profitable than first imagined. Interestingly, sometimes the largest customers in terms of sales generated are among the least profitable in terms of gross margin. Why? Because big customers demand more and better service and often drive harder deals on price, which leads to lower profit margins.

As you can see, critical to an assessment of a customer's lifetime value is an analysis of the costs associated with doing business with that customer. The first step is to have up-to-date information on the real costs of doing business with that customer. Often this means assigning a number of costs that might normally be left as overhead to specific customers. In addition, and this is key to sales cost analysis, it is essential to determine the real cost of maintaining the customer relationship. Of course, this includes not only the salesperson's time but the amount of customer service contact, sales terms, and payment schedules.

The final assessment of a customer's value is based on short- and long-term company objectives. While some companies are not generating highly profitable sales now, it may be possible to increase profitability by applying more and better resources to the customer. Companies almost always want to have potential new big customers in development to ensure company growth and protect against the loss of current big customers.

Banks such as Bank of America have been aggressive in assessing lifetime customer value. As a result, they evaluate each customer in terms of the business they currently have with the bank, the costs of providing those services, and the potential for new business. In some cases, the results have been surprising. For example, Bank of America found that nearly half its retail customers were unprofitable based on the services provided, funds deposited, and current fees being charged to customers. At the other end, banks are also targeting their best customers by offering more and better services such as platinum credit cards and low-interest home equity lines.

need data to assist them in calculating important customer metrics in the Innovation box.)

Marketing cost analysis can help identify opportunities for increasing the effectiveness of marketing expenditures. Sales are achieved at some cost, and marketing productivity focuses on the sales or profit output per unit of marketing effort input. Unfortunately, it is often difficult for a firm to know what the output/input relationships are without detailed analyses.

Most firms today produce many products, which they sell in multiple markets. For each product and market, the mix of marketing elements differs. Only by analyzing specific relationships among these products and markets can the firm hope to identify situations where marketing input should be increased or altered, where it should remain at historic levels, and where it should be decreased. These insights are simply not produced by the information that flows from normal accounting operations. Similarly, to deploy the firm's salespeople most effectively, the sales manager needs to appreciate the output/input relationships by product, territory, customer, channel of distribution, and so on. Marketing cost analysis estimates these relationships.

COST ANALYSIS DEVELOPMENT

Sales management has been somewhat slower to adopt cost analysis (or as it is sometimes called, profitability analysis) than sales analysis for managing the sales function. The empirical evidence indicates that if they do it at all, firms are more likely to conduct product profitability analyses and less likely to do it for customers. Only about half of all companies do it at all, and less than a third analyze costs by products, territories, salespeople, and customers. Interestingly, companies do focus on a salesperson's pricing authority, which is a key factor in determining the overall profitability of each customer.[2]

Historically, one reason for this was that most accounting systems were not designed to meet the needs of marketing management but, rather, to report the aggregate effects of a firm's operations to creditors and stockholders. They were subsequently modified to provide a better handle on the production operations of the firm. Even today many accounting systems are still oriented toward external reporting and production cost analysis.

However, the integration of company information systems over the last 10 years enables accounting systems to identify and include the types of cost and profitability data needed by sales executives. For a sales manager, the key is to understand how costs are allocated so that the true profitability of any particular customer, geographic area, product, or market can be determined. Any accounting system can take the direct cost of supplies and components and add those together to come up with the cost of a product. The challenge is adding management costs, office supplies, warehousing, IT, and so forth. There are three approaches to cost allocation: full costing, contribution analysis, and activity-based costing (ABC). The choice of which costing approach to use is very important to sales managers. For example, territories have been mistakenly cut because the accounting information used by managers didn't allocate costs appropriately.

Full Cost versus Contribution Margin

The more popular and traditional accounting methods are the full-cost (or as it is sometimes called, net profit) approach and the contribution margin approach. The argument over which should be used has generated controversy through the years.[3] To appreciate the controversy fully, it is helpful to understand the differences between direct and indirect costs as well as specific and general expenses.

A direct cost can be specifically identified with a product or a function.[4] The cost is incurred because the product or function exists or is contemplated. If the product or function were eliminated, the cost would also disappear. An example is inventory carrying costs for a product.

An indirect cost is a shared cost because it is tied to several functions or products. Even if one of the products or functions were eliminated, the cost would not be. Rather, the share of the cost previously borne by the product or function that was eliminated would shift to the remaining products or functions. An example of an indirect cost is the travel expenses of a salesperson selling a multiple product line. Even if one product the rep sells is eliminated, the travel cost would not be.

The *profit/loss or net income statement* typically distinguishes between costs and expenses. The term cost is often restricted to the materials, labor, power, rent, and other miscellaneous items used in making the product. The cost of goods sold on the following conceptual net income statement reflects these costs.

	Sales
Less:	Cost of goods sold
Equal:	Gross margin
Less:	General administrative and selling expenses
Equal:	Profit or net income before taxes

The expenses reflect the other costs incurred in operating the business, such as the cost of advertising and of maintaining branches. Expenses cannot be tied nearly as well as costs to specific products, since they are general expenses associated with doing business. In marketing cost analysis, the distinction between costs and expenses is not nearly so clear, and the terms are often used interchangeably.

Just like costs, expenses can be classified into two broad categories: specific and general expenses. A specific expense is just like a direct cost—it can be identified with a specific product or function. The expense would be eliminated if the product or function were eliminated. If the product were eliminated, for example, the specific expense of the product manager's salary need not be incurred.

A general expense is like an indirect cost—it cannot be identified directly with a specific object of profit measurement such as a territory, salesperson, or product. Thus, the expense would not be eliminated if the specific object were eliminated. An example is the sales manager's salary when the object of measurement is a product in a multiple-product company. The elimination of the product would not eliminate this salary.

A particular cost or expense may be direct for some measurement purposes and indirect for others. The object of the measurement determines how the cost should be treated.

If it is a product line, costs directly associated with the manufacture and sales of the product line are direct. All other costs in the business are indirect. If the object of measurement shifts to a sales territory, some of the costs of product-line measurement, which were direct, will remain direct costs now associated with the territory; some will become indirect; and others that were indirect will become direct. For example:[5]

| | Object of Measurement | |
Cost	Product	Territory
Sales promotion display	Direct	Direct
Sales rep compensation	Indirect	Direct
Product-line manager's salary	Direct	Indirect
Corporate president's salary	Indirect	Indirect

As mentioned, there is controversy about whether one should use a full-cost or contribution margin approach in marketing cost analysis. Proponents of the full-cost or net profit approach argue that all costs should be assigned and somehow accounted for in determining the profitability of any segment (e.g., territory, product, and salesperson) of the business.

Under this approach, each unit bears not only its own direct costs but a share of the company's cost of doing business, referred to as indirect costs. Full-costing advocates argue that many of the indirect costs can be assigned to the unit being assessed on the basis of a demonstrable cost relationship. If a strong relationship does not exist, the cost must be prorated on a reasonable basis. Under the full-costing approach, a net income for each marketing segment can be determined by matching the segment's revenue with its direct and indirect costs.[6]

Contribution margin advocates argue, on the other hand, that it is misleading to allocate costs arbitrarily. They suggest that only those costs that can be specifically identified with the segment of the business should be deducted from the revenue produced by the segment to determine how well the segment is doing. Any excess of revenues over these costs contributes to the common costs of the business and thereby to profits. The contribution margin approach does not distinguish where the costs are incurred but rather simply whether they are variable or fixed. Thus, the difference between sales and all variable costs, whether they originate in manufacturing, selling, or some administrative function, are subtracted from revenues or sales to produce the contribution margin of the segment.

The net profit approach does attempt to determine where the costs were incurred. The difference in perspectives is highlighted in Exhibit 12.1. Not only is segment net income derived differently in the two approaches, but also advocates of the contribution margin approach do not even focus on net income when evaluating the profitability of a segment of the business. Rather, they focus on the contribution produced by the segment after subtracting the costs directly traceable to it from its sales.

The contribution margin advocates are winning the controversy. Although the early emphasis in accounting for distribution costs was on full-cost allocation, the recent emphasis is on the contribution margin approach.[7] The contribution margin approach has unmistakable logic. If the costs associated with the segment are not removed with the elimination of the segment, why should they be arbitrarily allocated? That just confuses things and provides a blurred, distorted picture for management decision making. The costs still have to be borne after the segment is eliminated, but they must be borne by other segments of the business. Such allocation can simply tax the ability of these other segments to remain profitable. Exhibits 12.2 and 12.3 illustrate this phenomenon.

The example involves a department store with three main departments. The administrative expenses in Exhibit 12.2 are all fixed costs; they were allocated to departments on the basis of the total percentage of sales accounted for by each department. This is a common allocation basis about which more will be said later. Those who embrace the full-cost approach would argue that Department 1 should be eliminated because of the net loss of $12,500.

Note what would happen if this were pursued. First, the sales of the department would be lost, but $12,500 of selling expenses would also be eliminated. However,

EXHIBIT 12.1 Differences in perspective between full-cost and contribution margin approaches to marketing cost analysis	**Full-Cost Approach**		**Contribution Margin Approach**	
		Sales		Sales
	Less:	Cost of goods sold	Less:	Variable manufacturing costs
	Equal:	Gross margin	Less:	Other variable costs directly traceable to the segment
	Less:	Operating expenses (including the segment's allocated share of company administration and general expenses)	Equal:	Contribution margin
			Less:	Fixed costs directly traceable to products Fixed costs directly traceable to the market segment
	Equal:	Segment net income	Equal:	Segment net income

EXHIBIT 12.2 Profit and loss statement by department using a full cost approach		**Totals**	**Department 1**	**Department 2**	**Department 3**
	Sales	$500,000	$250,000	$150,000	$100,000
	Cost of goods sold	400,000	225,000	125,000	50,000
	Gross margin	100,000	25,000	25,000	50,000
	Other expenses				
	Selling expenses	25,000	12,500	7,500	5,000
	Administrative expenses	50,000	25,000	15,000	10,000
	Total other expenses	75,000	37,500	22,500	15,000
	Net profit (loss)	25,000	(12,500)	2,500	35,000

EXHIBIT 12.3 Profit and loss statement if Department 1 were eliminated		**Total**	**Department 2**	**Department 3**
	Sales	$250,000	$150,000	$100,000
	Cost of goods sold	175,000	125,000	50,000
	Gross margin	75,000	25,000	50,000
	Other expenses			
	Selling expenses	12,500	7,500	5,000
	Administrative expenses	50,000	30,000	20,000
	Total other expenses	62,500	37,500	25,000
	Net profit (loss)	12,500	(12,500)	25,000

the $25,000 of fixed costs must now be borne by the other departments. Allocating these costs on the basis of percentage of sales suggests that Department 2 is unprofitable (see Exhibit 12.3). If one used the same argument as before, it too should be considered for elimination. Then the $50,000 of administrative expenses would be borne entirely by Department 3, making Department 3 (the entire store) unprofitable. That would suggest the store be closed, meaning management would close a profitable store simply because one department displayed a small dollar loss—a loss that could be attributed to an arbitrary allocation of fixed costs. Department 1, in fact, makes a positive contribution to profits, as the contribution margin statement in Exhibit 12.4 shows.

A contribution margin versus a full-cost profitability analysis is also supported by the recognition that most marketing phenomena are highly interrelated. For example, the demand for one product in a multiproduct company is often influenced by the availability of others, while the absence of a product may cause the sale of another product to decline.

The entire product line may be greater than the sum of its parts in terms of sales and profits. The same argument applies to other elements of the marketing mix. They have interdependent effects. The contribution margin approach implicitly recognizes this synergy through its emphasis on the contribution of each segment or part.

In sum, allocations of indirect costs for segment performance evaluation are generally inappropriate. That is, any measure of segment performance that includes allocated shares of indirect costs includes factors that do not really reflect performance in the segment as a separate entity. Hence, indirect cost allocations should not be made if the purpose is to measure true performance.

ABC Accounting

Over the last decade there has been a significant shift in the way accountants and managers view costs. Rather than focus on the reason for the cost (labor hours to produce a product), this new approach identifies and delineates the cause-and-effect relationship between costs and desired organizational outcomes. As a result, marketing decision makers can get answers to questions such as: How profitable is it to do business with this customer? or What level of customer service will make this customer unprofitable?

Activity-based costing (ABC) is based on the simple premise that almost all company activities are in support of manufacturing (or producing), marketing, and delivering goods and services to the customer. As presented in Exhibit 12.5, an ABC system consists of three basic informational components related to the company: resources, activities, and cost objects. Cost objects are associated with products, channels, and customers, all of which are particularly relevant to marketers. Critical to the analysis is an understanding that company resources (people, money, and organizational assets) are used to drive the activities that are needed to develop, produce, market, and service products for the customer. As an example, to make a sales call on a customer several resources are needed, such as a salesperson's time

	Totals	Department 1	Department 2	Department 3
Sales	$500,000	$250,000	$150,000	$100,000
Variable costs				
Cost of goods sold	400,000	225,000	125,000	50,000
Selling expenses	25,000	12,500	7,500	5,000
Total variable costs	425,000	237,500	132,500	55,000
Contribution margin	75,000	12,500	17,500	45,000
Fixed costs				
Administrative expenses	50,000			
Net profit	25,000			

EXHIBIT 12.4
Contribution margin by departments

(a human resource) and organizational assets (car, computer, cell phone, and other supplies). After resources have been identified, they are assigned to activities. For example, consider the number of service calls a company makes on a customer. Intuitively, it makes sense that customers requiring frequent service calls cost the company more than the customer who rarely requests service. Unfortunately, it was not possible for traditional cost accounting systems to capture those differences.[8]

Let's consider an example: A company manufactures two products and has one sales team for both products. Each product accounts for 50 percent of sales. The single most important activity to consider in evaluating the cost structure of the two products is the number of sales calls per product. The Widget takes three sales calls to close the sale while the Zidget takes two sales calls to close, which means that the number of

EXHIBIT 12.5
A diagram of activity-based costing[9]

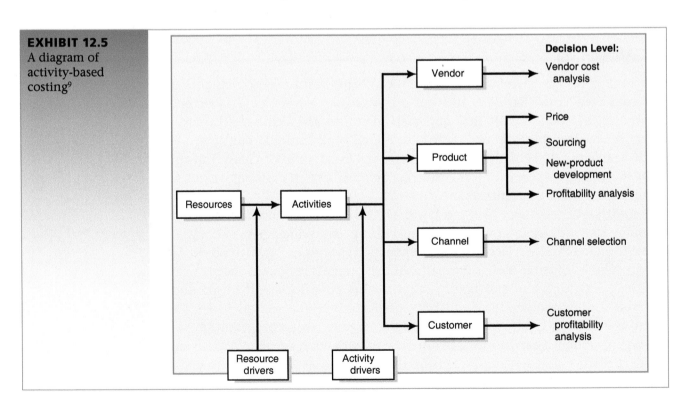

sales calls needed to close one sale for each product is five—3 (Widget) + 2 (Zidget) = 5. With the activity-based costing approach the Widget is allocated 60 percent of the office costs since it is more difficult to sell while the Zidget gets the remaining 40 percent. However, using a contribution or full-cost approach, the allocation would be 50 percent for each product based on sales volume. Note the difference in income in Exhibit 12.6. As a sales manager what types of decisions would be affected by the difference in income using the ABC method versus the contribution method.

PROCEDURE

The general procedure followed in conducting a cost or profitability analysis first involves specifying the purpose for which the cost study is being done. Knowing the purpose helps to determine the functional cost centers. The next step is to spread the natural account costs to these functional cost centers. Then the functional costs are allocated to appropriate segments using some reasonable basis. Finally, the allocated costs are summed, and the contribution of the segment is determined. Incidentally, the term *segment* is used here to mean a portion of the business, not in the normal sense of market segment.

The process is shown in Exhibit 12.7. Although the diagram is simple, its execution is difficult. Hard decisions about what sales costs or expenses are to be treated as fixed, semifixed, or variable and how various costs should be allocated to segments must be made.

As mentioned, the first step in a marketing profitability analysis is to determine the purpose for which it is being done. Is it designed to investigate the profitability of the various products in the line? Or is it designed to determine the profitability of sales branches, customers, or individual salespersons? The decision is essential because the treatment of the various costs and expenses depends on the purpose.

	Widget	Zidget	Widget	Zidget
Sales	$750	$750		
Less variable costs[i]	440	461		
Contribution margin	$310	$289		
	ABC Method		**Contribution Method**	
Less fixed manufacturing costs[ii]	$119	$21	$70	$70
Less fixed selling costs[iii]	$60	$40	$50	$50
Income using ABC	$131	$228		
Income using contribution			$190	$169

EXHIBIT 12.6
Comparison of contribution and ABC methods[10]

i Includes direct variable manufacturing and shipping costs as well as sales commissions paid to salespeople.

ii Total fixed manufacturing costs = $140. ABC allocates costs based on the complexity of the manufacturing process for each product.

iii Total fixed selling costs (includes administrative expenses and sales expenses) = $100. ABC allocates costs taking the longer selling cycle for Widgets (3 sales calls instead of two).

EXHIBIT 12.7
Steps in conducting a marketing profitability analysis

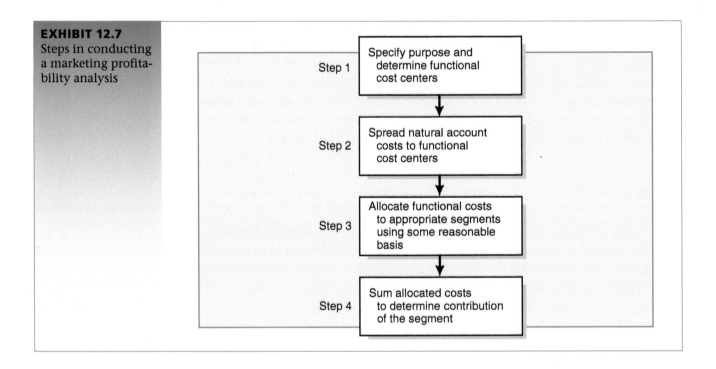

Step 1 — Specify purpose and determine functional cost centers

Step 2 — Spread natural account costs to functional cost centers

Step 3 — Allocate functional costs to appropriate segments using some reasonable basis

Step 4 — Sum allocated costs to determine contribution of the segment

Ideally, the firm would want to break all its costs or revenues into small building blocks or modules. These elements would be as small as possible and yet still be meaningful.[11] Such a breakdown allows the firm to aggregate these building blocks as needed to produce profitability analyses for various segments of the business. An example of a basic building block or module of cost is a regional sales manager's salary, which is a general expense when the profitability of various product lines is at issue. But that same sales manager's salary is a specific expense and needs to be considered when determining the contribution to profit of the region.

Thus, good profitability analyses require that the various costs be partitioned into direct and indirect expenses so the proper aggregations can be made. What is properly treated as direct and what should be treated as indirect or general depend on the study's purpose. Sales managers typically are most concerned with the profitability of various regions, branches, salespeople, and customers; they are only remotely concerned with the profitability of various products. Thus, a salesperson's salary is more likely to be treated as more of a direct than an indirect expense, whereas a product manager's salary is likely indirect, when the profitability of regions, branches, salespeople, and customers is at issue. Investigation of the profitability of the product line requires just the opposite treatment, which again illustrates the importance of specifying the purpose of the study.

In the second step of a profitability analysis, natural account costs need to be spread to the functional cost centers. Natural accounts are the categories of cost used in the normal accounting cycle. These costs include such things as salaries, wages, rent, heat, light, taxes, auto expenses, raw materials, and office equipment/supplies. They are called *natural accounts* because they bear the name of their expense categories.

Natural accounts are not the only way of classifying costs. In manufacturing cost accounting, for example, costs are often reclassified according to the purpose for which they were incurred. Thus, production wages might be broken into the cost categories of forging, turning, grinding, milling, polishing, and assembling. These categories are functional account categories because they recognize the function performed, which is the purpose for incurring the cost. Marketing cost analysis has a similar orientation. It recognizes that marketing costs are incurred for some purpose, and it recognizes general selling and administrative expenses according to their purposes or functions.

The salaries paid in a branch office, for example, could go to perform such functions as direct selling, advertising, order processing, and customer service. A functional cost analysis would involve spreading the total salaries paid in the office to these various functions. Exhibit 12.8 lists the major functional accounts that are useful in marketing cost analyses.

As Exhibit 12.7 indicates, the third step in conducting a cost or profitability analysis is to allocate the functional costs to the various segments of the business. One needs to recognize immediately that the bases for allocation are not fixed. Rather, they depend on the discretion of the decision maker and what he or she feels are "reasonable" bases.

One basis often used is to divide the expenses according to volume attained, which is in line with traditional cost accounting. Thus, if a regional sales manager was responsible for six branch offices, and one office produced 25 percent of the sales in the region, it would be charged with one-fourth of the sales manager's salary and expenses. This method is often used because of its simplicity.[12]

Allocating costs by sales volume is an erroneous method, however, in that it fails to recognize the purpose for which the regional sales manager's costs were incurred, which is the reason for a functional cost analysis. Maybe the branch was troublesome to manage and consumed 50 percent of the manager's time. In this case, it should bear half his salary. Alternatively, it may have run smoothly. The manager rarely had to get involved with the branch activities, so it consumed only 10 percent of his time and effort. In this case, only one-tenth of the regional sales manager's salary should be charged against the branch in determining its profit contribution. As Horngren, the eminent cost accountant, stated years ago, "The costs of efforts are independent of the results actually obtained, in the sense that the costs are programmed by management, not determined by sales. Moreover, the allocation of costs on the basis of dollar sales entails circular reasoning."[13] Thus, the trend is toward activity-based cost allocations.

The technology box highlights one example of the benefits associated with appropriate, thorough cost analysis. The causal relationships used can, and most likely will, be different for different questions.

Exhibit 12.9 shows some common bases for allocating functional costs to product groups, account size classes, and sales territories. The Leadership box on p. 387 shows how important appropriate breakdowns can be in managing salespeople's activities.

TECHNOLOGY The Hidden Costs of Trade Promotion

There is a great deal of variance in the promotional spending of consumer-packaged goods companies, some companies spend as little as 5 percent while others spend close to 25 percent of revenue. Unfortunately, substantial research suggests that promotional spending is, to a large degree, ineffective. This has led to a strong belief that much of the money spent on promotions can be better allocated to more significant growth drivers and brand equity. While some of these CPG companies use sophisticated post-promotion analysis technologies to determine return on investment, most do not go to any length to discover the unnecessary costs. The challenge is that many of those costs can be avoided with a more disciplined process and identifying inefficiencies in the supply chain used to outsource activities like production.

A closed-loop promotional process is the leading practice for managing trade show promotion. In this process, excess costs are pushed out of the supply chain through tightly managed planning and execution to find and eliminate waste. Common inefficiencies include promotional demand planning, partner or vendor planning, event execution, production and distribution, and retailer compliance.

For example, one company identified redundant costs of more than 10 percent of the company's trade promotion production costs. The company found the hidden costs after discovering current inefficiencies and implementing process improvements. These improvements led to new projected savings and organizational benefits that included reduced: 1) trade promotion production costs, and 2) personnel required for executing promotions.

EXHIBIT 12.8 Major functional accounts that are useful in marketing cost analysis	• Direct selling • Advertising and sales promotion • Product and package design • Technical product services • Sales discounts and allowances • Credit extension • Warranty costs • Marketing research	• Warehousing and handling • Inventory • Packaging, shipping, and delivery • Order processing/information technology • Customer service • Billing and recording of accounts receivable • Returned merchandise

The fourth step in the process is to sum the costs allocated to the segment. Costs for which there is no direct causal relationship remain unallocated in determining the contribution of the segment. A comparison of the contributions of like segments then indicates the remedial action that might be taken, if any.

THE PROCESS ILLUSTRATED

To illustrate the process of conducting a cost or profitability analysis, consider the situation encountered by the Hurricane Performance Bicycle Company in Exhibit 12.10, which was faced with a loss in its Orlando branch of more than $160,000. Suppose the sales manager is interested in further analyzing the branch to see whether the loss can be traced to particular sales reps or customers.

The sales manager has completed the first step in a cost analysis—the manager has decided the purpose of the analysis is to isolate the profit contributions of the various sales representatives in the branch. The next thing the manager must do is spread the general selling and administrative expenses incurred by the branch in the

ETHICAL MOMENT   The Ethics of Indirect Costs

This chapter highlights the importance of having a clear understanding of sales function costs. While it is relatively easy to assign certain costs, such as the cost of a sales call, other costs are more difficult to determine. However, how those costs are allocated can have a significant impact on a salesperson's performance evaluation.

The challenge is that some costs, such as sales administrative costs or training costs, are difficult to assign to a particular individual or account. As a result, allocating them becomes more subjective and ultimately more problematic. Companies invest a lot of resources to accurately assign costs, and accounting tools such as Activity Based Accounting help determine how costs should be assigned, but in the end, management must simply choose among various cost allocations methods.

Why is this important for the sales person? Because how and what costs are allocated can take a profitable sale and turn it into a marginally profitable or even unprofitable sale. Since salespeople are increasingly evaluated, at least in part, on their profitability to the firm, this becomes a big deal. In many companies salespeople take a direct interest in how the costs are allocated because they realize the impact of sales allocation on the performance evaluation.

Question to Ponder:

- Should sales managers be concerned with allocating indirect costs when evaluating individual salesperson performance? If so, how would you do it? If not, how then would you account for these costs?

Functional Cost Group	Basis of Allocation			
	To Product Groups	**To Account Size Classes**	**To Sales Territories**	
1. Selling—Direct Costs				**EXHIBIT 12.9**
Personal calls by salespeople and supervisors on accounts and prospects; sales salaries, incentive compensation, travel, and other expenses	Selling time devoted to each product, as shown by special sales call reports or other special studies	Number of sales calls times average time per call, as shown by special sales call reports or other special studies	Direct	Functional cost groups and bases of allocation
2. Selling—Indirect Costs				
Field supervision, field sales office expense, sales administration expenses, sales personnel training, sales management; market research, new-product development, sales statistics, determining services, sales accounting	In proportion to direct selling time, or time records by project	In proportion to direct selling time, or time records by project	Equal charge for each sales rep	
3. Advertising				
Media costs such as TV, radio, billboards, Internet, newspaper, magazine; advertising production costs; advertising department salaries	Direct, or analysis of space and time by media, other costs in proportion to media costs	Equal charge to each account, or number of ultimate consumers and prospects in each account's trading area	Direct, or analysis of media circulation records	

(continued)

EXHIBIT 12.9 Functional cost groups and bases of allocation (continued)			(continued)
4. Sales Promotion Consumer promotions such as coupons, patches, premiums; trade promotions such as price allowances, point-of-purchase displays, cooperative advertising	Direct, or analysis of source records	Direct, or analysis of source records	Direct, or analysis of source records
5. Transportation Railroad, truck, barge, etc., payments to carriers for delivery of finished goods from plants to warehouses and from warehouses to customers; traffic department costs	Applicable rates times tonnages	Analysis of sampling of bills of lading	Applicable rates times tonnages
6. Storage and Shipping Storage of finished goods inventories in warehouses; rent (or equivalent costs), public warehouse charges, fire insurance and taxes on finished goods inventories, etc; physical handling, assembling, and loading out of rail cars, trucks, barges for shipping finished products from warehouses and mills to customers; labor, equipment, space, and material costs.	Warehouse space occupied by average inventory; number of shipping units	Number of shipping units	Number of shipping units
7. Order Processing Checking and processing of orders from customers, shipping dates, coordination with production planning, transmittal to production, pricing customer invoices; freight accounting; credit and collection; handling cash receipts; provision for bad debts; salary, supplies, space, and equipment costs (computers, printers, etc.)	Number of order lines	Number of order lines	Number of order lines

profit and loss statement to the various functional accounts. To keep the example simple, the costs incurred in manufacturing will not be separated, although a more sophisticated contribution margin analysis would reflect such differences. Rather, the cost of goods sold is assumed to be a fixed charge to the Orlando branch, meaning the manager needs to concentrate on spreading only the selling and administrative expenses of functional cost groups.

Exhibit 12.11 lists the functional cost categories across the top and the natural account categories along the side. The individual entries indicate how a total natural cost is apportioned according to purpose. Note that the sum of all the functional costs in a row equals the natural cost for that row; that is, all natural costs are accounted for in the spread.

The details in the division of costs depend on the operation of the branch. In this case, the branch in the previous year paid $309,000 in salaries. They were distributed in the following way: branch manager—$78,000; four salespeople—$179,000; warehouse clerk—$24,000; and a clerical person handling order processing and billing—$28,000. The salaries of the branch manager and salespeople are charged against direct selling expenses because that is the purpose for which they were incurred.

Similarly, the office and warehouse clerk salaries are charged against their main functions. The functional account direct selling is also charged with the commissions earned by the four representatives; in addition to their base salaries, all salespeople were paid a commission equal to 1 percent of sales. Advertising charges reflect both a natural account cost and a functional account cost. Advertising charges are typically maintained in a separate category in the normal accounting cycle, and their name speaks to their purpose. The same is true of transportation charges.

The postage and supplies the office consumed were used to support the order processing and billing functions, and thus they are assigned to this category. Similarly, packaging material costs are assigned to warehousing and shipping because

---

LEADERSHIP   **Ripping Off the Company Using the T&E Expense Account**

Susan Yeaple never meant to eavesdrop on her employees, but as she casually sat at her desk on that Friday afternoon she could not help but overhear a conversation that gave her great concern. To her surprise, she learned it was common practice for salespeople to apply the "10 percent rule" in completing their expense reports for the company. Put simply, the rule meant that all expenses (meals, mileage, etc.) were increased by 10 percent. She pondered her options and chose to remain quiet; however, she went to payroll and asked that 10 percent be withheld from each salesperson's paycheck to send the message that this practice would not be tolerated in the future.

Ms. Yeaple's experience is much more common than many people think, as almost every sales manager has at least one story about salespeople cheating on their expense reports. Indeed, fraud related to travel and entertainment (T&E) has grown, more specifically nearly 60 percent of sales managers report catching a salesperson cheating on an expense report.

Not surprisingly, managers believe it is critical to review expense reports. Nearly six in ten sales managers review expense reports every month for their entire sales force, while another third do it occasionally. Less than one in ten indicate they never evaluate the expense reports of their salespeople.

There are two common frauds associated with T&E accounts. The first is *mischaracterized expenses*. This occurs when salespeople have a personal dinner or buy a personal item and charge it as a business expense. Companies have instituted detailed analyses of call reports and work schedules against T&E expenses. Increasingly, managers are also requiring a comprehensive explanation of expenses that includes what, when, and where the item was purchased. If the expense is a dinner or some other entertainment, the customer's name should be identified in the report. The second T&E fraud is *overstated expenses*. As the name implies, it means making a $50 dinner a $100 expense on the T&E report. Of course, requiring a receipt goes a long way to minimizing this kind of problem.

EXHIBIT 12.10
Example profit and
loss statement

Profit and Loss Statement for
HURRICANE PERFORMANCE BICYCLE COMPANY
Orlando Office

Sales		$4,963,500
Cost of goods sold		4,061,000
Gross margin		902,500
Selling and administrative expenses		
Salaries	$309,000	
Commissions	49,635	
Advertising	254,000	
Postage and office supplies	980	
Packaging materials	60,840	
Transportation charges	182,520	
Travel expenses	76,000	
Rent	130,000	
Total selling and administrative expenses		1,062,975
Net profit (loss)		$(160,475)

EXHIBIT 12.11
Allocation of
natural accounts to
functional accounts

Natural Accounts		Functional Accounts				
		Direct Selling	Advertising	Warehousing and Shipping	Order Processing and Billing	Transportation
Salaries	$309,000	$257,000		$24,000	$28,000	
Commissions	49,635	49,635				
Advertising	254,000		$254,000			
Postage and supplies	980				980	
Packaging materials	60,840			60,840		
Transportation charges	182,520					$182,520
Travel expenses	76,000	76,000				
Rent	130,000	28,000		95,000	7,000	
	$1,062,975	$410,635	$254,000	$179,840	$35,980	$182,520

that is the function for which they are used. Travel expenses reflect the food, lodging, and other expenses incurred by the sales representatives in carrying out their
main function of selling; thus, these costs are so assigned.

Perhaps the one natural account cost that requires the most explanation
is rent. The company was paying $70 per square foot for office space and $20
per square foot for warehouse space. These costs are spread to the functional
accounts in proportion to the space used by each activity. More particularly, the
order processing and selling functions used 100 of the 500 square feet of office
space the company rented; the salespeople and sales manager used the remainder.

The $95,000 assignment of rent to warehousing and shipping costs reflects the 4,750 square feet of warehouse space the company rented at $20 per square foot.

To assess the profit contribution of each salesperson, it is necessary to allocate all relevant functional costs to salespeople. Costs that bear some causal relationship to the level of activity should be allocated; these include salaries, commissions, and travel expenses. Conversely, costs that are not affected by the level of activity are not allocated. Office rent is an example. Even if one salesperson were fired, this cost would not change; thus, it should not be allocated.

Exhibit 12.12 provides much of the data on which the allocations to generate the profitability analysis by salesperson in Exhibit 12.13 are based. Exhibit 12.13 lists the gross margin by salesperson. From this, all direct expenses are subtracted to derive the contribution to profit by salesperson. Let us consider each expense category.

Direct Selling

For direct selling, the salary and commission items need little explanation; they reflect what each representative is paid and the 1 percent commission each earned on what was sold. Travel expenses per sales rep were determined by dividing total travel expenses by the number of calls to generate the cost per call, or $190. Branch accounting records allowed the identification of travel expenses by sales representative. Contact management software, such as ACT, enables sales managers and salespeople to track their sales calls by type (such as new account calls, cold calls, customer calls), so sales managers can use the software to track the time they spend with field salespeople. This cost is not allocated in the example because this information was not available, and in its absence, there is not a reasonable cause-and-effect basis for making the allocation.

A. Information by Product

Products	Selling Price per Unit	Cost per Unit	Gross Margin per Unit	Number Sold in Period	Sales in Period	Advertising Expenditures
A	$230	$180	$50	6,450	$1,483,500	$120,000
B	180	150	30	10,060	1,810,800	80,000
C	120	100	20	13,910	1,669,200	54,000
				30,420	$4,963,500	$254,000

B. Information by Salesperson

Salesperson	Number of Sales Calls	Number of Orders	Number of Units Sold A	B	C	Total
Nicholls	75	50	1,400	2,210	3,410	7,020
Pogue	125	65	1,725	2,725	3,515	7,965
Vilwock	100	50	1,711	2,609	3,506	7,826
Tucker	100	80	1,614	2,516	3,479	7,609
	400	245	6,450	10,060	13,910	30,420

EXHIBIT 12.12
Basic data used for allocations

	Total	Nicholls	Pogue	Vilwock	Tucker
EXHIBIT 12.13					
Profitability analysis by salesperson					
Sales					
Product A	$1,483,500	$322,000	$396,750	$393,530	$371,220
Product B	1,810,800	397,800	490,500	469,620	452,880
Product C	1,669,200	409,200	421,800	420,720	417,480
Total Sales	4,963,500	1,129,000	1,309,050	1,283,870	1,241,580
Cost of Goods Sold					
Product A	1,161,000	252,000	310,500	307,980	290,520
Product B	1,509,000	331,500	408,750	391,350	377,400
Product C	1,391,000	341,000	351,500	350,600	347,900
Total COGS	4,061,000	924,500	1,070,750	1,049,930	1,015,820
Gross Margin	902,500	204,500	238,300	233,940	225,760
Expenses					
Direct selling					
Salary	179,000	40,000	45,000	46,000	48,000
Commissions	49,635	11,290	13,091	12,839	12,416
Travel	76,000	14,250	23,750	19,000	19,000
Advertising					
Product A	120,000	26,047	32,093	31,833	30,028
Product B	80,000	17,575	21,670	20,748	20,008
Product C	54,000	13,238	13,646	13,611	13,506
Warehousing and shipping	60,840	14,040	15,930	15,652	15,218
Order processing	980	200	260	200	320
Transportation	182,520	42,120	47,790	46,956	45,654
Total Expenses	802,975	178,759	213,229	206,837	204,149
Contribution to Profit (Loss)	$99,525	$25,741	$25,071	$27,103	$21,611

Advertising

Panel A of Exhibit 12.12 lists the amount spent on advertising for each product. When these amounts are divided by the number of units sold, the following advertising charges per unit are generated:

A. $120,000 ÷ 6,450 units = $18.60/unit

B. $ 80,000 ÷ 10,060 units = $ 7.95/unit

C. $ 54,000 ÷ 13,910 units = $ 3.88/unit

The advertising expenses borne by each salesperson are determined by multiplying these per-unit advertising charges by the number of bicycles of each model that each rep sold.

The number of units of the product sold is a very common basis for allocating advertising expenses. Two other common bases are the number of prospects secured and the number of sales transactions. The decision to allocate advertising expenses on the basis of the number of units sold is controversial. While the per-unit-of-product-sold approach is popular, it is not hard to develop an argument against it. One could argue, for example, that advertising expenses are fixed for a period, and since they are fixed costs, productive salespeople should not have to assume a larger advertising burden than unproductive salespeople. One could also argue that the per-unit approach treats advertising as a consequence of sales, rather than as a cause, and therefore the scheme violates the control principle alluded to earlier that one should search for factors that control the functional cost.

While both of these arguments have merit, we will use the per-unit-of-product basis for allocating advertising expenses here for three reasons: (1) the per-unit approach is one of the most popular; (2) there is no clearly preferred alternative in the literature; and (3) the example is designed to illustrate the cost analysis process, not to provide the last word on all possible nuances. Yet you should be aware that the decision as to how to allocate advertising expenses or any of the expense categories can change the fundamental conclusions one draws about the profitability of a particular segment.

Warehousing and Shipping

In regard to warehousing and shipping costs, the profitability analysis by sales representatives does not include an allocation for the warehouseperson's salary because that salary would continue regardless of what the sales rep sold. Rather, all that is allocated to the salespeople are the packaging costs per unit, which amounted to $2 per bicycle.

Order Processing

The office clerk's salary is not allocated to salespeople because there is no causal link between an individual representative's sales and that salary. The office rent charged to this activity is similarly not allocated. The order processing costs that are allocated are the direct expenses for postage and supplies. Order processing costs are most directly linked to the number of orders, which produces an allocation of $4 per order.

Transportation

Transportation charges amounted to $6 per bike. These are charged against the individual sales representatives according to the number of bicycles each sold. When all these expenses are aggregated and subtracted from gross margin, it is found that each representative is contributing to profits. Such a result poses a dilemma for the company sales manager. The branch is not profitable, but each salesperson in the branch is contributing to profits. Admittedly, the sales reps may not be making a large enough contribution. If there were a profit standard for each salesperson, performance could be compared to the standard. This example demonstrates the difference between a performance analysis in which a standard of comparison is established beforehand and a straight cost and profitability analysis.

The company sales manager could compare the contributions to profit of the representatives in the Orlando branch with those of other sales representatives by doing a similar analysis for other branches. If the Orlando salespeople were found to be low, it might indicate the payroll in the Orlando branch was too high for the number of bicycles sold. The sales manager might then consider removing one or more reps from the territory. Alternatively, the manager might consider increasing the number of calls or changing the salary/commission mixture in the salespeople's compensation package. Still other strategies would be to close the warehouse associated with the branch or to close the branch. The profit implications of each strategy would be different. They could be calculated, however, if the company maintains sales and cost records by small units. Conversely, when basic records are aggregated into larger totals and are stored that way in the company's accounting system, such isolate-and-explode analyses are precluded.

Suppose the sales manager felt that for strategic reasons, she did not wish to close the branch or the warehouse. Rather, she wished to consider reassigning one representative in the branch to another office and territory. Since there are typically significant company costs and personal disruptions to the rep in such a switch, the sales manager did not take these reassignments lightly. Suppose, therefore, she wanted to ascertain the profitability of each account to the salesperson and the company.

Exhibit 12.14 and Exhibit 12.15 contain, respectively, the activity levels of Tucker, the worst-performing representative in terms of the analysis contained in Exhibit 12.12, broken down by account and the resulting profit contribution of each account based on the same allocation criteria used previously. The analysis illustrates the operation of the iceberg principle.

Although Tucker overall contributes to profit, one account is generating a loss. The loss can be traced to the number of bicycles ordered by Cooper. Cooper orders every time Tucker calls, but the average order size is very low. Less frequent calls might be the answer; fewer calls might produce the same net sales but reduce Tucker's travel expenses charged to Cooper. The analysis also reveals that although Allen purchased the most bikes, Brown was the most profitable account Tucker had. Again, these insights would be impossible to generate if Hurricane Performance Bicycle Company did not use modularized marketing cost analyses.

The profitability analyses by marketing segment do not tell the sales manager of Hurricane Performance Bicycle Company or any other manager what to do. They do, however, provide managers with some basic information for making intelligent choices.

Promise and Problems

The preceding example, while basic, reveals both the promise and some of the problems associated with marketing cost analysis. The real benefit is the opportunity it provides managers to isolate segments of the business that are most profitable as well as those that generate losses. This information allows those involved to improve their planning and control of the firm's activities. When combined with proper sales analysis techniques discussed in Chapter 13, it provides sales managers with a formidable analytical weapon for managing the personal selling function.

The example also illustrates the problems associated with the technique. Sales analysis requires that data be available in the proper detail. Some data can be costly to generate and expensive to maintain, but sophisticated information systems like enterprise software and contact management software can lower the cost. The system must be able to select and aggregate only those inputs appropriate to the segment of the business being analyzed. As the example indicates, there is often a question as to which costs should be allocated and what bases should be used to allocate these costs. The most appropriate allocation bases can generate spirited discussion among those involved. Allocations cannot be taken lightly because they

Customers of Tucker	Number of Sales Calls	Number of Orders	Number of Units Purchased				
			A	**B**	**C**	**Total**	
Allen	50	35	807	1,258	1,567	3,632	
Brown	25	20	645	880	1,043	2,568	
Cooper	25	25	162	378	869	1,409	
Total	100	80	1,614	2,516	3,479	7,609	

EXHIBIT 12.14 Activities of Tucker broken down by account

	Total	Allen	Brown	Cooper
Sales				
Product A	$371,220	$185,610	$148,350	$37,260
Product B	452,880	226,440	158,400	68,040
Product C	417,480	188,040	125,160	104,280
Total Sales	1,214,580	600,090	431,910	209,580
Cost of Goods Sold				
Product A	290,520	145,260	116,100	29,160
Product B	377,400	188,700	132,000	56,700
Product C	347,900	156,700	104,300	86,900
Total COGS	1,015,820	490,660	352,400	172,760
Gross Margin	225,760	109,430	79,510	36,820
Expenses				
Direct selling				
Salary	48,000	24,000	12,000	12,000
Commissions	12,416	6,001	4,319	2,096
Travel	19,000	9,500	4,750	4,750
Advertising				
Product A	30,028	15,014	12,000	3,014
Product B	20,008	10,004	6,998	3,006
Product C	13,506	6,083	4,049	3,374
Warehousing and shipping	15,218	7,264	5,136	2,818
Order processing	320	140	80	100
Transportation	45,654	21,792	15,408	8,454
Total Expenses	204,149	99,798	64,740	39,611
Contribution to Profit (Loss)	$21,611	$9,632	$14,770	$(2,791)

EXHIBIT 12.15 Profitability analysis for Tucker broken down by customer

ultimately affect the profitability of a segment; at the same time, however, there are usually no perfect answers as to how costs should be allocated. Thus, setting up a good marketing cost system can take a good deal of expensive executive time.

The benefits outweigh the higher costs. A growing number of companies are profiting from implementing market cost analysis.[14]

Return of Assets Managed

Sales and cost analyses provide the sales manager with two important financial techniques for controlling the personal selling function. The first measures the results achieved and the second the cost of producing those results. The important financial ingredient left out of those analyses is the assets needed to produce those results. At a minimum, the company will be committing working capital in the form of accounts receivable and inventories to support the sales function. The return produced on the assets used in each segment of the business provides sales managers with a useful variation of more traditional cost analysis procedures for evaluating and controlling various elements of the personal selling function.

The formula for return on assets managed (ROAM) reflects both the contribution margin associated with a given level of sales and asset turnover.[15] It is as follows:

$$\text{ROAM} = \text{Contribution as a percentage of sales} \times \text{Asset turnover rate}$$

The formula indicates that the return to a segment of the business can be improved either by increasing the profit margin on sales or by maintaining the same profit margin and increasing the asset turnover rate. The formula can then

	Branch A	Branch B
Sales	$2,500,000	$1,500,000
Cost of Goods Sold	2,000,000	1,275,000
Gross Margin	500,000 (20%)	225,000 (15%)
Less Variable Branch Expenses		
Salaries	155,000	80,000
Commissions	25,000	10,000
Office expenses	30,000	20,000
Travel and entertainment	40,000	20,000
	250,000	130,000
Branch Contribution to Profit	250,000	95,000
Branch investments		
Accounts receivable	500,000	150,000
Inventories	750,000	225,000
	1,250,000	375,000
Earnings as a Percentage of Sales	10.0%	6.3%
Turnover	2.0	4.0
Branch Percentage Return on Assets Managed	20.0%	25.2%

EXHIBIT 12.16 Analysis of return on assets managed

be used to evaluate segments or to select the best alternative from strategies being considered.

Think of, for example, the use of ROAM to evaluate the performance of two sales branches. Exhibit 12.16 contains the basic financial data. Note that Branch A sold more than Branch B and the gross margin on these sales was higher, both in total and as a percentage of sales, because of the mix of products. Furthermore, the contribution to total company profits was higher for Branch A than for Branch B, and earnings as a percentage of sales were 10.0 percent in Branch A and only 6.3 percent in Branch B. By all these standards, Branch A performed better.

These criteria, however, ignore the assets needed to produce these results. Consider that when the investment in assets, which in the example consists of accounts receivable and inventories for each branch, is factored into the analysis, the picture changes. Branch B required a smaller commitment of the firm's capital. Consequently, Branch B was able to affect an asset turnover twice as large as Branch A, so the return on investment was higher in Branch B than in Branch A.

While the basic ROAM formula can be used to provide useful management information, the managerial insights it affords can be magnified by breaking the basic formula down by its components. The first component—contribution as a percentage of sales—equals the ratio of net contribution divided by sales. The second component—the asset turnover rate—equals sales divided by the assets needed to produce those sales. Each of these second-level components could be expanded. One could, for example, break down the sales component by product or salesperson and could similarly break down the assets to assess the impact of each product or salesperson on profitability. Alternatively, one might choose to explode into its detailed elements only one of the second-level components of net contributions, sales, and assets. Exploding one or more of the components of the equation allows management to trace the impact of a number of "what if" scenarios.

Exhibit 12.17, for example, diagrams the return on assets model, with the asset component exploded. Each of the boxes applies to the segment of the business being analyzed. Previously, we saw, for example, that Branch B produced a higher ROAM than Branch A. With the exploded model, management can quickly explore what might be done to bring the returns into line. Exhibit 12.16 indicates, for example, that the amount invested in receivables and inventories as a percentage of sales varies across the two branches and that, in particular,

	Branch A	**Branch B**
Receivables as a percentage of sales	$\dfrac{\$150,000}{1,500,000} = 20\%$	$\dfrac{150,000}{1,500,000} = 10\%$
Inventories as a percentage of sales	$\dfrac{750,000}{2,500,000} = 30\%$	$\dfrac{225,000}{1,500,000} = 15\%$

Management might logically ask what would happen to ROAM in Branch A if receivables or inventories as a percentage of sales or both were reduced to the levels existing in Branch B. Exhibit 12.18 traces the implication of what a reduction

EXHIBIT 12.17
Expanded return on assets managed (ROAM) model

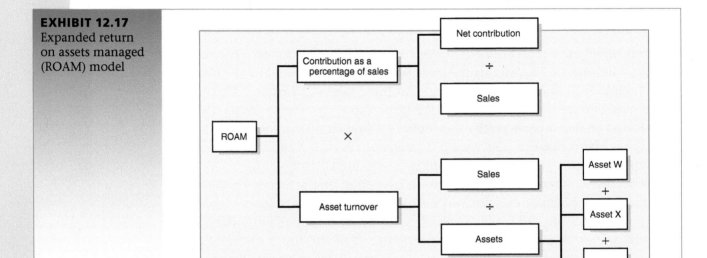

in accounts receivable to 10 percent of sales (to $250,000) in Branch A through better billing and follow-up procedures might do for its profitability. The example, which assumes no lost sales because of these billing efforts, demonstrates the returns could be brought directly in line with this one change. Management could just as easily assess the profit implications of, say, 5, 10, and 15 percent declines in sales to determine how sensitive the branch returns might be to a change in the billing procedures.

In sum, assets managed add another important dimension to the financial control picture. The investment required for a venture needs to be recognized because long-run profits can be maximized only if the optimal level of investment in each asset is achieved. Unfortunately, the point was made earlier that marketers have been slower to embrace cost analysis than sales analysis. Clearly, despite their compelling intuitive appeal, cost or profitability analysis and asset return analysis have a way to go before they match the popularity of sales analysis in managing the personal selling function.

SUMMARY

Marketing cost analysis attempts to isolate the costs incurred in producing various levels of sales to determine the profitability of sales by segment of the business. Marketing cost analysis can be used to advantage by sales managers to investigate the profitability of regions, branches, territories, customers, or various channels of distribution.

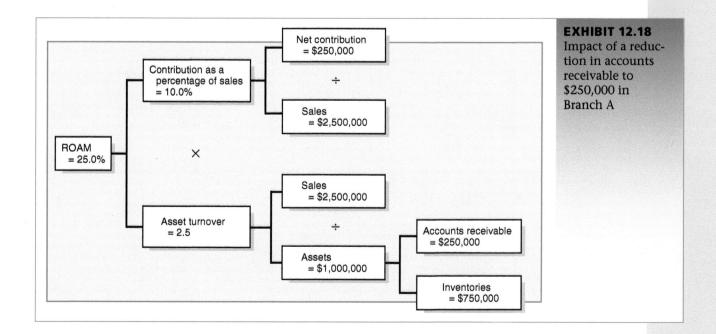

EXHIBIT 12.18
Impact of a reduction in accounts receivable to $250,000 in Branch A

Most firms have been slower to embrace cost analysis than sales analysis for studying their marketing activities. Part of this lag can be explained by the fact that many costs associated with doing business are not entered in the firm's accounting system in their most useful form for decision making. Thus, it is necessary to rework these costs so they are more useful. The adoption of activity-based cost (ABC) accounting systems is helping to increase the use of cost analysis.

A marketing cost analysis can be conducted using either a full-cost, a contribution margin, or an activity-based cost approach. The full-cost approach allocates all the costs of doing business, even fixed costs, to one of the operating segments. The contribution margin approach holds that only those costs that can be specifically identified with the segment of the business should be deducted from the revenue produced by the segment. The contribution margin approach is more logically defensible from a decision-making perspective. An activity-based cost approach is similar to contribution, but the cost of each activity is defined and allocated.

There are four steps in conducting a marketing cost analysis. First, the purpose of the study must be specified. Second, the natural account costs must be spread to functional cost centers. Next, the functional costs must be allocated to appropriate operating segments using some reasonable bases. Here one looks for those factors that bear a cause-and-effect relationship with the cost. Finally, the allocated costs are summed so the contribution of the segment can be determined.

Return on assets managed provides the sales manager with still another financial tool for controlling the personal selling function. Return on assets managed is the product of contribution to profit as a percentage of sales multiplied by asset turnover. Asset turnover is found by dividing sales by the assets needed to produce those sales. The formula recognizes that the sales manager has only limited assets with which to work. He or she can maximize the profits produced by the personal selling function only if each asset is put to its highest and best use. Return on assets managed is currently less popular than either sales or cost analysis in managing the personal selling function.

KEY TERMS

full-cost accounting	sales costs	*order processing*
contribution margin	*direct selling*	*transportation*
accounting	*advertising*	return on assets managed
activity-based costing	*warehousing and shipping*	(ROAM)
(ABC)		

BREAKOUT QUESTIONS

1. "Our costs are out of control," claimed Rosemary Harper, chief financial officer of Broadway United. "In particular, I am really concerned about the level of marketing costs, especially for the sales force." With a 235-person sales force, Broadway sells computer hardware and software packages to financial institutions. Harper supports the recommendations of a sales consulting firm to reduce the sales force by 50 percent and to hire a new "sales force" consisting of manufacturers' agents who would be paid on a straight commission basis. The reduction in the sales force would mean that 10 district sales managers would lose their jobs. The sales training manager position would be eliminated as well since manufacturers' agents do not need training according to the sales consultant. Harper intended to keep only the best sales reps and eliminate the others in the 50 percent reduction process. "Those experienced sales reps that remain with Broadway will not need enough training to justify keeping Broadway's training department," noted Harper. What are the advantages and disadvantages of the sales consultant's proposal? Is it possible for a company to cut costs too far?

2. Advertising has a synergistic effect. For example, in the Hurricane Performance Bicycle Company case, the $254,000 advertising expenditure for product A had a positive impact on products B and C and on the company as well. Besides, dollars spent in one period have a carryover effect to future periods. What recommendations would you make to handle these situations?

3. The Rite-Way Corporation, a manufacturer of a line of writing instruments, has completed a ROAM analysis for all products. The deluxe model in its line of fountain pens sells for $5.50 but produces a ROAM of 8.3 percent, well below the 23.5 percent average for the other products. Management believes rising raw material costs, such as gold and silver prices, are beyond Rite-Way's control. Should Rite-Way drop its deluxe product? Should Rite-Way eliminate commissions paid to sales representatives for deluxe sales?

4. The sales manager of Branch A (Exhibit 12.16) was dismayed with the results. The 20 percent ROAM for the branch was below expectations. The sales manager's response was "OK, they want better results, then we'll increase sales by at least 10 percent. But we'll have to cut prices by 5 percent to do this." Will this benefit Branch A?

5. Accounts receivable are too high for Branch A in Exhibit 12.16. One sales analyst recommends giving credit and collection responsibilities to the sales force. Sales reps

would be provided with delinquency objectives aimed at reducing accounts receivables by 20 percent. Those meeting their objectives would earn an additional 1 percent of sales for commission. Will this work? Another analyst contends that since the sales force has no training in credits and collections, accounts receivable should be excluded from ROAM calculations. Do you agree? What would happen to Branch A's ROAM if accounts receivable were excluded?

6. Given the following profit and loss statement for the XYZ Company, allocate the natural accounts to the functional accounts:

XYZ Company
Profit and Loss Statement
2015

Sales		$1,676,000
Cost of goods sold		1,003,000
Gross margin		$673,000
Selling and administrative expenses		
Salaries		
Salespeople	$120,000	
Sales manager	30,000	
Office personnel	38,000	
Warehouse personnel	30,000	
Commissions	16,760	
Advertising	93,800	
Postage	450	
Supplies		
Office	200	
Warehouse	500	
Packaging	30,000	
Transportation	80,290	
Travel expenses	40,000	
Rent		
Sales	15,000	
Warehouse	35,000	
Order processing	10,000	
Heat and electricity		
Sales	7,000	
Warehouse	18,000	
Order processing	5,000	
Total selling and administrative expenses		$570,000
Net profit (loss)		$103,000

7. Nancy Troyer, the sales manager for InterCraft, a manufacturer and distributor of picture frames and supplies, was in the midst of a heavy discussion with representatives from the company's accounting department. The discussion revolved around the new cost system the accounting department was developing so the sales function could be managed more effectively. The topic at the moment was how each salesperson's automobile expenses should be allocated, given that salespeople were handling eight

product lines and selling to three different types of outlets—office supply stores, bookstores, and arts and crafts specialty supply outlets. The situation was complicated further because sales reps were also expected to prospect for new accounts and attend trade shows in their own and contiguous territories. How would you recommend the costs be allocated if Troyer wanted to determine the profitability of each salesperson? Each product line? Each customer?

8. You are given the following information on two salespeople: Salesperson A earns a $22,000 salary; salesperson B earns $23,000. Both earn 1 percent commission. Advertising costs $3 per unit. Shipping expenses are $2 per unit. Order processing costs total $1 per order. Travel expenses amount to $0.50 per call. Your task is to calculate the contribution to profit (loss) made by each salesperson.

Salesperson	Number of Calls	Number of Orders	Units Sold	Total Sales	Cost of Goods Sold
A	200	250	15,000	$750,000	$600,000
B	295	230	18,000	900,000	720,000

9. As the sales manager of the M.N.O. Company, you are trying to evaluate the performance of two districts. You have decided to look at how each district has managed its assets employed in the selling function. Your task is to determine each district's ROAM.

	District 1	District 2
Sales	$800,000	$500,000
Cost of goods sold	624,000	390,000
Gross margin	176,000	110,000
Variable district expenses:		
Salaries	$49,600	$31,000
Commissions	8,000	5,000
Office expenses	9,600	6,000
Travel	12,800	8,000
Total expenses	80,000	50,000
Net profit (loss)	96,000	60,000
District investment in assets:		
Accounts receivable	120,000	45,000
Inventories	200,000	80,000
Earnings as a percentage of sales	0.12	0.12
Turnover	2.5	4.0

10. Sylvie Faivre, sales analyst for the Bouvre Cheese Company, had completed her analysis of one of the southern districts. The district was a candidate for consolidation because management believed sales were not as expected. Sylvie suggested she should first determine the district's return on assets managed before any decisions were made concerning territory modification. The following provides the data needed to calculate ROAM for the district:

Sales		$4,500,000
Cost of goods sold		4,000,000
Gross margin		500,000
Less variable branch expenses		
Salaries		$175,000
Commissions		30,000
Office expenses		35,000
Travel and entertainment		55,000
		295,000
District contribution to profit	$205,000	
District investments		
Accounts receivable	750,000	
Inventories	900,000	
	$1,650,000	

Determine the ROAM for the district. What would happen if inventories were reduced by 20 percent? How much would sales have to increase to obtain the company average ROAM of 25 percent? Bouvre's management believes salaries are too high and is considering a 15 percent reduction. Assuming no impact on sales, how would this affect district ROAM?

11. Ethical Question. As a sales manager, you have been reviewing the travel expense reports for your sales team and noticed a discrepancy with the travel expenses turned in by your top performing salesperson. After further review, you determine that the salesperson has been submitting personal travel expenses (hotels, gas, etc.) on the company expense account for several months. What would you do and why?

LEADERSHIP CHALLENGE: THAT SALE WAS EXPENSIVE, I THINK

Barry Jefferson could not understand why he was having a problem getting the information. As the regional vice president of sales (North America) for Digital Dimension Manufacturing he wanted to know how much it was costing the company for a salesperson to make a customer call. Certainly the company would know how much it costs to make a sales call. Unfortunately, the more he investigated the problem, the more he realized Digital Dimension did not have a good handle on its sales costs.

Digital Dimension was an established manufacturer of high-technology components based in Munich, Germany. Its products were used in a variety of products from computers to high-technology appliances, (refrigerators, dishwashers, etc.). Practically any product that required a computer chip could use the products offered by the company. As such, the company dealt with a wide range of customers, from the very large to medium-sized companies. Digital Dimension sold all over the world and had manufacturing plants in Germany, the United States, China and Malaysia.

Barry had 150 salespeople in 10 customer-focused sales groups across North American (100 in the United States, 30 in Canada, and 20 in Mexico). He knew the cost of making a sale varied a great deal across the sales force. Nearly half of the sales force was assigned to single customers; indeed, some even had offices inside their customers' businesses. For the very largest customers, Digital Dimension had as many as four salespeople dedicated to a single account. Others, mostly new salespeople, were responsible for calling on smaller, less-established customers as well as generating new business from potential clients.

He had spoken with his counterpart, Kim Reese, regional VP of sales (Europe), and she had confirmed her frustration with the current lack of information as well. She indicated support for a meeting with Grace Hart, executive vice president of sales, to discuss how Digital Dimension could get a better handle on the cost of doing business. As Barry sat in his office he considered how the meeting would go.

Questions

1. You are Barry Jefferson. What do you think would be important to discuss in a meeting with Grace Hart about the sales costs at Digital Dimension?

2. What information would you need to know in order to estimate the cost of making a sales call at the company?

3. If you were Grace Hart, what questions would you ask Barry Jefferson about implementing a cost analysis plan?

ROLE-PLAY: CANDO COFFEE SERVICE

Situation

Levita Wampley assumed the position of vice president of sales for the CanDo Coffee Service seven months ago. Before joining CanDo, Levita served for 12 years in various selling and sales management positions for a major restaurant food service provider. CanDo serves principally medium to large offices and factories, providing coffee pots, coffee, filters, and cups to various break rooms at their clients' places of business. The geographic area served is the state of Florida, with concentrations in the major metropolitan areas. In total, CanDo has about 2,100 established clients and a sales force of 25, plus two sales managers. Salespeople typically call on each client once every two weeks to ensure everything is going well with the service, to clean the equipment as needed, and to replenish supplies. Salespeople drive a CanDo van, which they must keep stocked appropriately from their local CanDo warehouse. CanDo operates with a very healthy margin of profit, as it is essentially providing a turnkey service to its clients—who are quite willing to pay well for avoiding the bother of performing this task.

Levita has become convinced that she must address the following problem. It seems that because of differing travel requirements for salespersons' routes, varying distances from salespersons' homes to the local CanDo warehouse, differences in the nature of the facilities of clients (size, layout, ease of access, etc.), and variation in the number of break rooms in each facility that must be serviced, a growing feeling of inequity is being experienced by the CanDo sales force. The salespeople are paid on a combination of salary and commission, and the commission is based on the profitability of each sales territory. Fixed and variable costs associated with the territory are allocated to arrive at the profit component. And to complicate things more, there is also a potential for a bonus component based on signing up new customers. This compensation mix is not the problem: the problem is effectively arriving at the territory profit figure monthly so that commission payments are fair and equitable across the different client situations and travel requirements.

In the past, the bottom-line profit has been calculated using a contribution margin approach with indirect costs allocated on the basis of overall sales volume of the territory as a percentage of total sales. Levita certainly realizes this is potentially problematic and has recently been reading up on activity-based costing as one way of dealing with issues such as this. She calls a meeting with the two sales managers, Ryan Roan and Fernando Perez, to discuss how they might restructure the calculations of the profit component of the salesperson incentive plan.

Characters in the Role-Play

Levita Wampley, VP of sales for CanDo Coffee Service
Ryan Roan, sales manager for northern Florida (roughly from I-4 northward)
Fernando Perez, sales manager for southern Florida (roughly everything south of I-4)

Assignment

Break into groups of three, with one student playing each character. It doesn't matter what the actual gender mix of your group is. Before you stage the meeting, work separately using the material in your chapter to come up with your own recommendation for a new approach to calculating the territory profit figures monthly. You can make some assumptions about the potential bases for allocation, and you can be creative in your solutions, so long as they are realistic. You will need to be prepared to justify your recommendations in the meeting. Then get together and role-play the meeting among Levita, Ryan, and Fernando. In the end, you want to come out of the meeting with a unified plan for changing this important input to their incentive program. Above all else, be sure your new system for calculating the territory profit component is fair and equitable to the CanDo salespeople. Note: Do not recommend changing their compensation/incentive plan. Assume that you are to simply fix the profit calculation.

MINICASE: TAKAMATSU SPORTS

Takamatsu Sports is a Japanese sporting goods company based in Osaka, Japan, that manufactures and sells tennis equipment. It sells three different tennis racquets: the Nomo, the Ichiro, and the Matsui. The company experienced a loss last year for the first time, and founder and CEO Hiroshi Takamatsu is interested in analyzing the company's financial data to determine a cause for the loss. Takamatsu's profit and loss statement for last year is as follows:

Profit and Loss Statement for Takamatsu Sports (in USD)

Sales		$2,253,370
Cost of goods sold		1,754,630
Gross margin		$498,770
Selling and administrative expenses		
Salaries	$156,000	
Commissions	22,534	

Advertising	176,890
Postage and office supplies	342
Packaging materials	20,527
Transportation charges	51,318
Travel expenses	42,000
Rent	120,000
Total selling and administrative expenses	589,611
Net profit (loss)	($90,871)

Takamatsu Sports has three sales representatives: Daisuke Chimura, Akihide Fujita, and Yoko Ota. Mr. Chimura and Mr. Fujita, both men, have been with the company for years and have successful sales records. However, the newest sales representative, Ms. Ota, is female and yet unproven, and the decision to hire her was a big change from traditional Japanese culture, because in the past it was rare for women to hold such positions. Mr. Takamatsu felt when hiring her that she was highly qualified, but he was concerned that she would face a challenge in communicating to customers because the customers might be uncomfortable working with a woman. In fact, early indications are that Ms. Ota is not making as many sales calls as the other two representatives. This troubles Mr. Takamatsu because at Takamatsu Sports, and in Japan in general, selling is based on a relationship-selling model, where relationships between seller and customer are paramount and may be built for months before an overture of buying products even is made.

Mr. Takamatsu decided to do a cost analysis with the purpose of determining the profitability of the three sales representatives. He then allocated natural accounts to functional accounts as follows:

Natural Accounts		Functional Accounts				
		Direct Selling	Advertising	Warehousing	Orders/ Billing	Transportation
Salaries	$156,000	$120,000		$ 19,000	$17,000	
Commissions	22,534	22,534				
Advertising	176,890		$176,890			
Postage and supplies	342				342	
Packaging materials	20,527			20,527		
Transportation charges	51,318					
Travel expenses	42,000	42,000			$51,318	
Rent	120,000	32,800		82,000	5,200	
Totals	$589,611	$217,334	$176,890	$121,527	$22,542	$51,318

He then gathered the following sales data to use in the profitability analysis:

A. Information by Product

Products	Selling Price per Unit	Cost per Unit	Gross Margin per Unit	Number Sold in Period	Sales in Period	Advertising Expenditures	Advertising Expenditures per Unit
Nomo	$45	$35	$10	16,742	$753,390	$29,500	$1.76
Ichiro	70	55	15	10,543	738,010	60,210	5.71
Matsui	110	85	25	6,927	761,970	87,180	12.59
				34,212	$2,253,370	$176,890	

B. Information by Salesperson

Salesperson	Number of Sales Calls	Number of Orders	Number of Units Sold			
			Nomo	Ichiro	Matsui	Total
Chimura	45	30	5,902	3,409	2,410	11,721
Fujita	40	20	5,100	3,510	1,890	10,500
Ota	35	30	5,740	3,624	2,627	11,991
	120	80	16,742	10,543	6,927	34,212

Mr. Takamatsu also determined the following data for making the cost allocations:

- Each salesperson was paid a $40,000 salary with a 1 percent commission on what was sold.
- Each salesperson was allotted an annual travel expense budget of $14,000, which was fully used by each salesperson.
- Advertising cost was allotted by the number of units sold by each salesperson.
- Packaging and shipping for the warehousing cost is $0.60 per unit sold.
- Order processing cost is $.01 per unit sold.
- Transportation cost is $1.50 per unit sold.

Mr. Takamatsu has now come to you, his trusted managerial accountant, with the preceding data and has asked you to perform the profitability analysis for the three sales representatives.

Questions

1. Develop a profitability analysis by salesperson based on the model of Exhibit 12.12 in the textbook.

2. Who is the most profitable sales representative? The least? Are Mr. Takamatsu's concerns about Ms. Ota's performance valid?

3. Based on your analysis, what recommendation(s) can you give to Mr. Takamatsu to return his company to profitability?

CHAPTER 13

Evaluating Salesperson Performance

LEARNING OBJECTIVES

Performance evaluations should be a process that provides a forum for dialogue between a salesperson and the sales manager, focused on gaining the impetus for future professional development and performance success. In order to successfully execute a performance review, sales managers must have a strong working knowledge of different measures of performance that are appropriate to a particular selling situation. Then they must conduct the appraisal in a manner that allows the salesperson to build on current strengths and proficiencies and make performance improvements where warranted.

After reading this chapter, you should be able to

- Explain the difference between performance and effectiveness.
- Identify objective measures of salesperson performance, both output and input.
- Utilize ratio analysis as an objective approach to salesperson performance measurement.
- Discuss key issues related to subjective measurement of salesperson performance and the forms that might be used to administer such an evaluation.
- Understand how a sales manager can make the performance review process more productive and valuable for the salesperson.

PERFORMANCE VERSUS EFFECTIVENESS

A key issue in evaluating the performance of salespeople is the distinction among the concepts of behavior, performance, and effectiveness.[1] Although role perceptions, aptitude, skill level, and motivation level were discussed in Chapter 6 as being directly linked to performance, it is also important to understand that they are directly linked to behavior as well.

Behavior refers to what salespeople do—that is, the tasks on which they expend effort while working. These tasks might include calling on customers, writing orders, preparing sales presentations, sending follow-up communication, and the like. These are the sales activities discussed in Chapter 2.

Think of performance as behavior evaluated in terms of its contribution to the goals of the organization. In other words, performance has a normative element reflecting whether a salesperson's behavior is good or bad, appropriate or inappropriate, in light of the organization's goals and objectives. Note that behavior and performance are both influenced by relevant sales activities. Of course, these activities in turn depend on the types of sales jobs in question.

Before we discuss salesperson evaluation further, let's also distinguish between performance and effectiveness. By definition, effectiveness refers to some summary index of organizational outcomes for which an individual is at least partly responsible. Examples include sales volume, market share, profitability of sales, and customer retention rate. The crucial distinction between performance and effectiveness is that the latter does not refer to behavior directly; rather, it is a function of additional factors not under the individual salesperson's control. These include such things as top management policies, sales potential or difficulty of a territory, and actions of competitors.

It is generally agreed that salespeople should be evaluated solely on those phases of sales performance over which they exercise control and should not be held responsible for factors beyond their control. If a company's method of measuring salesperson performance is to result in valid comparisons, serious consideration must be given to distinguishing between factors within a salesperson's control versus those outside his or her control in developing yardsticks for objective or subjective evaluation. The Leadership box presents a classic theory of motivation, attribution theory, that is quite relevant to this managerial dilemma.

One could argue that a sales manager's careful specification of performance standards by territory should eliminate inequities across territories. For example, percentage of quota attained should be an acceptable measure of performance because quotas supposedly consider variations in environmental factors across territories. Admittedly, a comparison of salespeople with respect to percentage of quota attained is a better measure of their performance than is a comparison that simply looks at each representative's level of absolute sales or market share, assuming the quotas were done well. However, assuming that quotas are done well is a big "if"— sometimes quotas are not so well developed. In some instances, they are arbitrary and are not necessarily based on an objective assessment of all the factors that facilitate or constrain a salesperson's ability to make a sale. This is especially true if quota development relies too heavily on historical trends and not enough on emerging trends in a given sales territory.

Even when quotas are done well, the measure "percentage of quota attained" still omits much with respect to a salesperson's performance. For one thing, it ignores the profitability of sales. Sales reps can be compared with respect to profitability, or the return they produce on the assets under their control. Establishing quotas that accurately consider the many factors affecting the level of sales a representative should be able to produce in a territory is difficult, but determining the appropriate standards of profitability for each territory is even more difficult.

Even if good sales and profit standards could be developed, the problem of evaluating salespeople would not be solved because neither measure incorporates activities that may have no short-term payout but still have substantial consequences to the firm in the long run. These include the time devoted to laying the groundwork for a long-term client relationship, particularly when developing a potentially large

LEADERSHIP   Attributions and Salesperson Performance Evaluation

Evaluating the performance of a salesperson is all about the sales manager attributing causes of that performance. That is, managers seek out why a salesperson's effectiveness is diminished or enhanced so that appropriate reinforcing or remedial actions may be taken. This process of attributing causes of outcomes has been studied extensively under the rubric of attribution theory, an approach quite relevant to sales management practice.

Psychologist Fritz Heider developed the cornerstone concept that evaluators tend to operate as "naïve psychologists" when they observe and analyze the behavior of others. He classified variables used by evaluators to interpret the actions of others into three categories: (1) a performance variable (i.e., task success, or effectiveness); (2) environmental variables (task difficulty and luck); and (3) person, or dispositional, variables (ability and effort). Heider proposed that evaluators assess performance based on the following relationships among these factors:

1. Ability = Task difficulty/Effort
2. Performance = (Ability × Effort) ± Task difficulty

According to equation 1, if two salespeople put forth the same amount of effort, the one who performs the more difficult task is expected to have the greater ability. Also, if two salespeople accomplish the same task with equal levels of performance, the one who expends the least effort is expected by the rater to have the higher ability. According to equation 2, a sales manager's perception of a salesperson's performance is a function of ability times effort, plus or minus the effects of differing task difficulty.

In the context of salesperson evaluation, Heider's concept of task difficulty may be easily translated to territory difficulty. Territory difficulty is important because rarely, if ever, in professional selling does one find any two territories that are equal in all respects. Therefore, sales managers must adjust performance ratings by taking into account the differences in territory difficulty among the salespeople they supervise. Unfortunately, this if often neglected when sales managers complete performance evaluations. A phenomenon known as the fundamental attribution error predicts that contextual or background information (such as differences in territories among salespeople in a sales manager's unit) will be systematically ignored by evaluators, and instead their ratings will be based on "person" factors such as perceived ability and effort. Heider proposed that background situational (contextual) information is less salient to evaluators than is person (appraisee) information, which is analogous to the Gestalt concept of figure against ground. In the context of salesperson evaluations, such thinking suggests that an evaluation bias may arise in which sales managers focus on dispositional factors, such as the salesperson's ability and effort (the "figure") and ignore contextual factors (the "ground"), such as territory difficulty and luck.

Sales organizations must work hard to guard against this form of evaluation bias. Assuming equal performance, over time a salesperson who is evaluated equally or lower than a peer whose territory is less difficult may become dissatisfied and feel unfairly treated, resulting in a very effective salesperson leaving the company. Firms must train their sales managers to fully consider all contextual and person factors when making their evaluations. By doing so, sales managers can avoid succumbing to the fundamental attribution error.

account. Other activities that often go unmeasured are building long-term goodwill for the company and developing a detailed understanding of the capabilities of the products being sold. Thus, other measures beyond sales and profits are needed to more directly reflect salesperson performance.

The other measures firms use to evaluate salespeople fall into two broad categories: (1) objective measures and (2) subjective measures.[2] *Objective measures* reflect statistics the sales manager can gather from the firm's internal data. These measures are best used when they reflect elements of the sales process. *Subjective measures* typically rely on personal evaluations by someone inside the organization, usually the salesperson's immediate supervisor, of how individual salespeople are doing.

Subjective measures are generally gathered via direct observation of the salesperson by the manager but may involve input from customers or other sources.[3]

OBJECTIVE MEASURES

Objective measures fall into three major categories: (1) output measures, (2) input measures, and (3) ratios of output or input measures. Exhibit 13.1 lists some of the more common output and input measures, and Exhibit 13.2 provides some of the more commonly used ratios.

The use of outputs, inputs, and ratios to measure salesperson performance is a recognition of the nature of the relationship selling process. As we have learned, some sales processes, especially those experienced by salespeople seeking to secure, build, and maintain long-term relationships with profitable customers, can take months or years. Within the relationship selling process, salespeople engage in activities with (or in pursuit of) the prospect or buyer. The manager can measure those activities and compare the activities with results for each stage. By examining this performance evidence, managers can pinpoint potential areas for improvement by each salesperson, or identify changes that should be made in the sales strategy so that it is aligned with how buyers want to buy.

Output Measures	Input Measures	**EXHIBIT 13.1** Common output and input measures used to evaluate salespeople
Orders	Calls	
Number of orders	Total number of calls	
Average size of orders	Number of planned calls	
Number of canceled orders	Number of unplanned calls	
Accounts	Time and time utilization	
Number of active accounts	Days worked	
Number of new accounts	Calls per day (call rate)	
Number of lost accounts	Selling time versus nonselling time	
Number of overdue accounts	Expenses	
Number of prospective accounts	Total	
	By type	
	As a percentage of sales	
	As a percentage of quota	
	Nonselling activities	
	E-mails to prospects	
	Phone calls to prospects	
	Number of formal proposals developed	
	Advertising displays set up	
	Number of meetings held with distributors/dealers	
	Number of training sessions held with distributor/dealer personnel	
	Number of calls on distributor/dealer customers	
	Number of service calls made	
	Number of overdue accounts collected	

EXHIBIT 13.2
Common ratios used to evaluate salespeople

Expense Ratios

- Sales expense ratio = $\dfrac{\text{Expenses}}{\text{Sales}}$

- Cost per call ratio = $\dfrac{\text{Total costs}}{\text{Number of calls}}$

Account Development and Servicing Ratios

- Account penetration ratio = $\dfrac{\text{Accounts sold}}{\text{Total accounts available}}$

- New-account conversion ratio = $\dfrac{\text{Number of new accounts}}{\text{Total number of accounts}}$

- Lost account ratio = $\dfrac{\text{Prior accounts not sold}}{\text{Total number of accounts}}$

- Sales per account ratio = $\dfrac{\text{Sales dollar volume}}{\text{Total number of accounts}}$

- Average order size ratio = $\dfrac{\text{Sales dollar volume}}{\text{Total number of orders}}$

- Order cancellation ratio = $\dfrac{\text{Number of cancelled orders}}{\text{Total number of orders}}$

- Account share = $\dfrac{\text{Salesperson's business from account}}{\text{Account's total business}}$

Call Activity or Productivity

- Calls per day ratio = $\dfrac{\text{Number of calls}}{\text{Number of days worked}}$

- Calls per account ratio = $\dfrac{\text{Number of calls}}{\text{Number of accounts}}$

- Planned call ratio = $\dfrac{\text{Number of planned calls}}{\text{Total number of calls}}$

- Orders per call (hit) ratio = $\dfrac{\text{Number of orders}}{\text{Total number of calls}}$

Output Measures

Output measures represent the results of the efforts expended by the salesperson.

Orders

The number of orders each salesperson secures is often used to assess the rep's ability to ultimately close sales. Although the number of orders a salesperson secures is important, the average size of those orders is equally so. Having many orders may mean the orders are small and may indicate the person is spending too much time calling on small, low-potential customers and not enough time calling on large, high-potential customers.

Still another related measure is the number of canceled orders. A salesperson who loses a large proportion of total orders to subsequent cancellation may be using high-pressure tactics in sales presentations rather than engaging in relationship selling.

Accounts

The various account measures provide a perspective on the equity of territory assignments and also on how the salesperson is handling the territory. Attention to these measures can help the sales manager overcome the tendency to discount territory difficulty information as discussed in the Leadership box on p. 408. One popular measure focuses on the number of active accounts in the salesperson's customer portfolio. Various definitions of an active account are used. For example, it may be any customer that has placed an order in the past six months or in the past year. A salesperson's performance in one year may be compared with performance in past years by contrasting the number of active accounts. Closely related to this yardstick is a measure that tracks the number of new accounts a salesperson develops in a given time. Some companies even establish new-prospect quotas for salespeople that allow a ready comparison of performance to standards in this area of evaluation.

As with the number of new accounts, the number of lost accounts can be a revealing statistic, since it indicates how successfully the salesperson is satisfying the ongoing needs of the established accounts in the territory. Still other account measures by which salespeople can be compared are the number of overdue accounts, which might indicate the level to which the salesperson is following company procedures in screening accounts for their creditworthiness, and the number of prospective accounts, which assesses the salesperson's ability to identify potential target customers.

Input Measures

Many objective measures of performance evaluation focus on the efforts sales representatives expend rather than the results of those efforts. These efforts are input measures of performance. Input measures are important for two key reasons. First, efforts or desirable behaviors are much more directly controllable than results in the short term. If a rep's sales fall short of quota, the problem may lie with the person, the quota, or a change in the environment. On the other hand, if the number of calls a salesperson makes falls short of the target, it is much clearer that the problem lies more directly with the individual.[4] Second, in relationship selling a time lag frequently exists between inputs and outputs. A particularly large sale may be the result of several years of effort. Thus, a focus on the efforts (behaviors) themselves affords the sales manager the opportunity to evaluate and coach the salesperson during the relationship selling process into making changes that can positively affect the output (results).

Calls

The number of current customer or prospect calls is often used to decide whether a salesperson is covering the territory properly. The number of calls on each account is an important factor in the design of territories and also should be used to evaluate the salesperson assigned to the territory. After all, sales calls are a resource with finite supply—they represent a resource that is time-sensitive in that the time available to make them evaporates if it is not used.

CRM software systems integrate customer contacts by salespeople into their information collection, analysis, and reporting capabilities. Also, contact and customer management software, such as GoldMine by FrontRange and Act! by Sage, automates the call report process. In a record established for each account, the salesperson can input information about each call. This information can be summarized by the software for a report made available to the sales manager either by e-mail or Web access. Of course, if the CRM software resides on a shared network, the sales manager can access the information directly. Such technological advances minimize the time spent preparing paperwork and help salespeople maximize their time in front of buyers; they also serve as a great aid to sales managers in performance evaluation.

Time and Time Utilization

The number of days worked and the calls per day (or call rate) are routinely used by many companies to assess salespeople's efforts since the product of the two quantities provides a direct measure of the extent of customer contact. If the amount of customer contact by a salesperson is low, one can look separately at the components to see where the problem lies. Perhaps the salesperson has not been working enough because of extenuating circumstances, a situation that would show up in the number of days worked. Alternatively, perhaps the salesperson's total time input was satisfactory, but the salesperson was not using that time wisely and, consequently, had a low call rate.

Comparing salespeople's division of time between sales calls, traveling, office work, and other job aspects offers a useful perspective. For the most part, the firm would want salespeople to maximize the time in face-to-face customer contact at the expense of the other two factors. Sales organizations want salespeople to minimize unproductive time. Of course, *telecommuting*, or working from a home office, is not new in the field of professional selling. Through necessity (e.g., no company facility from which to work in the salesperson's headquarters city) or convenience, many salespeople maintain their primary office space in their home.

Analysis of time utilization requires detailed input on how each salesperson is spending time, and collecting and analyzing this data can be expensive and can itself be time-consuming. Some companies, however, routinely conduct such analysis because the benefits are deemed to outweigh the costs.

Expenses

The objective inputs discussed so far for evaluating salespeople (calls; time and time utilization) focus mainly on the extent of a salesperson's efforts. Another key emphasis when evaluating salespeople is the cost of those efforts. Many firms keep records detailing the total expenses incurred by each salesperson. Some break these expenses down by type, such as automobile expenses, lodging expenses, entertainment expenses, and so forth. Sales managers might look at these expenses in total or as a percentage of sales or quota by salesperson and then use these expense ratios as part of the salesperson's performance evaluation.

Nonselling Activities

In addition to assessing the direct contact of salespeople with customers, some firms monitor indirect contact. They use indexes such as the number of letters written, number of telephone calls made, and number of formal proposals developed.

As we have learned, in relationship selling a salesperson's activities go beyond what might be considered a pure selling emphasis. For example, companies that sell to retailers may ask salespeople to help monitor and stock shelves, create displays, help retailers advertise, and engage in a number of other nonselling activities as part of an ongoing client relationship. In such instances, firms often try to monitor the extent of these duties, using such indexes as the number of promotional or advertising displays set up, the number of dealer meetings, the number of training sessions for distributor personnel held, the number of calls the salesperson made on dealer customers, the number of service calls made, the number of customer complaints received, and the number of overdue accounts collected. Some of this information can be gathered from the salesperson's reporting system, but it is becoming increasingly commonplace to gain feedback on elements of salesperson performance directly from customers. This trend is discussed in a later section of this chapter on 360-degree performance feedback.

Ratio Measures

As we have learned, a focus on outputs other than straight sales volume and profit can provide useful information on how salespeople are performing. So can analysis of input factors. Additional insights may also be gathered by combining the various outputs or inputs in selected ways, typically in the form of various ratio measures. As mentioned earlier, Exhibit 13.2 lists some of the ratios commonly used to evaluate salespeople. These are grouped by expense ratios, account development and servicing ratios, and call activity or productivity ratios.

Expense Ratios

The sales expense ratio combines both salespeople's inputs and the results produced by those inputs in a single number. Salespeople can affect this ratio either by making sales or by controlling expenses. The ratio can also be used to analyze salesperson expenses by type. Thus, a sales/transportation expense ratio that is much higher for one salesperson than others might indicate the salesperson is covering his or her territory inefficiently. However, it is important that the sales manager recognize territory difficulty differences when comparing these ratios, as the salesperson who has an out-of-line ratio may simply have a larger, more geographically dispersed sales territory to cover.

The cost per call ratio expresses the costs of supporting each salesperson in the field as a function of the number of calls the salesperson makes. The ratio can be evaluated using total costs, or the costs can be broken down by elements so that ratios such as expenses per call and travel costs per call can be computed. Not only are these ratios useful for comparing salespeople from the same firm, but they can also be compared with those of other companies in the same industry to assess the efficiency of the firm's selling effort. Such comparative data may be available from trade or professional associations.

Account Development and Servicing Ratios

A number of ratios concern accounts and orders that reflect on how well salespeople are capturing the potential business that exists in their territories. The account penetration ratio, for example, measures the percentage of accounts in the territory from which the salesperson secures orders. It provides a direct measure of whether the salesperson is simply skimming the cream of the business or is working the territory systematically and hard. It can also aid management in identifying both underperforming accounts and accounts that have low lifetime value to the sales organization.

The new-account conversion ratio similarly measures the salesperson's ability to convert prospects to customers. The lost account ratio measures how well the salesperson maintains active customers, reflecting how well the rep is serving the established accounts in the territory.

The sales per account ratio indicates the salesperson's success per account on average. A low ratio could indicate the salesperson is spending too much time calling on small, less profitable accounts and not enough time calling on larger ones. One could also look at the sales per account ratios by class of account, which can reveal the strengths and weaknesses of each salesperson. For example, a salesperson who has a low sales per account ratio for large, high-potential accounts might need help in learning how to sell to a buying center.

The average order size ratio can also reveal the salesperson's patterns of calling on customers. A very low average order size might suggest that calls are too frequent and the salesperson's productivity could be improved by spacing them more. The order cancellation ratio reflects on the salesperson's method of selling. A very high ratio could mean the salesperson is using high-pressure tactics to secure orders rather than pursuing relationship selling approaches and handling customers in a consultative manner.

A key measurement in some types of businesses, particularly those that provide supplies and raw materials, is account share. Account share is the percentage of the account's business that the salesperson gets. Many buyers will split their business among a number of vendors, believing (often erroneously) that they get better service and lower prices when sellers have to compete for the business. In industries where such buying practices are prevalent, the number of accounts is less important to salespeople than the share of each account. As account share increases, economies of scale increase, which raises the profit of the account. Similarly, the measure is an indication of the strength of the relationship with the account.

Call Activity or Productivity Ratios

Call activity ratios measure the effort and planning salespeople put into their customer call activities and the successes they derive from it. The measures might be used to compare salesperson activities in total—such as when using calls per day or when using calls per total number of accounts, or by type of account. The planned call ratio could be used to assess if the salesperson is systematically planning territory coverage or whether the representative is working the territory without an overall game plan. The orders per call ratio bears directly on the question of whether the salesperson's calls on average are productive. This ratio is sometimes called the hit ratio or batting average, since it captures the number of successes (hits or orders) in relation to the number of at-bats (calls).

SUMMARY OF OBJECTIVE MEASURES

As Exhibits 13.1, 13.2, and the preceding discussion indicate, many objective output measures, input measures, and ratio measures are available by which salespeople may be evaluated and compared. As you probably sense, many of the measures are somewhat redundant in that they provide overlapping information on salesperson effectiveness. A number of other ratios could be developed by combining the various outputs, inputs, or ratios in different ways. For example, one combination that is often used to evaluate salespeople is the following equation:

$$\text{Sales} = \text{Days worked} \times \frac{\text{Calls}}{\text{Days worked}} \times \frac{\text{Orders}}{\text{Calls}} \times \frac{\text{Sales}}{\text{Orders}}$$

or

$$\text{Sales} = \frac{\text{Days}}{\text{worked}} \times \frac{\text{Call}}{\text{rate}} \times \frac{\text{Batting}}{\text{average}} \times \frac{\text{Average}}{\text{order size}}$$

The equation highlights nicely what a salesperson can do to increase sales. The representative can increase the (1) number of days worked, (2) calls made per day, (3) level of success in securing an order on a given call, and (4) size of those orders. Thus, the equation can be used to isolate how an individual salesperson's performance could be improved. Such an equation, though, focuses on the results of the salesperson's efforts and ignores the cost of those efforts. Similarly, many of the other measures that have been reviewed could be combined via similar equations, but these too would probably ignore one or more elements of salesperson success. Bottom line: No single measure exists that can fully capture the scope of salesperson effectiveness.

In concluding this discussion of objective measures of salesperson performance, two essential points deserve mention. First, just as measuring straight sales volume and profit have advantages and disadvantages for use in evaluating salespeople, so do all of these other objective measures of performance. Rather than relying on only one or two of the measures to assess performance, the methods are more productively used in combination. Second, and also very important, all of the indexes are an aid to judgment, not a substitute for it. For example, the United States Army Recruiting Command (the part of the Army that sells young people on joining) once overrelied on conversion ratios (the percentage of prospects who actually ended up joining the army) to evaluate recruiters' performance. Orders were issued that calls of certain types had to be increased by a high percentage. The problem was that while the calls could be increased, quality could not be maintained. Recruiting effectiveness not only did not increase but actually went down as recruiter morale declined. The comparisons allowed by the various indexes should be the beginning, not the conclusion, of any analysis aimed at assessing how well individual salespeople or the entire sales force are doing.

SUBJECTIVE MEASURES

A useful conceptual distinction exists between the quantitative nature of objective measures of performance discussed in the preceding section and the qualitative nature of the subjective measures discussed here. Quantitative measures of performance focus on the outputs and inputs of what salespeople do, whereas qualitative measures reflect behavioral or process aspects of what they do and how well they do it. This difference in what is being measured creates some marked differences in the way objective and subjective measurements are taken and how they are used.

In many ways, it is more difficult to assess the quality rather than the quantity of a salesperson's performance. Quantity measures can require a detailed analysis of a salesperson's call report, an extensive time utilization analysis, or an analysis of the type and number of nonselling activities employed. However, once the measurement procedure is set up, it typically can be conducted with less bias and inconsistency than can quality measurement. On the other hand, when assessing qualitative performance factors, even a well-designed measurement process that is firmly in place leaves much more room for bias in the evaluation. Bias refers to performance evaluations that differ from objective reality, usually based on errors by the evaluator. Even well-designed systems must invariably rely on the personal judgment of the individual or individuals charged with evaluation—in our case, the sales manager. Typically, these judgments are secured by having the manager rate the salesperson on a performance appraisal form on each of a number of attributes using some type of rating scale. The attributes most commonly evaluated using performance evaluation forms include the following:

1. *Sales results.* Volume performance, sales to new accounts, and selling the full product line.

2. *Job knowledge.* Knowledge of company policies, prices, and products.

3. *Management of territory.* Planning of activities and calls, controlling expenses, and handling reports and records.

4. *Customer and company relations.* The salesperson's standing with customers, associates, and company.

5. *Personal characteristics.* Initiative, personal appearance, personality, resourcefulness, etc.

Note that these include a mix of objective and subjective performance measures. In fact, it is true that most formal performance evaluations of salespeople involve a combination of these two types of evaluative criteria.[5]

Forms Used for Subjective Measurement

Exhibit 13.3 shows a typical salesperson evaluation form for various subjective performance criteria. The specific evaluative criteria should match those identified as key success factors for the position (see Chapter 2 for a discussion of the identification of key success factors for sales positions). Such evaluations may be completed annually, semiannually, or quarterly, depending on the firm's human resource management policies. These evaluations supplement the objective performance data generated for the same time frame to provide an overall evaluation of salesperson performance. The form in Exhibit 13.3 is better than many of those in use because it contains anchors or verbal descriptors for the various points on the scale. Another favorable feature of this example form is the space provided for comments, which can enhance understanding of the ratings supplied. The form contains a section where needed improvements and corrective actions may be detailed. All in all, the form should facilitate a constructive dialogue between the salesperson and sales manager and help the salesperson understand his or her strengths and weaknesses and develop approaches to improve performance.

The worst type of rating forms simply list the attributes of interest along one side of the form and the evaluation adjectives along the other. Little description is provided, thus the potential for much ambiguity exists in the evaluation. Exhibit 13.4 illustrates such a poor form. Of course, this type of form can be completed very easily since the evaluator simply checks the box for the adjective that most clearly describes his or her perceptions of the salesperson's performance on each attribute. Unfortunately, such forms are quite common in sales organizations, and they work very poorly in practice and do little to stimulate a constructive dialogue between the salesperson and sales manager. Salespeople typically receive little useful information on improving performance when forms such as Exhibit 13.4 are used.

Problems with Subjective Performance Measurement

Some common problems with performance appraisal systems that rely on subjective rating forms, particularly those using the simple checklist type, include the following:[6]

1. *Lack of an outcome focus.* The most useful type of performance appraisal highlights areas of improvement and the actions that must be taken to implement such improvements. For this to occur, the key behaviors in accomplishing the tasks assigned must be identified. Unfortunately, many companies have not taken this step. Rather, they have simply identified attributes thought to be related to performance, but they have not attempted to systematically assess whether the attributes are key. One type of performance appraisal called BARS (behavioral anchored rating scale) helps overcome this weakness. A BARS system attempts to identify behaviors that are more or less effective with respect to the goals established for the person. BARS will be discussed in more detail shortly.

2. *Ill-defined personality traits.* Many performance evaluation forms contain personality factors as attributes. In the case of salespeople, these attributes might include such things as initiative and resourcefulness. Although these attributes are intuitively appealing, their actual relationship to performance is open to question.[7]

3. *Halo effect.* A halo effect is a common phenomenon in the use of any performance evaluation form. It refers to the fact that the rating assigned to one characteristic may significantly influence the ratings assigned to all other characteristics, as well as the overall rating. The halo effect holds that a sales manager's overall evaluations can be predicted quite well from their rating of the salesperson on the single performance dimension they believe is the most important. Different branch or regional managers might have different beliefs about what is most important, compounding the problem.

4. *Leniency or harshness.* Some sales managers rate at the extremes. Some are very lenient and rate every salesperson as good or outstanding on every attribute, whereas others do just the opposite. This behavior is often a function of their own personalities and their perceptions of what comprises outstanding performance, and no fundamental differences may exist in the way the salespeople under each of the managers are actually performing. The use of different definitions of performance depending on the manager can seriously undermine the whole performance appraisal system.

5. *Central tendency.* Some managers err in the opposite direction in that they never, or very rarely, rate people at the ends of the scale. Rather, they use middle-of-the road or play-it-safe ratings. One learns very little from such ratings about true differences in performance, and such ratings can be particularly troublesome when a company attempts to use a history of poor performance as the basis of a termination decision.

EXHIBIT 13.3
Sample subjective performance evaluation form

SALES PERSONNEL
INVENTORY

Employee's Name _____ Territory _____

Position Title _____ Date _____

INSTRUCTIONS (Read Carefully)

1. Base your judgment on the previous six-month period and not on isolated incidents alone.
2. Place a check in the block that most nearly expresses your judgment on each factor.
3. For those employees who are rated at either extreme of the scale on any factor—for example, outstanding, deficient, limited—please enter a brief explanation for the rating in the appropriate space below the factor.
4. Make your rating an accurate description of the person rated.

FACTORS TO BE CONSIDERED AND RATED:

1. **Knowledge of work** (includes knowledge of product, knowledge of customers' business)	☐ Does not have sufficient knowledge of products and application to represent the company effectively.	☐ Has mastered minimum knowledge. Needs further training	☐ Has average amount of knowledge needed to handle job satisfactorily.	☐ Is above average in knowledge needed to handle job satisfactorily.	☐ Is thoroughly acquainted with our products and technical problems involved in this application.

Comments _____

_____

2. **Degree of acceptance by customers**	☐ Not acceptable to most customers. Cannot gain entry to their offices.	☐ Manages to see customers but not generally liked.	☐ Has satisfactory relationship with most customers.	☐ Is on very good terms and is accepted by virtually all customers.	☐ Enjoys excellent personal relationship with virtually all customers.

Comments _____

_____

3. **Amount of effort devoted to acquiring business**	☐ Exceptional in the amount of time and effort put forth in selling.	☐ Devotes constant effort in developing business.	☐ Devotes intermittent effort in acquiring moderate amount of business.	☐ Exerts only minimum amount of time and effort.	☐ Unsatisfactory. Does not put forth sufficient effort to produce business.

Comments _____

_____

(continued)

EXHIBIT 13.3 Sample subjective performance evaluation form (continued)	**4. Ability to acquire business**	☐ Is able to acquire business under the most difficult situations.	☐ Does a good job acquiring business under most circumstances.	☐ Manages to acquire good percentage of customer's business if initial resistance is not too strong.	☐ Able to acquire enough business to maintain only a minimum sales average.	☐ Rarely able to acquire business except in a seller's market.
		Comments _____ _____				
	5. Amount of service given to customers	☐ Rarely services accounts once a sale is made.	☐ Gives only minimum service at all times.	☐ Services accounts with regularity but does not do any more than called on to do.	☐ Gives very good service to all customers.	☐ Goes out of the way to give outstanding service within scope of company policy.
		Comments _____ _____				
	6. Dependability— amount of supervision needed	☐ Always thoroughly abreast of problems in the territory, even under most difficult conditions. Rises to emergencies and assumes leadership without being requested to do so.	☐ Consistently reliable under normal conditions. Does special as well as regular assignments promptly. Little or no supervision required.	☐ Performs with reasonable promptness under normal supervision.	☐ Effort occasionally lags. Requires more than normal supervision.	☐ Requires close supervision in all phases of job.
		Comments _____ _____				
	7. Attitude toward company— support given to company policy	☐ Does not support company policy—	☐ Gives only passive support to company policy—does	☐ Goes along with company policy on most	☐ Adopts and supports company policy in	☐ Gives unwavering support to the *(continued)*

blames the company for factors that affect customers unfavorably.	not act as member of a team.	occasions.	all transactions.	company and company policy to customers even though he/she personally may not agree with the policy.	**EXHIBIT 13.3** Sample subjective performance evaluation form (continued)

Comments _____

_____

8. Judgment

☐	☐	☐	☐	☐
Analyses and conclusions subject to frequent error and are often based on bias. Decisions require careful review by supervisor.	Judgments usually sound on routine, simple matters but cannot be relied on when any degree of complexity is involved.	Capable of careful analyzing of day-to-day problems involving some complexity and rendering sound decisions. Decision rarely influenced by prejudice or personal bias.	Decisions can be accepted without question except when problems or extreme complexity are involved. Little or no personal bias enters into judgment.	Possesses unusual comprehension and analytical ability. Complete reliance may be placed on all judgments irrespective of degree of complexity. Decisions and judgments are completely free of personal bias or prejudice.

Comments _____

_____

9. Resourcefulness

☐	☐	☐	☐	☐
Work is consistently characterized by marked originality, alertness, initiative, and imagination. Can be relied on to develop new ideas and techniques in solving the most difficult problems.	Frequently develops new ideas of merit. Handling of emergencies is generally characterized by sound decisive action.	Meets new situations in satisfactory manner. Occasionally develops original ideas, methods, and techniques.	Follows closely previously learned methods and procedures. Slow to adapt to changes. Tends to become confused in new situations.	Requires frequent reinstruction. Has failed to demonstrate initiative or imagination in solving problems.

(continued)

EXHIBIT 13.3
Sample subjective performance evaluation form (continued)

Comments _____
_____

10. Based on the above evaluation, this employee should:

1. Be given additional instruction on _____
_____

2. Be given additional experience such as _____

3. Study such subjects as _____

4. Change attitude as follows _____

5. There is nothing more that I can do for this employee because _____

6. Remarks _____
_____
_____

EXHIBIT 13.4
Sample of a poorly constructed subjective performance evaluation form

	Poor	Fair	Satisfactory	Good	Outstanding
Knowledge of work	☐	☐	☐	☐	☐
Degree of acceptance by customers	☐	☐	☐	☐	☐
Amount of effort devoted to acquiring business	☐	☐	☐	☐	☐
Ability to acquire business	☐	☐	☐	☐	☐
Amount of service given to customers	☐	☐	☐	☐	☐
Dependability, amount of supervision needed	☐	☐	☐	☐	☐
Attitude toward company, support for company policies	☐	☐	☐	☐	☐
Judgment	☐	☐	☐	☐	☐
Resourcefulness	☐	☐	☐	☐	☐

6. *Interpersonal bias.* Interpersonal bias refers to the fact that our perceptions of others and the social acceptability of their behaviors are influenced by how much we like or dislike them personally. Many sales managers' evaluations of sales reps are similarly affected. Furthermore, research suggests a salesperson can use personal influence or impression management strategies on the manager to bias evaluations upward.

7. *Organizational uses influence.* Performance ratings are often affected by the use to which they will be put within the organization. If promotions and monetary payments hinge on the ratings, a tendency may exist toward leniency on the part of the manager who values the friendship and support of subordinates who press for higher ratings. It is not difficult to imagine the dilemma of a district sales manager if other district sales teams received consistently higher compensation increments and more promotions than his or her sales group. On the

other hand, when appraisals are used primarily for the development of subordinates, managers tend to more freely pinpoint weaknesses and focus on what is wrong and how it can be improved.[8]

By now, it should be clear that performance evaluation may be fraught with opportunities for biases and inaccuracies to creep into the process. The Leadership box describes one form of potential evaluator bias in more detail, the outcome bias. An outcome bias occurs when a sales manager allows the outcome of a decision or a series of decisions made by a salesperson to overly influence the performance ratings made by the manager.

Avoiding Errors in Performance Evaluation

To guard against the distortions introduced in the performance appraisal system by problems such as those listed earlier, many firms provide extensive training and guidelines to sales managers on completing the forms and conducting the appraisal process. Some common instructions issued with such forms include,

1. Read the definitions of each trait thoroughly and carefully before rating.

2. Guard against the common tendency to overrate.

3. Do not let personal likes or dislikes influence your ratings. Be as objective as possible.

4. Do not permit your evaluation of one factor to influence your evaluation of another.

5. Base your rating on the observed performance of the salesperson, not on potential abilities.

6. Never rate an employee on several instances of good or poor work, but rather on general success or failure over the whole period.

7. Have sound reasons for your ratings.[9]

These admonitions can help, particularly when the evaluator must supply the reasons for ratings. However, they do not resolve problems related to the selection of attributes for evaluation and how the resulting items are presented on the form. A trend in performance appraisal directed at resolving this issue is the BARS (behaviorally anchored rating scale).

Using a BARS System

A BARS system attempts to concentrate on the behaviors and other performance criteria that can be controlled by the individual. The system focuses on the fact

LEADERSHIP   Outcome Bias in Salesperson Performance Evaluations

By nature, professional selling is focused on bottom-line results. Persons who are successful in sales tend to like meeting tough goals and thrive on the immediacy, regularity, and visibility of feedback on their results. Thus, it is common for results (or outcomes) in sales to be viewed by management as a surrogate for the behavioral side of salesperson performance. In short: Make your quota, you must be doing things right; but miss your quota and, boy, are you ever doing the wrong things.

These "things" we are talking about are all the process steps that go into the job of selling. On a very basic level, they are all the decisions made by the salesperson over the course of a day, week, month, quarter, and year that add up to that person's performance (remember, earlier in this chapter we defined performance in terms of behavior evaluated in the context of its contributions to the goals of the organization).

Sometimes the outcomes and the process leading to those outcomes match: for example, a salesperson has a great sales quarter and also was great at doing all the things that are part of the sales job (presentations, customer care, administration, etc.). Clearly, the sales manager should recognize and reward this achievement. And in the opposite case, where a salesperson has a lousy sales quarter and also is struggling with the process elements of the job, clearly the sales manager needs to document the poor performance and a developmental plan needs to be put in place.

But what about the mixed cases? Consider the salesperson who has a great sales quarter but is not cutting the mustard in the day-to-day elements of the job. Maybe the favorable outcome was due to an unexpected windfall from a client, an easy territory, or some other event not directly attributable to much of anything the salesperson actually did to earn the business. Evaluating this salesperson favorably overall, based strictly on his or her performance outcome, can open a huge can of worms in a sales unit, as peer salespeople will see this person as a slacker who got lucky. And finally, perhaps the worst case of all, consider the salesperson who has a lousy sales quarter but has done absolutely everything right. If this salesperson is evaluated as a poor performer, based strictly on the outcome, chances are the organization will lose him or her.

The outcome bias is that evaluators tend to overlook process and rate performers based on outcomes. As illustrated in the mixed-case examples here, this tendency of outcome to overwhelm process can lead to poor morale, ill will, and turnover within the sales force.

It should be mentioned, however, that one school of thought in sales is that a bias toward outcomes isn't really a bias at all. That is, salespeople know when they get into the profession that bottom-line sales volume is the key to success. This perspective may be somewhat valid in straight commission selling situations. But in most of today's relationship-driven professional sales jobs, it is folly to utilize performance evaluation systems that ignore good, or bad, behavioral aspects of performance in favor of just the short-run bottom line. As we have learned, much of what constitutes success in relationship-driven sales organizations involves a complex set of actions inside and outside the selling firm, and the true outcome of these activities may not be realized for a long time. Fortunately, most modern sales organizations understand the threat of the outcome bias and work to integrate multiple aspects of performance into the evaluation process. One approach that addresses this is the BARS system, which is discussed in this chapter.

that a number of factors affect any employee's performance. However, some of these factors are more critical to job success than are others, and the key to evaluating people is to focus on these *critical success factors* (CSFs).[10] Implementing a BARS system for evaluating salespeople requires identifying the behaviors that are key to their performance. Also, the subsequent evaluation of a salesperson's performance must be conducted by rating these key behaviors using the appropriate descriptions.[11]

The process of developing a BARS system goes as follows. First, the key behaviors with respect to performance are identified using critical incidents. *Critical incidents* are occurrences that are vital (critical) to performance. To use the critical incident technique, those involved could be asked to identify some particularly outstanding examples of good or bad performance and to detail the reasons why.[12] The performances identified are then reduced to a smaller number of performance dimensions.

Next, the group of critical incidents is presented to a group of sales personnel who are asked to assign each critical incident to an appropriate performance dimension. An incident is typically kept in if 60 percent or more of the group assigns it to the same dimension as did the instrument development group. The sales personnel group is also asked to rate the behavior described in the critical incident on a 7- or 10-point scale with respect to how effectively or ineffectively it represents performance on the dimension. Incidents that generate good agreement in ratings, typically indicated by a low standard deviation, are considered for the final scale. The particular incidents chosen are determined by their location along the scale, as measured by the mean scores. Typically, the final scale has six to eight anchors. An example of a BARS scale that resulted from such a process for the attribute "promptness in meeting deadlines" is shown in Exhibit 13.5.

A key advantage of a BARS system is that it requires sales managers to consider in detail a wide range of components of a salesperson's job performance. It must also include clearly defined anchors for those performance criteria in specific behavioral terms, leading to thoughtful consideration by managers of just what comprises performance. Of course, by nature a BARS emphasizes behavior and

Very high This indicates the more-often-than-not practice of submitting accurate and needed sales reports.	10.0 ___ 9.0 ___ 8.0 ___ 7.0 ___	Could be expected to promptly submit all necessary field reports even in the most difficult of situations. Could be expected to promptly meet deadlines comfortably in most report completion situations.
Moderate This indicates regularity in promptly submitting accurate and needed field sales reports.	6.0 ___ 5.0 ___ 4.0 ___	Is usually on time and can be expected to submit most routine field sales reports in proper format. Could be expected to regularly be tardy in submitting required field sales reports.
Very low This indicates irregular and unacceptable promptness and accuracy of field sales reports.	3.0 ___ 2.0 ___ 1.0 ___ 0.0	Could be expected to be tardy and submit inaccurate field sales reports. Could be expected to completely disregard due dates for filing almost all reports. Could be expected to never file field sales reports on time and resist any managerial guidance to improve this tendency.

EXHIBIT 13.5
A BARS scale with behavioral anchors for the attribute "promptness in meeting deadlines"

ETHICAL MOMENT Ethical Challenges in Evaluation

Few sales management activities are more important to a salesperson than performance evaluation. And while the ultimate metric—sales volume—is the most widely used metric of salesperson performance, as you have read it is clearly not the only one that has value. The reality is that salespeople need to be evaluated across a broad range of metrics to assess their overall effectiveness. For example, a salesperson may drive huge sales numbers but also have higher expenses, and in the end that individual's overall profit contribution to the company could be poor.

Once evaluative criteria move past objective performance measures things get particularly tricky for sales managers. On the subjective measure side of the coin, it is easy to allow personal feelings to enter the evaluation process, creating a distorted viewpoint of the salesperson's actual performance. The question, from the sales manager's perspective, is can he or she put aside personal feelings about an individual and overcome inherent potential biases to accurately evaluate performance? Put another way, it's easy to review the sales numbers and other objective metrics and make a determination but how do you effectively assess important activities like willingness to help colleagues or customer service? Key to an effective evaluation process is the belief by the salesperson that the process is fair—it can be tough but if it is fair it goes a long way to removing questions or doubts about the process.

Companies are aware of this issue and work hard to train sales managers on implementing the performance evaluation process. Also, if a change in the performance evaluation criteria is anticipated, as you might imagine sales organizations and their managers must take care to clearly explain those changes well in advance of when the new "rules of the game" kick in. Otherwise it can be unfair to the sales force and negatively impact salesperson motivation and performance

Question to Ponder:

- How might personal subjectivity influence the sales performance evaluation process? As a sales manager how would you work to minimize the problem of bias entering the evaluation process?

---

performance rather than effectiveness. When used in tandem with appropriate objective measures (sales and profit analyses and output, input, and ratio measures), a BARS approach provides an attractive means of handling subjective evaluation criteria and thus providing as complete a picture as possible of a salesperson's overall performance and effectiveness.

BARS systems are not without their limitations, though. For one thing, the job-specific nature of the scales they utilize suggests they are most effective in evaluating salespeople performing very similar functions. They might be effective in comparing one key account rep to another key account rep or two territory representatives against each other, but they could suffer major shortcomings if used to compare a key account rep against a territory salesperson because of differences in responsibilities in these positions. BARS systems also can be relatively costly to develop since they require a good deal of up-front time from multiple people.[13]

360-DEGREE FEEDBACK IN PERFORMANCE EVALUATION

As we learned in Chapter 3, one important attraction of CRM systems to firms is the inherent capability of such systems to provide feedback from a wide range of constituents and stakeholders. Although the usage focus of much of this information is on product development and formulation of the overall marketing message, CRM systems typically also facilitate the gathering, analysis, and dissemination of a great deal of information directly relevant to the performance of the sales force.

In order for a sales organization to take full advantage of the available information generated by enterprise software such as CRM, the firm as a whole must embrace the philosophy that the customer is a customer of the *company*, not just of the individual salesperson. We have seen that the complex and often lengthy process of developing and managing customer relationships almost always involves more than just a salesperson and purchasing agent. An effective CRM system should be gathering data at all the important touchpoints where members of a selling organization interact with members of a buying organization, or members of a selling organization interact internally in order to forward a business relationship with a customer.

Such a comprehensive information management process allows for a rethinking of the nature of input data for use in salesperson performance evaluation. Rather than relying on purely objective measures or on subjective measures generated by one person (the sales manager), information for performance evaluation may come from multiple sources simultaneously. This concept of 360-degree performance feedback opens the door to a new era in using the performance appraisal process as an effective tool for salesperson development and improvement. Among the sources of feedback that would be useful to salespeople are external customers, internal organization members who serve as resources in serving external customers (this group is often referred to as internal customers), other members of the salesperson's selling team, any direct reports the sales manager may have (such as sales assistants), and of course the sales manager.[14] Integrating feedback from these and other relevant sources of performance information into the formal evaluation process (and thus onto the evaluation form) can provide the impetus for a more productive dialogue between the sales manager and salesperson when performance review time comes around.

One other issue deserves mention related to 360-degree feedback—self-evaluation. Sales organizations should encourage salespeople to prepare an honest assessment of their own performance against the established objective and subjective performance criteria, and this should be prepared *prior* to the formal performance review session with the sales manager.[15] The best sales organizations use this process to begin the dialogue of sales unit goal-setting for the next period, and especially to establish a professional development program to help move the salesperson toward the fulfillment of his or her personal goals on the job. We learned in Chapter 11 that intrinsic rewards are among the most powerful motivators—things such as feelings of accomplishment, personal growth, and self-worth. Allowing the salesperson to have direct input in establishing personal growth goals on the job, and then institutionalizing the achievement of those goals via the formal performance evaluation process, goes a long way toward providing a workplace atmosphere in which intrinsic rewards may be realized by salespeople.

It is particularly important to involve salespeople directly in all phases of the performance appraisal process. When appraisals provide clear criteria, the criteria meet with the salesperson's approval, and the appraisals are perceived as fair and used in determining rewards, salesperson job satisfaction increases. Thus, the critical determinants of appraisal effectiveness are not purely criteria-driven but rather are largely determined by appraisal process factors that managers can influence, such as buy-in by those being appraised and fairness with which the appraisal process is administered.[16]

An old adage in human resource management holds that if an employee is surprised by anything he or she is told during a formal performance review, the manager providing the evaluation is not doing a very good job. Performance evaluation should not be simply one cathartic event that happens periodically. Such a view can cause great trepidation on the part of both employees and managers, and it often results in managers procrastinating in conducting the review and minimizing the time spent with the employee during the review. In contrast, great sales organizations use the performance evaluation process to facilitate *ongoing* dialogue between salespeople and their managers. The key goal of the process should be facilitating professional and personal development—providing the salesperson the feedback and tools necessary to achieve his or her goals in the job. To make this happen, sales managers must be prepared to carry on the dialogue beyond just the periodic formal appraisal event and into day-to-day communication with the salesperson. Importantly, this developmental perspective on performance evaluation requires

---

INNOVATION   Making Appraisals More Effective

Appraisals can be a powerful tool if used correctly. Many managers dread the prospect of giving their staff honest feedback in the formal setting of the performance appraisal. The following are three steps to follow that should make the appraisal process more productive for both manager and employee:

1. Preparation—Have the reps rate themselves in the same areas that will be addressed in the appraisal. Focus on questions such as, Why is our organization a better place because you work here? In what areas do you need more support? What are your goals for the upcoming period?

2. Appraisal Interview—Make it clear that salary will not be discussed; use a separate meeting for this. The preparation work in step 1 will ensure that there is plenty to talk about. Focus on the areas where there may be differences in the answers to the preparation questions.

3. Post-appraisal—Hold a follow-up meeting and share the formal review documents. If salary is discussed be sure to provide a clear connection between decisions in this area and the issues that arose in the appraisal.

While pointing out flaws or areas that could be improved, do not neglect the power of acknowledgment for a job well done. While appraisals are an opportunity for a manager to improve the sales staff, the chance to build morale through positive reinforcement should not be missed.

that sales managers not just *give* feedback but also listen and respond to feedback and questions from the salesperson. The Innovation box provides insight on how sales managers can best use the performance appraisal process to the benefit of both the salesperson and manager.

Ultimately, sales organizations need to work toward developing a performance management system. To do so requires a commitment to integrating all the elements of feedback on the process of serving customers so that performance information is timely, accurate, and relevant to the customer management aspects of the firm.[17] The pieces of the performance puzzle are integrated in such a way that the salesperson does not have to wait on the manager for a formal validation of performance. Instead, under a performance management approach, salespeople take the lead in goal setting, performance measurement, and adjustment of their own performance.[18] The concept of performance management is analogous to TQM approaches that advocate the empowerment of employees to take ownership of their own jobs and conduct their own analyses of performance against goals, creating a culture of self-management. To successfully implement a performance management system, sales managers must shift their leadership style to that of a partner in a mutually shared process.

SUMMARY

Performance and effectiveness are different concepts. Performance may be thought of as a salesperson's behavior evaluated in terms of its contribution to the goals of the organization. On the other hand, effectiveness is an organizational outcome for which a salesperson is at least partly responsible, usually examined across a variety of indices.

Salespeople may be evaluated on the basis of objective and subjective criteria. Objective measures reflect statistics a sales manager can gather from a firm's internal data and other means and may be categorized as output measures (the results of the efforts expended by the salesperson) and input measures (the efforts they expend in achieving the results). Objective measures also may take the form of ratios that combine various outputs or inputs. On the other hand, subjective measures typically rely on personal evaluations of how the salesperson is doing, usually as viewed by the sales manager. In most cases, sales managers should pay attention to both objective and subjective measures in evaluating salespeople.

A variety of potential pitfalls exist in performance measurement, particularly utilizing subjective measures. These problems frequently take the form of various errors or biases in the evaluation, which result in an inaccurate performance appraisal that is perceived (rightly so) as unfair by the salesperson. Sales organizations and their managers must take great care to ensure that the performance evaluation process is conducted in as fair and accurate a manner as possible. Utilizing 360-degree feedback in the performance review, including a strong component of self-evaluation by the salesperson, can be very helpful in improving the usefulness of the performance evaluation process.

KEY TERMS

behavior	subjective measures	self-evaluation
performance	bias	performance management
effectiveness	outcome bias	system
attribution theory	BARS (behaviorally	
objective measures	anchored rating scale)	
output measures	360-degree performance	
input measures	feedback	
ratio measures	internal customers	

BREAKOUT QUESTIONS

1. Kevin Harrison, sales rep for Allied Steel Distributors, had an appointment with his sales manager to discuss his first-year sales performance. Kevin knew that the meeting would not go well. One of Allied's major accounts had changed suppliers due to problems with Kevin. The purchasing agent claimed that "personality differences" were so serious that future business with Allied was not possible. Kevin knew that these so-called personality differences involved his unwillingness to entertain in the same style as the previous sales rep. The previous sales rep frequently took the purchasing agent and others to a local topless bar for lunch. The rep told Kevin that this was expected and that if he wanted to keep the business, it was necessary. Besides, tickets to the professional basketball games didn't count anymore. What are the short- and long-range implications of this type of customer entertaining? What would you do in a similar situation? How should Kevin's sales manager react?

2. A large corporation notices an irregular decrease in the sales of a particular representative. The sales rep, normally in very high standing among other salespeople and quotas, has of late failed to achieve her own quota. What can be done by the sales manager to determine whether the slump in the sales curve is the responsibility of the representative or due to things beyond her control?

3. Given the following information from evaluations of the performance of different sales representatives, what possible conclusions can be made about why the sales reps are not achieving quota (assume each is not making quota)?

   a. Representative 1: Achieved goals for sales calls, telephone calls, and new accounts; customer relations good; no noticeable deficiencies in any areas.

   b. Representative 2: Completed substantially fewer sales calls than goal. Telephone calls high in number, but primarily with one firm. Time management analysis shows the sales rep to be spending a disproportionately large amount of time with one firm. New accounts are low; all other areas good to outstanding.

   c. Representative 3: Number of sales calls low, below goal. Telephone calls, letters, proposals all very low and below goal. Evaluation shows poor time utilization. Very high amount of service-related activities in sales representative's log; customer relations extremely positive; recently has received a great deal of feedback from customers on product function.

4. Is sales "just a numbers game," as one sales manager states? She believes that all you have to do is make the right number of calls of the right type, and the odds will work in your favor. Make 10 calls, get one sale. So to get two sales, make 20 calls. Is this the right approach? Why or why not?

5. Jackie Hitchcock, recently promoted to district sales manager, faced a new problem she wasn't sure how to resolve. The district's top sales rep is also the district's number-one problem. Brad Coombs traditionally leads the company in sales but also leads the company in problems. He has broken every rule, bent every policy, deviated from guidelines, and been less than truthful. Jackie knew Brad had never done anything illegal, but she was worried that something serious could happen. Other problems with Brad include not preparing call reports on time, failing to show up at trade shows, and not attending sales training programs. How should Jackie handle this problem? How does a sales manager manage a maverick sales rep? Specifically, how can the performance evaluation process help Jackie deal with Brad?

6. Ethical Moment. As sales manager for the largest sales region in your company (covering all of Asia), you are responsible for 20 salespeople that are widely geographically dispersed. The VP of sales has called you and told you that sales expenses must be reduced by 20 percent for the next fiscal year. This has a big impact on your sales team as they have high travel expenses due to the size of their territories. While you believe this 20 cut is unfair to your salespeople, the VP still expects you to implement the change. What should you do? Explain your rationale.

LEADERSHIP CHALLENGE: UNDERSTANDING SALESPERSON PERFORMANCE

Mike Hunt had been in sales for 20 years, and, as sales manager for Market First Distributors, he was confident of his ability to evaluate salespeople. Market First was a regional distributor of food products to restaurants. It competed with large distributors such as Sysco and had developed a very good reputation for great service and reasonable prices. The company had a sales force of 70 in six districts across five midwestern states. A formal evaluation process had been implemented nine years ago. The process focused on salespeople meeting specific targets on account development (sales per account and average order size) and call activity (calls per account). However, while the process had been successful in the past and everyone understood the expectations under the current system, Mike felt that something was missing.

Market First had begun to notice an increase in complaints with customers across all the sales districts. While the specific nature of the complaints varied, some themes showed up consistently. Customers were complaining that salespeople did not spend as much with them as they used to and were not as interested in the relationship.

Mike, as well as senior management, believed that it was time to broaden the performance evaluation process. They felt that by setting standards for territory management and customer satisfaction, the company could assess how well the sales force was doing in these critical areas. At this point, however, he was unsure how to set up such a system. As he sat in his office considering the options, he wondered if this would do more harm than good in the long run.

Questions

1. You are Mike Hunt. How would you measure a salesperson's territory management skills and his or her relationship with the customer?

2. Mike has asked you to come in and explain the strengths and weaknesses of objective versus subjective measures for territory management and relationships with customers. What would you say?

ROLE-PLAY: HARVEY INSURANCE AGENCY

Situation

Harvey Insurance Agency sells an extensive line of policies, representing several major insurance companies. Principal agent Bill Harvey started the business in 1993 with one office assistant, and since then the company has grown to become one of the largest independent insurance agencies in the Los Angeles area. Besides the original office, Bill now has two satellite offices around the metro area, each with a managing agent. Across the three locations he also employs 14 other agents and 27 staff people who primarily assist with clerical duties and follow-up.

Bill has always treated his people well, and as the agency has grown he has continued to pride himself on the family feeling of the business. Yet recently he has begun to question whether his performance evaluation system is appropriate. Yes, sales have continuously grown and he has had very little turnover, but success in the industry (which has always been oriented toward relationship selling) is becoming more and more about securing, building, and maintaining long-term relationships with profitable customers. Relationship selling necessitates many activities on the part of the agents to support sales.

Until now, Bill's annual performance review of his agents has focused almost exclusively on a few objectives: principally, sales volume, number of new customers, number of calls per week, and number of policies sold by line versus goals. The agents make commission and bonuses, plus a base salary. Bill likes this compensation plan because it allows him to financially reward agents for volume and for selling specific items, and it still affords him the opportunity, through the salary component, to have influence on their nonselling activities.

Bill sees his present challenge as follows: The focus on relationship selling necessitates maintaining the current compensation plan with the salary component. But his performance evaluation system doesn't match up well with the realities of his business, because it focuses only on a few objective performance measures. He sees the opportunity to incorporate some appropriate subjective measures of performance into the evaluation process and perhaps even add or change some of the objective measures. Bill calls a meeting with Chip Landers and Connie Perez, the managing agents of his satellite offices, to brainstorm ideas for changing the performance evaluation system for the agents.

Characters in the Role-Play

Bill Harvey, principal agent for Harvey Insurance Agency
Chip Landers, managing agent for the San Fernando Valley office
Connie Perez, managing agent for the Orange County office

Assignment

Break into groups of three, with one student playing each character. It doesn't matter what the actual gender mix of your group is. Before you stage the meeting, work separately using the material in your chapter to come up with your own recommendation for a new set of objective and subjective measures of agent performance. You will need to be prepared to justify your recommendations in the meeting. Then get together and role-play the meeting among Bill, Chip, and Connie. In the end, you want to come out of the meeting with a unified plan for changing the performance evaluation system for agents at Harvey Insurance Agency.

MINICASE: WEST MIDLANDS RESTAURANT APPLIANCES

West Midlands Restaurant Appliances (WMRA), headquartered in Birmingham, UK, sells large, industrial appliances such as refrigerators, freezers, and dishwashers to restaurants all over Great Britain. For several years, the company has been second in UK market share to industry leader Thames Restaurant Services, but it has been gaining share in recent years.

WMRA is especially optimistic about catching Thames this year because of the rise of its star sales manager, David Epstein, an energetic 31-year-old who has been with the company since he was 22. Epstein is popular with the sales staff, but he also is aggressive and demands high performance. One of his initiatives is to make all salespeople accountable by strictly evaluating performance using ratios as well as purely objective measures. In particular, he has collected performance data for each of his seven sales representatives as follows:

Sales Rep	Previous Sales	Current Sales	Current Quota	Number of Accounts	Number of Orders	Expenses	Number of Calls	Number of Days Worked
Derek Francona	£480,000	£481,000	£575,000	1,100	780	£9,300	1,300	235
Johnny Schilling	750,000	883,000	835,000	1,600	1,970	12,300	1,800	223
Daphne Gellar	576,000	613,000	657,000	1,150	1,020	7,500	1,650	228
Robert Smythe	745,000	852,000	850,000	1,350	1,650	11,000	1,700	230
Jennifer McCarver	765,000	860,000	850,000	1,300	1,730	11,300	1,750	232
Manuel Lopez	735,000	835,000	825,000	1,400	1,790	11,500	1,750	220
Samantha Kerrey	665,000	670,000	720,000	1,600	960	10,800	1,550	200
Erin McCloud	775,000	925,000	875,000	1,700	1,910	12,800	1,850	225

Epstein would like to see an analysis of salesperson performance using the following ratios: sales growth, sales to quota, sales per account, average order, sales expense, calls per day, orders per call.

Most of the salespeople are happy to be evaluated, but a few are dubious and fearful of the consequences. Robert Smythe, for one, feels that his territory, which includes some of the more rural areas in western England is more difficult to sell in because there are fewer restaurants and he has only been a salesperson for about a year. In addition, one of Derek Francona's largest customers recently went out of business, and he feels that his numbers slipped as a result. Both are close to quitting because they feel they are being evaluated unfairly.

Epstein wants to beat Thames very badly this year and feels that improving salesperson performance is the key. Therefore, his performance evaluation system is of the utmost importance.

Questions

1. Using the data given, calculate the performance ratios requested by Epstein and rank the salespeople accordingly.

2. What advice or guidance should Epstein give to each of the salespeople to improve performance?

3. What are the limitations of this evaluation system? What adjustments or additions could Epstein make to more accurately evaluate salesperson performance?

Endnotes

1 Introduction to Sales Management in the Twenty-First Century

1. Rolph R. Anderson, "Sales Management in the New Millennium," *Journal of Personal Selling & Sales Management* 16 (Fall 1996), pp. 17–32.
2. David W. Cravens, "The Changing Role of the Sales Force," *Marketing Management* 4 (Fall 1995), pp. 49–57.
3. Thomas L. Powers, J'Aime C. Jennings, and Thomas E. DeCarlo, "An Assessment of Needed Sales Management Skills," Journal of Personal Selling & Sales Management 34 (Issue 3, Summer 2014), pp. 206–222; Christian Schmitz, Lee You-Cheong, and Gary L. Lilien, "Cross-Selling Performance in Complex Selling Contexts: An Examination of Supervisory- and Compensation-Based Controls," *Journal of Marketing* 78 (May 2014), pp. 1–19.
4. Neil Rackham and John DeVincintis, *Rethinking the Sales Force* (New York: McGraw-Hill, 1999).
5. Adapted from Koka Sexton, "Business Must Have: Social CRM Apps," May 15, 2012, www.business 2community.com/mobileapps/business-must-have-social-crm-apps-0179264, accessed May 16, 2012.
6. Thomas G. Brashear, Danny N. Bellenger, James S. Boles, and Hiram C. Barksdale, Jr., "An Explanatory Study of the Relative Effectiveness of Different Types of Sales Force Mentors," *Journal of Personal Selling & Sales Management* 26 (Winter 2006), pp. 7–18.
7. Charles H. Schwepker, Jr. and Roberta J. Schultz, "Influence of the Ethical Servant Leader and Ethical Climate on Customer Value Enhancing Sales Performance," *Journal of Personal Selling & Sales Management* 35 (Issue 2, Spring 2015), pp.93–107; Fernando Jaramilloa, Belén Bande, and Jose Varela, "Servant Leadership and Ethics: A Dyadic Examination of Supervisor Behaviors and Salesperson Perceptions," *Journal of Personal Selling & Sales Management* 35 (Issue 2, Spring 2015), pp.108–124.
8. Adapted from ideas on the website of the Robert K. Greenleaf Center for Servant Leadership, www.greenleaf.org.
9. Stephen A. Samaha, Joshua T. Beck, and Robert W. Palmatier, "The Role of Culture in International Relationship Marketing," Journal of Marketing 78 (September 2014), pp. 78–98.
10. Jay P. Mulki, Jorge Fernando Jaramillo, and William B. Locander, "Critical Role of Leadership on Ethical Climate and Salesperson Behaviors," *Journal of Business Ethics* 86 (May 2009), pp. 125–131.
11. Lawrence B. Chonko, John F. Tanner, Jr., and Ellen Reid Smith, "The Sales Force's Role in International Marketing Research and Marketing Information Systems," *Journal of Personal Selling & Sales Management* 11 (Winter 1991), pp. 69–79.
12. O. C. Ferrell, John Fraedrich, and Linda Ferrell, *Business Ethics*, 7th ed. (New York: Houghton Mifflin, 2006).
13. Nicholas McClaren, "The Personal Selling and Sales Management Ethics Research: Managerial Implications and Research Directions from a Comprehensive Review of the Empirical Literature," *Journal of Business Ethics* 112 (January 2013), pp 101–125; Connie Bateman and Sean Valentine, "The Impact of Salesperson Customer Orientation on the Evaluation of a Salesperson's Ethical Treatment, Trust in the Salesperson, and Intentions to Purchase," *Journal of Personal Selling & Sales Management* 35 (Issue 2, Spring 2015), pp. 125–142; John E. Cicala, Alan J. Bush, Daniel L. Sherrell, and George D. Deitz, "Does Transparency Influence the Ethical Behavior of Salespeople?," *Journal of Business Research* 67 (September 2014), pp. 1787–1795; James B. DeConinck, "Outcomes of Ethical Leadership Among Salespeople," *Journal of Business Research* 68 (May 2015), pp. 1086–1093.
14. Colin B. Gabler, Adam Rapp, and Glenn Richey, "The Effect of Environmental Orientation on Salesperson Effort and Participation: The Moderating Role of Organizational Identification," *Journal of Personal Selling & Sales Management* 34 (Issue 3, Summer 2014
15. Leonard L. Berry, *On Great Service: A Framework for Action* (New York: The Free Press, 1995).

2 The Process of Selling and Buying

1. David W. Cravens, "The Changing Role of the Sales Force," *Marketing Management* 4 (Fall 1995), pp. 49–57.
2. This classic line of research on job satisfaction of salespeople was initiated by Gilbert A. Churchill, Jr., Neil M. Ford, and Orville C. Walker, Jr., in the article "Organizational Climate and Job Satisfaction of the Sales Force," *Journal of Marketing Research* (November 1976), pp. 323–332. Measurement approaches and study results within this domain have remained relatively stable for over 30 years.
3. http://www.bls.gov/ooh/management/sales-managers.htm
4. Thayer C. Taylor, "Going Mobile," *Sales & Marketing Management* (May 1994), pp. 94–101.
5. Greg W. Marshall, Daniel J. Goebel, and William C. Moncrief, "Hiring for Success at the Buyer–Seller Interface," *Journal of Business Research* 56 (April 2003), pp. 247–255.
6. Thorsten Gruber, Alexander Reppel, Isabelle Szmigin, and Roediger Voss, "Revealing the Expectations and Preferences of Complaining Customers by Combining the Laddering Interviewing Technique with the Kano Model of Customer Satisfaction," *Qualitative Market Research* 11, no. 4 (2008), pp. 400–413. See also Rosemary P. Ramsey and Ravi S. Sohi, "Listening to Your Customers: The Impact of Perceived Salesperson Listening Behavior on Relationship Outcomes," *Journal of the Academy of Marketing Science* 25 (Spring 1997), pp. 127–137.
7. Adam Rapp, Raj Agnihotri, and Lukas P. Forbes, "The Sales Force Technology–Performance Chain: The Role of Adaptive Selling and Effort," *Journal of Personal Selling & Sales Management* 28 (Fall 2008), pp. 335–350.
8. Emily A. Goad and Fernando Jaramillo, "The Good, the Bad and the Effective: A Meta-Analytic Examination of Selling Orientation and Customer Orientation on Sales Performance," *Journal of Personal Selling & Sales Management* 34 (Issue 4, Fall 2014), pp. 285–301.
9. Adapted from Neil Mahoney, "Telling Isn't Selling: Earning Prospects' Respect Is a Quiet Process," February 19, 2012, http://salesandmarketing.com/article/telling-isnt-selling, accessed June 4, 2012.
10. William C. Moncrief, Greg W. Marshall, Felicia G. Lassk, "A Contemporary Taxonomy of Sales Positions," *Journal of Personal Selling & Sales Management*, 26 (January 2006), pp. 56–65.
11. Derek A. Newton, *Sales Force Performance and Turnover* (Cambridge, MA: Marketing Science Institute, 1973), p. 3.
12. Mary M. Long, Thomas Tellefsen, and J. David Lichtenthal, "Internet Integration into the Industrial 449 Selling Process: A Step-by-Step Approach," *Industrial Marketing Management* 36 (July 2007), pp. 676–689.
13. Adapted from Aleksi Grym and Rahul Dhingra, "Who Are You After? Get a Better Handle on Your Customers before Outsourcing Sales Prospecting," May 1, 2012, http://salesandmarketing.com/article/who-are-you-after, accessed June 6, 2012.
14. Benson P. Shapiro, *Sales Program Management: Formulation and Implementation* (New York: McGraw-Hill, 1977), p. 160.
15. Christopher R. Plouffe, Willy Bolander, and Joseph A. Cote, "Which Influence Tactics Lead to Sales Performance? It Is a Matter of Style," *Journal of Personal Selling & Sales Management* 34 (Issue 2, Spring 2014), pp. 141–159.
16. Milt Grassell, "What Purchasing Managers Like in a Salesperson . . . and What Drives Them up the Wall," *Business Marketing* (June 1986), pp. 72–77. See also Edith Cohen, "The View from the Other Side," *Sales & Marketing Management* (June 1990), pp. 108–110; and "Ten Ways to Lose a Sale," *Sales & Marketing Management* (December 1992), p. 35.
17. Goutam Challagalla, R. Venkatesh, and Ajay K. Kohli, "Proactive Postsales Service: When and Why Does It Pay Off ?" *Journal of Marketing* 73 (March 2009), pp. 70–87.
18. Donald W. Jackson, Jr., Janet E. Keith, and Richard K. Burdick, "Purchasing Agents' Perceptions of Industrial Buying Center Influence: A Situational Approach," *Journal of Marketing* (Fall 1984), pp. 75–83.
19. Richard G. Jennings and Richard E. Plank, "When the Purchasing Agent Is a Committee: Implications for Industrial Marketing," *Industrial Marketing Management* 24 (November 1995), pp. 411–419.
20. Vince-Wayne Mitchell, "Buy-Phase and Buy-Class Effects on Organizational Risk Perceptions and Reductions in Purchasing Professional Services," *Journal of Business and Industrial Marketing* 13, no. 6 (1998), pp. 461–471.
21. Jennings and Plank, "When the Purchasing Agent Is a Committee."
22. Mark A. Moon and Susan Forquer Gupta, "Examining the Formation of Selling Centers: A Conceptual Framework," *Journal of Personal Selling & Sales Management* 17 (Spring 1997), pp. 31–42.
23. Louis V. Gerstner, Jr., *Who Says Elephants Can't Dance?* (New York: Harper Business, 2004).
24. Wesley J. Johnston and Jeffrey E. Lewin, "Organizational Buying Behavior: Toward an Integrative Framework," *Journal of Business Research* 35 (January 1996), pp. 1–15.

3 Linking Strategies and the Sales Role in the Era of CRM and Data Analytics

1. Ajay K. Kohli and Bernard J. Jaworski, "Market Orientation: The Construct, Research Propositions, and Managerial Implications," *Journal of Marketing* 54 (April 1990), pp. 1–18; John C. Narver and Stanley F. Slater, "The Effect of a Market Orientation on Business Profitability," *Journal of Marketing* (October 1990), pp. 20–35.

2. Chally Group Worldwide, *The World Class Excellence Report: The Route to the Summit* (Dayton, OH: HR Chally Group, 2007).

3. The Data Warehouse Institute, Industry Study 2000 Survey, p. 1.

4. www.PricewaterhouseCoopers.com.

5. Gabriel R. Gonzalez, Danny P. Claro, and Robert W. Palmatier, "Synergistic Effects of Relationship Managers' Social Networks on Sales Performance," *Journal of Marketing* 78 (January 2014), pp. 76–94.

6. Don Peppers and Martha Rogers, *One to One B2B: Customer Development Strategies for the Business-to-Business World* (New York: Doubleday, 2001).

7. Ronald S. Swift, *Accelerating Customer Relationships: Using CRM and Relationship Technologies* (Upper Saddle River, NJ: Prentice Hall PTR, 2000), p. 42.

8. Adapted from Tim Handorf, "Sales Mobility: What Your Sales Reps and Customers Need," September 22, 2011, www.salesandmarketing.com/article/sales-mobility-what-your-sales-reps-and-customers-need, accessed June 13, 2012.

9. Stanley A. Brown, ed., *Customer Relationship Management: A Strategic Imperative in the World of E-Business* (Toronto: John Wiley & Sons Canada, 2000), pp. 8–9.

10. Robert E. Carter, Conor M. Henderson, Inigo Arroniz, and Robert W. Palmatier, "Effect of Salespeople's Acquisition–Retention Trade-Off on Performance," *Journal of Personal Selling & Sales Management* 34 (Issue 2, Spring 2014), pp. 91–111.

11. Sharad Borle, Siddharth S. Singh, and Dipak C. Jain, "Customer Lifetime Value Measurement," *Management Science* 54 (January 2008), pp. 100–114.

12. Swift, "Accelerating Customer Relationships," pp. 39–42.

13. Ray McKenzie, *The Relationship-Based Enterprise: Powering Business Success through Customer Relationship Management* (New York: McGraw-Hill, 2001), pp. 7–8.

14. Ibid., p. 8.

15. Lori Wizdo, "Buyer Behavior Helps B2B Marketers Guide the Buyer's Journey," *Forrester,* October 2012, http://blogs.forrester.com/lori_wizdo/12-10-04-buyer_behavior_helps_b2b_marketers_guide_the_buyers_journey.

16. William C. Moncrief, Greg W. Marshall, and John M. Rudd, "Social Media and Related Technology: Drivers of Change in Managing the Contemporary Sales Force," *Business Horizons* 58 (January–February 2015), pp. 45–55.

17. SAS Website, "Big Data, Bigger Marketing," May 2015, http://www.sas.com/en_us/insights/big-data/big-data-marketing.html.

18. UBM Tech, "Acquire, Grow and Retain Customers—The Business Imperative for Big Data and Analytics," December 2013, http://www-01.ibm.com/common/ssi/cgi-bin/ssialias?infotype=SA&subtype=WH&htmlfid=NIL12362USEN#loaded.

19. Timothy M. Smith, Srinath Gopalakrishna, and Rabikar Chatterjee, "A Three-Stage Model of Integrated Marketing Communications at the Marketing-Sales Interface," *Journal of Marketing Research* 43 (November, 2006), pp. 564–579.

20. Michael T. Krush, Raj Agnihotri, Kevin J. Trainor, and Edward L. Nowlin, "Enhancing Organizational Sensemaking: An Examination of the Interactive Effects of Sales Capabilities and Marketing Dashboards," *Industrial Marketing Management* 42 (July 2013), pp. 824–835; Douglas E. Hughes, Joël Le Bon, and Adam Rapp, "Gaining and Leveraging Customer-Based Competitive Intelligence: The Pivotal Role of Social Capital and Salesperson Adaptive Selling Skills," *Journal of the Academy of Marketing Science* 41, (January 2013), pp. 91–110; Jeff Foreman, Naveen Donthu, Steve Henson, and Amit Poddar, "The Performance Implications of Planning, Implementation, and Evolution of Firms' Customer and Competitor Orientations," *Journal of Marketing Theory and Practice* 22 (Fall 2014), pp. 349–366.

21. Dominique Rouziès and John Hulland, "Does Marketing and Sales Integration Always Pay Off? Evidence From a Social Capital Perspective," *Journal of the Academy of Marketing Science* 42 (September 2014), pp. 511–527.

22. Daniel G. Simpson, "Why Most Strategic Planning Is a Waste of Time and What You Can Do about It," *Long Range Planning* 31, no. 3 (1998), pp. 476–480.

23. Timothy N. Nolan, Leonard D. Goodstein, and Jeanette Goodstein, *Applied Strategic Planning: An Introduction* (San Francisco: Pfeiffer, 2008).

24. Michael E. Porter, *Competitive Strategy* (New York: The Free Press, 1998), Chapter 2.

25. Raymond E. Miles and Charles C. Snow, *Organizational Strategy, Structure and Process* (New York: McGraw-Hill, 1978). Miles and Snow also identified a fourth category of businesses, which they called "reactors." However, because reactors are businesses with no clearly defined or consistent competitive strategy, we do not discuss them further here.

26. For a more detailed discussion of how a business's competitive strategy influences its marketing and sales strategies and programs, see Orville C. Walker, Jr., and Robert W. Ruekert, "Marketing's Role in the Implementation of Business Strategies: A Critical Review and Conceptual Framework," *Journal of Marketing* (July 1987), pp. 15–33.

27. Chally Group Worldwide (2012); Dennis B. Arnett and C. Michael Wittmann, "Improving Marketing Success: The Role of Tacit Knowledge Exchange Between Sales and Marketing," *Journal of Business Research* 67 (March 2014), pp. 324–331; Gaurav Sabnis, Sharmila C. Chatterjee, Rajdeep Grewal, and Gary L. Lilien, "The Sales Lead Black Hole: On Sales Reps' Follow-Up of Marketing Leads," *Journal of Marketing* 77 (January 2013), pp. 52–67; Virpi Turkulainen, Jaakko Kujala, Karlos Artto, and Raymond E. Levitt, "Organizing in the Context of Global Project-Based Firm—The Case of Sales–Operations Interface," *Industrial Marketing Management* 42 (February 2013), pp. 223–233;

28. Neil Rackham and John DeVincintis, *Rethinking the Sales Force* (New York: McGraw-Hill, 1999).

29. Annie Liqin Zhang, Roger Baxter, and Mark S. Glynn, "How Salespeople Facilitate Buyers' Resource Availability to Enhance Seller Outcomes," *Industrial Marketing Management* 42 (October 2013), pp. 1121–1130.

30. Christian Homburg, Torsten Bornemann, and Max Kretzer, "Delusive Perception—Antecedents and Consequences of Salespeople's Misperception of Customer Commitment," *Journal of the Academy of Marketing Science* 42 (March 2014), pp. 137–153.

31. John F. Tanner, Jr., "Users' Role in the Purchase: Their Influence, Satisfaction, and Desire to Participate in the Next Purchase," *Journal of Business & Industrial Marketing* 13, no. 6 (1998), pp. 479–491.

32. Jeff S. Johnson and Scott B. Friend, "Contingent Cross-Selling and Up-Selling Relationships with Performance and Job Satisfaction: an MOA-theoretic Examination," *Journal of Personal Selling & Sales Management* 35 (Issue 1, Winter 2015), pp. 51–71.

33. Christian Schmitz, "Group Influences of Selling Teams on Industrial Salespeople's Cross-Selling Behavior," *Journal of the Academy of Marketing Science* 41 (January 2013), pp. 55–72.

34. James P. Morgan and Shirley Cayer, "Working with World-Class Suppliers: True Believers," *Purchasing* (August 13, 1992), pp. 50–52.

35. Ronald Jelinek, "Beyond Commitment: Entrenchment in the Buyer–Seller Exchange," *Journal of Personal Selling & Sales Management* 34 (Issue 4, Fall 2014), pp. 272–284.

36. For example, see David A. Aaker, *Managing Brand Equity* (New York: The Free Press, 1991); Linda M. Keefe, "Corporate Voice in Relation to Product Brands," *Design Management Journal* 6 (1995), pp. 45–49.

37. Vishag Badrinarayanan and Debra A. Laverie, "The Role of Manufacturers' Salespeople in Inducing Brand Advocacy by Retail Sales Associates," *Journal of Marketing Theory & Practice* 21 (Winter 2013), pp. 57–70.

38. For a more detailed discussion of the role of personal selling and other promotional tools in building long-term relationships with channel members, see James A. Narus and James C. Anderson, "Turn Your Industrial Distributors into Partners," *Harvard Business Review* (March–April 1986), pp. 66–71; F. Robert Dwyer, Paul H. Schurr, and Sejo Oh, "Developing Buyer–Seller Relationships," *Journal of Marketing* (April 1987), pp. 11–27; Jan Heide and George John, "Do Norms Matter in Marketing Relationships?" *Journal of Marketing* (April 1992), pp. 32–44.

39. Bill Saporito, "Behind the Tumult at P&G," *Fortune* (March 7, 1994), pp. 74–82. For other examples involving B2B goods, see Joseph B. Fuller, James O'Conor, and Richard Rawlinson, "Tailored Logistics: The Next Advantage," *Harvard Business Review* (May–June 1993), pp. 87–98; W. David Gibson, "Holy Alliances," *Sales & Marketing Management* (July 1993), pp. 85–87.

40. Frederick F. Reichheld, "Loyalty and the Renaissance of Marketing," *Marketing Management* 2 (1994), pp. 10–21.

41. Ibid.

42. Louis V. Gerstner, *Who Says Elephants Can't Dance?* (New York: Harper Business, 2004).

4 Organizing the Sales Effort

1. Patricia Sellers, "How to Remake Your Sales Force," *Fortune* (May 4, 1992), pp. 96–102.

2. Christian Schmitz and Shankar Ganesan, "Managing Customer and Organizational Complexity in Sales Organizations," *Journal of Marketing* 78 (November 2014), pp. 59–77.

3. Charles Shaw, "The Rep and the Future—Which Is Now," *Agency Sales Magazine* (January 2001), pp. 28–30.

4. Dan Hanover, "Independents Day," *Sales & Marketing Management* (April 2000), pp. 65–68. Endnotes 451.

5. Jayashree Mahajan, G. A. Churchill, Jr., N. M. Ford, and O. C. Walker, Jr., "A Comparison of the Impact of Organizational Climate on the Job Satisfaction of Manufacturers' Agents and Company Salespeople: An Exploratory Study," *Journal of Personal Selling & Sales Management* (May 1984), pp. 1–10.

6. David I. Gilliland and Stephen K. Kim, "When Do Incentives Work in Channels of Distribution?," *Journal of the Academy of Marketing Science* 42 (July 2014) pp. 361–379; Karen E. Flaherty, James M. Pappas, and Lee Allison, "The Influence of an Optimal Control System on Salesperson Performance and Championing," *Industrial Marketing Management* 43 (February 2014), pp. 304–311.

7. Allen M. Weiss and Erin Anderson, "Converting from Independent to Employee Salesforces: The Role of Perceived Switching Costs," *Journal of Marketing Research* (February 1992), pp. 101–115.

8. Bernard J. Jaworski, "Toward a Theory of Marketing Control: Environmental Context, Control Types, and Consequences," *Journal of Marketing* (July 1988), pp. 23–39.

9. Erin Anderson, "The Salesperson as Outside Agent or Employee: A Transaction Cost Analysis," *Marketing Science* 4 (1985), pp. 234–254.

10. Erin Anderson and Barton Weitz, "The Use of Pledges to Build and Sustain Commitment in Distribution Channels," *Journal of Marketing Research* (February 1992), pp. 18–34.

11. Robert W. Ruekert, Orville C. Walker, Jr., and Kenneth J. Roering, "The Organization of Marketing Activities: A Contingency Theory of Structure and Performance," *Journal of Marketing* (Winter 1985), pp. 13–25.

12. Jeff S. Johnson and Ravipreet S. Sohi, "The Curvilinear and Conditional Effects of Product Line Breadth on Salesperson Performance, Role Stress, and Job Satisfaction," *Journal of the Academy of Marketing Science* 42 (January 2014), pp. 71–89.

13. Harri Terho, Andreas Eggert, Alexander Haas, and Wolfgang Ulaga, "How Sales Strategy Translates into Performance: The Role of Salesperson Customer Orientation and Value-Based Selling," *Industrial Marketing Management* 45 (February 2015), pp. 12–21.

14. Francy Blackwood, "Did You Sell $5 Million Last Year?" *Selling* (October 1995), pp. 44–53.

15. Adapted from Susan J. Campbell, "Telemarketing Software Drives the Capture of Effective Sales Data," August 22, 2011, http://telemarketing-software.tmcnet.com/articles/210460-telemarketing-software-drives-capture-effective-sales-data.htm, accessed June 21, 2012.

16. David A. Andelman, "Betting on the 'Net,'" *Sales & Marketing Management* (June 1995), pp. 47–59.

17. William C. Moncrief, Charles W. Lamb, Jr., and Terry Dielman, "Developing Telemarketing Support Systems," *Journal of Personal Selling & Sales Management* (August 1986), pp. 43–49.

18. Robert J. Hershock, "Notes from the Revolution," in *Reinventing the Sales Organization* (New York: The Conference Board, 1995), pp. 10–13.

19. Arun Sharma, "Who Prefers Key Account Management Programs? An Investigation of Business Buying Behavior and Buying Firm Characteristics," *Journal of Personal Selling & Sales Management* (Fall 1997), pp. 27–39. See also Catherine Pardo, "Key Account Management in the Business to Business Field: The Key Account's Point of View," *Journal of Personal Selling & Sales Management* (Fall 1997), pp. 17–26.

20. Frederick F. Reichheld, "Loyalty and the Renaissance of Marketing," *Marketing Management* 2 (1994), pp. 10–21; Rahul Jacob, "Why Some Customers Are More Equal than Others," *Fortune* (September 19, 1994), pp. 215–224; Sangit Sungupta, Robert E. Krapfel, and Michael Pusateri, "Switching Costs in Key Account Relationships," *Journal of Personal Selling & Sales Management* (Fall 1997), pp. 9–16.

21. Ian A. Daies, Lynette J. Ryals, "The effectiveness of Key Account Management practices," *Industrial Marketing Management* 43 (October 2014), pp. 1182–1194.

22. Benson P. Shapiro and Rowland T. Moriarity, Organizing the National Account Force (Cambridge, MA: Marketing Science Institute, 1984), pp. 1–37; Jerome A. Colletti and Gary S. Tubridy, "Effective Major Account Sales Management," *Journal of Personal Selling & Sales Management* (August 1987), pp. 1–10.

23. Scott B. Friend, Carolyn F. Curasi, James S. Boles, and Danny N. Bellenger, "Why Are You Really Losing Sales Opportunities? A Buyers' Perspective on the Determinants of Key Account Sales Failures," *Industrial Marketing Management* 43 (October 2014), pp. 1124–1135.

24. Seigyoung Auh, Stavroula Spyropoulou, Bulent Menguc, and Aypar Uslu, "When and How Does Sales Team Conflict Affect Sales Team Performance?," *Journal of the Academy of Marketing Science* 42 (November 2014), pp. 658–679.

25. Mark A. Moon and Susan Forquer Gupta, "Examining the Formation of Selling Centers: A Conceptual Framework," *Journal of Personal Selling & Sales Management* (Spring 1997), pp. 31–42.

26. Andy Cohen, "Top of the Charts—Lear Corporation," *Sales & Marketing Management* (July 1998), p. 40.

27. Geoffrey Brewer, "Lou Gerstner Has His Hands Full," *Sales & Marketing Management* (May 1998), pp. 36–41.

28. Dan T. Dunne, Jr., and Claude A. Thomas, "Strategy for Systems Sellers: A Team Approach," *Journal of Personal Selling & Sales Management* (August 1986), pp. 1–10. See also C. Jay Lambe, Kevin L. Webb, and Chiharu Ishida, "Self-Managing Selling Teams and Team Performance: The Complementary Roles of Empowerment and Control," *Industrial Marketing Management* 38 (January 2009), pp. 5–16.

29. Andy Cohen, "Top of the Charts—Pfizer," *Sales & Marketing Management* (July 1998), p. 41.

30. Yingli Wang, Andrew Potter, and Mohamed Naim, "Electronic Marketplaces for Tailored Logistics," *Industrial Management & Data Systems* 107, no. 8 (2007), pp. 1170–1187.

31. Barry Farber and Joyce Wycoff, "Customer Service: Evolution and Revolution," *Sales & Marketing Management* (May 1991), pp. 44–51.

32. Jesse N. Moore, Mary Anne Raymond, and Christopher D. Hopkins, "Social Selling: A Comparison of Social Media Usage Across Process Stage, Markets, and Sales Job Functions," *Journal of Marketing Theory and Practice* 23 (Winter 2015), pp. 1–20.

33. For a discussion of advantages and disadvantages of outsourced selling, see Andris A. Zoltners, Prabhakant Sinha, and Greggor A. Zoltners, *The Complete Guide to Accelerating Sales Force Performance* (New York: AMACOM, 2001), p. 34.

34. Michele Marchetti, "Can You Build a Sales Force?" *Sales & Marketing Management* (January 2000), pp. 56–61.

5 The Strategic Role of Information in Sales Management

1. For a discussion of some other, less common forecasting techniques, see Spyros Makridakis, Steven C. Wheelwright, and Rob J. Hyndman, *Forecasting: Methods and Applications* (New York: John Wiley & Sons, 1997).

2. See also David M. Georgoff and Robert Murdick, "Manager's Guide to Forecasting," *Harvard Business Review* 64 (January–February 1986), pp. 110–120, which contains a chart that rates 20 forecasting techniques on 16 evaluative dimensions.

3. C. L. Jain, "Delphi-Forecast with Experts' Opinion," *Journal of Business Forecasting* 4 (Winter 1985–86), pp. 22–23.

4. Peter J. Brockwell and Richard A. Davis, *Introduction to Time Series and Forecasting* (New York: Springer-Verlag, 1996).

5. Spyros Makridakis et al., "The Accuracy of Extrapolation (Times-Series) Methods: Results of a Forecasting Competition," *Journal of Forecasting* 1 (April–June 1982), pp. 111–153.

6. Spyros Makridakis and Michele Hibon, "Accuracy of Forecasting: An Empirical Investigation," *Journal of the Royal Statistical Society* 142, pt. 2 (1979), pp. 97–145. See also Robin M. Hogarth and Spyros Makridakis, "Forecasting and Planning: An Evaluation," *Management Science* 27 (February 1981), pp. 115–138.

7. Mark M. Moriarity and Arthur J. Adams, "Management Judgment Forecasts, Composite Forecasting Models, and Conditional Efficiency," *Journal of Marketing Research* 21 (August 1984), pp. 239–250.

8. Pierre Wack, "Scenarios: Shooting the Rapids," *Harvard Business Review* 63 (November–December 1985), p. 146. See also Peter W. Beck, "Debate over Alternate Scenarios Replaces Forecasts at Shell U.K.," *Journal of Business Forecasting* 3 (Spring 1984), pp. 2–6.

9. www.businessdictionary.com/definition/buying-power-index-BPI.html.

10. Wack, "Scenarios: Shooting the Rapids."

11. Alan J. Dubinsky and Thomas E. Barry, "A Survey of Sales Management Practices," *Industrial Marketing Management* 11 (April 1982), pp. 133–141.

12. Raymond W. LaForge, David W. Cravens, and Clifford E. Young, "Using Contingency Analysis to Select Selling Effort Allocation Methods," *Journal of Personal Selling & Sales Management* 6 (August 1986), pp. 19–28.

13. Walter J. Talley, Jr., "How to Design Sales Territories," *Journal of Marketing* 25 (January 1961), pp. 7–13.

14. Donald L. Brady, "Determining the Value of an Industrial Prospect: A Prospect Preference Index Model," *Journal of Personal Selling & Sales Management* 7 (August 1987), pp. 27–32.

15. Walter J. Semlow, "How Many Salesmen Do You Need?" *Harvard Business Review* 37 (May–June 1959), pp. 126–132. See also Charles B. Weinberg and Henry C. Lucas, Jr., "Semlow's Results Are Based on a Spurious Relationship," *Journal of Marketing* 41 (April 1977), pp. 146–147.

16. Zarrell Lambert and Fred W. Kniffen, "Response Functions and Their Applications in Sales Force Management," *Southern Journal of Business* 5 (January 1970), pp. 1–9.

17. A. Parasuraman, "An Approach for Allocating Sales Call Effort," *Industrial Marketing Management* 11 (1982), pp. 75–79; Renato Fiocca, "Account Portfolio Analysis for Strategy Development," *Industrial Marketing Management* 11 (1982), pp. 53–62; Rosann L. Spiro and William D. Perreault, Jr., "Factors Influencing Sales Call Frequency of Industrial Salespersons," *Journal of Business Research* 6 (January 1978), pp. 1–15.

18. Fiocca, "Account Portfolio Analysis for Strategy Development"; Raymond W. LaForge and David W. Cravens, "Steps in Selling Effort Deployment," *Industrial Marketing Management* 11 (1982), pp. 183–194; David W. Cravens and Raymond W. LaForge, "Salesforce Deployment Analysis," *Industrial Marketing Management* 12 (July 1983), pp. 179–192; Alan J. Dubinsky and Thomas N. Ingram, "A Portfolio Approach to Account Profitability," *Industrial Marketing Management* 13 (February 1984), pp. 33–41.

19. Raymond W. LaForge and David W. Cravens, "Empirical and Judgment-Based Sales-Force Decision Models: A Comparative Assessment," *Decision Sciences* 16 (Spring 1985), pp. 177–195.

20. Adrian B. Ryans and Charles B. Weinberg, "Territory Sales Response Models: Stability over Time," *Journal of Marketing Research* 24 (May 1987), pp. 229–233.

21. "Sales Analysis," *Studies in Business Policy*, no. 13 (New York: National Industrial Conference Board, 1965), p. 3.

6 Salesperson Performance: Behavior, Role Perceptions, and Satisfaction

1. This chapter borrows heavily from the following: Orville C. Walker, Jr., Gilbert A. Churchill, Jr., and Neil M. Ford, "Motivation and Performance in Industrial Selling: Present Knowledge and Needed Research," *Journal of Marketing Research* 14 (May 1977), pp. 156–168. See also Steven P. Brown, William Cron, and John W. Slocum, Jr., "Effects of Goal-Directed Emotions on Salesperson Volitions, Behavior, and Performance: A Longitudinal Study," *Journal of Marketing* (January 1997), pp. 39–50; C. Fred Miao and Kenneth R. Evans, "The Impact of Salesperson Motivation on Role Perceptions and Job Performance—A Cognitive and Affective Perspective," *Journal of Personal Selling & Sales Management* 27 (Winter 2007), pp. 89–101.

2. For studies of how role perceptions can affect salespeople's job satisfaction and performance, see Douglas N. Behrman and William D. Perreault, Jr., "A Role Stress Model of the Performance and Satisfaction of Industrial Salespeople," *Journal of Marketing* 48 (Fall 1984), pp. 9–21; George J. Avlonitis and Nikolaos G. Panagopoulos, "Role Stress, Attitudes, and Job Outcomes in Business-to-Business Selling: Does the Type of Selling Situation Matter?" *Journal of Personal Selling & Sales Management* 26 (Winter 2006), pp. 68–77; Charles E. Pettijohn, Linda S. Pettijohn, and A. J. Taylor, "Does Salesperson Perception of the Importance of Sales Skills Improve Sales Performance, Customer Orientation, Job Satisfaction, and Organizational Commitment and Reduce Turnover?" *Journal of Personal Selling & Sales Management* 27 (Winter 2007), p. 75; Kenneth R. Evans, Timothy D. Landry, Po-Chien Li, and Shaoming Zou, "How Sales Controls Affect Job-Related Outcomes: The Role of Organizational Sales-Related Psychological Climate Perceptions," *Academy of Marketing Science Journal* 35 (September 2007), p. 445.

3. R. Kenneth Teas, "Supervisory Behavior, Role Stress, and the Job Satisfaction of Industrial Salespeople," *Journal of Marketing Research* 20 (February 1983), pp. 84–91; Ajay K. Kohli, "Some Unexplored Supervisory Behaviors and Their Influence on Salespeople's Role Clarity, Specific Job Esteem, Job Satisfaction, and Motivation," *Journal of Marketing Research* 22 (November 1985), pp. 424–433. See also Goutam N. Challagalla and Tasaddug A. Servani, "Dimensions and Types of Supervisory Control Effects of Salesperson Performance and Satisfaction," *Journal of Marketing* (January 1996), pp. 89–105; Thomas E. DeCarlo, R. Kenneth Teas, and James C. McElroy, "Salesperson Performance Attributions Process and the Formulation of Expectancy Estimates," *Journal of Personal Selling & Sales Management* (Summer 1997), pp. 1–17; Douglas Amyx and Bruce L. Alford, "The Effects of Salesperson Need for Achievement and Sales Manager Leader Reward Behavior," *Journal of Personal Selling & Sales Management* 25 (Fall 2005), pp. 346–359 ; Tará Lopez and Amy McMillan-Capehart, "Elements of Salesperson Control: An Organization Theory Perspective," *The Journal of Business & Industrial Marketing* 24 (2009), p. 98.

4. Guenzi, Paolo, Luigi M. DeLuca, and Gabriele Troilo, "Organizational Drivers of Salespeople's Customer Orientation and Selling Orientation," *Journal of Personal Selling & Sales Management* 31 (Summer 2011), pp. 269–286. Barton A. Weitz, "A Critical Review of Personal Selling Research: The Need for Contingency Approaches," in *Critical Issues in Sales Management*, eds. Albaum and Churchill, Jr., pp. 76–126; John Andy Wood, "NLP Revisited: Nonverbal Communications and Signals of Trustworthiness," *Journal of Personal Selling & Sales Management* 26 (Spring 2006), pp. 198–204 ; Arun Sharma, Michael Levy, and Heiner Evanschitzky, "The Variance in Sales Performance Explained by the Knowledge Structure of Salespeople," *Journal of Personal Selling & Sales Management* 27 (Spring 2007), p. 169.

5. Siew Meng Leong, Paul S. Busch, and Deborah Roedder John, "Knowledge Bases and Salesperson Effectiveness: A Script-Theoretic Analysis," *Journal of Marketing Research* 26 (May 1990), pp. 164–178; Richard G. McFarland and Blair Kidwell, "An Examination of Instrumental and Expressive Traits on Performance: The Mediating Role of Learning, Prove, and Avoid Goal Orientations," *Journal of Personal Selling & Sales Management* 26 (Spring 2006), pp. 143–159.

6. R. Kenneth Teas, "An Empirical Test of Models of Salespersons' Job Expectancy and Instrumentality Perceptions," *Journal of Marketing Research* 18 (May 1981), pp. 209–226. For empirical evidence regarding the things that motivate salespeople in the United States versus salespeople in other countries, see Alex Palmer, "Success in Small Steps," *Incentive* 183 (February 2009), pp. 44–46.

7. Artur Baldauf, David W. Cravens, and Nigel F. Piercy, "Examining Business Strategy, Sales Management, and Salesperson Antecedents of Sales Organization Effectiveness," *Journal of Personal Selling & Sales Management* (Spring 2001), pp. 109–122; Ken Grant, David W. Cravens, George S. Low, and William C. Moncrief, "The Role of Satisfaction with Territory Design on Motivation, Attitudes, and Work Outcomes of Salespeople," *Journal of the Academy of Marketing Science* (Spring 2001), pp. 165–78; John W. Barnes, Donald W. Jackson, Jr., Michael D. Hutt, and Ajith Kumar, "The Role of Culture Strength in Shaping Sales Force Outcomes," *Journal of Personal Selling & Sales Management* 26 (Summer 2006), pp. 255–270.

8. "Take a Right and . . ." *Sales & Marketing Management* (September 1997), pp. 91–96.

9. Sunny Baker, and Kim Baker, "Divide and Conquer," *Journal of Business Strategy* 20, no. 5 (Sep/Oct 1999), pp. 16–19; Gilbert A. Churchill, Jr., Neil M. Ford, and Orville C. Walker, Jr., "Motivating the Industrial Salesforce: The Attractiveness of Alternative Rewards," *Journal of Business Research* 7 (1979), pp. 25–50; William L. Cron and John W. Slocum, Jr., "The Influence of Career Stages on Salespeople's Job Attitudes, Work Perceptions, and Performance," *Journal of Marketing Research* 23 (May 1986), pp. 119–129; Lawrence B. Chonko, John F. Tanner, and William A. Weeks, "Selling and Sales Management in Action: Reward Preferences of Salespeople," *Journal of Personal Selling & Sales Management* 12 (Summer 1992), pp. 67–75; William A. Weeks & Terry W. Loe, Lawrence B. Chonko, Carlos Ruy Martinez, and Kirk Wakefield, "Cognitive Moral Development and the Impact of Perceived Organizational Ethical Climate on the Search for Sales Force Excellence: A Cross-Cultural Study," *Journal of Personal Selling & Sales Management* 26 (Spring 2006), pp. 206–217.

10. Scott B. Friend, Jeff S. Johnson, Brian N. Rutherford, and G. Alexander Hamwi, "INDSALES Model: A Facet-level Job Satisfaction Model Among Salespeople," Journal of Personal Selling and Sales Management, 33, (Issue 4, Fall 2013), pp. 419–438. Rosemary R. Lagace, Jerry R. Goolsby, and Jule B. Gassenheimer, "Scaling and Measurement: A Quasi-Replicative Assessment of a Revised Version of Indsales," *Journal of Personal Selling & Sales Management* 13 (Winter 1993), pp. 65–72.

11. Te-Lin Chung, Brian Rutherford and Jungkun Park, "Understanding multifaced job satisfaction of retail employees," *International Journal of Retail and Distribution Management* 40, no 9 (2012), pp. 699–716. Steven P. Brown and Robert A. Peterson, "Antecedents and Consequences of Salesperson Job Satisfaction: Meta-Analysis and Assessment of Causal Effects," *Journal of Marketing Research* 30 (February 1993), pp. 63–77.

12. Ryan Mullins, Niladri Syam, "Manager-Salesperson Congruence in Customer Orientation and job Outcomes: The Bright and Dark Sides of Leadership in Aligning Values," *Journal of Personal Selling and Sales Management*, 34, (Issue 3, Summer 2014), pp. 188–205; Nadia Pomirleanu and Babu John Mariadoss, "The Influence of Organizational and Functional Support on the Development of Salesperson Job Satisfaction," *Journal of Personal Selling and Sales Management*, 35, (Issue 1, Winter 2015), pp. 33–50; Bashar S. Gammoh, Micahel L. Malling, and Ellen Bolman Pullins, "Antecedents and Consequences of Salesperson Identificaiton with the Brand and Company," *Journal of Personal Selling and Sales Management*, 34, (Issue 1, Winter 2014), pp. 3–18.

13. See Alan J. Dubinsky et al., "Salesforce Socialization," *Journal of Marketing* 50 (October 1986), pp. 192–207, for discussion of the socialization process.

14. Christophe Fournier, William A. Weeks, Christopher P. Blocker, and Lawrence B. Chonko, "Polychronicity and Scheduling's role in Reducing Role Stress and Enhancing Sales Performance," *Journal of Personal Selling and Sales Management*," 33, (Issue 2, Spring 2013), pp. 197–210.

15. Grant, Stephen E. and Alan J. Bush, "Salesforce Socialization Tactics: Building Organizational Value Congruence," *Journal of Personal Selling & Sales Management* 16 (Summer 1996), pp. 17–32; Todd D. Donovan, Xiang Fang, Neeli Bendapudi, Surendra N. Singh, "Applying Interactional Psychology to Salesforce Management, a Socialization Illustration," *Qualitative Market Research* V. 7 (2004), pp. 139–152; Sparks, John R. and Joseph A. Schenk, "Socialization Communication, Organizational Citizenship Behaviors, and Sales in a Multi-level Organization," *Journal of Personal Selling & Sales Management* 26 (Spring 2006), pp. 161–180; Cynthia D. Fisher and Richard Gitelson, "A Meta-Analysis of the Correlates of Role Conflict and Ambiguity," *Journal of Applied Psychology* 68 (May 1983), pp. 320–333. See also Rosemary Ramsey Lagace, "Role Stress Differences between Salesmen and Saleswomen: Effect on Job Satisfaction and Performance," *Psychological Reports* 62 (June 1988), pp. 815–825; Jagdip Singh, "Boundary Role Ambiguity: Facets, Determinants, and Impacts," *Journal of Marketing* 57 (April 1993), pp. 11–31; James S. Boles, John Andy Wood, and Julie Johnson, "Interrelationships of Role Conflict, Role Ambiguity, and Work–Family Conflict with Different Facets of Job Satisfaction and the Moderating Effects of Gender," *Journal of Personal Selling & Sales Management* 23 (Spring 2003), p. 99.

16. Fernando Jaramillo, Jay Prakash Mulki, and James S. Boles, "Workplace Stressors, Job Attitude, and Job Behaviors: Is Interpersonal Conflict the Missing Link?," *Journal of Personal Selling & Sales Management* 31 (Spring 2011, pp. 339–356; and William Connors, "RIM Objects to Survey Showing Weak BlackBerry Developer Outlook," *Wall Street Journal*, July 26, 2012, http://blogs.wsj.com/canadarealtime/2012/07/13/rim-objects-to-survey-showing-weak-blackberry-developer-outlook/

17. This discussion was based on the following articles: Goutam Challagalla, Tasaddug Shervani, and George Huber, "Supervisory Orientations and Salesperson Work Outcomes: The Moderating Effect of Salesperson Location," *Journal of Personal Selling & Sales Management* 20 (Summer 2000), pp. 161–171; Daniel Tynan, "Out of the Office, But Never Out of Reach," *Sales & Marketing Management* 155 (January 2003), pp. 18–19.

18. Neil M. Ford, Orville C. Walker, Jr., and Gilbert A. Churchill, Jr., "Expectation-Specific Measures of the Intersender Conflict and Role Ambiguity Experienced by Industrial Salesmen," *Journal of Business Research* 3 (April 1975), pp. 95–112; Kris Maher, "Stressed Out: Can Workplace Stress Get Worse?" *The Wall Street Journal* (January 16, 2001), p. B-6; Greg W. Marshall, Daniel J. Goebel, and William C. Moncrief, "Hiring for Success at the Buyer–Seller Interface," *Journal of Business Research* 56 (April 2003), p. 247.

19. Douglas N. Behrman and William D. Perrault, Jr., "A Role Stress Model of the Performance and Satisfaction of Industrial Salespeople," *Journal of Marketing* 48 (Fall 1984), pp. 9–21; Richard P. Bagozzi, "The Role of Social and Self-Conscious Emotions in the Regulation of Business-to-Business Relationships in Salesperson–Customer Interactions," *The Journal of Business & Industrial Marketing* 21 (2006), p. 453.

20. Kahn et al., *Organizational Stress*, pp. 72–95; Ajay K. Kohli, "Some Unexplored Supervisory Behaviors and Their Influence on Salespeople's Role Clarity, Specific Self-Esteem, Job Satisfaction and Motivation," *Journal of Marketing Research* 22 (November 1985), pp. 424–433; Louis W. Fry, Charles M. Futrell, A. Parasuraman, and Margaret Chmielewski, "An Analysis of Alternate Causal Models of Salesperson Role Perceptions and Work-Related Attitudes," *Journal of Marketing Research* 23 (May 1986), pp. 153–163; Jeffrey Sager, "A Structural Model Depicting Salespeople's Job Stress," *Journal of the Academy of Marketing Science* 22 (Winter 1994), pp. 74–84.

21. R. Kenneth Teas, John G. Wacker, and R. Eugene Hughes, "A Path Analysis of Causes and Consequences of Salespeople's Perceptions of Role Clarity," *Journal of Marketing Research* 16 (August 1979), pp. 355–369; Richard P. Bagozzi, "The Nature and Causes of Self-Esteem, Performance, and Satisfaction in the Sales Force: A Structural Equation Approach," *Journal of Business* 53 (1980), pp. 315–331; Gary K. Rhoads, Jagdip Singh, and Phillips W. Goodell, "The Multiple Dimensions of Role Ambiguity and Their Impact upon Psychological and Behavioral Outcomes of Industrial Salespeople," *Journal of Personal Selling & Sales Management* 14 (Summer 1994), pp. 1–24; Vincent Onyemah, "Role Ambiguity, Role Conflict, and Performance: Empirical Evidence of an Inverted-U Relationship," *Journal of Personal Selling & Sales Management* 28 (Summer 2008), p. 299.

22. William A. Weeks, and Christophe Fournier, "The Impact of Time Congruity on Salesperson's Role Stress: A Person-Job Fit Approach," *Journal of Personal Selling & Sales Management* 30 (Summer 2010), pp. 209–222; Charles M. Futrell and A. Parasuraman, "The Relationship of Satisfaction and Performance to Salesforce Turnover," *Journal of Marketing* 48 (Fall 1984), pp. 33–40; George H. Lucas, Jr., et al., "An Empirical Study of Salesforce Turnover," *Journal of Marketing* 51 (July 1987), pp. 34–59; Terence L. Holmes and Rajesh Srivastava, "Effects of Job Perceptions on Job Behaviors: Implications for Sales Performance," *Industrial Marketing Management* 31 (August 2002), p. 421.

23. James B. DeConinck, and Julie T. Johnson, "The Effects of Perceived Supervisor Support, Perceived Organizational Support, and Organizational Justice on Turnover Among Salespeople," *Journal of Personal Selling & Sales Management* 29 (Fall 2009), pp. 333–351. Richard P. Bagozzi, "Salesforce Performance and Satisfaction as a Function of Individual Difference, Interpersonal, and Situational Factors," *Journal of Marketing Research* 15 (November 1978), pp. 517–531; Ryan D. Zimmerman and Todd C. Darnold, "The Impact of Job Performance on Employee Turnover Intentions and the Voluntary Turnover Process; A Meta-Analysis and Path Model," *Personnel Review* 38 (2009), p. 142; Wouter Vandenabeele, "The Mediating Effect of Job Satisfaction and Organizational Commitment on Self-Reported Performance: More Robust Evidence of the PSM-Performance Relationship," *International Review of Administrative Sciences* 75 (March 2009), p. 11.

24. Rapp, Adam, Raj Agnihotri, and Thomas L. Baker, "Conceptualizing Salesperson Competitive Intelligence: An Individual Level Perspective," *Journal of Personal Selling & Sales Management* 31 (Spring 2011), pp. 141–156; Lawrence B. Chonko, Roy D. Howell, and Danny N. Bellenger, "Consequence in Sales Force Evaluation: Relation to Sales Force Perceptions of Conflict and Ambiguity," *Journal of Personal Selling & Sales Management* 6 (May 1986), pp. 35–48.

25. Orville C. Walker, Jr., Gilbert A. Churchill, Jr., and Neil M. Ford, "Organizational Determinants of the Role Conflict and Ambiguity Experienced by Industrial Salesmen," *Journal of Marketing* 39 (January 1975), pp. 32–39; Ellen Bolman Pullins, Leslie M. Fine, and Wendy L. Warren, "Identifying Peer Mentors in the Sales Force: An Exploratory Investigation of Willingness and Ability," *Academy of Marketing Science Journal* 24 (Spring 1996), pp. 125–136.

26. C. Fred Maio, and Kenneth R. Evans, "The Interactive Effects of Sales Control Systems on Salesperson Performance: a Job Demands–Resources Perspective," *Journal of the Academy of Marketing Science*, 41 (January 2013), pp. 73–90.

27. Lawrence B. Chonko, "The Relationship of Span of Control to Sales Representatives: Experienced Role Conflict and Role Ambiguity," *Academy of Management Journal* 25 (June 1982), pp. 452–456; Shelby D. Hunt and Arturo Z. Vasquez-Parraga, "Organizational Consequences, Marketing Ethics, and Salesforce Supervision," *Journal of Marketing Research* 30 (February 1993), pp. 78–90; Linda S. Hartenian, Farrand J. Hadaway, and Gordon J. Badovick, "Antecedents and Consequences of Role Perceptions: A Path Analytic Approach," *Journal of Applied Business Research* 10 (Spring 1994), pp. 40–50.

28. Sean, Valentine, "Ethics Training, Ethical Context, and Sales and Marketing Professionals' Satisfaction with Supervisors and Coworkers," *Journal of Personal Selling & Sales Management* 29 (Summer 2009), pp. 227–242; Susan Powell Mantel, "Choice or Perception: How Affect Influences Ethics Choices among Salespeople," *Journal of Personal Selling & Sales Management* 25 (Winter 2005), pp. 43–55. Paul Busch, "The Sales Manager's Bases of Social Power and Influence upon the Sales Force," *Journal of Marketing* 44 (Summer 1980), pp. 91–101; Ronald E. Michaels, William L. Cron, Alan J. Dubinsky, and Erich A. Joachimsthaler, "Influence of Formalization on the Organizational Commitment and Work Alienation of Salespeople and Industrial Buyers," *Journal of Marketing Research* 25 (November 1988), pp. 376–383.

29. Pradeep K. Tyagi, "The Effects of Stressful Organizational Conditions on Salesperson Work Motivation," *Journal of the Academy of Marketing Science* 13 (Winter–Spring 1985), pp. 290–309; Susan M. Keaveney and James E. Nelson, "Coping with Organizational Role Stress: Intrinsic Motivational Orientation, Perceived Role Benefits and Psychological Withdrawal," *Journal of the Academy of Marketing Science* 21 (Spring 1993), pp. 113–124; C. Fred Miao and Kenneth R. Evans, "The Impact of Salesperson Motivation on Role Perceptions and Job Performance: A Cognitive and Affective Perspective," *Journal of Personal Selling & Sales Management* 27 (Winter 2007), p. 89; Rutherford, Brian, JungKun Park, and Sang-Lin, "Increasing Job Performance and Descreasing Salesperson Propensity to Leave: An Examination in an Asian Sales Force," *Journal of Personal Selling & Sales Management* 31 (Spring 2011), pp. 171–184.

30. Greg W. Marshall, William C. Moncrief, and Felicia G. Lassk, "The Current State of Sales Force Activities," *Industrial Marketing Management* 28 (1999), pp. 87–98; William C. Moncrief, "Selling Activity and Sales Position Taxonomies for Industrial Salesforces," *Journal of Marketing Research* 23 (August 1986), pp. 261–270; Robert E. Hite and Joseph A. Bellizzi, "Differences in the Importance of Selling Techniques between Consumer and Industrial Salespeople," *Journal of Personal Selling & Sales Management* 5 (November 1985), pp. 19–30.

7 Salesperson Performance: Motivating the Sales Force

1. Suzy Ramlal, "Review of Employee Motivation Theories and Their Implications for Employee Retention within Organizations," *Journal of American Academy of Business* 5 (September 2004), pp. 52–64.

2. For a discussion of motivational theories and their interrelationships, see James L. Gibson, John M. Ivancevich, and James H. Donnelly, Jr., *Organizations: Behavior, Structure, Processes*, 7th ed. (Homewood, IL: Richard D. Irwin, 1991); Mary D. Stecher and Joseph G. Rosse, "Understanding Reactions to Workplace Injustice Through Process Theories of Motivation: A Teaching Module and Simulation," *Journal of Management Education* 31 (December 2007), pp. 777–796.

3. Barton A. Weitz, Harish Sujan, and Mita Sujan, "Knowledge, Motivation, and Adaptive Behavior: A Framework for Improving Selling Effectiveness," *Journal of Marketing* (October 1986), pp. 174–191. See also Harish Sujan, "Smarter versus Harder: An Exploratory Attributional Analysis of Salespeople's Motivation," *Journal of Marketing Research* (February 1986), pp. 41–49; Kirk Smith, Eli Jones, and Edward Blair, "Managing Salesperson Motivation in a Territory Realignment," *Journal of Personal Selling & Sales Management* 20 (Fall 2000), pp. 215–226; Dana James, "Web Conferencing, Talk Eases Salespeople's Fears," *Marketing News* (November 19, 2001), pp. 4–5.

4. Leff Bonney, Christopher R. Plouffe, and Jeremy Wolter, "I Think I Can, I Think I Can: The Impact of Perceived Selling Efficacy and Deal Disclosure on Salesperson Escalation of Commitment," Industrial Marketing Management, 43, (July 2014), pp. 826–839.

5. The argument is often advanced, for example, that salespeople should be given pricing flexibility in that they are closest to the customers and have the best perspective on the price that will be needed to make the sales. Interestingly, one study found that among a sample of 108 firms, those firms that gave salespeople the highest degree of pricing authority generated the lowest sales and profit performance. See P. Ronald Stephenson, William L. Cron, and Gary L. Frazier, "Delegating Pricing Authority in the Sales Force: The Effects on Sales and Profit Performance," *Journal of Marketing* (Spring 1979), pp. 21–28. See also Richard Kern, "Letting Your Salespeople Set Prices (Sort Of)," *Sales & Marketing Management* (August 1989), pp. 44–49; Thomas E. DeCarlo, R. Kenneth Teas, and James C. McElroy, "Salesperson Attribution Process and the Formation of Expectancy Estimates," *Journal of Personal Selling & Sales Management* 17 (Summer 1997), pp. 1–17.

6. Abraham K. Korman, "Expectancies as Determinants of Performance," *Journal of Applied Psychology* 55 (1971), pp. 218–222; Roy D. Howell, Danny N. Bellenger, and James B. Wilcox, "Self-Esteem, Role Stress, and Job Satisfaction among Marketing Managers," *Journal of Business Research* (February 1987), pp. 71–84. See also Jeffrey Sager, Junsub Yi, and Charles M. Futrell, "A Model of Depicting Salesperson's Perceptions," *Journal of Personal Selling & Sales Management* 18 (Summer 1998), pp. 1–22; Marc-André Reinhard and Oliver Dickhäuser, "Need for Cognition, Task Difficulty, and the Formation of Performance Expectancies," *Journal of Personality and Social Psychology* 96 (May 2009), p. 1062.

7. Rosemary Lagace, Stephen B. Castleberry, and Rick Ridnour, "An Exploratory Salesforce Study of the Relationship between Lead–Member Exchange and Motivation, Role Stress, and Manager Evaluation," *Journal of Applied Business Research* (Fall 1993), pp. 110–119; Julia Chang, "Happy Sales Force, Happy Returns," *Sales & Marketing Management* 158 (March 2006), pp. 32–34.

8. Fernando Jaramillo, Douglas B. Grisaffe, Lawrence B. Chonko, and James A. Roberts," Examining the Impact of Servant Leadership on Sales Force Performance," *Journal of Personal Selling & Sales Management* 29 (Summer 2009), pp. 257–276, James B. DeConinck, "The Effects of Leader-Member Exchange and Organizational Identification on Performance and Turnover Among Salespeople," *Journal of Personal Selling & Sales Management* 31 (Winter 2011), pp. 21–34. Edward E. Lawler III, *Pay and Organizational Effectiveness: A Psychological View* (New York: McGraw-Hill, 1971); Malcolm Fleschner, "Manager as Motivator," SellingPower.com (June 13, 2001); *Sales & Marketing Management* (August 2001), p. 62.

9. Alfie Kohn, *Punished by Rewards* (New York: Houghton Mifflin, 1993). Also see William Keenan, Jr., "Breaking with Tradition," *Sales & Marketing Management* (June 1994), pp. 94–99.

10. For example, see Thomas N. Ingram and Danny N. Bellenger, "Personal and Organizational Variables: Their Relative Effect on Reward Valences of Industrial Salespeople," *Journal of Marketing Research* (May 1983), pp. 198–205; Lawrence B. Chonko, John F. Tanner, Jr., and William A. Weeks, "Reward Preferences of Salespeople," *Journal of Personal Selling & Sales Management* (Summer 1992), pp. 67–76; Thomas E. DeCarlo, R. Kenneth Teas, and James C. McElroy, "Salesperson Performance Attribution and Processes and Formation of Expectancy Estimates," *Journal of Personal Selling & Sales Management* (Summer 1997), pp. 1–17; Alexander D. Stajkovic and Fred Luthans, "Differential Effects of Incentive Motivators on Work Experience," *Academy of Management Journal* 4, no. 3 (2001), pp. 580–590. For an interesting cross-cultural comparison of reward valences—as well as expectancy and instrumentality perceptions—across salespeople in the United States, Korea, and Japan, see Alan J. Dubinsky, Masaaki Kotabe, Chae Un Lim, and Ronald E. Michaels, "Differences in Motivational Perceptions among U.S., Japanese, and Korean Sales Personnel," *Journal of Business Research* 30 (1994), pp. 175–185; Jennifer Gilbert, "What Motivates Me," *Sales & Marketing Management* 155 (February 2003), pp. 30–35.

11. C. Fred Miao, and Kenneth R. Evans, "The Impact of Salesperson Motivation on Role Perceptions and Job Performance: A Cognitive and Affective Perspective," *Journal of Personal Selling & Sales Management* 27 (Winter 2007), pp. 89–101; *Sales & Marketing Management* (March 2001), p. 14

12. Gilbert A. Churchill, Jr., Neil M. Ford, and Orville C. Walker, Jr., "Predicting a Salesperson's Job Effort and Performance: Theoretical, Empirical, and Methodological Considerations," in *Sales Management: New Developments from Behavioral and Decision Model Research*, ed. Richard P. Bagozzi (Cambridge, MA: Marketing Science Institute, 1979), pp. 3–39; Gordon T. Gray and Stacia Wert-Gray, "Decision-Making Processes and Formation of Salespeople's Expectancies, Instrumentalities, and Valences," *Journal of Personal Selling & Sales Management* 19 (Summer 1999), pp. 53–59.

13. For a study focused on industrial salespeople, see Richard L. Oliver, "Expectancy Theory Predictions of Salesmen's Performance," *Journal of Marketing Research* (August 1974), pp. 243–253.

14. Abraham H. Maslow, *Motivation and Personality*, 2nd ed. (New York: Harper & Row, 1970); David L. Rennie, "Two Thoughts on Abraham Maslow," *The Journal of Humanistic Psychology* 48 (October 2008), p. 445.

15. Frederick Herzberg, Bernard Mauser, and Barbara Snyderman, *The Motivation to Work*, 2nd ed. (New York: John Wiley & Sons, 1959). See also Robert Berl, Terry Powell, and Nicholas C. Williamson, "Industrial Salesforce Satisfaction and Performance with Herzberg's Theory," *Industrial Marketing Management* (February 1984), pp. 11–19; David D. Shipley and Julia A. Kiely, "Industrial Salesforce Motivation and Herzberg's Dual Factor Theory: A U.K. Perspective," *Journal of Personal Selling & Sales Management* (May 1986), pp. 9–16; David Hackett, "Bespoke Bonus," *Marketing Week* 24, no. 12 (2001), p. 45.

16. Clayton P. Alderfer, "An Empirical Test of a New Theory of Human Needs," *Organizational Behavior and Human Performance* 4 (1969), pp. 142–175; Larry E. Pate, "Understanding Human Behaviour," *Management Decision* 25 (1987), pp. 58–64.

17. Gilbert A. Churchill, Jr., Neil M. Ford, and Orville C. Walker, Jr., "Personal Characteristics of Salespeople and the Attractiveness of Alternative Rewards," *Journal of Business Research* 7 (1979), pp. 25–50; Robert L. Berl, Nicholas C. Williamson, and Terry Powell, "Industrial Salesforce Motivation: A Critique and Test of Maslow's Hierarchy of Needs," *Journal of Personal Selling & Sales Management* (May 1984), pp. 33–39.

18. See Lawler, *Pay and Organizational Effectiveness*, especially, pp. 46–59; Maslow, *Motivation and Personality*, 2nd ed. (New York: Harper & Row, 1970).

19. Wesley J. Johnston and Keysuk Kim, "Performance, Attribution, and Expectancy Linkages in Personal Selling," *Journal of Marketing* (October 1994), pp. 68–81; Thomas E. DeCarlo, R. Kenneth Teas, and James C. McElroy, "Salesperson Performance Attribution Process and the Formation of Expectancy Estimates," *Journal of Personal Selling & Sales Management* 17 (Summer 1997), pp. 1–17.

20. David C. McClelland, John W. Atkinson, Russell A. Clark, and Edgar L. Lowell, *The Achievement Motive* (New York: Appleton-Century-Crofts, 1953); John W. Atkinson, *An Introduction to Motivation* (Princeton, NJ: Van Nostrand, 1964); Murray R. Barrick, Greg L. Steward, and Mike Piotrowski, "Personality and Job Performance: Test of the Mediating Effects of Motivation Among Sales Representatives," *Journal of Applied Psychology* 87 (February 2002), p. 43.

21. See, for example, E. E. Lawler III, "Job Attitudes and Employee Motivation: Theory, Research, and Practice," *Personnel Psychology* 23 (1970), pp. 223–237; Julian B. Rotter, "Generalized Expectancies for Internal versus External Control of Reinforcement," *Psychological Monographs: General and Applied* (1966), p. 80; Michael L. Mallin and Michael Mayo, "Why Did I Lose? A Conservation of Resources View of Salesperson Failure Attributions," *Journal of Personal Selling & Sales Management* 26 (Fall 2006), p. 345; J. K. Sager, H. D. Strutton, and D. A. Johnson, "Core Self-Evaluations and Salespeople," *Psychology & Marketing* 23 (February 2006), p. 95.

22. J. K. Sager, H. D. Strutton, and D. A. Johnson, "Core Self-Evaluations and Salespeople," p. 95.

23. Abraham K. Korman, "Expectancies as Determinants of Performance," *Journal of Applied Psychology* 55 (1971), pp. 218–222; Lawler, "Job Attitudes," pp. 223–237; Anonymous, "The 'Outcomes' Approach to Motivation," *Manager's Magazine* 59 (November 1984), pp. 32–35.

24. Ingram and Bellenger, "Personal and Organizational Variables," pp. 203–204.

25. R. Kenneth Teas and James C. McElroy, "Causal Attributions and Expectancy Estimates: A Framework for Understanding the Dynamics of Salesforce Motivation," *Journal of Marketing* (January 1986), pp. 75–86; DeCarlo, Teas, and McElroy, "Salesperson Performance Attribution Processes"; Johnston and Kim, "Performance, Attribution, and Expectancy Linkages"; Andrea L. Dixon, Rosann L. Spiro, and Maqbul Jamil, "Successful and Unsuccessful Sales Calls: Measuring Salesperson Attributions and Behavioral Intentions," *Journal of Marketing* 65, no. 3 (2001), pp. 64–78.

26. Karen E. Flaherty and James M. Pappas, "Using Career Stage Theory to Predict Turnover Intentions among Salespeople," *Journal of Marketing Theory and Practice* 10 (Summer 2002), pp. 48–57. See also Sujan, "Smarter versus Harder."

27. William L. Cron, "Industrial Salesperson Development: A Career Stages Perspective," *Journal of Marketing* (Fall 1984), pp. 41–52; William L. Cron and John W. Slocum, Jr., "The Influence of Career Stages on Salespeople's Job Attitudes, Work Perceptions, and Performance," *Journal of Marketing Research* (May 1986), pp. 119–129; William L. Cron, Alan J. Dubinsky, and Ronald E. Michaels, "The Influence of Career Stages on Components of Salesperson Motivation," *Journal of Marketing* (January 1988), pp. 78–92; William L. Cron, Ellen F. Jackofsky, and John W. Slocum, Jr., "Job Performance and Attitudes of Disengagement Stage Salespeople Who Are about to Retire," *Journal of Personal Selling & Sales Management* (Spring 1993), pp. 1–13.

28. Vaibhav Chawla and Sridhar Guda "Workplace Spirituality as Precursor to Relationship Oriented Selling Characteristics," Journal of Business Ethics, 115, (June 2013), pp. 63–73.

29. Douglas E. Hughers, "This Ad's For You: The Indirect Effect of Advertising Perceptions on Salesperson Effort and Performance," Journal of the Academy of Marketing Science, 41, (January 2013), pp. 1–18.

30. Bashar S. Gammoh, Michael L. Mallin, and Ellen Bolman Pullins, "Antecedents and Consequences of Salesperson Identification with the Brand and Company," *Journal of Personal Selling and Sales Management*, 34, (Issue 1, Winter 2014), pp. 3–18.

31. C. Fred Miao, Donald J. Lund, and Kenneth Evans, "Re-Examining the Influence of Career Stages on Salesperson Motivation: A Cognitive and Affective Perspective," *Journal of Personal Selling & Sales Management* 29 (Summer 2009), pp. 101–112; Robin T. Peterson, "Beyond the Plateau," *Sales & Marketing Management* (July 1993), pp. 78–82.

32. Michael Ahearne, Till Haumanm, Floria Kraus, Jan Wieseke, "Its a Matter of Congruence: How Interpersonal Identification Between Sales Managers and Salespersons Shapes Sales Success," *Journal of the Academy of Marketing Science*, 41 (November 2013), pp. 625–648.

33. Gilbert A. Churchill, Jr., Neil M. Ford, and Orville C. Walker, Jr., "Organizational Climate and Job Satisfaction in the Sales Force," *Journal of Marketing Research* (November 1976), pp. 323–332; Pradeep K. Tyagi, "Relative Importance of Key Job Dimensions and Leadership Behaviors in Motivating Salesperson Work Performance," *Journal of Marketing* (Summer 1985), pp. 76–86. See also Susan K. DelVecchio, "The Quality of Salesperson–Manager Relationship: The Effect of Latitude, Loyalty and Competence," *Journal of Personal Selling & Sales Management* (Winter 1998), pp. 31–48; Vincent Alonzo, "Perks for Jerks," *Sales & Marketing Management* (February 2001), pp. 38–40; C. David Shepherd, Armen Tashcian and Rick E. Ridnour, "An Investigation of the Job Burnout Syndrome in Personal Selling," *Journal of Personal Selling & Sales Management* 31 (Fall 2011), pp. 397–410.

8 Personal Characteristics and Sales Aptitude: Criteria for Selecting Salespeople

1. Julia Chang, "Born to Sell?" *Sales & Marketing Management* (July 2003), pp. 34–38. For a more complete discussion of current research on salesperson performance criteria, see William I. Cron, Greg W. Marshall, Jagdip Singh, Rosann L. Spiro, and Harish Sujan, "Salesperson Selection, Training, and Development: Trends, Implications, and Research Opportunities," *Journal of Personal Selling & Sales Management* 25 (Spring 2005), pp. 123–136; Thomas E. DeCarlo, Sanjeev Agarwal, and Shyman B. Vyas, "Performance Expectations of Salespeople: The Role of Past Performance and Casual Attributions in Independent and Interdependent Cultures," *Journal of Personal Selling & Sales Management* 27 (Spring 2007), pp. 133–147; Ronald Jelinek and Michael Ahearne, "The Enemy Within: Examining Salesperson Deviance and Its Determinants," *Journal of Personal Selling & Sales Management* 26 (Fall 2006), pp. 327–344; Blair Kidwell, Richard G. McFarland, and Ramon A. Avila, "Perceiving Emotion in the Buyer–Seller Interchange: The Moderated Impact on Performance," *Journal of Personal Selling & Sales Management* 27 (Spring 2007), pp. 119–132.

2. Arthur Bragg, "Are Good Salespeople Born or Made?" *Sales & Marketing Management* (September 1988), p. 74.

3. Gilbert A. Churchill, Jr., Neil M. Ford, Steven W. Hartley, and Orville C. Walker, Jr., "The Determinants of Salesperson Performance: A Meta-Analysis," *Journal of Marketing Research* (May 1985), pp. 103–118. See also Neil M. Ford, Orville C. Walker, Jr., and Gilbert A. Churchill, Jr., "Selecting Successful Salespeople: A Meta-Analysis of Biographical and Psychological Selection Criteria," in *Review of Marketing*, ed. Michael J. Houston (Chicago: American Marketing Association, 1988), pp. 90–131; Goutam Challagalla and Tasaddug A. Shervani, "Dimensions and Types of Supervisory Control: Effects on Sales Performance and Satisfaction," *Journal of Marketing* (January 1996), pp. 47–60; Fernando Jaramillo, Jay Prakash Mulki, and Greg W. Marshall, "A Meta-Analysis of the Relationship between Organizational Commitment and Salesperson Job Performance: 25 Years of

Research," *Journal of Business Research* 58 (June 2005), p. 705; Verbeke, Willem, Bart Dietz, and Ernst Verwaal, "Drivers of Sales Performance: A Contemporary Meta-Analysis, Have Salespeople Become Knowledge Brokers?", *Journal of the Academy of Marketing Science* 39 (2011), p. 407.

4. Christen P. Heide, *Dartnell's 30th Sales Force Compensation Survey* (Chicago: Dartnell Corporation, 1999), p. 187. See also HR Chally, "Applying Total Quality Management to Managing Talent" (2006), p. 5.

5. Jeffrey K. Sager, "Recruiting and Retaining Committed Salespeople," *Industrial Marketing Management* (May 1991), pp. 99–103.

6. Heide, *Dartnell's 30th Sales Force Compensation Survey*, p. 143.

7. Ibid.

8. Stan Moss, "What Sales Executives Look For in New Salespeople," *Sales & Marketing Management* (March 1978), pp. 43–48; Thomas Rollins, "How to Tell Competent Salespeople from the Other Kind," *Sales & Marketing Management* (September 1990), pp. 116–117, 145–146; Michael K. Rich and Daniel C. Smith, "Determining Relationship Skills of Prospective Salespeople," *The Journal of Business & Industrial Marketing* 15 (2000), p. 242.

9. Ford et al., "Selecting Successful Salespeople," pp. 90–131.

10. Ford et al., "Selecting Successful Salespeople." Also see Seymour Adler, "Personality Tests for Salesforce Selection: Worth a Fresh Look," *Review of Business* (Summer 1994), pp. 27–31.

11. Heide, *Dartnell's 30th Sales Force Compensation Survey*, p. 170.

12. C. David Shepherd and James C. Heartfield, "Discrimination Issues in the Selection of Salespeople: A Review and Managerial Suggestions," *Journal of Personal Selling & Sales Management* (Fall 1991), pp. 67–75; James M. Owens, Glenn M. Gomes, and James F. Morgan, "Broadening the Definition of Unlawful Retaliation Under Title VII," *Employee Responsibilities and Rights Journal* 20 (December 2008), pp. 249–260.

13. Bobbi Linkemer, "Women in Sales: What Do They Really Want?" *Sales & Marketing Management* (January 1989), pp. 61–65; Heide, *Dartnell's 30th Sales Force Compensation Survey*, p. 169.

14. John E. Swan, David R. Rink, G. E. Kiser, and Warren S. Martin, "Industrial Buyer Image of the Saleswomen," *Journal of Marketing* (Winter 1984), pp. 110–116. See also Myron Gable and B. J. Reed, "The Current Status of Women in Professional Selling," *Journal of Personal Selling & Sales Management* (May 1987), pp. 33–39; Lucette B. Comer, J. A. F. Nicholls, and Leslie J. Vermillion, "Diversity in the Sales Force: Problems and Challenges," *Journal of Personal Selling & Sales Management* (Fall 1998), pp. 1–20; Nigel F. Piercy, David W. Cravens, and Nikala Lane, "The New Gender Agenda in Sales Management," *Business Horizons* 46 (July–August 2003), p. 39; James S. Boles, John Andy Wood, and Julie Johnson, "Interrelationships of Role Conflict, Role Ambiguity, and Work–Family Conflict with Different Facets of Job Satisfaction and the Moderating Effects of Gender," *Journal of Personal Selling & Sales Management* 23 (Spring 2003), p. 99.

15. Lucette B. Comer and Marvin A. Jolson, "Perceptions of Gender Stereotypic Behavior: An Exploratory Study of Women in Selling," *Journal of Personal Selling & Sales Management* (Winter 1991), pp. 43–59. See also Judy A. Siguaw and Earl D. Honeycutt, Jr., "An Examination of Gender Differences in Selling Behaviors and Job Attitudes," *Industrial Marketing Management* 24 (1995), pp. 45–52; Arun Sharma, Michael Levy, and Heiner Evanschitzky, "The Variance in Sales Performance Explained by the Knowledge Structures of Salespeople," *Journal of Personal Selling & Sales Management* 27 (Spring 2007), p. 169.

16. Franklin Evans, "Selling as a Dyadic Relationship—A New Approach," *American Behavioral Scientist* (May 1963), pp. 76–79; Sean Dwyer, Orlando Richard, and C. David Shepherd, "An Exploratory Study of Gender and Age Matching in the Salesperson–Prospective Customer Dyad: Testing Similarity–Performance Predictions," *Journal of Personal Selling & Sales Management* 18 (Fall 1998), pp. 55–69.

17. Gilbert A. Churchill, Jr., Robert H. Collins, and William A. Strang, "Should Retail Salespersons Be Similar to Their Customers?" *Journal of Retailing* (Fall 1975), pp. 29–42. See also Barton A. Weitz, "Effectiveness in Sales Interactions: A Contingency Framework," *Journal of Marketing* (Winter 1981), pp. 85–103.

18. Rene Y. Darmon, "Where Do the Best Sales Force Profit Producers Come From?" *Journal of Personal Selling & Sales Management* 3 (Summer 1993), pp. 17–29; Heide, *Dartnell's 30th Sales Force Compensation Survey*; Judy Rose, "English Isn't Enough in Real Estate Sales: Agents Need Foreign Language Skills," *Washington Post* (April 21, 2001), p. H22.

19. Andrew J. Vinchur, Jeffrey S. Schippmann, Fred S. Switzer III, and Philip L. Roth, "A Meta-Analytic Review of Predictors of Job Performance for Salespeople," *Journal of Applied Psychology* 83 (August 1998), p. 586; Adler, "Personality Tests for Salesforce Selection"; Cengiz Yilmaz and Shelby D. Hunt, "Salesperson Cooperation: The Influence of Relational, Task, Organizational, and Personal Factors," *Journal of the Academy of Marketing Science* 29, no. 4 (2001), pp. 335–357.

20. Kirby J. Shannahan, Alan J. Bush, and Rachelle J. Shannahan, "Are You Salespeople Coachable? How Salesperson Coachability, Trait Competitiveness and Transformation Leadership Enhance Sales Performance," *Journal of the Academy of Marketing Science*, 41 (January 2013), pp. 40–54.

21. Belen Bande, Pilar Fernandez-Ferrin, Jose A. Varela, and Fernando Jaramillo, "Emotions and Salesperson Propensity to Leave: The Effects of Emotional Intelligence and Resilience," *Industrial Marketing Management*, 44 (January 2015), pp. 142–153

22. Raj Agnihotri and Michael T. Krush, "Salesperson Empathy, Ethical Behaviors, and Sales Performance: the Moderating Role of Turst in ONe's Manager," *Journal of Personal Selling and Sales Management*," 35 (Issue 2, Spring 2015), pp. 164–174.

23. Chien Chung and Fernando Jaramillo, "The Double-Edged Effects of Emotional Intelligence on the Adaptive Selling-Salesperson-Owned Loyalty Relationship," *Journal of Personal Selling and Sales Management*, 34, (Issue 1, Winter 2014), pp. 33–50.

24. Eric G. Harris, Daniel M. Ladik, Andrew B. Artis, and David E. Fleming, "Examining the Influence of Job Resourcefullness on Sales Performance," *Journal of Marketing Theory and Practice*, 21, (Fall 2013), pp. 405–414.

25. Adapted from *Sales & Marketing Management*, www.salesandmarketing.com, June 2015.

26. While another study examines job-specific abilities, it focuses on only one type of sales job—missionary selling. See Dan C. Weilbaker, "The Identification of Selling Abilities Needed for Missionary Type Sales," *Journal of Personal Selling & Sales Management* (Summer 1990), pp. 45–58.

27. Derek A. Newton, "Get the Most out of Your Salesforce," *Harvard Business Review* (September–October 1969), pp. 130–143. See also Weilbaker, "The Identification of Selling Abilities."

9 Sales Force Recruitment and Selection

1. Thomas Rollins, "How to Tell Competent Salespeople from the Other Kind," *Sales & Marketing Management* (September 1990), pp. 116–118, 145–146; Gigi Dryer, "Building a Successful Team," *Custom Retailer* 7 (July 2008), p. 45.

2. Byunghwa Yang, Youngchan Kim, and Richard G. McFarland, "Individual Differences and Sales Performance: A Distal-Proximal Mediation Model of Self Efficacy, Conscientiousness, and Extraversion," *Journal of Personal Selling & Sales Management* 31 (Fall 2011), pp. 371–382.

3. Claudia M. Van Der Heijde and Beatrice I. J. M. Van Der Heijden, "A Competence-Based and Multidimensional Operationalization and Measurement of Employability," *Human Resource Management* 45 (Fall 2006), p. 449.

4. pp. 75–85; Barry Farber, "Start at the Beginning," *Sales & Marketing Management* (March 1996), pp. 24–25; Carole Ann King, "Frustration Mounts as Recruiting Gets Harder," *National Underwriter* (March 19, 2001), pp. 6–7; Tali Arbel, "Saying Goodbye to the Want Ad," *Sales & Marketing Management* 158 (October 2006), p. 46.

5. Lin Grensing-Pophal, "Internal Selections," *HR Magazine* 51 (December 2006), pp. 75–78.

6. Daniel C. Feldman, William O. Bearden, and David M. Hardesty, "Varying the Content of Job Advertisements: The Effects of Message Specificity," *Journal of Advertising* 35 (Spring 2006), pp. 123–121.

7. Ibid.

8. Audrey Bottjen, "The Benefits of College Recruiting," *Sales & Marketing Management* (April 2001), p. 20. For a more in-depth discussion of university sales programs refer to "Top University Sales Education Programs," SellingPower.com., June 2007.

9. For a detailed discussion of salesperson selection, training, and development, reference William L. Cron, Greg W. Marshall, Jagdip Singh, Rosann L. Spiro, and Harish Sujan, "Salesperson Selection, Training, and Development: Trends, Implications, and Research Opportunities," *Journal of Personal Selling & Sales Management* 25 (Spring 2005), pp. 123–136; Anonymous, "Think 'Slow and Steady' for Snaring Top Hires," *Sales & Marketing Management* 160 (July–August 2008), p. 6.

10. For a discussion of the validity of different selection procedures as applied to the evaluation of salespeople, see Neil M. Ford, Orville C. Walker, Jr., and Gilbert A. Churchill, Jr., "Selecting Successful Salespeople: A Meta-Analysis of Biographical and Psychological Selection Criteria," in *Review of Marketing*, ed. Michael J. Houston (Chicago: American Marketing Association, 1988), pp. 90–131; Jose M. Cortina, Nancy B. Goldstein, Stephanie C. Payne, H. Kristl Davison, and Stephen W. Gilliland, "The Incremental Validity of Interview Scores Over and Above Cognitive Ability and Conscientiousness Scores," *Personnel Psychology* 53 (Summer 2000), pp. 325–351.

11. J. Craig Wallace and Stephen J. Vodanovich, "Personnel Application Blanks: Persistence and Knowledge of Legally Inadvisable Application Blank Items," *Public Personnel Management* 33 (Fall 2004), pp. 331–349.

12. Patrick M. Wright, Philip A. Lichtenfels, and Elliot D. Pursell, "The Structured Interview: Additional Studies and a Meta-Analysis," *Journal of Occupational Psychology* 62 (September 1989), pp. 191–199.
13. William Keenan, Jr., "Who Has the Right Stuff?" *Sales & Marketing Management* (August 1993), pp. 28–29.
14. Anonymous, "References Influence Interview Outcomes," *USA Today* 132 (December 2003), p. 12.
15. C. David Shepherd and James C. Heartfield, "Discrimination Issues in the Selection of Salespeople: A Review and Managerial Suggestions," *Journal of Personal Selling & Sales Management* (Fall 1991), p. 71. See also Allison Lucas, "Race Matters," *Sales & Marketing Management* (September 1996), pp. 50–62.
16. Seymour Adler, "Personality Tests for Salesforce Selection: Worth a Fresh Look," *Review of Business* (Summer 1994), pp. 27–31.
17. J. Denrell, "Selection Bias and the Perils of Benchmarking," *Harvard Business Review*, April 2005, pp. 114–119.
18. www.eeoc.gov, July 2015.
19. For a detailed discussion of the procedures required to validate employment tests, visit the Equal Employment Opportunity Commission, *www.eeoc.gov.*

10   Sales Training: Objectives, Techniques, and Evaluation

1. Ashraf M. Attia, Earl D. Honeycutt, Jr., and Mark P. Leach, "A Three-Stage Model for Assessing and Improving Sales Force Training and Development," *Journal of Personal Selling & Sales Management* 25 (Summer 2005), pp. 253–268; Holly Dolezalek, "Making the Buy So They Can Sell," *Training* 43 (August 2006), pp. 34–37; Felicia G. Lassk, Thomas N. Ingram, Florian Kraus, and Rita D. Mascio, "The Future of Sales Training: Challenges and Related Research Questions," *Journal of Personal Selling & Sales Management* 32, (Fall 2012), pp. 141–154.
2. Annual Report for Alcatel-Lucent, 2015, www.alcatel-lucent.com. For a more complete discussion on the use of self-directed training and its effect on performance, see Andrew B. Artis and Eric G. Harris, "Self-Directed Learning and Sales Force Performance: An Integrated Framework," *Journal of Personal Selling & Sales Management* 27 (Winter 2007), pp. 9–24; Mark P. Leach, Annie H. Liu, and Wesley J. Johnston, "The Role of Self-Regulation Training in Developing the Motivation Management Capabilities of Salespeople," *Journal of Personal Selling & Sales Management*, 25 (Summer 2005), pp. 269–281; Brad Huisken, "How Do I Set Up a Productivity Improvement Program?" *Jewelers Circular Keystone (JCK)* 178 (October 2007), p. 140.
3. Chia-Yi Cheng, "A Longitudinal Study of Newcomer Job Embeddedness and Sales Outcomes for Life Insurance Salespersons," *Journal of Business Research*, 67, (July 2014), pp. 1430–1438.
4. Jeffrey B. Boichuk, Williy Bolander, Zachary R. Hall, Michael Ahearne, William J Zahn, and Melissa Nieve, "Learned Helplessness Among Newly Hired Salespeople and the Influence of Leadership, *Journal of Marketing*, 78, (January 2014), pp. 95–111.
5. Judy A. Wagner, Noreen M. Klein, and Janet E. Keith, "Selling Strategies: The Effects of Suggesting a Decision Structure to Novice and Expert Buyers," *Journal of the Academy of Marketing Science* 29, no. 3 (2001), pp. 289–306; Trent Wachner, Christopher R. Plouffe, and Yany Grégoire, "SOCO's Impact on Individual Sales Performance: The Integration of Selling Skills as a Missing Link," *Industrial Marketing Management* 38 (January 2009), p. 32.
6. "Top Training Priorities?" *Training* (February 2004), pp. 26–32; V. Kumar, Rajkumar Venkatesan, and Werner Reinartz, "Performance Implications of Adopting a Customer-Focused Sales Campaign," *Journal of Marketing* 72 (September 2008), p. 50.
7. Sean Valentine, "Ethics Training, Ethical Context, and Sales and Marketing Professionals' Satisfaction with Supervisors and Coworkers," *Journal of Personal Selling & Sales Management* 29 (Summer 2009), pp. 227–242; See also Alan J. Dubinsky, "Sales Training and Education: Some Assumptions about the Effectiveness of Sales Training," *Journal of Personal Selling & Sales Management* (Summer 1996), pp. 67–76.
8. Shikhar Sarin, Trina Sego, Ajay K. Kohli, and Goutam Challagalla, "Characteristics That Enhance Training Electiveness in Implementing Technological Change in Sales Strategy: A Field-Based "Exploratory Study," *Journal of Personal Selling & Sales Management* 30 (Spring 2010), pp. 143–156; The following discussion is based to a large extent on "Top Training Priorities?" *Training* (February 2004), pp. 26–32.
9. Ibid., p. 38; Christen P. Heide, *Dartnell's 30th Sales Force Compensation Survey* (Chicago: Dartnell Corp., 1999), p. 142.
10. Kathleen McLaughlin, "Training's Top 50 Edward Jones," *Training* (March 2001), p. 20.
11. John Boe, "Time Is Money," *The American Salesman* 54 (January 2009), pp. 3–5.
12. www.caterpillar.com, July 2015.

13. Ellen Bolman Pullins, T.S. Ragu-Nathan, Monideepa Tarafdar, "Examining Impacts of Technostress on the Professional Salesperson's Behavioral Performance," *Journal of Personal Seling and Sales Management*, 34, (Issue 1, Winter 2014), pp. 51–69.

14. Thomas W. Leigh, Thomas E. DeCarlo, David Albright, and James Lollar, "Salesperson Knowledge Distinctions and Sales Performance," *Journal of Personal Selling and Sales Management*, 34, (Issue 2, Spring 2014), pp. 123–140.

15. Priscilla Donovan, "Selling Right and Left," *Sales & Marketing Management* (June 3, 1985), pp. 62–63.

16. Willem Verbeke and Richard Bagozzi, "Sales Call Anxiety: Exploring What It Means When Fear Rules the Sales Encounter," *Journal of Marketing* 64 (2000), pp. 88–101; Michele Marchetti, "Cold Feet," *Sales & Marketing Management* 155 (October 2003), p. 17.

17. Ned Miller, "Creating a Learning Environment: Tips for Sales Managers," *The RMA Journal* (July–August 2006), pp. 44–46; Heide, Dartnell's, p. 140.

18. Kevin Dobbs, "When Learning Really Happens," *Sales & Marketing Management* (November 2000), p. 98; Rebecca Aronauer, "Big Shoes to Fill," *Sales & Marketing Management* 158 (November–December 2006), p. 11.

19. Ross Wigham, "Off-Loading the Burden," *Training & Coaching Today* (February 2008), pp. 7–8.

20. Nathaniel N. Hartman, Brian N. Rutherford, G. Alexander Hamwi, and Scott B. Friend, "The Effects of Mentoring on Salesperson Commitment," *Journal of Business Research*, 66, (November 2013), pp. 2294–2300.

21. Kevin Dobbs, "Training on the Fly," Sales & Marketing Management (November 2000), pp. 92–98; Hyochang Lim, Sang-Gun Lee, and Kichan Nam, "Validating E-Learning Factors Affecting Training Effectiveness," *International Journal of Information Management* 27 (February 2007), p. 22.

22. Ibid., p. 96.

23. "Industry Report 2011," *Training*, July 2012, www.trainingmag.com

24. Ibid; Anonymous, "Get Value from Online Training," *Security* 45 (July 2008), pp. 78–79.

25. Robert C. Erffmeyer, K. Randall Russ, and Joseph F. Hair, Jr., "Needs Assessment and Evaluation in Sales-Training Programs," *Journal of Personal Selling & Sales Management* 11 (Winter 1991), pp. 17–31.

26. Fernando Jaramillo, Francois A. Carrillat, and William B. Locander, "A Meta-Analytic Comparison of Managerial Ratings and Self-Evaluations," *Journal of Personal Selling & Sales Management* 25 (Fall 2005), pp. 315–328.

27. Thomas L. Powers, Thomas E. DeCarlo, Gouri Gupte, "An Update on the Status of Sales Management Training," *Journal of Personal Selling & Sales Management* 30 (Fall 2010), pp. 319–326.

11 Salesperson Compensation and Incentives

1. Adapted from Malcolm Fleschner, "Should You Outsource Incentives?", February 17, 2010, http://www.sellingpower.com/magazine/article.php?i=49&ia=8989, accessed July 6, 2012.

2. Xin Liang, Sibin Wu, and Joo Y. Jung, "Recoupling Compensation-Performance Relationship: A Mediating Role of Performance," *International Journal of Human Resources Development and Management* 9, no. 4 (2009), pp. 317–333.

3. Leslie M. Fine and Janice R. Franke, "Legal Aspects of Salesperson Commission Payments: Implications for the Implementation of Commission Sales Programs," *Journal of Personal Selling & Sales Management* (Winter 1995), pp. 53–68.

4. Adapted from Stephanie Faris, "Sales Compensation Planning Is a Pain: Tech Help Is Here," February 20, 2012, www.smallbiztechnology.com/archive/2012/02/sales-compensation-planning-is-a-pain-tech-help-is-here.html/, accessed June 29, 2012.

5. Joanna L. Y. Ho, Anne Wu, and Ling-Chu Lee, "How Changes in Compensation Plans Affect Employee Performance, Recruitment, and Retention: An Empirical Study of a Car Dealership," *Contemporary Accounting Research* 4 (Spring 2009), pp. 167–199.

6. Arun Sharma, "Customer Satisfaction-Based Incentive Systems: Some Managerial and Salesperson Considerations," *Journal of Personal Selling & Sales Management* (Spring 1997), pp. 61–70.

7. Bulent Menguc, Seigyoung Auh, and Aypar Uslu, "Customer Knowledge Creation Capability and Cerformance in Sales Teams," *Journal of the Academy of Marketing Science* 41 (January 2013), pp. 19–39.

8. Joel Silver, "Building an Effective Sales Incentive Program," www.saleslobby.com, January 2002.

9. Ibid.; Audrey Bottjen, "Incentives Gone Awry," *Sales & Marketing Management* (May 2001), p. 72.

10. Karen Renk, "The Age-Old Question: Cash vs. Merchandise?" *Occupational Health and Safety* (September 2002), pp. 60–62.

11. Ibid.

12. Mark McMaster, "Personalized Motivation," *Sales & Marketing Management* (May 2002), p. 16.

13. Kerr's original article was updated and republished as follows—Steven Kerr, "On the Folly of Rewarding A, While Hoping for B," *Academy of Management Executive* 9, no. 1 (1995), pp. 7–14.

14. Soumaya Ben Letaifa and Jean Perrien, "The Impact of E-CRM on Organisational and Individual Behavior: The Effect of the Remuneration and Reward System," *International Journal of E-Business Research* 3 (April–June 2007), pp. 13–21.

15. Arun Sharma and Dan Sarel, "The Impact of Customer Satisfaction-Based Incentive Systems on Salespeople's Customer Service Response: An Empirical Study," *Journal of Personal Selling & Sales Management* (Summer 1995), pp. 17–29.

16. Christian Homburg, Torsten Bornemann, and Max Kretzer, "Delusive Perception—Antecedents and Consequences of Salespeople's Misperception of Customer Commitment," Journal of the Academy of Marketing Science 42 (March 2014), pp. 137–153; Jan Wieseke, Sascha Alavi, and Johannes Habel, "Willing to Pay More, Eager to Pay Less: The Role of Customer Loyalty in Price Negotiations," *Journal of Marketing* 78 (November 2014), pp. 17–37.

17. HR Chally Group, *The Great Business Challenges of the New Millennium* (Dayton, OH: HR Chally Group, 2007).

18. S. Scott Sands, "Ineffective Quotas: The Hidden Threat to Sales Compensation Plans," *Compensation and Benefits Review* 32 (March–April 2000), pp. 35–42.

19. Kemba J. Dunham, "Back to Reality: To Lure Workers, Dot-Coms Are Having to Focus on Something Besides Options, Such as Salaries," *The Wall Street Journal* (April 12, 2001), p. R5.

20. Susan L. Dustin and Ariel R. Belasen, "The Impact of Negative Compensation Changes on Individual Sales Performance," *Journal of Personal Selling & Sales Management* 33 (Issue 4, Fall 2013), pp. 403–417.

12 Cost Analysis

1. Robert Dwyer and John F. Tanner, Jr., *Business Marketing: Connecting Strategy, Relationships, and Learning* (New York: McGraw-Hill, 2009); HR Chally Group, *"The Great Business Challenges of the New Millenium* (Dayton, OH: HR Chally Group, 2007), p. 7.

2. Kissan Joseph, "On the Optimality of Delegating Pricing Authority to the Sales Force," *Journal of Marketing* (January 2001), pp. 62–70. See also Birendra K. Mishra and Ashutosh Prasad, "Centralized Pricing versus Delegating Pricing to the Salesforce under Information Asymmetry," *Marketing Science* 23 (Winter 2004), pp. 21–27.

3. Makoto Matsuo, "The Influence of Sales Management Control on Innovativeness of Sales Departments," *Journal of Personal Selling & Sales Management* 29 (Fall 2009), pp. 321–332.

4. Sanford R. Simon, *Managing Marketing Profitability* (New York: American Management Association, 1969), p. 37. All serious students of marketing cost analysis are urged to read this classic book on marketing profitability analysis. It illustrates the process that should be followed in carrying out a marketing cost analysis and the insights gained from doing so with detailed examples. Much of this and the following section rely heavily on this excellent book. See also Robin Cooper and Robert S. Kaplan, "Profit Priorities from Activity-Based Costing," *Harvard Business Review* 69 (May–June 1991), pp. 130–135.

5. Simon, *Managing Marketing Profitability*, pp. 37–38.

6. Gayle Rayburn, "Accounting Tools in the Analysis and Control of Marketing Performance," *Industrial Marketing Management* 6 (1977), pp. 175–182.

7. Robin Cooper and Robert S. Kaplan, "Measure Costs Right: Make the Right Decision," *Harvard Business Review* 66 (September–October 1988), pp. 96–103.

8. Daniel J. Goebel, Greg W. Marshall, and William B. Locander, "Activity Based Costing: Accounting for a Market Orientation," *Industrial Marketing Management* 27 (November 1998), pp. 497–510; David Bukovinsky, Hans Sprohge, and John Talbott, "Activity-Based Costing for Sales and Administrative Costs: A Case Study," *The CPA Journal* 70 (April 2000), pp. 70–72.

9. Adapted from Ashford C. Chea, "Activity Based Costing in the Service Sector: A Strategic Approach for Enhancing Managerial Decision Making and Competitiveness," *International Journal of Business and Management* 6, no. 11 (November 2011), pp. 3–10.

10. Robert A. Dwyer and John F. Tanner, Jr., *Business Marketing: Connecting Strategy Relationships and Learning 4e* (New York: McGraw-Hill, 2009).

11. Robin Cooper and Robert S. Kaplan, "Activity-Based Systems: Measuring the Cost of Resource Usage," *Accounting Horizons* 6 (September 1992), pp. 1–13. For another method of dividing revenue (customers) into segments, see the discussion on decile analysis in Dwyer and Tanner, *Business Marketing*, chap. 5.

12. Douglas M. Lambert and Jay U. Sterling, "What Types of Profitability Reports Do Marketing Managers Receive?" *Industrial Marketing Management* 16 (November 1987), pp. 295–304.

13. Charles R. Horngren, George Foster, Srikant M. Datar, Madhav Rajan, and Chri Ittner, *Cost Accounting: A Managerial Emphasis*, 13th ed. (Englewood Cliffs, NJ: Prentice Hall, 2008), p. 381. See also Fred Selnes, "Analyzing Marketing Profitability: Sales Are a Dangerous Cost-Driver," *European Journal of Marketing* 26, no. 2 (1992), pp. 15–26.

14. Thomas M. Petro, "Profitability: The Fifth 'P' of Marketing," *Basic Marketing* 22 (September 1990), pp. 48–52.

15. J. S. Schiff and Michael Schiff, "New Sales Management Tool: ROAM," *Harvard Business Review* 45 (July–August 1967), pp. 59–66. For the application of ROAM to evaluating sales territories, see J. S. Schiff, "Evaluating the Sales Force as a Business," *Industrial Marketing Management* 12 (April 1983), pp. 131–137. One problem with the return on assets managed measure for evaluating segment performance is that it neglects the firm's opportunity costs for the capital invested in the assets. Residual income analysis is a preferred alternative on these grounds for evaluating the profitability of the personal selling effort. See William L. Cron and Michael Levy, "Sales Management Performance Evaluation: A Residual Income Perspective," *Journal of Personal Selling & Sales Management* 7 (August 1987), pp. 57–66.

13 Evaluating Salesperson Performance

1. Nigel F. Piercy, David W. Cravens, and Nikala Lane, "Enhancing Salespeople's Effectiveness: When Is More Sales Management Control Better Sales Management Control?" *Marketing Management* 16 (September–October 2007), pp. 18–25.

2. David W. Cravens, Felicia G. Lassk, George S. Low, Greg W. Marshall, and William C. Moncrief, "Formal and Informal Management Control Combinations in Sales Organizations: The Impact on Salesperson Consequences," *Journal of Business Research* 57 (March 2004), pp. 241–248.

3. Manoshi Samaraweera and Betsy D. Gelb, "Formal Salesforce Controls and Revenue Production: A Meta-Analysis," *Journal of Personal Selling & Sales Management* 35 (Issue 1, Winter 2015), pp. 23–32.

4. David W. Cravens, Thomas N. Ingram, Raymond W. LaForge, and Clifford E. Young, "Behavior-Based and Outcome-Based Salesforce Control Systems," *Journal of Marketing* 57 (October 1993), pp. 47–59.

5. Ryan R. Mullins, Michael Ahearne, Son K. Lam, Zachary R. Hall, and Jeffrey P. Boichuk, "Know Your Customer: How Salesperson Perceptions of Customer Relationship Quality Form and Influence Account Profitability," *Journal of Marketing* 78 (November 2014), pp. 38–58.

6. Benton Cocanougher and John M. Ivancevich, "'BARS' Performance Rating for Sales Force Personnel," *Journal of Marketing* 42 (July 1978), pp. 87–95.

7. Lyndon E. Dawson, Jr., Barlow Soper, and Charles E. Pettijohn, "The Effects of Empathy on Salesperson Effectiveness," *Psychology and Marketing* 9 (July–August 1992), pp. 297–310. See also Neil M. Ford, Orville C. Walker, Jr., Gilbert A. Churchill, Jr., and Steven W. Hartley, "Selecting Successful Salespeople: A Meta-Analysis of Biographical and Psychological Selection Criteria," in *Annual Review of Marketing*, ed. Michael J. Houston (Chicago: American Marketing Association, 1987), pp. 90–131.

8. Cocanougher and Ivancevich, "'BARS' Performance Rating for Sales Force Personnel," p. 89

9. Greg W. Marshall, John C. Mowen, and Keith J. Fabes, "The Impact of Territory Difficulty and Self versus Other Ratings on Managerial Evaluations of Sales Personnel," *Journal of Personal Selling & Sales Management* 12 (Fall 1992), pp. 35–47.

10. Aharon Tziner, Christine Joanis, and Kevin R. Murphy, "A Comparison of Three Methods of Performance Appraisal with Regard to Goal Properties, Goal Perception, and Ratee Satisfaction," *Group and Organization Management* 25 (June 2000), pp. 175–190.

11. Cocanougher and Ivancevich, "'BARS' Performance Rating for Sales Force Personnel," pp. 90–99.

12. Mary Jo Bitner, Bernard H. Booms, and Mary Stanfield Tetreault, "The Service Encounter: Diagnosing Favorable and Unfavorable Incidents," *Journal of Marketing* 54 (January 1990), pp. 71–84.

13. Roger J. Placky, "Appraisal Scales that Measure Performance Outcomes and Job Results," *Personnel* 60 (May–June 1983), pp. 57–65.

14. Nihal Mamatoglu, "Effects on Organizational Context (Culture and Climate) from Implementing a 360-Degree Feedback System: The Case of Arcelik," *European Journal of Work and Organizational Psychology* 17 (December 2008), pp. 426–449.

15. "Give Yourself a Job Review," *American Salesman* (May 2001), pp. 26–27.

16. Charles E. Pettijohn, Linda S. Pettijohn, and Michael d'Amico, "Characteristics of Performance Appraisals and Their Impact on Sales Force Satisfaction," *Human Resource Development Quarterly* 12 (Summer 2001), pp. 127–139.

17. William Fitzgerald, "Forget the Form in Performance Appraisals," *HR Magazine* 40 (December 1995), p. 134.

18. Helen Rheem, "Performance Management: A Progress Report," *Harvard Business Review* (March–April 1995), p. 11.

Index